THE ELGAR COMPANION TO RECENT ECONOMIC METHODOLOGY

The Elgar Companion to Recent Economic Methodology

Edited by

John B. Davis

Professor of History and Methodology of Economics, University of Amsterdam, The Netherlands, Professor of Economics, Marquette University, USA and co-editor, Journal of Economic Methodology

D. Wade Hands

Professor of Economics, University of Puget Sound, USA and co-editor, Journal of Economic Methodology

Edward Elgar
Cheltenham, UK • Northampton, MA, USA

Published by
Edward Elgar Publishing Limited
The Lypiatts
15 Lansdown Road
Cheltenham
Glos GL50 2JA
UK

Edward Elgar Publishing, Inc.
William Pratt House
9 Dewey Court
Northampton
Massachusetts 01060
USA

A catalogue record for this book
is available from the British Library

Library of Congress Control Number: 2011926837

ISBN 978 1 84844 754 7 (cased)

Typeset by Servis Filmsetting Ltd, Stockport, Cheshire
Printed and bound by MPG Books Group, UK

Contents

Contributors

Anna Alexandrova, University of Cambridge, Cambridge, UK.

Eric Angner, George Mason University, Fairfax, VA, USA.

Roger E. Backhouse, University of Birmingham, Birmingham, UK.

Bradley W. Bateman, Denison University, Granville, OH, USA.

Paul L. Borrill, REPLICUS Software Corporation, Palo Alto, CA, USA.

Luigino Bruni, Bicocca University, Milan, Italy.

David Colander, Middlebury College, Middlebury, VT, USA.

John B. Davis, University of Amsterdam, Amsterdam, The Netherlands; Marquette University, Milwaukee, WI, USA.

Kurt Dopfer, University of St Gallen, St Gallen, Switzerland.

Pedro Garcia Duarte, University of São Paulo, São Paulo, Brazil.

D. Wade Hands, University of Puget Sound, Tacoma, WA, USA.

Daniel M. Haybron, St Louis University, St Louis, MO, USA.

Floris Heukelom, Radboud University, Nijmegen, The Netherlands.

Geoffrey M. Hodgson, University of Hertfordshire, Hatfield, UK.

Katarina Juselius, University of Copenhagen, Copenhagen, Denmark.

Uskali Mäki, University of Helsinki, Helsinki, Finland.

Caterina Marchionni, University of Helsinki, Helsinki, Finland.

Tiago Mata, Duke University, Durham, NC, USA.

Philip Mirowski, University of Notre Dame, Notre Dame, IN, USA.

Pier Luigi Porta, Bicocca University, Milan, Italy.

Don Ross, University of Cape Town, Cape Town, South Africa; Georgia State University, Atlanta, GA, USA.

Ana C. Santos, University of Coimbra, Coimbra, Portugal.

Leigh Tesfatsion, Iowa State University, Ames, IA, USA.

Paola Tubaro, University of Greenwich, London, UK.

K. Vela Velupillai, University of Trento, Trento, Italy.

Jack Vromen, Erasmus University, Rotterdam, The Netherlands.

L. Randall Wray, University of Missouri – Kansas City, Kansas City, MO, USA.

Stefano Zambelli, University of Trento, Trento, Italy.

1 Introduction: the changing character of economic methodology
John B. Davis and D. Wade Hands

In the slightly more than half century from the late 1930s, when economic methodology began to be seen as a distinct domain of investigation and a separate field within economics (Hutchison, 1938), to well into the 1990s, philosophy has played a dominant role in determining how economic methodology was understood by its practitioners. Indeed the history of economic methodology during this period can be broadly understood as the successive application of series of different philosophical views regarding the nature of good scientific theorizing: the early embrace of logical positivist thinking, the move to a Popperian falsificationism, its replacement by the Lakatosian research program approach, the turn to language and rhetoric, and most recently the arguments for realism (Blaug, 1992 [1980]; Caldwell, 1994 [1980]; Davis et al., 1998; Hands, 2001; Davis et al., 2004; Kincaid and Ross, 2009; Boumans and Davis, 2010). Thus the field of economic methodology has traditionally been defined in terms of doctrines that have come from outside of economics, primarily the philosophy of natural science, that were simply (often simplistically) applied to economic theorizing. But by the late 1990s economic methodology had begun to be pursued differently. Economic methodologists began to set aside the normative methodological agendas associated with philosophical imports, and increasingly sought to elicit and describe the methodological reasoning they found implicit in economists' thinking. This has now made what goes on inside of economics more central to the field of economic methodology than what comes from outside of it, and has arguably made research in economic methodology more immediate to the concerns of economists themselves.

At the same time, this shift in orientation has coincided with the emergence of renewed interest in methodological reasoning – if not in the field itself – on the part of economists involved in a number of influential new research programs, including experimental economics, behavioral economics, neuroeconomics, evolutionary economics, complexity and computational economics, ecological economics, and the subjective well-being approach. In each of these new research programs practitioners have sought to differentiate their programs from the post-war economics

1

mainstream associated with neoclassical economics and classical game theory, not only by marking out their theoretical differences from standard views, but also by emphasizing their own departures from standard methodological strategies (Davis, 2007). In some instances this has involved a reappropriation of well-known figures in the history of economic methodology and the philosophy of science. Vernon Smith (2008), for example, has referred to Karl Popper and Imre Lakatos to defend experimentalism. Colin Camerer (2006) has defended the realism of behavioral economics by criticizing the 'as if' instrumentalist reasoning of Milton Friedman. Others have emphasized the methodological reasoning of past economists, as for example in Luigino Bruni and Robert Sugden's (2007) reappraisal of Pareto's thinking as a way of appreciating behavioral economics, and in Paul Zak's (2008) return to Adam Smith's early ideas in his defense of neuroeconomics. Many have simply set out methodological arguments as ways of introducing how their research programs are different from more conventional ones. Thus Alan Kirman (2011) explains complexity economics in terms of the different ways in which knowledge is produced, Geoffrey Hodgson and Thorbjørn Knudsen (2010) apply Darwin's evolutionary reasoning to recast economic systems as evolutionary, and Amartya Sen (2009) argues for a new methodological strategy for incorporating justice into normative economics.

The emergence of the new research programs in recent economics, however, has a further significance for economic methodology in that many of these programs borrow significantly from thinking in other sciences, and thus draw on and translate practitioner reasoning in these other sciences into explanatory concerns that occupy economists. Behavioral economics has its origins in psychology, experimental economics applies laboratory methods to economics long employed in many sciences, neuroeconomics is based on neuroscience, evolutionary economics comes from evolutionary biology, complexity reasoning is widespread throughout science, and the capability approach makes use of anthropological reasoning. Thus the economic methodology associated with these recent research programs employs a diverse array of different types of scientific thinking. On the one hand, there are new strategies of empirical investigation based on the different ways in which laboratory techniques and simulation methods have been adapted to economics; on the other hand, there are concepts new to (or little used in) economics, such as reference points and endowment effects (behavioral economics), emergence (evolutionary and complexity economics), happiness (subjective well-being), sustainability (ecological economics), and the brain (neuroeconomics).

An important set of issues, consequently, that has been added to the domain of economic methodology concerns how explanations in economics reflect relationships between different types of reasoning employed in economics and other sciences. This contrasts with the first half century or so of the history of the field when its subject of investigation – the nature of explanation in economics – was developed in terms of a general, 'one size fits all' understanding of scientific explanation appropriate in essentially the same way to all sciences. Recent explanations in economics that incorporate the influences of other sciences upon economics lack this sort of conceptual uniformity, since they show how disparate conceptual resources associated with different sciences get combined in hybrid types of explanations.

A precursor example of this kind of explanation, where the direction of influence rather runs in the opposite direction from economics to other sciences, are those explanations of economics imperialism in the 1980s that focused on the export of Chicago School and Public Choice School rational choice explanations to other social sciences (see Mäki, 2008). But these explanations generally focused less on conceptual relationships between reasoning in economics and in other fields than on how economists sought to simply replace existing explanations in other sciences with ones from economics. That is, they ignored the processes of hybridization that occur when sciences accommodate and adapt concepts and methods from other sciences within the scope of their existing disciplinary concerns.

The more recent 'reverse' imperialism phenomenon, in which concepts and principles from others sciences have been adopted and deployed in the new research programs in economics, involves a process in which the traditional concerns of economics have been modified to make space for new concepts and methods from other sciences. This raises many issues regarding what the definition and core concerns of economics as a science can be said to be (Davis, 2010), so the methodological examination of this recent history offers many avenues for research and future investigation.

This volume provides a selection of significant chapters that reflects the expanding horizons of economic methodology. Their authors draw on a wide range of contributions to the various subfields in economics that experienced significant change during the last two decades, while also surveying and explaining many of the recent new developments in methodological thinking stimulated by these research programs. In general, the emphasis in these chapters rests on understanding the thinking of the practitioners, but the authors of these chapters also bring to bear the more than a half century of careful thinking about the nature of methodological thinking in economics.

The volume is divided into six parts, each focusing on a few aspects of the recent economic literature. Part I is concerned with one of the areas of economics that has exhibited both significant growth and profound change during the last few decades: the literature on individual or agent choice associated with behavioral economics, experimental economics, neuroeconomics, and related fields.

Chapter 2 by Floris Heukelom provides a methodologically focused historical overview of behavioral economics and the psychological literature that influenced it. Starting in the 1950s he traces certain ideas from the research on behavioral decision research in psychology – the work of Ward Edwards, Eric Wanner, Daniel Kahneman, Amos Tversky, and others – and their influence on recent behavioral economics (both as a descriptive scientific theory and also in its more welfare-oriented forms such as libertarian paternalism). One of Heukelom's main themes is the importance of the distinction between rational choice theory as a scientific descriptive or positive theory of individual behavior and as a normative theory of rationality: what one ought to do in order to be rational. He shows that this distinction was emphasized early in the psychological literature and continues to be endorsed by recent behavioral economists. The standard behavioral criticism of textbook rational choice theory is that it repeatedly fails to predict and/or explain the behavior of real economic agents (hence the many well-known 'anomalies'), and yet in the policy domain – in nudging and such – it continues to be the standard for how economic agents ought to (or ought to be encouraged to) act. Heukelom argues that this is a direct carry-over from the earlier psychological literature on behavioral decision theory.

Ana C. Santos's Chapter 3 reflects on the major methodological debates within recent experimental economics. Starting with the early experiments versus theory literature that focused on testing various aspects of standard microeconomic theory, through the debate over internal and external validity, to the more recent emphasis on policy intervention, the field of experimental economics has always been characterized by active methodological engagement. In some cases resources from the philosophy of natural science (for example falsificationism) have been directly involved, but more often the debates are quite naturalistic and driven by the actual (although changing) practices of the field itself. Santos employs the distinction between technological experiments (concerned with knowledge claims about institutions and structures) and behavioral experiments (emphasizing knowledge claims about behavior, particularly anomalous behavior) as a general framework for helping us to understand these various methodological debates.

Don Ross writes about neuroeconomics from the vantage point of someone with experience as an economist, a philosopher of mind, and a practitioner of neuroeconomic research. His Chapter 4 is a critical review of the methodological issues raised during the first decade of this rapidly expanding field. He argues that two fundamentally different approaches to neuroeconomics have emerged during its short history: the approach of Paul Glimcher and others in the early literature on neuroeconomics which is associated with computational learning theory; and a later approach – revisionist behavioral economics – that uses the technologies of neuroscience, particularly functional magnetic resonance imaging (fMRI), to test standard rational choice-based theories of individual behavior. The latter literature has discovered numerous anomalies and is generally quite critical of mainstream economic theory, while the former is methodologically much closer to what Ross calls 'standard, not revisionist, microeconomics'. Ross defends the scientific potential, and in certain cases progress, of the more pro-rational choice program of Glimcher, and criticizes the approach to neuroeconomics taken by behavioral economists. In the last portion of the chapter Ross explains the most recent developments in the Glimcher approach – his subjective value theory – and gives a general endorsement of the research program (although he remains skeptical about certain aspects).

The last chapter in Part I overlaps a bit with the welfare and policy-based literature discussed in Part II, but also addresses recent developments in the economics of behavior and choice. Chapter 5 by Anna Alexandrova and Daniel M. Haybron assesses the revival of the subject of happiness within recent economics. They suggest that a positivist-inspired skepticism about subjective states – methodological minimalism – moved economists away from happiness and experienced utility during much of the twentieth century. The result, they argue, was a microeconomic theory of behavior and choice that focused on utility, but utility that was devoid of the hedonistic subjective states of the earlier theory and simply identified utility with choice. They call this approach – the mainstay of economic minimalism – 'revealed preference methodology' (although 'contemporary revealed preference methodology' might be a better term). They argue that this methodological approach was parsimonious and amenable to mathematical formalism, but sacrificed fidelity to the economic world that the discipline was trying to explain. In the second half of the chapter they use this methodological framework to discuss a number of recent developments in the economics of happiness and related literature.

Part II contains four chapters on a variety of topics related to welfare economics and microeconomic policy. Some of these chapters overlap a bit with chapters in Part I, but generally have more of a welfare and policy focus, and are less concerned with the prediction and explanation of individual behavior.

In Chapter 6 Erik Angner examines the recent movement toward subjective measures of well-being and away from the more traditional individual preference satisfaction view of welfare. He argues that these two contested frameworks are based on two fundamentally different views of measurement. The traditional view of welfare is based on a measurement-theoretic approach that is deductive, emphasizes individual preference satisfaction, and relies on observable choice data. Alternatively, the newer subjective approach to welfare – often, but not exclusively associated with experimental psychology and behavioral economics – is based on a psychometric approach to measurement. It is more inductive, focuses on mental states, and utilizes questionnaires and other types of survey data. Angner argues that while there is no evidence that one approach has a clear advantage over the other – on the grounds of realism, 'realisticness' or fidelity – recognition of the fact that they are based on quite different notions of measurement helps to explain many features of, and positions taken in, the ongoing debate between these two approaches to welfare.

Chapter 7 by Luigino Bruni and Pier Luigi Porta addresses some of the same issues as Chapter 5, but offers a different take on the material. Bruni and Porta examine the recent revival of experienced utility and happiness from a historical and methodological perspective. They discuss experienced utility in section 7.2 and then turn to the related research on happiness in section 7.3 of the chapter. In section 7.2 they trace the literature on hedonistic experienced utility in economics from Jeremy Bentham, through a number of early neoclassicals, and on to the recent revival by Daniel Kahneman and others. They argue that there were two phases to Kahneman-inspired work on experienced utility: an early descriptive research focusing on framing and reference-dependence; and the later more welfare-focused literature linked directly to hedonism and informed by the recent literature on neuroeconomics. In section 7.3 Bruni and Porta discuss the Easterlin paradox and make the case that such empirical results about the relationship between income and happiness can be (and usually are) interpreted in hedonistic utilitarian terms, but they can also be interpreted in terms of Aristotle's Eudaimonia. They close the chapter by making the case for thinking about happiness in an Aristotlian way.

David Colander examines the methodological history of welfare economics in Chapter 8. The central thesis of his chapter is that 'classical' welfare economics (which includes the welfare economics of some neoclassical economists such as Marshall and Robbins) was quite different from the neoclassical welfare economics that has dominated economic theory since the end of World War II. In particular, the classical economists did not assume that it was possible to go directly from abstract economic models to policy recommendations. For the classicals the economic world is quite subtle and complex, making it impossible to do effective policy analysis without considering various social, political and philosophical (particularly ethical) issues, and without understanding the historical and institutional details of the particular situation. For them abstract economic theory was useful for policy analysis, but it was only one piece of the policy puzzle. Neoclassical welfare economics harbors no such doubts about the adequacy of economic theory; it is assumed that Walrasian welfare economics is sufficiently general to subsume all of the important issues and can be applied to policy in a fairly straightforward manner. One of the examples discussed in the chapter is Abram Bergson; Colander argues that he made a sharp distinction between economic welfare and social welfare – with the former being just one small part of the latter – while the generation of welfare economists that elaborated and extended his analytical framework effective ignored this (classical) distinction. Colander closes the chapter with a plea for history, history of economic thought and moral philosophy (an education more like the classicals received) in the graduate education of contemporary economists in order to help them better understand the complexities of the policy realm.

Chapter 9 by Uskali Mäki and Caterina Marchionni examines the field of geographical economics which emerged during the 1990s as the result of work by Paul Krugman and others. The central message of the chapter is that any simplistic methodological dichotomy that either praises geographical economics for its real-world and empirical focus, or (as is more often the case) criticizes it for its emphasis on disciplinary conventions and pure theory, will fail to understand the field, particularly the complexity of its methodology and standard practices. Although geographical economics is 'constrained by the characteristic disciplinary conventions of conventional economics' and it is therefore 'pretty much economics as usual', these features are not necessarily in conflict with it being 'world-oriented' or partly shaped by 'matters of fact'. Much of the chapter examines the three key achievements of geographical economics – the recovery of space, its grounding in microfoundations, and its ability to unify a number of previously disparate subjects – and the role that its particular (contrastive) explanatory strategy has played in the development of the field (particularly with respect to unification).

Part III contains three chapters on recent developments in complexity theory and computational economics. The omnipresence and range of powers of the digital computer has opened the door to new modeling techniques in economics that were simply not available to the economists of previous generations. In some cases these new tools are complements to the traditional tools of economic analysis and provide new techniques for modeling long-standing economic questions, and in other cases they are substitutes that radically transform the economic questions being considered. The chapters discuss a variety of methodological questions associated with this recent computer-based literature.

In Chapter 10 Paola Tubaro examines some of the methodological issues associated with the rapidly growing field of agent-based computational economics (ACE). ACE is a broad class of computer models that explain various aggregate stylized facts as emergent properties of the repeated interactions of individual heterogeneous agents. The field is broadly interdisciplinary with applications in the other social sciences, ecology, biology, and a number of other fields in addition to economics. In general the results that emerge from agent-based computational models in economics are 'profoundly different' from the properties of the equilibria in 'received economic theories'. Tubaro discusses four main methodological issues in ACE: how it functions as an experimental methodology; the variety of different decision rules employed within ACE; the question of whether ACE can, or how it can, be validated and/or verified (and how it provides explanations); and the broad diversity of modeling techniques employed in ACE. Various applications of ACE are discussed including research on loyalty, reputation and endogeneity of preferences.

The following chapter by Paul L. Borrill and Leigh Tesfatsion (Chapter 11) also discusses agent-based modeling and covers some of the same methodological issues discussed by Tubaro. The main difference is that Borrill and Tesfatsion focus on agent-based modeling (ABM) in general rather than ACE in particular. They argue that classical mathematics is often inappropriate for the social sciences, and the ABM approach to modeling systems 'as collections of autonomous interacting entities' often provides a much more useful tool for analyzing complex social interactions. The agents or entities in ABM are both distributed and connected; distributed in the sense that each agent responds to local interactions (with path-dependency so that two agents, that are initially the same, can end up quite different after a number of interactions), and connected because each is embedded in a network of interactions with other entities. The result is a type of 'controlled computer experiment' that allows the experimenter to 'investigate how large-scale effects arise from the micro-level interactions of dispersed autonomous agents'. Borrill and Tesfatsion end their detailed methodological discussion of ABM with two illustrative examples: a model of wholesale electrical power markets and an agent-based model of the storage and management of information.

K. Vela Velupillai and Stefano Zambelli's Chapter 12 is a broad historical and methodological discussion of computation in economics and computational economics. It begins with a history of the origins of computational economics – particularly the Cambridge Growth Project – and a discussion of the methodological issues associated with the use of digital (as opposed to analog) computers in economic modeling. One of the arguments is that most contemporary economists – even those working within computational economics – do not realize that there exists a long and extremely diverse 'noble tradition of computation in economics'. The main body of the chapter is a detailed discussion of four specific topics in the epistemology of economic computation: the connection with behavioral economics (classical and recent); the literature on computable general equilibrium theory; the topic of computable economics more generally; and the literature on agent-based computational economics examined in the previous two chapters. Much of the discussion of these four topics is critical. Two of the main themes are that classical behavioral economics (associated with the work of Herbert Simon and others) was very computationally oriented – seeking 'computable foundations for boundedly rational choice and satisficing decisions' – and that this computational aspect has been lost by contemporary behavioral economists. And that neoclassical-based computational economics – such as Arrow–Debreu-based computable general equilibrium theory – rests on inadequate computational and constructivist foundations. These, and other criticisms, reflect contemporary economists' 'lack of anchoring in the noble traditions broached by the pioneers'.

One of the recent growth areas in economics has been the intersection of economics and evolutionary biology. Although the field has origins going back to the early twentieth century it has exploded in a variety of different directions in recent years. There now exists a number of quasi-autonomous research programs with the broad field of evolutionary economics. Some of these subfields have linkages to topics discussed in previous chapters – behavioral economics, neuroeconomics and computational economics in particular – but some of the literature draws on resources from evolutionary biology and philosophy of biology that are not directly connected with these other areas of recent development within economics. Part IV contains three chapters on various topics in the history and philosophy of this evolutionary literature.

Geoffrey M. Hodgson provides a philosophically focused survey of evolutionary economics focusing on ontological issues in Chapter 13. After a brief discussion of the history of the field, emphasizing its broad diversity, Hodgson turns to the major ontological divergences among contemporary evolutionary economists. He examines debates on dualism versus monism and the plurality regarding demarcated entities, but the main focus is 'generalized Darwinism'. Generalized Darwinism – a modification of Richard Dawkins's 'universal Darwinism' – is the thesis that the core Darwinian principles of random variation and selective retention 'have a wider application than to biology alone'. In section 13.7 of the chapter Hodgson argues for a middle ground – a 'strategy of reconciliation' – between the two main positions in the debate: identifying generalized Darwinism with reduction to biology and treating these Darwinian ideas as mere analogies with no ontological force.

In Chapter 14 Kurt Dopfer provides an alternative interpretation of the evolution of evolutionary economics. He opens the chapter with a discussion of Richard Nelson and Sidney Winter's *An Evolutionary Theory of Economic Change* (1982) as the origin of many of the current debates within contemporary evolutionary economics. Evolutionary economics 'deals with the structural evolution of knowledge of economic operations', whereas neoclassical economics 'analyzes ongoing economic operations under the assumption of given knowledge'. Dopfer explores the question of economics as a cultural science and (following the author's earlier work) offers *Homo sapiens oeconomicus* as proper characterization of the economic agent in evolutionary economics, and argues that the field of evolutionary economics itself should be a subset of complexity-based evolutionary archaeology. Much of the second half of the chapter is concerned with the 'meso' level of processes, situated between the micro and the macro, and how the investigation of such processes by evolutionary economics would give us a much better understanding of economic dynamics, particularly economic growth, as an 'endogenously self-generating, self-adapting and continuously self-restructuring process'.

In the third and final chapter in this part, Chapter 15, Jack Vromen offers yet another interpretation of recent debates within evolutionary economics – including the generalized Darwinism discussed by Hodgson in Chapter 13. Vromen argues that many of the efforts to strengthen the application of Darwinian ideas to the social and cultural sciences render the evolutionary approach so general and abstract that they end up being a Darwinism 'not worth fighting for'. Much of the chapter is a discussion of recent arguments by Peter Godfrey-Smith and how they might be used to improve the current received view within evolutionary economics: generalized Darwinism and formal models of replicator dynamics in particular. With respect to generalized Darwinism, Vromen argues that giving the three Darwinian principles of variation, replication and selection an abstract generalized interpretation leads to explanatory weakness and too much reliance on auxiliary hypotheses. With respect to replicator dynamics, he makes the case that such mathematical models place too much emphasis on technique and not enough on empirical relevance. The chapter ends by supporting the Godfrey-Smith approach, but also offering some suggestions about where it too may have problems.

Unlike the previous sections, Part V is concerned with macroeconomic theory and policy. Outside of a few periods when one particular research program dominated the field – such as IS-LM Keynesianism during the 1960s and dynamic stochastic general equilibrium (DSGE) models quite recently – macroeconomics has traditionally been a very contested field: theoretically, empirically and methodologically. Whether it was Keynesianism versus monetarism, new classical versus new Keynesian, or other debates, one strategy has often been to capture the epistemological high ground by challenging the scientific credibility of the opposition. The four chapters in this section take very different points of view, but they all suggest that the recent macroeconomic and financial crisis has reopened the door to a host of debates within macroeconomics. Some of these debates have been with the profession since the early years of the Keynesian revolution and others are quite recent, but they all involve methodological issues in a serious way.

Pedro Garcia Duarte's Chapter 16 examines the DSGE approach to business cycles. He explains that as the DSGE literature evolved during the late 1990s and early 2000s it involved a combination of ideas from both real business cycle and new Keynesian theorizing. He explains the class of facts that these models attempt to explain, and the basic impulse response approach that they take to such explanation. After a detailed discussion of the basic theoretical structure of the standard DSGE model – emphasizing the representative agent microfoundations and the absence of any financial sector – Duarte turns to some specific methodological issues. He examines the debate over calibration versus estimation in the empirical implementation of DSGE models and argues that the general tendency has been away from the former and toward the latter. He also discusses the debate over the use of the representative agent, with supporters arguing that it provides a 'natural objective' for social welfare – the social welfare being the utility of the representative agent – and critics noting how problematic it is for policy analysis and also that it conflicts with earlier theoretical results in both social choice theory and (heterogenerous agent) Walrasian models. Duarte closes the chapter with a discussion of the many criticisms that have been raised against the DSGE model in the aftermath of the recent financial crisis and concludes that it is too early to know the outcome of the debate.

Katarina Juselius's Chapter 17 examines the recent literature on empirical macroeconomics. The central thesis is that the theory-first approach that currently dominates empirical macroeconomics should be replaced by the more data-based approach of cointegrated vector autoregressive (CVAR) models that give 'the data a rich context in which they are allowed to speak freely'. Theory-first standard practice starts with a static mathematical model and then expands it to include stochastic components, while CVAR starts with a statistically well-specified model that is more capable of dealing with disequilibrium and the non-stationarity of data. In addition to being more true to the data than the dominant approach, Juselius argues that the CVAR methodology is more falsificationist (and less verificationist) oriented and more effective in detecting regime shifts. A substantial portion of the chapter is dedicated to criticizing the real business cycle (RBC) based models of Peter Ireland that employ a vector autoregressive (VAR) approach to empirics. She also argues that the macroeconomic data is more consistent with the theoretical framework offered by imperfect knowledge economics (IKE) than with most rational expectations-based models. She closes the chapter with a defense of CVAR as a partial solution to the problem of the poor performance of DSGE-based models in predicting or explaining the recent financial crisis.

Roger E. Backhouse and Bradley W. Bateman explore various methodological issues in the history of Keynesian macroeconomics in Chapter 18. After noting the financial crisis-induced revival of Keynesian ideas, they trace through the main methodological debates that have occurred in the history of the Keynesian literature. They note that while the monetarist critique of the 1960s was critical of Keynesian policy, it accepted the general methodological framework of the (then) dominant IS-LM model. This was not the case with the rational expectations, new classical, and real business cycles macroeconomics that came later. In these cases the challenge – particularly the microfoundations challenge – was methodologically more serious. The three main Keynesian responses were the 'disequilibrium' approach, the new Keynesian methodology, and post-Keynesianism. The disequilibrium approach was relatively short-lived, but the other two continue to be established Keynesian frameworks: the new Keynesian is more mainstream (essentially 'bolting' Keynesian ideas on to the core DSGE model) and post-Keynesian is more anti-neoclassical. In addition to these three versions of Keynesian macroeconomics, they also discuss the more politically and philosophically focused revival of Keynesian theory initiated by Keynes's biographer Robert Skidlesky, and the recent Keynesian literature that draws on some of insights from behavioral economics. Backhouse and Bateman ultimately conclude that it is the behavioral approach – in both behavioral macroeconomics and behavioral finance – that 'resonates most closely with the way Keynes argued in the *General Theory*', but maintain an 'eclectic view' about how the Keynesian research program will evolve and how it will influence macroeconomic theorizing in the near future.

L. Randall Wray presents a defense of a particular interpretation of Keynesian economics in Chapter 19. After a rather sharp attack on the inability of various neoclassical-based macroeconomic theories to predict, offer insight into the causes of, or recommend policies for the recent financial crisis, Wray turns to the particular Hyman Minsky-inspired version of Keynesian macroeconomics that he defends. He argues that the central thesis of the *General Theory* was that firms produce 'what they expect to sell' and there is no reason to believe that these decisions will be 'consistent with the full employment level of output in the short run or in the long run'. He then discusses Minsky's financial instability thesis in detail, emphasizing how its key assumptions regarding the way that market economies operate differs from those of neoclassical-inspired macroeconomic theory. The main instabilities for Minsky involve the difference between private and public default risk and the financial sector's 'tendency toward explosive euphoria'. The last part of the chapter focuses on policy, in particular how much Wray's interpretation of Keynes's policy recommendations differ from the textbook, pump-priming view. The chapter closes with the argument that Keynesian economists, unlike neoclassical macroeconomists, did in fact 'see it coming'.

Part VI contains two chapters discussing the (current) relationship between the economics profession and the general public. Chapter 20 by Philip Mirowski concerns the economic profession's overall response to the financial crisis – particularly in contact with the media – and emphasizes how this response differs from what most discussions of economic methodology might lead one to expect. The final chapter by Tiago Mata examines recent changes in the economic profession through the window of the new world of economic blogs.

Philip Mirowski starts by reviewing the 'shellacking' that the economics profession has taken over its seeming inability to predict, explain or recommend policy solutions for the financial crisis, but the main focus of the chapter is the profession's response to these criticisms. Mirowski's general framework for his analysis of the response is a combination of the theory of cognitive dissonance from social psychology, and the Duheimian underdetermination thesis from philosophy of science. He argues that the 'failure to predict' indictment was particularly hard hitting since the profession has long paid lip service to Friedman's methodological claim that the accuracy of a theory's predictions is the only thing that matters to the success of a scientific theory, and also because recent macroeconomics has been so focused on expectations and perfect foresight (some of the things that Keynesian theory ostensibly lacked). The second half of the chapter is an extended discussion of the three main disciplinary 'responses' to the crisis-based criticism: rejection of the perfect rationality assumption by behavioral economists; a renunciation of the efficient market hypothesis; and the argument for the abandonment of the DSGE model. Mirowski examines each of these responses in detail, but generally concludes – consistent with cognitive dissonance and the Duheim thesis – that the majority amount to relatively minor modifications within the protective belt of neoclassical economics rather than substantive attempts to forge a new paradigm.

Tiago Mata in Chapter 21 uses the framework of contagion, conformity, paranoia and alienation to examine the rise of economics blogs during the last few years. He provides information about who is writing for blogs, who is reading the blogs, the topics covered, and the characteristics of the blogs that are most successful. He discusses a number of important, and perhaps rather surprising, features of the economic blogosphere. One is that even though they are technically quite public conversations, they often end up being relatively inward-looking (bloggers writing to/for other bloggers). Another feature is that the economists involved in blogging do not seem to be alienated from, or shunned by, the profession in other aspects of their professional lives. It remains to be seen if this new and growing means of communication among economists and with the general public will fundamentally alter the discipline's theory, practice or methodology.

REFERENCES

Blaug, Mark (1992), *The Methodology of Economics or How Economists Explain*, 2nd edn, Cambridge: Cambridge University Press; 1st edn (1980).

Boumans, Marcel and John B. Davis (2010), *Economic Methodology: Understanding Economics as a Science*, Basingstoke: Palgrave Macmillan.

Bruni, Luigino and Robert Sugden (2007), 'The Road Not Taken: How Psychology Was Removed from Economics, and How it Might Be Brought Back', *Economic Journal*, 117(516), 146–173.

Caldwell, Bruce (1994), *Beyond Positivism: Economic Methodology in the Twentieth Century*, London: Routledge; 1st edn (1980).

Camerer, Colin (2006), 'Behavioral Economics', in R. Blundell, W. Newey and T. Persson (eds), *Advances in Economics and Econometrics*, Cambridge: Cambridge University Press, pp. 181–214.

Davis, John B. (2007), 'The Turn in Economics and the Turn in Economic Methodology', *Journal of Economic Methodology*, 14 (September), 275–290.

Davis, John B. (2010), 'Mäki on Economics Imperialism', Marquette University Economics Department, WP 2010-04.

Davis, John B., D. Wade Hands and Uskali Mäki (eds) (1998), *The Handbook of Economic Methodology*, Cheltenham, UK and Lyme, NH, USA: Edward Elgar.

Davis, John B., Alan Marciano and Jochen Runde (eds) (2004), *The Elgar Companion to Economics and Philosophy*, Cheltenham, UK and Northampton, MA, USA: Edward Elgar Publishing.

Hands, D. Wade (2001), *Reflection without Rules: Economic Methodology and Contemporary Science Theory*, Cambridge: Cambridge University Press.

Hodgson, Geoffrey and Thorbjørn Knudsen (2010), *Darwin's Conjecture: The Search for General Principles of Social and Economic Evolution*, Chicago, IL: University of Chicago Press.

Hutchison, Terence W. (1938), *The Significance and Basic Postulates of Economic Theory*, London: Macmillan.

Kincaid, Harold and Don Ross (2009), *Oxford Handbook of Philosophy of Economics*, Oxford: Oxford University Press.

Kirman, Alan (2011), *Complex Economics: Individual and Collective Rationality*, London: Routledge.

Mäki, Uskali (2008), 'Economics Imperialism: Concept and Constraints', *Philosophy of the Social Sciences*, **9**(3), 351–380.

Nelson, R. and J. Winter (1982), *An Evolutionary Theory of Economic Change*, Cambridge, MA: Harvard University Press.

Sen, Amartya (2009), *The Idea of Justice*, Cambridge, MA: Belknap Press of Harvard University Press.

Smith, Vernon (2008), *Rationality in Economics: Constructivist and Ecological Forms*, Cambridge: Cambridge University Press.

Zak, Paul (2008), *Moral Markets: The Critical Role of Values in the Economy*, Princeton, NJ: Princeton University Press.

PART I

ECONOMICS OF BEHAVIOR AND CHOICE

2 Behavioral economics
Floris Heukelom

2.1 INTRODUCTION

Behavior as a concept encapsulating all acts of the human being – and, more controversially, of the animal being – originates in the United States of the early twentieth century (Danziger, 1997). Subsequently, this new concept of behavior provided the basis for the label of the new approach to psychology baptized 'behaviorism' (Mills, 1998). Behaviorism in its strictest sense is a scientific program commenced and developed by John Broadus Watson, Burrhus Frederick Skinner and others, which reigned psychology in the 1920s and 1930s. In addition, behaviorism forms part of a broader characteristic of twentieth-century American social science and society, namely to 'think behavioristically' (Mills, 1998, p. 1; see also for example Ross, 1991). To think behavioristically is to equate 'theory with application, understanding with prediction, and the workings of the human mind with social technology' (Mills, 1998, p. 2). Although the behavioral economics discussed in this chapter does not directly relate to behaviorism, it is part of the twentieth-century American focus on thinking behavioristically.

It was after World War II that behavior's adverbial conjugation 'behavioral' was introduced in relation to science and economics. The usage of 'behavioral economics' was initially popularized at the University of Michigan's Survey Research Center in the late 1940s, where George Katona understood behavioral economics as investigating economic behavior, that is, the subclass of behavior produced in the course of the agent's activities in the economy (for example Festinger and Katz, 1953, Juster, 2004). Other users of the adverb 'behavioral' included Ward Edwards, also at the University of Michigan, who, starting in the late 1950s, employed it as the name of his branch of operations research called behavioral decision research (Edwards, 1954, 1961); and Herbert Simon, who from the late 1950s advanced what he labeled behavioral economics as an alternative to the dominant neoclassical school in economics (Simon, 1959, 1986). The label of behavioral economics was later picked up by economists who sought to reform the dominant neoclassical view of the day along the lines set out by Simon, establishing a thriving, albeit non-mainstream economic research program. During the early 1980s, behavioral economics was furthermore claimed by Eric Wanner – first at the Alfred P. Sloan Foundation and from 1986 onwards as President of the Russell Sage Foundation – when he brought together a group of psychologists and economists in a program aimed at applying insights from behavioral decision research to economics. Individuals involved in this program from the first included Amos Tversky, Daniel Kahneman, Richard Thaler, Robert Shiller, Lawrence Summers, and others. After a number of years on the margin of economics, this 'new' program of behavioral economics (Sent, 2004) became influential in the 1990s, and developed into one of the key contenders for replacing the no longer dominant neoclassical economic theory in the 2000s – as exemplified among others by Kahneman's Nobel Prize in 2002 (Kahneman, 2003). While not denying the importance and lasting influence of Katona, Simon and their many followers and associates, the rest of this chapter will focus on this last, new program of behavioral economics – which, for reasons of convenience, shall simply be referred to in this chapter as behavioral economics.[1]

A central feature of behavioral economics has been its – to economists – new use of the terms 'normative' and 'descriptive' (or 'positive'). Normative has been defined ethically in economics at least since the publication of John Neville Keynes's *Scope and Method of Political Economy* (1890). In the normative domain one discussed what was good, fair, just, or ethical in other ways (Hands, 2001, p. 30). Positive first of all meant *not* value-based, and secondly referred in a general sense to the empirical basis of a value-free science of economics. Behavioral economists, by contrast, introduced to economists the definition of normative as used by behavioral decision researchers, mathematical psychologists, mathematicians, philosophers and others, namely: normative as the rubric under which to discuss how one ought to behave if one wants to behave rationally.

2.2 HISTORICAL AND METHODOLOGICAL BACKGROUND

To understand behavioral economics, a useful starting point is 1948. In that year, Milton Friedman co-published an article in the *Journal of Political Economy* with Leonard 'Jimmie' Savage, a brilliant young mathematician five years his junior. The paper, entitled 'The Utility Analysis of Choice Involving Risk', sought to rationalize human beings' simultaneous purchases of risk-seeking lotteries and risk-avoiding insurance. The authors' solution – a wiggly concave–convex utility–wealth curve – is less important than the methodological justification on which they grounded their solution. Friedman's subsequently famous 'as if' reasoning (Friedman, 1953) was already clearly present in the article:

> [The wiggly concave-convex utility–wealth curve asserts that] in making a particular class of decision, individuals behave *as if* they calculated and compared expected utility and *as if* they knew the odds. The validity of this assertion does not depend on whether individuals know the precise odds, much less on whether they say that they calculate and compare expected utilities or think that they do, or whether psychologists can uncover any evidence that they do, but solely on whether it yields sufficiently accurate predictions about the class of decision with which the hypothesis deals. (Friedman and Savage, 1948, p.298, emphasis in the original)

In other words, it does not matter that people do not actually make their decisions on the basis of a wiggly utility curve, as long as their behavior can be accurately rationalized as if they do so. But also Savage's methodological position clearly emerged in between the lines: normal, healthy adults want to make their decisions on the basis of sound reasoning, and when doing so carefully are capable of doing so.

During the late 1940s and early 1950s, Savage was also working on a more encompassing project, a book in which he sought to establish a set of axioms describing rational behavior under uncertainty, based on work by, among others, Frank Ramsey, Bruno de Finetti and, in particular, John von Neumann and Oskar Morgenstern ([1944] 2004). The book was nearing its completion when in the spring of 1952 Savage attended a seminar in Paris organized by Maurice Allais and also attended by, among others, Milton Friedman and Kenneth Arrow. During the seminar Allais famously confounded Savage's axioms by presenting Savage with a decision problem in which the American mathematician, after careful thinking, made the non-rational decision, according to his own set of axioms (Jallais and Pradier, 2005). Forced to choose between two unappealing options – either his theory was invalid or he had made an irrational decision – Savage chose the latter, thus admitting that even very smart people when thinking carefully through a decision problem could make the wrong decision. To accommodate this unsettling conclusion, Savage enriched his manuscript with a new distinction between a normative and an empirical theory. The normative theory explained how normal healthy adults would want to make their decisions, and how they would make their decisions if the different options had been well explained to them and they had thought them through carefully. Savage considered his own set of axioms to be such a normative theory. Under the heading of the empirical theory, Savage argued, psychologists and other empirical social scientists could investigate under which circumstances people are prone or likely to make mistakes relative to the normative theory, and how these mistakes are most effectively corrected. With the addition of the normative–empirical distinction, *The Foundations of Statistics* was published in 1954.

Savage's book was picked up by experimental psychologist Ward Edwards, who, like many mathematically oriented social scientists at the time, admired Savage as one admires a genius (Krantz – Interview, 2008; Dawes – Interview, 2008). At the University of Michigan's Human Performance Center, Edwards set up his own Engineering Psychology Laboratory in 1958 to investigate his own version of operations research, labeled behavioral decision research (Philips and von Winterfeldt, 2006; Pachella – Interview, 2009). Edwards understood Savage's normative–empirical distinction in terms of the experimental psychological distinction between an objective stimulus set by the experimenter (objective in the sense that the stimulus – say the brightness of a lamp bulb – is objectively measured by a measurement instrument), and the subjective perception of that objective stimulus by the human subject in the laboratory. Thus, Edwards substituted for the brightness of lamp bulbs rational decision making under uncertainty and experimentally investigated when, how, and why normal healthy adults make mistakes with respect to the normative theory of Savage.

Edwards focused on decision making under uncertainty in which the uncertainty was given and unchanging (and therefore often defined as risk, as opposed to the strategic uncertainty of game theory). However, he considered Savage's theory to be naturally aligned with game theory, which he classified as decision making under strategic uncertainty. On the other hand, Edwards understood Savage and his own research as linking to decision making under certainty, by which he meant the indifference curve economics of Edgeworth, Pareto, Fisher, Samuelson, and other familiar names. Edwards was somewhat puzzled by the fact that the economists did not empirically investigate their normative theory of decision making under certainty, implicitly assuming that the economists could not possibly think that people always behave exactly according to the dictates of the normative theory. But despite his evidently extensive knowledge of neoclassical economics, and despite his urging students and fellow psychologists to acquaint themselves with the economic literature, Edwards continued to focus his own research on decision making under given uncertainty.

Throughout his career, Edwards was of the opinion that although people may be prone to mistakes in their decision making, they are ultimately capable of avoiding doing so given the right amount of information and sufficient time. Moreover, he was convinced that people want to comply with (what he understood as) the normative theories of indifference curves,

Bayesian statistics, decision theory and game theory. The latter assumption continued to be a firm pillar of behavioral decision research, but starting in the early 1970s some of Edwards's students began to question the first assumption. Amos Tversky in particular questioned whether people indeed, by and large, behave in accordance with the normative theories. Tversky's celebrated work with fellow Israeli psychologist Daniel Kahneman, which became known as the heuristics and biases program, assumed that people make their decisions on the basis of decision heuristics instead of Savage's axioms, and that the use of these heuristics often produces systematic and predictable biases from the predictions of the normative theory.

A full-fledged alternative behavioral theory appeared in 1979 as 'Prospect Theory: An Analysis of Decision under Risk', published in *Econometrica*. In the article Kahneman and Tversky maintained utility maximizing and the other theories of rational decision making of the economists and mathematicians as the universal, normative benchmarks by which all decision making was to be judged. But in addition they argued that economists had focused too much on the normative theories, and that they should devote more energy to developing descriptive accounts of human decision behavior. In the second part of the article, Kahneman and Tversky provided their own detailed theory of how people actually make their decisions – the now famous prospect theory, which argued that after a first heuristics-based editing phase, the human being makes her decision from the perspective of a context-determined reference point and based on a preference for risk-avoiding in the gain-domain and a preference for risk-seeking in the loss-domain. Prospect theory was picked up by a few economists, the young Richard Thaler first among them, but in 1979 the paper was not immediately the blockbuster article it would later become.

2.3   THE MAKING OF BEHAVIORAL ECONOMICS

An important catalyst for Kahneman and Tversky's success in economics was Eric Wanner's new behavioral economic program. In 1982, as a former Harvard psychology PhD, Wanner left Harvard University Press for the Alfred P. Sloan Foundation. At Sloan, Wanner explored the possibility of a program that would apply cognitive psychology to financial decision making. As part of his explorations he asked Kahneman and Tversky whether they thought such a program would have any potential. Kahneman and Tversky were not very optimistic, arguing that to get the economists' attention psychologists would have to be more economically sophisticated than they actually were, and they advised Wanner not to spend too much money on the project (see also Kahneman, 2002). In addition, there was the towering presence of Herbert Simon, who despite his Nobel memorial prize in 1978, was generally considered not to have had a large impact on economists' thinking about human decision making. Nevertheless, Wanner proposed to his superiors at the Sloan Foundation that they make a small endowment for a 'high risk, high return' program that would be successful where others had failed.

Early in 1984, Wanner invited psychologists Robert Abelson and Leon Festinger and economists William Baumol and Thomas Schelling to form the behavioral economics advisory committee. In mid-1984 Wanner and the advisory committee invited psychologists and economists possibly interested in the program, and announced the organization of three meetings for those interested. The list of some forty invited researchers included, among others, Vernon Smith from the University of Arizona; Daniel Kahneman and George Akerlof from the University of California, Berkeley; Charles Plott and David Grether from the Californian Institute of Technology; Robyn Hogarth and George Loewenstein from the University of Chicago; Herbert Simon, Robyn Dawes and Baruch Fischhoff from Carnegie Mellon University; Richard Thaler and Robert Frank from Cornell University; Larry Summers, Richard Zeckhauser and Howard Raiffa from Harvard University; Thomas Juster from the University of Michigan; Colin Camerer from Penn State University; Amos Tversky, Kenneth Arrow and James March from Stanford University; Robert Shiller, Sidney Winter and Richard Nelson from Yale; and Paul Slovic, and Sarah Lichtenstein from the Oregon Research Institute (Behavioral Economics Advisory Committee meeting, 13 November 1984, RSF, New York, RAC). Over the course of the following year more names were added to the list, such as Fisher Black from Goldman Sachs, and Franco Modigliani from the Massachusetts Institute of Technology.

This first list of invited researchers thus comprised all the researchers now familiarly associated with the Sloan and Russell Sage behavioral economics program, and thus with behavioral economics. But it also included a number of scientists who at the end of the first decade of the twenty-first century are not normally associated with this program. For the most part these were researchers who simply never responded to Wanner's invitation, including Slovic, Winter, Nelson, Juster, Dawes, Grether, and Plott. Some were initially more or less engaged, but left later on. Smith, Lichtenstein, and Hogarth, for instance, were among the first to receive a behavioral economics grant in 1986, but later lost interest or received less favorable reception. Furthermore, of the Kahneman and Tversky tandem, it seems that from the start Kahneman was the more active participant in the behavioral economic program. In addition, a peculiar history developed between the new behavioral economic program and Herbert Simon.

After expressing his initial enthusiasm for the new program in a letter to Wanner in December 1984, Simon turned very skeptical during 1985. He concluded rather pessimistically that 'behavioral economics is "largely a promise," but that mainline economists continue to ignore vast bodies of relevant evidence in their preferred pursuit of armchair model building', and hence that there did not seem to be much point in the new Sloan Foundation program (Simon's letter to Wanner, 4 January 1986, RAC). Wanner asked the behavioral economics advisory committee what to do with Simon's arguments and how to respond. Without any apparent prior discussion, the members of the advisory committee[2] were surprisingly unanimous in their response. For instance, Baumol bluntly told Wanner that 'I read the note by my friend Herb Simon with interest, but I disagree with him in this case rather completely' (Baumol's letter to Wanner, 20 January 1986, RAC). Thus, after a conciliatory discussion and drinks with Wanner and the advisory committee, Simon was no longer consulted or invited.

Meanwhile Thaler rapidly moved to the center of the new behavioral economic program. After the first of the behavioral economics grants was given to Thaler in 1984, Wanner and the advisory committee awarded four more grants in 1985, one of them to, again, Thaler (see Heukelom, forthcoming, for details of the Sloan and Russell Sage grants). Moreover, around mid-1985, Wanner and the advisory committee decided to focus the program on anomalies in financial markets, already very much the research topic of Thaler. In the summer of 1985, Wanner sent out invitations for a third behavioral economics meeting on financial anomalies. It was no more than natural that Wanner should appoint Thaler to chair the meeting.

Thus, the core of the behavioral economics program that rose to prominence in the 1990s and 2000s had clearly begun to emerge during 1985. Yet, the program's future was anything but secure. The Sloan Foundation's trustees told Wanner they would provide funds for 1986, but only on the condition that the Foundation's staff would 'stay in fairly close contact with all projects on the 1986 round', that all grantees would agree to occasional 'visits by Foundation staff and/or the program's advisory committee', and would agree to the possible request 'that grantees hold a brief symposium on their work-in-progress'. The year 1986 was important for other reasons as well. Around the middle of that year Wanner left Sloan to become President of the Russell Sage Foundation, which put him in a position to further strengthen the support for behavioral economics. A first step was to involve the Russell Sage Foundation in the behavioral economics program, where the board of trustees after a few rounds of negotiations agreed to a small amount of financial support.

Thus, the behavioral economics program could proceed, now supported by two foundations. As a way of stimulating further progress, in late 1986 Wanner agreed to form three 'interdisciplinary groups': one on 'the psychology of inter-temporal choice and its economic consequences' led by George Loewenstein and Jon Elster; one led by Kahneman and Don Courcey on 'the effects of individual decision biases on experimental markets'; and one 'on behavioral approaches to financial markets', led by Thaler (Wanner's letter to the Behavioral Economics Advisory Committee, 18 February 1987, RAC). It is the research that came out of these three groups that would define much of the behavioral economics research of the 1990s and 2000s.

A second crucial development that involved Thaler was his anomalies columns for the *Journal of Economic Perspectives*. Sometime in 1986 Thaler 'happened to be having dinner with Hal Varian' (email Thaler to author, 14 January 2009), a prospective member of the editorial board of the soon to-be-created *Journal of Economic Perspectives*. As the new journal was intended to address economists in general, rather than specialists in a particular field, Thaler and Varian conceived of the idea of a 'regular feature on Anomalies' (ibid.). Thaler published two series of 'anomalies' columns for the *Journal of Economic Perspectives* that had the sole purpose of proclaiming that economics had serious problems regarding its theory of economic behavior.[3] Thaler's anomalies are prominent examples of behavioral economics research of the 1980s and 1990s. The first series contained 14 anomalies articles and appeared from the first issue of the journal in 1987 through to 1991.[4] The second series contained four publications and appeared between 1995 and 2001. The first anomaly article in 1987 documented 'the January effect'. When the market for stocks is in efficient equilibrium, in the neoclassical world the average monthly return should be equal for each month. There is no reason to expect that stocks would perform better just because it happens to be a certain month. However, this was exactly what was observed in the case of January. Especially for smaller firms stock returns were substantially higher in January compared with other months. How could this January effect be possible, given the theory of efficient markets? The answer was that it was not possible, and that one needed a theory such as Kahneman and Tversky's prospect theory to account for the findings.

Loewenstein and Thaler (1989) then showed that many similar anomalies existed in and outside the economy that have to do with intertemporal choice. For example, people prefer to pay too much tax in advance and receive some back when the year is over instead of the reverse, even when the first option is subject to costs in terms of lost interest. Schoolteachers who can choose between being paid in nine months (September–June) or in twelve (September–August), choose the second option although from a profit-maximizing perspective the first is more rational, they argued. But Loewenstein and Thaler also cited the dermatologist who lamented that her patients were unwilling to avoid the sun when she told them about the risks of skin cancer, but who were quick to stay out of the sun when she told them about the risk of getting 'large pores and blackheads'. This example, Loewenstein and Thaler argued, was also a violation of economic theory because it showed myopia in patients which they should not have if they acted rationally. The implicit reasoning was that economic theory could be applied to every aspect of our lives, and that therefore also violations of economic theory could be drawn from every corner of life.

In 1992, the Russell Sage Foundation's board of trustees no longer accepted the promise of possible future success, and asked Wanner to terminate the program. In an attempt to save something of the program, Wanner sent out letters to close to a hundred economists asking them to evaluate the program. As it happened, the letters were quite positive; positive enough in any case for Wanner to negotiate a compromise with the board of trustees in which the Russell Sage Foundation would continue to endow the program with some money – $100,000 annually – on the condition that the Foundation's staff would no longer be spending any time on it. In response Wanner set up a committee composed of former recipients of behavioral economic grants, and gave them the fancy label of 'behavioral economics roundtable'. Half of the members would be appointed by the board of trustees, while the other half would be elected by the recipients. The newly elected members of the roundtable chose to use the money to organize a bi-annual summer institute to attract young researchers to the field, and to set up a small grants program in which young researchers could receive up to $5000 for a project. This new arrangement worked out quite well. The Russell Sage Foundation's board of trustees wanted to pull out at the very moment when behavioral economics started to gain momentum, but through Wanner's efforts a core group of behavioral economists had been created; a growing number of behavioral economic studies had been published which started to attract the attention of the economic community at large; and a growing number of PhD candidates and other young scholars had chosen behavioral economics as the field of their academic career, among them Matthew Rabin, David Laibson, and Sendhil Mullainathan.

2.4 CONTEMPORARY THEMES

During the 1990s and 2000s, behavioral economists gradually built their program into a stable and well-defined mainstream economic program.

In this process, the main question was how to construct the descriptive theory of human decision behavior. To answer that question, behavioral economists explored a range of different scientific disciplines and methods. At the same time, however, they remained faithful and always came back to the normative–descriptive framework introduced by Savage and Edwards and later amended by Kahneman and Tversky. This conceptual core determined how behavioral economists understood the economic world, it determined the welfare implications they drew, and finally it determined how they pulled back when their explorations diverged too far from this conceptual core. The new terminology of rationality laid the foundation for discussing behavioral economists' new paternalistic stance on economic policy advice which developed from the early 2000s, and the growth of behavioral economics from the mid-1990s onwards led behavioral economists to distinguish themselves more clearly from psychology and experimental economics. Following a steady growth of the program in the 1990s, the big recognition for the field came with the Nobel memorial prize in economics for psychologist Kahneman (Tversky had died in 1996). With Kahneman's Nobel Prize, behavioral economics became a household name in contemporary economics and a prominent program within the broad mainstream of the economic discipline, perhaps best exemplified by the number of behavioral economists purportedly in US President Obama's economic team (Grunwald, 2009). A few themes have come to the fore as behavioral economists' main areas of interest.

2.4.1 Theoretical Developments

The research on intertemporal choice extended Thaler's research on financial anomalies. First, a piece of standard neoclassical economics was examined; in this case the assumption of exponential discounting. Subsequently, it was shown that this piece of the neoclassical theory failed descriptively. In the next step, the piece of neoclassical economics as descriptive theory was adjusted to be compatible again with the empirical facts; in this case the linear exponential discount function was transformed into a hyperbolic discount function. The behavioral economists' way of dealing with intertemporal choice described human behavior as the outcome of two systems or processes striving for dominance (for example Harris and Laibson, 2001; Loewenstein et al., 2001). Some behavioral economists linked this dual system solution to research in neuroscience and neurobiology, thus contributing to the creation of a new sub-field called neuroeconomics (Camerer et al., 2003). This literature maintained the normative–descriptive distinction, but nevertheless slightly reinterpreted the distinction by supposing that the two sides of the distinction represent two sides of human behavior. In other words, the normative was reduced from something external to the individual to one of two faculties innate to human nature that strive for dominance (for example McClure et al., 2004; Kahneman, 2003).[5]

The incorporation of the distinction between the rational norm and its imperfect realization in the economic agent considerably broadened the scope of behavioral economics. However, there seemed to be limits to broadening the scope as well. This can be illustrated by behavioral economists' cooperation with anthropologists on the subject of the emergence of preference. The research was a large-scale interdisciplinary study of the ultimatum game in 15 small-scale societies. It was published in a number of journals. The most extensive discussion can be found in the book devoted to it, Joseph Henrich et al.'s *Foundations of Human Sociality* (2004). In the book, the researchers concluded that differences found in the behavior of individuals belonging to the different societies should be attributed to differences in the environment in which they lived. As a consequence, preferences were not understood as exogenous, but as determined by the environment. Taking this approach and the results of the experiments seriously would imply not only that individual preferences to a large extent are determined by the environment and by learning, but it would also undermine the notion of fixed norms in behavioral decision research and well-defined rationality in economics. It is perhaps due to these extensive implications that in spite of plans to continue the research, follow-up studies and further elaboration of the implications of the experiments by this diverse group of economists and anthropologists to date have not been worked out.

2.4.2 Normative versus Descriptive

As will be evident from the brief history set out above, the normative–descriptive distinction that provided the methodological basis for behavioral economics is clearly at odds with the traditional, ethical definition of normative and descriptive (or positive) in economics. In behavioral economics, the difference between normative and descriptive is the difference between the universal rules of rational decision making provided by mankind's best rational reasoning in mathematics, economics, philosophy and other branches of science, and the empirically grounded theories of how human beings actually go about their decision making.

This new way of conceiving of human behavior and of science's relation to it has had two important implications for economics. First of all, it has turned the traditional conception of economics, and of the relation of economics to the economic world, on its head. Before, neoclassical mainstream economists prided themselves on the positivist understanding of economists as neutral or value-free describers of economic behavior. With the arrival of behavioral economics, they have had to acknowledge that in fact economics does a very bad job at describing economic behavior. But more important, secondly, is that the new methodological basis of behavioral economics implies that economists cannot be value-free observers of economic reality, but have an obligation to help economic actors to behave more in accordance with the principles of the normative theory of full rationality.

In the early 2000s, the concept of bounded rationality was adopted from Simon and together with the concept of full rationality was employed to rephrase Kahneman and Tversky's normative–descriptive distinction. Gradually, what before was understood as the normative decision now became the full rationality decision. Similarly, when the actual decision made by the individual deviated from the full rationality decision, it was now deemed boundedly rational instead of descriptive. In one smooth argument, Kahneman and Tversky's distinction between the concepts of normative–descriptive was replaced by concepts more appropriate in an economic context, and at the same time Simon was appropriated as an authoritative source for the use of these concepts.

Note the ingenuity of this fundamental methodological realignment. In contrast to for instance Simon, Kahneman and Tversky, and later the behavioral economists, did not demand a complete revision of the traditional neoclassical mainstream, but offered it an honorable way out. There is nothing wrong with traditional neoclassical reasoning, they argued. It is just that it is only a theory of how people should behave, not of how they actually behave. There is nothing wrong with neoclassical economics, they argued, it merely needs to be amended. This ingenuous methodological realignment is one key reason for the tremendous success of behavioral economics (Heukelom, 2011c). It is not clear where this position will take behavioral economics and the economic community more generally in the mid to longer term. But in the short run it has at the very least resulted in a behavioral economics which has descended from the ivory tower of general equilibrium theory and constrained utility maximizing to become a more applied and more engaged social science.

2.4.3   Paternalism

Also starting in the early 2000s, the normative–descriptive foundation of behavioral economics has given rise to a new perspective on welfare economics. For instance, behavioral economists discovered that people often save much less for their pensions than they should, and that when they do save, they do not diversify their portfolios optimally. Following on these results, programs have been set up to investigate how people can be induced to save more for retirement and better diversify their stock portfolios (for example Cronqvist and Thaler, 2004; Thaler and Benartzi, 2004). Another example concerns the use of medication. It has often been found that people who need to take drugs on a regular basis are very lax at doing so. Even when the risks are substantial and potential costs in terms of health very great, such as in the case of medication that reduces the chance of having a second stroke, people are very lax at taking their medication properly. To solve this problem, programs have been set up that investigate how insights from behavioral economics can be used to design incentive mechanisms that induce people to take their medication (for example Badger et al., 2007). Finally, behavioral economists have turned their attention to development economics, with the purpose of using insights from behavioral economics to improve the functioning of development programs. It is for instance suggested that being poor is cognitively more difficult than not being poor, because the poor individual constantly has to weigh pros and cons of possible expenditures. As a result, poor individuals may be more susceptible to misleading information and be less cognitively capable of making long-term decisions, simply because of the fact of being poor (see for example Bertrand et al., forthcoming a, b).

Behavioral economists have framed and defended this research in a number of closely related ways. Well-known is Thaler and Sunstein's (2003) 'Libertarian paternalism', in 2008 followed up by *Nudge: Improving Decisions About Health, Wealth, and Happiness* (Thaler and Sunstein, 2008). Libertarian paternalism can be understood as a paternalism that does not restrict individual freedom of choice. Thaler and Sunstein distinguished themselves explicitly from the traditional neoclassical stance towards welfare issues:

> We clearly do not always equate revealed preference with welfare. That is, we emphasize the possibility that in some cases individuals make inferior choices, choices that they would change if they had complete information, unlimited cognitive abilities, and no lack of willpower. (Thaler and Sunstein, 2003, p. 175)

In the behavioral economics paternalism debate, the justification for paternalistic policies has been the fact that the decisions people actually make, their 'revealed preferences', do not always match with their 'true' preferences. Behavioral economists have thus constructed a distinction between 'revealed' and 'true' preferences. However, this does not mean that preferences are context dependent. Rather, it means that it depends on the context and on the individual's willpower whether the true preferences can and will be revealed appropriately.

A more detailed and elaborate explication and defense of this new branch of behavioral economics can be found in Camerer et al. (2003), 'Regulation for Conservatives: Behavioral Economics and the Case for "Asymmetric Paternalism"'. In this article, the five authors (Camerer, Issacharoff, Loewenstein, O'Donoghue, and Rabin) made a case for what they labeled 'asymmetric paternalism', where: '[a] regulation is asymmetrically paternalistic if it creates large benefits for those who make errors, while imposing little or no harm on those who are fully rational' (Camerer et al., 2003, p. 1212). Behavioral economics, then, 'describes ways people sometimes fail to behave in their own best interests' (Camerer et al., 2003, p. 1217). These 'apparent violations of rationality [. . .] can justify the need for paternalistic policies to help people make better decisions and come closer to behaving in their own best interests' (Camerer et al., 2003, p. 1218). The definition of asymmetric paternalism resembles the Paretean improvement argument: 'asymmetric paternalism helps those whose rationality is bounded from making a costly mistake and harms more rational folks very little' (Camerer et al., 2003, p. 1254). Another way of putting it, Camerer et al. argued, is to see the boundedly rational individual as imposing negative externalities on his or her own demand curve. 'When consumers make errors, it is as if they are imposing externalities on themselves because the decisions they make as reflected by their demand do not accurately reflect the benefits they derive' (Camerer et al., 2003, p. 1221). Hence, there is a need for a policy maker who can remove the externalities and redirect behavior in such a way that the externalities disappear. Camerer et al. furthermore noted that firms could either consciously or unconsciously use the irrationality of individuals to gain more profit.

A detailed example has been provided by Grubb (2006), who showed that cellphone companies could permanently increase their profits by using the phenomenon of overconfidence. When consumers systematically underestimate the number of minutes that they will use their cellphones for each month, it is profitable for firms to charge the marginal costs per minute up to the number of minutes that consumers expect they will use their cellphones. After this point, they can greatly increase their rates. Consumers will not mind because they do not expect to be using their phones that much. But the cellphone company knows that the consumers are overconfident, and thus know the customers will use some of these expensive minutes. Thus the cellphone company increases its profit by exploiting consumers' overconfidence. The example shows that firms in the market can use the bounded rationality of individuals and thus not produce efficient outcomes. Moreover, the example shows that it might be more in the interest of companies to maintain or even amplify the bounded rationality of individuals. It suggests that firms are apt to look for ways to increase the irrationality of individuals, and that as a result the market, instead of producing an efficient equilibrium, could even produce greater irrationality. Behavioral economists thus argued that deviations from full rationality not only persist in markets, but that markets can even increase this deviating behavior.

Under the rubric of 'experienced utility', Kahneman and a number of associates have taken the debate on behavioral economics and policy making a step further by arguing for a return to the hedonistic utilitarianism of Jeremy Bentham (for example Kahneman et al., 1997; Kahneman and Sugden, 2005). Such an approach requires a measurement of the individual's perceived pleasure and pain – or happiness or subjective well-being in contemporary terms (for example Kahneman et al., 1999; Edwards, 2010). But while the question how to determine the individual's true preferences remains one of the most salient questions in behavioral economics, most behavioral economists seem reluctant to roam that far into psychological and philosophical territory.

Behavioral economists have attempted to solve mankind's bounded rationality problem by using phenomena similar to those that formed the basis for behavioral economics to begin with. The reason that they could do so was that behavioral economics had remained faithful to Kahneman and Tversky's approach. The most important phenomenon in this regard is what is most commonly known in behavioral economics as framing. One of the central findings of Kahneman and Tversky's behavioral decision research and behavioral economics was that people are susceptible to the way in which a choice is presented to them. Depending on the 'reference point', in Kahneman and Tversky's terms, or 'frame', the term Thaler favored for behavioral economics, people may change their preferences. The example taken from Thaler and Sunstein (2003, 2008) is of the cafeteria manager who can either place the desserts before the fruits or vice versa. If she frames this decision as fruits-before-desserts, the fruit will be chosen more often. Thus, framing is used to influence people's behavior without affecting their freedom to choose in any significant way. Changing the default option from not participating to participating in pension saving schemes is another often-quoted example.

By exploring how policies can be designed to solve the bounded rationality of individuals, behavioral economists have taken the full rationality versus bounded rationality framework (that is, the normative versus descriptive) and the experimental results of psychologists and economists to their ultimate consequences. Behavioral economic paternalism is very much an economics solution to bounded rationality, emphasizing incentive mechanisms and monetary rewards.

2.4.4   Methodological Eclecticism

One should always beware of rhetoric or bending of the truth when scientists provide historical and methodological overviews of their own field. Yet, in describing their field as methodologically eclectic (for example Camerer and Loewenstein, 2004), the behavioral economists are essentially right. Although behavioral economics took its initial inspiration from the laboratory experiments of the behavioral psychologists, economists quickly broadened their methodological toolbox to include analysis of data from a wide range of sources (stock markets, government salary pay-outs, pension saving); field experiments; simulations on the basis of assumptions, experimental outcomes or economic data; and modeling on the basis of the existing mathematical techniques employed by economists. In contrast to experimental economics, behavioral economists have not defined their field in terms of one method. Instead, behavioral economics has always been defined methodologically in terms of the normative–descriptive or full rationality–bounded rationality distinction (see also Heukelom, 2011a).

That said, despite a growing emphasis on mathematical modeling since the mid-1990s, behavioral economics is first of all grounded in empirical research. Where the neoclassical mainstream of the post-war period claimed to be empirically based but in practice often relied only on mathematical reasoning, behavioral economics is first of all an empirical program which employs mathematical modeling mainly to adhere to and not lose contact with its neoclassical heritage.

This eclectic, or perhaps one should say pragmatic, methodology of behavioral economics is not revered by all. A recent biting criticism was provided by Gul and Pesendorfer (2008), who among others firmly rejected all theories and observations below the level of individual choices as irrelevant for economic theorizing, and who urged behavioral economists to retreat from their strong paternalistic and normative claims. However, Gul and Pesendorfer's blunt objections were immediately countered by a number of behavioral economists who, rather than retreating, suggested behavioral economics had not yet advanced far enough (see the contributions to Caplin and Schotter, 2008). It induced Loewenstein and Haisley, for instance, to argue for a new conception of the economist as a therapist who helps people make the rational choices based on their 'true' preferences (Loewenstein and Haisley, 2008).

It will have to be a topic of future research to determine what this all implies for the development of behavioral (and experimental) economics. One possible development is the gradual integration of behavioral and experimental economics. It seems, however, equally possible that the proliferation of the use of methods and theories from other disciplines in behavioral economics at some point will be countered by a desire to define behavioral economics more explicitly as an economic program. But regardless of what happens, that is of course what makes behavioral economics an interesting and rewarding topic of investigation.

2.5   CONCLUDING REMARKS

This chapter has briefly set out how behavioral economics grew out of a branch of psychology called behavioral decision research, what its main methodological characteristics are, and how it relates to and builds upon the dominant neoclassical economics of the post-war decades. In a larger picture one might argue that behavioral economics forms part of an empirical turn in microeconomics that started roughly in the early 1980s and includes, besides behavioral economics, experimental economics, evolutionary economics, neuroeconomics, and happiness and well-being research.

Given the financial and economic crisis of the recent past and a variety of evident behavioral and institutional fallacies, the paternalistic research strand within behavioral economics is likely to receive further attention. One clear indication, for instance, is the interest expressed by US President Obama and his economic advisors in a number of proposals put forth by the behavioral economists (Grunwald, 2009). Much will however depend on the yet-to-be proven efficacy of the paternalistic policies and on the public's support for policies which nudge you in a certain direction without necessarily explaining why you should go there. That is, it remains to be seen how far policy makers and the public are willing to go with policies that are based on the premise 'trust us, we're economists'.

Finally, a reasonable prediction for the near future is that the boundaries between, on the one hand, the different new empirically based microeconomic programs and, on the other hand, the new programs and the traditional neoclassical position on microeconomics will gradually dissolve and that one new mainstream will emerge. Already, it is increasingly difficult to classify economists as only behavioral, experimental or neuroeconomists, with many contributing to two or more fields. In addition, economists within these fields seem increasingly unwilling to define these different fields and the boundaries between them. However, what such a new microeconomic consensus would look like remains to be seen.

NOTES

1. In addition to the sources referred to, this chapter draws on Heukelom (2011a, 2011b, 2011c, forthcoming).
2. The advisory committee consisted of psychologists Leon Festinger and Robert Abelson, and economists Thomas Schelling and William Baumol.
3. Each column had a length of about 4000 words, making it perhaps more a short article than a column.
4. The anomalies of the first series have been collected in *The Winners Curse* (1992).
5. One may wonder how compatible this new neuroeconomic perspective is with the Savage–Edwards and Kahneman–Tversky tradition.

REFERENCES

Non-published Sources

David Krantz – interview with the author, Columbia University, New York, 20 June 2008.
Richard Thaler – email to author, 14 January 2009.
Robert Pachella – interview with the author, University of Michigan, Ann Arbor, 8 April 2009.
Robyn Dawes – interview with the author, Carnegie Mellon University, Pittsburgh, 23 June 2008.
Rockefeller Foundation Archives, Rockefeller Archive Center, Sleepy Hollow, New York (RAC).

Published Sources

Badger, G.J., W.K. Bickel, L.A. Giordano, E.A. Jacobs, G. Loewenstein and L. Marsh (2007), 'Altered States: The Impact of Immediate Craving on the Valuation of Current and Future Opiods', *Journal of Health Economics*, **26**, 865–876.
Bertrand, M., S. Mullainathan and E. Shafir (forthcoming a), 'Behavioral Economics and Marketing in Aid of Decision-Making among the Poor', *Journal of Public Policy and Marketing*.
Bertrand, M., S. Mullainathan and E. Shafir (forthcoming b), 'A Behavioral Economics View of Poverty'.
Camerer, C., S. Issacharoff, G. Loewenstein, T. O'Donoghue and M. Rabin (2003), 'Regulation for Conservatives: Behavioral Economics and the Case for "Asymmetric Paternalism"', *University of Pennsylvania Law Review*, **151**, 1211–1254.
Camerer, C. and G. Loewenstein (2004), 'Behavioral Economics: Past, Present, Future', in C. F. Camerer, G. Loewenstein and M. Rabin (eds), *Advances in Behavioral Economics*, Princeton, NJ: Princeton University Press, pp. 3–52.
Caplin, A. and A. Schotter (eds) (2008), *The Foundations of Positive and Normative Economics: A Handbook*, Oxford: Oxford University Press.
Cronqvist, H. and R. Thaler (2004), 'Design Choices in Privatized Social-Security Systems: Learning from the Swedish Experience', *American Economic Review*, **94**(2), 424–428.
Danziger, K. (1997), *Naming the Mind: How Psychology Found its Language*, London: SAGE Publications.
Edwards, J.M. (2010), 'Joyful Economists: Remarks on the History of Economics and Psychology from the Happiness Studies Perspective', doctoral thesis, Economics Department, Université Paris I Panthéon-Sorbonne, Paris.

Edwards, W. (1954), 'The Theory of Decision Making', *Psychological Bulletin*, **51**, 380–417.
Edwards, W. (1961), 'Behavioral Decision Theory', *Annual Review of Psychology*, **12**, 473–498.
Festinger, L. and D. Katz (eds) (1953), *Research Methods in the Behavioral Sciences*, Fort Worth, TX: Dryden Press.
Friedman, M. (1953), *The Methodology of Positive Economics. Essays in Positive Economics*. Chicago: Chicago University Press.
Friedman, M. and L. Savage (1948), 'The Utility Analysis of Choice Involving Risk', *Journal of Political Economy*, **56**(4), 279–304.
Grubb, M.D. (2006), 'Selling to Overconfident Consumers', Working Paper, Stanford University.
Grunwald, M. (2009), 'How Obama is Using the Science of Change', *Time*, New York. 2 April.
Gul, F. and W. Pesendorfer (2008), 'The Case for Mindless Economics', in A. Caplin and A. Schotter (eds), *The Foundations of Positive and Normative Economics: A Handbook*, Oxford: Oxford University Press, pp. 3–39.
Hands, D.W. (2001), *Reflection without Rules: Economic Methodology and Contemporary Science Theory*, Cambridge: Cambridge University Press.
Harris, C. and D. Laibson (2001), 'Dynamic Choices of Hyperbolic Consumers', *Econometrica*, **69**(4), 935–957.
Henrich, J., R. Boyd, S. Bowles, C. Camerer, E. Fehr, H. Gintis and R. McElreath (2004), *Foundations of Human Sociality: Economic Experiments and Ethnographic Evidence from Fifteen Small-Scale Societies*, Oxford: Oxford University Press.
Heukelom, F. (2011a), 'Building and defining behavioral economics', in J.E. Biddle and R.E. Emmet (eds), *Research in History of Economic Thought and Methodology, Vol. 29*. Bingley, UK: Emerald, pp. 1–30.
Heukelom, F. (2011b), 'What to Conclude from Psychological Experiments: The Contrasting Cases of Experimental and Behavioral Economics', *History of Political Economy*, forthcoming.
Heukelom, F. (2011c), 'Three Explanations for the Kahneman–Tversky Programme of the 1970s', *European Journal of the History of Economic Thought*, forthcoming.
Heukelom, F. (forthcoming), 'A Sense of Mission – The Alfred P. Sloan and Russell Sage Foundations' Behavioral Economics Program, 1984–1992', *Science in Context*.
Jallais, S. and P.-C. Pradier (2005), 'The Allais Paradox and its Immediate Consequences for Expected Utility Theory', in P. Fontaine and R. Leonard (eds), *The Experiment in the History of Economics*, New York: Routledge, pp. 25–49.
Juster, F.T. (2004), 'The Behavioral Study of Economics', in J.S. House, F.T. Juster, R.L. Kahn, H. Schuman and E. Singer (eds), *A Telescope on Society, Survey Research and Social Science at the University of Michigan and Beyond*, Ann Arbor, MI: The University of Michigan Press, pp. 119–130.
Kahneman, D. (2002), 'Autobiography', from http://nobelprize.org/economics/laureates/2002/kahneman-autobio.html.
Kahneman, D. (2003), 'Maps of Bounded Rationality: Psychology for Behavioral Economics', *The American Economic Review*, **93**(5), 1449–1475.
Kahneman, D., E. Diener and N. Schwarz (eds) (1999), *Well-Being, The Foundations of Hedonic Psychology*, New York: Russell Sage Foundation.
Kahneman, D. and R. Sugden (2005), 'Experienced Utility as a Standard of Policy Evaluation', *Environmental & Resource Economics*, **32**, 161–181.
Kahneman, D. and A. Tversky (1979), 'Prospect Theory: An Analysis of Decision under Risk', *Econometrica*, **47**, 313–327.
Kahneman, D., P. Wakker and R. Sarin (1997), 'Back to Bentham? Explorations of Experienced Utility', *The Quarterly Journal of Economics*, **112**(2), 375–405.
Keynes, J.N. (1890), *The Scope and Method of Political Economy*, London: Macmillan.
Loewenstein, G. and E. Haisley (2008), 'The Economist as Therapist: Methodological Ramifications of "Light" Paternalism', in A. Caplin and A. Schotter (eds), *Perspectives on*

the Future of Economics: Positive and Normative Foundations, Oxford: Oxford University Press, 210–245.

Loewenstein, G. and R. Thaler (1989), 'Anomalies: Intertemporal Choice', *Journal of Economic Perspectives*, **3**, 181–193.

Loewenstein, G., E. Weber, C. Hsee and N. Welch (2001), 'Risk as Feelings', *Psychological Bulletin*, **127**, 267–286.

McClure, S.M., D. Laibson, G. Loewenstein and J. D. Cogen (2004), 'Separate Neural Systems Value Immediate and Delayed Monetary Rewards', *Science*, **306**, 503–507.

Mills, J.A. (1998), *Control: A History of Behavioral Psychology*, New York: New York University Press.

Neumann, J. von and O. Morgenstern ([1944] 2004), *Theory of Games and Economic Behavior*, Princeton, NJ: Princeton University Press.

Phillips, L.D. and D. von Winterfeldt (2006), 'Reflections on the Contributions of Ward Edwards to Decision Analysis and Behavioral Research', Working Paper LSEOR 06.86. London, LSE.

Ross, D. (1991), *The Origins of American Social Science*, Cambridge: Cambridge University Press.

Savage, L.J. (1954), *The Foundations of Statistics*, New York: John Wiley & Sons.

Sent, E.-M. (2004), 'Behavioral Economics: How Psychology Made its (Limited) Way Back into Economics', *History of Political Economy*, **36**(4), 735–760.

Simon, H.A. (1959), 'Theories of Decision-Making in Economics and Behavioral Sciences', *American Economic Review*, **49**(1), 253–283.

Simon, H.A. (1986), 'The Behavioral Foundations of Economic Theory', *The Journal of Business*, **59**(4), S209–S224.

Thaler, R. (ed.) (1992), *The Winners Curse : Paradoxes and Anomalies of Economic Life*, New York: Free Press.

Thaler, R.H. and S. Benartzi (2004), 'Save More Tomorrow: Using Behavioral Economics to Increase Employee Saving', *Journal of Political Economy*, **112**, S164–187.

Thaler, R.H. and C.R. Sunstein (2003), 'Libertarian Paternalism', *The American Economic Review*, **93**(2), 175–179.

Thaler, R.H. and C.R. Sunstein (2008), *Nudge: Improving Decisions About Health, Wealth, and Happiness*, New Haven, CT: Yale University Press.

3 Experimental economics
Ana C. Santos[1]

3.1 INTRODUCTION

Not so long ago economics was considered to be a non-experimental science. This generalized perception has marked the experimental field of economics since its early years. In the 1950s, when experiments started to be carried out in a more systematic way, the profession did not see the purpose and the relevance of laboratory experiments. Given the skepticism towards experimentation, the pioneers concentrated on producing a variety of examples of their work before arguing for the relevance and practical usefulness of economics experiments.[2] The strategy paid off. It contributed to the rapid stabilization of the field's aims, standards, benchmarks and techniques, and as a result, to the fast growth of experimental economics research.[3] In the early 1980s experimental economics had already turned into Kuhnian 'normal' science in that researchers had a set of established standards for guiding the selection of problem-situations that could be solved with available conceptual and instrumental tools. In 2002 its official recognition arrived with the award of the Nobel memorial prize to Daniel Kahneman and Vernon Smith for their pioneering experimental work, the former in the study of human judgment and decision-making under uncertainty, and the latter in the study of alternative market mechanisms.[4]

As is often the case with new fields of research, the methodological reflections on the experimental endeavor have lagged behind the rapid growth and the various uses and applications of experimental tools and results. Methodological debate might have been held back by the strong skepticism toward laboratory experimentation in economics. Experimental economists might have felt the need to wait for a more favorable timing to address legitimate criticisms openly and acknowledge the limitations of the experimental method. Whatever their reasons might have been, as experimental economics became an established field of research, concern about the insufficient degree of critical discussion and the premature stabilization of standard practices began to be voiced by experimenters (for example Starmer, 1999; Schram, 2005; Barsley et al., 2010). At the same time experimental economics started to attract the interest of other students of science (for example Guala, 1998, 2002, 2005; Morgan, 2002, 2003, 2005; Mäki, 2005).

The time is now ripe for the methodological study of economics experiments, undoubtedly a fertile subject matter for economic methodology. Unsatisfactorily answered questions still abound on fundamental issues, such as the external validity of economics experiments, that is, the possibility of generalizing laboratory findings to real-world economic phenomena. And new questions have been formulated, stimulated by the application of experimental results to policymaking as experimental findings and tools began to be used in the resolution of practical problems, especially so since the 1980s, with the processes of market deregulation. At first, experiments were used in the design of new market arrangements for a number of sectors in restructuration (McCabe et al., 1989; Plott, 1997; Binmore and Klemperer, 2002); more recently experimental findings have been inspiring the proposal of 'debiasing' policies for assisting consumers in complex decision-making (Jolls et al., 1998). These applications are now becoming popular beyond the discipline's boundaries, fueling new research areas such as the performativity of economics (Callon, 2007).

The present chapter reviews methodological reflections on experimental economics. It examines the defense of experiments as tests of theories within a hypothetico-deductive methodology, most overtly defended by Vernon Smith (1982, 1989, 2002, 2008), and the recent justification of experiments as tools for the exploration of empirical regularities in inductive inquiry by Robert Sugden (2005, 2008) and his colleagues (Bardsley et al., 2010). It shows how methodological reflections in the field have struggled with the external validity issue, which is still considered the most challenging issue of experimental economics. It argues that the ability of economics experiments to provide meaningful knowledge of real-world situations is not best addressed as an external validity issue. And it advocates the analysis of the use of experiments in policymaking as a fruitful topic of research for improving understanding of experimental investigations in economics and, thus, as a research agenda for the methodology of economics.

3.2   THE EARLY METHODOLOGY OF EXPERIMENTAL ECONOMICS

The first methodological reflections in experimental economics (Smith, 1982) had falsificationism, a very popular methodology among economists at the time, as the model of good scientific practice. Falsificationism (Popper, 1959 [1934], 1965 [1963]) provided economists with a framework that could render economics experiments comprehensible to the economics profession as falsifying tools of economic theory. Later, awareness that falsificationism does not provide the most adequate methodology to account for and guide experimental practice has led economists gradually to revise their conception of science. Experimental economists then recognized the difficulties entailed by the Duhem–Quine thesis (Bardsley et al., 2010; Smith, 1989; Smith et al., 1991), namely that the confrontation of theory with evidence is not simply a logical exercise. The test of any theory always involves a test system: a conjoint test of a target hypothesis (that is, the hypothesis derived from theory) together with a variety of auxiliary hypotheses necessary to implement, construct and execute the test. Thus, when experimenters obtain disconfirming data for the hypothesis under test they do not know which hypothesis/hypotheses is/are falsified. This means that a clash between theory and evidence does not have the decisive disproving force suggested by falsificationism. This is especially the case when the theory is well established because scientists will tend to question empirical results instead of the theory itself. By the same token, a confirming test result does not provide definitive support for the target hypothesis, for the positive result may be explained by factors other than the validity of the hypothesis under test.

From falsifying instruments economics experiments then became tools for producing 'extensions in the theory that increase its empirical content' (Smith, 1989, p. 152) within the framework of the Lakatosian methodology of scientific research programs (Lakatos, 1970), the new model of good scientific practice. The more tenable methodology of scientific research programs could better account for the practice of economists, who seldom reject well-established theories on the basis of experimental evidence alone. Lakatos could more easily allow construing experimental economics as a progressive research program. Whatever the results of experiments, the ultimate goal is to increase the theory's empirical content, which can be done either by pushing the edge of the theory's validity when it survives the test, or by modifying the theory in the light of disconfirming evidence.

The conception of economics experiments continued to evolve, however, and in the course of his subsequent methodological reflections, Smith (2002, 2008) integrated into his arguments the actual practices of experimental economists, who generally did not follow any particular set of strict rules. That the philosophy of science has been unable to articulate what Smith calls a 'rational constructivist' methodology capable of guiding scientists, or of explaining what they do, is for him an indication of the failure of the rational constructivist accounts, not of science. According to Smith, if methodology is rational it follows a kind of 'ecological rationality', which 'rightly and inevitably grows out of the rule-governed norms, practices, and conversation that characterize meaningful interactions in the scientific community' (Smith, 2008, p. 284). In other words, rationality in science stems from the collective processes of production and validation of scientific knowledge which establish common practices and guide the critical interactions of the scientists.

Thus, the call for an experimental method for economics has forced Smith to address methodological issues and acquaint himself with ongoing philosophical debates. He eventually followed the naturalistic turn in the philosophy of science, and grounded his arguments on the actual practices whereby economists produce knowledge by experimental means. The focus on the role of experiments as tests of theory forced him to recognize that empirical testing is not merely a logical exercise based on the confrontation of theoretical hypotheses with the hard facts discovered in the laboratories. The construction of test systems and the interpretation of experimental results require evaluative judgments by the community of researchers, based on the practices, norms and evolving institutional rules governing the critical interactions of scientists. In experimental economics, these evaluative judgments lead to the design of new experiments to explore how results are, or are not, influenced by changes in procedures, context, instructions and control protocols. This is in the end what makes experimental economics a rational collective enterprise.[5]

3.3   EXPERIMENTS AS TESTS OF ECONOMIC THEORY

Early methodological reflections focused on the relation between experiment and theory; namely, on how experiments were to provide empirical tests of economic theory (Smith, 1980, 1982; Wilde, 1981; Plott, 1982, 1991).The initial focus on theory testing is understandable given the generalized adoption of the hypothetico-deductive method at the time, which privileged theoretical work, and theoretical work of a particular kind. Theories were to be built deductively from a priori assumptions about, rather than from observations of, human behavior, and have their predictions tested against evidence from the real world (Sugden, 2008; Bardsley et al., 2010, Ch. 4).

The use of experiments as theory tests, as falsifying tests in particular, was justified by the possibility afforded by the laboratory of designing experimental situations that bear closely on theoretical hypotheses, and by the participation of experimental subjects that renders the laboratory 'a far richer and more complex set of circumstances than is parameterized in our theories', thus providing 'ample possibilities for falsifying any theory we might wish to test' (Smith, 1982, p. 936). Smith argued that the participation of experimental subjects renders experiments 'real' systems in the sense that in the laboratory, 'real economic agents exchange real messages through real property right institutions that yield outcomes redeemable in real money' (ibid.). Smith did not spell out how and to what extent the 'reality' of economics experiments enhances the falsifying potential of the experimental system. But underlying his argument seems to be the fact that experimental subjects may behave differently from the behavior postulated by economic theories and thus generate results that disconfirm theoretical predictions (Santos, 2010, Ch.7).

Charles Plott (1991), another prominent experimental economist, introduced the argument that economics experiments are suitable to test general theories. Because general theories depict economies 'found in the wild' by representing their structure and by using 'basic principles intended to have applicability independent of time and location' (p. 905), they must also apply to the laboratory. If the theory fails in these special cases, so it was argued, it also fails in the complex economies found in the wild. On this view, then, the simplified nature of economics experiments reinforces the epistemic weight of negative evidence for general theories. If the theory does not predict well in simple environments, then it should be discarded or modified. However, this argument limits the use of experiments to tests of a particular kind of theory, namely, general theories which ought to apply to the laboratory.

The pioneers of experimental economics provided very general arguments to justify the role of experiments as tests of economic theory. No methodological prescriptions were advanced, except the vague appeal to develop 'extensions in the theory that increase its empirical content' (Smith, 1989, p. 152). This issue has been recently taken up by Robin Cubitt (2005) and his co-authors (Bardsley et al., 2010, Ch. 2).

Cubitt and his co-authors propose a framework to guide economists in the design of experimental tests and assist them in judging the implications of experimental tests for theory. The goals are twofold: to promote laboratory tests by extending the testing conditions for theory; and to promote adequate interaction between experiment and theory by imposing restrictive conditions on admissible responses to disconfirming tests. They take as their starting point Smith's and Plott's arguments – that experiments may closely correlate with theoretical concepts and that (some) theories may be interpreted to be general. And they argue that any laboratory environment in the 'base domain' of an economic theory (defined by the possible phenomena to which application of the theory seems reasonably unambiguous *ex ante*) should be presumed to provide legitimate testing conditions for that theory (for example a theory that refers without quali-fication to markets is held to apply to all markets, including laboratory markets). Laboratory environments are particularly convenient because they can be purposefully designed so as to be in the base domain of rel-evant theories, establishing a direct correspondence between laboratory constructs and the formal concepts of the theory. But the laboratory can no longer be expected to offer adequate test conditions if it differs from the 'intended domain' of the theory (defined by the phenomena to which the theory is deemed to apply for understanding or predicting those phenom-ena) such that conformity of behavior with the theory does not obtain (for example tests of equilibrium predictions that specify equilibrating mecha-nisms, say arbitrage, must implement them, otherwise they fail belonging to the theory's intended domain).

Disconfirming experimental evidence cannot be dismissed by simply pointing out that the laboratory does not belong to the intended domain of the theory. Reasons must be given as to why differences between the laboratory and the intended domain of the theory should be relevant. These reasons must also be suggestive of testable hypotheses. If empiri-cally supported, defenders of a particular theory must accept the resulting contraction of the domain of application. Experimental tests beyond the theory's intended domains are nonetheless encouraged because they allow us better to map and understand the contexts where the theory succeeds and fails.

The justification of experiments as tests of economic theory within hypothetico-deductive frameworks does not tell us about other uses of economic experiments. Even though Smith's and Plott's arguments were part and parcel of the wider discussion about the relevance of economic experiments to provide meaningful knowledge of 'real-world' economies, the focus on theory testing avoided the issues generally labeled as the 'blame-the theory' argument.[6] As long as an experiment aims at testing a theory, or at discriminating between alternative theories, so the argument goes, the experiment does not need to reproduce a concrete situation, and no presumption need be made about its connection to the more complex 'real-world' context. It only needs to be relevant to the theory or theories being tested. Given that an experiment can be at least as 'realistic' as the theory being tested, charges of 'unrealisticness', if empirically grounded, spotlight a failure of the theory which should then be revised (Smith, 1980, 1982).[7]

As experiments have had other uses, experimental economists felt increasing pressure to shift their attention from the relation between experiments and theory to that between experiments and real-world situations.

3.4   ECONOMICS EXPERIMENTS AND THE 'REAL WORLD'

Even though early experiments had theory testing as their stated goal, their results inspired the design of novel experiments to explore the phenomena produced by experimental means. Gradually the discipline started 'to treat experimental observations as part of the material that it is to explain', marking a 'momentous methodological step' in a discipline that has long been a hypothetico-science (Bardsley et al., 2010, p. 167). Economics experiments have in this way acquired a life of their own, generating a list of 'stylized facts', which are now being used as empirical basis for the (re) construction of economic theory.

As mentioned above when referring to theory testing, experimental results are not self-evident. They are often amenable to various, if not conflicting, interpretations. They are particularly controversial when they contradict well-established theories. Experimentalists then check those results that they regard as surprising by designing and conducting further experiments to settle the points of contention. A general pattern can be identified. At first, follow-up experiments investigate whether the experimental phenomenon is to be attributed to an artifact of the experimental procedure. This normally calls for the re-examination of the standard procedures of experimental economics (for example experimenters check instructions for lack of clarity, subjects' inexperience, adequacy of the reward structure, and other conventional sources of 'error').[8] If the phenomenon remains recalcitrant, attention is directed to investigating its causes. Experimentalists then obtain a more precise specification of the phenomenon under scrutiny and of the conditions in which it is more likely to be observed. At a later stage, when the phenomenon is better understood, experimenters try to put forward and test tentative explanatory hypotheses. Earlier results may then be reinterpreted, areas of disagreement narrowed down, and what were apparently conflicting results may eventually be integrated into a more general and complete account. Or, on the contrary, the conditions under which the phenomenon occurs may be more narrowly defined and earlier conclusions may be substantially revised.

Given the profession's initial skepticism toward the use of experiments in economics, and the dominance of the hypothetico-deductive methodology, experimental economists seem to have been reluctant to advance arguments to justify the use of experiments as tools of inductive research (Bardsley et al., 2010). While the use of experiments as tests of theory could be partially justified on the basis of the close correspondence between experimental constructs and theoretical concepts, and also on the possibility of observing disconfirming behavior in the laboratory, the use of experiments as tools for investigating empirical regularities requires addressing two criticisms: the 'simplicity criticism', which targets the simplicity of the laboratory and its failure to capture the complexity of 'real-world' environments; and the 'artificiality criticism', which casts doubt on the possibility of obtaining any meaningful knowledge from the artificial conditions of the laboratory (Santos, 2010, pp. 102–8). This is so because an economics experiment is necessarily a fairly simple and artificial situation, as are other laboratory experiments in the natural or human sciences.

Experiments are used in science precisely because naturally occurring phenomena are either too complex to understand 'in the wild' or do not occur in conditions that allow for close scrutiny. Experimenters have thus to engage in the production of the phenomenon of interest in order to study it under the favorable controlled and artificial conditions of the laboratory, which shields the phenomenon of interest from the interference of factors that may have an effect on it but are not the object of study.

To conduct a controlled experiment in economics is to design and enforce the set of rules that regulate the actions of the participants in the course of the experiment, and the reward structure that induces prescribed monetary value on participants' actions (Smith, 1976, 1982). For instance, in double auction experiments (Smith, 1962, 1964) subjects are randomly assigned the roles of sellers or buyers. Sellers are endowed with a unit of a fictitious commodity and told that they can earn the difference between the price at which that unit is sold and its reservation price (set by the experimenter). Similarly, buyers are told that purchases of this commodity may result in earnings equal to the difference between the reservation price (set by the experimenter) and the actual paid price. Subjects are then asked to engage in multilateral bargaining by orally stating intentions to buy or sell one unit of the commodity to the whole group of traders. Whenever a match is reached, a binding contract is closed for the agreed contract price. The same conditions apply for each subject in every trading period. When the experiment ends, each subject receives the earnings made from trading.

Hence, in an economics experiment, participants are asked to solve fairly simple decision-problems, generally in conditions of anonymity, and are paid on the basis of their performance. Besides defining a salient reward structure capable of inducing economic motives in experimental subjects, economists carefully create fairly neutral and abstract problem-situations to avoid the interference of individuals' subjective perceptions of the context of interaction, and thereby prevent subjects from acting in conformity (or defiance) of whatever they think is the goal of the experiment (for example in the double auction subjects are trading a fictitious good and ignore that the purpose of the experiment is to test the equilibrium prediction of competitive price theory). The practice of deceiving experimental subjects is also banned, to assure subjects that they can trust what they are told, enhancing the efficacy of the experimental instructions. Finally, experimenters give subjects the opportunity to acquaint themselves with the task at hand in advance to make sure that participants fully understand the experiment as intended.

In summary, an economics experiment creates a simple and neutral context of interaction in which subjects guided by induced economic motives make fairly abstract decisions. In real-world contexts, in contrast, human motivations are heterogeneous and may be dependent on the specificity of the situation. The attention that experimenters dedicate to the design of the experiment demonstrates this. An important part of experimental design is to control subjects' motives, which are multiple and often context-dependent.

Besides the simplified tasks and the various controls used to make certain that participants understand the experimental situation as intended, the laboratory differs in a more fundamental way from 'real-world' situations: subjects know that they are taking part in an experiment. This introduces an artificial element that can substantially alter the behavior elicited in the lab. As Nikos Siakantaris (2000, pp. 274–5) put it, the 'laboratory is not a socially neutral context, but is itself an institution with its own formal or informal, explicit or tacit rules', and one distorted by 'the idea of experimenting with humans'.

The pioneer experimentalists acknowledged that economics experiments involve simple contexts. They claimed, as we have seen above, that the simple circumstances of the laboratory are epistemically valuable, providing strong falsifying evidence. If the theory does not predict well there, it will also fail in the more complex real world. But they have dismissed the artificiality criticism straight off by stressing that economics experiments are as real as 'real-world' economies and, hence, the principles of economics that apply to natural contexts also apply to the laboratory:

> [E]conomies created in the laboratories might be very simple relative to those found in nature, but they are just as real. Real people motivated by real money make real decisions, real mistakes and suffer real frustrations and delights because of their real talents and real limitations. Simplicity should not be confused with reality. Since the laboratory economies are real, the general principles and models that exist in the literature should be expected to apply with the same force to these laboratory economies as to those economies found in the field. (Plott, 1991, p. 905)

Clearly, this response does not fully address what is at stake. 'Real' experimental subjects may behave differently in the lab than they do in the field.

Plott's evasive response, however, is rather revealing. There transpires a genuine difficulty in justifying the ability of experimental results to provide understanding of real-world economies. Plott went as far as delimiting the use of experiments to theory testing, stating that the full understanding of the 'simple' laboratory worlds do not allow the extrapolation of their results to more 'complex' cases, and hence: '[e]conomies found in the wild can only be understood by studying them in the wild' (Plott, 1991, p. 918). Smith, however, believed that experimental results may apply to other contexts provided the 'parallelism' precept is satisfied: '(p)ropositions about the behavior of individuals and the performance of institutions that have been tested in laboratory microeconomies apply also to nonlaboratory microeconomies where similar *ceteris paribus* conditions hold' (Smith, 1982, p. 936). But Smith did not elaborate on this any further. Parallelism is an empirical matter that demands investigating whether similar *ceteris paribus* conditions hold.

Notwithstanding the difficulty in responding to the criticisms that challenge the relevance of experiments to provide understanding of real-world situations, experimental economists have de facto used experiments in inductive inquiry. In inductive research, experiments have been depicted as 'exhibits', recording the discovery of interesting phenomenon in a form that other scientists can verify or challenge (Sugden, 2005, 2008; Bardsley et al., 2010).

Experimental economics has recently produced a substantial list of exhibits, most of which have produced surprising results in the light of extant theory, fueling empirical investigations oriented toward further understanding the discovered regularities. The most famous exhibits include the common ration effect, preference reversals, the endowment effect, the ultimatum game, and the public goods game, which have all inspired theoretical developments that attempt to account for observed behavior. 'Prospect theory' (Kahneman and Tversky, 1979), for example, explains the endowment effect (overvaluation of the goods one possesses) in terms of people's aversion to losses. The 'theory of fairness, competition and cooperation' (Fehr and Schmidt, 1999), to give another example, explains pro-social behavior observed in the ultimatum game and the public goods game in terms of people's tendency to reciprocate. It is thus in this way that exhibits are taken to invert the relationship between experiment and theory, where theory is built inductively from evidence.

But a careful justification for the use of experiments in inductive science is still missing. We have seen that the pioneers evaded the criticisms that pointed to differences between the lab and the contexts to which experimental results could potentially apply. More recently, the concerns entailed by these criticisms have been recognized and closely scrutinized by a younger generation of experimental economists (Starmer, 1999; Bardsley, 2005; Schram, 2005; Bardsley et al., 2010). However, no argument has yet been offered to justify the ability of economics experiments to provide meaningful knowledge of real-world situations, and thus the use of economics experiments in inductive inquiry.[9] As I will explain below, part of the difficulty of coming up with such an articulated argument may be found in the framing of the relation between experiment and the real world as the issue of 'external validity'.

3.5   THE EXTERNAL VALIDITY OF ECONOMICS EXPERIMENTS

The generalization of experimental findings is the most challenging methodological issue experimenters confront. It requires justifying the possibility of obtaining meaningful knowledge about human behavior and socio-economic institutions from the simple and artificial circumstances of the laboratory.

In methodological discussions, the possibility of generalizing experimental findings has been addressed as an empirical issue, one that requires assessing the external validity of economics experiments, that is, determining whether the internally valid inferences obtained from a given experiment apply outside the laboratory (Guala, 1998, 2002, 2005). In particular, it requires adducing experimental and field evidence to evaluate whether the similar observed features of the experimental system and its target (the concrete situation in the real world to which experimental findings allegedly apply) are generated by similar data-generating processes. The mere observation of the same outcomes does not suffice to demonstrate external validity because the same data may be generated by different causal processes.

Given the controls required to obtain internally valid inferences, which ultimately account for the simplicity and artificiality of experiments, it comes as no surprise that the 'safest way' to obtain externally valid inferences is by 'exporting the lab' to real-world contexts (Guala, 2005, pp. 187–9). That is, confidence that the 'artificial' experimental results can be brought to bear on 'real' economic phenomena is best achieved (when the experiment can be recreated outside the laboratory world) by the possibility of implementing in the real world the experimental socio-economic situation. Insofar as it is only under the controlled conditions of the laboratory that experimenters achieve internally valid inferences, which must be obtained before exporting them to the outside world, it should also be under fairly controlled conditions that the same results are observed elsewhere. Thus, mere analysis of the experimental method suggests that the target system must also be a reasonably controlled system so that experimental results apply therein, and hence that the same observed outcomes are generated by the same data generating process.

The illustrations used when discussing the external validity of economics experiments indeed refer to observed regularities that occur in fairly circumscribed environments, namely auctions, which experimenters have designed and tested in the lab and then carefully implemented in the field so as to ensure that the same or similar outcomes occurred outside the laboratory (for example the FCC auction, see Guala, 2001). This suggests not only that external validity claims are inferences from experimental systems to similar targets, but also that achieving external validity is a complex engineering endeavor. It requires intervening both in the target and in the experimental systems to make them resemble each other. The external validity of experimental results is hence a local and context-specific achievement, which explains why the record of externally valid inferences is rather low.

Not surprisingly, this state of affairs has been met with apprehension. While the growing documentation of empirical regularities is adding to the 'library of phenomena' of experimental economics, their relevance, so it is claimed, still awaits demonstration in concrete applications (Guala, 2005, pp. 229–30). Concerns thus build up that experimentalists are not moving beyond their created worlds (Schram, 2005).

But rather than indulging in the exploration of created worlds, the difficulty of obtaining externally valid inferences might indicate that the concepts of internal and external validity do not capture all types of inference that economists can obtain from experiments, or that external validity is not the sole criterion to evaluate the ability of economic experiments to provide knowledge of economic behavior and socio-economic institutions.

3.6   THE PRACTICAL RELEVANCE OF ECONOMICS EXPERIMENTS

Regardless of the intended goals of experiments, economists obtain stable empirical regularities with them, which they then try to understand and explain. Based on this accumulated knowledge, theories have been developed and policy recommendations have been drawn from, and applied to, real-world situations. That is, economics experiments have been considered relevant to understanding and intervening in real-world situations. The analysis of theoretical developments inspired by experimental research and their policy implications thus seems to constitute a fruitful enterprise for developing arguments that justify the relevance of experiments in economics.

In order to show this, I now draw on the epistemic distinction between two kinds of economics experiments – technological and behavioral experiments – according to the content of the knowledge claims that can be derived from them (Santos, 2007, 2010).

3.6.1 Technological Experiments

Technological experiments produce knowledge claims about microeconomic institutions (Santos, 2007, 2010); falling within this category are most market experiments in the subfields of industrial organization, asset markets and auctions (Kagel and Roth, 1995) that investigate the institutional characteristics of particular industries, special markets, or the transaction of commodities with singular properties.

Smith (1962) launched this research program with his first double auction experiments, aimed at testing competitive price theory. Because this required specifying the process rules and procedures of the market mechanism, which were left unspecified in economic theory, it called Smith's attention to the importance of market rules to both individual behavior and market performance. In short, it made Smith acknowledge that 'institutions matter'. Experimental economists have been particularly interested in studying the incentive-compatibility of market mechanisms (Smith, 1982), that is, whether the set of market rules lead each economic agent to choose the action that is the best utility-maximizing response to the other agents' actions, and whether a social optimum obtains in the sense that no one can increase his utility without decreasing that of others (in other words, if the market is capable of generating a Nash equilibrium whose outcomes are Pareto optima).

Technological experiments have since produced a vast list of stylized facts regarding various mechanisms and their respective performances (for example Holt, 1995). They have also been used as engineering tools for building new markets from scratch. That is, they have been used for building 'economic machines' which 'are supposed to work for several years, in different contexts and without constant supervision of their manufacturer' (Guala, 2001, p. 464) or 'testbeds' of 'a working prototype of a process that is going to be employed in a complex environment' (Plott, 1997, p. 605). In sum, this strand of research has turned experiments into engineering tools for economic design (Roth, 2002; Santos and Rodrigues, 2009). This is in fact what explains the label attributed to this category of experiments.

It is clear from the various accounts of the applications of technological experiments that the success of mechanism design depends on the possibility of controlling the actions of market participants. It depends on the feasibility of designing and testing in the laboratory market mechanisms which, when implemented in the economy, tame the actions of economic agents such that the desirable outcomes produced in the lab are also observed in the real economic situation. This is a complex and difficult engineering endeavor. While experimenters can achieve a high level of control in the lab, this control is very difficult to obtain outside of the laboratory. This is why it is extremely difficult that the inferences obtained in laboratory worlds are also valid in the economy.

As Smith (2008, p. 129) describes, mechanism design is a 'rational constructivist' exercise, one that begins with a theoretically 'optimal' design that applies reason to both individuals and the rule system. These proposed mechanisms are not 'ecologically fit' because not all relevant factors can be taken into account in abstract modeling. Nor can they be identified in experimental testbeds. In implementation, unconsidered and unaccounted factors interfere, calling for a 'rule fix', to introduce further constraints on individual behavior. This may then give rise to unexpected problems demanding a new cycle of rule adjustment.

Part of the difficulty of mechanism design in generating ecologically fit institutions lies in the fact that it concentrates on the 'technical' issues, namely those pertaining to the incentive structure and the strategic nature of the problem-situation (Roth, 2002; Chen and Ledyard, 2010), thus overlooking the political nature of the process of (re)building new socio-economic institutions. The Federal Communications Commission (FCC) auctions, for example, aimed to organize the decisions of economic agents in particular ways (by promoting the revelation of bidders' true valuations) while controlling for anticipated undesirable actions on their part (for example collusive behavior). The failures later identified indicate that control was not complete. The regulator could not fully control the influence of big companies on the building of the auction and during its operation after it was implemented. As a result, the licenses for the use of the airwave spectrum were acquired at lower prices than expected, and the market became more concentrated in the hands of a few large corporations (see Santos and Rodrigues, 2009 and the references therein). The higher the stakes, the more the (re)creation of a new market will give rise to an intense struggle for influence over the collective definition of the new market rules. The final outcome will be uncertain and will depend on the political power of those involved and their capacity to bring forward their favored solutions.

3.6.2   Behavioral Experiments

Behavioural experiments produce knowledge claims about human behavior (Santos, 2007, 2010). Within this category of experiments fall individual decision-making and game theory experiments (Kagel and Roth, 1995) that have studied individual preferences, the processes by which people select and apply rules, strategies or social norms for dealing with particular individual and collective problems, and how these decisions are influenced by the overall context of social interaction. Behavioral experiments have in fact contributed to the establishment of the field of behavioral economics, which grew with the accumulation of results from other empirical inquiries, and from other disciplines, namely from cognitive and social psychology (Camerer and Loewenstein, 2004).

Behavioral experiments have been prolific in generating so-called 'anomalies', that is, patterns of judgment and choice that are inconsistent with the traditional model of utility maximization and challenge the neoclassical assumptions of unbounded rationality, unbounded self-interest and unbounded willpower.[10] Economists have since introduced amendments to standard rational choice theory so as to account for some types of anomalous behavior: for example, by introducing revisions to the axioms of expected utility theory, making rationality demands less stringent (for example Loomes and Sugden, 1982), or by introducing other-regarding motives in individual utility functions (for example Fehr and Schmidt, 1999).

These observations have been explained in various ways. Whichever is the privileged interpretation, there is the general sense that the proposed explanation accounts for human behavior both in and outside the laboratory. The observation of reciprocity – cooperative and retaliatory costly responses in social interactions that yield neither present nor future material rewards (in the ultimatum, the gift exchange and in the public good games) – has inspired the construction of behavioral models that are taken to apply to real-world behavior (for example Rabin, 1993; Fehr and Schmidt, 1999; Fehr and Gächter, 2000). Cooperative behavior observed in public goods experiments, to give an example, is taken to have improved our understanding of collective action problems, showing how cooperation depends on the formation of shared beliefs about the appropriate behavior in concrete circumstances and the presence of informal mechanisms of reward and punishment that enforce prescribed behavior. The relevance of these experiments is deemed to lie in: 'the analytical structure of the public good problem [which] is a good approximation to the question of how social norms are established and maintained' (Fehr and Gächter, 2000, p. 166). Even though these results are not used to account for any particular concrete socio-economic situation, they are taken to illuminate the class of situations where individuals may be willing and able to reward or punish the actions of others. This is not to say that these findings cannot provide fruitful insights for understanding concrete situations. The point is instead that their relevance does not depend on assessing whether the internally valid inferences obtained in these games also apply to concrete real-world situations.

In fact, given the difficulty of obtaining or demonstrating external validity, experimental findings might, in fact, be insightful precisely when it is not easy (or not relevant) to disentangle the actual causal factors in operation in the messier real-world situations. For instance, even though the downward rigidity of nominal wages might be explained by various factors, the reciprocal behavior observed in the experimental games has shed light on understanding the resistance of employers to reducing wages in periods of recession from fear of retaliation on the part of the workers (Fehr and Gächter, 2000).

To give another example, experiments on individual decision-making have shown that people are prone to mistakes when facing particularly difficult and complex decision-problems, such as intertemporal choices. Under these circumstances, people struggle to process relevant information accurately, or having processed it correctly, they may fail to act on it due to self-control problems. These results have inspired the behavioral approach to law and economics that aims to replace the standard rational choice approach in the economic analysis of law (Jolls et al., 1998), revealing that economists and legal scholars believe that the results obtained in the artificial conditions of the laboratory provide understanding of human behavior that is of practical relevance, namely, 'to improve the law's ability to move society toward desired outcomes' (ibid., p. 1522). In more recent years the same researchers have proposed so-called 'soft paternalistic' approaches to individual decision-making (Camerer et al., 2003; Thaler and Sunstein, 2003, 2008), devoted to helping people make choices more in line with maximizing behavior, while avoiding as much as possible causing harm to those who behave rationally. Again, these uses of experiments have not been supported by demonstrations of external validity. In fact, the experimental results are mobilized in the proposal of policies that attempt to prevent undesirable behaviors in situations where people may be prone to make decisions that they later regret (for example overconsumption). In these cases, the relevance of experiments lies in the possibility of understanding the contexts and circumstances that render people particularly prone to unreflective and careless decision-making, say by making more salient to them the costs of their choices (for example in terms of the interest rates on credit cards).

This brief exposition of recent applications of experimental results in policymaking testifies to the relevance of economics experiments, both technological and behavioral. The potential of technological experiments relies on the possibility of designing market rules that attempt to organize individual actions so as to bring about socially desirable outcomes. The potential of behavioral experiments is more subtle. They too aim at directing human behavior toward desirable directions. However, they allow a higher degree of individual choice. Rather than constraining the range of options available to economic agents, desirable behaviors are promoted by improving the access to and the processing of relevant information, helping individuals to make choices more aligned with their preferences; or by eliciting important values or social norms, and thereby triggering informal mechanisms of social rewarding and punishment. The effectiveness of these proposals hence depends on how they are tailored to people's psychological and sociological make-up rather than on their capacity to constrain undesirable behaviors.

To conclude, the use of experimental findings in policymaking supports the relevance of experimental claims to knowledge even though they may fall short of the external validity condition. They also show that external validity might be too high a standard to apply to experimentation in the social sciences. This is not to say that the concerns evoked in discussions about the simplicity and artificiality of experimental environments are not important. The point is that external validity is not the only criterion to assess the relevance of economics experiments.

3.7   CONCLUDING REMARKS

This chapter has reviewed methodological reflection in experimental economics. It shows that the long-held view that economics is a non-experimental science conditioned the development of experimental economics. Economists first presented experiments within a hypothetic-deductive methodological framework, in which experiments were to provide empirical tests of economic theories. This justification allowed economists to evade the more complex issue of how the simple and artificial conditions of the laboratory can provide understanding of the real world. But experiments gained a life of their own. Experimental economists gradually began to conduct experiments to explore their laboratory worlds. The more they did so, the more they felt pressured to address the external validity of economics experiments, which has been taken as the most challenging methodological issue of experimental economics.

Experimental economists still build on the distinction between the purposes of experiments in their deductive and inductive enterprises. In deductive inquiry, experiments dialogue with theory, making it possible to define and circumscribe more precisely the domain of application of economic theory. In inductive research, experiments must establish a more direct relation to real-world environments. But economics experiments will hardly fulfill conditions of external validity defined by the generalization of the internally valid laboratory inferences to non-laboratory environments. An economics experiment is a controlled socio-economic system that isolates particularly interesting causal relations for scientific research. The results obtained in these environments will apply to equally controlled and isolated systems. Yet experimental economists insist that more research should be devoted to improve the external validity of economics experiments, suggesting that this can be done by forging a more direct resemblance between the laboratory and real-world situations.

The low external validity of economics experiments is an inescapable feature of experimentation. But from this it does not follow that experimental findings do not provide meaningful knowledge. The applications of experimental findings in policymaking deny that. While these applications do not seem particularly encouraging to the external validity aspirations of experimental economics, they may suggest alternative criteria that better justify and assess the relevance of economics experiments. The study of the uses of experiments in policymaking thus constitutes a fruitful topic of research for improving understanding of experimental investigations in economics, and thus, a relevant research agenda for the methodology of economics.

NOTES

1. I am grateful for the helpful comments and suggestions of John B. Davis, D. Wade Hands and Caterina Marchionni. The usual disclaimers apply.
2. For a first-hand account of this resistance see Smith (1982, 1991, 1992).
3. Smith's (1976, 1982) methodological papers have played a great part in fixing the main tenets of experimental economics.
4. The rapid growth of experimental economics is well documented by its gradual institutionalization, namely with the foundation in 1986 of its official association, the Economic Science Association, the launch in 1998 of its specialized journal *Experimental Economics* and, since the mid-1990s, the regular publication of experimental economics textbooks, handbooks and various compilations of seminal work (for example Davis and Holt, 1993; Friedman and Sunder, 1994; Kagel and Roth, 1995). At present we may discern a qualitative change in the expansion of experimental research with the emergence of specialized subfields (for example experimental labour economics; experimental microeconomics, see Durlauf and Blume, 2010), and the

participation of experimental methods in interdisciplinary investigations (for example neuroeconomics, see Camerer et al., 2005).

5. Santos (2010) offers an account of experimental economics along this line, highlighting the epistemic value of the collective processes of knowledge production, namely its role in the identification and test of the effect of consciously and unconsciously held beliefs and the arbitrariness of decisions taken in the course of experimental practice. It pays equal attention to economists' practical engagements with their objects of study, and in particular, to the participation of human subjects in experiments.

6. To be discussed below.

7. The complete argument is as follows: 'Experiments are sometimes criticized for not being "realistic" . . . There are two appropriate responses to this criticism: First, if the purpose of the experiment is to test a theory, are the elements of alleged unrealism in the experiment parameters of the theory? If not, then the criticism must be directed to the theory as much as to the experiment. Laboratory experiments are normally as "rich" as the theories they test. Second, are there field data to support criticism, i.e. data suggesting that there may be differences between laboratory and field behavior. If not, then the criticism is pure speculation; if so, then it is important to parameterize the theory to include the behavior in question' (Smith, 1980, p. 350).

8. To be developed below.

9. Such attempts have, however, been made by non-experimentalists, highlighting the materiality of economics experiments. Francesco Guala (2005, p. 214), for instance, takes experiments to be epistemically superior to simulations because laboratory systems are made of the same 'stuff' of their real-world counterparts. Hence, whereas the correspondence relation between the experiment and the relevant real world situation 'holds at a 'deep', 'material' level', in simulations, 'the similarity is admittedly only abstract and formal' (see also Guala, 1998, 2002; Morgan, 2002, 2003, 2005; Santos, 2007, 2010).

10. Richard Thaler has had an important role introducing these results to economists in the column 'anomalies' of the *Journal of Economic Perspectives*, from 1987 to 1990. Thaler's (1992) *The Winner's Curse: Paradoxes and Anomalies of Economic Life*, collects some of these experimental results. See also Camerer (1995).

REFERENCES

Bardsley, N. (2005), 'Experimental Economics and the Artificiality of Alteration', *Journal of Economic Methodology*, **12**, 239–251.

Bardsley, N., R. Cubitt, G. Loomes, P. Moffat, C. Starmer and R. Sugden (2010), *Experimental Economics: Rethinking the Rules*, Princeton, NJ: Princeton University Press.

Binmore, K. and P. Klemperer (2002), 'The Biggest Auction Ever: The Sale of the British 3G Telecom Licenses', *Economic Journal*, **112**, C74–C96.

Callon, M. (2007), 'What Does it Mean to Say that Economics is Performative?', in D. MacKenzie, F. Muniesa and L. Siu (eds), *Do Economists Make Markets? On the Performativity of Economics*, Princeton, NJ: Princeton University Press, pp. 311–357.

Camerer, C.F. (1995), 'Individual Decision Making', in J.H. Kagel and A.E. Roth (eds), *The Handbook of Experimental Economics*, Princeton, NJ: Princeton University Press, pp. 587–703.

Camerer, C.F., S. Issacharof, G. Loewenstein, T. O'Donoghue, and M. Rabin (2003), 'Regulation for Conservatives: Behavioral Economics and the Case for Asymmetric Paternalism', *University of Pennsylvania Law Review*, **151**, 1211–1254.

Camerer, C.F. and G. Loewenstein (2004), 'Behavioral Economics: Past, Present, Future', in C.F. Camerer, G. Loewenstein and M. Rabin (eds) *Advances in Behavioral Economics*, Princeton, NJ, USA and Oxford, UK: Princeton University Press, pp. 3–51.

Camerer, C.F., G. Loewenstein and D. Prelec (2005), 'Neuroeconomics: How Neuroscience can Inform Economics', *Journal of Economic Literature*, **43**, 9–64.

Chen, Y. and J.O. Ledyard (2010), 'Mechanism Design Experiments', in S.N. Durlauf and L.E. Blume (eds), *Behavioural and Experimental Economics*, New York: Palgrave Macmillan, pp. 191–205.

Cubitt, R. (2005), 'Experiments and the Domain of Economic Theory', *Journal of Economic Methodology*, **12**, 197–210.

Davis, D. and C. Holt (1993), *Experimental Economics*, Princeton, NJ: Princeton University Press.

Durlauf, S.N. and L.E. Blume (2010), *Behavioural and Experimental Economics*, New York: Palgrave Macmillan.

Fehr, E. and S. Gächter (2000), 'Fairness and Retaliation: The Economics of Reciprocity', *Journal of Economic Perspectives*, **14**, 159–181.

Fehr, E. and K.M. Schmidt (1999), 'A Theory of Fairness, Competition, and Cooperation', *Quarterly Journal of Economics*, **114**, 817–868.

Friedman, D. and S. Sunder (1994), *Experimental Methods*, Cambridge: Cambridge University Press.

Guala, F. (1998), 'Experiments as Mediators in the Non-laboratory Sciences', *Philosophica*, **62**, 901–918.

Guala, F. (2001), 'Building Economic Machines: The FCC Auctions', *Studies in History and Philosophy of Science*, **32**, 453–477.

Guala, F. (2002), 'Models, Simulations, and Experiments', in L. Magnani and N.J. Nersessian (eds), *Model-Based Reasoning: Science, Technology, Values*, New York: Kluwer, pp. 59–74.

Guala, F. (2005), *The Methodology of Experimental Economics*, New York: Cambridge University Press.

Holt, C.A. (1995), 'Industrial Organization: A Survey of Laboratory Research', in J.H. Kagel and A.E. Roth (eds), *The Handbook of Experimental Economics*, Princeton, NJ: Princeton University Press, pp. 349–443.

Jolls, C., C.R. Sunstein and R.H. Thaler (1998), 'A Behavioral Approach to Law and Economics', *Stanford Law Review*, **50**, 1471–1550.

Kagel, J.H. and A.E. Roth (eds) (1995), *The Handbook of Experimental Economics*, Princeton, NJ: Princeton University Press.

Kahneman, D. and A. Tversky (1979), 'Prospect Theory: An Analysis of Decision Under Risk', *Econometrica*, **47**, 263–291.

Lakatos, I. (1970), 'Falsification and the Methodology of Scientific Research Programmes', in I. Lakatos and A. Musgrave (eds), *Criticism and the Growth of Knowledge*, Cambridge: Cambridge University Press, pp. 91–196.

Loomes, G. and R. Sugden (1982), 'Regret Theory: An Alternative Theory of Rational Choice under Uncertainty', *Economic Journal*, **92**, 805–824.

Mäki, U. (2005), 'Models are Experiments, Experiments are Models', *Journal of Economic Methodology*, **12**, 303–315.

McCabe, K., S.J. Rassenti and V.L. Smith (1989), 'Designing 'Smart' Computer-Assisted Markets: An Experimental Auction for Gas Networks', *European Journal of Political Economy*, **5**, 259–283.

Morgan, M. (2002), 'Model Experiments and Models in Experiments', in L. Magnani and N.J. Nersessian (eds), *Model-Based Reasoning: Science, Technology, Values*, Dordrecht: Kluwer, pp. 41–58.

Morgan, M. (2003), 'Experiments without Material Intervention: Model Experiments, Virtual experiments and Virtually Experiments', in H. Radder (ed.), *The Philosophy of Scientific Experimentation*, Pittsburgh, PA: University of Pittsburgh Press, pp. 216–235.

Morgan, M. (2005), 'Experiments versus Models: New Phenomena, Inference and Surprise', *Journal of Economic Methodology*, **12**, 317–329.

Plott, C.R. (1982), 'Industrial Organization Theory and Experimental Economics', *Journal of Economic Literature*, **20**, 1485–1527.

Plott, C.R. (1991), 'Will Economics Become an Experimental Science?', *Southern Economic Journal*, **57**, 901–919.

Plott, C.R. (1997), 'Laboratory Experimental Testbeds: Application to the PCS Auction', *Journal of Economics and Management Strategy*, **6**, 605–638.

Popper, R.K. (1959), *The Logic of Scientific Discovery*, New York: Basic Books (translation of Popper, 1934).

Popper, R.K. (1965 [1963]), *Conjectures and Refutations*, 2nd edn, New York: Harper and Row.

Rabin, M. (1993), 'Incorporating Fairness into Game Theory and Economics', *American Economic Review*, **83**, 1281–1302.

Roth, A.E. (2002), 'The Economist as Engineer: game theory, experimentation, and computation as tools for Design Economics', *Econometrica*, **70**, 1341–1378.

Santos, A.C. (2007), 'The 'Materials' of Experimental Economics: technological versus behavioral experiments', *Journal of Economic Methodology*, **14**, 311–337.

Santos, A.C. (2010), *The Social Epistemology of Experimental Economics*, London: Routledge.

Santos, A.C. and J. Rodrigues (2009), 'Economics as Social Engineering? Questioning the Performativity Thesis', *Cambridge Journal of Economics*, **33**, 985–1000.

Schram, A. (2005), 'Artificiality: The Tension Between Internal and External Validity in Economics Experiments', *Journal of Economic Methodology*, **12**, 225–237.

Siakantaris, N. (2000), 'Experimental Economics under the Microscope', *Cambridge Journal of Economics*, **24**, 267–281.

Smith, V.L. (1962), 'An Experimental Study of Competitive Market Behaviour', *Journal of Political Economy*, **70**, 322–323.

Smith, V.L. (1964), 'Effect of Market Organization on Competitive Equilibrium', *Quarterly Journal of Economics*, **78**, 181–201.

Smith, V.L. (1976), 'Experimental Economics: Induced Value Theory', *American Economic Review*, **66**, 274–279.

Smith, V.L. (1980), 'Relevance of Laboratory Experiments to Testing Resource Allocation Theory', in J. Kmenta and J.B. Ramsey (eds) *Evaluation of Econometric Models*, New York: Academic Press, pp. 345–377.

Smith, V.L. (1982), 'Microeconomic Systems as an Experimental Science', *American Economic Review*, **72**, 923–955.

Smith, V.L. (1989), 'Theory, Experiment and Economics', *Journal of Economic Perspectives*, **3**, 151–69.

Smith, V.L. (1991), 'Experimental Economics at Purdue', in Vernon L. Smith (ed.), *Papers in Experimental Economics*, Cambridge: Cambridge University Press, pp. 369–373.

Smith, V.L. (1992), 'Game Theory and Experimental Economics: Beginnings and Early Influences', in E.R. Weintraub (ed.), *Toward a History of Game Theory*, Annual Supplement to Vol. 24, *History of Political Economy*, Durham, NC: Duke University Press, pp. 241–282.

Smith, V.L. (2002), 'Method in Experiment: Rhetoric and Reality', *Experimental Economics*, **5**, 91–110.

Smith, V.L. (2008), *Rationality in Economics: Constructivist and Ecological Forms*, Cambridge: Cambridge University Press.

Smith, V.L., K. McCabe and S. Rassenti (1991), 'Lakatos and Experimental Economics', in N. de Marchi and M. Blaug (eds), *Appraising Economic Theories*, Aldershot, UK and Brookfield, VT, USA: Edward Elgar, pp. 197–226.

Starmer, C. (1999), 'Experiments in Economics: Should we Trust the Dismal Scientists in White Coats?', *Journal of Economic Methodology*, **6**, 1–30.

Sugden, R. (2005), 'Experiments as Exhibits and Experiments as Tests', *Journal of Economic Methodology*, **12**, 291–302.

Sugden, R. (2008), 'The Changing Relationship between Theory and Experiment in Economics', *Philosophy of Science*, **75**, 621–632.

Thaler, R. (1992), *The Winner's Curse: Paradoxes and Anomalies of Economic Life*, Princeton, NJ: Princeton University Press.

Thaler, R.H. and C. Sunstein (2003), 'Libertarian Paternalism', *American Economics Review*, **93**, 175–179.

Thaler, R.H. and C.R. Sunstein (2008), *Nudge: Improving Decisions About Health, Wealth, and Happiness*, New Haven, CT and London, UK: Yale University Press.
Wilde, L.L. (1981), 'On the Use of Laboratory Experiments in Economics', in J.C. Pitt (ed.), *The Philosophy of Economics*, Dordrecht: Reidel, pp. 137–148.

4 Neuroeconomics and economic methodology

Don Ross

4.1 INTRODUCTION

Paul Zak, a leading researcher among self-described neuroeconomists, declares without qualification that 'economic decisions are made in the brain', and 'the brain is an economic system' (2008, p. 301). These propositions can usefully be regarded as the two basic operative assumptions that drive the subdiscipline of neuroeconomics. As I will show in the present chapter, the relationship between them, and the empirical research programs that they underwrite, are more complicated than is generally appreciated. Many commentators take it to be self-evident that economic decisions are made in the brain. Zak signals this view when he adds '(not the toe or elbow)' after the first quoted remark above. However, I will argue that on its most interesting interpretation, the claim is a contingent empirical one that might or might not be true; the second foundational assumption, I will maintain, looks safer and may better underwrite a distinctive and fecund research program.

Neuroeconomics as a sociological phenomenon arises from three distinct intellectual currents: computational learning theory, behavioral economics and functional neuroanatomy. Most current neuroeconomic research emphasizes only one or two of these influences, and in that way the subfield remains disunified. I will organize the coming discussion in terms of the first two of these distinguishable threads, weaving the third through both of the others. At the end, I will assess prospects for stronger synthesis.

Because of this organization, my methodological survey of neuroeconomic research will be out of chronological order. The historically earliest – and, I will argue, strongest and most promising – roots of neuroeconomics lie in computational learning theory. However, the prominence of neuroeconomics is mainly attributable to its links with behavioral economics. Many economists may indeed be familiar with neuroeconomics only through this link. I therefore begin with it.

4.2 BEHAVIORAL ECONOMICS IN THE NEUROIMAGING SCANNER

The first generation of marginalist economists, especially including Jevons and Edgeworth, expected psychologists eventually to provide direct observational foundations for their basic assumptions, in particular for the decreasing marginal utility of a consumption commodity. Jevons the engineer presumed that technologies would someday be developed that would allow observations of working brains, and so he would not have been surprised by the invention of the modern methods of neuroimaging and recording. He would have encouraged the use of these technologies to search for substantiation of the core principles of economics, and he would have been confident in the success of this search.

However, other founders of the neoclassical tradition developed microeconomics in a direction leading away from, rather than into, the brain. Three milestones in this process are most noteworthy. First, following Wicksteed's lead, all forms of value were generalized by reference to an abstract concept of utility. Second, Pareto, Fisher and Hicks led the recognition that downward-sloping compensated demand need not be grounded in a psychological principle of diminishing marginal satisfaction, but can be derived simply from consequences of scarcity and of non-satiation for the substitutability of consumption bundles. Third, Samuelson's revealed preference theory aimed, semantic irony notwithstanding, to eliminate the preference construct from economics, insofar as preferences were conceived as latent states of mind, in favor of attention to the logical consistency of observable choices. This is the intellectual background to the fact that some current economists, notably Gul and Pesendorfer (2008), deny as a matter of principle that anything can be learned about economics by studying brains. According to Gul and Pesendorfer, the task of positive economics is to predict choices as functions of changes in incentives and opportunity sets. Such choices are abstract constructs rather than directly observable phenomena, as are all relationships into which they enter. Though Gul and Pesendorfer concede that the mechanics of choice presumably involve neural computations, they see this as no more relevant to the economics of choice than is the fact that every choice must be made at some particular point on the surface of the planet. The intended value of such extreme abstraction lies in achieving generalizations of maximum scope.

The Gul and Pesendorfer critique has been extensively evaluated elsewhere. (See the papers in Caplin and Schotter, 2008, and also Harrison and Ross, 2010). I mention it here only to indicate why resistance to neuroeconomics has become associated with the conservative side of the disciplinary establishment, notwithstanding the continuity of neuroeconomics with the views of the earliest neoclassicists, as pointed out above. This ideological alignment might have been different had researchers motivated by traditional economists' concerns (as opposed to neuroscientists' concerns, as we will see later) 'looked into' brains and taken themselves to have observed neurons computing minima of opportunity costs given fully utilized resource budgets. But traditionally minded economic theorists were not motivated to 'look into' brains in the first place. Their polemical anti-establishment critics, the behavioral economists, were so motivated. What they thought they saw was certainly not constrained optimization under rational expectations.

In 2005, Camerer, Loewenstein and Prelec published a manifesto for neuroeconomics as revisionist microeconomics in the *Journal of Economic Literature*. They argued that, because of the nature of their brains, individual people's economic responses do not and cannot respect the principles of rational choice (that is, of Savage expected utility theory) except under highly unusual circumstances. The main force that stands in the way is emotion: 'brain mechanisms combine controlled and automatic processes, operating using cognition and affect. The Platonic metaphor of reason as a charioteer, driving twin horses of passion and appetite, is on the right track – except reason has its hands full with headstrong passions and appetites' (p. 56).

We will return to consider the empirical basis for this claim shortly. Let us first take note of a methodological point. The idea that reason battles for control against unruly passions is, as Camerer et al. say, an old and hugely influential part of the Western intellectual tradition. In principle, it can serve as the basis for two possible attitudes to applied microeconomics that differ sharply in their rhetorical valence, (though perhaps much less in their practical implications):

1. Models of people as rational utility maximizers are false, because people are not rational.
2. Economic models of people should try to estimate correctly and factor in the costs that are imposed on them by the presence of emotional impulses operating through their brains, in particular, the costs of impulsive actions that are subsequently regretted, and of energy spent in resisting temptations to such actions.

An example of this distinction in application can be found in economists' models of addiction, a behavioral pattern that challenges revealed preference assumptions because it seems manifestly inconsistent. We find one family of models (for example Loewenstein, 1999; Prelec and Bodner,

2003) that explains addiction by hypothesizing compromised inferential rationality, and another family (for example Gul and Pesendorfer, 2001; Benhabib and Bisin, 2004) that features rational agents facing costs due to exogenous temptations arising as 'itches in their brains'. The latter models are most interesting in the context of neuroeconomics, because they conceptually locate the brain, or at least part of the brain, outside the agent. This conception of the agent–brain relationship simply represents theoretical abstraction, not dualism. It implies a role for neuroscience as a deliverer of input data to economics, but across a principled boundary between the disciplines.

What confuses this picture is increasing reluctance, following the psychological investigations of Damasio (1994) and a highly influential book by the economist Robert Frank (1988), to regard emotions as contra-rational influences. The 'somatic marker hypothesis' (SMH) refers to the idea that emotions aid decisions by focusing or stabilizing preferences. A mini-tradition of behavioral experiments on which this hypothesis was mainly based relies on the Iowa Gambling Task (IGT), in which subjects earn monetary rewards by drawing cards from rigged decks. Experimenters following Bechara et al. (1997) found that subjects with damage to the orbitofrontal cortex (OFC) had difficulty learning to prefer decks that delivered higher expected pay-offs with lower variance to decks that delivered lower expected payoffs with higher variance. This was widely interpreted as showing that emotions are endogenous to choice because OFC was thought to be part of the limbic system. However, the integrity of this general construct has come under strong pressure as functional neuroanatomy has progressed: emotions as traditionally understood do not appear to reside in a particular part of the brain, or exclusively in older brain areas, but are instead widely distributed. Damage to the OFC could impair IGT performance by a number of pathways other than interference with emotional response (Dunn et al., 2006).

This problem clouds interpretation of neuroeconomic investigations based on the SMH. For example, Talmi et al. (2008) conditioned subjects to a CS+ and a CS-, then administered a standard extinction protocol. During the extinction phase subjects expressed their binary preferences over available rewards by squeezing handgrips. Subjects were observed to squeeze harder when presented with the irrelevant CS+, suggesting (very indirectly) that expectation of gain increases intensity of preference expression. This was also correlated with higher levels of activity in the dopamine reward circuit, especially the nucleus accumbens (NAcc), which many studies have indicated as a main site of reward anticipation and comparative valuation. This only seems to suggest a comment on the impact of emotion to the extent that reward system activation is regarded as an emotional response. However, most current models of the reward system rely on denying the identification of 'wanting' with the kind of subjective 'liking' historically associated with arational hedonic response (Berridge and Robinson, 1998; McClure et al., 2003). Of course, yearning and craving are strong affective states that often accompany preference. But such accompaniment is not evidence that the reward system's computation of comparative reward values are endogenous to emotional states.

Reviewing neuroscientific evidence for the SMH and for the sensitivity of preferences to emotional states, Phelps (2009) agrees that one cannot infer the latter merely from observation that a brain area that has been associated with emotional states is active during performance of preference elicitation tasks. This 'fallacy of reverse inference' (Poldrack 2006) is implicated unless one has independent evidence that the brain area in question is highly selective in its response. However, in the case of emotional response, such selectivity has not been established for any brain area (including the famous amygdala). We can find this criticism applied directly by one group of neuroeconomists against others, and against a flagship hypothesis of revisionary behavioral economics to the effect that imminence of 'visceral' rewards often sets people into 'hot' states that boost the subjective value of their consumption (Loewenstein, 1999). McClure et al. (2004) take neuroimaging data from a delay-discounting experiment that they ran as confirming the visceral salience hypothesis. However, Glimcher (2009) points out that two of the regions that have been identified as being associated with 'emotional' decision-making in these tests, the basal ganglia and the medial prefrontal cortex (MPFC), have also been shown by others to be associated with traditionally 'rational' functions such as the encoding of monetary and primary rewards, and the expression of ordinal preference.

Revisionist behavioral economists who continue to interpret emotions as contra-rational influences on choice might find neuroeconomic evidence for their position easier to come by. Suppose we begin by distinguishing between preferences which a specified person would cognitively and publicly affirm (for example, 'I would prefer, and pay a cost, not to be around a live snake') from preferences that person expresses in weakly self-monitored behavior but which she would not rationally affirm or knowingly pay costs to avoid (for example, 'I don't like to see pictures of snakes'). No one, as far as I am aware, denies that dispositions of the latter kind importantly influence human behavior. These influences furthermore, are the kind most likely to be associated with localized responses in older brain areas. Again, however, concerning appeals to facts about brains to score points in battles between orthodox and heterodox economists, we seem to face a set of interlocked modeling decisions that cannot be settled empirically. The approach defended by Gul and Pesendorfer treats the outputs of older, cognitively impenetrable brain areas as external influences on agents' opportunity sets and budget constraints, and/or as causes of exogenous preferences, rather than as selectors of normative strategies from strategy sets. Gul and Pesendorfer then assign their study to psychologists rather than economists.

As we will see in a later section of the present chapter, this basis for black-boxing some or all of the brain in economics cannot evade the implications of empirical discoveries about how subjective valuations are neurally processed. But these considerations lead us to the strand of neuroeconomics that is not motivated by one set or another of philosophical precommitments concerning the appropriate scope of economics.

Before we turn to this, we must consider a second major basis for the association between revisionist behavioral economics and neuroscience. With drumbeat regularity, revisionist behavioral economists stress that non-sociopathic people's individual utility functions are not narrowly self-regarding. Much of this literature greatly exaggerates the extent to which orthodox economic theorists have supposed, or have ever had any good reason to suppose, otherwise (Hausman and McPherson, 2006; Binmore, 2009; Ross, 2005, 2012). However, in the present context, we are interested in a more narrowly focused question: to what extent do neuroeconomists' observations of and experiments with functional properties of brain responses reveal features of human preferences that support challenges to economic models that are based on relatively asocial motivations?

Space prohibits any attempt at an overview of the large empirical literature in this area. I will instead follow one illustrative thread of experiments that Fehr (2009) uses to construct a complex hypothesis about the influence of different brain areas on an aspect of social preference processing, namely, a person's choice of response to perceived unfair treatment. Our primary interest here is in the nature of the reasoning by which Fehr works up his favored hypothesis from the observations. Many revisionist behavioral economists promote the idea that people often do not act like rational economic agents because different parts of their brains pursue incompatible objectives, and more farsightedly rational parts enjoy only highly imperfect and erratic control over other, more myopic, parts. In the reasoning I will follow, Fehr develops a case for a specific instantiation of this general idea. He is attracted to the hypothesis that in situations in which people could enforce a norm for generous or other pro-social behavior by punishing narrowly selfish actions at cost to themselves, older brain areas may get in the way by favoring narrowly self-interested cost–benefit maximization, while newer brain areas encourage pro-social

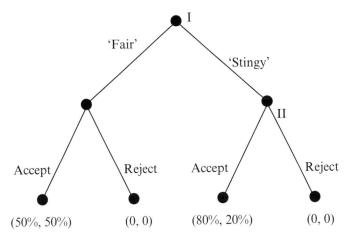

Figure 4.1   The Sanfey et al. (2003) ultimatum game protocol

choices – which, in the instance I will review, are ironically choices traditionally regarded as impulsive, namely, choices aimed at gaining revenge.

Fehr begins with an experiment in which Sanfey et al. (2003) had subjects play sequential one-shot ultimatum games (UGs), as shown in Figure 4.1, while being scanned using functional magnetic resonance imaging (fMRI). Each participant was introduced to ten people who would be their partners. Five offered 'Fair' ($5:$5) splits. The other five played differing variations on a 'Stingy' strategy, offering $9:$1, $9:$1, $8:$2, $8:$2 and $7:$3 respectively. Players also received ten offers from a partner they were told was a computer. Participants' brains were interpreted as showing significantly greater activation to 'Stingy' offers from people than to 'Fair' offers and to 'Stingy' offers from computers in the anterior insula (AI), dorsolateral prefrontal cortex (DLPFC) and anterior cingulate (AC). AI was also interpreted as showing correlation between activity levels and degree of offer stinginess (for example, more activation in response to $9:$1 than to $8:$2). In another experiment (Rilling et al., 2007), AI activation levels predicted retaliation by players who suffered defection in repeated prisoner's dilemmas.

Commenting on these results, Fehr suggests that the AC activation associated with receipt of stingy offers may be related either to emotional resentment or to motivational conflict between desire to punish and desire to harvest a reward, with increased activation reflecting the effort of cost comparison. Given background knowledge about the DLPFC, Fehr speculates that its activation in the experiment indicates cognitive control of an impulse to inflict punishment.

Fehr interprets subsequent experiments, especially work performed by his own group, as shedding light on this interpretive dichotomy. In particular, Knoch et al. (2006) used transcranial magentic stimulation (TMS) to interfere with DLPFC activation during UG play. Instead of increasing the rejection rate on stingy offers, as the original impulse control hypothesis predicts, the acceptance rate went up. Furthermore, attenuation of DLPFC activation had less impact on acceptance rates of stingy offers generated by computer opponents. On this basis two further (rival) hypotheses are constructed: (1) disruption of the DLPFC interferes with subjects' disposition to perceive stingy offers as unfair; (2) disruption of the DLPFC interferes with subjects' dispositions to control their selfish impulses. The second hypothesis is supported by evidence that TMS interference with the DLPFC does not disrupt subjects' verbally reported judgments about unfairness.

Fehr next seeks an explanation of AI activation observed during the UG experiments. He notes that, according to Knutson et al.'s (2007) interpretation of their observations of consumption choices under fMRI, AI is 'linked to' the emotional representation of purchase costs. Fehr then claims that AI activation is also 'linked to' the emotional cost of accepting unfair offers, though no specific basis for this is cited. This then leads to the suggestion that: 'perhaps the disruption of right DLPFC reduces a subject's ability to process this cost information or to integrate this cost information with the monetary benefits that are associated with the acceptance of unfair offers' (Fehr, 2009, p. 224).

Let us note several features of this reasoning. First, it involves reverse inference as described earlier and as criticized by Poldrack and Phelps; no one, to my knowledge, has tried to show or argue that the exclusive function of AI is to represent emotional costs of actions under consideration. Indeed, the relation Fehr suggests is only the vague one of 'linkage'. Second, the reverse inference is ampliative, in the sense that the impairment suggested to be caused by disruption of the right DLPFC is more functionally specific than what the reverse inference would directly support if it were deemed valid.

Hypothesis construction continues in this vein. Various experiments are cited to establish that the ventromedial PFC (VMPFC) is 'involved in' the emotional representation of differences between costless and costly strategic action and consumption. We are told that this 'provides nice support for the integration hypothesis' (p. 224). In addition, the 'VMPFC is involved in emotional processing and moral judgment' (ibid.). The next inference presupposes that these 'involvements' must form an integrated process: 'the . . . studies suggest a general role of VMPFC in integrating emotional feelings about costs and benefits, regardless of whether these choices involve economic consumption goods or "non-economic" goods such as the subjective value of rejecting an unfair offer' (ibid.). Finally, all of the inferential pieces are assembled as follows: 'It seems possible that low-frequency TMS of right DLPFC induces an impairment in the integration of the emotional cost of accepting an unfair offer. Such impairment could be caused by possible network effects of TMS that diminish the functioning of the VMPFC' (ibid.).

This reasoning borders on unconstrained word association. No doubt the hypothesized effect is possible. Reasons for believing that it is actual are scant in the extreme. The chain of repeated ampliative reverse inferences is not the only problem here. The alert reader may wonder how the VMPFC comes to be factored into the explanation in the first place, given that no reference to it features in the reports of the UG experiments. fMRI, if and when all goes well statistically, indicates brain areas that were, during a given observed timeframe, more active than their own baseline rates outside that frame. Thus one cannot infer from the fact that VMPFC activation was not correlated with any tested ultimatum game condition that the VMPFC was inactive during the experiments. Its introduction into the already elaborate and overcooked hypothesis is a pure guess. Finally, since the brain is massively interconnected in both circuitry and function, if we can invoke speculative 'network effects' on areas not mentioned in null hypotheses that we test, then we grant ourselves an open ticket to invent stories that outrun our data.

Reasoning of this kind unfortunately seems to be standard in efforts by behavioral economists to 'ground' their preferred interpretations of behavioral experiments by 'finding' their processing components directly in neuroimaging data. Proponents of revisionist behaviorist neuroeconomics might respond by saying that they are merely canvassing possibilities for subsequent investigation, something properly indicated by Fehr's cautious formulations ('Perhaps . . .'; 'It seems possible that . . .', and so on). However, Harrison and Ross (2010) describe two general problems with this defense, which will be indicated more briefly here.

First, interpretations of fMRI output cannot play the role of manifest observational data that we can use for testing among alternative interpretations of gross behavioral patterns. Rabe-Hesketh et al. (1997, pp. 217–26) nicely summarize the chains of epistemically risky estimations that are required to move from changes in magnetic pulses to conclusions about hemodynamics inside the head, then to estimations of the probability that neural activity at a specific spatial location differed significantly from baseline along a specific time course, then to identifications of the spatial locations in question with hypothesized functional units. The fact that fMRI data are time series, in which point estimates from one stage are taken as data in the next stage, raises particular complications, because standard errors of estimates at later stages are likely to overstate estimate precision. As Harrison (2008) documents, neuroeconomic reports often reveal significant understatement of standard errors on estimates of effects, implying significant overstatement of statistically significant differential activation. Of course one should not object to any ongoing scientific activity on grounds that it is hard. The point for now is merely that fMRI interpretation, involving the testing of models in which all variables are risky estimates, is very far indeed from straightforward measurement of first-order data. Thus the image of the behavioural economist testing her inferred explanations of behavioural hypotheses by 'opening the bonnet and looking at the engine' are deeply misleading.

This concern is closely related to a second one. Behavioural economists (for example Zak, 2008) sometimes say that because all economic decisions must be computed by brains, and because brains are characterized by complex functional anatomy, differences in processing biases in different parts of the brain simply must be relevant to economic generalizations. However, this presupposes a reductionist faith in economic patterns as direct expressions of individual people arriving at and applying valuations individually, using, as it were, the resources of their own raw brains. It ignores what Gigerenzer et al. (1999) and Smith (2007) call 'ecological rationality', the use of culturally evolved and socially salient structures to constrain both representations of and solutions to economic problems. What the philosopher Clark (1997) and the anthropologist Hutchins (1995) call 'cognitive scaffolding' is invisible to the behavioral neuroeconomist because it is found out in the environment rather than in the brain.

A very simple example can illustrate the point. Most people avoid becoming addicted to drugs. Some may do this because the interaction between their behavior and their baseline brain chemistry maintains high equilibrium levels of the neurotransmitters serotonin and gamma-aminobutyricacid (GABA), which inhibit control of consumption by midbrain dopamine systems that are vulnerable to obsessive attention on short reward cycles (Ross et al., 2008). Other people may avoid addiction by living in strict religious communities or by becoming airline pilots, thereby facing extreme sanctions for indulgence (Heyman, 2009). The economic behavior of these various groups of people with respect to drugs may be the same, but the neuroeconomist's methods will not predict this.

The intended upshot here is certainly not that neuroscience is irrelevant to economics. The simple example above underscores that point too: economic behavior would be very different if most people, as opposed to only some people, were cursed with 'addiction genes' that promote very rapid attenuation of GABA circuits on exposure to brief experiences of intoxication or gambling. I suggest that we should look forward to a day in the near future when standard models of microeconomic choice include independent variables for conditions in people's brains. However, even Gul and Pesendorfer accept that much; on this picture of interdisciplinary relations, economists accept data from neuroscientists, but do not set out to discover or parameterize these data themselves. I am therefore so far unconvinced that neuroeconomics has furnished, or will furnish, new reasons to invest in the revisionist behavioral project in economics.

Fortunately for the future reputations of neuroeconomists, hopes of remaking the rational economic agent as a bug-hobbled cyborg are not the only, or the best, motivation for combining the skills and knowledge of economists and neuroscientists. Neuroeconomics is methodologically Janus-faced, and I will now review the more handsome side.

4.3 ECONOMIC MODELS OF REWARD LEARNING IN THE BRAIN

People and other animals whose behavior is not strictly determined by local environmental contingencies must constantly make decisions under time pressure: to eat or not to eat this possible source of nutrition or that one; to attend to and pursue a cue for a possible mating opportunity or a cue for a possible meal, where both cannot be pursued at once; to signal presence, size and health to potential rivals and mates at the risk of alerting predators, or to remain silent and concealed. In social animals, and especially in people, culturally evolved scaffolding may greatly facilitate such decisions, but ultimately they must involve selective neural attention and neural preparation and guidance of motor systems. Furthermore, in non-stationary environments the comparative values of different stimuli for attention and action change, and these changes in relative values must be learned. For the past several decades in the cognitive sciences, modeling of these processes, often at an abstract level, has been the preoccupation of computational learning theory.[1]

A reward signal in the brain is regarded as 'pure' if it does not reflect specific facts about the sensory properties of the reward cue or expectation, and if it does not vary with the type of action appropriate to harvesting the reward; either source of 'impurity' must complicate the organism's ability to compare alternatives on a single scale. The majority of midbrain dopamine neurons, the circuit running from the ventral tegmental area (VTA) through the ventral striatum (VS) including the NAcc, and forward to the OFC, appear to be 'almost pure' reward signalers in this sense.[2] They fall short of 'true' purity because they send signals that prepare the motor system for one or another member of a set of broad action types. It is possible to set claims like these on reasonably solid empirical ground because the midbrain and its gross subparts are anatomically distinctive, and because its responses seem relatively impenetrable to control by newer cognitive systems, at least on short timescales.

We should not be surprised to find purity or near-purity in mammalian reward systems. A mobile animal, as noted above, must make many quick decisions that involve choices between, and therefore comparisons of value amongst, different kinds of contingencies that have no non-abstract feature dimensions in common. This would seem to require polysensory processing and a common internal currency. The processing in question must be adaptive: common currency values must fluctuate as evidence arrives that indicates changes in comparative reward values due to shifts in supply, demand or risk.

A major scientific breakthrough of the 1980s and early 1990s was the discovery, over the course of many experiments using invasive single-neuron probes of working monkey and rat brains, that midbrain dopamine neurons implement a form of reinforcement learning. The form in question had already been modeled by computational learning theorists as 'temporal difference (TD) learning', or, in a more general variant, 'Q-learning' (Sutton and Bartow, 1998). The history of these developments is extremely well documented; the reader can find a compact survey in Schultz (2009), and a detailed, thesis-length one in Daw (2003).

TD learning is an algorithm that estimates a value function V^*, that is, a rule for taking a stream of possible information as input and turning it into a stream of advance relative value estimates as output. More technically, the rule denotes a family of functions that relate a situation at a particular time s_t to a time-discounted sum of expected rewards (idealized as numeric measures r of received utility) that can be earned into the future. Suppose, following McClure et al. (2003), that t, $t+1$, $t+2$ and so on represent times on some arbitrary measurement scale. Let g be a discount parameter between 0 and 1 that varies with the interval between the time of valuation and the expected time of reward consumption. Then the TD equation is:

$$V^*(s_t) = E[r_t + \gamma r_{t+1} + \gamma^2 r_{t+2} + \gamma^3 r_{t+3} + \ldots]$$

which we close by writing:

$$V^*(s_t) = E[r_t + \gamma V^*(s_{t+1})]$$

This describes the procedure by which the algorithm continuously inputs new information to keep refining its estimate of V^* to get a particular stream of actual temporal valuations V. From this we can define a measure δ of the extent to which the value estimates of two successive states and a reward experienced by the system are consistent with one another:

$$\delta(t) = r_t + \gamma V(s_{t+1}) - V(s_t),$$

where δ is an error signal that pushes $V(s)$ towards better estimates as it gets more data. If $V(s_{t+1})$ turns out to be better than expected, then $\delta(t)$ will be positive, thus indicating that $V(s_t)$ needs to be adjusted upward. If $V(s_{t+1})$ turns out to be worse than expected, $\delta(t)$ will be negative and $V(s_t)$ will be adjusted downwards. If $\delta(t) = 0$ then no learning occurs (as it should not, since the system has received no new information).

The TD algorithm presupposes substantial advance knowledge by the system of the structure of its learning space. Yet the dopamine reward system is not flummoxed by unfamiliar learning contexts. To model learning in situations where there is not yet a rich representation of the relationships between possible actions and values, computational learning theorists have developed a generalization of TD learning called Q-learning, which models a family of algorithms for learning value functions over state (S) and action (a) pairs (Howard, 1960; Watkins, 1989; Sutton and Bartow, 1998, pp. 148–151; Montague et al., 2006; Niv and Montague, 2009). The learning rule is:

$$Q(S_t, a_t)_{new} = Q(S_t, a_t)_{old} + \eta\delta(t).$$

There are two forms of the TD prediction-error term. The first form:

$$\delta(t) = r_t + \max_a \gamma Q(S_{t+1}, a) - Q(S_t, a_t)$$

compares what happens to the best action that was possible. This is 'off policy' learning, and so presumes capacity for simulation. The alternative form of the TD prediction-error term:

$$\delta(t) = r_t + \gamma Q(S_{t+1}, a_{t+1}) - Q(S_t, a_t)$$

compares the outcome with the action actually chosen. This is an efficient way to learn in an environment in which trial-and-error learning is relatively less dangerous.

The hypothesis that single neurons or groups of neurons in the dopamine reward circuit implement a reinforcement learning algorithm is empirically testable, and has provided the basis for studies based on single-cell recording in monkeys and fMRI experiments with humans. Knutson et al. (2000), McClure et al. (2003) and O'Doherty et al. (2003) were key early studies that all suggested a similar conclusion: firing rates observed in the human VMPFC correlate with relative reward values, while VS neurons seem to track the error term in the TD algorithm. A more recent experiment by Hampton et al. (2006) comparatively tests the simple TD rule against a more sophisticated, state-sensitive version of Q-learning, and finds the latter to be better confirmed by the neuroimaging data.

More precise localization of reward learning within the VS, and identification of the error-response mechanism with dopamine, traces most directly to a highly influential contribution by Montague and Berns (2002). They reported an experiment in which human subjects under fMRI learned that light flashes predicted squirts of liquid. No interesting response differences in midbrain dopamine neurons were observed upon receipt of juice compared with water. But much of interest was seen in responses to the predictor cues. The following conditions were varied: (1) predictability of the reward type (juice or water); (2) predictability of the reward timing; and (3) whether subjects were active or passive. Variation (3) made no difference, which Montague and Berns take to indicate that the dopamine response is not a post-evaluative coding for decisions to act. Subjects exhibited strong hemodynamic variations in the VS in accordance with the hypothesis that their brains were predicting the expected times of squirts. This was important in light of a long-established result from conditioning literature that animals learn more efficiently and remember training for longer when stimulus–response intervals vary.

Exhibiting a principle familiar for some time to cognitive modelers of animal learning, a stimulus that is paired with a fully predicted reward does not elicit variation in dopamine neuron response, and so does not become a reward predictor; such a stimulus is said to be blocked. No dopamine depression will follow its presentation without the reward, and dopamine activation will follow reward delivery after it is presented alone. The results of variance in Montague and Berns's first and second conditions are taken to indicate that the reward valuation encoded by dopamine signals is relatively abstract. In particular, the system is not sensitive to differences between combinations of magnitude and probability that combine to yield identical values. Value is operationalized by about 65 percent of the neurons as mean divided by the standard deviation; thus the same level of activation will occur to the highest mean-valued reward within any given distribution (Schultz, 2009). The remaining 35 percent of neurons are reported to be increasingly active as variance increases; thus these neurons can code for risk levels (ibid.).

One naturally wonders at this point what the system as modeled does when reward timing is random, or too irregular to be learned against the system's sampling window of < 2 seconds. Montague and Berns hypothesize and model a rule by which the system could evaluate its reliance on the output of its reward predictor. Suppose $R(x,n)$ estimates the value of a reward distributed at various possible times $x, y, z, \ldots, n$ in the future, scaled according to the uncertainty attending to the intervals between the estimation point and each time, as in:

$$R(x, n; D) = \int_{-\infty}^{+\infty} dy \, G(x - y, (x - n)D)r(y)$$

where $G(z, b) = (2\pi b)^{-1/2} \exp\{-z^2/2b\}$ and D is a constant. Then the value $F(n)$ the brain attaches to getting a particular predictor signal for a reward with estimated point value r at perceptual time n is given by:

$$F(n) = \int_{n}^{+\infty} dx \, e^{-q(x-n)} \int_{-\infty}^{+\infty} dy \, G(x - y(x - n)D)\rho(y)$$

$$= \int_{n}^{+\infty} dx \, \{e^{-q(x-n)}\} \, \{R(x, n; D)\} = \int_{n}^{+\infty} dx$$

{discounted future time x relative to perceptual time n} · {diffused version of reward estimate ρ (x) for some x and n}

The diffusion term reflects the idea that as time to reward increases, the probability of error increases with it.

There is no direct empirical evidence that this predictor-valuation (PV) model is implemented in the brain. Montague and Berns note that it is structurally isomorphic to the Black–Scholes model of pricing risky assets in efficient markets, which serves to emphasize the essentially normative – and characteristically economic – principles of reasoning by which it is derived. It tells us how an efficient reward seeker facing scarcity and uncertainty and equipped with a relatively general-purpose reinforcement learning apparatus could avoid wasting its time trying to learn the unlearnable. This enterprise differs importantly from the style of neuroeconomics described in section 4.1, which is closer to the tradition of psychology in being descriptive, and in tending to report contingent impediments, arising from the brain's evolutionary history, to the implementation of principles of the kind represented by the PV model.

In this respect, the PV model is typical of the neuroeconomics literature that descends mainly from computational learning theory. Indeed, as Niv and Montague (2009, p. 332) emphasize, all reinforcement learning models are normative in character, beginning from the assumption that the learning system is evolved to optimize some function. Other functions that have featured in neuroeconomic models include algorithms for maximizing expected value and for minimizing risk. The extent to which real neural circuits actually optimize in their performance must be determined by comparison of predictions based on the normatively derived functions with empirical data. This is, of course, standard operating procedure in economics. Neuroeconomists focused on reward value learning devote considerable energy, like other economists, to theoretical explorations of the properties of formal models. This does not justify critics in leaping directly to the conclusion that the research program is unconstrained by empirical data.

As a nice illustration of the role of idealization in neuroeconomics, which is logically identical to its function in economics generally, Niv and Montague note that standard reinforcement learning models implicitly assume that prediction errors are applied uniformly to the values of cue stimuli. Though this has been known for decades to be an extreme simplification, the method that neuroeconomists have adopted for relaxing it does not simply involve adding parameters derived from empirical measurements. Normative reasoning is reapplied: the Kalman filter model of Dayan et al. (2000) is based on asking how weighting of predictor cues in learning would optimally vary with the reliability and frequency of the cues. Resort to such abstract theoretical considerations, however, need not involve ignoring facts about the brain. Thus, for example, Yu and Dayan (2005) review evidence that high acetylcholine levels in striatum signal expected uncertainty, that is, known variability in the environment, while high norepinephrine levels signal unexpected uncertainty, unknown variability. If this is right, then prediction errors in phasic dopamine signals carry different implications depending on the acetylcholine–norepinephrine ratio. Where acetylcholine dominates, prediction errors would indicate unexpected changes in the environment. Where norepinephrine dominates, prediction errors would indicate higher expected variability.

A further illustration of the sensitivity of theoretically motivated reward learning models to empirical observations is the recognized need to explain why midbrain dopamine neurons respond to novel stimuli that, being novel, justify no predictions. Kakade and Dayan (2002) suggest that animals should be encouraged to explore their environments by finding novelty rewarding in itself. This could be implemented by a learning algorithm that optimistically takes novelty as predictive of reward, that is, that satisfies the condition:

$$r_{new}(t) = r_t + novelty(S_t).$$

The principal contribution of Kakade and Dayan's paper is their argument that this condition would account for specific properties of the reported novelty response in dopamine signaling, for example dips in firing rates below baseline following novelty bursts. Ng et al. (1999) had previously shown that this complication does not significantly change the qualitative learning properties of a TD learning system.

In addition to learning to predict the magnitudes, probabilities and expected times of rewards, animals must also learn to select behaviors. When they can estimate the comparative expected values (EVs) of outcome states associated with alternative actions, then TD learning can suffice: the rational animal should simply estimate the EVs of outcomes and take whatever action is linked to the outcome with the highest value. But how might the system learn about variations in links between actions and outcomes in the first place?

As discussed by Niv and Montague (2009), a standard response to this problem in artificial intelligence is to build an 'actor-critic model'. Such a model comprises two units, where the units can be computers of any level of complexity, but might be as simple as individual neurons. One unit, the adaptive critic element, implements reinforcement learning to estimate values of states of the environment. These estimates are used to train the second unit, the associative search element, which learns to optimize actions by trial and error. For a typical animal in a typical environment, this will be very dangerous unless the animal can test the consequences of its actions in simulations that its brain can run. Dennett (1997) is among several authors who hypothesize that this is the basic source of evolutionary pressure for the development of cognition. In some environments actor-critic models will fail to converge, in which cases an animal learning in this way will not be well modeled as an economic agent. In other environments, actor-critic models can get stuck in local maxima (suboptimal equilibria).

Niv and Montague hypothesize that dopamine signals in the reward circuit implement the critic in an actor-critic model, while a circuit that projects from pars compacta of substantia nigra (SNPC) to dorsal striatal areas implements the actor. Evidence specifically to support this hypothesis has not yet been forthcoming. However, it is clearly testable.

Reinforcement learning models have also recently been applied to animals' choices of rates of behavioral response. The net rate of reward partly determines (along with relative energy costs) the opportunity cost of a given behavioral policy for an animal. Consider two alternative policies A and B, and suppose that A is chosen over B. The higher the reward rate from B, the more vigorously A should be pursued by an economically rational animal. There is overwhelming evidence that reward delivery rates are represented by animals with brains, and are crucial variables in many learning rules (Gallistel and Gibbon, 2002). Niv and Montague hypothesize that tonic dopamine levels – slow-changing general dopamine levels prevailing across the whole reward circuit – represent associations between net rates of reward and environments. Because tonic changes are undetectable by neuroimaging, such limited evidence for this hypothesis as currently exists comes from biochemical manipulations and studies of damaged and diseased brains.

The history of development and testing of models of reward learning in the brain thus demonstrate the kind of careful interanimation of normative-theoretical and positive-descriptive work that characterizes good economics. This is not to claim that its horizons are unclouded by any general methodological challenges. A notable one can be derived from Wilcox (2006). He shows, in connection with learning in repeated games, that if tests of learning models begin from pooled observations of the players, and if there is heterogeneity among players' response functions, then overwhelming bias may be introduced in favor of any reinforcement learning model that is compared with an alternative model based on rational conjectures rather than players' past track records. The intuitive basis of the problem is straightforward: both models will yield prediction errors correlated with past choices of heterogeneous players, because these will carry idiosyncratic parameter information; but because reinforcement models are directly conditioned on players' lagged choices, they will tend automatically to fit the pooled data better. But of course such a basis for confirmation is a methodological artifact. Two considerations make this problem relevant to neuroeconomic theories of reward learning: (1) neuroeconomists use pooled time-series data consisting of multiple observations from a few brains; and (2) both neural complexity and a long tradition in psychology (see, for example, Ainslie, 2001) suggest that within-person heterogeneity in response functions likely reflects empirical reality. Wilcox shows that use of random parameter estimators instead of pooled estimators tend to mitigate the problem. It is unclear how this leverage might be put to work in interpretation of fMRI data collected using standard neuroeconomic protocols; but neuroeconomists might benefit from studying Conte et al. (2007).[3]

Wilcox's problem resembles all of the currently most interesting methodological challenges in economics in being drawn from the frontiers of our understanding of statistical inference techniques. This frontier has been a rapidly moving one, especially thanks to fast and powerful computing. The posing and solving of problems along it has been highly productive, and characteristic of a healthy research program.

The first research that was self-consciously 'neuroeconomic' was explicit in deriving its methodology from standard, not revisionist, microeconomics. If there is a single source that merits being regarded as the founding document of neuroeconomics, it is Paul Glimcher's 2003 book *Decisions, Uncertainty and the Brain* (Glimcher, 2003a).[4] Glimcher devotes the first half of the book to the following methodological argument. The Sherringtonian tradition in neuroscience of trying to infer neural functions directly from observation of neuroanatomical pathways ultimately fails, because the brain exploits cross-cutting channels of communication that are far more complex than the workings of an electrical circuit, the metaphor on which the traditional conception relied. In the face of this complexity, the more appropriate philosophy of neuroscience is derived from Marr (1982). This involves first identifying problems that the brain and its functional subunits, including individual neurons, must solve, and specifying algorithms that could compute the solutions. This informs the empirical search for mechanisms that could perform the relevant computations.

A methodological point which Glimcher does not address, but which nothing in his arguments tells against, is that there is no reason why all computations relevant to functional neuroscience must rely exclusively on causal mechanisms located entirely 'in the head'. Consider one pathway by which information might be transferred from one part of my brain to another: I detect an instance of an abstract pattern, and name it by its type as discovered and modeled by scientists. My silent representation of the English name for the pattern type is processed in auditory cortex trained to respond to scientific English. Output from this system facilitates association of the pattern with others that are linked to it by textbooks and scientific papers I have read. The Marr–Glimcher methodology for neuroscience raises no barrier against the idea that this process implements a computational mechanism that involves neurons, textbooks, papers and the encoding of information in the social structures of scientific English. For discussions of this leading recent theme in the philosophy of cognitive science, see Menary (2010).

The work we have reviewed so far in the current section on reward learning algorithms and mechanisms reflects the Marr–Glimcher approach, which, as Glimcher makes explicit, is essentially an adaptation to neuroscience of the standard methods of contemporary microeconomists and game theorists. Caplin and Dean (2008a, 2008b) complete the implementation of this standard methodology by providing an axiomatic model of dopamine reward valuation. If the course of empirical science turns out to vindicate Glimcher's (2009) speculation that all reward valuation in the brain is represented in the currency of dopaminergic response, then Caplin and Dean's axioms are the foundations of a genuine neurocellular economics. These initial axioms are the frame of a building that awaits furnishing, but the hope is that the axioms will constrain future work and will be elaborated upon but not revised. If this hope is satisfied, then neurocellular economics will constitute another instance of the program that mainstream microeconomics has pursued since Samuelson (1947).

In Glimcher's 2003 book, the pre-axiomatic aspects of the program are illustrated by his own group's early research into the value computations of individual neurons. This work, which has given rise to a progressive set of experimental protocols that have fanned out across several laboratories, has two important advantages as a methodological exemplar: (1) it is based originally on single-cell recordings in monkeys, rather than fMRI, thus being immune from the main criticisms of Harrison (2008); (2) it models outputs of learning rather than learning processes per se, thus not being on foundational 'probation' pending deeper exploration into Wilcox's problem.

In Glimcher's basic paradigm, monkeys are trained to implement choices by directing their gaze to one member of a set of colored flashes on a computer screen. These choices are sometimes moves in simple games. While the monkeys do this, activity in single neurons in the lateral intra-parietal area (area LIP) is recorded. Neurons in this area encode salience of visual targets, and thereby direct attention to them. They deliver output to parts of the visuomotor system that plan and execute eye saccades. Thus it is hypothesized that area LIP neurons do not compute, but are closely correlated with, the monkeys' decisions about where to look. One of Glimcher's early breakthrough experiments (Glimcher 2003b) found that, when monkeys played the inspection game shown in Figure 4.2, firing rates of LIP neurons were equal for each pure strategy that was mixed in Nash equilibrium (NE). If the neurons were tracking probabilities of movement instead of expected utility, this should not have been observed. This interpretation of the observations was greatly strengthened and enlarged in importance by a subsequent experiment (Dorris and Glimcher, 2004) in which monkeys learned changing reward values in the same game. Trial-by-trial fluctuations in LIP activity correlated with trial-by-trial behavioral estimates of expected utility. Given recent skepticism from behavioral economists about NE as a solution concept that people actually implement, it is striking to find evidence of monkey neurons directly computing it. (For discussion, see Vromen, 2010.)

Other researchers have fruitfully applied Glimcher's experimental paradigm. Lee et al. (2004) investigated the performance of non-human primates in the Matching Pennies game (Figure 4.3) by having monkeys play against computers running three different algorithms. Algorithm 0 played the mixed NE strategy unilaterally, without looking for patterns to be exploited in the monkeys' responses. In such cases monkeys show strong biases toward one or another of the pure strategies. (The source of these biases in the experiments is unknown and was not investigated.)

	Inspect	Don't inspect
Work	2, 2	2, 4
Shirk	–2, –2	4, –4

NE = (randomize, randomize)

Figure 4.2 The inspection game

	H	T
H	–2, 2	2, –2
T	2, –2	–2, 2

NE = (randomize, randomize)

Figure 4.3 Matching Pennies

Algorithm 1 detects such biases and counteracts them by driving the computer toward the opposite bias. Monkeys respond by dynamically conditioning switches between pure strategies on specific wins and losses. This 'win-stay, lose-switch' (WSLS) strategy is an implementation of matching behavior. It is as good a strategy as any other against Algorithm 1. Finally, Algorithm 2 looks for patterns in recent histories of monkey play compared with the monkey's gains and losses, and exploits any such patterns. The only NE response to Algorithm 2 is randomization between pure strategies. Monkeys learn this.

A follow-up experiment (Lee et al., 2005) applied the same protocol to the familiar Rock–Paper–Scissors (R–P–S) game. In response to Algorithm 0, monkeys tended to settle on a preferred pure strategy. In response to Algorithm 1, they played the Cournot best response, biasing their choices in each round n by reference to the pure strategy that would have won or did win in round $n - 1$. Monkey response to Algorithm 2 was especially interesting in R–P–S. They approximated but did not quite achieve randomization. In particular, they came as close to randomization as a TD learning rule can get. (Note that possible availability of a PV mechanism is irrelevant here, since as the best response approaches randomization, the value of the predictor approaches 0.)

These results motivate search for a neural mechanism that will adjust stochastic response frequencies toward WSLS when the environment strategically adapts to it but does not model it, and implements reinforcement learning when the environment strategically models it. Direct recording identified individual neurons in the DLPFC that modulate their activity in ways that allow for trial-by-trial comparison of two alternatives, as in Matching Pennies (Barraclough et al., 2004; Seo et al., 2007). Crucially, some DLPFC neurons store 'eligibility traces', that is, modulate their response probabilities in light of results of previous responses. This would be necessary in a neural system able to learn best (or near-best) replies to Algorithm 2. (Note that the DLPFC receives signals from the VS.) Individual neurons in the anterior cingulate cortex (ACC) were also studied. Their activity co-varied with calculated reward prediction errors, but not with changes in value functions (Seo and Lee, 2007).

Lee and Wang (2009) review models of processes by which some individual dLPFC neurons might adjust their stochastic response probabilities in such a way as to implement WSLS when randomization does not improve on it, and randomize when the environment responds as if strategically modeling the organism's behavior. The first is a specific type of 'ramping-to-threshold' model based on drift-diffusion. Suppose we have two alternatives X_1 and X_2 for comparison, where $X = X_1 - X_2$. Then the dynamics of X are modeled by drift diffusion if:

$$dX/dt = \mu + \omega(t)$$

where μ is the drift rate and $\omega(t)$ is a white noise of zero mean and standard deviation σ. μ represents a bias in favor of one alternative X_1 or X_2. The system is a perfect integrator of the input

$$X(t) = \mu t + \int^{t} \omega(t') dt'$$

and terminates whenever $X(t)$ reaches a positive threshold θ (choice 1) or $-\theta$ (choice 2). If μ is positive then choice 1 is correct, while choice 2 is an error; otherwise the opposite. If m is 0 the system is 'set' to randomize.

Can neural circuits implement this model? Lee and Wang point out that they can not perfectly integrate inputs, because they 'leak' – that is, drift with time independently of μ. (That is to say, they forget.) However, Wang (2001, 2002) and others have demonstrated that this can be corrected by recurrent activation. So as long as input meets some persistence threshold, and the neuron is embedded in a network that receives stabilizing feedback from elsewhere in the brain (that is, there is recurrence), then a neuron's stochastic response rate can systematically adjust in the way approximately described by the drift diffusion model. If neurons ramp to threshold, then learning must involve adjustments to the thresholds (for example, to θ in the model). Lee and Wang suggest that this is what the striatal dopamine signal does.

We can shift to a less abstract level of modeling – but constrained by the higher-level models – in search of greater biophysical accuracy. A 'spiking network' model takes account of the specific rise-times and decay-times of synapses. Lee and Wang point out that: 'synaptic dynamics turn out to be a crucial factor in determining the integration time of a neural circuit dedicated to decision making, as well as controlling the stability of a strongly recurrent network' (2009, p. 499).

In general, what holds stochastic neural firing frequencies within stable but adjustable bands are presumed to be network properties that create complex dynamics with multiple attractors. Pairs of neural networks linked to one another by both excitatory and inhibitory connections decide between two alternatives A and B, with C_A and C_B denoting recurrence of input favoring A and B respectively, according to the softmax function:

$$P_A(C_A - C_B) = 1/(1 + \exp(-(C_A - C_B))/\sigma$$

where σ denotes the 'extent of' stochasticity' in the network. Such a system will decide between A and B even when absolute magnitudes of C_A and C_B are small, and when $C_A = C_B$. Lee and Wang claim that the function performs well in describing monkey behavior in the Matching Pennies game, but has not yet been tested on single neuron responses in the DLPFC during game play. However, Lee and Wang report that it has produced good fits in estimating firing rates in area LIP when monkeys learned to anticipate stochastic changes in visual displays. As reported in Lee and Wang (2009) these imprecise claims cannot be evaluated. For present purposes the point is to once again display the continuous dynamic interplay between normatively derived models and empirical tests.

Lee and Wang do not discuss possible ways of generalizing the softmax function to describe dynamic attraction that would incorporate choices among more than two alternatives, as in their R–P–S experiment. Nor do they mention any test of a relationship between their model and the reported pattern of monkey play in R–P–S.

Lee and Wang introduce an additional methodological strategy by using their model to generate a simulation of neural learning of the monkeys' task in the Matching Pennies experiment. It captures the broad characteristics of the observed behavior, though it underpredicts the monkeys' frequency of use of WSLS against Algorithm 1. To reproduce this, Lee and Wang adjust the model by using 'a different learning rule, according to which synapses onto both neural populations (selective for the chosen and unchosen targets) are modified in each trial. This is akin to a "belief-dependent learning rule"' (p. 498). They report that the model used for the simulation required different parameters for play against each of the three algorithms, and that they 'incorporated a meta-learning rule proposed by Schweighofer and Doya (2003) that maximizes long-term rewards' (ibid.). Thus the simulation really tests a joint hypothesis: that some neurons (somewhere in the brain) tune their response probabilities by ramping to thresholds via strongly recurrent dynamics, thereby learning strategically superior stochastic behaviors, and parameters that govern applications of this learning model are themselves learned by some so far unspecified neural process somewhere else in the brain that implements the Schweighofer–Doya meta-learning rule. It would seem, from the methodological point of view, that the main value of the simulation lies – as is generally the case with simulations – in its potential for suggesting more refined models. To the extent that these require more parameters, a loss of generalization is implied.

4.4   GLIMCHER'S PROGRAM FOR FUTURE NEUROECONOMIC RESEARCH

I have argued in this chapter that neuroeconomic research activity divides into two sets: (1) searches for brain mechanisms that explain respects in which evolution has failed to produce rational decision makers; and (2) efforts to model the processes of value learning in the brain's reward system. The former approach, based largely on applications of fMRI, do not yet seem to have produced results to justify the excitement that typically accompanies popular reports of the research. The second approach has all of the hallmarks of standard, sound economic research. Models are constructed on a normative basis, their formal properties are compared, and their consequences under various parameterizations are derived. They are examined in light of empirical data, but the relationship between models and evidence is not a simple matter of deducing predictions and attempting to refute or confirm them directly. Relationships between theoretical models and data models are mediated by sophisticated statistical inference principles of which we do not, in principle, have complete understanding. The relevant understanding steadily improves, however.

A concrete and ambitious research agenda for the second strand of neuroeconomics has been outlined by Glimcher (2009). I will close by summarizing this program. In light of the boldness of its underlying hypothesis, it represents a route by which the pursuit of 'sound but dull' neuroeconomics (type 2) could eventually transform microeconomics, though not in the way promoted by revisionist behavioral economists. I am doubtful that the underlying hypothesis is true, but think that it is very much worth pursuing for the sake of the knowledge to be gained in the chase.

Glimcher sketches a 'back-pocket' neuroeconomic model of choice. By this he means a general form of model that investigators can carry around from experiment to experiment, from which each new investigation can begin, and which each investigator can aim to refine and elaborate upon. He makes clear that he expects a boot-strapping process to occur here; that is, he expects that efforts to refine the model will ultimately lead to its replacement by a better one. He has, he says 'certain knowledge that the details of the following framework are wrong' (p. 504). This emphasizes that the point of the exercise is to outline a research program rather than propound a theory that runs ahead of evidence. Nevertheless, the program is based on an underlying, and very strong, empirical hypothesis.

The first element of the hypothesis is that choice occurs at the neural level through the chaining together of two distinct processes. First, a valuation mechanism ranks sets of options. Then a choice mechanism selects items from such sets and directs actions aimed at consuming the items in question. The basic evidence for this two-stage model is straightforward: repeatedly observed groups of neurons in the VS and PFC fire in patterns that linearly co-vary with previously learned values of rewards even under conditions when animals face no relevant choices among actions. Distinct neural areas, especially in the parietal cortex (PC), are active in choice, and receive input from the valuation system.

Economic theory is to be used to define objects that 'serve . . . as mapping rules that connect existing theoretical tools to the empirical measurements of neuroscience' (p. 506). The central such relationship is the interpretation of value-in-the-brain as something conceptually resembling utility that often exactly mimics it. By 'utility' Glimcher understands the proper concept as defined by the Savage axioms. He is nicely unequivocal about the point and value of these axioms: '[they] are not some set of strange and arbitrary assumptions about how people *must* behave . . . The axioms are a statement not about people (or the brain) in any sense; the axioms are a precise definition of a theory' (p. 507). 'Theory' is here being used in the sense that mainstream economists understand, as a device that precisely defines the relationships within a family of models. Some of the models in question might describe some aspects of empirical reality more or less closely; this we can determine only by measurement and testing.

Glimcher defines a new, distinctively neuroeconomic, object that he calls 'subjective value' (SV). SVs are real numbers ranging from 0 to 1000. Their units are action potentials per second. They are defined as the mean firing rates of specific populations of neurons, so they are linearly proportional to the blood-oxygen-level dependence (BOLD) signals measured by fMRI in the populations in question. SVs are always stochastically consistent with choice, even when expected utilities are not. (For ease of subsequent discussion, let us call this 'Property*'.) SVs have a unique reference-dependent anchoring point called the baseline firing rate. All SVs are encoded cardinally in firing rates relative to this baseline. SVs cannot take negative values, and have finite range and finite, but large variance. Thus if SV determines choice, choice will be stochastic and error-ridden.

Among the reasons that SV cannot be equated with utility, even though it conceptually resembles utility, is that SV does not respect the independence axiom of expected utility theory. For this same reason, measurement of SVs does not have 'clear' welfare implications. On the other hand, axiomatization of SV should specify the exact network of formal relationships between utility and SV. If, as Glimcher hypothesizes, SVs determine choice behavior, then the precise mapping between SV and utility will allow us to explain and model the respects in which human choice behavior departs from pure economic agency. In cases where utility theory does predict choice, we will have grounded the relationship – will no longer need to resort to 'as if' formulations – in the isomorphism between utility and SV.

Glimcher first summarizes his underlying hypothesis as follows: 'SV is encoded directly in the valuation mechanisms of the human brain, and . . . existing economic theory tells us much about how this representation *must* behave' (p. 510). Subsequently, this hypothesis is strengthened consider-ably when Glimcher suggests that all the neurons we need to study to find the SV for any object are in the VS and PFC. Unsurprisingly, he proposes that: 'one central goal of neuroeconomics should be to develop a complete theory of SV' (ibid.).

He defines the basic elements of that theory: First, the relative SV (*RSV*) of an option *j*:

$$RSV_j = \frac{SV_j}{\sum_i SV_i + c}$$

where *i* is the set of all options in the choice set, and *c* is an empirically measurable normalization constant derived from neuroscience. Glimcher argues that choices between options are made by comparison of their RSVs.

Next, obtained SV (*ExperSV*): the SV of the state of the world that results from a choice. 'The neural location of ExperSV is not known, though the activity of dopamine neurons provides overwhelming evidence that it is present as one of the midbrain inputs to those neurons' (ibid.).

Reward prediction error, in terms of values defined so far:

$$RPE = \alpha(SV_{forecast} - ExperSV)$$

There are two sources of stochasticity relevant to choice: in valuation, cor-responding to random utility distributions, and in the choice mechanism, corresponding to the game-theoretic notion of a trembling hand:

- SV variability is a random term drawn from a Gaussian distribution and added to mean SV to yield SV.
- Cortical noise before choice is a random term drawn from a Poisson distribution and added to RSV as a stochastic time series before choice. It reflects the physics of cortical neurons.

Pulling all this together, the SV of an option *j* is the sum:

$$SV_j = \frac{\sum_i \omega_i x_{ij}}{\sum_i \omega_i}$$

where *i* indexes each neuron in the brain, x_i is the firing rate of the *i*th neuron, and ω_i is a weight ranging from 0 to 1 describing the additive contribution of the *i*th neuron to the SV of *j*.

Glimcher identifies two questions that he calls 'paramount' for a scientist looking for some SV_j in the brain:

1. In cases where utility predicts choice, can we identify a firing rate (or a proxy for it, for example BOLD activation) of some neurons that is linearly correlated with the utility of actions or options that the subject chooses?
2. What is the smallest group of neurons that can maintain this linear correlation (that is, the smallest group for which $\omega_i \neq 0$?

Glimcher hypothesizes that dopamine neurons directly compute SV under conditions indicated by the following model:

$$SV_{jt} = SV_{j(t-1)} + \alpha(ExperSV - SV_{j(t-1)})$$

Aspects of the computation of reinforcement effects occur in basal ganglia. However, Glimcher interprets the weight of fMRI and other evidence as indicating that the SV of an action or good is encoded by the mean activity in the medial PFC and the VS. He speculates that the medial PFC stores goods valuation and the VS stores action valuation.

Because neurons have finite rates of stochasticity, SV estimates must be drawn from an underlying distribution. Therefore, their estimation is said to be more closely analogous to random utility estimation than to von Neumann–Morgenstern calculation. However, random utility models share the von Neumann–Morgenstern assumption that the decision-maker has perfect discrimination capability.

We might agree – I do agree – that developing a rigorous and complete theory of SV, strictly comparable to the theory of utility, should be the organizing master goal of neuroeconomics, even if we are unpersuaded – as I am unpersuaded – by Glimcher's strong underlying hypothesis.

I will indicate the basis of my doubts. Glimcher argues that the leading alternative to his hypothesis of a uniform basis of neural valuation – of SV – is the 'multiple self' model that has been proposed by a number of revisionist behaviorists, and whose flagship experiment is McClure et al. (2004). Glimcher summarizes the model as follows: '[T]he basal ganglia and the medial prefrontal cortex form an emotional decision-making module which interacts (additively) with a second system organized around posterior parietal cortex and the dorsolateral prefrontal cortex, which form a rational decision-making module' (p. 518). His strongest reason for rejecting this model is empirical: replicating the McClure et al. experiment with a superior design, he and his collaborators obtained results that directly confuted it (Kable and Glimcher 2007; Glimcher et al., 2007). However, this evidence does not bear against a different kind of multiple-self model with which the McClure et al. model might be confused, namely, the picoeconomic model promoted by Ainslie (1992, 2001). In a chapter devoted to neuroeconomics, it would carry me too far off topic to explain the deep differences between these two types of multiple self framework; the reader can consult Ross et al. (2010), as well as Ross et al. (2008, Ch. 8). To summarize very briefly, picoeconomic models distinguish between personal (or 'molar') utility, which may be partly calculated by the person in conjunction with external systems in the environment, and value-in-the-brain. Picoeconomics grants that SV or something much like it is a crucial input to personal choice, but also allows for other sorts of input, many of which are simply 'choice-governing tracks' laid out in the subject's cultural, social or market environment and which the brain may never explicitly evaluate. Picoeconomists welcome the evidence against dual valuation systems at the neural level, but also take seriously the 'ecological rationality' of Vernon Smith (2007) and others, and so doubt that economic choice is 'all in the head'. This implies doubt that any neural process has what I dubbed Property*, the property of always being stochastically consistent with choice. We think that doubt about Property* is most consistent with the idea of revealed preference. Often people 'make choices', in the sense of doing things they would not have done had incentives (for example, prices) been different, in ways that do not involve their brains computing any relative values among the items in the choice set. (Of course, their brains must always do something to produce the behavior that implements the choice.)

This basis for skepticism about Glimcher's strong hypothesis is wholly compatible with the postulated existence of SV, and with the call to neuroeconomists to organize their research around developing and testing a more complete model of it in light of the most cleverly obtained neural data they can get. In my opinion, to the extent that neuroeconomics remains tightly associated with revisionist behavioral economics it will fail to sustain the popular excitement it has aroused; to the extent that it takes Glimcher's proposed research program as its mission (and reduces its excessive reliance on fMRI, as technological developments will surely allow), it will add a vibrant new wing to the proud edifice of modern economics.

NOTES

1. For a classic survey of computational learning theory as it reached maturity of methods and fundamental framework, see Gallistel (1993).

2. Dopamine neurons in the OFC appear to be less pure reward signalers than dopamine neurons in the midbrain.
3. Conte et al. begin from the point, established in a previously circulated paper by Harrison and Rutström (published as 2009), that mixture models – models that avoid imposing a common objective function to fit all choice data – can be used to discriminate between maximization of expected utility and other functions. To this Conte et al. introduce random coefficients, including on the mixing probability. They are explicit that they are motivated as much to accommodate within-subject heterogeneity as to accommodate between-subject heterogeneity.
4. Glimcher (personal communication) wanted to title the book *Neuroeconomics*. His editor at MIT Press feared that this neologism would not be understood and would depress sales.

REFERENCES

Ainslie, G. (1992), *Picoeconomics*, Cambridge: Cambridge University Press.
Ainslie, G. (2001), *Breakdown of Will*, Cambridge: Cambridge University Press.
Barraclough, D., M. Conroy and D. Lee (2004), 'Prefrontal Cortex and Decision-Making in a Mixed Strategy Game', *Nature Neuroscience*, **7**, 404–410.
Bechara, A., H. Damasio, D. Tranel and A. Damasio (1997), 'Deciding Advantageously Before Knowing the Advantageous Strategy', *Science*, **275**, 1293–1295.
Benhabib, J. and A. Bisin (2004), 'Modeling Internal Commitment Mechanisms and Self-control: A Neuroeconomics Approach to Consumption-Saving Decisions', *Games and Economic Behavior*, **52**, 460–492.
Berridge, K. and T. Robinson (1998), 'What is the role of dopamine in reward: Hedonic impact, reward learning, or incentive salience?', *Brain Research Reviews*, **28**, 309–369.
Binmore, K. (2009), *Rational Decisions*, Princeton, NJ: Princeton University Press.
Camerer, C., G. Loewenstein and D. Prelec (2005), 'Neuroeconomics: How Neuroscience can Inform Economics', *Journal of Economic Literature*, **43**, 9–64.
Caplin, A. and M. Dean (2008a), 'Economic Theory and Psychological Data: Bridging the Divide', in A. Caplin and A. Schotter (eds), *The Foundations of Positive and Normative Economics: A Handbook*, Oxford: Oxford University Press, pp. 336–371.
Caplin, A. and M. Dean (2008b), 'Dopamine, reward prediction error, and economics', *Quarterly Journal of Economics*, **123**(2), 663–701.
Caplin, A. and A. Schotter (eds) (2008), *The Foundations of Positive and Normative Economics: A Handbook*, Oxford: Oxford University Press.
Clark, A. (1997), *Being There*, Cambridge, MA: MIT Press.
Conte, A., J. Hey and P. Moffatt (2007), 'Mixture Models of Choice under Risk', Discussion Papers 07/06, Department of Economics, University of York, http://www.york.ac.uk/depts/econ/documents/dp/0706.pdf.
Damasio, A. (1994), *Descartes' Error*, New York: Putnam.
Daw, N. (2003), 'Reinforcement Learning Models of the Dopamine System and Their Behavioral Implications', doctoral dissertation, Carnegie Mellon University, Pittsburgh, PA, USA.
Dayan, P., S. Kakade and P.R. Montague (2000), 'Learning and Selective Attention', *Nature Neuroscience*, **3**, 1218–1223.
Dennett, D. (1997), *Kinds of Minds*, New York: Basic Books.
Dorris, M. and P. Glimcher (2004), 'Activity in Posterior Parietal Cortex is Correlated with the Relative Selective Desirability of Action', *Neuron*, **44**, 365–378.
Dunn, B., T. Dalgleish and A.D. Lawrence (2006), 'The Somatic Marker Hypothesis: A Critical Evaluation', *Neuroscience and Biobehavior Review*, **30**, 239–271.
Fehr, E. (2009), 'Social Preferences and the Brain', in P. Glimcher, C. Camerer, E. Fehr and

R. Poldrack (eds), *Neuroeconomics: Decision Making and the Brain*, London: Elsevier, pp. 215–232.

Frank, R. (1988), *Passions Within Reason*, New York: Norton.

Gallistel, C.R. (1993), *The Organization of Learning*, Cambridge, MA: MIT Press.

Gallistel, C.R. and J. Gibbon (2002), *The Symbolic Foundations of Conditioned Behavior*, Mahweh, NJ: Lawrence Erlbaum.

Gigerenzer, G., P. Todd and the ABC Research Group (1999), *Simple Heuristics That Make Us Smart*, Oxford: Oxford University Press.

Glimcher, P. (2003a), *Decisions, Uncertainty and the Brain*, Cambridge, MA: MIT Press.

Glimcher, P. (2003b), 'The Neurobiology of Visual-Saccadic Decision Making', *Annual Review of Neuroscience*, **26**, 133–179.

Glimcher, P. (2009), 'Choice: Towards a Standard Back-Pocket Model', in P. Glimcher, C. Camerer, E. Fehr and R. Poldrack (eds), *Neuroeconomics: Decision Making and the Brain*, London: Elsevier, pp. 503–521.

Glimcher, P.W., J.W. Kable and K. Louie (2007), 'Neuroeconomic Studies of Impulsivity: Now or Just as Soon as Possible?', *American Economic Review*, **97**, 142–147.

Gul, F. and W. Pesendorfer (2001), 'Temptation and Self Control', *Econometrica*, **69**, 1403–1436.

Gul, F. and W. Pesendorfer (2008), 'The Case for Mindless Economics', in A. Caplin and A. Schotter (eds), *The Foundations of Positive and Normative Economics: A Handbook*, Oxford: Oxford University Press, pp. 3–39.

Hampton, A., P. Bossaerts and J. O'Doherty (2006), 'The Role of the Ventromedial Prefrontal Cortex in Abstract State-based Inference during Decision-making in Humans', *Journal of Neuroscience*, **26**, 7836–8360.

Harrison, G. (2008), 'Neuroeconomics: A Critical Reconsideration', *Economics and Philosophy*, **24**, 303–344.

Harrison, G. and D. Ross (2010), 'The Methodologies of Neuroeconomics', *Journal of Economic Methodology*, **17**, 185–196.

Harrison, G. and E.E. Rutström (2009), 'Expected Utility and Prospect Theory: One Wedding and a Decent Funeral', *Experimental Economics*, **12**, 133–158.

Hausman, D. and M. McPherson (2006), *Economic Analysis, Moral Philosophy and Public Policy*, Cambridge: Cambridge University Press.

Heyman, G. (2009), *Addiction: A Disorder of Choice*, Cambridge, MA: Harvard University Press.

Howard, R. (1960), *Dynamic Programming and Markov Processes*, Cambridge, MA: MIT Press.

Hutchins, E. (1995), *Cognition in the Wild*, Cambridge, MA: MIT Press.

Kable, J. and P. Glimcher (2007), 'The Neural Correlates of Subjective Value during Intertemporal Choice', *Nature Neuroscience*, **10**, 1625–1633.

Kakade, S. and P. Dayan (2002), 'Dopamine: Generalization and Bonuses', *Neural Networks*, **15**, 549–559.

Knoch, D., A. Pascual-Leone, K. Meyer, V. Treyer and E. Fehr (2006), 'Diminishing Reciprocal Fairness by Disrupting the Right Prefrontal Cortex', *Science*, **314**, 829–832.

Knutson, B., S. Rick, G. Wimmer, D. Prelec and G. Loewenstein (2007), 'Neural Predictors of Purchases', *Neuron*, **53**, 147–156.

Knutson, B., A. Westdorp, E. Kaiser and D. Hommer (2000), 'fMRI Visualization of Brain Activity during a Monetary Incentive Delay Task', *NeuroImage*, **12**, 20–27.

Lee, D., M. Conroy, B. McGreevy and D. Barraclough (2004), 'Reinforcement Learning and Decision Making in Monkeys during a Competitive Game', *Cognition and Brain Research*, **22**, 45–48.

Lee, D., M. Conroy, B. McGreevy and D. Barraclough (2005), 'Learning and Decision Making in Monkeys during a Rock–Paper–Scissors Game', *Cognition and Brain Research*, **25**, 416–430.

Lee, D. and X.-J. Wang (2009), 'Mechanisms for Stochastic Decision Making in the Primate Frontal Cortex: Single-Neuron Recording and Circuit Modeling', in P. Glimcher,

C. Camerer, E. Fehr and R. Poldrack (eds), *Neuroeconomics: Decision Making and the Brain*, London: Elsevier, pp. 481–501.

Loewenstein, G. (1999), 'A Visceral Account of Addiction', in J. Elster and O.-J. Skog (eds), *Getting Hooked: Rationality and Addiction*, Cambridge, MA: Cambridge University Press, pp. 235–264.

Marr, D. (1982), *Vision*, San Francisco, CA: W.H. Freeman.

McClure, S., N. Daw and R. Montague (2003), 'A Computational Substrate for Incentive Salience', *Trends in Neuroscience*, **26**, 423–428.

McClure, S., D. Laibson, G. Loewenstein and J. Cohen (2004), 'Separate Neural Systems Value Immediate and Delayed Monetary Rewards', *Science*, **306**, 503–507.

Menary, R. (ed.) (2010), *The Extended Mind*, Cambridge, MA: MIT Press.

Montague, P.R. and G. Berns (2002), 'Neural Economics and the Biological Substrates of Valuation', *Neuron*, **36**, 265–284.

Montague, P.R., B. King-Cassas and J. Cohen (2006), 'Imaging Valuation Models in Human Choice', *Annual Review of Neuroscience*, **29**, 417–448.

Ng, A., D. Harada and S. Russell (1999), 'Policy Invariance under Reward Transformations: Theory and Application to Reward Shaping', in I. Bratko and S. Dzeroski (eds) *Proceedings of the Sixteenth Annual Conference on Machine Learning*, San Francisco, CA: Morgan Kaufmann, pp. 278–287.

Niv, Y. and P.R. Montague (2009), 'Theoretical and Empirical Studies of Learning', in P. Glimcher, C. Camerer, E. Fehr and R. Poldrack (eds), *Neuroeconomics: Decision Making and the Brain*, London: Elsevier, pp. 331–352.

O'Doherty, J., P. Dayan, K. Friston, H. Critchley and R. Dolan (2003), 'Temporal Difference Models and Reward-Related Learning Models in the Human Brain', *Neuron*, **38**, 329–337.

Phelps, E.A. (2009), 'The Study of Emotions in Neuroeconomics', in P. Glimcher, C. Camerer, E. Fehr and R. Poldrack (eds), *Neuroeconomics: Decision Making and the Brain*, London: Elsevier, pp. 233–250.

Poldrack, R.A. (2006), 'Can Cognitive Processes be Inferred from Neuroimaging Data?', *Trends in Cognitive Science*, **10**, 59–63.

Prelec, D. and R. Bodner (2003), 'Self-Signaling and Self-Control', in G. Loewenstein, D. Read and R. Baumeister (eds), *Time and Decision*, New York: Russell Sage Foundation, pp. 277–298.

Rabe-Hesketh, S., E. Bullmore and M. Brammer (1997), 'The Analysis of Functional Magnetic Resonance Images', *Statistical Methods in Medical Research*, **6**, 215–237.

Rilling, J.K., A.L. Glenn, M.R. Jairam, G. Pagnoni, D.R. Goldsmith, H.A. Elfenbein and S.O. Lilienfeld (2007), 'Neural Correlates of Social Cooperation and Non-Cooperation as a Function of Psychopathy', *Biological Psychiatry*, **6**, 1260–1271.

Ross, D. (2005), *Economic Theory and Cognitive Science: Microexplanation*, Cambridge, MA: MIT Press.

Ross, D. (2012), 'The Economic Agent: Not Human, but Important', in U. Mäki (ed.), *Handbook of Philosophy of Science, Vol. 13: Economics*, London: Elsevier (forthcoming).

Ross, D., G. Ainslie and A. Hofmeyr (2010), 'Self-control, Discounting and Reward: Why Picoeconomics is Economics', Working Paper, University of Cape Town, http://uct.academia.edu/DonRoss/Papers/172669/SElf-control--discounting-and-reward--Why-picoeconomics-is-economics.

Ross, D., C. Sharp, R. Vuchinich and D. Spurrett (2008), *Midbrain Mutiny*, Cambridge, MA: MIT Press.

Samuelson, P. (1947), *Foundations of Economic Analysis*, Cambridge, MA: Harvard University Press.

Sanfey, A., J. Rilling, J. Aronson, L. Nystrom and J. Cohen (2003), 'The Neural Basis of Economic Decision-making in the Ultimatum Game', *Science*, **300**, 1755–1758.

Schultz, W. (2009), 'Midbrain Dopamine Neurons: A Retina of the Reward System?', in P. Glimcher, C. Camerer, E. Fehr and R. Poldrack (eds), *Neuroeconomics: Decision Making and the Brain*, London: Elsevier, pp. 323–329.

Schweighofer, N. and K. Doya (2003), 'Meta-Learning in Reinforcement Learning', *Neural Networks*, **16**, 5–9.

Seo, H., D. Barraclough and D. Lee (2007), 'Dynamic Signals Related to Choices and Outcomes in the Dorsolateral Prefrontal Cortex', *Cerebral Cortex*, **17**, 110–117.

Seo, H. and D. Lee (2007), 'Temporal Filtering of Reward Signals in the Dorsal Anterior Cingulate Cortex during a Mixed-Strategy Game', *Journal of Neuroscience*, **27**, 8366–8377.

Smith, V. (2007), *Rationality in Economics: Constructivist and Ecological Forms*, Cambridge: Cambridge University Press.

Sutton, R. and A. Bartow (1998), *Reinforcement Learning: An Introduction*, Cambridge, MA: MIT Press.

Talmi, D., B. Seymour, P. Dayan and R. Dolan (2008), 'Human Pavlovian-Instrumental Transfer', *Journal of Neuroscience*, **28**, 360–368.

Vromen, J. (2010), 'On the Surprising Finding that Expected Utility is Literally Computed in the Brain', *Journal of Economic Methodology*, **17**, 17–36.

Wang, X.-J. (2001), Synaptic Reverberation Underlying Mnemonic Persistent Activity', *Trends in Neuroscience*, **24**, 455–463.

Wang, X.-J. (2002), 'Probabilistic Decision Making by Slow Reverberation in Cortical Circuits', *Neuron*, **36**, 955–968.

Watkins, C. (1989), 'Learning With Delayed Rewards', doctoral dissertation, Cambridge University, Cambridge.

Wilcox, N. (2006), 'Theories of Learning in Games and Heterogeneity Bias', *Econometrica*, **74**, 1271–1292.

Yu, A. and P. Dayan (2005), 'Uncertainty, Neuromodulation, and Attention', *Neuron*, **46**, 681–692.

Zak, P. (2008), 'The Brains behind Economics', *Journal of Economic Methodology*, **15**, 301–302.

5 High-fidelity economics
Anna Alexandrova and Daniel M. Haybron[1]

5.1 INTRODUCTION[2]

Happiness is returning to economics. Not long ago, such a proposition might have seemed no more plausible than the canned food Homer Simpson once retrieved from his kitchen cupboard: 'Nuts and Gum: Together at Last!' No doubt the combination of economics and happiness remains nuts and gum to some economists. Yet happiness is, indeed, returning to economics after a long hiatus. The literature on economics and happiness is fast-growing and includes a number of leading economists, Nobel laureates among them. One of the pioneers in this venture, Swiss economist Bruno Frey, has gone so far as to title a recent book, *Happiness: A Revolution in Economics* (2008).

Revolution or no, change is afoot, and the incursions of research on the psychology of well-being into economics are bringing new values and methods into the fold. This research is wide-ranging, covering not just happiness but also the study of human judgment and choice processes in behavioral economics and allied fields, which bears on individuals' ability to pursue their interests effectively. Because all of this work concerns the psychology of well-being, or what philosophers call prudential value, we will place it under the common rubric of prudential psychology (Haybron, 2008). It remains to be seen how far the discipline will be changed by these developments, but they seem to us to promise an economics that is at once messier and yet more faithful to the realities of human life. Less exact, but higher fidelity. Or so we shall argue in what follows. In particular, we argue that the renewed focus on the psychology of well-being is stimulating improvements in economic methodology by moving it away from a view we call minimalism and toward greater methodological openness and diversity. This claim has two parts:

1. The methodology of positive economics is undergoing a significant change, whether or not it constitutes a revolution. While the standard methodology of revealed preference is not being abandoned (at least not entirely), it is being supplemented by a growing, and entirely appropriate, interest in psychological processes.
2. These changes have deep repercussions for normative economics.

Economists are learning to live with a less idealized and more realistic picture of human nature. As old assumptions about well-being and its promotion are being challenged, economists are actively exploring a 'new interventionism'. The dominant optimism about the prospects for advancing human well-being through a singular focus on expanding people's options is giving way, at least in some circles, to a more sober approach to liberal policy.

We do not claim that these changes affect all fields of economics, or that these changes are being accepted without controversy. We merely claim that they are significant enough to prompt a broad re-evaluation of the philosophical foundations of economics. Nor do we assert, or believe, that happiness is the sole constituent of well-being (indeed much of our discussion, regarding behavioral economics, requires no assumptions about happiness at all). Our discussion will be compatible with almost all extant theories of well-being, including many preference satisfaction accounts. We will help ourselves only to the commonsense notion that how happy a person is, understood in psychological terms, is an important aspect of most individuals' well-being.[3]

In section 5.2 we explain the methodological orthodoxy in economics – a view we call 'minimalism'. Section 5.3 argues in general terms for the importance of psychology in positive economics. Section 5.4 discusses the challenges raised for minimalism by recent work in the psychology of well-being, focusing mainly on normative economics. The chief policy consequence of these changes is a move toward a more interventionist approach to policy, a development we explore in section 5.4.4.

5.2   THE MINIMALIST LEGACY

The standard disciplinary narrative about the rise of happiness research in economics is that economists used to, at least for most of the twentieth century, be rightly suspicious of reference to subjective states; but now that psychologists have developed good measurement instruments to gauge them, happiness can legitimately return to economics.

There is reason to be suspicious of this story, as measurement of subjective mental states is not new to psychology, and much of the research now cited by economists employs techniques that have been around for some time, or did not require any great technical advances to devise (Angner, 2005). Happiness has been largely absent from economics in the twentieth century not because there were no measures of it, but because of the more general philosophical orientation of the discipline: a kind of methodological minimalism,[4] born of the positivist doctrines that prevailed for much of the last century. In a nutshell, economics has tended to stress a radical form of observability, favoring choice behavior over inner psychological states; explanatory parsimony, embodied for instance in Milton Friedman's claim that 'a hypothesis is important if it "explains" much by little';[5] and a thoroughgoing assimilation of intellectual rigor to mathematical precision, to the extent that ideas not expressed in mathematical terms tend not to be taken seriously (and simple ideas not needing a mathematical formalization often get the treatment anyway).

It is generally agreed that there is no single criterion on which to evaluate scientific theories. Among the criteria traditionally discussed by philosophers of science are empirical adequacy, consistency, parsimony, mathematical precision, explanatory scope and possibly others. The real question is what weight should be given to each of these virtues and how they ought to trade off against each other. The minimalist view in economics assigns a great deal of weight to parsimony and mathematical precision. It does so by postulating that only a certain kind of evidence is available to economists (choice behavior, but not survey, experimental or neural data), and sometimes also by restricting the range of phenomena that fall within the purview of economics (aggregate but not individual choice behavior, as Friedman did). The minimalist's commitment to parsimony and mathematization is manifested in the drive to represent all the relevant behavior with the same core assumptions in formal deductive models.

Precision, parsimony and a firm grounding in observable reality are all desirable features of scientific theories, to a point. But taken too far, they can be bought at the expense of fidelity to the reality we are trying to understand. It is good to explain a lot with a little, but sometimes a little only explains a little, or nothing at all. Positivist epistemology, which eschews everything but observable behavior – and thus throws out the baby, much of our best physics, and all good sense with the bathwater – has long since been consigned to the flames elsewhere in the academy. For that matter, we doubt many economists believe it any more. We suspect, and certainly hope, that the continued prominence of 'mindless economics', as two of its practitioners dubbed it,[6] has more to do with the ability of researchers to do meaningful work within that paradigm than any real devotion to behaviorist psychology.

Precision too is good, often essential, but must not be confused with rigor. A rigorous argument is careful and thorough in setting out the case for its conclusion; it does not claim to show more than it has in fact shown. But it need not be precise, certainly not mathematically precise, and some of the most acute analysis in philosophy and even the sciences – and even, we dare say, economics; see Adam Smith – is neither mathematical nor particularly exact. As Aristotle long ago observed, the appropriate degree of precision depends of the character of the subject matter. Demand more than the topic allows and we run afoul of Marshall's dictum: pruning the object of study to fit our analytical tools until there is little left of it.[7] Mathematical precision in particular requires a highly simplified accounting of reality, at least if it is to be tractable, and the richer the reality you are trying to model, the greater the risk that your formalization will leave out so much that the theory fails to get very much of it right. Precision, that is, can sometimes come at the expense of fidelity to the phenomena, and theorists need to find the right balance for the task at hand. Economics, we think, is particularly susceptible to this sort of worry, since probably few realities are richer than the ceaseless efforts of humanity to advance the manifold dimensions of well-being, and other values besides, through economic activity.

A number of threads of recent economic work, especially research drawing on the psychology of well-being, point to a style of economics that is less mindless, less parsimonious and less focused on formal precision, yet no less rigorous. And, in our view, more faithful to the realities of human life.

Minimalism, finally, includes 'normative minimalism': keeping value commitments to a minimum, if not avoiding them altogether, notably by orienting normative economics solely toward the satisfaction of preferences, and thus (ostensibly) deferring to individuals' own value judgments. Normative minimalists may adopt a preference satisfaction theory of well-being or welfarism, the view that only well-being is morally significant. But here we put aside these views and concentrate on one facet of normative minimalism: the assumption that only choice behavior, and not happiness, is a valid, or a valid enough,[8] indicator of well-being. It is this view that we take to be especially undermined by the current changes.

We recognize that minimalism is a complex package, which does not need to be accepted or rejected as a whole. There are many different permutations depending on how finely one partitions the minimalist space of possibilities. Here we concentrate especially on two crucial parts of the package: the revealed preference view and the deference to choice behavior as a guide to well-being.

5.3 WHY POSITIVE ECONOMICS NEEDS PSYCHOLOGY

The revealed preference methodology (hereafter RPM) is the mainstay of economic minimalism.[9] Proposed in the 1930s, the heyday of behaviorism and operationalism, it is one of the most influential methodological ideas in economics. In its strong form the view takes any psychological phenomena to be, by definition, outside the scope of economics. Alternatively RPM can take the evidential form that choice behavior is the only admissible evidence in economics. Rather than providing a comprehensive critique of RPM, here we have two goals. The first goal is to show that the recent attempts at defending RPM fail and with them the efforts to keep psychology out of economics. Secondly, the sensible revisions of RPM currently being pioneered need not involve a revolution in economics.

One strong claim associated with RPM is that as far as economics is concerned preferences are just choices. On this view, the term 'preference' in economics refers to observed behavior, not to the psychological state that may cause or explain this behavior, and the term 'utility' refers just to the numerical representation of these choices. Students of economics are thus traditionally cautioned: an agent chooses an option not because it has greater utility, rather it has greater utility because the agent chooses it. (Strictly speaking, RPM dispenses even with choices – any form of selection behavior will do. If Gandhi sleepwalks to the store, drops a wad of cash on the counter, walks out with a bottle of fortified wine, and returns to bed, he has thereby revealed his 'preference' for rotgut. Likewise if his puppet-master walks him through the same motions. RPM applies to zombies and thermostats no less than ordinary humans.)

This thesis is then used to give an interpretation of the standard utility theory of microeconomics – that it is a theory aiming at describing behavior with certain useful formalisms, not at explaining it by appeal to psychological states. Because of this, this theory cannot be challenged by any facts, new or old, about how people make decisions, but only by some facts about their choice behavior. Here are some of the most recent endorsements of this idea:

> The modern theory of utility . . . abandons any attempt to explain *why* people behave as they do. Instead of an explanatory theory, we have to be content with a descriptive theory, which can do no more than say that a person will be acting inconsistently if he or she did such-and-such in the past, but now plans to do so-and-so in the future. (Binmore, p. 542)

> Economic phenomena consist of individual choices and their aggregates and do not include hedonic values of utilities or feelings. Therefore, it is not relevant for an economic model to explore the feelings associated with economic choices. The point of revealed preference theory is to separate the theory of decision making from the analysis of emotional consequences of decisions. (Gul and Pesendorfer, 2008, p. 40)

And more strikingly: 'Populating economic models with "flesh-and-blood human beings," was never the objective of economists.' (Ibid., p. 43).

This view of economics does not sit happily with the growing prominence of research on the psychology of well-being.[10] Gul and Pesendorfer are explicitly skeptical about the possibility of peaceful coexistence between standard economics and prudential psychology as it is now conceived: 'Greater psychological realism is not an appropriate modeling criterion for economics and therapeutic social activism is not its goal' (ibid., p. 44); and '[Welfare economics] does not try to improve the decision-maker but tries to evaluate how economic institutions mediate (perhaps psychologically unhealthy) behavior of agents' (ibid., p. 3).

The advocates of RPM often claim that any reading of economic theory that interprets it as making claims about psychological processes fundamentally 'misunderstands' the nature and the subject matter of economics (Gul and Pesendorfer, 2008; Binmore, 2009). What is absent is a good argument for why this is the right view of economics. We will return to why this is a poor view of normative economics. On the positive side, apart from appeals to convention, we are told that this makes positive economics more flexible and less dependent on the vagaries of research in psychology. Economics should not commit itself to a controversial and most probably false theory of the mind (that is, the mind as a mechanism that calculates utility) (Binmore, 2009, p. 542).

The implicit reasoning seems to be as follows: utility maximization is clearly false as a psychological theory and yet we cannot reject utility maximization, so we have to define it in an apsychological way. In our view this is an ostrich strategy, akin to a recommendation that biology ignore chemistry if biological models are contradicted by evidence from chemistry. Furthermore, flexibility is only one virtue of scientific theories, a virtue that needs to be weighed against other important virtues such as empirical adequacy. Tautologies are flexible, but they are not scientific theories. Gul and Pesendorfer claim that another virtue of the 'mindless' approach is that it facilitates specialization of different disciplines, here economics and psychology (Gul and Pesendorfer, 2008, p. 9). Again, we grant that specialization can be valuable, but not in itself and not infinitely.

A more sophisticated defense of RPM is given by Don Ross (Ross, 2005, 2010). Like Binmore, and Gul and Pesendorfer, Ross does not deny the validity of a psychological study of human valuation and choice and hence of the findings of behavioral and experimental economics. He objects only to the claim that these results undermine traditional economic theory. There is a good reason to treat economic theory as concerning not flesh-and-blood people, but rather as formal descriptions of 'emergent systems of production, consumption and exchange, in a context of agnosticism about who or what the *ultimate* units of these activities are' (Ross, 2010, p. 7). This definition allows us to apply economic theory to agents other than human intentional agents, such as groups, animals, neurons and so on. Indeed insects, by virtue of their unchanging preferences, appear to behave very much like neoclassical agents (Ross, 2005). Any of these systems can implement economic agency and, if they do, economic generalizations, but perhaps not psychological ones, will apply to them.

Ross takes inspiration from an approach in philosophy of science called ontic structural realism, which takes our best science to be concerned with structural relations, where the relata themselves are not individuals (Ladyman and Ross, 2007). Whether or not this is a fruitful approach for some cases, the question remains whether or not it is a good interpretation of economics in general. We remain open-minded that sometimes it may be useful to subscribe to such a minimalist interpretation of economic theory, such as when this theory is successfully applied to agents without minds. The question is whether this interpretation should define the discipline of economics and its subject matter. Whether it should is not an a priori matter.[11] Rather it depends on the empirical pay-off of such an approach. Surely, the reasons to be realist about the particular structural network studied by economics on the revealed preference interpretation must come from the empirical successes of this research program. (This is why structural realism is defensible in the case of physics.) It is these reasons that we, along with many behavioral economists, fail to see. The rise of behavioral economics is precisely a response to failures of standard economics to explain and to predict human choices. Elsewhere one of us argued that from the point of view of history of science, RPM is a poor strategy because it insulates economics from empirical progress in the study of causal mechanisms and erects walls of incommensurability between it and the related disciplines such as psychology, anthropology and neuroscience which are crucial for this study (Craver and Alexandrova, 2008). Rejecting such insulation and tearing down such walls is precisely what made possible the empirical success of twentieth-century neuroscience, to cite just one example.

When economic theory is applied successfully by any reasonable standard, it is often truly steeped in psychology. Some of the best current practices of economics, even independently of the work involving happiness, cannot be understood without an explicit reference to psychological mechanisms. For example, the growing field of design economics (Roth, 2002), which currently comprises the center stage of empirical application of microeconomics, attests to this fact. When economists are called to construct reliable incentive-compatible institutions – for example, an auction that distributes spectrum licenses to telecommunication firms – they do so by testing a number of different causal claims. A specific kind of auction under specific conditions, which include agents' beliefs and desires, causes a specific distribution of goods and revenue generation. Crucially, in design economists' accounts of how they use models, the RPM approach to economic models is conspicuously absent (Plott, 1997; Guala, 2005). This is because this attitude does not fit the goal of design economics – to create mechanisms whose behavior we can more or less understand and control. Part of these mechanisms are preferences and expectations understood psychologically, not behavioristically.

Of course, an advocate of minimalism could dig in her heels and insist that to the extent that these projects require psychological theorizing, they are not genuinely economic projects. For Ross, for example, this research should be called 'psychology of valuation' (2010, p. 17), rather than economics. But exactly what scientific pay-off is achieved by this stipulation is far from clear. Presumably, our definition of the subject matter of a science should be sensitive to the state of our empirical knowledge and to its capacity to play the roles it is designed to play (explanation, prediction and control). If these constraints played no role, we would still be committed to the Aristotelian view that celestial phenomena are not within the purview of physics, despite the amazing success of Newton's unification.

The examples of the latest outbreaks in RPM advocacy that we cite here are instructive because they signal that the view Binmore, Gul and Pesendorfer, and Ross are so keen to deem 'standard' and 'mainstream', is no longer.[12] It is precisely because the larger paradigm in economics is changing that there is even any need to reaffirm the traditional revealed preference view, especially in such uncompromising terms. We think that RPM – either as a claim about what economics is, or what evidence is and is not available to economists – is on the wane. Economists are branching out. They are eagerly building conjectures about the mechanisms of evaluation and decision-making and treat these hypotheses as integral to their projects in economics (Kahneman et al., 1997; Beshears et al., 2008; Kahneman and Krueger, 2006; Ariely et al., 2006 along with many others). This does not mean that RPM is invalid, just that it is no longer definitive of economics.

Our second claim is that rejecting RPM as discussed above need not involve a revolution in economic methodology. Choice may not be the only evidence for inferring preferences and assessing utility functions, but the project started by Paul Samuelson that studies the conditions under which observed choices are compatible with utility maximization is far from dead. In fact this project is currently being enriched by economists who do take happiness and psychology seriously.

An essential part of the classic revealed preference theory is the assumption of rationality which in this case takes the following form: if the agent chooses A over B when both are available, then she prefers A over B (ignoring the possibility of indifference). Paul Samuelson's work has been widely used as a method[13] that, assuming rationality, makes it possible to infer utility functions from choices between two goods if the agent's choices satisfy the 'weak axiom of revealed preference' (which stipulates that the agent should not choose A over B when both are available in one case but not in another). Further axioms and techniques have been developed to infer utility functions in more complex settings (see Varian, 2006 on the state of the art). Since economists have traditionally adopted a preference satisfaction view of well-being, this project has been central to welfare economics.

Arguments against the universal applicability of RPM have been around for a while (Sen, 1993), recently underscored by doubts about rationality emanating from the heuristics and biases research program in psychology. Now concerns about happiness and well-being are bringing these doubts to the forefront. Economists are rethinking RPM to accommodate the need for psychological plausibility and their concern with well-being. Most are doing so in a non-revolutionary way that preserves useful elements of RPM while rejecting others.

Two questions raised recently about the relationship between well-being and revealed choices illustrate this approach. What are the general conditions in which choices do not, in all plausibility, reveal a person's well-being? Can we usefully summarize the social, environmental and psychological factors that bring about these conditions?

Botond Köszegi and Matthew Rabin explore the first question. They propose a framework for eliciting mistakes through choice behavior where mistakes are various failures of rationality and errors of statistical reasoning (for example, the gambler's or the projection fallacy). Once a person reveals that she makes certain errors, her preferences can be inferred given her erroneous beliefs (Köszegi and Rabin, 2008a, 2008b). It turns out that something like a weaker revealed preference approach can still be useful even without assuming rationality in the sense of utility maximization and faultless reasoning.

Where rationality is a reasonable assumption to make (and economists generally believe that there are many such contexts), Köszegi and Rabin show that choices will still fail to reveal preferences wherever the utility of an outcome depends on the context of choice. Examples include choices that vary with framing effects, 'social preferences' involving envy and other choices which may or may not be irrational. Köszegi and Rabin understand these situations as cases in which the happiness connected with an outcome varies with the circumstances of this outcome. When preferences exhibit such context-dependence, no amount of empirical data on the choice behaviors is sufficient to reveal the person's preference.

Crucially, Köszegi and Rabin wish to keep parts of RPM, since context-dependence is not always an issue. They only seek to limit its applicability.

More broadly, what are the social and psychological conditions under which revealed preferences should not be treated as a good guide to well-being? Beshears et al. (2008) argue that this happens: (1) whenever people make passive rather than active choices; (2) whenever the choice problems involve many options or long horizons; (3) whenever people have limited experience making this kind of decision; (4) whenever third-party marketing is involved; and (5) often when they have to make choices about how valuable future outcomes are. Although there are methods consistent with revealed preference that can detect some preferences indicative of well-being, psychological measures must be admitted into the pool of evidence. Once again, we see here an explicit attempt to unify the traditional and the new sources of evidence without entirely abandoning the old paradigm.

This is a dramatic development and it is not isolated (see, for example, Loewenstein and Haisley, 2008). Economists are becoming more and more accepting of the idea that one kind of indicator (traditionally, income or growth, which they have taken to be fallible but decent proxies for actual preference satisfaction) is insufficient to evaluate well-being (for example, Stiglitz et al., 2009). Dramatic as they are, these developments do not unambiguously amount to a revolution.[14] No Kuhnian succession of incommensurable paradigms is taking place. Economists are reassessing and supplementing RPM, not rejecting it wholesale.[15] However, they are aware of its limitations and do not take these limitations to be unimportant or exceptional. In other words, economics is becoming more methodologically open.

5.4   ECONOMICS MEETS THE PSYCHOLOGY OF WELL-BEING

5.4.1   Historical Background: Liberal Optimism

The next section will examine more directly the psychological findings in the well-being literature that have proven inhospitable to the revealed preference orthodoxy. First we need to set this research in historical context. Note that while the discussion in these sections mainly focuses on normative economics, much of it bears directly on positive economics as well, as we explain in section 4.4.3.

By and large, the mood of modernity has had an optimistic tone – optimistic, particularly, about the rational powers of the human individual. Casting off the dark medieval picture of a dim-witted populace damaged by original sin, Enlightenment thinkers came to believe that each of us has the ability to choose rationally for ourselves, correctly discerning our interests and making prudent choices in their pursuit. Liberating individuals for the personal pursuit of well-being accordingly became a central priority of the modern world – and indeed, became for many the sole purpose, more or less, of government. In liberty lies our salvation; and salvation, for those of us blessed with sufficient liberty, lies well within our grasp. Allow us adequate resources to pursue our goals, leave us be, and watch us flourish.

This inspiring vision typifies the liberal ethos that has dominated the modern political and intellectual scene, and the optimism it embodies might thus be termed 'liberal optimism'.[16] A bit less roughly, liberal optimism maintains that freedom is good for us, the more freedom the better. And given sufficient freedom to shape our lives as we wish, we will tend to do pretty well, and largely through the prudent exercise of that freedom. The freedom in question is 'option freedom': having as wide a range of options, with as little encumbrance on choosing among them, as possible (again, roughly speaking).

It is easy to see why economics should have come to such prominence in this era, and why economic thinking should tend to embody the spirit of liberal optimism. Economics is arguably a science of freedom, concerned as it is with allocating the resources needed for people to have meaningful options in life. What money does for us, after all, is free us to do and have many of the things we want, and many other things besides. It gives us options. Indeed, in the standard revealed preference framework, I am made better off when I gain a new option, x, and I choose x over my existing options (under the typical assumptions of rationality and full information). As Edward Glaeser recently put it, 'the only way that economists know that utility has increased is if a person has more options to choose from, and that sounds like freedom to me'[17] (2007). Economic growth, being an advancement of freedom, will naturally seem a potent – perhaps the superlative – means of promoting human welfare.

Liberal optimism has a good deal more to recommend it than the illiberal pessimism that ruled the premodern world. Flogging the peasants is off the list of approved methods for advancing the public weal, hopefully for good. But liberal optimism is not the sole alternative to its grim precursor, and it rests on a series of bold assumptions that are increasingly coming up for scrutiny. Increasingly, it seems that they are not going to hold up. A new sobriety is taking root.

Two of these assumptions have been particularly important within mainstream economics in the last century, offering crucial support for its minimalist methodology. First, a heavily freighted version of the preference satisfaction view of well-being – the freight being (roughly) that preferences are well-defined, fixed and independent of others' tastes and attainments, and generally revealed through agents' choices. Unofficially it is often assumed that happiness[18] depends entirely on the satisfaction of preferences, thus understood (and indeed the abandonment of happiness in favor of preferences in economics was originally motivated in part by the idea that preference satisfaction could serve as a proxy for happiness[19]). Intuitively, the idea is that people have their own priorities in life, and their well-being is a matter of success in getting what they want. The second assumption is that people have a high degree of aptitude for making prudent choices (Haybron, 2008).[20] People have the psychological endowments needed to choose well in pursuit of their interests, and will indeed do so reliably under most circumstances, including when they enjoy broad freedom to shape their lives as they wish. Within economics, the standard assumption is that people are perfectly rational, or close enough to it that we can get away with assuming as much.

5.4.2 Challenges from the Psychology of Well-being

These are not empirically modest assumptions, and the relevant science has been looking more and more hostile to them. The aptitude assumption has come under fire from many directions, notably behavioral economics, which has documented numerous 'anomalies' – departures from standard notions of rationality, such as loss aversion – in human judgment and choice.[21] Also significant is research on happiness documenting systematic errors in affective forecasting and recall, so that many choices reflect false information about happiness (Kahneman et al., 1993; Gilbert, 2006). So numerous, predictable and pervasive are these effects that they are coming to seem less than anomalous. Default assumptions about human functioning may need to change, yielding a more nuanced image of pluralistic motivation in which rational choice is not the sole, or perhaps even dominant, determinant of behavior. And what once seemed to be anomalies may turn out to be utterly typical, expectable features of human psychology.[22]

There has been considerable debate over the threat this research actually poses for mainstream economics, but there is substantial and growing acceptance of the need for economics to adjust to the findings on heuristics and biases and other idiosyncrasies of human judgment and choice. It is important to note as well that what counts as a reasonable assumption will depend on our purposes. In some contexts, for instance predicting many kinds of market behavior, the standard rationality assumption may be a useful approximation. But in others, like determining the impact of policies on human welfare across the lifespan, it may not. For even if you choose prudently 99.9 percent of the time, a single mistake can wreck your life. The fact that you tend to buy less of things when they get more expensive will not insulate you from spending your golden years eating dog food because you failed to save for retirement, the reason being that that was not the default option, and having a tolerable senescence would have required you to lift your pen and check a box.[23] We suspect that much of the dispute over the import of behavioral economics reflects different emphases on these perspectives.

The second assumption, concerning the character of well-being, has likewise met with heavy resistance, embodied most notoriously in the surprisingly modest correlations between money and self-reports of happiness (Biswas-Diener, 2008). If well-being is getting what you want, and money essentially a form of freedom to get what you want, then monetary gains should yield comparably greater well-being. Such improvements in well-being should, in turn, involve happiness gains of roughly similar magnitude, or so many have assumed. Yet studies of happiness are widely taken to show that such gains have not been forthcoming. The most striking claim to this effect may be the Easterlin Paradox: the standard story here is that within nations, wealthier people appear to be happier; but wealthier nations – above a relatively low threshold – do not seem to be much happier than poorer nations; and importantly, economic growth may not make nations happier (Easterlin, 1974). In light of this and similar claims, the usual take on the happiness research is that, above a certain threshold where basic needs are met, absolute levels of income have little impact on happiness, whereas the relative level of income within nations has a modest influence. The idea is that what matters for happiness, and well-being in turn, is not how much money you have in absolute terms, but how much you have relative to others in your society (again, above a minimum).

This, if true, is a most unwelcome result for mainstream welfare economics,[24] and indeed for the traditional Enlightenment project of bettering the human condition via the proliferation of ever more options. In the United States, for instance, real per capita gross domestic product (GDP) has tripled since 1950, representing a massive increase in the options available to the average American. Yet reported happiness has arguably declined, remaining flat at best (Diener and Seligman, 2004). Better positioned to satisfy our desires than any peoples in history, Americans seem no happier for it. This, at least relative to the common understanding of happiness' importance, is pretty disappointing stuff.[25]

This conclusion has recently become the subject of vigorous debate, with other research suggesting that happiness does increase with absolute income, at all income levels (for example, Stevenson and Wolfers, 2008). It is not yet clear how this dispute will play out, but even the objectors seem to be positing a relatively small effect. (Though what counts as a 'big' or 'small' effect in this literature is itself a matter of some contention.) At the present time, the conventional reading of the happiness research continues to be that money and happiness, above a certain point, are only modestly related. It bears remarking as well that no one disputes the existence of numerous outliers: comparatively poor societies with high levels of reported happiness – higher, often, than many of the most affluent nations, and indeed sometimes topping the rankings of happiest nations. In short, the connection between money and happiness appears to be substantially weaker than one would expect from the traditional economic view of human welfare.

What explains these results? One possibility is bad data: perhaps the self-report measures are just wrong, overlooking real increases in happiness as people get wealthier. It may be, for instance, that the many boons of modern living really do make our lives more pleasant, but we have grown so accustomed to them that we fail to register them when judging how happy we are (Wilkinson, 2007). The self-report measures do, however, correlate fairly well with a wide range of other indicators, including friends' reports, longevity, and so on (Pavot, 2008). This is compatible with fairly serious errors, like systematic inflation, but it at least suggests that the measures are not wildly erroneous. As well, errors can cut both ways: perhaps common opinion is right that life became more stressful as our incomes multiplied, yet a kind of adaptation keeps that information from impacting self-reports. It is plausible, too, that valence biases – tendencies to skew positive or negative in making happiness judgments – introduce some slippage between real and reported happiness, and probable that these are not entirely independent of economic achievement.[26] We suspect that economic growth very often promotes positivity biases, for instance because people with high-wage careers have a greater stake in seeming happy. If so, then self-reports of happiness will tend in that respect to overstate the benefits of economic growth.

It is unlikely that the apparent economic paradoxes of happiness are purely artifacts of measurement error. But why should happiness be so insensitive to income? We suspect a number of causes, but two plausible culprits have been widely cited in the literature:[27] adaptation and position-sensitivity. In the case of adaptation, or habituation, people get used to things – handicaps, winning the lottery, and so on – and cease to respond as strongly to them, or even to respond at all. Monetary and other material gains appear to be especially susceptible to adaptation: get a big raise and you'll be delighted for a while; but eventually it simply becomes the new normal, and no longer does much for your mood. This seems to have happened on a society-wide basis in many cases of economic growth, and is strikingly illustrated by studies finding material aspirations rising in lockstep with material gains (Easterlin, 2003).

Position-sensitivity, on the other hand, is meant to explain why richer people seem to be happier within countries: people assess their lives relative to local standards, and naturally the richer tend to be doing better by those benchmarks, at least on many dimensions, than their poorer neighbors. The point is often put in terms of our being rivalrous – we are status-conscious, and like to be doing better than the next person – but we need not look to envy to explain the society-wide correlations. To a great extent, position-sensitivity may simply reflect the different income demands of different societies: you need more income to meet your perceived needs in wealthier societies, and those who are struggling to get by will plausibly tend to be less happy than those who are not. One variant of this is the 'nice suit' problem: those with more money buy nicer suits; to keep up and look relatively presentable, the rest of us need to spend more on our own suits (Frank, 1999). We need not be rivalrous to get sucked into this game; we need only to value gainful employment in offices that require suits. Multiply this scenario enough times and it is going to wear on the psyches of those less able to keep up – to wit, those with less income.

5.4.3   The Upshot

How to respond to it all? One possibility is to rethink the importance of happiness. Maybe happiness is merely, as Becker and Rayo recently put it, one of many commodities in the utility function (2008). Getting what we want is ultimately what matters, and if that does not do much for happiness, then so much the worse for happiness. Indeed it is eminently plausible that people care about things other than their own happiness, or even their own well-being. That said, we would be precipitate to dismiss happiness as merely one commodity in our utility functions; that is certainly not how the general run of humanity views it. It is, at the very least, a very important and central commodity. If your best efforts to improve the human condition can do nothing to boost happiness, or even ameliorate the considerable unhappiness that afflicts so many, then it is not entirely clear how much you have to brag about.

Note that while we are sympathetic to the view that pecuniary gains are surprisingly unreliable sources of well-being, our case does not rest on this claim. Happiness research would arguably warrant substantial changes in economic methodology even if we regard happiness as merely one among many human goods, and even if we dismiss entirely the claimed paradoxes of happiness. For it is quite plausible that happiness research, understood broadly to include any research on the psychological aspects of well-being, can provide significant information about well-being that cannot easily be gotten solely through monetary and other 'mindless' indicators. (Stevenson and Wolfers themselves accept a substantial role for happiness research in economics.) Even within a preference framework, we might see happiness both as a useful indicator of preference satisfaction and as a major object of preference. No one, for instance, disputes the existence of non-market goods, and efforts to impute preferences in such cases are notoriously fraught with peril. In fact it does not matter what your theory of well-being is; if you want your economic policies to be sensitive to the welfare impact of, say, a resultant increase in social fragmentation, you had probably best not blind yourself to the entire corpus of research about its impact on people's psychological conditions.

The potential significance of psychological well-being research is clearest for normative economics, a question we will take up in the next section. But it matters for positive economics as well: most obviously, evidence of systematic irrationality bears on the accuracy of our models of choice behavior. But even the happiness literature impacts positive economics, in at least two ways. First, forecasting errors and related mistakes about what will make us happy indicate that many choices are, in predictable ways, poorly informed with respect to the happiness of those making the choices. Second, the happiness research suggests that the variables tracked by standard economic models, such as income or choice behavior, may not correspond very well to the variables that actually matter. Presumably, economists should study not just any old economic phenomena, or what someone has arbitrarily stipulated to be 'economic phenomena', but (at least) the economic phenomena that human beings care about. Among those phenomena, surely, are the effects of economic institutions and policies on human happiness. Good science studies matters of importance, not trivia.

5.4.4   Liberal Sobriety and the New Interventionism

Many economists are taking the psychological research seriously and concluding that our policies need to change. The traditional policy imperative of generating ever more options for people, by swelling GDP, has not produced the hoped-for results. The old liberal optimism is moderating into a new sobriety – not illiberal, nor necessarily pessimistic, but less enamored of the prospects for promoting human welfare through nothing more than the elimination of constraint. Accordingly, many economists are becoming more interventionist in their approach to public policy, advocating measures that correct for irrational tendencies or steer our societies to paths more conducive to happiness.[28] These interventions take two broad forms, corresponding to the findings on imprudence and the paradoxes of happiness, respectively.

In response to systematic imprudence, economists are not, by and large, recommending heavy-handed state coercion. They are rather suggesting a variety of 'nudges' to steer people toward choices that better serve their interests, while leaving it wholly open for the individual to choose otherwise. To compensate for the biases that lead people to privilege default options, for example, it is suggested that default options for important choices like retirement savings be set to what most people will recognize to be a prudent value, such as 'set aside something for retirement'. Such measures may indeed be paternalistic,[29] but in a way that advocates think should worry no one, and they accordingly refer to this sort of approach as 'light paternalism', 'libertarian paternalism' or 'asymmetric paternalism'.[30] Whether libertarian or not, such nudges do not seem obviously incompatible with traditional liberal strictures on paternalistic interference. Whether more aggressive measures will gain support among mainstream economists remains to be seen.

In response to the paradoxes of happiness, a variety of policies have been suggested. Some depart relatively little from tradition, such as the suggestion that governments prioritize reductions in unemployment, which is well known to have serious and lasting impacts on happiness, over economic growth (for example, Oswald, 1997). Others are more revisionary, for instance restrictions on television advertising, or on performance-related pay, to reduce position-related dissatisfaction (Layard, 2005). Progressive consumption taxes have been recommended to discourage positional 'arms races', and progressive income taxes to reduce incentives for overwork, thus making more time for relationships (Frank, 1999; Layard, 2005). And so on.

George Loewenstein and Peter Ubel coin the term 'new interventionism' to describe efforts to compensate for mistakes, but the rubric could well be extended to include policies directly aimed at promoting happiness (Loewenstein and Ubel, 2008). All these policies depart from traditional economic thinking in attempting to promote well-being more directly, and not simply by expanding people's options so they can more easily choose what they want (or rather, what they are inclined to choose). They are interventionist in the sense that they aim directly at promoting certain outcomes, rather than leaving the choice of outcomes entirely up to individuals; they are 'outcome-based', we might say, rather than 'option-based'. Implicit in this project is the recognition that freedom alone will not yield the dividends anticipated by the Enlightenment's optimistic architects. Some constraints, and assists, may be necessary for a flourishing society.[31]

These developments signal a new openness to engaging seriously with questions of value. Once we grant that choice behavior is a dubious guide to well-being, we have to decide what does matter. Normative economics is effectively a branch of ethics, and it is therefore odd that the minimalist orthodoxy has tended to eschew substantial consideration of the ethical literature, assuming a stripped-down value theory that few if any living ethicists would endorse.[32] Economists have been understandably desirous to defer to the individual as much as possible on matters of value – and on that point we are substantially in agreement – but such deference is itself a controversial ethical stance. As well, it is hardly obvious that limiting ourselves to an austere diet of revealed preference, the Pareto principle, standard-issue cost–benefit analyses – in short, an ethical framework that very many individuals would strenuously *reject* – is the way to defer to people's own values. Minimalism in fact imposes a highly sectarian and controversial set of values on the ostensible beneficiaries of economic policy. Such an imposition might sometimes be defensible, but at the very least it demands careful reflection on our ethical principles. This means engaging with the vast literature in ethical and political philosophy.[33] It also means taking seriously humanity's profound and abiding concern for allegedly occult matters like 'intrinsic rights to certain goods, moral reasons, social concerns', not offhandedly consigning them to the dustbin of frivolous objections, as World Bank chief economist Lawrence Summers did in the course of recommending pollution policies that may well have been repugnant even to most of their beneficiaries.[34]

In any event, the illusion of deference to the sovereign consumer is no longer easy to maintain, since the research on behavioral economics and subjective well-being is making manifest the gap between citizens' priorities and the outcomes promoted by minimalist ideals. People care immensely about happiness, for instance, and yet increasing their choice set apparently pays undersized dividends in this department. People want a comfortable retirement, yet many choose not to have one, often for utterly inane reasons. In response, economists are grappling with a variety of deep normative issues: what matters, if not (just) satisfying people's actual preferences, as revealed by choice? Informed or otherwise sanitized preferences? Pleasure? Life satisfaction? Capabilities? The choice among these and other options is not an easy one, but just to be asking such questions is to make considerable progress. Economists rightly worry about the fact that even ethicists disagree about so much, a point that counsels caution before lashing policy to any particular ethical framework. But we can be mindful of ethical theory without committing ourselves to a full-blooded ethical system.[35] (It is helpful that the vast majority of ethicists, Utilitarians and Kantians alike, agree that something like traditional deontological constraints against rights violations, and so on, should be employed in practice. We doubt that any living ethicist believes that policy should always be decided by explicitly consequentialist reasoning.)

As economists come to grips with the complexities of human valuing, some are no longer insisting on a single standard of value of the sort that would allow decision-making through straightforward cost–benefit calculations, and allow that decisions will sometimes require a balancing act among incommensurable values.[36] Many economists understandably worry that such an approach offers policymakers less scientific guidance than we might like, and leaves decision-making vulnerable to unsavory influences. But it has always been possible, and not terribly hard, to rig the calculations in one's favor, and it seems more important to get it roughly right, as the old saw goes, than to get it exact but wrong.[37] In the end, there is no substitute for human judgment.

A more salient worry, it seems to us, is whether the new normative engagement in economics goes far enough. For even economists who take normative questions seriously still tend to assume a consequentialist ethic involving, among other things, a maximizing approach to value. This assumption is problematical given the controversy attending it, especially as a procedure for ordinary decision-making. If neither ordinary morality nor a majority of ethicists endorses such an approach to deliberation, then it is at least open to question whether economists are entitled simply to assume it when making policy recommendations. Given the traditional wariness of economists about imposing alien values on the public, we are hopeful that such questions will, in due course, receive the attention they deserve.

5.5   CONCLUSION

Economists are broadening their methodological repertoire, going beyond the psychological and normative minimalism of the past to incorporate a richer understanding of human psychology and values in their inquiries. This manner of proceeding is indeed messier, but this is arguably less a deficiency of the new economics than a frank acknowledgment of the untidiness of human life, and a recognition that the minimalist approach leaves out far too much. Economics, we would suggest, is getting better at representing the real economy – the one populated with people, who have minds. Sometimes less precise and less elegant, yes, but also less wedded to idealization, less prone to float off into the Platonic ether. Closer to Earth, and higher fidelity.

NOTES

1. The authors' names are listed in alphabetical order. They are equally and jointly responsible for the content of this chapter.
2. This chapter benefited greatly from comments by Dan Hausman, Erik Angner, Francesco Guala, Wade Hands, John Davis and Paul Dolan, as well as audiences at the 2010 St Louis Area Philosophy of Science Association conference and the 2010 Philosophy of Social Science Roundtable.
3. In fact it is plausible that happiness often serves as a proxy for well-being in ordinary discourse – for example, knowing that someone is happy or unhappy is typically taken to license an inference that the person is doing well or badly (Haybron, 2008). We do not commit here to any theory of happiness, but take the main contenders to be hedonistic, life satisfaction, emotional state and hybrid (for example, subjective well-being) theories (Haybron, 2008).
4. Caplin (2008) uses the term 'minimalism' similarly, although he goes on to propose an extension of this approach that allows for the use of psychological data in economic modeling.
5. Friedman (1953, p. 14).
6. Gul and Pesendorfer (2008). These authors clearly are not committed to behaviorist psychology.
7. 'Many important considerations . . . do not lend themselves easily to mathematical expression: they must either be omitted altogether, or clipped and pruned till they resemble the conventional birds and animals of decorative art. And hence arises a tendency towards assigning wrong proportions to economic forces; those elements being most emphasized which lend themselves most easily to analytical methods . . . It is a danger which more than any other the economist must have in mind at every turn' (Alfred Marshall, *Principles of Economics*, 1890, pp. 801–802).
8. Choice behavior is traditionally recognized not to capture perfectly the degree of actual preference satisfaction in cases of public goods and externalities, but here we are concerned with the deeper failures of this method.
9. For a view on exactly how long it has been dominant and in what form see Hands (2008).
10. Binmore contends that the revealed preference view of utility may in fact be compatible with concern about happiness (Binmore, 2009, p. 542), but he does not explain how.
11. Though see Sen (1993) and Hausman (1992) for more philosophical objections to RPM, the revealed preference theory.
12. See the largely critical responses to Gul and Pesendorfer in Caplin and Schotter (2008).
13. For an account of what Samuelson actually intended to do in his 1938 and 1948 writings, see Hands (2008).
14. See Frey (2008) for an argument that it is indeed a revolution. We see elements of both revolutionary and normal science in the recent developments in the economics of happiness. The ordinal revolution is known as such in part because it expunged psychology out of economics. The current development is not completely undoing the effects of the ordinal revolution, just correcting its excesses. We thus stop short of calling it a revolution.
15. For more on the continuity between traditional economics and the economics of happiness see Layard (2008).
16. For further discussion, see Haybron (2008). Naturally, liberals and economists have varied in their views here, as on most matters discussed in this chapter. Economists

need not accept all tenets of liberal optimism; for instance, they could be 'cruel world' liberals, thinking people unlikely to do well under any regime – merely better given greater option freedom than lesser. But the dismal science has rarely seemed so dismal as that.

17. We take Glaeser to be saying only that having more options is a necessary condition for an increase in utility. He is not claiming that any increase in options, however inferior, suffices for an increase in utility.

18. Again, we use the term in its psychological, not evaluative, sense to denote a positive inner state. The precise characterization of this state (Haybron, 2008) is immaterial to the goals of this chapter.

19. For example, Pigou (1932).

20. Though see Hausman and McPherson (2009) for a weaker formulation of this assumption that might be sufficient for some purposes.

21. The literature here is vast and well-enough known that we will not discuss it in any detail. For references, see Haybron (2008, p. 308n4).

22. For a discussion of the psychological literature suggesting as much, see Haybron (2008, pp. 242–251).

23. On default options, see Thaler and Sunstein (2008).

24. While mainstream economic theory does not explicitly claim anything about happiness, its viability depends on making believable assumptions about human well-being, which the happiness data seriously call into question. We elaborate below. For a detailed defense of the importance of happiness for well-being, see Haybron (2008).

25. It is possible that factors unrelated to economic growth have cancelled out real improvements in happiness brought about by economic gains, though we have seen little evidence for this. Of course, economic growth may benefit people without making them happier, if only by increasing longevity. But most people would, *ex ante*, have expected economic growth to pay off primarily in terms of happiness, and it is not clear what the other benefits are that would make up for the weak happiness dividends; that case, if there is one, needs to be made explicitly. Even regarding longevity, it is likely that economic growth in Western nations has far exceeded that needed to secure long lives; and the recent health trends in the United States are, notoriously, uninspiring. (If anything, they suggest a further well-being paradox.) We are grateful to Dan Hausman for pointing out the need for clarification here.

26. For discussion, see Haybron (2007; 2008, Ch.10).

27. For example, Easterlin (2003), Frank (1999), Layard (2005).

28. For an excellent overview, see the papers collected in the August 2008 issue of the *Journal of Public Economics*.

29. However, cf. Hausman and Welch (2010).

30. Camerer et al. (2003), Loewenstein and Haisley (2008), Sunstein and Thaler (2003).

31. See the discussion of 'contextualism' in Haybron (2008), especially pp. 263–267.

32. There are of course exceptions to the orthodoxy, particularly in development economics, for example Sen (1987) and Dasgupta (2001).

33. An excellent starting point would be Hausman and McPherson's book on the subject (Hausman and McPherson, 2006), which should probably be required reading, and rereading, for all economists.

34. For discussion, see Hausman and McPherson (2006).

35. Layard has notably made such an endorsement explicit, advocating a classical Utilitarian moral theory (Layard, 2005). We note that a recent poll of philosophers at 99 leading departments found only 23 percent of specialists in normative ethics ($n = 139$) endorsing or leaning toward any kind of consequentialism, and 24 percent of philosophers overall ($n = 931$). Results available at http://philpapers.org/surveys/.

36. Sunstein (2000), Loewenstein and Haisley (2008), Loewenstein and Ubel (2008), Stiglitz et al. (2009), Adler and Posner (2008), Dolan and White (2007), Frey (2008).

37. The old saw, paraphrased here, hails from Read (1898).

REFERENCES

Adler, M. and E.A. Posner (2008), 'Happiness Research and Cost–Benefit Analysis', *Journal of Legal Studies*, **37**(s2), S253–S292.

Angner, Erik (2005), 'The Evolution of Eupathics: The Historical Roots of Subjective Measures of Well-being', manuscript, University of Alabama, Birmingham.

Ariely, D., G. Loewenstein and D. Prelec (2006), 'Tom Sawyer and the Construction of Value', *Journal of Economic Behavior and Organization*, **60**, 1–10.

Becker, G.S. and L. Rayo (2008), 'Comments on Stevenson and Wolfers, Economic Growth and Subjective Well-Being: Reassessing the Easterlin Paradox', *Brookings Papers on Economic Activity*, **1**, 88–95.

Beshears, J., J. Choi, D. Laibson and B. Madrian (2008), 'How Are Preferences Revealed?', *Journal of Public Economics*, **92**(8–9), 1787–1794.

Binmore, K. (2009), 'Interpersonal Comparison of Utility', in H. Kincaid and D. Ross (eds), *Oxford Handbook of Philosophy of Economics*, New York: Oxford University Press, pp. 540–559.

Biswas-Diener, R. (2008), 'Material Wealth and Subjective Well-Being', in M. Eid and R.J. Larsen (eds), *The Science of Subjective Well-Being*, New York: Guilford Press, pp. 307–323.

Camerer, C., S. Issacharoff, G. Loewenstein, T. O'Donoghue and M. Rabin (2003), 'Regulation for Conservatives: Behavioral Economics and the Case for "Asymmetric Paternalism"', *University of Pennsylvania Law Review*, **151**, 1211–1254.

Caplin, A. (2008), 'Economic Theory and Psychological Data: Bridging the Divide', in A. Caplin and A. Schotter (eds), *The Foundations of Positive and Normative Economics: A Handbook*, Oxford: Oxford University Press, pp. 336–372.

Caplin, A. and A. Schotter (eds) (2008), *The Foundations of Positive and Normative Economics: A Handbook*, New York: Oxford University Press.

Craver, C.F. and A. Alexandrova (2008), 'No Revolution Necessary: Neural Mechanisms for Economics', *Philosophy and Economics*, **24**(3), 381–406.

Dasgupta, P. (2001), *Human Well-being and the Natural Environment*, Oxford, UK and New York, USA: Oxford University Press.

Diener, E. and M. Seligman (2004), 'Beyond Money: Toward an Economy of Well-being', *Psychological Science in the Public Interest*, **5**(1), 1–31.

Dolan, P. and M.P. White (2007), 'How can Measures of Subjective Well-being be Used to Inform Public Policy?', *Perspectives on Psychological Science*, **2**(1), 71–85.

Easterlin, R. (1974), 'Does Economic Growth Improve the Human Lot?', in P.A. David and M.W. Reder (eds), *Nations and Households in Economic Growth: Essays in Honor of Moses Abramovitz*, New York: Academic Press, pp. 89–125.

Easterlin, R. (2003), 'Explaining Happiness', *Proceedings of the National Academy of Sciences of the United States of America*, **100**(19), 11176–11183.

Frank, R. (1999), *Luxury Fever*, New York: Simon & Schuster.

Frey, B.S. (2008), *Happiness: A Revolution in Economics*, Cambridge, MA: MIT Press.

Friedman, M. (1953), 'The Methodology of Positive Economics', in M. Friedman (ed.), *Essays in Positive Economics*, Chicago, IL: University of Chicago Press, pp. 3–43.

Gilbert, D. (2006), *Stumbling on Happiness*, New York: Knopf.

Glaeser, E.L. (2007), 'Coercive Regulation and the Balance of Freedom', *Cato Unbound*, 11 May, http://www.cato-unbound.org/2007/05/11/edward-glaeser/coercive-regulation-and-the-balance-of-freedom/.

Guala, F. (2005), *Methodology of Experimental Economics*, Cambridge: Cambridge University Press.

Gul, F. and W. Pesendorfer (2008), 'The Case for Mindless Economics', in Andrew Caplin and Andrew Shotter (eds), *The Foundations of Positive and Normative Economics*, Oxford: Oxford University Press, pp. 3–42.

Hands, W. (2008), 'Introspection, Revealed Preference and Neoclassical Economics: A Critical Response to Don Ross on the Robbins-Samuelson Argument Pattern', *Journal of the History of Economic Thought*, **30**, 1–26.

Hausman, D.M. (1992), *The Inexact and Separate Science of Economics*, Cambridge: Cambridge University Press.

Hausman, D.M. and M.S. McPherson (2006), *Economic Analysis, Moral Philosophy, and Public Policy*, New York: Cambridge University Press.

Hausman, D.M. and M.S. McPherson (2009), 'Preference Satisfaction and Welfare Economics', *Economics and Philosophy*, **25**, 1–25.

Hausman, D.M. and B. Welch (2010), 'Debate: To nudge or not to nudge', *Journal of Political Philosophy*, **18**(1), 123–136.

Haybron, D.M. (2007), 'Do We Know How Happy We Are?', *Nous*, **41**(3), 394–428.

Haybron, D.M. (2008), *The Pursuit of Unhappiness: The Elusive Psychology of Well-Being*, New York: Oxford University Press.

Kahneman, D., B.L. Fredrickson, C.A. Schreiber and D.A. Redelmeir (1993), 'When More Pain Is Preferred to Less: Adding a Better End', *Psychological Science*, **4**(6), 401–405.

Kahneman, D. and A. Krueger (2006), 'Developments in the Measurement of Subjective Wellbeing', *Journal of Economic Perspectives*, **20**(1), 3–24.

Kahneman, D., P.P. Wakker and R.K. Sarin (1997), 'Back to Bentham? Explorations of Experienced Utility', *Quarterly Journal of Economics*, **112**, 375–405.

Koszegi, B. and M. Rabin (2008a), 'Choices, Situations, and Happiness', *Journal of Public Economics*, **92**(8–9), 1821–1832.

Koszegi, B. and M. Rabin (2008b), 'Revealed Mistakes and Revealed Preferences', in Andrew Caplin and Andrew Schotter (eds), *The Foundations of Positive and Normative Economics*, New York: Oxford University Press, pp. 193–209.

Ladyman, J. and D. Ross (with David Spurrett and John Collier) (2007), *Every Thing Must Go: Metaphysics Naturalized*, Oxford: Oxford University Press.

Layard, R. (2005), *Happiness: Lessons from a New Science*, New York: Penguin.

Layard, R. (2008), 'Introduction', *Journal of Public Economics*, **92**(8–9), 1773–1777.

Loewenstein, G. and E. Haisley (2008), 'The Economist as Therapist: Methodological Ramifications of "Light" Paternalism', in A. Caplin and A. Schotter (eds), *The Foundations of Positive and Normative Economics*, New York: Oxford University Press, pp. 210–248.

Loewenstein, G. and P.A. Ubel (2008), 'Hedonic Adaptation and the Role of Decision and Experience Utility in Public Policy', *Journal of Public Economics*, **92**(8–9), 1795–1810.

Marshall, A. (1890), *Principles of Economics*, London: Macmillan.

Oswald, A.J. (1997), 'Happiness and Economic Performance', *Economic Journal*, **107**(445), 1815–1831.

Pavot, W. (2008), 'The Assessment of Subjective Well-Being: Successes and Shortfalls', in M. Eid and R.J. Larsen (eds), *The Science of Subjective Well-Being*, New York: Guilford Press, pp. 124–140.

Pigou, A.C. (1932), *The Economics of Welfare*, London: Macmillan.

Plott, C.R. (1997), 'Laboratory Experimental Testbeds: Application to the PCS Auction', *Journal of Economics and Management Strategy*, **6**(3), 605–638.

Read, C. (1898), *Logic, Deductive and Inductive*, London: Grant Richards.

Ross, D. (2005), *Economic Theory and Cognitive Science: Microexplanation*, Cambridge, MA: MIT Press.

Ross, D. (2010), 'The Economic Agent: Not Human, but Important', in U. Mäki (ed.), *Handbook of the Philosophy of Science, Vol. 13, Philosophy of Economics*, Oxford: Elsevier, pp. 627–671.

Roth, A. (2002), 'The Economist as Engineer: Game Theory, Experimental Economics and Computation as Tools of Design Economics', *Econometrica*, **70**(4), 1341–1378.

Sen, A. (1987), *On Ethics and Economics*, Oxford: Basil Blackwell.

Sen, A.K. (1993), 'Internal Consistency of Choice', *Econometrica*, **61**(3), 495–521.

Stevenson, B. and J. Wolfers (2008), 'Economic Growth and Subjective Well-Being: Reassessing the Easterlin Paradox', National Bureau of Economic Research, Inc.

Stiglitz, J.E., A. Sen and J.-P. Fitoussi (2009), 'Report of the Commission on the Measurement of Economic Performance and Social Progress', http://www.stiglitz-sen-fitoussi.fr.

Sunstein, C.R. (2000), 'Cognition and Cost–Benefit Analysis', *Journal of Legal Studies*, **29**(2), 1059–1103.
Sunstein, C.R. and R.H. Thaler (2003), 'Libertarian Paternalism Is Not an Oxymoron', *University of Chicago Law Review*, **70**(4), 1159–1202.
Thaler, R.H. and C.R. Sunstein (2008), *Nudge: Improving Decisions about Health, Wealth, and Happiness*, New Haven, CT: Yale University Press.
Varian, H. (2006), 'Revealed Preference', in M. Szenberg, A. Gottesman and L. Ramrattan (eds), *Samuelsonian Economics and the 21st Century*, New York: Oxford University Press, pp. –115.
Wilkinson, W. (2007), 'In Pursuit of Happiness Research: Is it Reliable? What Does it Imply for Policy?', Cato Institute Policy Analysis Series (590).

PART II

WELFARE AND MICROECONOMIC POLICY

6 Current trends in welfare measurement
Erik Angner[1]

6.1 INTRODUCTION

Welfare or well-being – I will use the terms interchangeably – is 'what we have when our lives are going well for us, when we are living lives that are not necessarily morally good, but good *for us*' (Tiberius, 2006, p. 493). Because the concept of well-being is frequently assumed to capture what is – ultimately and not just instrumentally – good for individuals and for groups, it is also supposed to capture that which we have reason to promote – as an end and not just as a means – in our own lives and in the lives of others (Scanlon, 2000, pp. 108–9). Hence, it is widely assumed that well-being is one (or *the* one) consideration that should serve as an end – and not just a means – for public policy. 'A full consideration of taxes, subsidies, transfer programs, health care reform, regulation, environmental policy, the social security system and educational reform', Daniel T. Slesnick writes, 'must ultimately address the question of how these policies affect the well-being of individuals' (Slesnick, 1998, p. 2108).

Given the importance of the concept of welfare, it is unsurprising that the measurement of welfare should be a central concern of modern economics – both theoretical and applied – and of public policy analysis (Slesnick, 1998, p. 2108). To develop a working definition of 'measurement', I will follow David H. Krantz, R. Duncan Luce, Patrick Suppes, and Amos Tversky: 'When measuring some attribute of a class of objects or events, we associate numbers (or other familiar mathematical entities, such as vectors) with the objects in such a way that the properties of the attribute are faithfully represented as numerical properties' (Krantz et al., 1971, p. 1). Thus, loosely speaking, measurement is the process of assigning numbers or other mathematical entities to objects so as to represent some attribute of those objects; a measure is a function from a set of objects to a set of numbers or other mathematical entities. In the context of welfare measurement, the attribute of interest is welfare; the objects are individuals (in the case of individual welfare measurement) or groups (in the case of social welfare measurement).

Welfare measurement has been central to economics at least since the time of A.C. Pigou, author of *The Economics of Welfare* (1952; 1st edn 1920). Pigou, who believed that 'economic welfare . . . is the subject-matter of economic science', made it a crucial goal to develop practicable welfare measures (Pigou, 1952, pp. 10–11). Pigou drew a distinction between 'total welfare' and 'economic welfare', where the latter is 'that part of social welfare that can be brought directly and indirectly into relation with the measuring-rod of money' (Pigou, 1952, p. 11). Yet, he proceeded to argue that 'qualitative conclusions about the effect of an economic cause upon economic welfare will hold good also of the effect on total welfare' (Pigou, 1952, p. 20), which would entail that for practical purposes the difference between economic and total welfare can be ignored and that measures of economic welfare can be used as proxies for total welfare. These days, orthodox economic welfare measures – including measures of national income, consumer and producer surplus, as well as equivalent and compensating variation (see section 6.3 below) – remain by far the most commonly used measures of welfare.

In recent years, however, so-called subjective measures of well-being have increasingly been presented as substitutes for or complements to orthodox economic measures (Campbell, 1976; Diener, 2000, 2006; Diener et al., 2009; Diener and Seligman, 2004). Subjective measures of well-being – sometimes called measures of subjective well-being – are typically based on direct questions such as: 'Taking things all together, how would you say things are these days – would you say you're *very happy*, *pretty happy*, or *not too happy* these days?' (Gurin et al., 1960, p. 411). Answers to such questions are used to construct numerical measures of both individual and social well-being (Angner, 2009a, 2009b). Though subjective measures originated in psychology in the 1920s and 1930s, increasing numbers of bona fide economists are now endorsing their use (Blanchflower and Oswald, 2004; Clark and Oswald, 2002; Frey, 2008; Frey and Stutzer, 2002; Kahneman and Krueger, 2006; Kahneman et al., 2004a, 2004b; Krueger, 2009; Layard, 2005). Furthermore, policymakers appear to be paying attention. In a recent commencement address, for example, US Federal Reserve Chairman Ben S. Bernanke argued: 'Happiness research can be useful for individuals, but it also has implications for policy' (Bernanke, 2010, p. 10).

The rise of subjective measures represents at least two important trends in the measurement of welfare or well-being. The first trend, which has already received some attention in the literature, is a shift away from preference-satisfaction accounts of individual well-being and toward mental-state accounts (Adler and Posner, 2008; Angner, 2008, 2009b, 2010a).[2] Orthodox economic welfare measures are based on preference-satisfaction accounts of well-being, according to which a person is well off to the extent that his or her preferences are satisfied; that is, orthodox economic measures are designed to represent degrees of preference satisfaction. By contrast, subjective measures of well-being are based on mental-state accounts of well-being, according to which a person is well off to the extent that he or she is in some particular subjectively experienced mental state, like happiness or satisfaction; that is, subjective measures are designed to represent degrees of happiness, satisfaction, and the like. As one indication of the recent surge in interest in mental states like happiness, consider the fact that the first edition of the *New Palgrave Dictionary of Economics*, originally published in 1987, does not even have an entry for happiness (Eatwell et al., 1998), whereas the most recent (second) edition, published in 2008, dedicates almost six pages to the topic (Durlauf and Blume, 2008).

The shift from preference-satisfaction to mental-state accounts of well-being constitutes a major methodological transition. Since it is possible to be happy and/or satisfied even though one's preferences are not satisfied, and vice versa, a person who is well off according to the one account is not necessarily well off according to the other. It follows that the individual-welfare criteria proposed in literature on subjective measures of well-being are radically different from those used by orthodox economists, for example, in the two fundamental theorems of welfare economics. Indeed, the simultaneous endorsement of the two individual-welfare criteria would lead to inconsistency. Consider two states of the world x and y such that a person P strictly prefers x to y but is happier in y than in x. Here, the orthodox economic welfare criterion ranks x strictly above y in terms of P's welfare while the welfare criterion advocated in the literature on subjective measures ranks y strictly above x. Hence, the simultaneous endorsement of the two welfare criteria would entail that x is ranked strictly above and strictly below y, which is impossible. The fact that subjective and economic measures are based on different conceptions of individual well-being is frequently overlooked, which has generated a great deal of confusion (Angner, 2009b). Because this trend has been discussed elsewhere, however, it will not be my focus here.

The second trend, which has gone largely unnoticed, is a shift away from the measurement-theoretic (or representational) approach to measurement and toward the psychometric approach. In this chapter, I will argue that orthodox economic welfare measures and subjective measures of well-being are based not just on radically different conceptions of well-being, but on radically different approaches to measurement as well: whereas orthodox economic welfare measures are based on the measurement-theoretic approach, subjective measures are based on the psychometric approach. The difference helps explain why subjective measures are based on questionnaire data, while orthodox economic measures are based on observable choices; why proponents of subjective measures validate their measures by establishing construct validity, reliability, and so on, whereas orthodox economists tend to establish that a particular function is a utility function; why orthodox economists' approach to welfare measurement strikes proponents of subjective measures as terribly inadequate, and vice versa; and indeed, why subjective measures are based on mental-state accounts of well-being, whereas orthodox economic measures are based on preference-satisfaction accounts.

The shift from the measurement-theoretic to the psychometric approach to measurement, which I will argue is evident also outside of the literature on subjective measures, constitutes another major methodological transition. Since it is possible to satisfy the strictures imposed by the one approach to measurement without satisfying those imposed by the other, a measure that has been validated in accordance with the one approach has not necessarily been validated in accordance with the other. Indeed, the simultaneous endorsement of the two approaches to measurement would lead to inconsistency. As in the case of the underlying conceptions of well-being, a failure to notice the difference between the two approaches can generate a great deal of confusion. Although the trend away from the measurement-theoretic and toward the psychometric approach has not yet received much attention, the fact that it constitutes a radical methodological shift means that it is likely to have a significant impact on the shape of welfare economics and on the public policy that it informs, and could generate thoroughly novel and highly interesting avenues of research.

6.2   APPROACHES TO MEASUREMENT

It is widely recognized that there are, broadly speaking, two different approaches to measurement in social and behavioral science (Dawes and Smith, 1985; John and Benet-Martínez, 2000; Judd and McClelland, 1998; Krantz, 1991).[3] As Krantz (1991) puts it: 'One, which may be termed the *psychometric* approach, introduces latent [unobservable] variables to explain behavioral orderings' (Krantz, 1991, p. 2). This approach emphasizes latent constructs, reliability, and construct validity. Krantz continues: 'The second . . . treats the numerical representation of behavioral orderings axiomatically' (Krantz, 1991, p. 2). This approach emphasizes observable orderings, homomorphisms, and representation theorems. The second approach is sometimes – for example, in Robyn Dawes and Tom L. Smith (1985, pp. 511–512) – referred to as the *representational* approach. For the reason identified by Dawes and Smith – the fact that all measurement is at bottom about representation – I will call it the *measurement-theoretic* approach. In this section, I will discuss the two approaches in reverse order. We will see that the differences between the two approaches have deep implications for the nature of measurement in social and behavioral science.

6.2.1 The Measurement-Theoretic Approach

The measurement-theoretic approach was first articulated by Dana Scott and Suppes (1958) but received its canonical statement in the three-volume *Foundations of Measurement*, the first volume of which appeared in 1971 (Krantz et al., 1971). In order to develop a better idea of the nature of this approach, I will also rely on two articles by Krantz: 'Measurement Structures and Psychological Laws' (1972) and 'From Indices to Mappings: The Representational Approach to Measurement' (1991). As we will see, this approach emphasizes observable orderings, homomorphisms, and representation theorems.

Here is how the authors of *Foundations of Measurement* capture the essence of what I have called the measurement-theoretic approach: 'From this standpoint, measurement may be regarded as the construction of homomorphisms (scales) from empirical relational structures of interest into numerical relational structures that are useful' (Krantz et al., 1971, p. 9). In what follows, I will try to explain what this means. It helps to think of measurement in the context of an actual example, so let us follow Krantz et al. (1971) and consider the case of length measurement. In their words:

> Suppose that we have a set of straight, rigid rods whose lengths are to be measured. If we place the rods a and b side by side and adjust them so that one is entirely beside the other and they coincide at one end, then either a extends beyond b at the other end, or b beyond a, or they appear to coincide at that end also. We say, respectively, that a is longer than b, b is longer than a, or that a and b are equivalent in length. For brevity, we write, respectively, $a>b$, or $b>a$, or $a{\sim}b$. Two or more rods can be concatenated by laying them end to end in a straight line, and so we can compare the qualitative length of one set of concatenated rods with that of another by placing them side by side, just as with single rods. The concatenation of a and b is denoted $a{\circ}b$ and the observation that c is longer than $a{\circ}b$ is denoted $c>a{\circ}b$, etc. Many empirical properties of length comparison and of concatenation of rods can be formulated and listed, e.g., $>$ is transitive; $\circ$ is associative; if $a>b$, then $a{\circ}c>b$; etc. (Krantz et al., 1971, p. 2)

The fundamental idea is that a set A of objects, in this case rods, can be ordered with respect to length by means of an observable operation. That is, it can be determined how various rods are related to each other with respect to length by applying a series of simple operations like those described above. The ordering of rods will as a matter of fact satisfy a number of conditions, including that of transitivity: if a is longer than b, and b is longer than c, it follows that a is longer than c. These conditions, which can be established by empirical study, can be expressed as a set of axioms (Krantz et al., 1971, p. 6), which in turn can be seen as a set of empirical laws (Krantz et al., 1971, p. 13). Thus, 'fundamental measurements are based on certain qualitative physical laws' (Krantz, 1972, p. 1428).

The example illustrates what Krantz et al. mean by a relational structure: it is a set of objects along with certain relations on that set (Krantz et al., 1971, p. 8).[4] In this case, we have a set A of rods as well as two relations on that set: $>$, which is a binary relation, and o, which is ternary, holding between a, b, and $c=a \circ b$. The relational structure is referred to as $\langle A, >, \circ \rangle$. The relational structure is empirical in the sense that (1) the members of A are observable entities, and (2) the relations between these entities can be established by means of a series of observable operations. An empirical relational structure contrasts with a numerical relational structure, which is a set of mathematical objects like numbers along with relations on that set.

Given an empirical relational structure, we can construct a measure of length by assigning real numbers $\phi(a)$, $\phi(b)$, . . ., to rods a, b, . . ., in such a way that two conditions are satisfied (Krantz et al., 1971, p. 5). First, we require that the number assigned to a be greater than the number assigned to b just in case a in fact is longer than b; that is, for all a and b, $\phi(a) > \phi(b)$ if and only if $a > b$. Second, we require that the numbers assigned be additive with respect to concatenation; that is, for all b and c, $\phi(b \circ c) = \phi(b) + \phi(c)$. If we succeed in assigning numbers such that these two conditions are satisfied, the function $\phi(\cdot)$ is a homomorphism from the empirical relational structure into a numerical relational structure $\langle R, >, + \rangle$. This means that $\phi(\cdot)$ takes elements of A into the set R of real numbers in such a way that the corresponding relationships are preserved. That is, $a > b$ if and only if $\phi(a) > \phi(b)$, and $c = a \circ b$ if and only if $\phi(c) = \phi(a) + \phi(b)$.[5] Especially in the empirical literature, homomorphisms are often referred to as scales. This explains the view of Krantz et al. (1971, p. 9) that the process of measurement can be seen as the process of constructing homomorphisms, or scales, from empirical to numerical relational structures.

Not every empirical relational structure allows the construction of a homomorphism. As a result, it is useful to ask what conditions must be satisfied by the empirical relations $>$ and $\circ$ on A in order for it to be possible to construct a function $\phi(\cdot)$ with the desired properties. The question is important: 'A measurement procedure certainly is not adequately understood if it depends on properties that are not explicitly recognized' (Krantz et al., 1971, p. 6). The question can be approached formally, by asking what axioms are necessary and sufficient for it to be possible to construct a function $\phi(\cdot)$ with the desired properties (Krantz et al., 1971, p. 8). The answer is provided by a *representation theorem*, which 'asserts that if a given relational structure satisfies certain axioms, then a homomorphism into a certain numerical relational structure can be constructed' (Krantz et al., 1971, p. 9).

The measurement-theoretic point of view aspires to be, in a certain sense, ontologically non-committal. When measurement theorists talk about length, hunger, frustration, risk aversion, and so on, Krantz notes, it may seem as if they 'introduce ontological presuppositions' and presuppose the existence of unobservable entities (Krantz, 1991, p. 3). However, he argues, measurement theorists do not need to take a position on the issue of the ontological status of such entities; the only thing measurement theorists need to assume is the existence of an empirical relational structure, that is, a set of observable entities and an observable ordering satisfying certain conditions (Krantz, 1991, p. 3). In order to justify talk about length, then, the only thing that needs to be assumed is the existence of an empirical structure consisting of a set of rods and of relations satisfying the right conditions. It is important to notice, by the way, that measurement theory is not an attempt to provide operational definitions of theoretical terms in the manner of Percy W. Bridgman (1927). Krantz et al. write that to treat measures as 'objective definitions of unanalyzed concepts' is a temptation that must be resisted (Krantz et al., 1971, p. 32).

In sum, the measurement-theoretic approach emphasizes concepts like observable orderings, homomorphisms, and representation theorems. Those operating in accordance with the measurement-theoretic approach take as their starting point data concerning observable entities. The evidence employed consists of claims to the effect that a given relation satisfies certain axioms, which can be established empirically by applying a series of observable operations. From such evidence, those who use this approach reason deductively: they offer mathematical proofs or other forms of reasoning with the feature that if their premises are true then the conclusion must be true too. It is sometimes useful to think of the defense of a given measure as a matter of constructing an argument to the conclusion that the measure represents that which it purports to represent. If so, the measurement-theoretic approach requires a deductive argument from the premise that some observable ordering satisfies certain conditions to the conclusion that the measure represents that which it purports to represent.

6.2.2   The Psychometric Approach

The psychometric approach is due in large part to the American Psychological Association's 'Technical Recommendations for Psychological Tests and Diagnostic Techniques' (1954) but was further developed by Lee J. Cronbach and Paul E. Meehl (1955). In order to develop a better idea of the nature of the psychometric approach, I will rely on two standard textbooks: *Psychometric Theory*, by Jum C. Nunnally and Ira H. Bernstein (1994), and *The New Psychometrics*, by Paul Kline (1998). As we will see, this approach emphasizes latent constructs, reliability, and construct validity.

A central term of the psychometric approach is that of reliability. To say that a measure is reliable means that it is 'without variation regardless of when the measurement is made or who makes the measurement, provided only that the individual [taking the measurement] is sane, in possession of his or her faculties and trained to use the instrument' (Kline, 1998, p. 26). There are at least two kinds of reliability. A measure has test–retest reliability insofar as it yields 'the same score for each subject when he or she takes the test on another occasion, given that their status on the variable has not changed' (Kline, 1998, p. 29). A test has internal consistency insofar as 'each item [of the test administered] measures the same variable' (Kline, 1998, p. 30). If total test scores vary too much over time, or individual items of the test diverge too much from each other, the measures are considered unreliable.

Another central term in the psychometric approach is that of validity. As Kline puts it: 'A test is said to be valid if it measures what it purports to measure' (Kline, 1998, p. 34; cf. Nunnally and Bernstein, 1994, p. 83). Again, there are several types of validity, including face validity, concurrent validity, predictive validity, content validity and discriminant validity (Kline, 1998, pp. 34–37). Here I will focus on construct validity, which is sometimes described as subsuming the other kinds (Judd and McClelland, 1998, p. 203), and which at any rate is the form of validity most relevant for present purposes. Introducing the topic of construct validity, Nunnally and Bernstein (1994, p. 84) argue that the aim of science – including social and behavioral science – is to establish functional relationships between variables of different kinds. They continue:

> To the extent that a variable is abstract and latent rather than concrete and observable . . . it is called a 'construct' . . . A construct reflects a hypothesis (often incompletely formed) that a variety of behaviors will correlate with one another in studies of individual differences and/or will be similarly affected by experimental manipulations. Nearly all theories concern statements about constructs. (Nunnally and Bernstein, 1994, p. 85)

In this view, two of scientists' most important tasks are to develop measures of individual constructs and to establish functional relationships between such measures (Nunnally and Bernstein, 1994, p. 85). The process of construct validation helps scientists reach these goals.

In practical terms, construct validation – which is often described as an instance of ordinary hypothesis testing (Cronbach and Meehl, 1955, p. 300; Johnson, 2001, p. 11316) – has three phases:

> (1) specifying the domain of observables related to the construct; (2) determining the extent to which observables tend to measure the same thing, several different things, or many different things from empirical research and statistical analyses; and (3) performing subsequent individual differences studies and/ or experiments to determine the extent to which supposed measures of the construct are consistent with 'best guesses' about the construct. (Nunnally and Bernstein, 1994, pp. 86–87)

In what follows, I will discuss the three phases in order. First, scientists need to identify a class of observable variables that are potentially related to the construct. Nunnally and Bernstein argue that there is no algorithm that can be followed in this phase; instead, scientists must rely on intuition and preconceived ideas about how the construct relates to those variables. The identification of such a class of variables is a necessary condition for the second phase, which is to explore whether the different measures can be described as representing the same thing or not. This second phase is performed by 'determining how well the measures of observables "go together" (intercorrelate) empirically' (Nunnally and Bernstein, 1994, p. 88). Typically, this amounts to computing a range of correlation coefficients and examining the resulting patterns of variances and covariances. Nunnally and Bernstein add:

> The results of investigations like those described above lead to one of three conclusions. If all the proposed measures correlate highly with one another, it can be concluded that they all measure much the same thing. If the measures tend to split up into clusters such that the members of a cluster correlate highly with one another and correlate much less with the members of other clusters, they measure a number of *different* things . . . A third possibility is that the correlations among the measures all are near zero, so that they measure different things and there is no meaningful construct. (Nunnally and Bernstein, 1994, p. 90)

The third and final phase is to show that a set of highly correlated observables in a domain can legitimately be thought of as measures of the construct in which the scientist is interested. In the words of Nunnally and Bernstein: 'To the extent that the elements of such a domain [are intercorrelated], *some* construct may be employed to account for the interrelationships, but it is by no means certain that the construct name which motivated the research is appropriate' (Nunnally and Bernstein, 1994, p. 90). To see whether a set of intercorrelated variables can be assumed to represent a given construct like anxiety, stress or happiness, the scientist needs to explore whether the variables vary across conditions approximately as we would expect degrees of anxiety, stress or happiness to do. In all, Nunnally and Bernstein propose that construct validity obtains if 'the supposed measure(s) of the construct *behave as expected'* (Nunnally and Bernstein, 1994, p. 90).

In sum, the psychometric approach emphasizes concepts like latent constructs, reliability, and construct validity. Those operating in accordance with the psychometric approach take as their starting point data concerning measures of latent constructs and/or observable variables. The evidence employed consists of claims to the effect that the measures behave as expected, which can be established empirically by showing that the pattern of variances and covariances exhibited by the measures conforms to expectations. This approach, then, does not require the existence of observable orderings satisfying conditions like transitivity; it requires a set of assumptions about a latent, unobservable construct. From such evidence, those who use this approach reason inductively: they offer reasons that give good grounds for thinking that the measure is valid. If we think of the defense of a given measure as a matter of constructing an argument, the psychometric approach requires an inductive argument from the premiss that some measure behaves as expected to the conclusion that the measure represents that which it purports to represent.

6.2.3   Discussion

In this section, I have outlined the two approaches to measurement in social and behavioral science: the measurement-theoretic approach and the psychometric approach. We have seen that there are real differences between the two approaches. While those operating in accordance with the measurement-theoretic approach reason deductively from the claim that a given empirical relation satisfies certain axioms, those operating in accordance with the psychometric approach reason inductively from the claim that a given measure behaves as expected. Hence, when showing that a given measure represents that which it purports to represent – that is, when showing that a given measure is valid – the two approaches differ when it comes to the character of the data, the nature of the evidence, and the mode of inference.

The differences between the two approaches have deep implications for the nature of measurement in social and behavioral science. Since it is possible to satisfy the strictures imposed by the one approach to measurement without satisfying those imposed by the other, a measure that has been validated in accordance with the one approach has not necessarily been validated in accordance with the other. Moreover, the simultaneous endorsement of the two approaches to measurement would lead to inconsistency, since the measurement-theoretic approach entails that an observable ordering satisfying certain axioms is necessary for measurement whereas the psychometric approach entails that it is not. Like in the case of the underlying conceptions of well-being, a failure to notice the differences between the two approaches can generate a great deal of confusion; the confusion may concern the data, evidence, and mode of inference required to establish the validity of a given measure.

Some advantages and disadvantages associated with the two approaches are readily apparent. The fact that the measurement-theoretic approach relies on deductive reasoning is *ceteris paribus* an enormous advantage. A valid deductive argument is by definition truth-preserving, in the sense that it cannot lead from true premises to a false conclusion, and erosion-proof, in the sense that it cannot be made invalid by the introduction of new premisses; an inductive argument is neither truth-preserving nor erosion-proof (Salmon, 1992, p. 11). The Achilles heel of the measurement-theoretic approach, as we will see, is the fact that it requires observable orderings that satisfy strict axioms. The fact that the psychometric approach does not require the existence of such orderings, and can proceed from weaker premises, is its central advantage. The advantage can be ascribed to the fact that it relies on inductive reasoning. An inductive argument can proceed from weaker premises because it is 'ampliative', in the sense that its conclusion has informational content that goes beyond that of its premises; deductive reasoning is not (Salmon, 1992, p. 11).

6.3   APPROACHES TO WELFARE MEASUREMENT

As we saw in the introduction, orthodox economic welfare measures differ from subjective measures of well-being with respect to the underlying conception of well-being. But there are other differences as well. In this section, I will maintain that orthodox economic welfare measures – or economic measures, for short – and subjective measures of well-being are based on radically different approaches to measurement: whereas economic measures are based on the measurement-theoretic approach, subjective measures are based on the psychometric approach. As we will see below, the fact that different measures are based on different approaches to measurement has deep implications for the measurement of welfare.

6.3.1   Economic Welfare Measures

Orthodox economists' arsenal of welfare measures contains a variety of measures. Pigou himself favored the 'national dividend' – that is, 'that part of the objective income of the community, including, of course, income derived from abroad, which can be measured in money' (Pigou, 1952, p. 31). Measures of this general kind, like gross domestic product (GDP) per capita, have well-known shortcomings but continue to be widely used for public policy purposes (Nussbaum and Sen, 1993, p. 2). The importance of the national product as a measure of well-being helps explain the widespread concern with economic growth: since 'growth' is often used to refer to the first derivative of the national product, and 'growth rate' to refer to the second derivative, high growth (or growth rate) is thought to be an indication of future well-being.

An alternative way to evaluate the welfare consequences of policy interventions is in terms of consumer surplus (CS) and producer surplus (PS). The notion of consumer surplus goes back to Jules Dupuit, who in a paper originally published in 1844 wished to determine the conditions under which public works – such as the building of a bridge – can 'be declared of public utility' (Dupuit, 1969, p. 255). Dupuit's ideas were developed and popularized by Alfred Marshall (1920; 1st edn 1890), who defined the consumer surplus of a good as: '[the] excess of the price which [the consumer] would be willing to pay rather than go without the thing, over that which he actually does pay' (Marshall, 1920, p. 124). Measures of consumer and producer surplus are widely used to evaluate the consequences of public policy: 'Consumer surplus is the overwhelming choice as a welfare indicator' (Slesnick, 1998, p. 2110). Moreover, consumer/producer surplus is the tool preferred by many economics textbooks when evaluating the welfare consequences of interventions like price ceilings and trade restrictions (see Mankiw, 2001, 'Part III: Markets and Welfare').

Yet another set of measures revolve around the concepts of 'compensating variation' (CV) and 'equivalent variation' (EV). These notions were developed in a series of publications by John R. Hicks (for example 1943), who had noted certain technical difficulties associated with surplus measures. The CV is 'the amount of money which, when taken away from an individual after an economic change, leaves the person just as well off as before', while the EV is 'the amount of money paid to an individual which, if an economic change does not happen, leaves the individual just as well off as if the change had occurred' (Just et al., 2004, p. 9). CV and EV measures are used in many contexts to assess changes in welfare:

> In cost–benefit analysis and other exercises in applied welfare economics, *aggregate willingness-to-pay* – the simple sum of Hicksian compensating variations [–] is often used as a test. A positive sum is taken as evidence of a social improvement or an increase in economic efficiency. (Blackorby and Donaldson, 1990, pp. 471–472)

Though different, all these measures have much in common, including the fact that they are all based on the measurement-theoretic approach to measurement.

There is much evidence that orthodox economists operate with the measurement-theoretic approach. First, there is a purely historical connection, in that both orthodox economics and the measurement-theoretic approach were shaped by the same broadly speaking empiricist philosophy of science. Although economists during the early twentieth century were comfortable talking about mental states like pain and pleasure – Pigou (1952, p. 10), as a case in point, defined welfare in terms of 'states of consciousness and, perhaps, their relations' – economists soon, under the influence of logical empiricism in philosophy, behaviorism in psychology and operationalism in physics, came to see references to unobservable mental states as unscientific and at any rate dispensable (Angner and Loewenstein, 2012). Much for the same reason, the measurement-theoretic approach was explicitly designed in order to provide a solid foundation for measurement on the basis of observable relations such as '*x* is longer than *y*' while avoiding controversial 'ontological presuppositions'. As J.D. Trout points out, this approach 'has been developed in a way that displays the distinct and deep influence of empiricism' (Trout, 1998, p. 49). Moreover, as we will see shortly, the measurement-theoretic approach was in fact motivated in part by the problem of utility measurement (Krantz et al., 1971, p. 9).

Second, the manner in which economic measures are defended is consistent with the measurement-theoretic approach. In order to see how utility measurement is addressed within the measurement-theoretic framework, let us return to Krantz (1991), who discusses the issue explicitly. The assumption underlying the measurement of utility is that a choice structure – a set X of options and a choice relation R on X – is an empirical relational structure satisfying certain axioms. Though there are different ways to approach the topic, typically X is the set of all possible acts or commodity bundles, and R is a binary relation such that aRb means that a is chosen over b in a pair-wise choice in which both a and b are available. Krantz writes:

> Since 1960, there seems to have been general agreement concerning two main points about the measurement of utility. First, the empirical ordering

underlying utility is determined by actual choices; that is, the choice of one act over others is represented by a utility assigned to the chosen act that is higher than the utilities assigned to the other acts. (Krantz, 1991, p. 28)[6]

Krantz goes on: 'The first of these points reflects the view that it is actual choices that are the most trustworthy and most important data of a behavioral science' (Krantz, 1991, p. 28). This view, of course, also assumes that choices reflect preferences over the various options. Anyway, as Krantz notes, 'most utility theories cling to the idea that the ordering is based on observation of choice behavior' (Krantz, 1991, pp. 28–29).

In order for the representation theorem to work, the measurement theorist must assume that the choice structure $\langle X,R \rangle$ satisfies some set of conditions. Either one of several different sets of axioms will do the trick. However, there are some conditions that are shared by all axiomatizations of utility. As Krantz et al. (1971, pp. 21–22) note, transitivity is a necessary condition, in the sense that it is mathematically necessary for any representation theorem to work. Just like in the case of the measurement of length, the axioms are seen as empirical, descriptive laws; in this case, they are laws of choice. Thus, for instance, the famous axioms articulated by von Neumann and Morgenstern (1944) 'constitute a set of qualitative laws for "rational" decisions among risky options' (Krantz, 1972, p. 1428). Very often, of course, these axioms are treated as normative principles. In the present context, however, the normative status of the axioms is irrelevant: the point is that the representation theorem requires that they be true descriptive laws. For the theorem to apply, the choice structure must in fact satisfy the axioms, that is, the axioms must be true of the relevant empirical relational choice structure. As Norman Cliff puts the point: 'Axiomatic measurement theory holds that . . . the order relations . . . must display a strong kind of consistency' (Cliff, 1992, p. 187).

We can now see how the measurement of utility is supposed to relate to the example of length measurement. Instead of a set of rods we have a set of bundles or acts. Instead of an ordering determined by comparisons of rods placed side by side, we have an ordering determined by the choices of some agent. Just as in the case of length, measurement theory is supposed to allow us to remain agnostic about the existence of unobservable attributes; utility is understood as a measure, or index, of preference satisfaction, with no connection whatsoever with mental states or other unobservables. Thus, the measurement theorist claims to provide methodological foundations for talk about utility and preference in a manner that is ontologically non-committal, without, as the case is sometimes made, 'pretending to look into the head of the agent'. In order to allow the construction of a representation theorem, we need to identify a set of axioms, which are seen as empirical, descriptive laws of choice. One of these laws is the proposition that preferences are transitive. What the measurement theorist assumes is that choices determine an empirical relational structure with the appropriate properties; that is, that actual choices satisfy the appropriate axioms. Note, again, the importance of the consistency or transitivity condition: if this condition is not in fact satisfied, measurement theory offers no grounds for constructing a utility function on the set of available options.

When orthodox economists defend their welfare measures, their actual practice conforms to this picture. Those economists begin with the assumption that market choices satisfy certain axioms, and on the basis of the axioms, proceed to offer a formal proof that the measure is an index of preference, that is, a utility function. This is true for all three kinds of welfare measure discussed above. The proofs are available in any standard-issue graduate-level microeconomics textbook like Andreu Mas-Colell et al.'s *Microeconomic Theory* (Mas-Colell et al., 1995). Mas-Colell et al. demonstrate that given a number of assumptions, for example, about the rationality of individuals and the nature of the budget set, and holding prices fixed, it can be shown that utility (understood in terms of preference satisfaction) is strictly increasing in individual wealth, which is to say that under certain assumptions wealth is a utility function (Mas-Colell et al., 1995, p. 56). Given a similar set of assumptions, they also show that consumer surplus as well as compensating and equivalent variation are utility functions (Mas-Colell et al., 1995, pp. 81–83). Because this procedure establishes that the measure is a homomorphism, the actual practice of orthodox economists indicates a commitment to the measurement-theoretic approach to measurement.

Finally, orthodox economists show few signs of a commitment to the psychometric approach. They typically do not even mention latent constructs, reliability, or construct validity. Moreover, they make little to no effort to validate their measures in the manner required by the psychometric approach, that is, by showing that a given measure exhibits the appropriate pattern of variances and covariances. Certainly, Mas-Colell et al. (1995) waste no time or ink on such things. The reason why orthodox economists came to think of CS/PS measures as inferior to CV/EV measures, for example, is not that the former were found to have a lower validity coefficient than the latter in psychometric studies, but that in the presence of wealth effects standard consumer surplus measures may fail to be utility functions, that is, homomorphisms (Mas-Colell et al., 1995, pp. 88–91).

6.3.2   Subjective Measures of Well-Being

What I have called 'subjective measures' in fact includes a range of specific measures. For most of their history, subjective measures have been constructed on the basis of one or more straightforward questions like that of Gurin et al. (1960), quoted in the introduction. Sonja Lyubomirsky and Heidi S. Lepper (1999) offer four prompts of the form: 'In general, I consider myself . . .', and invite subjects to respond on a seven-point scale, where 1 represents '. . . not a very happy person' and 7 '. . . a very happy person' (Lyubomirsky and Lepper, 1999, p. 151). Others ask subjects 'How do you feel about your life as a whole?' and give them response categories ranging from 'Delighted', 'Pleased', and 'Mostly satisfied', through 'Mixed (about equally satisfied and dissatisfied)' to 'Mostly dissatisfied,' 'Unhappy' and 'Terrible' (Andrews and Withey, 1976, p. 18). Occasionally, researchers invite responses using graphic representations like horizontal lines (Watson, 1930), ladders and mountains (Cantril, 1965), or happy and sad faces (Andrews and Withey, 1976). Some of these questions were designed to represent affective states, some to represent cognitive states, and some to represent a combination of the two (Angner, 2010b).

A somewhat different approach has been developed by Daniel Kahneman (1999) and others under the heading of 'experience sampling'. Kahneman prompts his subjects every so often – for example with the use of hand-held electronic devices – to judge the 'quality of their momentary experience' along the 'good/bad dimension' (Kahneman, 1999, p. 7). The assumption is that, at every point in time, the brain rates the quality of experience in a manner that can be represented on a single numerical scale and which, furthermore, is accessible to the agent. What matters, at the end of the day, is the time integral (which Kahneman calls 'objective happiness') of the instant happiness rating (which Kahneman calls 'subjective happiness') (Kahneman, 1999, p. 5). The effort to produce a dense record of an individual's affective state as a function of time was pioneered by Hornell Hart (1940), the inventor of the 'euphorimeter': a device that would permit the quick assessment of an individual's level of happiness based on self-reports. Though Kahneman and co-authors have since developed other measures, they insist: 'Experience sampling is the gold standard' (Kahneman et al., 2004b, p. 1777).

More recently, Kahneman and Alan B. Krueger have suggested the use of a measure they call the 'U-index' (Kahneman and Krueger, 2006; cf. Krueger, 2009). Introduced under the heading of 'A Measure of Society's Well-Being', the U-index is clearly intended to be a measure of social well-being. The 'U' stands for 'unpleasant' or 'undesirable', and the index 'measures the proportion of time an individual spends in an unpleasant state', where an episode gets classified as pleasant or unpleasant depending on whether the strongest effect experienced during the episode is positive or negative (Kahneman and Krueger, 2006, pp. 18–19). The U-index was designed to overcome several perceived problems associated with other subjective measures, above all problems related to interpersonal comparability (Krueger, 2009, p. 3).

There is much evidence that proponents of subjective measures operate with the psychometric approach. First, there is a purely historical connection, in that both subjective measures and psychometrics grew out of personality psychology, which uses tests based on self-reports in order to assess individual differences in personality, and which emerged shortly after World War I. As personality psychologists grew confident that they could explore scientifically various personality characteristics, it was not long before they started asking questions about the determinants and distribution of positive or desirable mental states like happiness and satisfaction. And psychometrics too was a direct outgrowth of personality psychology: from its very beginnings, personality psychology was characterized by an emphasis on measurement and psychometrics, and by a desire to be useful to corporations and governments (Winter and Barenbaum, 1999, p. 5).

Second, the manner in which subjective measures are defended is consistent with the psychometric approach. In order to show this, I will rely on a 1999 review article by Ed Diener, Eunkook M. Suh, Richard E. Lucas and Heidi L. Smith. In defense of subjective measures, the authors write:

> These measures do possess adequate psychometric properties, exhibiting good internal consistency, moderate stability, and appropriate sensitivity to changing life circumstances. Furthermore, global reports show a moderate level of convergence with daily mood reports, informant reports, spouse reports, and recall for positive versus negative life events. People who score high on global life satisfaction are less likely to attempt suicide and to become depressed in the future. (Diener et al., 1999, pp. 277–278)[7]

The reasoning invoked here fits the schematic picture painted in section 6.2.2 very well. First, Diener et al. identify a set of variables – in this case, spouses' reports, the absence of suicides, and so on – that they take to reflect the same construct as self-reported happiness. Second, the authors explore the degree to which these variables intercorrelate (positively and negatively) with the self-reports. Third, because all these variables are found to correlate positively, Diener et al. conclude that they all represent the same construct. Moreover, Diener et al. check whether the construct behaves as expected: when they argue that self-reports exhibit 'appropriate sensitivity to changing life circumstances', what they mean is that the measure varies across conditions more or less as anticipated.

A more recent contribution makes the point even clearer. Ed Diener, Richard Lucas, Ulrich Schimmack, and John Helliwell dedicate a whole chapter to the thesis that 'Well-being measures are valid' (Diener et al., 2009, p. 67). The authors argue that the general procedures that must be followed when validating a scientific measure are straightforward and uncontroversial; that widely used happiness measures have passed the basic tests mandated by these procedures; and that those who would reject the validity of happiness measures have failed to marshal any empirical evidence against them. Specifically, Diener et al. point out that, '[a] key requirement for any measure is that it is reliable', and proceed to outline the evidence for the reliability of measures of subjective well-being (Diener et al., 2009, pp. 68–74). After that, the authors introduce the concept of validity – in the process describing face validity, content validity convergent validity, and discriminant validity – as well as the process of construct validation, and they proceed to argue that subjective measures are valid in the relevant sense (Diener et al., 2009, pp. 74–93).

In fact, efforts to validate measures of happiness in accordance with what we now call the psychometric approach are as old as the measures themselves. Throughout the history of these measures, proponents have postulated the existence of a construct like happiness, satisfaction, or similar; proposed a measure of it; and sought to confirm that the measure behaves as expected when compared to objective life circumstances, other people's judgment of subjects' happiness, measures of mental health, and so on (cf. Lyubomirsky and Lepper, 1999, p. 145). In an early review of the literature, Warner Wilson made the case by arguing that self-reported happiness scores were sufficiently correlated with the judgments of associates, teachers, professors, principals, psychologists and clinical judges, as well as with scores on elation–depression scales (Wilson, 1967, pp. 294–295). Hart found that happiness scores, tracked over time, changed as expected when participants fell in love, experienced the death of their mothers or contemplated suicide (Hart, 1940, pp. 19–25). Based on a 1997 review, subjective measures are sufficiently positively correlated with happiness ratings of friends and family, psychologists' judgments, amount of smiling; sufficiently negatively correlated with depression; and not overly correlated with general intelligence, current mood, humility and the language in which the question was asked (Diener and Suh, 1997, pp. 436–438).

Because the procedure followed by all these authors serves to establish the reliability and validity of measures of a latent construct, the manner in which proponents of subjective measures defend their measures exhibits the hallmarks of the psychometric approach. The contention that proponents of subjective measures operate with the psychometric approach to measurement is further supported by the fact that they explicitly refer to 'psychometric criteria' (Lyubomirsky and Lepper, 1999, p. 140) and 'psychometric properties' (Diener et al., 1999, p. 277). In brief, the actual practice of proponents of subjective measures indicates a commitment to the psychometric approach to measurement.

Finally, proponents of subjective measures show few signs of a commitment to the measurement-theoretic approach. They typically do not even mention observable orderings, homomorphisms, or representation theorems, and they make little to no effort to defend their measures in the manner favored by the measurement-theoretic approach, that is, by identifying an empirical relational structure and proving that their measures are homomorphisms.[8] Speaking about the measurement of attitudes – conceived of as cognitive, affective, or conative mental states – Dawes and Smith note: 'Representational measurement is rare in the field of attitude; instead this field is permeated by questionnaires and rating scales' (Dawes and Smith, 1985, pp. 511–512). Indeed, for reasons we will explore in section 6.4, within contemporary psychology, the measurement-theoretic approach is widely regarded as a failure and is not commonly used (Cliff, 1992, p. 189; John and Benet-Martínez, 2000, p. 341).

6.3.3 Why are Economic and Subjective Measures so Different?

So far, I have argued that orthodox economic welfare measures and subjective measures of well-being are based on radically different approaches to measurement: whereas economic measures are based on the measurement-theoretic approach, subjective measures are based on the psychometric approach. The thesis that economic and subjective measures are based on different approaches to measurement helps explain the fact that proponents of different kinds of measure go about measuring well-being so differently, and consequently end up with such different measures. The remarkable explanatory power of the thesis, by the way, constitutes additional evidence in its support.

First, the thesis helps account for the fact that proponents of different measures rely on such different data. As we have seen, proponents of subjective measures are comfortable using questionnaire and survey data, whereas orthodox economists tend to require data concerning observable choices. The contention that proponents of subjective measures adopt the psychometric approach helps explain why it comes so naturally for them to take questionnaire and survey data as their starting point: questionnaires and surveys have been part and parcel of the practice of psychometrics since the very beginning. The contention also explains why proponents of subjective measures admit self-reports: it is not that they unquestioningly believe that people know how happy they are, but rather that self-reports can constitute one of many measures of the latent construct of interest. Meanwhile, the contention that orthodox economists adopt the measurement-theoretic approach helps explain why it comes so naturally for them to take data about economic transactions like market choices as their starting point: since the very beginning, the measurement-theoretic approach has required observable orderings like those imposed on a set of alternatives by an agent's consistent choices. Orthodox economists' preference for observable choices is well documented. As Amartya Sen notes: 'Much of the empirical work on preference patterns [and therefore welfare] seems to be based on the conviction that [non-verbal] behaviour is the only source of information on a person's preferences' (Sen, 1982, p. 71). The reasoning underlying the exclusive reliance on choice data is neatly expressed in *The Welfare Economics of Public Policy* (Just et al., 2004). After pointing out that utility is not observable, the authors add: 'In most practical situations, the applied welfare economist can, at best, observe income and consumption decisions at various prices and then, on the basis of these economic transactions, try to compute some money-based measure of welfare effects' (Just et al., 2004, p. 98).

Second, the thesis helps account for the fact that proponents of different measures rely on such different evidence. As we have seen, proponents of subjective measures rely on evidence to the effect that subjective measures behave as expected, which can be established empirically by showing that the pattern of variances and covariances exhibited by the measures conforms to expectations, while orthodox economists rely on evidence to the effect that market-based choices satisfy certain axioms, which can be established empirically by applying a series of observable operations. The contention that proponents of subjective measures adopt the psychometric approach explains why it comes so naturally for them to use the kind of evidence they do: the comparison of patterns of variances and covariances with expectations forms the very heart of the approach. At the same time, the contention that orthodox economists adopt the measurement-theoretic approach explains why it comes so naturally for them to use the kind of evidence that they do: claims to the effect that certain orderings satisfy particular axioms are a critical part of the measurement-theoretic approach.

Third, the thesis that economic and subjective measures are based on different approaches to measurement helps account for the fact that proponents of different measures use such different arguments in support of their measures. As we have seen, proponents of subjective measures validate their measures by establishing reliability, construct validity, and so on, whereas orthodox economists prove that a particular function is a utility function. The contention that proponents of subjective measures operate with the psychometric approach helps explain why they believe that the use of a given measure has been justified when it has been shown that it behaves as expected when compared to measures of other latent constructs, observable behavior, and so on: this procedure, if successful, establishes reliability and construct validity, which is what the psychometric approach requires. Meanwhile, the fact that orthodox economists operate with the measurement-theoretic approach helps explain why they assume that the use of a given measure has been justified when it has been shown that it is based on market choices assumed to satisfy the relevant axioms in conjunction with a formal proof that shows that the measure is a utility function: this procedure, if successful, in fact establishes that the measure is a homomorphism, which is what the measurement-theoretic approach requires.

Fourth, the thesis explains why orthodox economists' approach to welfare measurement (including their choice of data, evidence, and mode of inference) strikes proponents of subjective measures as terribly inadequate, and vice versa. For anyone trained in the psychometric tradition, a person's income and market choices are likely to seem hopelessly indirect as measures of their welfare, independently of whether welfare means preference-satisfaction, happiness, or satisfaction. Those trained in psychometrics have been taught to reject measures not validated in the manner of the psychometric approach, and as we have seen, orthodox economists make no effort to validate their efforts in this manner. For somebody trained in the measurement-theoretic tradition, meanwhile, a person's answers to questionnaires and surveys are likely to appear inherently dubious. Those trained in this tradition have been taught to reject measures that have not been shown to be homomorphisms in the manner of the measurement-theoretic approach, and as we have seen, proponents of subjective measures make no effort to establish that their measures are homomorphisms based on observable orderings. Moreover, the inductive arguments required by the process of construct validation are likely to appear far inferior to the deductive reasoning required by the measurement-theoretic tradition.

Finally, the thesis helps account for the fact that orthodox economists, on the one hand, and psychologists and unorthodox economists, on the other, adopt such different accounts of well-being. As we saw in the introduction, whereas orthodox economists tend to adopt preference-satisfaction accounts of well-being, proponents of subjective measures tend to adopt mental-state accounts. Orthodox economists were originally drawn to preference-satisfaction accounts after convincing themselves that pleasure and pain could not be measured scientifically, whereas preference satisfaction could (Angner and Loewenstein, 2012, Section 2.2; Mandler, 1999, p. 6). Similarly, twentieth-century interest in happiness appears, at least in part, to be a result of traditional psychologists and unorthodox economists convincing themselves that mental states like happiness can, in fact, be scientifically measured. An uncharitable interpretation of these events suggests that economists and psychologists alike are like the drunken man who looks for his lost key not where he lost it, but where the light is. A more charitable interpretation of these events is that psychologists and economists alike believe that accounts or conceptions of well-being can be judged in part on the grounds of whether they permit the development of adequate measures of well-being. This idea is explicit in several prominent contemporary philosophers. James Griffin argues that we cannot 'first fix on the best account of "well-being" and independently ask about its measurement. One proper ground for choosing between conceptions of well-being would be that one lends itself to the deliberation that we must do and another does not' (Griffin, 1986, p. 1). Similarly, Christine M. Korsgaard maintains that an account of the quality of life may be assessed 'for its utility in determining actual political and economic policy – that is, whether it provides accurate enough measures to assess the effects of policy' (Korsgaard, 1993, p. 54).

If economists and psychologists alike believe that accounts of well-being can be judged in part on the grounds of whether they permit the development of adequate measures of well-being, this would go a long way toward explaining why orthodox economists tend to favor preference-satisfaction accounts whereas psychologists and unorthodox economists tend to favor mental-state accounts.[9] According to this hypothesis, the fact that orthodox economists operate with the measurement-theoretic approach to measurement helps explain why they reject mental-state accounts of well-being in favor of preference-satisfaction accounts. After all, their favored approach requires that measurement be based on observable orderings, but because they believe that no such ordering exists in the case of happiness measurement, they believe that happiness cannot be measured, which they take to be reason to reject mental-state accounts of well-being; at the same time, they believe that degrees of preference satisfaction can be measured based on an observable ordering, so they believe that degrees of preference satisfaction can be measured, which they take to be a reason to adopt some preference-satisfaction accounts of well-being. According to my hypothesis, meanwhile, the fact that psychologists and unorthodox economists operate with the psychometric approach helps explain why they, by and large, adopt mental-state accounts of well-being. After all, their favored approach requires measures that behave as expected rather than observable orderings; because they believe that existing measures of happiness, satisfaction, and so on do behave as expected, they believe that happiness, satisfaction, and so on can be measured, which they take to be a reason to adopt some mental-state accounts of well-being. In sum: the difference between the two approaches to measurement helps explain why subjective measures are based on mental-state accounts whereas orthodox economic measures are based on preference-satisfaction accounts of well-being.

6.3.4 Discussion

In this section, I have defended the thesis that economic measures are based on the measurement-theoretic approach while subjective measures are based on the psychometric approach. In addition, I have maintained that this thesis has remarkable explanatory power. The thesis that subjective and economic measures are based on different approaches to measurement serves to bring out radical differences between the two kinds of measure, *inter alia*, when it comes to the nature of the data, the character of the evidence, and the mode of inference. The thesis also helps explain orthodox economists' rejection of subjective measures, and vice versa, as well as why those who operate with the psychometric approach tend to favor mental-state accounts whereas those who operate with the measurement-theoretic approach tend to favor preference-satisfaction accounts. (As we will see below, however, the measurement-theoretic approach to measurement is logically consistent with a commitment to preference-satisfaction accounts of well-being.)

Notice that my thesis does not presuppose that those who are committed to the measurement-theoretic approach never use inductive reasoning, or that those who are committed to the psychometric approach never use deductive reasoning. Even for somebody fully committed to the measurement-theoretic approach, inductive reasoning might be necessary, for example, when trying to assess a person's preferences over an infinitely large set of alternatives (perhaps represented by a vector of real numbers) on the basis of a necessarily finite series of observable choices; moreover, deductive reasoning is widely used in all the sciences. Similarly, my thesis does not presuppose that those who rely on the psychometric approach never use observable-choice evidence: the psychometric approach permits, though it does not require, the use of such evidence. Hence, my thesis is not undercut by the observation that orthodox economists sometimes rely on inductive reasoning, that psychometricians sometimes use observable-choice evidence, and so on.

Attention to the differences between the two kinds of measure helps illuminate some of their advantages and disadvantages. The fact that economic measures are defended using deductive arguments is *ceteris paribus* a huge advantage, since (as pointed out in section 6.2.3) such arguments are both truth-preserving and erosion-proof. At the same time, however, the fact that these arguments proceed from the assumption that observable choices constitute an ordering satisfying strict axioms is a disadvantage, since that is a strong assumption indeed. The fact that subjective measures are defended using inductive arguments is *ceteris paribus* a disadvantage, since (as we also saw in section 6.2.3) such arguments are neither truth-preserving nor erosion-proof. Yet, because inductive reasoning is ampliative, these arguments do not require observable orderings and can proceed from the weaker assumption that certain measures behave as expected.

6.4   THE SHIFT TOWARD TO THE PSYCHOMETRIC APPROACH

Given the thesis that economic measures are based on the measurement-theoretic approach to measurement while subjective measures are based on the psychometric approach, it should not be surprising that the rise of subjective measures would be associated with a transition from the measurement-theoretic to the psychometric approach. In this section, I argue that this trend is evident also outside of the literature on subjective measures, among authors who apparently remain committed to preference-satisfaction accounts of well-being. Though this trend has gone largely unnoticed, there are exceptions. In his contribution to the previously mentioned volume about the U-index (Krueger, 2009), William Nordhaus remarks that the strategy of Krueger and co-authors 'uses a completely different approach to measuring the values associated with time uses – one based on surveys or other psychometric measurements' (Nordhaus, 2009, p. 127). Nordhaus's use of the term 'psychometric measurement' strongly suggests that he is drawing attention to a trend toward the psychometric approach to measurement.

The transition from the measurement-theoretic to the psychometric approach to measurement is most evident among economists who jettison orthodox economic welfare measures in favor of subjective measures of well-being. These economists exhibit a marked shift from observable choice data toward questionnaire and survey data; from evidence showing that some ordering satisfies strict axioms toward evidence showing that a given measure behaves as expected; from mathematical proofs and other forms of (truth-preserving, erosion-proof) deductive arguments toward (ampliative) inductive arguments; and from preference-satisfaction accounts of well-being toward mental-state accounts. As pointed out in section 6.3.4, the psychometric approach can make use of, though it does not require, measures of observable choices; deductive reasoning is widely used in all the sciences, and so on. My thesis offers a plausible account of the rise of subjective measures of well-being and the return of mental-state accounts of well-being, as both of these developments can be seen as resulting from a shift from the measurement-theoretic to the psychometric approach to measurement, in combination with mounting evidence of reliability and validity of subjective measures.

The trend from the measurement-theoretic toward the psychometric approach is evident also outside of the literature on subjective measures, among authors who apparently remain committed to preference-satisfaction accounts of well-being. In this sense, I will argue, current trends in economics mimic recent trends in psychology. In contemporary psychology (as mentioned in section 6.3.4 above), the measurement-theoretic approach is largely regarded as a failure and not widely used. The main reason is that in the social and behavioral sciences observable orderings satisfying conditions like transitivity are rare. As Cliff puts the problem: 'Measurement theory says that if certain conditions hold, then scales of a given kind are defined. If not, they are not. But data always contradict one or the other axiom' (Cliff, 1992, p. 189). By 1991, Krantz himself had come to a very similar conclusion. Under the heading 'The myth of utility', Krantz argues:

> Choice does indeed depend on the method of testing and depends especially on how options are *framed*. Results such as these show that ordering options by choices is no more determinate than ordering 'overall' reading skill by testing on a particular set of materials. (Krantz, 1991, p. 32)

Krantz points to empirical results by Tversky and Kahneman and their co-authors, whose work is widely interpreted as showing that real-life choices reflect what is often called 'normatively irrelevant' factors and consequently fail to satisfy the axioms. Krantz infers: 'Preference ordering is a behaviorist myth' (Krantz, 1991, p. 35). From our vantage point, if anything, the case for the empirical adequacy of the axioms of rational choice theory is even weaker than it was when Krantz wrote his retrospective two decades ago. Many different researchers claim to have uncovered evidence to the effect that people's choices, to a very significant extent, reflect incidental aspects of the decision situation rather than a stable, consistent preference ordering (Camerer and Loewenstein, 2004; Kahneman, 2003; Rabin, 2002).

While realizing that the measurement-theoretic approach is largely inapplicable due to the lack of relevant observable orderings, psychologists have become increasingly convinced of the adequacy of the psychometric approach. As Charles M. Judd and Gary H. McClelland put it:

> While the revolution of representative measurement was sputtering, psychometric measurement was faring better in its ability to make predictions and was making progress at getting its own house in order with respect to being able to test its measurement scales. (Judd and McClelland, 1998, p. 183)

Hence, contemporary psychologists have come to believe not just that the measurement-theoretic approach is inadequate, but that the psychometric approach has much to be said for it in terms of building theories with predictive ability. Consequently, the psychometric approach has come to dominate the field: 'Most measurement in social psychology consists of questionnaire and observational measures whose validity is established not by a set of axiomatic consistency tests but rather by the observed patterns of variances and covariances that they display' (Judd and McClelland, 1998, p. 201).

My thesis in this section is that a similar trend is apparent in contemporary economics. In the past few years, a number of economists have noticed the problem posed by non-standard choice behavior for welfare measurement, and have worked to make sense of the idea of welfare measurement in the absence of observable orderings satisfying the relevant axioms. In a 2007 working paper, for example, Jerry Green and Daniel Hojman (2007) develop a method that permits them to assess the welfare of a decision maker whether or not his or her choices satisfy the axioms of rational choice theory; the idea is to assume the existence of unobservable, simultaneously held preference relations, and use observable choices to estimate properties of those preference relations. In a similar vein, Ariel Rubinstein and Yuval Salant (2008) maintain that, given a domain of objects, economists need to distinguish what they call 'mental preference' – an unobservable 'mental attitude of an individual towards to objects' – from observable choice and to develop techniques to estimate the former based on the latter. In their view: 'There is no escape from including mental entities, such as the way in which an individual perceives the objects and his mental preferences, in economic models' (Rubinstein and Salant, 2008, p. 117). These papers represent a growing literature on how to do welfare analysis in the presence of non-standard choice behavior.

While there is much to be said about this development, what matters most for present purposes is that it shows clear evidence of a transition from the measurement-theoretic to the psychometric approach to measurement. These authors clearly reject the notion that measurement must take as its starting point an observable ordering satisfying strict axioms; instead, they take as their starting point some set of assumption about unobservable entities like 'mental preference', which psychometricians would call latent constructs. Moreover, these authors reject the notion that a measure of preference satisfaction must be shown to be a homomorphism based on some observable ordering; instead, they use observable evidence to make inductive inferences about the satisfaction of unobservable mental preferences. Insofar as these proposals take as their starting point an unobservable construct like a 'mental preference' and reason inductively from evidence other than observable orderings, the actual practice of these economists conforms more closely to the psychometric than to the measurement-theoretic approach. In fact, the realization that the measurement-theoretic approach is inapplicable in the absence of observable orderings of the relevant kind constitutes an implicit acknowledgement that the psychometric approach is the only game in town.

It might be objected that the economists mentioned here do not think of their work as representing a trend from the measurement-theoretic to the psychometric approach to measurement, and that this fact undercuts the thesis that such a trend is taking place. I have no reason to doubt that few of the economists mentioned here think of their activities in these terms. In fact, I think it is fair to say that many economists are unaware of the existence of two mutually inconsistent approaches to measurement, since the difference has received little attention in the literature. According to Judd and McClelland, 'there is almost no literature in psychology where the two measurement traditions have spoken to each other' (Judd and McClelland, 1998, p. 227), and much the same thing is true in economics. Nevertheless, the fact that a given economist does not think of his or her activities in these terms does not undercut my thesis. It is perfectly possible to operate with a given approach to measurement, and to shift from one approach to another, without being aware of it. Hence, the fact (if it is one) that few of the economists mentioned here think of their work as representing a trend from the measurement-theoretic to the psychometric approach to measurement does not undercut my thesis.

6.5   CONCLUSION

Why should anyone pay attention to issues of measurement? As Judd and McClelland put it: 'While the individual researcher can ignore measurement issues for the most part without consequence, the discipline as a whole suffers when theories and methods underlying measurement are undeveloped and unscrutinized' (Judd and McClelland, 1998, p. 180). Most practicing scientists can get along just fine without thinking seriously about issues of measurement, but there are times when attention to the nature of measurement is critical for understanding the nature, advantages and disadvantages of alternative approaches. It is my hope that the present discussion has served to illustrate the point in the case of welfare measurement.

In this chapter, I have argued that the rise of subjective measures of well-being represents two major trends in contemporary welfare economics: a shift from preference-satisfaction to mental-state accounts of well-being and a shift from the measurement-theoretic to the psychometric approach to measurement. The thesis that subjective and economic measures are based on different approaches to measurement serves to bring out radical differences between the two kinds of measure, *inter alia*, when it comes to the nature of the data, the character of the evidence, and the mode of inference. Attention to these differences helps illuminate some of the advantages and disadvantages associated with the two kinds of measure. Though I am not the only one to notice the shift from measurement-theoretic to the psychometric approach to measurement – which is evident also outside of the literature on subjective measures, among authors who apparently remain committed to preference-satisfaction approach – the fact that orthodox economic welfare measures and subjective measures of well-being are based on different approaches to measurement is seldom explicitly acknowledged. Both these trends constitute radical methodological transitions, which are likely to have a significant impact on the shape of welfare economics and on the public policy that it informs.

As in the case of underlying conceptions of well-being, the difference matters. Since it is possible to satisfy the strictures imposed by the one approach to measurement without satisfying those imposed by the other, a measure that has been properly validated in accordance with the one approach has not automatically been validated in accordance with the other. It is quite clear that the assessment of both orthodox economic welfare measures and subjective measures of well-being will hinge, to some extent, on the adequacy of the two approaches to measurement. Moreover, a failure to notice the difference between the two approaches can generate a great deal of confusion. For example, economists often reject subjective measures of well-being by saying that mental states like happiness simply cannot be measured. In his 1975 book *Two Cheers for the Affluent Society: A Spirited Defense of Economic Growth*, Wilfred

Beckerman dismissed efforts to measure happiness by declaring that '[the] concept of happiness is one for which there can be no scientific objective measure' (Beckerman, 1975, p. 53). This objection can be understood as presupposing that observable orderings are necessary for measurement, as the measurement-theoretic approach suggests. The criticism does not acknowledge that subjective measures – whatever their flaws – are defended in the manner of the psychometric approach, not the measurement-theoretic one. Similarly, psychologists sometimes criticize economists for failing to validate properly their measures in the manner of the psychometric approach. For instance, Diener et al. (2009) attack economists for failing to properly validate GDP as a measure of welfare, as they write that 'economists assumed that income is a valid indicator of well-being, but few studies have systematically tested this assumption' (Diener et al., 2009, p. 75). The objection can be understood as presupposing that measures must be validated in accordance with the psychometric approach. The critique does not acknowledge that economic measures – whatever their flaws – are defended in accordance with the measurement-theoretic approach to measurement, not the psychometric one.

It is important to notice what my thesis does not entail. There is no clear sense in which either one of the two trends per se represents a shift from less to more realism, that is, the view that science, in its theories, aims 'to provide a true description of the world' (Okasha, 2002, p. 59); from less to more 'realisticness', a cluster of arguably desirable properties of scientific theories, including plausibility and usefulness (Mäki, 1998); or from lower to higher fidelity, meaning 'messier and yet more faithful to the realities of human life' (Alexandrova and Haybron, Chapter 5 in this volume). The trends toward mental state accounts of well-being and the measurement-theoretic approach to measurement have no direct implications concerning the aims of science or the attributes of scientific theories at all. Moreover, I see no interesting sense in which mental-state accounts and the psychometric approach per se are messier and more faithful to human realities; indeed, the theory of measurement might strike an innocent observer as messy enough, given that it took the authors of *Foundations of Measurement* three volumes to spell it out in the detail required to capture the relevant phenomena. (That said, I do not deny that psychometrics and/or mental-state accounts when combined with other assumptions, for example, about the aim of science or the nature of theories, might have implications for realism, realisticness, or fidelity.)

The notion that well-being should serve as a goal – perhaps even the only goal – for public policy is hardly uncontroversial. After discussing the roles that the concept of well-being is frequently assumed to play, as mentioned in the introduction, Scanlon goes on to argue that 'it is a mistake to think that there is a single notion of well-being that plays all the roles I have mentioned' (Scanlon, 2000, p. 109). Yet, insofar as the concept of well-being plays any role at all in our political and other deliberations, there will be a need for a systematic way to assign numbers or other mathematical objects to individuals and groups; that is, there will be a need for measures of individual and social well-being. And if so, questions about the nature of measurement – for example, what it takes to be able to say that a given measure is a valid measure of well-being – will sooner or later have to be addressed. If it is indeed true that there is a strong trend away from the measurement-theoretic approach and toward the psychometric approach in contemporary economics, this would constitute a radical change in the methodological foundations of modern economics, which is likely to have a significant impact on the shape of welfare economics and on the public policy that it informs. In addition, if the methodological sophistication of psychometricians could be integrated with the statistical sophistication of econometricians, these trends could offer promising avenues of research indeed.

NOTES

1. I am grateful to the editors of this volume for constructive criticism of an earlier draft. Errors remain my own.
2. See Angner (2010b) for more about the conception of individual well-being implicit in literature on subjective measures of well-being. By contrast, subjective measures of well-being are based on the same conception of social well-being as orthodox economic measures (Angner, 2009a).
3. Denny Borsboom (2005) adds a third approach, *classical test theory*, which I will ignore here.
4. Krantz (1972) refers to relational structures as measurement structures, and Krantz (1991) as qualitative structures.
5. If a homomorphism $\phi(\cdot)$ is one–one, it is said to be an isomorphism. In the context of our example, this will occur if no two rods are equal with respect to length, so that each rod gets assigned a unique number.
6. The second point has to do with whether utility scales are ordinal or cardinal, which is a topic I will not go into here.
7. References have been omitted.
8. There are contributions to the literature on subjective measures that aspire to use an axiomatic approach, which makes them in this respect consistent with the measurement-theoretic approach (Kahneman et al., 1997). I thank Anna Alexandrova for pointing this out.
9. Below, we will see that there are exceptions to this rule, since there are economists who appear to gravitate toward the psychometric approach to measurement while remaining committed to preference-satisfaction accounts of well-being.

REFERENCES

Adler, M. and E. Posner (2008), 'Happiness Research and Cost–Benefit Analysis', *Journal of Legal Studies*, **37**(S2), S253–S292.

American Psychological Association (1954), 'Technical Recommendations for Psychological Tests and Diagnostic Techniques', *Psychological Bulletin*, **51**(2, Pt.2), 1–38.

Andrews, F.M. and S.B. Withey (1976), *Social Indicators of Well-Being: Americans' Perceptions of Life Quality*, New York: Plenum Press.

Angner, E. (2008), 'The Philosophical Foundations of Subjective Measures of Well-Being', in L. Bruni, F. Comim and M. Pugno (eds), *Capabilities and Happiness*, Oxford: Oxford University Press, pp. 286–298.

Angner, E. (2009a), 'The Politics of Happiness: Subjective vs. Economic Measures as Measures of Social Well-Being', in L. Bortolotti (ed.), *Philosophy and Happiness*, New York: Palgrave Macmillan, pp. 149–166.

Angner, E. (2009b), 'Subjective Measures of Well-Being: Philosophical Perspectives', in H. Kincaid and D. Ross (eds), *The Oxford Handbook of Philosophy of Economics*, Oxford: Oxford University Press, pp. 560–579.

Angner, E. (2010a), 'Are Subjective Measures of Well-Being "Direct"?', *Australasian Journal of Philosophy*, **89**(1), 115–130.

Angner, E. (2010b), 'Subjective Well-Being', *Journal of Socio-Economics*, **39**(3), 361–368.

Angner, E. and G. Loewenstein (2012), 'Behavioral Economics', in U. Mäki (ed.), *Handbook of the Philosophy of Science: Philosophy of Economics*, Amsterdam: Elsevier, pp. 641–690.

Beckerman, W. (1975), *Two Cheers for the Affluent Society: A Spirited Defense of Economic Growth*, New York: Saint Martin's Press.

Bernanke, B.S. (2010), 'Commencement Address: The Economics of Happiness', 8 May, http://www.federalreserve.gov/newsevents/speech/bernanke20100508a.pdf.

Blackorby, C. and D. Donaldson (1990), 'A Review Article: The Case Against the Use of the Sum of Compensating Variations in Cost–Benefit Analysis', *The Canadian Journal of Economics*, **23**(3), 471–494.

Blanchflower, D.G. and A.J. Oswald (2004), 'Well-Being over Time in Britain and the USA', *Journal of Public Economics*, **88**(7–8), 1359–1386.

Borsboom, D. (2005), *Measuring the Mind: Conceptual Issues in Contemporary Psychometrics*, Cambridge: Cambridge University Press.

Bridgman, P.W. (1927), *The Logic of Modern Physics*, New York: Macmillan.

Camerer, C.F. and G. Loewenstein (2004), 'Behavioral Economics: Past, Present, Future', in C.F. Camerer, G. Loewenstein and M. Rabin (eds), *Advances in Behavioral Economics*, New York and Princeton, NJ: Russell Sage Foundation and Princeton University Press, pp. 3–51.

Campbell, A. (1976), 'Subjective Measures of Well-Being', *American Psychologist*, **31**(2), 117–24.

Cantril, H. (1965), *The Pattern of Human Concerns*, New Brunswick, NJ: Rutgers University Press.

Clark, A.E. and A.J. Oswald (2002), 'A Simple Statistical Method for Measuring how Life Events Affect Happiness', *International Journal of Epidemiology*, **31**(6), 1139–1144.

Cliff, N. (1992), 'Abstract Measurement Theory and the Revolution that Never Happened', *Psychological Science*, **3**(3), 186–190.

Cronbach, L.J. and P.E. Meehl (1955), 'Construct Validity in Psychological Tests', *Psychological Bulletin*, **52**(4), 281–302.

Dawes, R. and T.L. Smith (1985), 'Attitude and Opinion Measurement', in G. Lindzey and E. Aronson (eds), *Handbook of Social Psychology*, Vol. 1, New York: Random House, pp. 509–566.

Diener, E. (2000), 'Subjective Well-Being. The Science of Happiness and a Proposal for a National Index', *American Psychologist*, **55**(1), 34–43.

Diener, E. (2006), 'Guidelines for National Indicators of Subjective Well-Being and Ill-Being', *Applied Research in Quality of Life*, **1**(2), 151–157.

Diener, E., R. Lucas, U. Schimmack and J. Helliwell (2009), *Well-Being for Public Policy*, New York: Oxford University Press.

Diener, E. and M.E.P. Seligman (2004), 'Beyond Money: Toward an Economy of Well-Being', *Psychological Science in the Public Interest*, **5**(1), 1–31.

Diener, E. and E.M. Suh (1997), 'Measuring Quality of Life: Economic, Social, and Subjective Indicators', *Social Indicators Research*, **40**(1–2), 189–216.

Diener, E., E.M. Suh, R.E. Lucas and H.L. Smith (1999), 'Subjective Well-Being: Three Decades of Progress', *Psychological Bulletin*, **125**(2), 276–302.

Dupuit, J. (1969), 'On the Measurement of Public Works', in K.J. Arrow and T. Scitovsky (eds), *Readings in Welfare Economics*, Homewood, IL: R.D. Irwin, pp. 255–283.

Durlauf, S.N. and L. Blume (eds) (2008), *The New Palgrave Dictionary of Economics*, 2nd edn, New York: Palgrave Macmillan.

Eatwell, J., M. Milgate and P. Newman (eds) (1998), *The New Palgrave: A Dictionary of Economics*, corrected paperback edn, London: Macmillan.

Frey, B.S. (2008), *Happiness: A Revolution in Economics*, Cambridge, MA: MIT Press.

Frey, B.S. and A. Stutzer (2002), *Happiness and Economics: How the Economy and Institutions Affect Well-Being*, Princeton, NJ: Princeton University Press.

Green, J. and D. Hojman (2007), 'Choice, Rationality and Welfare Measurement', November, Harvard Institute of Economic Research Discussion Paper No. 2144, KSG Working Paper No. RWP07-054, http://papers.ssrn.com/sol3/papers.cfm?abstract_id=1030342.

Griffin, J. (1986), *Well-Being: Its Meaning, Measurement, and Moral Importance*, Oxford: Clarendon Press.

Gurin, G., J. Veroff and S. Feld (1960), *Americans View Their Mental Health: A Nationwide Interview Survey*, New York: Basic Books.

Hart, H. (1940), *Chart for Happiness*, New York: Macmillan.

Hicks, J.R. (1943), 'The Four Consumer's Surpluses', *Review of Economic Studies*, **11**(1), 31–41.

John, O.P. and V. Benet-Martínez (2000), 'Measurement: Reliability, Construct Validation, and Scale Construction', in H.T. Reis and C.M. Judd (eds), *Handbook of Research Methods in Social and Personality Psychology*, New York: Cambridge University Press, pp. 339–369.

Johnson, J.A. (2001), 'Personality Psychology: Methods', in N.J. Smelser and P.B. Baltes (eds), *International Encyclopedia of the Social and Behavioral Sciences*, Vol. 16, Oxford: Pergamon, pp. 11313–11317.

Judd, C.M. and G.H. McClelland (1998), 'Measurement', in D.T. Gilbert, S.T. Fiske, and G. Lindzey (eds), *The Handbook of Social Psychology*, 4th edn, Vol. 1, New York: Oxford University Press, pp. 180–232.

Just, R.E., D.L. Hueth and A.L. Schmitz (2004), *The Welfare Economics of Public Policy: A Practical Approach to Project and Policy Evaluation*, Cheltenham, UK and Northampton, MA, USA: Edward Elgar.

Kahneman, D. (1999), 'Objective Happiness', in D. Kahneman, E. Diener and N. Schwarz (eds), *Well-Being: The Foundations of Hedonic Psychology*, New York: Russell Sage Foundation, pp. 3–25.

Kahneman, D. (2003), 'A Psychological Perspective on Economics', *American Economic Review*, **93**(2), 162–168.

Kahneman, D. and A.B. Krueger (2006), 'Developments in the Measurement of Subjective Well-Being', *Journal of Economic Perspectives*, **20**(1), 3–24.

Kahneman, D., A.B. Krueger, D. Schkade, N. Schwarz and A. Stone (2004a), 'Toward National Well-Being Accounts', *American Economic Review*, **94**(2), 429–434.

Kahneman, D., A.B. Krueger, D.A. Schkade, N. Schwarz and A.A. Stone (2004b), 'A Survey Method for Characterizing Daily Life Experience: The Day Reconstruction Method', *Science*, New Series, **306**(5702), 1776–1780.

Kahneman, D., P.P. Wakker and R. Sarin (1997), 'Back to Bentham? Explorations of Experienced Utility', *Quarterly Journal of Economics*, **112**(2), 375–405.

Kline, P. (1998), *The New Psychometrics: Science, Psychology, and Measurement*, London: Routledge.

Korsgaard, C.M. (1993), 'G.A. Cohen: Equality of What? On Welfare, Goods and Capabilities. Amartya Sen: Capability and Well-Being', in M.C. Nussbaum and A. Sen (eds), *The Quality of Life*, Oxford: Clarendon Press, pp. 54–61.

Krantz, D.H. (1972), 'Measurement Structures and Psychological Laws', *Science*, **175**(4029), 1427–1435.

Krantz, D.H. (1991), 'From Indices to Mappings: The Representational Approach to Measurement', in D.R. Brown and J.E.K. Smith (eds), *Frontiers of Mathematical Psychology: Essays in Honor of Clyde Coombs*, New York: Springer, pp. 1–52.

Krantz, D.H., R.D. Luce, P. Suppes and A. Tversky (1971), *Additive and Polynomial Representations*, Foundations of Measurement, Vol. 1, New York: Academic Press.

Krueger, A.B. (ed.) (2009), *Measuring the Subjective Well-Being of Nations: National Accounts of Time Use and Well-Being*, Chicago, IL: University of Chicago Press.

Layard, P.R.G. (2005), *Happiness: Lessons from a New Science*, New York: Penguin Press.

Lyubomirsky, S. and H.S. Lepper (1999), 'A Measure of Subjective Happiness: Preliminary Reliability and Construct Validation', *Social Indicators Research*, **46**(2), 137–155.

Mäki, U. (1998), 'Realisticness', in J.B. Davis, D.W. Hands and U. Mäki (eds), *The Handbook of Economic Methodology*, Northampton, MA: Edward Elgar, pp. 409–413.

Mandler, M. (1999), *Dilemmas in Economic Theory: Persisting Foundational Problems of Microeconomics*, New York: Oxford University Press.

Mankiw, N.G. (2001), *Principles of Microeconomics*, 2nd edn, Fort Worth, TX: Harcourt College.

Marshall, A. (1920), *Principles of Economics: An Introductory Volume*, 8th edn, London: Macmillan.

Mas-Colell, A., M.D. Whinston and J.R. Green (1995), *Microeconomic Theory*, New York: Oxford University Press.

von Neumann, J. and O. Morgenstern (1944), *Theory of Games and Economic Behavior*, Princeton, NJ: Princeton University Press.

Nordhaus, W. (2009), 'Measuring Real Income with Leisure and Household Production', in A.B. Krueger (ed.), *Measuring the Subjective Well-Being of Nations: National Accounts of Time Use and Well-Being*, Chicago, IL: University of Chicago Press, pp. 125–144.

Nunnally, J.C. and I.H. Bernstein (1994), *Psychometric Theory*, 3rd edn, New York: McGraw-Hill.

Nussbaum, M.C. and A. Sen (eds) (1993), *The Quality of Life*, Oxford: Clarendon Press.

Okasha, S. (2002), *Philosophy of Science: A Very Short Introduction*, Oxford: Oxford University Press.

Pigou, A.C. (1952), *The Economics of Welfare*, 4th edn, London: Macmillan.

Rabin, M. (2002), 'A Perspective on Psychology and Economics', *European Economic Review*, **46**(4–5), 657–685.

Rubinstein, A. and Y. Salant (2008), 'Some Thoughts on the Principle of Revealed Preference', in A. Caplin and A. Schotter (eds), *The Foundations of Positive and Normative Economics: A Handbook*, New York: Oxford University Press, pp. 115–124.

Salmon, W.C. (1992), 'Scientific Explanation', in M.H. Salmon, J. Earman, C. Glymour, J.G. Lennox, P. Machamer, J.E. McGuire, J.D. Norton, W.C. Salmon and K.F. Schaffner (eds), *Introduction to the Philosophy of Science*, Englewood Cliffs, NJ: Prentice Hall, pp. 7–41.

Scanlon, T. (2000), *What We Owe to Each Other*, Cambridge, MA: Belknap Press.

Scott, D. and P. Suppes (1958), 'Foundational Aspects of Theories of Measurement', *Journal of Symbolic Logic*, **23**(2), 113–128.

Sen, A. (1982), *Choice, Welfare, and Measurement*, Cambridge, MA: MIT Press.

Slesnick, D.T. (1998), 'Empirical Approaches to the Measurement of Welfare', *Journal of Economic Literature*, **36**(4), 2108–2165.

Tiberius, V. (2006), 'Well-Being: Psychological Research for Philosophers', *Philosophy Compass*, **1**(5), 493–505.

Trout, J.D. (1998), *Measuring the Intentional World: Realism, Naturalism, and Quantitative Methods in the Behavioral Sciences*, New York: Oxford University Press.

Watson, G. (1930), 'Happiness among Adult Students of Education', *Journal of Educational Psychology*, **21**(2), 79–109.
Wilson, W.R. (1967), 'Correlates of Avowed Happiness', *Psychological Bulletin*, **67**(4), 294–306.
Winter, D.G. and N.B. Barenbaum (1999), 'History of Modern Personality Psychology Theory and Research', in L.A. Pervin and O.P. John (eds), *Handbook of Personality: Theory and Research*, 2nd edn, New York: Guilford Press, pp. 3–27.

7 Happiness and experienced utility
Luigino Bruni and Pier Luigi Porta

7.1 INTRODUCTION

The term and concept of 'experienced utility' has been reintroduced by Daniel Kahneman as 'the meaning of utility that Jeremy Bentham introduced, and it was mostly retained by the economists of the nineteenth century' (Kahneman and Thaler, 2006). Edgeworth's *Mathematical Psychics* (1881), Kahneman and Thaler continue, provides an instance; that work 'was quite explicit about this, and even defined happiness as the temporal integral of momentary experienced utility'. However, those authors further observe, 'the notion of utility as an aspect of experience essentially disappeared from economic discourse at the beginning of the twentieth century, when utility came to be construed as decision utility'.

It is important to understand how and why the use of the idea of experienced utility is embedded in a revolution in method and content in economic theory, deploying itself through the last 40-odd years and gaining momentum at present. The revolution involves two main areas of economics: the use of the concept of rationality and the definition and measurement of welfare or well-being. Thereby the present chapter will be divided into two sections: we shall first discuss utility and its link with rationality, stressing the cognitive imperative for economics to part with the idea of optimizing; in the second half, which follows as an implication and a consequence from the first, we shall highlight the motives behind the impressive recent surge of happiness studies within economics.

7.2 UTILITY

7.2.1 Economics and Psychology

Dealing with the use of the concept of utility today leads to a focus on the renewed emphasis on the links between psychology and economics. This is a major turn in method and contents of latter-day economics. If we take a long-run perspective in looking at the relation between the two disciplines, it is easy to see that there is today a new approach emerging from a variety of sources. It is possible to argue that the renewed interdisciplinary link has been taking shape mainly as a result of the innovative approach to economic rationality established in particular by the researches of two psychologists, D. Kahneman and A. Tversky. The importance of that strand of research has been acknowledged also with the attribution of the Nobel Prize for Economics 2002.

Historically the relationship of economics and psychology has been a rather twisted one and this provides a case where the historico-analytic perspective becomes essential in order to capture the drift and the novelty of the current frontier of research. We shall proceed here by taking first of all a specific instance of the relationship, which will be outlined on the basis of the case of Daniel Kahneman. Daniel Kahneman stands out today as perhaps the most relevant scientific figure in the realm of the vigorous new wave of research on the widening common ground shared by economists and psychologists. The new approach, pioneered by Kahneman, has indeed given rise to such a vast array of applications that it would be impossible to hint at them all in the present contribution. If we wish to focus on fundamentals, Kahneman's case is going to provide an excellent guide.

It is also important to notice that Kahneman (surviving Tversky since 1996) has recently driven the approach toward a new way of studying utility and toward the rise of the economics of happiness. At the basis of both developments, now greatly enlarged and involving a number of diverse contributions, there is a substantially new approach to rationality, on which we have to dwell for a while in this chapter. As a matter of fact, through the final decades of the twentieth century, the new marriage of economics and psychology set in mainly as a reaction to the excesses of the perfectionist (sometimes called 'olympic') ground for rationality shared by economists and psychologists, but especially cherished by economists. Kahneman was singled out by the Royal Swedish Academy for the 2002 Nobel Prize 'for having integrated insights from psychological research into economic science, especially concerning human judgment and decision-making under uncertainty'. The rise of the subdiscipline of cognitive economics, under full development nowadays, could hardly be conceived without his own contributions to research.

The new approach embodies a retrieval of the tradition of classical utilitarianism, from Jeremy Bentham down to John Stuart Mill, to Francis Ysidro Edgeworth, to Maffeo Pantaleoni and others. New experimental instruments and a new conceptual apparatus have been designed in order to explore the world behind choices: the realm of preferences. In the language of economic theory, it is probably fair to say that the new cognitive discipline can be conceived of as an alternative to the behaviouristic approach implicit in the axiom of revealed preferences, on which the standard economic approach to human choice has long been based. That means that we have to emphasize experienced utility with respect to decision utility, a turn which implied – in Kahneman's view – a return to Bentham.[1] The new line of research is of comparatively recent development: think, for example, that it has very little place in a staple reference work on the state of economics as a discipline today such as the *New Palgrave*, published in the 1980s by Macmillan (admittedly the situation has somewhat improved with the second edition, 2008, of the *New Palgrave*).

The relationship of psychology and economics goes back to the link between pleasure and satisfaction on one side and economic value on the other in the philosophers of the ancient world. Relevant episodes in the relationship are provided through more recent times, for example, by the case of the famous 'St. Petersburg's paradoxes' putting forward a challenge to justify the finite value of an infinite sum game; a challenge taken up by Daniel Bernoulli in his famous *memoir* of 1738, 'Specimen Theoriae Novae de Mensura Sortis', and resolved by him precisely on the basis of a psychological notion of subjective value. More facts in the rich and complex developments of the relationship of the two disciplines crop up during the nineteenth and twentieth centuries. Heinrich Gossen, Stanley Jevons, Carl Menger, Maffeo Pantaleoni and Friedrich Hayek provide relevant examples on the economists' side; a further step is represented by the Allais and Ellsberg paradoxes during the 1950s.[2]

In spite of all the above developments, however, economics has ended up being conquered by a growing emphasis on separation and autonomy with respect to psychology. We cannot extend the discussion in the present context, and we simply recall here that such an emphasis reflects a line of thought stemming from very influential contributions, such as those of Vilfredo Pareto, John Hicks, Lionel Robbins, John von Neumann and Oskar Morgenstern. That, as an approach to the problem, still is largely part of the prevailing public image of economics as a scientific discipline.

That is why the logical and rhetorical strategy of the economic science has been based, at least since the second half of the nineteenth century and all through the twentieth century, on the assumption that each individual is endowed with stable and coherent preferences and that he or she rationally maximizes those preferences, following the well-known adage *de gustibus non est disputandum*, later called into question by several authors. Under uncertainty, given a set of options and probabilistic beliefs, an agent is supposed to maximize the expected value of a specified utility function. The canonical form of the economic problem then takes the shape of a problem of optimization – which is characteristic of the economic approach such as it is described in Lord Robbins's 1932 classic treatment. In that perspective, economics and psychology are disciplines altogether separate and working on independent statutes. Although that approach was often thought of in normative (rather than positive) terms, it is clear that economics has come to be based on a solid rational set-up which is what any student of economics is first taught even today in most university curricula. Vilfredo Pareto had even theorized of economics as the discipline of logical actions, that is, actions motivated by instrumental rationality, to be kept separate from sociology which deals with non-logical actions.

7.2.2   Forms of Rationality

The above perspective largely belongs to the past. We have travelled today to a new phase. It is one of the main recent achievements in scientific work to have brought back to the centre of the stage the view that the formal consistency requirements of the so-called economic rationality are psycho-logically impossible: they quite simply cannot be met by the human mind.

It would be a mistake, of course, to conceive of the new approach as a radical critique of rationality. The position rather implies that the sole realistic notion of rationality is the notion of bounded rationality, a concept introduced by Herbert Simon. Simon – an immensely crea-tive economist and certainly a non-mainstream figure in the profession, sometimes perhaps rather reductively mentioned as the father of artificial intelligence, and himself a Nobel laureate for economics in 1978 – would speak of a model of 'olympic' rationality for the standard case in the eco-nomic science (see his essay, 1983), a notion he contrasts with 'bounded rationality'; the latter leads to substitute 'satisficing' for optimization. With Simon's work the idea began to gain currency that what had con-stantly appeared to be the more robust, elegant and general scheme of analysis (that is, the 'olympic' one) had in fact to be set aside as insuffi-ciently specified and unable to bear the burden of providing a benchmark rule for economic theorizing. 'Bounded rationality' has since gradually turned familiar to a wide area of research spanning economics, psychology and the social sciences, and has become pivotal to a whole wave of new studies on psychological processes underpinning individual rationality and decisions.

However, it is only through Daniel Kahneman's research work that it has been possible to understand more thoroughly why and, above all, how rationality is limited and to explore the psychic mechanisms through which the actual beliefs and preferences of the agents are gener-ated. Daniel Kahneman's research presents a menu of important ways in which economics traditionally misunderstood human behaviour thus ending up to endorse, in the name of rationality, misleading arguments about human behaviour. A whole array of behavioural and experimental applications – in the fields of finance, organization, decision theory and so on – have proved the fruitfulness of the approach and have improved economic analysis by incorporating greater psychological realism. The research work in question has been in part developed in collaboration with other authors, notably with Amos Tversky and Richard Thaler. Kahneman's scientific work has increasingly become the object of research and scientific discussion all over the world.

7.2.3   From Bounded Rationality to the Hedonic Experience

Again following Kahneman's lead, it should be pointed out that it is possible to speak of two phases of Daniel Kahneman's scientific activity: a former phase is leading to the construction of the theory on the framing of decisions. In an important work first published in 1986 with Amos Tversky, 'Rational Choice and the Framing of Decisions', the authors argue that: 'alternative descriptions of a decision problem often give rise to different preferences, contrary to the principle of invariance that underlies the rational theory of choice'. The descriptive realism of the scheme of rational choice is called into question by the fact that it is impossible to stick to the classic 'invariance principle', which maintains a sort of 'neutrality' of preferences with respect to the frame which provides the setting of their formation and where the process of choice has its origin. There are rules that govern the framing of decisions and it is necessary to take into account the psychophysical principles of evaluation embodied in prospect theory. Kahneman and Tversky's prospect theory places the emphasis on a specific asymmetry in the process of evaluation and individual judgement and leads to the conclusion that different preferences take shape, according as a given problem – with a given outcome in terms of expected utility – is formulated in terms of possible gains rather than in terms of possible losses. At the same time two different modes, though logically equivalent, of specifying a problem can lead the decision makers to different choices. In particular, since agents are empirically more sensitive to losses than they are to gains (a principle later to be called 'loss aversion' by Kahneman and Tversky), a 'frame' which highlights the losses associated with a choice makes that choice less attractive.

We can understand that Kahneman's work consists of series of specifications, routines, maps of bounded rationality (following the title of his Nobel Lecture; Kahneman, 2003); specifications reflecting 'the *heuristics* that people use and the *biases* to which they are prone in various tasks of judgment under uncertainty', following a famous *Science* article (with

Amos Tversky) in 1974. What emerges is a new theory – which includes, at least in part, the formation of preferences – that provides an attack on the economic modelling of behaviour insofar as it is based on the application of olympic rationality (even if the latter were conceived in normative terms) on the basis of given preferences.

The use of the notion of olympic rationality contributes to build up a strong tendency to identifying the economic problem with a question of a relationship between agent and commodities. Under the spell of olympic rationality it is Robinson Crusoe – the man surviving on the desert island – that forms the prototype of the economic agent, the *Homo oeconomicus*. Kahneman and Tversky's approach, on the contrary, is fully open to a conception of economics as the study of relations among (personal) agents including the implied strategic perspectives.

Moreover, in Kahneman and Tversky's approach, the root of the insufficient descriptive power of 'classical' analysis of expected utility is also linked with an exclusive focus of the latter on final states or on the outcomes of a process of choice. Contrary to that, the logic of the new approach implies a principle of 'reference-dependence' whereby the carriers of value are gains and losses defined relative to a reference point. The transition from wealth to variations of wealth as carriers of utility is in fact made necessary precisely by that 'irrational' property of preferences that has been called 'loss aversion' as hinted above. The approach stems from a view of perception and judgement emphasizing that a general property of perceptual systems is that they are designed to enhance the accessibility of changes and differences.

7.2.4 Experienced Utility and Happiness

Both the above characteristics (emphasis on relations and emphasis on variations) taken together lead to outline a subsequent phase of Daniel Kahneman's work, which has special significance in the perspective of the present chapter. The latter phase rather more directly relates with the links of economics to happiness and adjoining fields. The conceptual apparatus of traditional neoclassical theory in economics is, in a sense, too poor to be helpful in that direction and that is a reason why studies on economics and happiness, now flourishing, exhibit a distinctive heterodox character. In particular, as hinted above, in Kahneman's view prevailing economic theory only takes decision utility into account, but it forgets about experienced utility. Decision utility implies a perfect continuity between preference and choice; preferences, indeed, are inferred from choices. Experienced utility brings us back to Bentham's concept of utility as a hedonic quality of human experience which can be studied and gauged independently of the process of choice. Experienced utility is the fundamental concept in the cognitive perspective.

Recent works by Daniel Kahneman have increasingly given relevance to a conceptual definition and measurement of well-being and happiness. We may mention here the collection of papers on well-being published by the Russell Sage Foundation in 1999, edited by Kahneman with Ed Diener and Norbert Schwartz.

Indeed a number of authors have either paved the way to Kahneman's results or stepped into the field at a later stage, as will be made clear in the subsequent section of the present chapter. Outstanding cases of predecessors are given by Scitovsky and Easterlin. Studies on economics and happiness were brought to renewed life by Tibor Scitovsky and by Richard Easterlin by the mid-1970s and they are now flourishing also as a result of a combination with Daniel Kahneman's contribution. Kahneman himself explains how and why Scitosvky had a scarce audience especially among economists, when he was trying to retrieve (in substance) Bentham's notion of experienced utility especially in order to explain the dramatic distorsions afflicting our economies nowadays. Such distortions (generating the 'joyless economy') are, in his view, the result of an excessive attention on comfort (involving a passive attitude of the consumer) to the detriment of stimulation and happiness (in turn implying creativity and active participation). As Easterlin notes: 'Scitovsky has argued that cultural goods . . . are less subject to hedonic adaptation than "comfort" goods'. The distinction is significant and relevant to latter-day theories on the issue. Scitovsky himself had drawn inspiration from Daniel Berlyne's studies on arousal and stimulation, as he made clear especially in his chapter on 'The Pursuit of Novelty' (Scitovsky, 1976, Ch. 3). Such macroscopic phenomena continue to be more or less 'invisible' to the income measures in macroeconomics.

It is also contended by Kahneman that a closer look at emotions, affections, sensations and in general at hedonic experiences is necessary today in order to offer a more solid and constructive basis for welfare and felicific calculus in terms of experienced utility, compared to the income and product calculations used in economics. This strand of research is likely to come close also to later developments in neuroeconomics, which are not taken up in the present treatment, however.

At the present moment such and similar researches on the subject of happiness aim at the practical result of finding an 'index of national welfare' to be substituted for income as a standard indicator. Kahneman's researches on the concept and measurement of objective happiness are of the utmost significance as a basis for that purpose.

As already hinted, the recent developments in studies on economics and happiness have emphasized the need for distinguishing the use of commodities and the involvement in human relations. If economics, from the discipline of optimization, is transformed into a discipline of personal relationships and interactions, this fact can be seen as an indication of a reconsideration of Adam Smith's system stressing the links between the *Wealth of Nations* and the *Theory of Moral Sentiments*, leading to a much richer image of him compared to the traditional neoclassical rationality view of Smith (see Gui and Sugden, 2005).

7.3   HAPPINESS

7.3.1   The Return of Happiness in Economics

Happiness is back in economics. The return of happiness is one of the most relevant methodological novelties in economics and social sciences today. Thanks to happiness studies, in contemporary economics there is also a new interest in the analysis of interpersonal relationships, because there is huge empirical evidence that genuine, not instrumental, i.e. intrinsically motivated sociality, is one of the heaviest components of subjective happiness (Bruni and Stanca, 2008). At the same time, contemporary economics is badly equipped for understanding the nexus between happiness and genuine sociality. In fact, mainstream economics considers genuine sociality as basically an extra-economic matter, or as an element to be taken into account in terms of externalities (Gui and Sugden, 2005).

The reason for economics' new interest in happiness is well expressed by Andrew J. Oswald, one of the three authors of the 1997 controversy in the *Economic Journal*: 'The importance of the economic performance is that it can be a means for an end. The economic matters interest only as far as they make people happier' (Oswald, 1997, p. 1815). The same idea is restated by the third author, Yew-Kwang Ng: 'We want money (or anything else) only as a means to increase our happiness. If to have more money does not substantially increase our happiness, then money is not so important, but happiness is' (Ng, 1997, p. 1849). By arguing that happiness should take a more central role in economics once again, economists like Oswald and Ng also call attention to one of the main assumptions of economics since the very beginnings of modern economics in the eighteenth century: the positive and direct nexus between wealth and welfare or 'public happiness'. Economics deals directly with wealth and by its concern for growth it indirectly aims to contribute to an economic policy of increasing the national well-being.[3]

Recent empirical findings however appear to falsify this assumption and urge economists to rethink the subject matter of economics. This section moves from a discussion of these empirical findings – phrased as the 'paradox of happiness' or the 'Easterlin paradox' – and then proceeds to spell out their impact on economists' agendas. A discussion of rivalling explanations will show how the paradox is giving rise to a revival of Aristotelian or eudaimonian approaches to happiness and economics.

7.3.2   The Easterlin Paradox

The rediscovery of happiness in economics is mainly a by-product of a process originating in psychology. In fact, the chapter published by Brickman and Campbell in 1971, under the telling title 'Hedonic Relativism and Planning the Good Society', can rightly be considered to be the starting point of the new studies on happiness and its paradoxes related to the economic domain. In their study, the two psychologists extend the 'adaptation level' theory to individual and collective happiness, concluding that bettering the objective conditions of life (income or wealth) bears no lasting effects on personal well-being. Such a thesis should have provoked a serious methodological discussion about the meaning of analysis of the nature and causes of the wealth of nations. Yet it did not; the study remained practically unknown in mainstream economics for years.

By utilizing empirical researches on people's happiness, Richard Easterlin managed to open the debate around the 'happiness paradox' – also today called the 'Easterlin paradox'. He made use of two types of empirical data. The first was supplied by the responses to a Gallup Poll type of survey in which a direct question was asked – a question which is still at the basis of most empirical analyses on happiness: 'In general, how happy would you say that you are – *very* happy, *fairly* happy, or *not very* happy?' (Easterlin, 1974, p. 91). The other data set that Easterlin made use of came from more sophisticated research carried out by the humanist psychologist Hadley Cantril (1965), another forerunner of contemporary studies on happiness, concerning people's fears, hopes and satisfaction in 14 countries. The subjects interviewed were asked to qualify their own 'life satisfaction' on a scale from 1 to 10.

Drawing on both types of data, Easterlin's seminal analyses produced several converging results:

1. Within a single country, at a given moment in time, the correlation between income and happiness exists and is robust. 'In every single

survey, those in the highest status group were happier, on the average, than those in lowest status group' (Easterlin, 1974, p. 100).

2. In cross-sectional data among countries, the positive wealth–happiness association, though present, is neither general nor robust, and poorer countries do not always appear to be less happy than richer countries. In other words, 'if there is a positive association among countries between income and happiness it is not very clear . . . The results are ambiguous' (Easterlin, 1974, p. 108).[4]

3. National time-series data collected in 30 surveys over 25 years (from 1946 to 1970 in the United States) show that per capita real income rose by more than 60 percent, but the proportion of people who rate themselves as 'very happy', 'fairly happy' or 'not very happy' remained virtually unchanged.

Today almost all scholars, irregardless of background, agree on the third thesis above, that is, the non-correlation between happiness and income in time series. There is, in fact, evidence that:

> over time and across OECD [Organisation for Economic Co-operation and Development] countries rises in aggregate income are not associated with rises in aggregate happiness . . . At the aggregate level, there has been no increase in reported happiness over the last 50 years in the US and Japan, nor in Europe since 1973 when the records began. (Layard, 2005, p. 148)

Many economists confirm Easterlin's finding that a causal correlation runs from income to happiness within a single country at a given moment in time and is robust (point (1) above).[5] Scholars disagree, however, with Easterlin's (1974) point (2) result, that is, with the cross-country income–happiness correlation. Using data from the World Values Survey, some economists argue that despite Easterlin's thesis a correlation does exist: 'Various studies provide evidence that, on average, persons living in rich countries are happier than those living in poor countries' (Frey and Stutzer, 2002, p. 19). Hagerty and Veenhoven (2003) claim that rising gross domestic product (GDP) is associated with greater happiness. Replying to this paper and defending his classical thesis, Easterlin (2005b) passes over Veenhoven's criticism of his thesis about international comparisons. Veenhoven (1991) plotted the same data as Cantril, though using the same scale on both axes, and showed that the relationship follows a convex pattern of diminishing returns.[6]

Notwithstanding the critiques, the idea of a very low correlation between happiness and income growth is still widely accepted among economists working on happiness. An example of recent research which confirms this idea is Layard (2005):

[I]f we compare countries, there is no evidence that richer countries are happier than poorer ones – so long as we confine ourselves to countries with incomes over [US] $15 000 per head . . . At income levels below $15 000 per head things are different, since people are nearer to the absolute breadline. At these income levels richer countries are happier than poorer ones. And in countries like India, Mexico and Philippines [*sic*], where we have time series data, happiness has grown as income levels have risen. (p. 149)[7]

7.3.3 On the Definition of Happiness

Before discussing explanations of the happiness paradox it is important to note that economists have no clear conceptual understanding of what happiness is in relation to other similar concepts. Ng (1997) defines happiness as 'welfare'; for Oswald (1997) happiness means 'pleasure' or 'satisfaction'. Easterlin is most explicit: 'I use the terms happiness, subjective well-being, satisfaction, utility, well-being and welfare interchangeably' (2001, p. 465). Frey and Stutzer (2002) argue that everybody should feel free to choose an idea of happiness. What is more, the way economists deal with happiness is mostly empirical, and their research is driven by the availability of self-reports on happiness or satisfaction with life. They rely on subjective responses to questionnaires simply asking people, 'How happy are you?'[8] It is fully self-reported without any need to define *ex ante* what happiness is or should be.

For a more concrete definition of happiness and a better understanding of the indicators used to measure it, we turn to psychology. In psychology, studies on happiness began in the 1950s, and psychologists generally use the expression 'happiness' with more precision than economists. Psychologists distinguish: (1) 'life satisfaction', which is a cognitive element; (2) 'affection', which is the affective component; and (3) 'subjective well-being' (SWB), defined as a 'state of general well-being, synthetic, of long duration, which includes both the affective and cognitive component' (Ahuvia and Friedman, 1998, p. 153).

It is important to note that in these studies of happiness there is a rivalry between two approaches to happiness. The first approach relates to the hedonistic/utilitarian views of Epicurus and Jeremy Bentham on humanity and society (Kahneman et al., 1997). More precisely, 'hedonism' (Kahneman et al. 2004) reflects the view that well-being is equivalent to feeling happy, that is, experiencing pleasure. 'Hedonism, as a view of well-being, has . . . been expressed in many forms and has varied from a relatively narrow focus on bodily pleasures to a broad focus on appetites and self-interests' (Deci and Ryan, 2001, p. 144). Sometimes this approach is labelled as 'subjectivist' or 'psychologistic' because of its almost exclusive reference to what people report about their own – subjectively experienced – feelings.

The second approach relates to Aristotle's ethics, in particular to his understanding of happiness as eudaimonia. According to Aristotle, happiness is about the good life and human flourishing, that is, the actualization of human potentials through intrinsically motivated activities in a context of interpersonal relationships. Until recently this approach was almost absent from economists' discussions of wealth and happiness (see Gui and Sugden, 2005 for a review). We shall return to this view on happiness after a discussion of explanations of the Easterlin paradox, based on hedonistic/utilitarian understandings of happiness.

7.3.4　Individual and Social Treadmills

The first economist who attempted to explain the paradox was Richard Easterlin himself, in his seminal 1974 paper. His explanation refers to Duesenberry's (1949) relative income theory. According to Duesenberry (1949, p. 32), we are constantly comparing ourselves to some group of people and what others buy influences our choices about what we want to buy. It is the 'keeping up with the Joneses' scenario. The consumption function is constructed upon the hypothesis that our consumption choices relate to our relative income – reflecting the difference between our level of income and others' income level – instead of our absolute income. The utility that individuals experience from a certain level of consumption depends on their budget relative to others' budgets.

Without going back to classical authors, who gave prominence to the social dimensions of consumption, at the end of nineteenth century Veblen introduced the notion of 'conspicuous goods', referring to goods that people purchase to impress others with their wealth. After all, the most significant acts of consumption are normally carried out in public, under others' gaze. In recent times, Tibor Scitovsky (1976) dealt with the relationship between consumption and status, and Fred Hirsch (1977) coined the term 'positional good'. Contemporary positional theory centres on the concept of externality: conspicuous commodities share some characteristics of 'demerit goods' (because they are private goods generating negative externalities), with the typical consequence of Pareto-inefficiency (for overconsumption). In other words, there is a problem of self-deception: people, because of self-deception, consume an excessive amount of conspicuous goods, and as a consequence, the amount of time devoted to 'inconspicuous consumption' is inefficient (too little) (Easterlin, 2005a).

Besides explanations based on the relative consumption hypothesis (Frank, 1997, 1999; Ng, 1997; Höllander, 2001; Layard, 2005), there are other explanations as well, based on the 'treadmill' concept introduced from research on happiness in the field of psychology.

The treadmill metaphor, coined by Brickman and Campbell (1971), imagines that one is running constantly and yet remains at the same place because of the treadmill, which is operating at the same pace – or even faster. Key concepts in individual treadmill explanations are 'hedonic adaptation' and 'set point'.

According to the set-point theory, there is a level of happiness which remains practically constant during one's lifetime, because personality and temperament variables seem to play a strong role in determining the level of happiness of individuals. Such characteristics are basically innate. In other words, in the long run, we are fixed at hedonic neutrality, and our efforts to make ourselves happier by gaining good life circumstances are only short-term solutions. Therefore, life circumstances including health and income often account for a very small percentage of variance in subjective well-being. People initially do react to events (positive as well as negative), but then they return to baseline levels of well-being that are determined by personality factors (Argyle, 2001; Lucas et al. 2002). Empirical studies (Lykken and Tellegen, 1996), for instance, conclude that more than 80 per cent of the variance in long-term stable levels of subjective well-being can be attributed to inborn temperament. It is on this basis that researchers have claimed people to have inborn subjective well-being 'set points'.[9] The various shocks that hit people in their lifetime affect their happiness only temporarily. We inevitably return – that is, there is a 'hedonic adaptation' – to our set point after a brief period.

Set-point theory explanations are popular in economics. Their proponents believe happiness to be essentially a congenital matter that mostly depends on subjective elements that are absolute, such as character, genes or the inherited capacity to live with and overcome life's hardships. In other words, there exists a given level of happiness, around which the various experiences of life gravitate. This approach is not far removed from the thesis of Herrnstein and Murray (1994), who in their *The Bell Curve* decry the uselessness of social programmes on the basis that people's innate level of intelligence cannot be permanently changed by education.

More recently, Kahneman et al. proposed distinguishing another type of treadmill, the satisfaction one, besides the treadmill based on hedonic adaptation. While 'hedonic treadmill' denotes the treadmill based on adaptation, 'satisfaction treadmill' is based on aspiration, 'which marks the boundaries between satisfactory and unsatisfactory results' (1999, p. 14). Frey and Stutzer (2005) make a similar distinction between the two treadmill effects: 'This process, or mechanism, that reduces the hedonic effects of a constant or repeated stimulus, is called *adaptation* . . .

According to aspiration level theory, individual well-being is determined by the gap between aspiration and achievement' (p. 125).

As their incomes rise, people are induced to seek continuous and ever more intense pleasures in order to maintain the same level of satisfaction. The satisfaction treadmill works in such a way that one's subjective happiness (self-evaluation) remains constant even when one's objective happiness improves. In this case, while Mr Brown gets a boost in his objective well-being, because he bought a new car, the fact that he has had a rise in income has also boosted his aspirations about which is the ideal car to own; so his subjective satisfaction level remains the same. This is true even though he may be objectively more comfortable in his new car. Frank (2005) and Layard (2005) suggest policies for offsetting distortions due to such self-deception; for example, that inconspicuous consumption be taxed less than conspicuous consumption.

7.3.5   Explanations from a Eudaimonian Perspective on Happiness

Relative consumption and treadmill explanations are based on a hedonic/utilitarian understanding of happiness: happiness is conceived as the effect of earning income aimed at purchasing commodities. From an Aristotelian eudaimonian[10] perspective this conception is too restrictive and – because of this restriction – even biased. Earning money and purchasing commodities in the context of a market economy is at best only an aspect of what eudaimonia stands for – a meaningful life or well-being in the sense of actualization of human potentials through intrinsically motivated activities in a context of interpersonal relationships.

The idea that happiness is in essence relational offers a hint to a different explanation of the Easterlin paradox: higher income does not contribute to a happier life when more income involves a tendency to overconsume commodities – produced and purchased in the market economy – and to underconsume relational goods. See, for example, Lane (2000) and Putnam (2000) indicating that time devoted to interpersonal relations is diminishing, crowded out by the extension of markets and in particular of the market economy itself. That latter creates greater mobility among jobs and areas but erodes 'spaces' for interpersonal relations, shifting the care of children and elderly from family to market (see Gui and Sugden, 2005). Antoci et al. (2008) claim to explain the underconsumption of relational goods by focusing on relational goods as public goods: people in developed countries intentionally consume too little relational goods which ends in a suboptimal equilibrium (like in a Prisoner's Dilemma game).

Scitovsky discussed this problem in his *Joyless Economy* (1976). As hinted above (see section 7.1), he argues that people in affluent societies consume too much comfort goods and too little stimulation goods, such as relational goods, since the relative price of comfort goods is lower and even decreases more because of economies of scales and technologically induced increases in productivity absent with stimulation goods. Today Bruni and Stanca (2008), among others, point out complementary causes of comfort goods driving out relational goods, including the presentation of comfort goods as surrogate relational goods, such as a TV programme or social networks.

7.4 FINAL REMARKS

The paradox of happiness, or the 'Easterlin paradox', questions the ethical justification of economic science. Economics – considered as political economy, that is, a branch of moral philosophy – achieved an autonomous statute with respect to moral theology in the eighteenth century, when the idea became commonsense that an increase in the 'wealth of nations' was synonymous with an increase in the 'welfare of nations' or even an increase in 'public happiness'. That was the underlying ethical claim of political economy through the classical era, from Smith to Mill; in some sense that can be extended also to John Maynard Keynes, Joseph Schumpeter and John Hicks. Even today that claim is present and pervasive in economics, when the discipline focuses on the causes and nature of the wealth of nations, mainly as a result of the still-strong belief that wealth is the main factor contributing to the amelioration of social well-being (see Friedman, 2005). The evidence from the paradox of happiness runs against that supposition, and therefore it invites a reassessment of the ethical foundations of the discipline. It makes it mandatory for contemporary economics to redefine its moral basis, if it still intends to contribute to the well-being of people.

Rethinking the ethical foundations of economics will bear also on other parts of the frame of reference of the discipline. The paradoxes of happiness, for example, affect the basic assumption of modern economics that the 'goods' which contribute to an increase of both individual and social well-being are fundamentally material commodities. This as an assumption was probably adequate for the societies of the first Industrial Revolution and for Fordist societies, since in those societies the scarce resources, indeed, were material goods, commodities, physical and/or financial capital.

In contemporary societies, however, the 'goods' turning increasingly scarce are 'relational goods', non-instrumental relationships. This is the real gist of the paradoxes of happiness. Rethinking happiness in an eudaimonian way – by giving a more central place to relational goods and intrinsic motivation – could usher in a new season in the dialogue between economics and ethics. The works of Amartya Sen (2009) and Martha Nussbaum (1986) offer interesting perspectives today in a Neo-Aristotelian, anti-utilitarian direction.

NOTES

1. In arguing that way, Kahneman fails to emphasize the issue of distinguishing possible qualitative differences in experienced utility. See Porta (2009).
2. On the links between the two disciplines in historical perspective, see Bruni and Sugden (2007).
3. The choice (by Adam Smith) of the word 'wealth' (from 'weal') instead of 'riches' is also a sign of the profound nexus, in his thinking, of wealth with public happiness.
4. Cantril's data showed, for instance, that Cuba and Egypt were more satisfied than West Germany (1965, p. 258). He plotted satisfaction against the log of income and thus construed a lack of relationship.
5. For example: 'When we plot average happiness versus average income for clusters of people in a given country at a given time . . . rich people are in fact a lot happier than poor people. It's actually an astonishingly large difference. There's no one single change you can imagine that would make your life improve on the happiness scale as much as to move from the bottom 5 percent on the income scale to the top 5 percent' (Frank 2005, p. 67), and, 'Of course within countries the rich are always happier than the poor' (Layard, 2005, p. 148).
6. A similar criticism has been put forward by Oswald (1997, p. 1817) and others.
7. Among psychologists the relation between income and happiness is even more controversial. Some, on the basis of data different from those of the World Values Survey, challenge the correlations (also when other variables are controlled for) between income and happiness in general (among countries, within a country and over time). For a review cf. Diener et al. (2004).
8. In the World Values Survey questionnaires there is also the information about 'life satisfaction', measured on a numerical 1-10 scale.
9. For a critique of this theory see Lucas et al. (2002, p. 4).
10. On eudaimonia see Bruni (2010).

REFERENCES

Ahuvia, A. and C. Friedman (1998), 'Income, Consumption, and Subjective Well-being: Toward a Composite Macromarketing Model', *Journal of Macromarketing*, **18**, 153–168.

Antoci, A., P.L. Sacco and L. Zarri (2008), 'Social Preferences and the Private Provision of Public Goods: A "Double Critical Mass" Model', *Public Choice*, **135**, 257–276.

Argyle, M. (2001), *The Psychology of Happiness*, New York: Taylor & Francis.

Bernoulli, D. (1738) 'Specimen Theoriae Novae de Mensura Sortis', English transl. (1954), 'Exposition of a New Theory on the Measurement of Risk', *Econometrica*, **22**, 23–36.

Brickman, P. and D.T. Campbell (1971), 'Hedonic Relativism and Planning the Good Society', in M. H. Apley (ed.), *Adaptation-Level Theory: A Symposium*, New York: Academic Press, pp. 287–302.

Bruni, L. (2010), 'The Happiness of Sociality', *Rationality and Society*, **28**, 383–406.

Bruni, L. and L. Stanca (2008), 'Watching Alone: Relational Goods, Happiness and Television', *Journal of Economic Behavior and Organization*, **65**, 506–28.

Bruni, L. and R. Sugden (2007), 'The Road Not Taken: How Psychology was Removed from Economics and How It Might Be Brought Back', *Economic Journal*, **117**, (January), 146–173.

Cantril, H. (1965), *The Pattern of Human Concerns*, New Brunswick, NJ: Rutgers University Press.

Deci, E.L. and R.M. Ryan (2001), 'On Happiness and Human Potentials: A Review of Research on Hedonic and Eudaimonic Wellbeing', *Annual Review of Psychology*, **52**, 141–46.

Diener, E., C.N. Scollon and R.E. Lucas (2004), 'The Evolving Concept of Subjective Wellbeing: The Multifaceted Nature Of Happiness', *Advances in Cell Aging and Gerontology*, **15**, 187–219.

Duesenberry, J. (1949), *Income, Saving and the Theory of Consumer Behaviour*, Cambridge, MA: Harvard University Press.

Easterlin, R. (1974), 'Does Economic Growth Improve Human Lot? Some Empirical Evidence', in P.A. Davis and M.W. Reder (eds), *Nation and Households in Economic Growth: Essays in Honor of Moses Abromowitz*, New York, USA and London, UK: Academic Press, pp. 89–125.

Easterlin, R. (2001), 'Income and Happiness: Towards a Unified Theory', *Economic Journal*, **111**, 465–484.

Easterlin, R. (2005a), 'Towards a Better Theory of Well-being', in L. Bruni and P.L. Porta (eds), *Economics and Happiness: Framings of Analysis*, Oxford: Oxford University Press, pp. 29–64.

Easterlin, R. (2005b), 'Feeding the Illusion of Growth and Happiness: A Reply to Hagerty and Veenhoven', *Social Indicators Research*, **74**(3), 429–443.

Frank, R. (1997), 'The Frame of Reference as a Public Good', *Economic Journal*, **107**, 1832–1847.

Frank, R. (1999), *Luxury Fever*, New York: Free Press.

Frank, R. (2005), 'Does Absolute Income Matter?', in L. Bruni and P.L. Porta (eds), *Economics and Happiness: Framings of Analysis*, Oxford: Oxford University Press, pp. 65–90.

Frey, B.S. and A. Stutzer (2002), *Happiness in Economics*, Princeton, NJ: Princeton University Press.

Frey, B.S. and A. Stutzer (2005), 'Testing Theories of Happiness', in L. Bruni and P.L. Porta (eds), *Economics and Happiness: Framings of Analysis*, Oxford: Oxford University Press, pp. 116–146.

Friedman, B.M. (2005), *The Moral Consequences of Economic Growth*, New York: Knopf.

Gui, B. and R. Sugden (2005), *Economics and Social Interactions*, Cambridge, UK: Cambridge University Press.

Hagerty, M.R. and R. Veenhoven (2003), 'Wealth and Happiness Revisited: Growing National Income Does Go with Greater Happiness', *Social Indicators Research*, **64**, 1–27.

Herrnstein, R.J. and C. Murray (1994), *The Bell Curve: Intelligence and Class Structure in American Life*, New York: Free Press.

Hirsch, F. (1977), *Social Limits to Growth*, London: Routledge.

Höllander, H. (2001), 'On the Validity of Utility Statements: Standard Theory versus Duesenberry's', *Journal of Economic Behaviour and Organization*, **45**, 227–249.

Kahneman, D. (2003), 'Maps of Bounded Rationality: Psychology for Behavioural Economics', *American Economic Review*, **93**(5), 1449–1475.

Kahneman, D., E. Diener and N. Schwartz (eds) (1999), *Well-Being: Foundations of Hedonic Psychology*, New York: Russell Sage Foundation.

Kahneman, D., A. Krueger, D. Schkade, N. Schwarz and A. Stone (2004), 'A Survey Method for Characterizing Daily Life Experience: The Day Reconstruction Method (DRM)', *Science*, **306**, 1776–1780.

Kahneman, D. and R.H. Thaler (2006), 'Utility Maximization and Experienced Utility', *Journal of Economic Perspectives*, **20**(1), pp. 221–234.

Kahneman, D. and A. Tversky (1974), 'Judgment under Uncertainty. Heuristics and Biases', *Science*, **185**, 1124–1131.

Kahneman, D. and A. Tversky (1986), 'Rational Choice and the Framing of Decisions', *Journal of Business*, **59** (4), Pt 2, 251–278.

Kahneman, D., P.P. Wakker and R. Sarin (1997), 'Back to Bentham? Explorations of Experienced Utility', *Quarterly Journal of Economics*, **112**, 375–405.

Lane, R. (2000), *The Loss of Happiness in the Market Democracies*, New Haven, CT: Yale University Press.

Layard, R. (2005), 'Rethinking Public Economics: The Implications of Rivalry and Habit', in L. Bruni and P.L. Porta (eds), *Economics and Happiness: Framings of Analysis*, Oxford: Oxford University Press, pp. 147–169.

Lucas, R.E., A.E. Clark, Y. Georgellis and E. Diener (2002), 'Unemployment Alters the Set-point for Life Satisfaction', Working Paper 17, Paris: Delta.

Lykken, D. and A. Tellegen (1996), 'Happiness is a Stochastic Phenomenon', *Psychological Science*, **7**, 186–189.

New Palgrave Dictionary of Economics (2008), S.N. Durlang and L.E. Alume (eds), 2nd edition, London: Palgrave Macmillan.

Ng, Y.K. (1997), 'The Cave for Happiness, Cardinalism and Interpersonal Comparability', *Economic Journal*, **107**, 1848–58.

Nussbaum, N. (1986), *The Fragility of Goodness: Luck and Ethics in Greek Tragedy*, Cambridge: Cambridge University Press.

Oswald, A.J. (1997), 'Happiness and Economic Performance', *Economic Journal*, **107**, 1815–1831.

Porta, P.L., (2009), 'What Kahneman Could Have Learnt From Pietro Verri', in R. Arena, S. Dow, M. Klaes (eds), *Open Economics, Economics in Relation to Other Disciplines*, London: Routledge, pp. 48–70.

Putnam, R. (2000), *Bowling Alone*, New York: Simon & Schuster.

Robbins, L.C. (1982), *An Essay on the Nature and Significance of the Economic Science*, London: Macmillan.

Scitovsky, T. (1976), *The Joyless Economy: An Inquiry into Human Satisfaction and Consumer Dissatisfaction*, Oxford: Oxford University Press.

Sen, A.K. (2009), *The Idea of Justice*, London: Allen Lane.

Simon, H. (1983), *Reason in Human Affairs*, Stanford, CA: Stanford University Press.

Veenhoven, R. (1991), 'Is Happiness Relative?', *Social Indicators Research*, **24**, 1–34.

8 Applied policy, welfare economics, and Mill's half-truths
David Colander

8.1 INTRODUCTION

The argument in this chapter is a simple one. It is that sometime around the 1930s the economics profession's use of models in thinking about economic policy changed. The result has been a tendency to draw unwarranted policy implications from models and theory, such as occurred in the recent financial crisis. The chapter argues that to prevent such misuse of models from occurring, the economics profession needs to return to the earlier methodological approach, which recognized the complexity of the economy and the relative simplicity of our formal models.

Up until the 1930s what might be called the Classical method predominated in applying models to policy.[1] This method assumed that the economy was too complicated for formal modeling, and that any formal model would have to be seen as providing at best what John Stuart Mill called half-truths (Mill, 1838 [1950]). These half-truths from models would have to be integrated into a much broader implicit theory before they could be applied to real-world policy. Because this broader implicit theory was so complicated, it was accepted that economists would focus only on the economic portion of that broader theory, leaving it to other social scientists, or to economists who were operating outside the science of economics, to add the other elements necessary to draw policy results from economic models. This meant that for Classical economists, welfare economics was not, and could not be, a stand-alone field. Only when these other elements were added could one arrive at policy conclusions.

Classical economists who specialized in methodology recognized that economists would have a tendency to justify their policy prescriptions by claiming the imprimatur of economic science. To help insure against that, Classical economic methodology maintained a strict separation between the science of economics and economic policy analysis. Science was concerned with understanding for the sake of understanding, and was not concerned with policy. This meant that if there was any welfare economics which gave prescriptions for policy, it was not part of the science of economics.

The Classical method reflected a skepticism of models and theory, and of what economics could contribute to policy. As an advocate of this Classical method, Lionel Robbins stated: 'What precision economists can claim at this stage is largely a sham precision. In the present state of knowledge, the man who can claim for economic science much exactitude is a quack' (Robbins, 1927, p. 176).

Put in modern context, Classical economists saw the economy as a highly complex and interrelated system that was impossible to model formally. This did not mean that they did not use models; it simply meant that they saw a model's results being blended together with philosophical views, feelings, sensibilities and institutional knowledge to arrive at a policy conclusion. For Classical economists applied policy was an art, not a science.

We can see this separation of policy from models early on in Classical methodological writing. For example, Nassau Senior, the earliest Classical economist who took a strong interest in methodology, writes:

> [An economist's] conclusions, whatever be their generality and their truth, do not authorize him in adding a single syllable of advice. That privilege belongs to the writer or statesman who has considered all the causes which may promote or impede the general welfare of those whom he addresses, not to the theorist who has considered only one, though among the most important of those causes. The business of a Political Economist is neither to recommend nor to dissuade, but to state general principles, which it is fatal to neglect, but neither advisable, nor perhaps practicable, to use as the sole, or even the principle [*sic*], guides in the actual conduct of affairs. (Senior, 1836 [1951], pp. 2–3)

For Senior, and for most early Classical economists concerned with methodology, the economic science of the time was a branch of logic. In the pure science of economics at the time one did theory, which meant that one developed theorems from almost self-evident principles. But, as Senior makes clear, economic theory was not meant to guide policy directly. To move from the theorems developed in the science of economics to the precepts of policy-relevant economics, Classical economists believed that one had to rely on commonsense judgment and institutional knowledge, and that discussing policy involved different skills than did doing economic theory.

This theory–policy divide can also be found in J.N. Keynes's famous summary of economists' methodology at the turn of the nineteenth century (J.N. Keynes, 1891). Like Senior, J.N. Keynes saw the pure science of economics, which he called positive economics, as a relatively narrow branch of economics, which needed to be strictly separated from the applied policy branch – which he called the art of economics. He argued that the two branches needed to be separated because they had quite different methodologies. He writes: 'a definitive art of political economy, which attempts to lay down absolute rules for the regulation of human conduct, will have vaguely defined limits, and be largely non-economic in character' (J.N. Keynes, 1891, p. 83).

8.2 'NEOCLASSICALS' FOLLOWING CLASSICAL METHODOLOGY

This separation of applied policy from the science of economics did not end with Classical economists. It also characterized the approach of numerous economists who are often classified as neoclassical. These include Alfred Marshall, Lionel Robbins, John Maynard Keynes and even A.C. Pigou. In my view, in terms of method (by which I mean methodological views about how economic theory and models relate to policy), all four of these writers belong much more in a Classical tradition than in what has become known as a neoclassical tradition. By that I mean that they maintained the same strict separation between policy and theory that Classical economists did, and saw models as aids to judgment, not as definitive guides to policy.

Consider Marshall and Pigou. While it is true that Marshall and Pigou both developed more formal models than did most earlier Classical economists, and used those models in discussions of policy, it is also true that they were very careful to add a large number of qualifiers that could change the results of the model. Like their Classical ancestors, they both saw economic policy as an art that involves issues outside the domain of economics, and not as a set of prescriptions that followed directly from models. They were careful in their writings to emphasize the limitations of their models. For example, in the core text of Marshall's *Principles* he carefully specifies the limitations of the models rather than developing the analytics of the models. Often, he placed his formal analytics in appendices, not in the core chapters. His *Principles* was designed to teach students how economists thought about policy issues, and to introduce them to some models that could help integrate economic reasoning into their thinking. His textbook was not designed to teach students about how to model the issues formally. Put another way, he was teaching students to be 'consumers' of theory, not 'producers' of theory.

Pigou, the economist most associated with the term 'welfare economics', also carefully limited the applicability of his models. He tells his readers that his analytic work provides only 'vague judgments' and 'instructed guesswork'.[2] He specifically does not draw definitive policy conclusions from his models. For example, in Pigou (1935) he argues that his formal model showing that certain policy actions will improve welfare 'only takes us a little way' in arriving at a policy view. He points out that there are many other issues that the model does not take into account, any of which could reverse the policy argument following from a model. He further states:

> The issue about which popular writers argue – the principle of laisser-faire versus the principle of State action – is not an issue at all. There is no principle involved on either side . . . Each particular case must be considered on its merits in all the detail of its concrete circumstance. (Pigou, 1935, pp. 127–128)

Contrary to popular opinion, Lionel Robbins also falls into this Classical methodological tradition of not drawing policy conclusions from formal models.[3] In his Ely Lecture (Robbins, 1981), Robbins reflects back on how his famous 1932 essay (Robbins, 1932) was incorrectly interpreted by the profession. He states explicitly that the economics profession needs a separate branch, which he calls political economy, to deal with policy. He writes that this policy branch of economics 'depends upon the technical apparatus of analytical Economics; but it applies this apparatus to the examination of schemes for the realization of aims whose formulation lies outside Economics' (Robbins, 1981, p. 8).

It was not only in microeconomic policy that the Classical methodology of strict separation of models and policy continued beyond what is generally thought of as the Classical period. It was also in macroeconomic policy. By that I mean that J.M. Keynes also followed this Classical method, and carefully did not derive policy conclusions from his models.[4] Instead, he used many different models and arrived at a policy conclusion through reasoned judgment. He writes:

> Economics is a science of thinking in terms of models joined to the art of choosing models which are relevant to the contemporary world . . . Good economists are scarce because the gift for using 'vigilant observation' to choose good models, although it does not require a highly specialized intellectual technique, appears to be a very rare one. (Keynes, 1938)

In summary, the economist's method through the 1930s was a method that separated applied policy work from formal models and theories. Applied economics was seen as an art that used economic models, but that also involved much more than those models. To arrive at any policy conclusion, one had to go beyond economic models. In the Classical method, any 'theory' of welfare economics was not a theory to be applied directly to policy. Instead, it was a guide to reasoned thought about applied policy issues. The results of theory were meant to be used with caution, judgment and knowledge of the institutional details. No policy conclusion followed directly from economic theory or from economic models. Consistent with this applied policy approach, discussions of applied policy were to carry warning labels about the limitations of the models. This approach did not mean that economists, in their role as private individuals or statesmen, could not or should not arrive at policy conclusions. What it meant was that if they did so, they should make it clear that they were not claiming economic science as underpinning their arguments.

8.3   THE ABANDONMENT OF THE CLASSICAL METHOD AND THE RISE OF THE NEOCLASSICAL METHOD

Beginning in the 1930s, that Classical 'strict separation' methodology became less and less strict, and by the 1970s it was replaced in the textbooks with a more direct approach of connecting models and policy. Instead of maintaining a strict separation between models and policy, and emphasizing the importance of broader issues in arriving at policy conclusions, models and policy prescriptions became blended into one. To contrast this direct blending of models and policy with the above described Classical methodological approach, I call it the neoclassical methodological approach.

The neoclassical method does not seem ever to have been formally defended in methodological writings, as the Classical method was. It simply evolved over time, as the strict separation qualifications that the Classical methodologists emphasized faded from memory and practice. A full explanation of why this occurred is beyond the scope of this chapter, but my initial thoughts are that the change was associated with a change in the institutional structure within which economists worked, and with the development of empirical methods, which allowed economists to hope that the models could be chosen on the basis of statistical tests, and hence could have empirical foundations that would not necessitate the subjective judgment that Classical economists believed that it did.

The change in institutional structure involved the development of economics as a separate discipline with its own separate training. Up until the 1930s, a majority of those who wrote on economics were not in economics departments. They either were not primarily employed as academics, or were in broader political philosophy departments. Increasingly after the 1930s that changed; economics became a separate academic discipline, and training in economics became narrower as it focused more on pure economic issues, and less on the broad social science and philosophical issues that characterized earlier training. As that narrowing happened, methodology no longer became a topic that economists studied. Instead, economists' work became more focused on the technical issues of modeling. As that happened the extensive discussions of scope and method of economics, which contained the caveats on the use of models in Classical writing, disappeared, either because the writers assumed that economists knew these caveats, and hence they did not require further discussion, or because such methodological issues were not for economists to discuss.

This institutional reason for the change was supplemented by a technological change in how economic analysis was done. Beginning in the 1930s, empirical methods of testing models expanded. This allowed economists to hope that the precision of the models could be increased beyond a 'sham precision'. With developments in econometric theory, there was hope that economics could become a positive science, in which theories and models could be tested, and shown to be true or false. That hope was largely unfulfilled, but the hopes for empirical work likely played a role in changing the economic method guiding applied policy work. If models could be selected on scientifically acceptable empirical grounds, then they could be considered scientific truths, and implications for policy could be drawn from those truths.

It was during this shift from Classical to neoclassical methodology that the formal subfield of welfare economics, which drew relatively firm policy precepts from economic models, developed. Welfare economics moved beyond Marshall's partial equilibrium approach in which models were used as a tool for reasoning about particular policy issues. In the Marshallian approach to applied policy the reasoning chains were kept short, and one would continually emphasize the limitations of the models. In the new welfare economics approach to policy this Marshallian partial equilibrium framework was replaced with a Walrasian general equilibrium framework. This Walrasian framework that pictured the economy as a system of 'solvable' simultaneous equations was much more mathematical than the Walrasian approach, and it drew out policy conclusions from models based on long chains of reasoning, with little to no discussion of the limitations of the models as they related to real-world policy.

These developments led to an enormous burst of creative technical work that extended the partial equilibrium models of Marshall to general equilibrium models. The limitations against using long lines of reasoning to arrive at policy conclusions faded away. In the 1930s and 1940s work in this area advanced economic theory enormously, and a wide range of theoretical issues were cleared up in the writings of economists such as John Hicks (1939), Paul Samuelson (1947) and Abba Lerner (1944). It was a change from a Marshallian economic vision of the economy as a complex system too complicated to model fully to a Walrasian economic vision that was captured by a formal model.

It was during this time period that most of the qualifications of models that Classical economists had emphasized were moved to the back of economists' minds. As I argue in 'The Sins of the Sons of Samuelson' (Colander and Rothschild, 2010), with each successive generation the qualifications about the use of models faded further and further back, and by the 1960s Classical methodology had been replaced by neoclassical methodology in young economists' thinking and in the textbooks.

Of the three economists mentioned above, Abba Lerner was the most likely to draw policy conclusions directly from models and, in many ways, the policy discussion in his *Economics of Control* (1944) served as the template for the teaching of both micro and macro policy starting in the 1950s and continuing until today. Lerner drew specific policy conclusions from his theoretical models in microeconomics and provided few discussions of nuances or limitations.[5] He framed microeconomic policy as a technical issue of meeting the appropriate marginal conditions that were to become the fundamental theorems of welfare economics. Instead of students being taught that models provided half-truths, they were taught that by following the rules of welfare economics that equated marginal social costs with marginal social benefits, policy makers could lead society to a Pareto optimum. These rules, which were known as the Lange–Lerner rules, became the guiding rules of welfare economics, and have become the central frame of undergraduate micro theory in the textbooks.

Similarly, Lerner framed macroeconomic policy as a technical issue of meeting what he called the rules of functional finance (Lerner, 1944). These rules structured macroeconomic policy as following directly from an IS/LM type model, which led to specific policy actions: if income is below what is desired, use expansionary fiscal policy; if income is above what is desired, use contractionary fiscal policy. Use monetary policy to set interest rates so as to yield the optimal amount of investment.

Lerner's rules of both microeconomic policy and macroeconomic policy, because of their simplicity and clearness, became the template for the textbook presentation of both micro and macro policy discussions.[6] These policy rules that Lerner developed were not presented in the texts as general guidelines to be used in combination with non-economic considerations, as were the policy precepts found in Marshall and Pigou. Instead, Lerner's policy rules were presented as firm rules following directly from economic theory. Models were presented as forming the basis of policy – the blueprints that governments should follow – if government wanted to work in the social interest. For example, in the introduction to his *Economics of Control* Lerner writes:

> [we] shall concentrate on what would be the best thing that the government can do in the social interest – what institutions would most effectively induce the individual members of society, while seeking to accomplish their own ends, to act in the way which is most beneficial for society as a whole . . . Here we shall merely attempt to show what is socially desirable. (Lerner, 1944, p. 6)

Unlike Marshall, and Pigou (1920), who carefully discussed the limitations of economic models when arriving at policy conclusions, following Lerner, the new pedagogical presentation of applied policy aggressively related theory and models to policy conclusions. The new pedagogical presentation did not make the Classical distinction between precepts (derived from the art of economics embodying value judgments in the theory) and theorems (derived from pure theory, and quite irrelevant for direct policy application).[7] Lerner's work was the core of much graduate teaching in the late 1940s. Then, as others expanded the models and developed more complicated models that showed the limitations of the arguments, Lerner's work simply became a stepping stone to a much wider range of increasingly complex models taught in graduate school. It remained, however, the central framework of undergraduate presentations of economic policy in both micro and macro, and thereby provided the frame that most economists who do not specialize in welfare economics bring to policy analysis.[8]

I am not arguing that the limitations of that framework were not known or understood. Although in Lerner's presentation, and in the textbook presentations of welfare economics that followed from it, there was little to no discussion of the nuances of application, in more technical advanced work there was a clear exposition of the limitations. Specialists in welfare economics fully understood that the formal models had little value for actual direct policy guidance. For example, in his *A Critique of Welfare Economics*, I.M.D. Little (1950) showed the limitations of the welfare economics as a guide for policy. Similarly, J. de V. Graaff concluded his famous consideration of welfare economics, *Theoretical Welfare Economics*, with the statement: 'the possibility of building a useful and interesting theory of welfare economics – i.e. one which consists of something more than the barren formalisms typified by the marginal equivalences of conventional theory – is exceedingly small' (Graaff, 1957, p. 169). Unfortunately that advanced work was not imprinted on the minds of most economists in the way that the limitations of the models for policy analysis were imprinted on Classical economists.

The decreasing emphasis given to the limitations of economic models for policy can also be seen in the evolution of the presentation of advanced social welfare theory, which abandoned the Pareto optimality approach to welfare economics found in Lerner's approach and replaced it with a social welfare function approach (Bergson, 1938). Analytically, the social welfare function approach was a major improvement; it solved the Hume's dictum problem that one cannot derive a 'should' from an 'is'. It recognized that to derive policy recommendations that involve value judgments, one must explicitly state what underlying value judgments one starts from. But it did so primarily in theoretical expositions, not in real-world applications. By that I mean that while this social welfare function approach helped to clarify the formal structure of the micro policy model, and more correctly specified the analytics of what policy implications could be drawn from the analytics of the model, it nonetheless lost many of the nuances about limitations of applying models to reality that the earlier strict-separation Classical method had maintained. Consider Bergson's initial discussion of the social welfare function (Bergson, 1938). In it, he distinguishes an economic welfare function, in which only economic variables are considered, from a social welfare function, in which all the variables which affect welfare are taken into account.

He emphasizes that his 1938 discussion is of an economic welfare function, not of a social welfare function, which means that he accepts that the economic welfare function approach is only a partial analysis which needed to be combined with insights of other social sciences and philosophy to arrive at a policy conclusion. He justifies his focus on economic variables in his article with the following argument: 'For relatively small changes in these variables, other elements in welfare, I believe, will not be significantly affected. To the extent that this is so a partial analysis is feasible' (Bergson, 1938, p. 314).

But Bergson went even further than that, and later questioned whether a useful separation could be made. In a later article (Bergson, 1954), he expanded on this distinction where he discusses new developments in welfare theory. In this article he repeats his earlier argument that welfare analysis 'must rest on "value judgments" no matter how broad or narrow the scope' (Bergson, 1954, p. 249) He also writes that his 'own ethical thinking has evolved in the course of time'. He states: 'If value criticism of a deep sort can be meaningful, I still feel that it is also largely philosophic, at least in the present primitive state of psychology.' He concludes: 'I cannot imagine any sensible alternative to ethical counseling.' By this, he meant that the conclusions of any of the economic models could not be translated into policy without their being placed in a broader philosophical and ethical context. Welfare economics as a separable branch of the science of economics could not exist, and policy advocacy had to integrate ethical and value considerations. The economics profession did not follow Bergson; instead, it moved further and further away from any discussion of broader issues and concentrated on drawing direct policy conclusions from formal economic models.

What is relevant about Bergson's qualifications and differentiation between the economic welfare function and the social welfare function were soon lost and forgotten in most economists' discussions of applied policy and in the textbooks. To my knowledge, no textbook differentiated an economic welfare function from a social welfare function and made the point that Bergson made that economic welfare was only a small part of social welfare, and policy had to be decided on social welfare grounds, not on economic welfare grounds. Instead microeconomists have translated their economic models' results into direct policy recommendations with few of the broader qualifications that were emphasized in the Classical and Bergson's method.

More advanced critiques of the economic welfare function frame, such as Graaff's and Bergson's, or later Amartya Sen's (1970), seldom made it to the textbooks even in watered-down form, and thus between the 1940s and 1960s there was a major change in how economics was taught and how most economists thought about applied policy. Robert Solow (1997) makes this difference in pedagogy clear in his comparison of 1940s textbooks and textbooks beginning in the 1960s. He writes that books through the 1940s were discursive in nature. He states: 'Most provide more institutional descriptions, very sensible discussions of economic policy, and serious looks at recent history as it would be seen by an economist . . . The authors ruminate more than they analyze' (p. 88). Solow continues:

> the student is not encouraged to make literal use of the apparatus of supply and demand curves. Both books spend time discussing monopolistic elements in real-world markets, but most of the discussion is institutional. Their reflections on the workings of economy are worth reading. They inspire bursts of nostalgia; words like 'civilized' came to mind. (Solow, 1997, p. 89)

Starting in the 1950s, following Samuelson's famous text (Samuelson, 1948), the textbook approach changed. The new style texts placed economics in a scientific framework with the microeconomic presentation organized around supply and demand graphs and a general Walrasian conception of the economy. While the principles-level microeconomic presentations did not present the full optimality presentations, the policy frame that they provided students was one that focused on marginal conditions, and micro policy was discussed in terms of models without significant discussion of the limitations of models. Similarly, its macroeconomics was organized around a Keynesian aggregate expenditures, aggregate production model, in which fiscal policy was needed to keep the economy at full employment, and monetary policy was used to set an optimal interest rate. Samuelson fully recognized the limitations of the models, and some discussion of those limitations show up in addenda in the text and the footnotes. But there is none of the discursive presentation emphasizing how other issues enter into the analysis. Neither are there any broad discussions of limitations of the models such as found in Marshall's *Principles* (1890) or in economic principles textbooks through the 1940s.

Other books followed Samuelson's lead, and that modeling presentation of policy became embedded in economists' thinking. Just how embedded can be seen in Solow's (1997) description of how economists approach problems today. He writes:

> Judicious discussion is no longer the way serious economics is carried out . . . In the 1940s, whole semesters could go by without anyone talking about building or testing a model. Today, if you ask a mainstream economist a question about almost any aspect of economic life, the response will be: suppose we model that situation and see what happens. (Solow, 1997, p. 89–90)

8.4 CONCLUSION

The above history demonstrates the changes to the economists' approach to applied economic policy, and to teaching applied economic policy, which occurred in the transition from Classical methodology to neoclassical methodology. In the Classical period and up until the 1940s in the neoclassical period, textbook presentations carefully developed economic policy as only a part of a broader philosophical or social policy; the books were focused on training students to be consumers of economic theory, not producers of economic theory, and the textbook authors saw their role as guiding students in being good consumers of economic reasoning. This meant pointing out the need for context and the limitation of models simultaneously as they taught the models. The narrower neoclassical methodological approach moved directly from economic models to economic policy recommendations. It concentrated on teaching students modeling and understanding the analytics of the model.

These differences are primarily pedagogical differences, and do not necessarily reflect deep changes in economic methodology specialists' beliefs in how economics relates to policy. But, over time, pedagogical decisions have effects, and in economics, they had an enormous effect. They led more and more economists to lose sight of the limitations of models and the need to be humble about what the models are telling us, and what implications can be drawn.

Even if one accepts that economic policy is part of moral philosophy, and that models have to be put in context, an argument can still be made to continue teaching as we do. The issue guiding what economics teaches its students involves practical trade-offs. Consider John Siegfried's consideration (2009) of Stephen Marglin's (2008) call to broaden economic teaching to include much more than the algorithmic knowledge taught in the neoclassical texts. Siegfried agreed with Marglin that teaching students about how models relate to economic policy required much more than what is currently taught, but argued that: 'a persuasive case for a concentrated dose of algorithmic knowledge in economics classrooms can spring from its scarcity elsewhere . . . In the absence of assurance that logical deduction will be emphasized elsewhere in the curriculum, maybe the best use of economics courses is to fill that gap aggressively' (Siegfried, 2009, p. 219).

The difficulty with this argument is that it assumes that students and economists are being trained on the limitations of models elsewhere. But that is not the case. Graduate economic programs provide little discussion of context, and instead concentrate heavily on teaching students modeling techniques. Economic training is geared to creating producers of models, not consumers of models who have the contextual and institutional knowledge, and the incentive to worry, about whether the model is the appropriate model for the purpose. Some economists of course, intuitively or through outside training, incorporate the nuances of applying models to policy problems. But that ability is neither selected for in the admission process, nor is it taught in terms of core content of graduate programs. Those programs emphasize the teaching of modeling techniques, not modeling interpretation. For applied policy, this presents a problem. As Keynes noted in his quotation above, an applied policy economist needs to know both how to model, and how to choose the right model.

The problem with our current approach to teaching models is that it leads to economists who are not trained in the subtleties of applying models to apply models, and to claim the imprimatur of economic science in doing so. Thus, for example, we can see two top macroeconomists, Chari and Kehoe (2006), writing in the AEA's *Journal of Economic Perspectives* that 'recent theoretical advances in macroeconomic theory have found their way into policy' and claiming that:

> The message of examples like these is that discretionary policy making has only costs and no benefits, so that if government policymakers can be made to commit to a policy rule, society should make them do so. (pp. 7–8)

and:

> Macroeconomists can now tell policymakers that to achieve optimal results, they should design institutions that minimize the time inconsistency problem by promoting a commitment to policy rules. (p. 9)

Such hubris about the strong policy implications of highly abstract models whose assumptions do not come close to fitting reality helped lead to the recent financial economic crisis. Such claims of policy certainty flowing directly from models do not sit well with economists trained in the Classical methodology that questions how well the model being used fits the situation being described. For example, Robert Solow, who was trained in the Classical methodology even though he strongly advocates a concentration on modeling, responded to their claims by arguing that their conclusions are totally spurious, and do not deserve to be taken seriously because the dynamic stochastic general equilibrium (DSGE) model that their claims are derived from is so far from the institutional setting of the real-world economy that lessons from the model cannot be directly applied to policy issues.

The primary recommendation following from the arguments in this chapter is that economics policy training could be improved by instituting specific training for applied policy and welfare economics that emphasizes the skills needed to interpret models. It would involve economic history, history of economic thought, real-world institutions, methodology and moral philosophy. This training could exist as a separate track for applied policy economists within economics departments, in public policy programs, in transdisciplinary programs, or in a separate program in political economy as distinct from economic science.

Such training would be much closer to the training that the Classical economists received. The training would involve discussions of technical models, but the goal of the training would be to provide students with a consumer's knowledge of theory and models, rather than with a producer's knowledge of theory and models. The graduates of these applied economics programs, or applied policy tracts, would be seen as the specialists in choosing among models produced by others, and these programs would have their own measures of output quite separate from the measures of output used by current graduate economics programs. Creating a cadre of economic policy specialists could go a long way toward restoring the humility about what claims can be made from our limited models in the face of the enormous complexity of the real-world economy that was expressed in Mill's recognition that analytic models provide at best half-truths.

NOTES

1. Although I call it the Classical method, as I discuss below, its use extended well into what is normally called the neoclassical period.

2. See Steven Medema (2010) for a nice discussion of how Pigou limited the applicability of his models.
3. For a further discussion of Robbins's approach, see David Colander (2009).
4. For a expansion of this issue, see Colander (2011).
5. Specifically, government should adjust resources until a set of marginal conditions are met (Lerner, 1944, p. 96). His rules on income redistribution did not become part of the textbook template. Lerner agreed that we had no basis for making interpersonal welfare comparisons, but argued that because of the uncertainty principle, redistribution was more likely to improve social welfare than hurt it, and thus he supported redistribution, and defined his welfare rules to include redistribution. Later developments switched to a welfare economics focus only on Pareto efficiency.
6. Lerner's early writing played an important role in the socialist calculation debate that was ongoing at the time, and very much concerned the arguments behind the role of the state in the economy. In that debate Lerner advocated market socialism, and argued that socialist planners could give directives to managers to set price at marginal costs, and thereby achieve maximum social welfare.
7. Lerner even extended the analysis to get around interpersonal comparisons of welfare by arguing that while interpersonal comparisons of welfare were impossible, 'probable comparisons' were not, and that redistribution policy should be based on 'probable total satisfaction' (Lerner, 1944, p. 29). Consistent with this view he drew out specific rules for how government could achieve the optimal distribution of income.
8. Ronald Coase's work provides an alternative frame, but few texts are structured around his more Marshallian approach.

REFERENCES

Bergson, Abram (1938), 'A Reformulation of Certain Aspects of Welfare Economics', *Quarterly Journal of Economics*, **52**(2), 310–334.
Bergson, Abram (1954), 'On the Concept of Social Welfare', *Quarterly Journal of Economics*, **68**(2), 233–252.
Chari, V.V. and Patrick J. Kehoe (2006), 'Modern Macroeconomics in Practice: How Theory is Shaping Policy', *Journal of Economic Perspectives*, **20**(4), 3–28.
Colander, David (2009), 'What Was "It" that Robbins was Defining?', *Journal of the History of Economic Thought*, **31**(4), 437–448.
Colander, David (2011), 'The Keynesian Method, Complexity, and the Training of Economists', in Arie Arnon, Jimmy Weinblatt and Warren Young (eds), *Perspectives on Keynesian Economics*, Heidelberg, Dordrecht, London and New York: Springer, pp. 183–201.
Colander, David and Casey Rothschild (2010), 'The Sins of the Sons of Samuelson: Vision, Pedagogy and the Zig-Zag Windings of Complex Dynamics', *Journal of Economic Behavior and Organization*, **74**(3), 277–290.
Graaff, J. de V. (1957), *Theoretical Welfare Economics*, Cambridge: Press Syndicate of the University of Cambridge.
Hicks, John (1939), *Value and Capital*, Oxford, UK and New York, USA: Oxford University Press.
Keynes, John Maynard (1938), Letter to Roy Harrod. 4 July, http://economia.unipv.it/harrod/edition/editionstuff/rfh.346.htm, accessed 15 March 2009.
Keynes, John Neville (1891), *The Scope and Method of Political Economy*, London: Macmillan.
Lerner, Abba (1944), *The Economics of Control*, New York: Macmillan.
Little, Ian Malcom David (1950), *A Critique of Welfare Economics*, Oxford: Clarendon Press.
Marglin, Stephen (2008), *The Dismal Science: How Thinking Like an Economist Undermines Community*, Cambridge, MA: Harvard University Press.

Marshall, Alfred (1890), *Principles of Economics*, London: Macmillan.

Medema, Steven G. (2010), *The Hesitant Hand: Taming Self-Interest in the History of Economic Ideas*, Princeton, NJ: Princeton University Press.

Mill, John Stuart (1838 [1950]), 'Essay on Bentham', in F.R. Leavis (ed.), *Mill on Bentham and Coleridge*, London: Chatto & Windus, pp. 39–98.

Pigou, Arthur Cecil (1920), *The Economics of Welfare London*, London: Macmillan.

Pigou, Arthur Cecil (1935), 'State Action and Laisser-Faire', *Economics in Practice: Six Lectures on Current Issues*, London: Macmillan, pp. 107–128.

Robbins, Lionel (1927), 'Mr Hawtrey on the Scope of Economics', *Economica*, **20**, 172–178.

Robbins, Lionel (1932), *An Essay on The Nature and Significance of Economic Science*, London: Macmillan.

Robbins, Lionel (1981), 'Economics and Political Economy', *American Economic Review*, **70**(2), 1–10.

Samuelson, Paul (1947), *Foundations of Economic Analysis*. Cambridge, MA: Harvard University Press.

Samuelson, Paul (1948), *Economics*, New York: McGraw Hill

Sen, Amartya Kumar (1970), *Collective Choice and Social Welfare*, San Francisco, CA: Holden-Day.

Senior, Nassau William (1836), *An Outline of the Science of Political Economy*. London: W. Clowes & Sons; reprinted (1951), New York: Augustus M. Kelley.

Siegfried, John (2009), 'Really Thinking Like an Economist', in David Colander and KimMarie McGoldrick (eds), *Educating Economists: The Teagle Discussion on Re-evaluating the Undergraduate Economics Major*, Cheltenham, UK and Northampton, MA, USA: Edward Elgar, pp. 215–224.

Solow, Robert Merton (1997), 'How Did Economics Get That Way and What Way Did It Get?', *Daedalus*, **126**, 39–58.

9 Economics as usual: geographical economics shaped by disciplinary conventions
Uskali Mäki and Caterina Marchionni[1]

9.1 INTRODUCTION

Is economics a proper science at all? Or if it qualifies as a science, does it underperform, does it fail to fulfil its scientific duties? Does it perhaps just pretend to proceed as a science by applying principles and techniques that are not suitable for addressing its proper subject matter and for meeting the legitimate expectations? There is a long and live tradition of economics-bashing and economics apology in posing and answering such questions.

One popular current in this tradition is to blame economics for being theory-driven or method-driven or driven by whatever else but the world or empirical evidence or observation. Economics thus does not care about the real world – indeed, being so deeply shaped by its favourite theories and methods disconnects economics from the world. The alternative to this gloomy scenario is for a discipline to be evidence-driven or world-oriented or to be guided by some such proper scientific ethos. Being theory-driven involves stressing scientific virtues such as simplicity, coherence, convenience, tractability, formal rigor, theoretical elegance, and so on. Being observation-driven or world-oriented means emphasizing the importance of truth, complexity, empirical testing, practical relevance, and so on. Sometimes the former is characterized as a deductive approach, in contrast to the latter inductive approach. Diagnosis of the failures of economics and advice for how to do better economics is often put in such dichotomous terms.

This popular way of framing the issues and debates is all too simplistic and outright distortive. It is often misled by the appearances and neglectful of the complex details of scientific practice in actual economic inquiry – characteristics that it denounces in the target of its criticism. Indeed, it looks like an example of the theory-driven approach at the meta-level. In the meta-inquiry that we offer here we adopt an approach that is closer to the approach that the critics recommend to the remedy of economics in that we acknowledge the complexity of the issues and use an empirical case study in supporting the claims we make. What we will find is that the simplistic dichotomy between theory-driven economics and world-oriented or data-driven economics indeed distorts. Among other things, we point out that being theory-driven and being world-oriented are not in necessary conflict with one another, and that being data-driven and being world-oriented should be kept separate and not be conflated with one another.

The empirical case that we examine is geographical economics. In many ways, it is an appropriate case to look at. It is a recent stream in mainstream economics. It has already been acknowledged with a Nobel Prize. Its major architects, most notably Paul Krugman, have been active in reflecting on some of the methodological issues surrounding it. It is at once a representative and unique case of what many would recognize as theory-driven development in economics, and indeed it has received its share of the sort of blame we outlined in the beginning. A closer look however reveals that being theory-driven can be a complex property that is compatible with being constrained by evidence and with being world-oriented.

We deal with geographical economics (GeoEcon) in terms of scientific conventions, virtues and constraints. We show that there are many kinds of constraining and enabling conventions that, by interacting with one another in a broad range of contingent ways, shape the trajectory of theory development. The conventions shaping GeoEcon are those of the conventional core of the discipline of economics. So there is nothing very unusual about its particular trajectory.

What we call disciplinary conventions define the enabling and constraining principles that shape scientific inquiry characteristic of a discipline or research field. They suggest what should and should not be done by setting the virtues of inquiry and its products that are to be pursued – such as truth, empirical confirmation, simplicity, coherence, unification, tractability, explanatory force, predictive reliability, policy relevance, and so on, variously interpreted and combined at different levels of abstraction and specificity.

Our goal is to identify the disciplinary conventions characteristic of GeoEcon and to show how they have shaped its emergence. In other words, we provide rudiments of the story about the troubled relationship between economics and geography, or the delayed rediscovery of space by economics: how and why economics first ignored geography, then managed to incorporate it into its theoretical framework. Among our observations are the following:

1. For a long time, conventional economists ignored geography because they were unable to incorporate it in the established (general equilibrium) theoretical framework.

2. The incorporation of geography in the core theory was finally made possible by the construction of a theoretical model that combined increasing returns to scale and monopolistic competition.
3. Its incorporation was deemed desirable because economists held the extra-theoretic belief that, as a matter of fact, geography makes a difference.
4. Its incorporation was guided by the desideratum of having mechanistic microfoundations for claims about aggregate-level phenomena.
5. Its incorporation was furthermore shaped by the ambition of explanatory unification in terms of common mechanisms.
6. The sort of explanatory unification that was sought required (implicitly) having rather narrow explananda and (explicitly) using rather strong tractability-enhancing theoretical assumptions.

9.2   A BRIEF SUMMARY OF GEOGRAPHICAL ECONOMICS

In 2008 Paul Krugman was awarded the Nobel Prize in economics for 'his analysis of trade patterns and location of economic activity'.[2] These are Krugman's crucial contributions to the creation of well-known fields within economics, namely 'new trade theory' and 'new economic geography', or as we prefer to call the latter, geographical economics (GeoEcon). Not surprisingly, the two developments are closely connected. In fact, it was a small modification to a new trade theory model that gave rise to the first model of GeoEcon, namely the core–periphery model laid out in Krugman (1991) (see Brakman et al., 2009, pp. 81–131).

Krugman (1991) derives the agglomeration of economic activity within a model in which there are two locations and two sectors in both locations, namely the manufacturing and the agricultural sector. The agricultural sector is perfectly competitive and its workers are evenly distributed across the two locations and are assumed not to move across them. The manufacturing sector is characterized by monopolistic competition and increasing returns to scale. Each firm produces a variety of a differentiated product, and products are subject to transportation costs. In this model, workers of the manufacturing sector are assumed to move across locations. Consumers' utility positively depends on the amount of each variety consumed, and on the number of varieties that is available in their location (love of variety).

The spatial economy is shaped by the relative strength of centripetal forces, that is, forces pushing towards agglomeration; and centrifugal forces, that is, forces that push towards dispersion. Centripetal forces arise from the presence of increasing returns to scale and transportation costs, which create an incentive for firms to locate close to the larger market (the larger market will be in the location which, due to some historical accident, happens to have a larger share of firms and workers) so as to minimize transportation costs. Workers, who are also consumers, likewise have an incentive to locate where the market is larger, for this decreases their living costs and allows them to benefit from a larger variety of products. Centrifugal forces emerge from the stronger competition firms face in the larger location, and from the need to serve the agricultural sector. Which force is stronger, and hence whether agglomeration or dispersion occurs, depends on the level of transportation costs, increasing returns to scale, and mobility of workers. There are multiple equilibria, that is, agglomeration can arise in either region, depending on which one happens to have the larger share of firms and workers and hence the larger market.

Suitably modified, the basic model laid out in Krugman (1991) is claimed by economists to 'offer insights' into agglomeration at different spatial scales such as core–periphery patterns, the location of industry, and the existence of cities. Later developments have sought to incorporate assumptions that could more realistically apply to a given level of spatial aggregation. For example, the assumption of the mobility of workers is quite unrealistic in many international contexts. Krugman and Venables (1995) replace it with the assumption that there are input–output linkages between firms that use each other's outputs as intermediate inputs. Combined with the other elements of the GeoEcon framework, this assumption gives rise to an analogous agglomeration mechanism: rather than workers' mobility, now the push towards agglomeration comes from the incentive that firms have to locate close to each other in order to save on the transport costs of intermediate inputs.[3] GeoEcon indeed has been built on the idea that the same kind of mechanisms, namely 'economic mechanisms yielding agglomeration by relying on the trade-off between various forms of increasing returns and different types of mobility costs' (Fujita and Thisse, 2002, p. 1), operate at all spatial scales, although with different degrees of strength.

GeoEcon has been celebrated for three interrelated achievements (Brakman et al., 2009, pp. 515–516):

- The recovery of space. GeoEcon has succeeded in bringing space back into the core of economics.[4]
- The provision of microfoundations. The GeoEcon models offer the desired microfoundations in that they can be used to endogenously derive agglomeration (and dispersion) from well-defined microeconomic parameters within a general equilibrium framework.

- The unification of phenomena and theories. Within one and the same framework GeoEcon provides explanatory insights into a variety of kinds of agglomeration phenomena, such as industry clusters, core–periphery patterns among countries and regions, cities and systems of cities, patterns of international trade and specialization, and the causes of economic growth and development. In unifying these phenomena, GeoEcon also paves the way for the long-awaited unification of international and regional economics (Ohlin, 1933).

In what follows we examine these achievements in terms of what we call disciplinary virtues and constraints, and show that the simplistic dichotomy we outlined in the beginning is indeed a major distortion.

9.3   THE RECOVERY OF SPACE

That space matters for economic activity was certainly no news at the time when Krugman (1991) came up with the first model of geographical economics. And yet previously space had been virtually ignored by the mainstream of the economics discipline. Economists and others actually believed that, as a matter of fact, space makes a difference, yet this belief did not show in mainline Anglo-American economic theory. There probably are a variety of reasons for this neglect. For example, the bulk of spatial economics was formerly done by the German location school of the likes of von Thünen, Lösch, Weber and others writing in German, and 'by and large economists then and now do not read economics written in foreign languages, and, even when they do, they rarely read it with the same attention as economics written in their own language' (Blaug, 1979, p. 24). A complementary explanation is that before the 1980s and 1990s economists lacked the theoretical tools needed for dealing with space within their own favourite framework. Spatial phenomena cannot be incorporated without dropping the assumptions of perfect competition and constant or decreasing returns in favour of those of increasing returns and imperfect competition. Earlier, economists did not have the tools for dealing with increasing returns and imperfect competition in a way that would satisfy the principles of general equilibrium theorizing. Adherence to these principles is among the disciplinary conventions that impose constraints on economic modelling by defining what is admissible and tractable. In other words, given the web of disciplinary conventions characteristic of mainline economics, spatial issues were not tractable, hence they were neglected.

Not only is Krugman himself well aware of this point, but he offers an interesting justification for it. The justification is in terms of an analogy, recounting the way in which important ideas about geography and development were first lost and then regained. In his Ohlin lectures entitled *Development, Geography and Economic Theory* (1995) Krugman compares the evolution of ideas in development and economic geography that culminated in GeoEcon with two episodes in the history of science: the evolution of European maps about Africa, and the evolution of the hypothesis of continental drift in geology. In the fifteenth century, maps of Africa were very detailed about the interior of the continent (including real cities, real rivers and real people), drawing on the information from first- and second-hand reports of travellers. On the other hand, those maps were very inaccurate about distances, coastlines and other such macroscopic matters. Over time, techniques of mapmaking improved thanks to the use of compasses and sextants, while second-hand descriptive reports ceased to be considered valid data. As a consequence, maps about Africa became increasingly more accurate about things such as distance, while at the same time all sorts of details about the interior disappeared (Krugman, 1995, pp. 1–2). In the (happy) end, further advances in mapmaking produced maps that were accurate about both distances and the interior of the continent, but Krugman's point is clear: for long periods of time, the improved rigour in mapmaking led to neglecting valuable information. Implying another disciplinary convention shared by most economists (viz. that rigour requires formal modelling), Krugman puts this in terms of modelling: 'the rich if unreliable insights of the early explorers . . . were eventually ruled inadmissible as evidence because those insights could not be clearly modeled' (Krugman, 1995, p. 33).

Similarly, mainstream geology pre-1960s could not account for both the existence of continents and their shape. It was only in the 1960s, with the discovery of seafloor spreading, that the theory of continental drift could be backed up by a suitable mechanism, and the whole set of questions regarding the existence of continents, their shape, and the shape of the earth's surface became relevant and were put on the agenda (Krugman, 1995, pp. 31–32). So again:

> the importance of the ability to model stands out . . . continental drift was an unacceptable, indeed almost incomprehensible, hypothesis because geologists could not think of how to model such a process. And the response of the geological profession was a remarkable, although typical one: virtually to ignore, even to deny the existence of questions that it was not prepared to answer. (1995, p. 32)

In these scientific episodes valuable information was neglected because scientists lacked the ability to include it in their maps and theories, given the technical and more substantive conventions that they subscribed to. According to Krugman, these developments parallel the history of dealing with spatial issues in economics: first ignored, then accommodated by the mainstream of the discipline. It was the advancement in modelling techniques within the accepted theoretical framework that allowed these old ideas to be regained. The workhorse of GeoEcon is the Dixit–Stiglitz model of imperfect competition (Dixit and Stiglitz, 1977), a mathematical tool suitable for tackling increasing returns to scale – in spite of, or perhaps thanks to, its highly simplifying assumptions. Geographical economists have sometimes referred to the Dixit–Stiglitz model as one of the 'modelling tricks' used in building GeoEcon models.[5]

The Dixit–Stiglitz model was first developed in the study of industrial organization, and then successively applied in the fields of international trade theory, macroeconomics and growth theory. There is a particularly tight relationship between the application of the Dixit–Stiglitz model in international trade theory that resulted in the 'new trade theory' and geographical economics. As was hinted above, the first model of GeoEcon arises from a modification to new trade theory models. Krugman and Venables (1990), a new trade theory model, contains most of the elements of Krugman (1991), the first model of GeoEcon. What makes the latter a GeoEcon model is the novel assumption that agents (workers and firms) can move across locations. This makes the size of the market endogenous and hence the agglomeration of economic activity can be derived within the model from the agents' locational choices (a detailed account of the theoretical linkage between the new trade theory and GeoEcon is in Brakman et al., 2009, pp. 59–68).

This way of telling the story might appear to support the view of those who blame economics for being more interested in fancy theoretical models than in any real-world systems that those models should represent. The suspicion is that there must be something wrong with a science that neglects important ideas only because they cannot be modelled in a way that economists happen to find appropriate within the received intellectual framework (for example Manicas, 2007). The suspicion is not at all dispelled by the fact that when they are finally modelled, use is made of tricks that have no other justification but their capacity to enhance tractability. All this, the charge goes, undermines the goals of explaining and understanding real-world phenomena. However, if considered merely from (what we might call) a non-moral epistemic point of view, this conclusion is too hasty. It ignores pervasive features of actual scientific practice that, when viewed in the short run, may indeed appear to act against progress in the scientific understanding of the real world. When considered in a long enough haul, however, the appearance may turn out to be misleading.

So, although the GeoEcon story can be told as one in which modelling techniques alone drive theoretical development, unconstrained by any concerns with real-world issues, there is another, equally plausible story. This alternative account talks of the interrelationship between beliefs about important matters of causal fact (whatever the source of these beliefs) and available research technology. What can be broadly conceived as available research technology imposes constraints on theory development, but this is consistent with the view that beliefs about matters of fact play a role in the process and that the aim of science is understanding and explaining real-world phenomena. In our case, prior to the emergence of GeoEcon, virtually everybody may have shared the factual belief that space makes a difference for many economic phenomena. This factual belief was in tension with the contents of standard economic theory that ignored such a causally important factor. This tension was then relieved by the invention of a formal tool and its employment in further modelling. This roundabout yet potentially progressive development was driven and constrained by both ontological conviction and conventions of tractability. Economics can be world-oriented and constrained by its modelling conventions at the same time.

Nor is it ruled out that such a pattern of roundabout development is favourable for scientific progress, not only in finally incorporating previously neglected factors but also in generating a better grasp of them. Philosopher of science Philip Kitcher (1993) argues that in the transitions from Aristotelian to Newtonian physics and from Priestley's to Lavoiser's chemistry progress was made by way of regaining and articulating previously neglected vague insights:

> The losses (if any) were vague insights that could not be articulated at that stage in the development of science; the gains, in both instances, were correct explanatory schemata that generated significant, *tractable*, questions, and the process of addressing these questions ultimately led to a recapturing of what was lost. (Kitcher, 1993, p. 117)[6]

So Kitcher is saying that when insights that were previously neglected are later recovered, they are sometimes dealt with more thoroughly, and in those cases this amounted to progress. Clearly it is not necessarily the case that first losing an insight and then regaining it leads to a more thorough articulation of it than would have been otherwise possible. Yet if Kitcher's analysis of these scientific episodes is correct, this further supports Krugman's observation that even if economics has neglected ideas that it could not deal with at the earlier stages of its development, this is not necessarily an obstacle to the field's progress.

9.4   THE PROVISION OF MICROFOUNDATIONS

Economists tend to prefer building models that provide some (what they call) 'insight' into phenomena. We interpret this notion as follows: to provide insight is to depict a mechanism that contributes to the production of the phenomenon to be explained, and depicting a mechanism is a task for a model. Reflecting the more substantive disciplinary conventions of conventional economics, the models that economists find genuinely explanatory are those in which a phenomenon is shown to derive from the decisions and interactions of rational agents. Failing to provide microfoundations conceived in such a way is viewed as a major reason for discontent with other accounts of agglomeration. Indeed, providing such microfoundations to theories of agglomeration within a general equilibrium framework is regarded as one of GeoEcon's achievements vis-à-vis the kind of spatial models that were previously dominant in economic geography and regional and urban economics. According to geographical economists, having microfoundations enables avoiding the risk of settling on non-explanatory accounts such as when saying that agglomerations exist because of agglomeration economies (for example Krugman, 1995, p. 52).

As we have seen in section 9.2, the GeoEcon agglomeration mechanism enables deriving agglomeration and dispersion of economic activity from the interplay between centripetal and centrifugal forces, whose relative strengths in turn depend on the level of key parameters such as increasing returns and transportation costs. Note that talking of *the* agglomeration mechanism may be confusing if not understood correctly. GeoEcon models come in clusters and each of them depicts a slightly different mechanism (see for instance Mäki and Marchionni, 2009, 2011). Still, those mechanisms can be regarded as more specific versions of the generic GeoEcon agglomeration mechanism. What all of them share is that agglomeration at the aggregate level is modelled as an equilibrium outcome between centrifugal and centripetal forces that arise from the actions and interactions by rational individuals.

The emphasis on the explanatory role of micro-level mechanisms suggests that (geographical) economists are not after event-regularities as argued by some critics of economics (see Lawson, 1997, for example). Economists are after mechanisms, but these are mechanisms of a special kind. Indeed, vis-à-vis the traditional practices in the other social sciences, the distinctiveness of conventional economics is that its mechanisms regularly involve rationality-cum-equilibrium, and this is so for GeoEcon too. This is a (contestable and actually contested) disciplinary norm that dictates how to proceed in modelling and explanation. According to this norm, phenomena should be explained as equilibrium outcomes of the interaction among rational agents. This is yet another characteristic of constrained theoretical development in economics that may contribute to the impression of a discipline where rather rigid a priori conventions about the strategies of modelling trump the more venerable scientific aim of understanding the world.

The role of disciplinary conventions in directing theoretical and empirical developments and in determining styles of explanation is not a peculiarity of economics, but a pervasive feature of science. Disciplinary conventions define a field's identity and its characteristic and appropriate ways of construing and resolving research problems. This feature as such does not necessarily hinder the aim of understanding and explaining the world – otherwise it would not be possible to make such discipline-based epistemic progress. At this point it is important to see that 'understanding and explaining the world' is too much to ask and expect: that is not what particular disciplines, fields, theories and pieces of inquiry aim at. They are more modest in their goals and instead focus on answering specific questions about small fragments of the world. Any assessment of a strategy must consider it relative to such specific goals.

No doubt some modelling or explanatory strategies are more effective than others in pursuing such more specific goals. A special challenge is to identify the strategies that work well (as well as those that do not) in certain contexts and for certain purposes (see Wimsatt, 2007). So we should ask whether the disciplinary conventions of economics hinder or enhance the attainment of some worthwhile epistemic goals. Do they function effectively as the means of understanding and explaining anything about the world for any decent epistemic purpose? How far can they get us?

Reductive mechanistic strategies of explanation are generally sound, and this is probably why they have been adopted and are being applied in a great deal of contemporary science dealing with complex systems. A large body of literature in the philosophy of science (for example, Glennan, 1996; Machamer et al., 2000; Bechtel and Abrahamsen, 2005; Craver, 2007) has shown that explanation in the biological sciences proceeds by identifying the lower-level mechanisms that bring the explanandum phenomena about, rather than by deriving the phenomena from general laws. If we understand mechanisms broadly as being composed of parts whose organized interaction produces or constitutes the phenomenon to be explained, then the search for microfoundations in economics amounts to a search for explanatory mechanisms.

One of the advantages of mechanistic explanation is that by identifying the relations of dependency between the micro-level and the macro-level, it shows how changes at the level of parts and their mode of organization affect changes at the level of the explanandum phenomenon. In so doing, explanation by mechanisms allows us to answer a wide range of 'what-if-things-had-been-different' questions, which according to recent theories of explanation amounts to greater explanatory power (Woodward, 2003; Craver, 2007). This is also what Krugman sees as a virtue of economic modelling, namely the 'ability to answer "what-if" questions: if something were different, how would that change the economic outcomes?' (Krugman, 2010, p. 6). In the context of GeoEcon, this amounts to saying that vis-à-vis other approaches to agglomeration, GeoEcon affords the ability to answer 'what-if' questions about how changes at the level of micro-parameters affect macro-level agglomeration (or dispersion).

So the incorporation of geography into the mainstream of the discipline of economics has been constrained by a disciplinary convention that dictates that explanatory models are those that derive the aggregate phenomenon to be explained (typically a stylized fact) as the equilibrium outcome of the actions and interactions of rational agents. That there is a disciplinary constraint is not reason enough for bashing economics. All scientific fields are defined by conventions regarding what are appropriate explanation-seeking questions and appropriate ways of answering them. Recognizing this commonality however is not an apology for economics either. But it directs our attention away from sweeping generalizations and simplistic dichotomies to the important question of when and for what purposes the search for microfoundations in general, and the maximization within an equilibrium framework in particular, can and cannot give satisfactory explanations of some well-defined real-world economic phenomena (see Marchionni, forthcoming).

9.5   THE UNIFICATION OF PHENOMENA AND THEORIES

Unification has been a major motivating and justifying virtue in the emergence and development of GeoEcon. Thanks to the Dixit–Stiglitz model, conjoined with various tractability-enhancing assumptions, GeoEcon has been able to bring under a common mathematical framework a number of stylized facts about agglomeration phenomena such as the emergence of international core–periphery patterns, the existence of cities and of industrial clusters. By doing so, GeoEcon has also paved the way for the unification of regional and international economics. The unification of both phenomena and theories has been celebrated as an important achievement.

The heavy reliance on a set of quite flexible and unrealistic modelling tricks however may raise doubts about whether GeoEcon is at all guided by beliefs about the world, or whether it is only a technical accomplishment. Elsewhere we have examined various characteristics of GeoEcon related to its unificationist ambitions (Mäki and Marchionni, 2009, 2011). What is most relevant to the current discussion is that although the GeoEcon unification does possess features of a technical achievement apparently having little or nothing to do with the search for explanation of real-world agglomeration, on closer inspection its unification is also shaped by ontological beliefs. In order to identify the respective roles of mathematical and ontological considerations, we have adopted a distinction between derivational and ontological unification (developed in Mäki, 2001).

Derivational unification is only a matter of applying the same abstract mathematical framework to phenomena in different domains, whereas ontological unification is also a matter of discovering that those different phenomena are actually caused by the same kind of mechanisms. The way in which unification in GeoEcon has unfolded is by means of the application of a small set of model types, which with only slight modifications could be used to derive stylized facts about agglomeration at the international, national or local scale. In itself this derivational achievement may be appreciated because it brings about cognitive economy, or because it increases simplicity and theoretical beauty, but it can hardly be regarded as a sufficient ground for a Nobel Prize in economics, or so we would hope.

Our suggestion is that behind this merely formal achievement lies the belief that the phenomena are united in the sense that they are (at least partly) the result of the operation of the same kind of economic mechanisms, namely: 'economic mechanisms yielding agglomeration by relying on the trade-off between various forms of increasing returns and different types of mobility costs' (Fujita and Thisse, 2002, p. 1). In other words, the GeoEcon unification is grounded on the belief that the derivational achievement can actually help capture the way things are in the world. And if the GeoEcon unification succeeds in capturing whatever degree of ontic unity exists among varieties of agglomeration phenomena, then the GeoEcon unification should be seen as advancing our understanding of real-world agglomerations.

Notice that we use the conditional above: 'if the GeoEcon unification succeeds'. Indeed it may well be that the kind of mechanisms GeoEcon postulates only operate in certain contexts and not in others, or they are irrelevant explanatory factors, or that the modelling tricks GeoEcon employs are so utterly unrealistic that the GeoEcon results about agglomeration become nothing but artefacts of those unrealistic assumptions.

Clearly these are issues that can only be addressed by means that include empirical investigation.

Thus far empirical evidence remains inconclusive. Although it is suggested by the proponents that there is evidence in support of the GeoEcon approach, they recognize two major open problems that would need to be resolved: first, currently available empirical studies generally cannot discriminate between GeoEcon and other theories of location and trade; and second, when the GeoEcon approach is applied in a multi-region context, conclusive testing becomes even harder (Brakman et al., 2009; Redding, 2010). No doubt these are serious issues, but we cannot anticipate whether they will be resolved and what the outcome of further empirical investigations might be. Under the circumstances, the message we wish to convey remains open but clear: the aim of understanding and explaining real-world phenomena can be hindered by an excessive emphasis on formal considerations, but this need not be so.

9.6   THE PRICE OF UNIFICATION

Unification comes at a price. The coin of unification has two sides. In order for a theory to unify many kinds of phenomena, only some limited aspects of those phenomena are to be explained by that theory. In other words, for a theory to have a broad range of explananda, those explananda must be conceived narrowly. This has been noted also in cases of unification in the natural and biological sciences: unification typically occurs by omitting specific information about the phenomena that are unified (for example Morrison, 2000). We can put this by saying that phenomena are theoretically unified only under a rather abstract description. This has consequences for the explanatory performance of the theory. A theory that unifies phenomena does not explain all their aspects, or all facts about them. It only answers a limited set of explanatory questions about the phenomena.

This also applies to geographical economics. In order for the GeoEcon models to be applicable to a large variety of kinds of phenomena of agglomeration at different spatial scales, GeoEcon ignores many features that are specific to each of the particular phenomena or their kinds (Mäki and Marchionni, 2009, 2011). There is a significant trade-off here. Reducing the range of features that are included in a model enables the application of the model to a broader range of phenomena on the one hand (gain in breadth or generality), but this results in a loss of information about aspects of specific phenomena on the other (loss in comprehensiveness or completeness). So we have a trade-off between breadth and comprehensiveness, and we face the challenge of striking a balance between them such that it serves some decent epistemic purposes. A good way of understanding the challenge is to make an erotetic turn and to start asking questions about questions.

In general, what is included in and what is excluded from a theory or model constrains the kinds of question that it can be used to address and answer. And the questions we want to answer constrain the contents of the model used for the task. No model explains everything about a phenomenon or a class of phenomena or a class of such classes. Explanatory services are always limited. One powerful method for identifying those limits – that is, what exactly a model or a set of models can and cannot explain – is the idea of contrastive explanation (Lipton, 1990; Garfinkel, 1981; Ylikoski, 2007).

The idea of the erotetic-contrastive perspective is to view explanations as answers to explanation-seeking questions that have a contrastive structure of the form: 'why *p* rather than *q*?', where *p* is the phenomenon to be explained and *q* is an alternative, typically exclusive, occurrence. Phenomena in fact are typically brought about by a multitude of causes, but explanations only pick out a subset of those causes. The contrastive explanandum provides the criterion for selecting which subset of causes is relevant for a particular explanatory request. The subset of factors that a model (or cluster of models) has isolated as doing the explanatory work determines the contrastive question that it can be used to address, and vice versa. So, attention to what the phenomenon is contrasted to serves to spell out what fact precisely is being explained about a phenomenon and hence to identify the actual (rather than intended) explanatory capacity of a model (Ylikoski, 2007).

The application of the idea of contrastive explanation to the GeoEcon case (Marchionni, 2006; Marchionni and Oinas, 2009) reveals that its generic explanandum is quite narrow. We can express the generic GeoEcon explanatory question as follows: 'why is economic activity agglomerated rather than evenly dispersed across space?' It is easy to see that this formulation does not specify any particular location or spatial scale, and it does not allow for alternatives other than those of (partial or full) agglomeration and dispersion. This implies that the GeoEcon models have little or nothing to say on other questions such as 'why did agglomeration occur in this particular location rather than another?', or 'why do firms agglomerate rather than join their activities into a larger single firm?'[7]

The erotetic formulation of the generic GeoEcon explanandum can be broken down into more precise contrastive questions. For example, models tailored to deal with a specific spatial scale (international, regional, urban) can address explananda that do include reference to features specific to that spatial scale. Furthermore, theoretical advances are likely to further increase the range of explanatory questions the theory can be used to answer. The generic explanandum however captures the most highly unifying aspect of GeoEcon, and its explanans corresponds to the generic agglomeration mechanism, which relies on the trade-off between increasing returns and mobility costs. Specifications of the generic mechanism are modelled to address more specific versions of the generic GeoEcon explanandum, such as: 'why does an international core-periphery pattern exist rather than economic activity being evenly dispersed across nations?'

The explanatory capacity of GeoEcon is broad in terms of kinds of phenomena it encompasses, but narrow in terms of the kinds of questions it can address about them. This combination of qualities is not as obviously appreciated by all disciplines. Consider economic geography. Its subject matter substantially overlaps with that of GeoEcon, but the field is more closely affiliated with the broad interdisciplinary endeavour of human geography than with economics, thus its guiding conventions tend to be different from those of economics. While economics has incorporated space by trading a broad range of explanandum phenomena for the comprehensiveness of their aspects, the disciplinary conventions of much of economic geography appear to value comprehensiveness more highly. So it is no surprise that economic geographers have criticized the GeoEcon models because they cannot address questions such as: 'why does agglomeration occur in particular places but not in others?'

This complaint partly reflects a commitment to a different set of explanatory virtues than those cherished by economists: when facing the trade-off between breadth and comprehensiveness, (some) geographers seem to prefer to sacrifice the former in favour of the latter. They believe this will enable them to explain a larger range of aspects of phenomena of agglomeration, including what happens in particular places and hence what renders particular cases of agglomeration different from others. Economic geographer Ron Martin for example stresses the importance of the diversity, empirical messiness and particularity of economic systems and argues that these are suppressed by the GeoEcon approach that is characterized by 'deductivist, mathematical demonstration' (Martin, 1999, p. 81). Now if cases of agglomeration are to be accounted for in their 'diversity, empirical messiness and particularity', unification of a broad range of kinds of phenomena obviously cannot serve as an overriding virtue.

So, this is yet another juncture at which disciplinary conventions enter the picture in that they determine the kinds of explanation-seeking questions that are perceived as more or less interesting, more or less relevant within a discipline, and the kind of explanations that are deemed appropriate. Conventional economics has a strong taste for unification, and in nurturing this taste, it is bound to sacrifice 'empirical messiness and particularity' and to compromise on the range of explanatory questions that it aspires or is able to answer. In order to unify – in order to be broad – a theory ends up being narrow on another dimension. The important point is that this does not undermine the possibility of attaining ontological unification (rather than merely derivational unification), so there is no necessary violation of being world-oriented. Even if narrow, the GeoEcon explananda may be real aspects of the world, and the GeoEcon mechanism may be causally connected to them. The disciplinary conventions of conventional economics settle the trade-off between breadth and comprehensiveness in a way that can be contested, but first it must be understood properly. There are many possible ways of being world-oriented, and attention to diversity, messiness and particularity is just one of them.

9.7   THEORY-DRIVEN ECONOMICS AS USUAL

Much of the development of economic theory is not prompted by a new empirical discovery or the collection of new empirical evidence or some new experimental result or some such. It is rather a matter of finding a way of deriving a known phenomenon or regularity or pattern from the basic principles of the received theoretical framework by making adjustments in auxiliary assumptions. The discovery is guided by conventions that favour providing mechanistic microfoundations that serve to unify as many kinds of phenomena as possible.

We have shown that geographical economics is representative of the above image. It is pretty much economics as usual, largely theory-driven and constrained by the characteristic disciplinary conventions of conventional economics. We have shown how the obsession with unifying micro mechanisms is connected to a broad explanatory reach with narrowly conceived explananda. We have also argued that these things are not in conflict with being world-oriented, or being partly shaped by an interest in matters of fact, or acquiring information about the world – and that being world-oriented does not presuppose being evidence-driven.

Not all of economics is economics as usual. For example, parts of experimental and behavioral economics are more flexible about theory and are open for making new empirical discoveries. Establishing preference reversals as a stable pattern required some experimental effort, and explaining the pattern has required some theoretical creativity, not completely constrained by standard theory, and has resulted in a number of possible theoretical explanations. Manifesting the disciplinary conventions dominant in economics, critics have complained that a proper 'theory' is missing in these endeavours, implying that no powerfully unifying theory has been proposed. This complaint is found less worrying by those leaning towards the disciplinary conventions of psychology.

None of what we have said implies that GeoEcon is economics as it should be; or that GeoEcon models are true or approximately true of their targets; or that GeoEcon explanations are scientifically excellent explanations; or, for that matter, that the disciplinary conventions observed by GeoEcon are somehow impeccable. What we do want to claim is that GeoEcon models and explanations are not and cannot be useful for all important epistemic and practical purposes, and that its characteristic conventions are not the only possible legitimate conventions guiding scientific work.

ACKNOWLEDGEMENTS

Thanks to the editors for their helpful suggestions. We gratefully acknowledge the financial support of the Academy of Finland.

NOTES

1. The authors have contributed equally to this work.
2. 'The Sveriges Riksbank Prize in Economic Sciences in Memory of Alfred Nobel 2008', Nobelprize.org, 7 December 2010, http://nobelprize.org/nobel_prizes/economics/laureates/2008/.
3. This model and its further extensions are now thought of as another core model of GeoEcon.
4. In trade theory models, there is no genuine locational choice. Regional and urban economics deal with spatial issues, but in contrast to geographical economics their models do not endogenously yield agglomeration within a general equilibrium framework.
5. The other modelling tricks are 'icebergs', namely that transportation costs are assumed to be of the iceberg form: a fraction of the good is assumed to melt in transit; 'evolution', viz. the use of evolutionary dynamics in static models; and 'the computer', viz. the use of numerical examples to aid analytical results (Fujita et al., 1999, pp. 6–9).
6. Backhouse and Laidler (2004) first noted the analogy between Krugman's recounting of the rediscovery of geography and Kitcher's analyses of (erotetic) progress in such episodes in the history of science.
7. To be more precise, GeoEcon both explains 'why agglomeration rather than dispersion occurs' as well as 'why dispersion rather than agglomeration occurs'. This is because the GeoEcon models can be used for identifying the conditions under which agglomeration occurs as well as those under which dispersion occurs.

REFERENCES

Backhouse, R. and D. Laidler (2004), 'What was Lost with IS-LM', *History of Political Economy*, **36** (Supplement), 25–56.

Bechtel, W. and A.A. Abrahamsen (2005), 'Explanation: A Mechanistic Alternative', *Studies in the History and Philosophy of the Biological and Biomedical Sciences*, **36**, 421–441.

Blaug, M. (1979), 'The German Hegemony of Location Theory: A Puzzle in the History of Economic Thought', *History of Political Economy*, **11** (1), 21–29

Brakman, S., H. Garretsen and C. van Marrewijk (2009), *The New Introduction to Geographical Economics: Trade, Location and Growth*, Cambridge: Cambridge University Press.

Craver, C. (2007), *Explaining the Brain: Mechanisms and the Mosaic Unity of Neuroscience*, Oxford: Oxford University Press.

Dixit, A.K. and J.E. Stiglitz (1977) 'Monopolistic Competition and Optimum Product Diversity', *American Economic Review*, **67**, 297–308.

Fujita, M., P. Krugman and A. Venables (1999), *The Spatial Economy: Cities, Regions and International Trade*, Cambridge, MA: MIT Press.

Fuijta, M. and J-F. Thisse (2002), *Economics of Agglomeration. Cities, Industrial Location and Regional Growth*, Cambridge: Cambridge University Press.

Garfinkel, A. (1981), *Forms of Explanation*, New Haven, CT: Yale University Press.

Glennan, S. (1996), 'Mechanisms and the Nature of Causation', *Erknntnis*, **44**, 49–71.

Kitcher, P. (1993), *The Advancement of Science*, Oxford: Oxford University Press.

Krugman, P. (1991), 'Increasing Returns and Economic Geography', *Journal of Political Economy*, **99**, 183–199.

Krugman, P. (1995), *Development, Geography and Economic Theory*, Cambridge, MA, USA and London, UK: MIT Press.

Krugman, P. (2010), 'The New Economic Geography, Now Middle-aged', prepared for presentation to the Association of American Geographers, 16 April 2010.

Krugman, P. and A. Venables (1990), 'Integration and Competitiveness of Peripheral Industry', in C. Bliss and J. Braga de Macedo (eds), *Unity with Diversity in the European Economy*, Cambridge: Cambridge University Press, pp. 56–75.

Krugman, P. and A. Venables (1995), 'Globalization and the Inequality of Nations', *Quarterly Journal of Economics*, **110**, 857–880.

Lawson, T. (1997), *Economics and Reality*, London, UK and New York, USA: Routledge.

Lipton, P. (1990), 'Contrastive Explanations', in D. Knowles (ed.), *Explanation and its Limits*, Cambridge: Cambridge University Press, pp. 247–266.

Machamer, P., L. Darden and C.F. Craver (2000), 'Thinking about Mechanisms', *Philosophy of Science*, **67**, 1–25.

Mäki, U. (2001) 'Explanatory Unification: Double and Doubtful', *Philosophy of the Social Sciences*, **31** (4), 488–506.

Mäki, U. and C. Marchionni (2009), 'On the Structure of Explanatory Unification: the Case of Geographical Economics', *Studies in History and Philosophy of Science*, **40** (2), 185–195.

Mäki, U. and C. Marchionni (2011), 'Is Geographical Economics Imperializing Economic Geography?', *Journal of Economic Geography*, **11**, 645–665.

Manicas, P. (2007), *A Realist Philosophy of Science: Explanation and Understanding*, Cambridge: Cambridge University Press.

Marchionni, C. (2006) 'Contrastive Explanation and Unrealistic Models: The Case of the New Economic Geography', *Journal of Economic Methodology*, **13** (4), 425–446.

Marchionni, C. (forthcoming), 'Geographical Economics and its Neighbours – Forces Towards and Against Unification', in U. Mäki (ed.), *The Handbook of the Philosophy of Economics*, Amsterdam: Elsevier.

Marchionni, C. and P. Oinas (2009), 'Contrastive Explanations and Interdisciplinarity: The Case of Explaining Spatial Industrial Clusters', paper presented at the Conference of the International Network for Economic Method, July.

Martin, R. (1999), 'The "New" Geographical Turn in Economics: Some Critical Reflections', *Cambridge Journal of Economics*, **23**, 65–91.

Morrison, M. (2000), *Unifying Scientific Theories*, Cambridge: Cambridge University Press.

Ohlin, B. (1933), *Interregional and International Trade*, Cambridge, MA: Harvard University Press.

Redding, S.T. (2010) 'The Empirics of New Economic Geography', *Journal of Regional Science*, **50** (1), 297–311.

Wimsatt, W.C. (2007), *Re-engineering Philosophy for Limited Beings*, Cambridge, MA: Harvard University Press.

Woodward, J. (2003), *Making Things Happen*, New York: Oxford University Press.

Ylikoski, P. (2007), 'The Idea of Contrastive Explanandum', in J. Persson and P. Ylikoski (eds) *Rethinking Explanation*, Dordrecht: Springer, pp. 27–42.

PART III

COMPLEXITY AND COMPUTATION IN ECONOMICS

10 Computational economics
Paola Tubaro

10.1 INTRODUCTION

Broadly speaking, computational economics is the use of computer-intensive tools and techniques in the study of economic problems, and is at the crossroads between economics and informatics; its models take the form of computer programs that can be run to simulate the behavior of the economic system under study. The origins of the field date back to the first development of calculators in the 1950s, and its areas of application have widened over time as computing power has grown. The core of computational economics used to be the search for numerical solutions of equation-based models and the exploration of new optimization techniques, as reflected in the first volume of the *Handbook of Computational Economics* (Amman et al., 1996). The dramatic rise in calculation capacity of the last two decades has not only strengthened this line of research, but also fostered the appearance of a novel approach to the study of decentralized market economies. The new subfield, which is central to the second volume of the *Handbook* (Tesfatsion and Judd, 2006), places emphasis on agents and the dynamics of their interactions, and is often referred to as 'agent-based computational economics' (ACE). Among the main lines of development of ACE are, in apparent contrast to conventional economic approaches, a non-Walrasian framework of analysis, spatially distributed transactions, bounded rationality together with agents' capacity to revise their decisions as interaction plays out, and learning processes.

This chapter focuses entirely on ACE. It presents the main features of this area of research and discusses similarities and differences with respect to previously existing work in economics in general, and in computational economics in particular. Based on that, it outlines the methodological characteristics of this approach, its most recent developments, and the challenges it currently faces; special emphasis is on its experimental character, possible options to model decision-making processes, validation and verification issues, and heterogeneity of modeling approaches. Examples are mainly drawn from research on markets, even though ACE can be applied to various topics ranging from economic growth to technological change, use of natural resources, and the environment. Finally, the chapter assesses the impact of ACE on the methodology of economics more generally.

10.2 ACE AS A SUBFIELD WITHIN ECONOMICS AND COMPUTATIONAL ECONOMICS

This section first outlines the main characteristics of ACE. Focus is on similarities and differences with respect to received economic theories and, more specifically, computational economics. Then, the section briefly presents the major influences and the milestones that have marked the development of ACE, at the interface between economics and neighboring disciplines, and its subsequent acceptance as a legitimate field within economics.

10.2.1 Similarities and Differences

In general terms, it can be said that ACE models aim to explain aggregate regularities as so-called 'emergent' properties of an economic system, arising over time from repeated interactions between autonomous, heterogeneous agents. Depending on the problem under study, the latter can be individuals or entities such as households, firms and organizations. The notion of emergence refers to cases in which the whole cannot be taken as the sum of its parts: put differently, individual behavior alone is insufficient to fully predict large-scale outcomes, and some understanding of how agents interact with one another is necessary to bridge the micro and macro levels of analysis. In turn, aggregate-level outcomes may induce changes in individual behavior, in a two-way feedback between the agent and the system. The perspective is clearly dynamic in the sense that the modeler first formulates hypotheses about the behavior of agents and their interactions with others, and then uses computer simulation to generate 'histories' that bring to light the implications of these hypotheses. Agents' behaviors and interactions usually depend on their past experience, and in many models, agents update their behavior based on that experience. This generates path-dependence, a property that can be related to heterogeneity of agents. Indeed even if the attributes of two agents are identical at the beginning, they may make different choices and evolve along distinct trajectories, so as to distinguish themselves progressively from each other (Rouchier, 2008).

With its focus on decentralized decision-making by a multitude of autonomous agents and the rise of non-fully predictable macro-level regularities from micro-level actions, ACE echoes a conception of the market system that has always been at the heart of economics. It appears as a modern rejoinder to the long-lasting reflection on the unintended social consequences of purposeful human action, with contributions ranging from Adam Smith's 'invisible hand' metaphor to Hayek's conception of the economic order and Walrasian general equilibrium. Yet ACE's insistence on path-dependence and heterogeneity of agents reveals how profoundly different it is from received economic theories. It is to some extent closer to evolutionary theory, which emphasizes adaptation of the individual to its environment and the development of interindividual and intergroup variation.

More to the point, standard utility maximization and perfect information assumptions are not normally present in ACE models, which rather tend to explore alternative notions of cognition, rationality and learning. Induction and calculation prevail over deduction; central issues are the acquisition, accumulation and use of information at individual level, and the circulation of information at system level. Accordingly, the core questions of ACE are closer to those of experimental and behavioral economics as well as game theory than to those of neoclassical economics. It can thus be said that this approach participates to some extent in the ongoing renewal of the economic theory of individual behavior.

ACE is not fully interchangeable with experimental or behavioral research, though: it cannot, say, test whether actual decision-makers violate rational choice theory, but it can provide insight into the possible consequences of an alternative behavioral assumption in a given social context. Its specificity is its focus on interpersonal social interactions in a dynamic perspective. As a matter of fact, the motivations for economists to explore agent-based modeling include dissatisfaction not only with utility maximization but also with mainstream economics' difficulty in deriving aggregate properties from individual behavior, the 'representative agent' being a particularly unsatisfactory solution (Kirman, 1992). Likewise, ACE's emphasis on the time factor can be seen as a response to the standard equilibrium approach and its inability of dealing with out-of-equilibrium situations. Awareness of these potential strengths is widespread among practitioners of the field, some of whom loudly promote ACE as an alternative to received wisdom (see for example Farmer and Foley, 2009; Buchanan, 2009).

Focus on agent interactions in a dynamic framework distinguishes ACE also from other types of computer-intensive work in economics; in a sense, the fact that all use computers is only a loose analogy (Axtell, 2000). One may go as far as to say that computational techniques play only a small part in the definition of ACE: indeed among the early contributions to this approach, many include the model of urban segregation that Thomas Schelling originally developed by moving dimes and pennies on a chessboard by hand (1978). The relatively greater importance of agents and their interactions with respect to the use of computer-based tools is also reflected in the name that Leigh Tesfatsion, a major contributor to the field, initially proposed for it: it was simply 'ABE', agent-based economics, later changed to ACE for clarity.[1] The similar denomination of ABM (agent-based modeling), also with no reference to computational tools, is still commonly used to denote this approach.

10.2.2   The Multidisciplinary Origins of ACE and its Integration into Economics

This terminological double-meaning reflects a specific trait of the field. While the ACE label refers explicitly to economics, ABM does not, and in fact discloses the multidisciplinary origins of this approach. It is true that Schelling, an economist, was a pioneer in showing how the complex pattern of interactions among agents in society may give rise to unexpected collective outcomes. Other recognized influences, however, include John Holland, whose book on adaptation (1975 [1992]) drew heavily on both evolutionary biology and computer science; and Robert Axelrod, a political scientist, with his work on the emergence of cooperation in an Iterated Prisoner's Dilemma game (1984). The influence of complex systems physics has also been important, with a major role for the Santa Fe Institute in bringing together economists and physicists (Anderson et al., 1988) and the development of the closely related 'econophysics' research program (Rosser, 2008). At least in the early days of the Santa Fe Institute, the approach even had the ambition to provide a unifying perspective to the study of nature, human life and society. Its development has also benefited from contributions of representatives of the wider social sciences, especially in Europe (Gilbert and Doran, 1994; Gilbert and Conte, 1995). Today, agent-based models are applied in a variety of disciplines, including not only economics but also management, political science, sociology, anthropology, geography, biology, ecology, and even archaeology and linguistics. Users of agent-based models form a well integrated multidisciplinary community, and share common outlets for their publications such as (especially in Europe) the web-based *Journal of Artificial Societies and Social Simulation.*[2]

While honoring its multidisciplinary origins, agent-based modeling has aroused much interest within economics since the first Santa Fe Institute (SFI) conference on The Economy as a Complex System was held in 1987, followed by the foundation of a new SFI economics program, and the publication of first research results in top journals (Arthur, 1991; Holland and Miller, 1991). Support from renowned economists including Kenneth Arrow, Alan Kirman and Axel Leijonhufvud contributed progressively to reinforcing the field. As early as 1996, Tesfatsion created a dedicated website,[3] which she has maintained since then and which has become a reference for agent-based modelers, especially in economics. ACE has now secured a place in the Society for Computational Economics and in specialized journals (*Computational Economics*, *Journal of Economic Dynamics and Control*), while remaining open to collaborations with like-minded researchers in neighboring disciplines. Though ACE has not experienced the extraordinary success of other emerging fields such as behavioral economics, it has stabilized as a subfield, enjoys an increasingly solid reputation, and is expanding its presence in both teaching and research programs worldwide.

10.3 THE UNIQUE METHODOLOGICAL CHARACTERISTICS OF ACE

To identify the strengths and weaknesses of ACE, this section first provides a few introductory details on the underlying logic and founding principles of agent-based models. On this basis, it aims to derive questions for a more in-depth methodological discussion. Specifically, attention is drawn to four main issues, namely: the interpretation of ACE as an experimental methodology; the choice between different models of decision-making, and their methodological implications; validation and verification issues; and finally, diversity of modeling approaches, assumptions, interpretations and objects of study within ACE.

10.3.1 The Structure of an ACE Model

At a very basic level, most models share a similar structure, even though with some variation. Given a population of agents situated in a predefined environment and/or social context, at the heart of a model is their decision-making process. As a rule, agents' decisions are about possible exchanges or interactions with others and may include both the choice of an action (for example the quantity of a good to buy or sell) and the choice of a partner (for example a seller for a buyer, or a buyer for a seller); in other cases, partners (buyers and sellers in this example) are matched randomly by the computer. Depending on the problem under study, the model may represent exchanges of goods or services but also communication, information-sharing, advice-seeking, and other cognitive or social processes. As mentioned above, the individual decision-making process and the ensuing interactions between agents are iterated many times; at each step, past decisions and actions shape new choices and in some models, agents change their behavior progressively, based on the results of past choices and the ensuing changes in the environment.

The social context may take various forms: for example, it may allow agents to interact with any other agent or with a selected subgroup, which in turn may be defined spatially as a neighborhood or in terms of a network of ties, and may change in size and composition as a result of agents' actions over time. The choice set may be either given or gradually discovered as the agent acquires and accumulates information, while choice-making rules may range from forms of strategic, rational behavior to some 'satisficing' criterion à la Simon and even to random choice, sometimes allowing for differences within the same population depending on the individual attributes of agents. Technically, there are many possibilities: for instance time may be continuous or discrete, choices may be simultaneous or sequential, and interactions may be bilateral or multilateral. It is the modeler who defines these and all other framing aspects, also including agents' attributes and the state of the system at time 0 (initialization). The modeler also needs to specify in advance some indicators of the properties (of agents and/or of the system as a whole) that are of interest for the investigation, for example patterns of transaction prices and quantities in a market model.

Then, the modeler lets agents interact repeatedly over time and refrains from any further intervention, typically until the system reaches a steady state. At the end, the modeler observes the values of indicators and derives from them answers to the questions under study. The simulation can be replicated for various values of the parameters and the initial conditions so as to learn how to fine-tune the model to yield different results. This approach, which limits the participation of the modeler to the definition of the starting point and the rules of action, is often referred to as 'bottom-up' in that the final result depends only on agent behavior with no imposition of equilibrium conditions from the outside ('top-down').

10.3.2   ACE as an Experimental Methodology

Drawing an analogy from biology, Tesfatsion compares the bottom-up approach of ACE to a 'culture-dish laboratory experiment' (2002). More generally, she and other practitioners of the field propose an interpretation of it as an experimental methodology, exploiting controlled conditions as a means of isolating the micro-level sources of macroeconomic phenomena. Running a computer simulation is comparable to performing an experiment on a model and in fact, ACE is similar to experimental economics in many respects: both generate their own data, rely on inductive rather than deductive reasoning, and make extensive use of computers to record data and allow replication. As mentioned above, the main difference between the two is the focus of ACE on the macro effects of micro behavior; nevertheless, many methodological similarities can be brought to light. Along these lines, agent-based simulation has been compared to the use of 'computational laboratories', both in the social sciences in general (Dibble, 2001) and in economics in particular (Tesfatsion, 2002; Duffy, 2006).

Indeed a particularly promising direction of research consists in coupling ACE models with human subject experiments (Tesfatsion, 2002; Duffy, 2006; Contini et al., 2006; Rouchier, 2007). Laboratory findings can provide rich information on agents' attributes, cognitive skills and behavior; they thus contribute to designing and fine-tuning the simulation. In turn, the latter can help us to better understand results from experiments with human subjects, for instance by allowing a very high number of repetitions of an experiment, or by providing insight into the possible large-scale effects of some observed behavior, which would be difficult to do in the laboratory. Agent-based models can also provide a benchmark: for example in market experiments, researchers can program software buyers and sellers to act according to some prespecified rule, and compare simulated prices and quantities to those that prevail with human subjects in the lab. By so doing, they can assess similarities and differences between observed human behaviors and those implied by the rule under study, so as to gain further insight into decision-making processes.

The similarities between agent-based modeling and experimental economics, and the increasingly diffuse practice of performing parallel experiments with human subjects and artificial agents, are among the reasons that account for the rise of ACE in recent years. To some extent, the subfield participates in the success of experimental research and its perceived potential to enrich economic knowledge.

10.3.3 Decision-making in ACE Models

To examine more closely the unique methodological characteristics of ACE, with its strengths and weaknesses, it is important to discuss the individual decision-making process. As mentioned above, researchers in this field overwhelmingly reject neoclassical utility maximization, under a variety of influences ranging from Herbert Simon's 'bounded rationality' approach to behavioral economists' claim that real decision-makers do not follow rational choice theory. The search for alternative models of rationality and cognition oscillates between the opposed principles of simplicity and complexity (Jager, 2000, p. 102). They frame the extremes on a continuum and many researchers adopt intermediate positions; nevertheless, debates among supporters of the two visions have often been lively, and for the sake of argument, it is useful to keep them separate. Simplicity has been widely popularized through Axelrod's KISS principle, which allegedly stands for the army slogan 'keep it simple, stupid', and is in fact a reformulation of Occam's razor. The idea is that as any other human being, the researcher has limited cognitive ability, so that it is crucial to understand everything that goes into the model in case a surprising result occurs. Simplicity at the agent level allows focusing on the dynamics of interactions among agents and on how they can, alone, lead to complex (and often, unexpected) outcomes at the aggregate level. In Axelrod's own words:

> The point is that while the topic being investigated may be complicated, the assumptions underlying the agent-based model should be simple. The complexity of agent-based modeling should be in the simulated results, not in the assumptions of the model. (Axelrod, 2007)

Simplicity is especially useful in models that need to separate out the effects of the structure of interaction from those of individual behavior. In particular the so-called 'Zero-Intelligence' agents research program on the functioning of markets, inaugurated by a seminal article by Gode and Sunder (1993), assumes random decision-making so as to obtain a high degree of simplicity at agent level, and exploits it to develop tractable models of the bearing of the institutional structure on price formation. Random choice should not be taken as a truthful representation of human behavior, but rather as an attempt to isolate the effects of the market structure in which transactions take place. With this approach, Sunder (2006a, 2006b) has advocated a new direction of research, focusing more on institutions and structures than on the detailed study of micro behavior that in his view characterizes much of today's economics. Along similar lines, researchers at the Santa Fe Institute are currently investigating the role of financial institutions in shaping the price formation process, independently of the behavior of individual traders.

Clearly, a drawback of simplicity is its lack of realism. This is not necessarily a concern: the 'as-if' arguments used in economics at least since Milton Friedman (1953) suggest that even if its assumptions are unrealistic, a theory does not need to be rejected provided its predictions are not contradicted. Yet too naive behavioral hypotheses may hinder the study of relevant issues, for instance in this case, the question of whether and how traders consent to abide by market rules and may even contribute to reshaping and improving them over time (Gode and Sunder, 1997; Tubaro, 2009).

A more realistic representation of individual decision-making requires some degree of complexity, endowing agents with relatively sophisticated behavioral and cognitive skills (see for example Conte and Paolucci, 2001; Edmonds and Moss, 2001; Sun and Naveh, 2004; Sun, 2006). For instance, there might be a fitness or utility function that enables the agent to evaluate the consequences of its past actions and take them as a basis to improve its choice criteria ('learn'), in a dynamic process. In more complex models, agents learn not only from their own experience but also from others, so that learning becomes a collective rather than an individual process (Vriend, 2000). Correspondingly, learning may take several forms, ranging from relatively simple stimulus–response learning (Arthur, 1991, 1993; Roth and Erev, 1995; Erev and Roth, 1998) to more sophisticated belief-based learning, which requires an agent to form, and regularly update, beliefs on other agents' actions (Cheung and Friedman, 1997). Even more complex forms of learning that are found in the literature are genetic algorithms and classifier systems, borrowed from the principles of population biology (Holland, 1975 [1992]).

On the whole, research along these lines places less emphasis on cognitive limits, and rather stresses the inadequacy of rational choice theory in the case of complex or ill-defined problems – the typical example is chess, where deduction alone does not lead to a solution and other cognitive capacities such as induction or calculation must intervene (Batten, 2000). Generally speaking, reliance on complexity is relatively more widespread in the growing literature that addresses cognitive and information-related issues, often (though not always) relying on insights from psychology or cognitive science. A reason for concern, though, is that simulations tend to be less transparent under these conditions, and may make it difficult to clearly identify the dynamics that relate macro-level outcomes to micro-level behavior.

10.3.4   Validation and Verification

Whether a modeler adopts simplicity or complexity, the question remains of what an explanation in an agent-based model is. How can computer simulation provide insight into a social phenomenon? In the early days of agent-based modeling, it was already a big step forward to generate a social phenomenon artificially:

> What constitutes an explanation of an observed social phenomenon? Perhaps one day people will interpret the question, 'Can you explain it?' by asking 'Can you *grow* it?' Artificial society modeling allows us to 'grow' social structures *in silico* demonstrating that certain sets of microspecifications are *sufficient to generate* the macrophenomena of interest. (Epstein and Axtell, 1996, p. 20).

While this approach allowed significant progress initially, many questions remained open. How to ensure that the model captures salient dimensions of the problem under study, and reproduces relevant social processes? How to compare it to previously existing theories, and how to test its findings against empirical data? How to check for robustness of results to changes in parameter settings, initial conditions and software implementation? These questions are all the more challenging as path-dependence and co-evolution of agent behavior and the environment often entail non-linearities or multiple equilibria, so that an analytical solution is hard or even impossible to find. More precisely, computer simulation does not provide proofs *stricto sensu* but only allows for inductive reasoning, so that it is more similar to engineering and the experimental sciences than to deductive logic or mathematics. It enables us to identify sufficient, but generally not necessary, conditions for a phenomenon to emerge. In a sense, simulation may even appear as a 'black box' in which the modeler defines the inputs (agents' attributes, initial conditions, rules of interaction) and observes the output (indicators), but may have limited understanding of the inner working of the system.

Such issues are behind the reservations of many non-ACE economists, who feel on more solid ground with conventional mathematical and statistical models. In response, the ACE community has become progressively more aware of methodological problems and has devoted increasing attention to validation and verification, with an exponential growth of contributions in recent years (Fagiolo et al., 2007b; Fagiolo et al., 2007a; Galán et al., 2009). A full account of the whole range of discussions pertaining to validation would be outside the scope of this chapter, which will simply outline some of the main lines of reflection; the interested reader is invited to refer to the specialized literature.

Broadly speaking, validation can be theoretical or empirical. The former is particularly appropriate in cases in which agent-based models are used for qualitative insight and theory generation, and basically consists in weighing model results against predictions derived from economic theory: for instance, the extent to which neoclassical supply-and-demand schemes are good predictors of decentralized market outcomes even if, say, exchanges do not follow *tâtonnement* rules, or agents do not maximize utility, can be assessed by comparing simulated prices and quantities to those that would prevail at the theoretical equilibrium point. Models with Zero-Intelligence agents in a general equilibrium framework are a case in point (Crockett et al., 2008).

Empirical validation can take several forms, but a common approach starts from identifying a set of 'stylized facts' in the real world, that is, following the definition of Nicholas Kaldor (1961), broad tendencies that summarize the empirical data, ignoring that individual detail may be subject to snags and qualifications; then, the modeler builds an agent-based environment and endeavors to reproduce the stylized facts in the simulation. Thus, choice of parameter values will be such that the simulated result is closest to the observed facts; put differently, it is the output of the model that is subject to validation, rather than its inputs. This approach is particularly appropriate for models that aim to explain some persistently observed empirical regularities, for instance models of financial markets (LeBaron, 2002; Tesfatsion, 2008). One problem that frequently arises with output validation, however, is that different combinations of parameters and initial conditions may be consistent with the set of stylized facts of interest, so that some kind of validation is also desirable for the micro structure of the model.

In fact validation may also concern inputs, especially for models that aim to design some new institutional mechanism or rule, in a normative perspective; in such cases, parameter values should reproduce the observed characteristics of individuals, their interactions and their local environment as closely as possible, so that the simulation can be trusted to yield plausible results. Examples of this type of research include design of matching mechanisms, of auctions (Sun and Tesfatsion, 2007) and of welfare benefit schemes (Pingle and Tesfatsion, 2003). However, with input validation, it may be the case that parameters and/or initial conditions cannot be easily estimated, due to lack of sufficiently rich microdata: in particular, statistical databases very rarely include any details on decision-making and learning rules (Fagiolo et al., 2007b).

One solution consists, as mentioned above, in performing parallel experiments with artificial and human subjects. They can provide much richer information on agent attributes, cognitive skills and behavior than other data sources; they thus contribute to defining the appropriate specification of agent behavior and the parameters of agent-based models. Still another approach to validation is based on involvement of stakeholders, who participate in the definition of the situation – usually, some social dilemma – and possible scenarios (Barreteau and others, 2003). Validation comes from actors' acceptance of the model as an adequate description of their problem and as a useful tool to address it. This approach is better than experiments in providing insight into agents' representations in the real world, but allows only limited control and replicability; its findings are often context-dependent, and accumulation of empirically based knowledge is relatively difficult (Rouchier, 2007). To date, stakeholder involvement models are less common in economics than in other social sciences.

10.3.5 Diversity of Modeling Approaches

Constrained maximization at individual level and equilibrium at collective level form the core principles of neoclassical economics and give it some degree of unity, despite the nuances and qualifications that apply to its particular components. In contrast, ACE models share only minimal commonalities and are in fact very diverse. One reason is that the standard utility maximization and perfect information hypotheses admit not one but many alternatives: hence, their removal opens the way to a variety of choice criteria ranging from Zero-Intelligence to sophisticated learning processes, and to differing assumptions about how agents collect, process and accumulate information. Although use of experimental or other data can restrict the range of possible options, no decision-making model has emerged as a universally valid alternative so far; rather, many researchers believe that the context of choice may determine which conception is most appropriate.

Modeling frameworks are also heterogeneous. For instance, ACE representations of the market often follow the experimental economics tradition of assigning reservation values to each buyer and seller, and then deriving aggregate supply and demand schedules by sorting seller values from lowest to highest, and buyer values from highest to lowest. While allowing for straightforward linkages between agent simulations and human subject experiments, this approach does not facilitate comparison with standard microeconomics arguments, typically framed in terms of preferences, utility functions and endowments. The main reason for this gap is that the experimental/ACE method draws heavily on Marshallian analysis, which was very much in the minds of the pioneers of market experiments such as Edward Chamberlin and Vernon Smith, but was at the same time losing ground elsewhere and has now virtually disappeared from microeconomics textbooks (Tubaro, 2009).

The community of agent-based modelers has recognized that heterogeneity of assumptions and frameworks of analysis may hinder comparability and transferability of knowledge between models (Fagiolo et al., 2007b). Because computer simulation does not allow proofs as in deductive logic or mathematics, but only inductive reasoning, the reliability of a result is higher if it is reproduced by different modelers and/or on different software and hardware platforms. Hence, many researchers insist on the need to replicate, rewrite and compare models more systematically (Hales et al., 2003), and some have gone as far as to propose a common protocol (Leombruni et al., 2006).

An issue that has been less widely discussed in the literature is ACE's distinctiveness in the choice of its objects of study. To be sure, some of them overlap with those of previous economic theories, for instance the general principles regulating price formation and the coordinating capacities of decentralized market economies (for example Gode and Sunder, 1993; Weisbuch et al., 2000; Axtell, 2005; Gintis, 2007). Yet they also include a broad range of less conventional issues. Specifically, ACE goes beyond the traditional neoclassical view in which all interindividual interactions are mediated by market prices, and explores a larger variety of coordinating processes and mechanisms. For instance, ACE draws on insights from game theory and experimental economics (Ostrom and Walker, 2005) to study how trust and reciprocity may appear in situations of imperfect information or uncertainty, in which agents can choose between cooperative or defecting behaviors. Under these conditions, an agent may accept being vulnerable to the actions of another based on the expectation that the other will cooperate; this is all the more likely as interactions are repeated over time and agents have the opportunity to reciprocate. Agent-based models of trust and reciprocity can be used to explain, among other things, the formation of long-term business relationships between firms and their suppliers and customers (for example Kim, 2009).

Other questions that ACE models deal with include loyalty, which may arise in cases in which heterogeneous agents interact repeatedly, and at each step choose which agent to interact with and which actions to perform. Loyalty has been especially explored in the study of perishable good markets (fruits, vegetables and fish), where buyer–seller interactions are repeated on a daily basis due to limited possibilities of forming stocks, and participants are very dependent on the regularity, and predictability, of their interactions. It has been shown that loyalty towards the same buyers or sellers increases predictability and thus market efficiency, while opportunism (that is, shopping around for the cheapest prices) makes transactions less predictable, lowers efficiency and increases waste (Rouchier, 2004; Kirman and Vriend, 2000). Reputation also has a place in ACE models of the market. It matters when buyers need to choose from among a group of sellers but have imperfect information on the quality of the goods or services on offer; in such cases, they can take the reputation of a seller, that is, other buyers' judgment, as an indicator of quality. This principle may give rise to complex dynamic interactions in which sellers endeavor to improve the image they convey to buyers and the latter exchange with each other information about sellers. In the absence of other sources of information, use of reputation as an indicator can lead to strong potential gains in terms of buyer and seller satisfaction (Rouchier, 2008). To give another example, agent-based models also consider endogeneity of consumer preferences due to social influence. The idea is that tastes and preferences may evolve following the marketing and advertising strategies of firms (Janssen and Jager, 2003) or peer influence, with social processes such as imitation, social comparison and status-seeking (Dosi et al., 1999; Kemp, 1999), which give rise in some cases to forms of conspicuous consumption as originally described by Veblen (Friedman and Ostrov, 2008).

Clearly, inclusion of non-traditional topics is not only due to linkages with experimental economics research; nor does it entirely derive from the specific assumptions of ACE and its emphasis on imperfect information, non-deductive reasoning and a non-Walrasian framework of analysis. It is also related to ACE's closeness with neighboring disciplines; in particular, sociology already has a long tradition of investigating relationships between market participants that are not mediated by prices, and may involve coexistence of forms of competition and cooperation (Smelser and Swedberg, 2005).

Combinations of new hypotheses, new tools and new topics allow ACE to explore a wider range of 'possible worlds', and by so doing enrich economists' understanding of the market mechanism. This perspective is all the more promising as an increasing amount of research is done in parallel with experimental and game-theoretic work, not to mention psychological and sociological research. Nevertheless, widening of topics together with inputs from other disciplines may hamper comparison with other parts of economics and make interpretation of ACE models less straightforward. This may discourage other economists from developing an interest in the field.

10.4   THE IMPACT OF ACE ON THE METHODOLOGY OF ECONOMICS

Based on the discussion conducted so far, it is now possible to frame a broad reflection on the relationships between ACE and economic methodology. A first issue is, of course, that computer simulation is commonly perceived as less rigorous than the logical deduction and mathematics that imposed themselves as primary tools for economic reasoning after World War II with the seminal contributions of Paul Samuelson and the Arrow–Debreu general equilibrium model. In this sense, computer simulation is bound to be suspicious for many mathematically trained economists.

Yet the ongoing tendency is to broaden the range of admissible methods of research in economics, and to lessen the centrality of the abstract, deductive mathematical method that was dominant until recently. Increasingly sophisticated statistical techniques, econometric methods, software tools and experimental design protocols have led to a remarkable diversification of permissible methodologies. Though not identical to pure mathematics, these methods are all based on some kind of quantitative reasoning and are increasingly demanding in terms of the technical and methodological skills needed to apply them – a reason that partly explains their perceived solidity and their newly earned status in economics. To the extent that computer simulation can be seen as part of this trend, it may benefit from it and contribute, in turn, to transforming economics.

Further, the growing amount of methodological reflection on validation and verification issues that has recently developed within the ACE community may have wider repercussions as it raises the very general questions of cross-model comparability, generation of cumulative knowledge, relationship between theory and data, and the interpretation of empirical findings. It may also cross-fertilize with what is currently being done in other fields, for instance concerning replication, data quality and reporting of results, which are also widely discussed in relation to (among other things) applied econometrics.

The preceding sections also show that ACE contributes to shaping a novel theory of individual economic behavior, taking into account human cognitive limits on the one hand, and the existence of decision-making situations for which pure deduction is inappropriate on the other hand. From this perspective, agent-based models appear as valuable complements to game theory and experimental and behavioral economics; more precisely, by studying interactions and two-way feedback effects, they provide insight into the possible implications of different behavioral assumptions in a given social context. In particular, a major result of ACE research is that neoclassical utility maximization and perfect information hypotheses are much less general than is usually thought, and apply in fact only to a subset of choice problems. Agent-based market models provide especially strong evidence that a number of standard economic results rely less on rational choice theory than is typically assumed. Indeed in single-market models, the same supply-and-demand equilibrium obtains both with utility-maximizing and with 'Zero-Intelligence' agents (Gode and Sunder, 1993, 1997). This result confirms that the familiar supply and demand model, of Marshallian origin, is a good predictor of market outcomes and is robust to changes in individual behavioral assumptions. In light of this result, computer simulation can be said to provide a new way to test the consistency of existing theories and to assess the role of their underlying assumptions.

Another feature of ACE which raises questions for the methodology of economics is its embeddedness in an interdisciplinary context. Major contributions to the methodological and substantive development of ACE have come from fields of research outside economics, and cross-disciplinary dialogue and exchange are widespread within the agent-based modeling community. This process has allowed ACE economists to absorb contents from other disciplines over time, and transform their work accordingly – in an attitude opposed to the infamous 'imperialist' tradition of the discipline. This tendency is now slightly declining and ACE is becoming relatively more closely connected to other parts of economics, albeit slowly. Interdisciplinary relationships enrich economic reflection with new research questions, variables and assumptions. The drawback is that insight from other disciplines may hinder comparison with intradisciplinary theories and results; as a result, it may be difficult to assess ACE findings and their contribution to a better understanding of economic phenomena. In the coming years, the challenge for ACE will be to strike a balance between the two opposite needs of maintaining interdisciplinary contacts and enhancing dialogue with other parts of economics. The extent to which it will succeed in doing so will determine its future place in a renewed but methodologically more highly demanding economics discipline.

NOTES

1. See http://www.econ.iastate.edu/tesfatsi/news0297.htm.
2. http://jasss.soc.surrey.ac.uk/JASSS.html.
3. http://www.econ.iastate.edu/tesfatsi/ace.htm.

REFERENCES

Amman, H.M., D.A. Kendrick and J. Rust (1996), *Handbook of Computational Economics*, Vol. 1, Amsterdam: Elsevier/North-Holland.
Anderson, P.W., K.J. Arrow and D. Pines (eds) (1988), *The Economy as an Evolving Complex System*, Reading, MA: Addison-Wesley.
Arthur, W.B. (1991), 'Designing Economic Agents that Act Like Human Agents: A Behavioural Approach to Bounded Rationality', *American Economic Review*, **81**, 353–359.
Arthur, W.B. (1993), 'On Designing Economic Agents that Behave like Human Agents', *Journal of Evolutionary Economics*, **3**, 1–22.
Axelrod, R. (1984), *The Evolution of Cooperation*, New York: Basic Books.
Axelrod, R. (2007), 'Advancing the Art of Simulation in the Social Sciences', in Rennard J.P. (ed.), *Handbook of Research on Nature Inspired Computing for Economics and Management*, Hersey, PA: Idea Group, pp. 90–100.
Axtell, R. (2000), 'Why Agents? On the Varied Motivations for Agent Computing in the Social Sciences', Center on Social and Economic Dynamics, The Brookings Institute, Working Paper 17, Washington, DC.
Axtell, R. (2005), 'The Complexity of Exchange', *Economic Journal*, **115**(504), 193–210.
Barreteau, O. and others (2003), 'Our Companion Modelling Approach', *Journal of Artificial Societies and Social Simulation*, **6**(1), http://jasss.soc.surrey.ac.uk/6/2/1.html.
Batten, D.F. (2000), *Discovering Artificial Economics: How Agents Learn and Economies Evolve*, Boulder, CO: Westview Press.
Buchanan, M. (2009), 'Meltdown Modeling: Could Agent-based Computer Models Prevent Another Financial Crisis?', *Nature – News*. **460**(6), 680–682.

Cheung, Y.W. and D. Friedman (1997), 'Learning in Evolutionary Games: Some Laboratory Results', *Games and Economic Behavior*, **19**, 46–76.

Conte, R. and M. Paolucci (2001), 'Intelligent Social Learning', *Journal of Artificial Societies and Social Simulation*, **4**(1), http://www.soc.surrey.ac.uk/JASSS/4/1/3.html.

Contini, B., R. Leombruni and M. Richiardi (2006), 'Exploring a New ExpAce: The Complementarities between Experimental Economics and Agent-based Computational Economics', LABORatorio R. Revelli Working Papers Series 45.

Crockett, S., S. Spear and S. Sunder (2008), 'Learning Competitive Equilibrium', *Journal of Mathematical Economics*, **44**(7–8), 651–671.

Dibble, C. (2001), 'Theory in a Complex World: GeoGraph Computational Laboratories', PhD Dissertation, Geography Department, University of California Santa Barbara.

Dosi, G., G. Fagiolo, R. Aversi, M. Meacci and C. Olivetti (1999), 'Cognitive Processes, Social Adaptation and Innovation in Consumption Patterns: From Stylized Facts to Demand Theory', in S.C. Dow and P.E. Earl (eds), *Economic Organizations and Economic Knowledge: Essays in Honour of Brian Loasby*, Cheltenham, UK and Northampton, MA, USA: Edward Elgar, pp. 139–144.

Duffy, J. (2006), 'Agent-based Models and Human Subject Experiments', in Tesfatsion L. and Judd K.L. (eds), *Handbook of Computational Economics*, Vol. 2, Amsterdam: Elsevier/North Holland, pp. 950–1011.

Edmonds, B. and S. Moss (2001), 'The Importance of Representing Cognitive Processes in Multi-Agent Models', in G. Dorffner, H. Bischof and K. Hornik (eds), *Artificial Neural Networks – ICANN'2001*, Lecture Notes in Computer Science, **2130**, Berlin: Springer-Verlag, pp. 759–766.

Epstein, J. and R. Axtell (1996), *Growing Artificial Societies: Social Science from the Bottom Up*, Cambridge, MA: MIT Press and Brookings Institution Press.

Erev, I. and A.E. Roth (1998), 'Predicting How People Play Games: Reinforcement Learning in Experimental Games with Unique, Mixed Strategy Equilibria', *American Economic Review*, **88**, 848–881.

Fagiolo, G., C. Birchenhall and P. Windrum (2007a), 'Empirical Validation in Agent-based Models: Introduction to the Special Issue', *Computational Economics,* **30**(3), 189–194.

Fagiolo, G., A. Moneta and P. Windrum (2007b), 'A Critical Guide to Empirical Validation of Agent-Based Models in Economics: Methodologies, Procedures, and Open Problems', *Computational Economics*, **30**(3), 195–226.

Farmer, J.D. and D. Foley (2009), 'The Economy Needs Agent-based Modeling', *Nature – Opinion*, **460**(6), 685–686.

Friedman, D. and D.N. Ostrov (2008), 'Conspicuous Consumption Dynamics', *Games and Economic Behavior*, **64**(1), 121–145.

Friedman, M. (1953), 'The Methodology of Positive Economics', in M. Friedman, *Essays in Positive Economics*, Chicago, IL: University of Chicago Press, pp. 3–43.

Galán, J.M., L.R. Izquierdo, S.S. Izquierdo, J.I. Santos, R. del Olmo, A. López-Paredes and B. Edmonds (2009), 'Errors and Artefacts in Agent-Based Modelling', *Journal of Artificial Societies and Social Simulation*, **12**(1), http://jasss.soc.surrey.ac.uk/12/1/1.html.

Gilbert, G.N. and R. Conte (eds) (1995), *Artificial Societies: The Computer Simulation of Social Life*, London: UCL Press.

Gilbert, N. and J. Doran (1994), *Simulating Societies: The Computer Simulation of Social Phenomena*, London: UCL Press.

Gintis, H. (2007), 'The Dynamics of General Equilibrium', *Economic Journal*, **117**(523), 1280–1309.

Gode, D.K. and S. Sunder (1993), 'Allocative Efficiency of Markets with Zero Intelligence Traders: Markets as a Partial Substitute for Individual Rationality', *Journal of Political Economy*, **101**, 119–137.

Gode, D.K. and S. Sunder (1997), 'What Makes Markets Allocationally Efficient?', *Quarterly Journal of Economics*, **112**, 603–630.

Hales, D., J. Rouchier and B. Edmonds (2003), 'Model-to-Model Analysis', *Journal of Artificial Societies and Social Simulation*, **6**(4), http://jasss.soc.surrey.ac.uk/6/4/5.html.

Holland, J.H. (1975), *Adaptation in Natural and Artificial Systems, An Introductory Analysis with Applications to Biology, Control and Artificial Intelligence*, Cambridge, MA: MIT Press; 2nd edn (1992).

Holland, J.H. and J.H. Miller (1991), 'Artificial Adaptive Agents in Economic Theory', *American Economic Review*, **81**, 365–370.

Jager, W. (2000), *Modeling Consumer Behaviour*, PhD dissertation, University of Groningen, http://irs.ub.rug.nl/ppn/240099192.

Janssen, M.A. and W. Jager (2003), 'Simulating Market Dynamics: Interactions between Consumer Psychology and Social Networks', *Artificial Life*, **9**, 343–356.

Kaldor, N. (1961), 'Capital Accumulation and Economic Growth', in F.A. Lutz and D.C. Hague (eds), *The Theory of Capital*, London: International Economic Association, pp. 177–222.

Kemp, J. (1999), 'Spontaneous Change, Unpredictability and Consumption Externalities', *Journal of Artificial Societies and Social Simulation*, **2**(3), http://www.soc.surrey.ac.uk/JASSS/2/3/1.html.

Kim, W.S. (2009), 'Effects of a Trust Mechanism on Complex Adaptive Supply Networks: An Agent-Based Social Simulation Study', *Journal of Artificial Societies and Social Simulation*, **12**(3), http://jasss.soc.surrey.ac.uk/12/3/4.html.

Kirman, A.P. (1992), 'Whom or What does the Representative Agent Represent?', *Journal of Economic Perspectives*, **6**(2), 117–136.

Kirman, A.P. and N.J. Vriend (2000), 'Learning to Be Loyal. A Study of the Marseille Fish Market', in D. Delli Gatti, M. Gallegati and A.P. Kirman (eds), *Interaction and Market Structure. Essays on Heterogeneity in Economics*, Lecture Notes in Economics and Mathematical Systems 484, Berlin: Springer, pp. 33–56.

LeBaron, B. (2002), 'Building the Santa Fe Artificial Stock Market', working paper, Brandeis University, June.

Leombruni, R., M. Richiardi, N. Saam and M. Sonnessa (2006), 'A Common Protocol for Agent-Based Social Simulation', *Journal of Artificial Societies and Social Simulation*, **9**(1), http://jasss.soc.surrey.ac.uk/9/1/15.html.

Ostrom, E. and J. Walker (2005), *Trust and Reciprocity: Interdisciplinary Lessons from Experimental Research*, New York: Russell Sage Foundation.

Pingle, M. and L. Tesfatsion (2003), 'Evolution of Worker–Employer Networks and Behaviors Under Alternative Unemployment Benefits: An Agent-Based Computational Study', in A. Nagurney (ed.), *Innovations in Economic and Financial Networks*, Cheltenham, UK and Northampton, MA, USA: Edward Elgar, pp. 256–285.

Rosser, J.B., Jr (2008), 'Econophysics', in S.N. Durlauf and L.E. Blume (eds), *The New Palgrave Dictionary of Economics*, 2nd edn, Palgrave Macmillan, http://www.dictionaryofeconomics.com/article?id=pde2008_E000253.

Roth, A.E. and I. Erev (1995), 'Learning in Extensive-form Games: Experimental Data and Simple Dynamic Models in the Intermediate Term', *Games and Economic Behavior*, **8**, 164–212.

Rouchier, J. (2004), 'Interaction Routines and Selfish Behaviours in an Artificial Market', Presentation at WEHIA, Workshop of Economics with Heterogenous Interacting Agents, Kyoto, 29–31 May.

Rouchier J. (2007), 'Data Gathering to Build and Validate Small Scale Social Models for Simulation', in J.P. Rennard (ed.), *Handbook of Research on Nature Inspired Computing for Economics and Management*, Hersey, PA: Idea Group, pp. 198–210.

Rouchier, J. (2008), 'Agent-based Simulation as a Useful Tool for the Study of Markets', GREQAM Working Paper n. 8.

Schelling, T. (1978), *Micromotives and Macrobehaviour*, New York: Nortin.

Smelser, N.J. and R. Swedberg (2005), *Handbook of Economic Sociology*, 2nd edn, Princeton, NJ: Princeton University Press.

Sun, R. (ed.) (2006), *Cognition and Multi-Agent Interaction: From Cognitive Modeling to Social Simulation*, Cambridge: Cambridge University Press.

Sun, R. and I. Naveh (2004), 'Simulating Organizational Decision-Making Using a

Cognitively Realistic Agent Model', *Journal of Artificial Societies and Social Simulation*, 7(3), http://jasss.soc.surrey.ac.uk/7/3/5.html.

Sun, J. and L. Tesfatsion (2007), 'An Agent-Based Computational Laboratory for Wholesale Power Market Design', *IEEE Proceedings*, Power and Energy Society General Meeting, Tampa, FL.

Sunder, S. (2006a), 'Determinants of Economic Interaction: Behavior or Structure', *Journal of Economic Interaction and Coordination*, 1(1), 21–32.

Sunder, S. (2006b), Economic Theory: Structural Abstraction or Behavioral Reduction', in P. Mirowski and D. Wade Hands (eds), *Agreement on Demand: Consumer Theory in the Twentieth Century*, annual supplement to *History of Political Economy*, 38, 322–342.

Tesfatsion, L. (2002), 'Agent-based Computational Economics: Growing Economies from the Bottom Up', *Artificial Life*, 8, 55–82.

Tesfatsion, L. (2008), *Detailed Notes on the Santa Fe Artificial Stock Market (ASM) Model*, http://www.econ.iastate.edu/classes/econ308/tesfatsion/SFIStockDetailed.LT.htm.

Tesfatsion, L. and K.L. Judd (2006), *Handbook of Computational Economics*, Vol. 2, *Agent-Based Computational Economics*, Amsterdam: Elsevier/North Holland.

Tubaro, P. (2009), 'Is Individual Rationality Essential to Market Price Formation? The Contribution of Zero-Intelligence Agent Trading Models', *Journal of Economic Methodology*, 16, 1–19.

Vriend, N. (2000), 'An Illustration of the Essential Difference Between Individual and Social Learning, and its Consequences for Computational Analyses', *Journal of Economic Dynamics and Control*, 24, 1–19.

Weisbuch, G., A. Kirman and D. Herreiner (2000), 'Market Organisation and Trading Relationships', *Economic Journal*, 110(463), 411–436.

11 Agent-based modeling: the right mathematics for the social sciences?
Paul L. Borrill and Leigh Tesfatsion

11.1 INTRODUCTION

As in the physical sciences, theoretical modeling in the social sciences typically entails the specification and analysis of parameterized systems of differential equations. Many critical insights have been obtained by social scientists using this powerful classical mathematics approach.

Nevertheless, it is extremely difficult to capture physical, institutional and behavioral aspects of social systems with empirical fidelity and still retain analytical tractability. Entities in social systems are neither infinitesimally small nor infinitely many, nor are their identities or behaviors necessarily indistinguishable from one another. Common simplifications, such as assumed homogeneous behaviors or the existence of single representative agents, are thus problematic. Moreover, the social sciences cannot separate observers from 'the real world out there'. Rather, social scientists must consider multiple observers in a continual co-evolving interaction with each other and with their environment.

This leads us to question whether other forms of traditional mathematics, or even new forms of mathematics, might better serve the purposes of social scientists. In short, what is the 'right' mathematics for the social sciences? Moreover, if a 'right' mathematics exists for the social sciences, what are the implications for the physical sciences? And what can the social and physical sciences learn from each other?

As elaborated in Bridges (2009), constructive mathematics is distinguished from classical mathematics by the strict interpretation of 'there exists' ($\exists$) as 'we can construct', classical mathematicans accept the law of the excluded middle (LEM): for any proposition P, either P is true or its negation is true; there is no middle ground that evades this decidability logic. Thus, classical mathematicians accept existence proofs based on proof by contradiction: if the negation of P is not true, then P must be true. In contrast, constructive mathematicians require a direct proof that P is true in the form of a computational procedure in order to rule out both the falseness and the undecidability of P. Constructive proofs can, in principle, be realized as computer programs. Constructive mathematics thus embodies the fundamental concepts of information, and the limitations on knowledge, implied by modern computability theory (Bridges, 1999; Eberbach et al., 2004).

This distinction provides a dramatically different perspective on how we perceive models in our mind in relation to the real-world systems they are intended to represent. For example, social system modelers using classical mathematics typically assume (explicitly or implicitly) that all modeled decision makers share common knowledge about an objective reality, even if there is no constructive way in which these decision makers could attain this common knowledge. In contrast, social system modelers advocating a constructive mathematics approach have argued that the 'reality' of each modeled decision maker ought to be limited to whatever that decision maker is able to compute (Velupillai, 2010).

In this chapter we argue that agent-based modeling (ABM) is an alternative and potentially more appropriate form of mathematics for the social sciences. Roughly, ABM is the computational modeling of systems as collections of autonomous interacting entities. As will be clarified in subsequent sections, ABM is a powerful blend of classical and constructive mathematical approaches.

Section 11.2 provides a basic introduction to the ABM methodology as an alternative form of mathematics, with a primary focus on its applicability for social science research.[1] Section 11.3 describes typical goals of ABM social science researchers and the 'culture-dish' nature of their computer experiments. It also provides pointers to active ABM social science research areas. The applicability of ABM for science more generally is considered in sections 11.4 and 11.5, with special attention to physics. This broader perspective highlights the conceptual similarity and applicability of agent representations across various scientific disciplines. Section 11.6 summarizes two ABM applications that illustrate concretely the duality of ABM: real-world systems cannot only be simulated with verisimilitude using ABM; they can also be efficiently and robustly designed and constructed on the basis of ABM principles. Concluding remarks are provided in section 11.7.

11.2 WHAT IS ABM?

11.2.1 ABM as an Alternative Form of Mathematics

Social systems consist of heterogeneous communicating entities in an evolving network of relationships. One branch of mathematics that deals with networks of relationships is graph theory, and significant new perspectives and results are emerging from that field (Albert and Barabási, 2002). Another is category theory, which specifies relationships (morphisms) among collections of objects as first-class citizens along with the objects themselves (MacLane, 1998). Category theory is being promoted as the intellectual successor to set theory, which for generations has been considered the foundation of mathematics.

Graph theory and category theory are powerful tools supporting deductive reasoning in many sciences, including the social sciences. Indeed, as discussed by Laubenbacher et al. (2009, section 6.3), certain classes of ABMs representable as finite dynamical system 'objects' with appropriately defined types of morphisms can be shown to constitute a category. Nevertheless, the classical idea that we can deduce solutions (or 'future states') for systems a priori, purely from a study of their structural characteristics, is beginning to be overshadowed by the realization that many systems are computationally irreducible (Laughlin and Pines, 2000).

More precisely, for systems that are strongly interactive and/or highly sensitive to initial conditions, it is often not practical (or even possible) to predict their global outcomes in advance of actual implementation even when their laws of motion are known. Examples include John Conway's Game of Life, Aristid Lindenmayer's L-systems, Benoit Mandelbrot's generated fractal sets, Stephen Wolfram's elementary cellular automata (class four), and a long list of other foundational contributions too numerous to mention. Social systems appear to be subject to this form of computational irreducibility. Not only in practice, but now also in theory, we have come to realize that the only option we have to understand the global properties of many social systems of interest is to build and run computer models of these systems and observe what happens.

The computer modeling approach advocated here is the relatively young and still-developing methodology known as ABM. In this approach, systems are modeled as collections of autonomous interacting entities ('agents') with encapsulated functionality that operate within a computational world.

As elaborated below, ABM combines constructive and classical modeling approaches. As is true for real people, agents can only acquire new data about their world constructively, through interactions. Nevertheless, again like real people, ABM agents can have uncomputable beliefs about their world that influence their interactions. These uncomputable beliefs can arise from inborn (initially configured) attributes, from communications received from other agents, and/or from the use of non-constructive methods (for example, proof by contradiction) to interpret acquired data. These uncomputable beliefs enable agents to make creative leaps, to come up with new ideas about their world not currently supportable by measurements, observations, or logical extrapolations from existing information – in short, to be Smolin's seers (Smolin, 2002, Chapter 18).

The import of this ABM blending of constructive and classical mathematics depends upon the purpose at hand. For example, for descriptive purposes, it permits human behavior to be captured with greater fidelity than simple algorithmic representations. For optimization purposes, it permits a deeper and more creative exploration of large domains, a melding of experience-tempered guesswork with step-by-step computation that could vastly extend the power of traditional finite search methods.

ABMs with no run-time interaction with external systems are Turing computable; hence, in principle, they can be equivalently expressed as finite systems of discrete-time recursive equations over finite state domains (Axtell, 2003, section 2.1; Epstein, 2006, Chapter 2; Laubenbacher et al., 2009). However, ABMs can also be constructed to support persistent run-time interactions between computer agents and real-world entities via general types of input–output data streams. That is, ABMs can be data-driven dynamic applications systems (Darema, 2005).

Data-driven ABMs are a form of interactive system called Super-Turing Machines by Eberbach et al. (2004) and Goldin et al. (2006). The latter authors argue that Super-Turing Machines constitute a new class of computation models capable of going beyond Turing Machines and algorithms. This claim is disputed in part by Prasse and Rittgen (1998). Nevertheless, the possibility of constructing ABMs as open systems with external run-time interactions and information flows has exciting practical ramifications even if the full computational and philosophical implications remain controversial (LeBaron and Tesfatsion, 2008).

Finally, as will be illustrated concretely in section 11.6.3, ABM is more than a modeling methodology; ABM principles can also be used to construct real-world systems. Examples include shopbots, automated Internet auctions, smart-grid electronic devices and data storage systems. The resulting real-world systems can, in turn, be simulated by ABMs that mimic their basic architecture and constituent agent types. This natural duality affords researchers an opportunity, perhaps for the first time in history, to match faithfully the behavior of computer models to real deployed systems. This should permit unprecedented predictive power, well beyond that achievable with either analytical models or traditional simulations.

We therefore view ABM as a bona fide member of the mathematician's toolbox, suitable for the study of complex interactive processes in all scientific disciplines. Nevertheless, ABM is particularly congruent to social systems because of the ease of mapping agents to recognizable social entities and the natural hierarchical self-organization readily seen in social

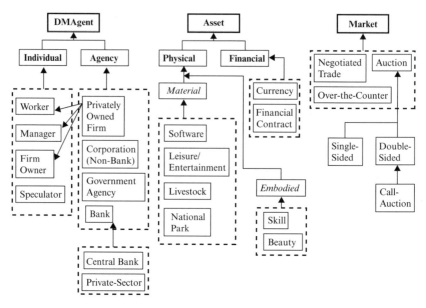

Note: Upward-pointing arrows denote 'is a' relationships and downward-pointing arrows denote 'has a' relationships.

Figure 11.1   Illustrative partial agent hierarchy for an economic ABM

systems. We thus see the social sciences, including economics, as among the most promising areas for ABM application.

11.2.2   ABM Agents

Agents in ABM are entities that encapsulate data as well as methods that act on this data.[2] As illustrated in Figure 11.1, ABM agents can represent a broad spectrum of entities ranging from passive physical materials governed by relatively simple dynamical methods, such as physical decay, to individual or group decision-making agents (DMAgents) with social capabilities.

ABM provides wide latitude when it comes to specifying the complexity and plasticity of agent representations. Analytical tractability is no longer a valid excuse for simplifications. Rather, for any particular purpose at hand, ABM researchers must decide the most appropriate level for their initial agent representations, the degree to which individual agent representations can undergo structural change over time, and the degree to which agent populations can evolve over time.

For example, an individual ABM agent can have a small number of simple fixed methods resulting in a relatively small range of if–then individually expressed behaviors within its world, similar to the fixed rules in cellular automata (von Neumann, 1951; Wolfram, 2002). Just as the simple fixed rules of a chess game can produce an enormously large space of different games through player interactions, so the simple fixed methods of individual agents within ABMs can produce unexpectedly rich global system behaviors through agent interactions.

Alternatively, individual ABM agents can have methods permitting more complex behaviors characteristic of people in real life. These behaviors can include: state-conditioned adaptive response (if this happens, what should I do?); anticipatory learning (if I do this, what will happen?); intertemporal planning; social communication; goal-directed learning leading to changes in state-conditioned responses; and reproduction (birth and death) leading to changes in the composition of agent populations.

The goals guiding goal-directed learning and action choice for ABM agents can be inborn or evolved. Moreover, these goals can be open-ended in form: for example, 'maintain high power status', or 'avoid bankruptcy', or 'earn as much as possible' for oneself or for a group. An ABM agent with open-ended goals is more aptly described as a tracker rather than as an optimizer or satisficer, and its goal-seeking methods have no natural finite termination point apart from the termination of the agent itself.

The data and methods of each ABM agent are encapsulated in the sense that their form and content can be hidden from other agents. An agent communicates with other agents only through its public interface, the subset of its data and methods that other agents are permitted to see.

Agent encapsulation gives ABMs a striking resemblance to real-world systems. Information hiding (state containment) results in uncertainty in agent interactions, in the sense that agents can never be entirely certain how other agents will behave. Even if an agent is acting in accordance with a fixed private behavioral method, it can appear as a 'different entity' in different interactions at different times due to the differences in its expressed behaviors induced in these interactions.

Moreover, in any ABM that is closed – that is, without external run-time interactions – agent encapsulation enforces the real-world constraint that all calculations must be carried out by the agents that actually reside within the ABM world. Free-floating procedures and restrictions influencing ABM world outcomes, such as global continuity or equilibrium conditions externally imposed across agents, are not permitted. Conversely, the procedures and restrictions encapsulated in the methods of a particular ABM agent can only be implemented using the particular resources available to that agent. An ABM agent that exhausts its resources is constrained in its future ability to act effectively within its world. Thus, relative to traditional equation-based modeling, agent encapsulation in ABM permits a more realistic representation of real-world systems composed of interacting distributed entities with limited information, limited possible responses, limited material resources and limited computational capabilities.

A key aspect of decision-making agents (DMAgents) in ABM is their increased autonomy relative to the decision makers appearing in analytical social science models. This increased autonomy arises from agent encapsulation. DMAgents can self-activate and self-determine their actions on the basis of hidden internal data and methods. These methods can include pseudo-random number generators (PRNGs)[3] permitting randomizations of behaviors and decisions. For example, DMAgents might use 'coin flips' to decide among equally preferred actions or action delays, mixed strategies in game situations to avoid exploitable predictability, and mutations (random perturbations) of normal routines to explore new possibilities. Moreover, the data and methods of DMAgents can change over time as they interact within their world and learn from these interactions.

Indeed, DMAgents in ABMs should be able to pass the following constructive replacement test: given any DMAgent interacting within an ABM through its public interface, it should be feasible to replace this DMAgent with a person that interacts through this same public interface. This leads naturally to the idea of a constructive Turing test: would a person interacting within an experimental framework involving a mixture of human and computer-agent participants be able to discern which were human and which were computer-generated? (Barr et al., 2008).

These proposed tests reflect the dual ability of ABMs to both represent and synthesize real-world systems. Already in ABM we are seeing a blurring of the lines between direct human control of computer-agent representatives (avatars), modeling of human behaviors via computer agents, and self-directed behaviors by autonomous computer agents. These advances in human–computer interfaces could ultimately revolutionize the theory and practice of social science.

11.2.3   ABM Horizontal and Hierarchical Organization

ABM agents are distributed in the sense that each agent experiences its own explicit or implicit locality within its larger world. Even if ABM agents are initially specified to be structurally identical, they can change or evolve over time to have widely varying data and methods supporting persistent cross-sectional behavioral diversity.

On the other hand, ABM agents are connected in the sense that each agent is embedded in a network of links representing some form of interaction (communication, trades . . .) with other agents. The form and strength of these interaction networks can evolve over time through necessity (for example, the death of agents) as well as through choice and chance.

ABMs are horizontally scalable. An ABM initially developed on a single computer with a small number of interacting agents to facilitate debugging and compilation can subsequently be expanded to include larger numbers of interacting agents distributed across multiple machines on a network with the additional memory and CPU cores used to accelerate the simulation (Axtell, 2003). Indeed, in principle, 'cloudbursting' an ABM onto cloud-computing infrastructures would allow scaling out an ABM to any arbitrary size.[4]

In addition, ABM facilitates the modeling of hierarchical constructions. ABM agents can include other agents as members. Examples include household agents with multiple family members, community agents with multiple households as members, and nation agents with multiple communities as members. Moreover, member agents can reason about the larger agent of which they are a constituent part. Consequently, ABM enables the modeling of systems encompassing nested self-referential subsystems as commonly seen in the real world.

ABM also permits a more realistic modeling of changes in horizontal and hierarchical organization (Chang and Harrington, 2006). For example, real-world firms often modify their internal organization over time to compete better with other firms. The standard economic modeling of firms by means of parameterized equations is therefore problematic. In contrast, in ABM a firm can be represented as an agent that includes other agents as members. As depicted in Figure 11.1, these member agents might include 'workers', 'managers' and a 'firm owner'. The horizontal extent and hierarchical organization of these member agents can then evolve naturally over time through hiring, firing, lay-offs, resignations and internal reorganization decisions.

The ability of ABM to model fluidity in horizontal and hierarchical organization in turn facilitates the modeling of complex real-world innovation processes (Chen and Chie, 2007; Dawid, 2006; Gilbert et al., 2001). Consider Google. A key aspect of Google's competitive position is the continual development of new search algorithms, new ways of advertising, and so forth. This innovation occurs in at least two distinct ways. Google continually hires new employees that bring new ideas into Google from other places. Also, existing Google employees are encouraged through the local rules of their collective to generate new ideas. Indeed, Google has claimed that half of its new products come from ideas generated by engineers during the 20 percent worktime during which they are free to work on whatever they wish. The structure and behavior of Google thus exhibits fundamental change over time even as Google continues to maintain its identity within the world as 'Google'.

These types of innovation processes are not easily modeled in terms of parameterized equations. ABM on the other hand is particularly well suited for the modeling of shifting landscapes involving changes in the behavioral methods of individual agents as well as evolutionary changes in the composition of agent populations.

11.3　ABM AS AN EXPLORATORY RESEARCH TOOL

11.3.1　ABM Research Goals

Normative ABM research commonly addresses two basic 'what if' questions with regard to system changes. First, do intended consequences actually arise? Second, under what conditions might a system change give rise to unintended consequences?

For example, would a change in the pricing rule for a market generate more efficient outcomes over time, as desired? Or would the change in fact lead to inefficiency as strategic participants within the system waste resources in their attempts to exploit the changed pricing rule for their own advantage? Would a change in a standard operating procedure or a human resource policy lead to improved profits for a firm, as planned? Or would the change in rules in fact reduce the firm's profits due to unanticipated incompatibilities with the corporate culture?

A common goal of descriptive ABM research is to provide possible 'generative explanations' for observed empirical regularities (Epstein, 2006). Can an observed empirical phenomenon be reliably generated by a particular form of ABM starting from particular forms of initial conditions? For example, can the empirically observed thick tails for stock return distributions be reliably reproduced within ABM stock market frameworks that include suitably heterogeneous trader agents?

Other forms of ABM research involve qualitative insight. Under what conditions might a system give rise to unanticipated behaviors that lead to deeper intuitions about its nature? The quintessential example here is the venerable yet still unresolved concern of economists such as Adam Smith (1776 [1976]) and Friedrich von Hayek (1948) to understand the surprising ability of traders in decentralized market economies to self-organize into resilient trade networks.

The ideal goal of qualitative ABM research is to characterize the complete dynamic landscape for a system. This includes the behaviors exhibited at any equilibria that might exist as well as the behaviors exhibited in the basins of attraction associated with these equilibria. It also includes a characterization of any phase transitions exhibited by a system in response to changes in its structural form or scale. Examples include the transition of water from steam to liquid to ice in response to reduced temperature, the transition from unpredictable to predictable outcomes in minority games as the ratio of the number of resolvable past play histories to the number of agents increases (Farmer et al., 2005), and the bifurcation of chaotic systems into foliations of distinct possible long-run behaviors in response to small perturbations in their parameter values (Devaney and Keen, 1989).

Whatever the exact nature of their objectives, ABM researchers must also address challenging model verification and empirical validation issues (Tesfatsion, 2010c). Verification concerns consistency with objectives: does an ABM do what a researcher intends, or is there some form of logical or conceptual programming error? Empirical validation concerns consistency with empirical reality: does an ABM appropriately capture the salient characteristics of a real-world system of interest, and does it provide outcomes that cohere with empirical observations?

11.3.2 ABM Research as Culture-Dish Experimentation

ABM researchers use controlled computer experiments to investigate how large-scale effects arise from the micro-level interactions of dispersed autonomous agents. In principle, as in wetware culture-dish experimentation, the only intervention permitted by ABM researchers is the setting of initial experimental conditions.

In carrying out an ABM experiment, an ABM researcher typically implements the following eight steps in sequence:

- Step One: Develop an experimental design for the systematic exploration of a theoretical issue of interest.
- Step Two: Construct a computer world ('culture dish') consisting of a collection of constituent agents appropriate for the study of this theoretical issue.
- Step Three: Configure the computer world in accordance with the experimental design.
- Step Four: Compile and run the computer world with no further external interference and record world outcomes of interest.
- Step Five: Repeat this 'same' computer experiment multiple times for multiple PRNG seed values to generate an ensemble of runs from which sample distributions for recorded world outcomes can be derived.

- Step Six: Repeatedly iterate steps three through five until the full range of configurations specified under the experimental design has been explored.
- Step Seven: Analyze the resulting sample distributions for recorded world outcomes and summarize their theoretical implications.
- Step Eight: Use these theoretical summaries to form hypotheses (conjectures) that can be brought to historical or real-time data for testing and empirical validation.

The intended meaning of some of these steps is more fully explained below.

In Step One, for example, a researcher might be interested in exploring whether differences in learning have systematic effects on the formation of stock price bubbles. To examine this issue, the researcher might develop an experimental design in which traders with variously specified mixes of learning capabilities engage in a sequence of stock market trades.

With regard to Step Two, the initial data and methods of the computer world determine the initial physical realm (for example, spatial landscape) within which the constituent agents interact as well as simulation controls such as simulation stopping rules and non-perturbational instrumentation devices (for example, pause buttons). The initial data and methods of the constituent agents determine the initial sequencing of their actions as well as the initial pattern of their interactions. For scientific investigations of real-world phenomena, these constructions should correspond to actual or proposed real-world counterparts and should reflect the physical, institutional and behavioral aspects of these real-world counterparts.

The configuration in Step Three typically includes the initial number of constituent agents, the specification of fixed agent attributes (for example, learning capabilities), initial settings for variable agent attributes (for example, available resources), and the initial spatial or social network determining permissable channels for initial agent interactions. It also includes the specification of seed values for any pseudo-random number generators (PRNGs) appearing in agent methods. The (initial) state of the world then consists of the (initially configured) data and methods for the world and for each of its constituent agents.

In Step Four the initial state of the world is permitted to evolve, driven solely by agent interactions. The only further role permitted for the external ABM researcher in this evolutionary process is the non-perturbational observation and recording of world outcomes of interest.

In Step Seven the theoretical summaries of experimental findings can often be enhanced by graphical visualizations. For example, grey-scale or color heatmaps can be used to display large data sets to facilitate discovery of any emergent global patterns.

11.3.3 ABM Research Areas

The range of ABM research is now extensive. Only a few areas of study relevant for social scientists are noted here to indicate the versatility of the methodology.

Within economics, ABM research areas that have been particularly active in recent years include agricultural and environmental economics, automated markets, business and management, electricity markets, financial economics, industrial organization, labor markets, macroeconomics, political economy and economic network formation. A list of pointers to ABM research sites in these areas can be accessed at Tesfatsion (2010d).

Within the social sciences more generally, highly active ABM research areas include emergence of collective behavior, evolution of cooperation and trust, innovation, institutional design, learning, norms, social influence and social network formation. Pointers to selected work in these areas can be accessed at Axelrod and Tesfatsion (2010).

Finally, ABM interdisciplinary application areas relevant for social scientists include ecological systems (Grimm and Railsback, 2005), epidemiology (Epstein, 2006, Ch. 12), health care management (Huang et al., 1995), information storage and management (Borrill, 2005, 2008), land use (Parker et al., 2003), military planning (Cioppa et al., 2004), transportation systems (Nagel and Wagner, 2006) and urban planning (Batty, 2005).

11.4 ALTERNATIVE MODELING MODALITIES

11.4.1 God's-Eye View or Local Observer View?

Science has traditionally been explored by means of analytical models based on classical mathematical principles. These models have been used to amplify human intuition about the way our world works. Computer models have frequently been seen as a poor substitute, a tool for determining approximate solutions to intractable analytical models.

Yet there is another side to this story. In analytical modeling, as well as in computer modeling used as an approximation tool, systems are typically represented from a God's-Eye View (GEV). The mathematician or programmer presides over the modeled world like some form of Laplace's demon, able in principle to discern the entire course of world events based on a complete understanding of the initial state of the world as well as its laws of motion.

Recently, however, it has been proven that Laplace was wrong to claim the future can be predicted without error given sufficient knowledge of the present, even in a classical non-chaotic universe (Binder, 2008; Wolpert, 2008). The capabilities of physical inference devices are inherently limited, not because of chaotic dynamics or quantum mechanical indeterminism, but rather due to a 'Cantor diagonalization' demonstration that at least some portion of knowledge will always remain unavailable to any one inference device.

Constructive mathematics is well-matched to this reality because it relies solely upon a Local-Observer View (LOV). The data that a constructive mathematician can acquire about a system is limited to what the mathematician can obtain by means of computations.[5] As developed by Errett Bishop, constructive mathematics is based on intuitionistic logic (Bridges, 1999), a deductive system[6] $\mathcal{D}$ that does not include the law of the excluded middle ($P \wedge \neg P$) among its rules of inference. Intuitionistic logic permits three logical possibilities for a proposition: true, false, or undecidable. A proposition is true (or false) relative to $\mathcal{D}$ if its truth (or falsity) can be established by a computation within $\mathcal{D}$. A proposition whose truth or falsity cannot be established by a computation within $\mathcal{D}$ is said to be undecidable relative to $\mathcal{D}$. In addition, the logical status of a proposition can be open relative to $\mathcal{D}$ in the sense that its classification within $\mathcal{D}$ has not been established. The uncountably large class of undecidable and open propositions (problems) relative to $\mathcal{D}$ dominates the attention of many current constructive mathematicians (Ambos-Spies and Fejer, 2006).

ABM supports an LOV modeling approach in the sense that the 'reality' of each ABM agent is confined to the network of agents within which it interacts. An ABM agent starts with a configuration of data and methods constituting its initial understanding of its world. The agent can then migrate from one part of its world to another, redefining its locality within this world by adding and deleting links with other agents; yet it is always restricted to interactions with other agents only one link away. Communication in ABM is thus a percolation process, and it is only through such percolation processes that new data about the world are acquired and global properties emerge.

On the other hand, although ABM agents acquire new data constructively through interactions, they can be configured so that portions of their initial data represent GEV (uncomputable) assertions about their world. They can also believe GEV assertions communicated to them by other agents, and they can have methods for interpreting data that entail the use of non-constructive deductions (for example, proof by contradiction). Thus, as is true for real people, the content and timing of the constructive actions that ABM agents take within their world can be influenced by uncomputable beliefs.

11.4.2 Time and Asynchronicity in ABM

An important theoretical and practical concern for ABM researchers is how to specify the relative timing of agent interactions and the methods by which agents update their internal states based on these interactions. Careless treatments of these timing issues can induce undesirable artifacts in simulation outcomes, hide important potential system behaviors, and even result in a complete inability to generate empirically relevant results (Axtell, 2001; Newth and Cornforth, 2009; Tosic, 2005).

In particular, considerable care must be exercised when running ABM simulations on conventional computer architectures – for example, on existing high performance computing (HPC) platforms – or even on commodity (multiple-vendor open-standard) hardware platforms that use a non-uniform memory architecture (NUMA). These basic computer hardware configurations can impose hidden constraints on temporal relationships among agents that a modeler does not intend, beyond simple variations in the behavior of the cache/memory hierarchy from one simulation run to the next.

For example, key areas of a computing infrastructure in which unintended distributed simultaneity assumptions can arise include: pre-emptive schedulers in the operating system when running multiple processes on a single processor; multithreading within each process; communication through a shared memory bus on a symmetric multiprocessor; a common clock driving multiple cores at once on the same chip; and a single isochronous global clock in a single-instruction multiple-data (SIMD) graphic processing unit used for agent modeling in an array. If this listing leaves the reader with the impression that it is almost impossible not to have some potentially problematic simultaneity assumptions lurking somewhere in their computational infrastructure, then a crucial point will have been effectively conveyed.

More fundamentally, resolution of timing issues forces ABM researchers to think deeply about the nature of the reality they are supposedly modeling. Conventional modeling of dynamical systems is frequently based on an implicit assumption that there exists a global (absolute or Newtonian) clock. This clock permits the perfectly synchronized updating of all components of the system state vector at each successive time step, where a time step is represented as an instant or interval along a real time line. The empirical artificiality of global clocks permitting perfect synchronization is abundantly clear. Most real systems are massively asynchronous in nature, and any implied simultaneity across distributed systems has long since been proven false in physics. Yet to what extent, and in what manner, should ABM researchers work to achieve a more empirically compelling modeling of time and true asynchronicity?

Unfortunately, even the best available theories from physicists (Barbour, 2001, 2009; Markopoulou, 2000; Rovelli, 2008; Smolin, 2002) and philosophers (Markosian, 2010; Price, 1996) provide little definitive insight into the nature of time; like the quantum measurement problem, it continues to be an enigma. Computer scientists appear to be even further behind in their understanding, typically endorsing a pre-relativistic and pre-quantum Newtonian concept of a background time (Herlihy and Shavit, 2008, Ch. 2.1).

This leaves ABM researchers with a conundrum. If the computer platforms available for ABM simulations, as well as the very theoretical foundations on which ABM simulations are built, embody empirically questionable notions of time and simultaneity, what can an ABM researcher do?

This is where the fundamental role of 'interactions' in ABM comes into play. Each ABM agent can have an entirely independent sense of time that bears no relation to the flow or passage of time perceived by other agents. Nevertheless, the agents can still experience 'change' as a result of the interactions between them, and they can observe an ordering of events (generally unique to each observer). The changes experienced by each agent can be accumulated in the information retained by the agent, and also in the instrumentation provided to observe and record system outcomes.

In particular, running ABMs as genuinely asynchronous interactive systems could permit them to reflect the forms of self-synchronization observed in many natural phenomena (Strogatz, 2003) and in spatial game situations (Newth and Cornforth, 2009). For example, consider an ABM consisting of a collection of fully independent agents in a weakly asynchronous interaction network. It might be utterly intractable to 'synchronously' explore the random sequential execution of agents with anything but a coarse resolution in time: imagine a 100 microsecond primary cycle, and consider how long it would take to explore combinatorial alternatives down to a 1 microsecond or even a 1 nanosecond resolution. However, running the ABM as a genuinely asynchronous simulation might permit self-synchronization to arise as a natural temporal phenomenon rather than as an artifact of a synchronous straight-jacket imposed to simplify implementation at the expense of empirical fidelity. Genuinely asynchronous modeling remains an important research topic for ABM researchers (Tosic, 2005).

In summary, the explicit and implicit restrictions on timing and updating in the implementation of ABMs should be brought to the fore in the analysis and publication of ABM research results. This would permit peer researchers to examine the robustness of reported outcomes to seemingly inconsequential changes in these restrictions.

11.4.3 Simple or Complex Modeling of Human Behaviors?

A scientific model should be a condensed representation of some phenomenon: as simple as possible but no simpler. By stripping away unnecessary details, the modeler seeks to identify the salient conditions that enable the model to faithfully reflect the phenomenon under investigation. Stripping away superfluous detail allows the modeler to expose deeper principles driving the observed outcomes.

For descriptive studies, two approaches can be distinguished. The first approach is to start with simple behaviors, adding more complex behaviors only as needed to explain an observed regularity. The second approach is to start with the types of complex behaviors observed in natural settings, field experiments, or human-subject laboratory experiments, and then to progressively simplify the behaviors until the ability to generate an observed regularity is lost.

On the other hand, normative (goal-oriented) studies require different considerations. For such studies, agent behavior becomes an experimental treatment factor rather than a descriptive representation.

For example, suppose the goal is robust system performance. A researcher will then need to examine system performance under a wide range of possible scenarios, including stress-tests involving low-probability events having highly adverse social impacts. Ideally, the agent representation of human behavior under these alternative scenarios should span the full range of possibilities. What if people respond calmly? What if they panic? Moreover, what might be the longer-term effects on system performance if people learn from their experiences and modify their future behaviors?

Alternatively, suppose the goal is successful individual performance within a specified system setting. A researcher will then need to conduct a series of 'what if' experiments involving alternative individual strategies, possibly including newly envisioned strategies never before tried in practice. Moreover, these individual strategies might have to involve learning and even learning-to-learn aspects to permit flexible response to the possible behaviors of other system participants.

In view of these considerations, ABM researchers are exploring a wide range of behavioral and learning specifications for the agents included in their models (Tesfatsion, 2010e). These specifications take into account the behaviors actually observed in field and lab studies, but they also permit the study of new kinds of behaviors potentially suitable for achieving variously specified goals.

11.5   IS ABM THE RIGHT MATHEMATICS FOR THE PHYSICAL SCIENCES?

The traditional goal of physics has been to explain properties of matter that are relatively free of historical contingency (Farmer et al., 2005). The greatest scientific achievements of physicists have involved issues arising in the very large (gravity and cosmology) and in the very small (quantum level). 'Observers' in these two extreme realms measure and assign states to the systems they observe. However, these observers have traditionally been interpreted as external moving spatial frames of reference rather than any form of conscious being localized in some space.

The social sciences occupy a middle ground between these two extreme realms. Social scientists, by definition, must address the problem of human interaction impinging on world events. These interactions leave traces on the human interactors themselves, changing their memories, their knowledge, their future interaction patterns, and their expressed behaviors in these future interactions. In consequence, social systems are intrinsically heterogeneous and path-dependent. This has led some physical scientists to question the scientific status of the social 'sciences'.

Nevertheless, many physicists have expressed the belief that physics cannot be considered complete until it provides a unified theory that encompasses all of nature, from general relativity to quantum physics. Understanding a natural world such as ours – a world that contains living entities – would require confronting the difficulties posed by having multiple observers imbedded within this world whose measurements are necessarily local and relative to each other and whose interactions can potentially alter its dynamic course.

In particular, physicists recognize the observer-dependent nature of cosmological knowledge (Döring and Isham, 2010; Markopoulou, 2000; Smolin, 2002). For example, Smolin (2002, p. 32) writes:

> we should not be surprised if both cosmology and social theory point us in the same direction. They are the two sciences that cannot be formulated sensibly unless we build into their foundations the simple fact that all possible observers are inside the system they study.

Also, recent developments in quantum physics have focused on the modeling of interactions (information exchange) among relative entities rather than the measurement of absolute physical properties by some omniscient observer. In particular, according to the recently developed theory of relational quantum mechanics (RQM) there are no observer-independent states (Rovelli, 1996). The distinctions between observer and observed, and between cause and effect, are replaced by a symmetric notion of mutual observers interacting with each other and leaving behind their informational footprint as irreversible processes that dissipate energy when information is erased.

RQM thus interprets quantum mechanics to be a theory describing the information one system can have about another, acquired only through interactions, rather than a theory providing a GEV perspective on the physical states of systems (Smerlak, 2006; van Fraassen, 2010). A further implication of RQM is insight into the non-commutative matrix mechanics characteristic of quantum theory, which implies that the order of events defines the reality of what is measured. In RQM, the history (or order of events) measured by each observer creates the reality that this observer perceives as the evolution of the system.

These developments in physics support a key concept that appears to be mirrored in all of our fundamental laws of physics: there is no preferred frame of reference for any measurement. Rather, all frames are equally valid; and each observer will register a unique view of any measurement, including the order of observed events, from its own relative vantage point.

In addition, the implication of physical theories relying on 'symmetry breaking' is that the properties of even very basic physical systems can be determined in part by historical conditions. For example, remarking on the multiple low-energy states of a polymer of amino acids, Laughlin et al. (2000, section IV) note: 'The property of having such a set of low-energy states is connected with the idea of replica symmetry breaking: Different copies of the same system may well fall into different long-lived states through accidents of detailed molecular motion.'

In summary, physics shares with the social sciences an interest in understanding the complicated interactions of entities composed of more elementary entities behaving in accordance with potentially simpler rules. Physics also shares with the social sciences the need to account for multiple observers with different perspectives on reality whose measurements necessarily entail perturbative interactions with persistent (information flow) traces. Finally, physical theories based on broken symmetries suggest that systems of interest to physicists can display what social scientists refer to as 'path dependencies', that is, dependencies on historical conditions.

These aspects of physical reality are precisely the kind of complexity that ABM tools and ABM design principles have been developed to handle. ABM permits the modeling of asynchronous interactions among heterogeneous hierarchically nested agents, each operating in terms of its own local coordinate system. Each ABM agent acquires data about its world through interactions with other agents and uses these data to build and maintain a coherent picture of a world centered about itself.

The question then arises whether the modeling problems faced by physicists attempting to derive unified theories of nature are in fact all that different from the modeling problems faced by social scientists. If not, ABM methods now being adopted for social science research might ultimately have a fundamental role to play within a larger scientific realm.

11.6   TWO ILLUSTRATIVE ABM APPLICATIONS

11.6.1   Overview

This section briefly describes two ABM applications to illustrate concretely the dual ability of ABM to both simulate and synthesize real-world systems. The first application involves the development and use of an ABM testbed for the performance evaluation of restructured wholesale power markets. The second application involves the use of ABM design principles to develop a new type of architecture for the storage and management of information.

11.6.2   Electricity Market Design

In 2003 the US Federal Energy Regulatory Commission (FERC) recommended the adoption of a common market design for US wholesale power markets (FERC, 2003). As indicated in Figure 11.2 and elaborated in Joskow (2006), versions of this design have been implemented (or adopted for implementation) in North American energy regions in the Midwest, New England, New York, the Mid-Atlantic States, California, the Southwest and Texas.

A core feature of FERC's design is a reliance on locational marginal pricing (LMP) to manage transmission grid congestion. Under this pricing system, the price charged to wholesale buyers and received by wholesale sellers at a particular transmission grid bus location at a particular point in time is the least cost to the system of providing an additional increment of power at that bus location at that time.

For the past several years a group of researchers at Iowa State University has been developing and using an agent-based testbed AMES (Agent-based Modeling of Electricity Systems) to explore the performance

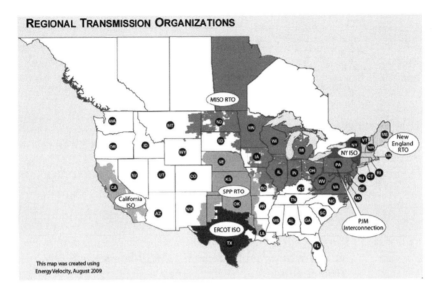

Source: www.ferc.gov/industries/electric/indus-act/rto/rto-map.asp.

Figure 11.2   North American energy regions that have adopted versions of FERC's wholesale power market design

characteristics of wholesale power markets operating under FERC's design (Tesfatsion, 2010f). As indicated in Figure 11.3 AMES models strategic trading among a dispersed collection of load-serving entities (LSEs) who bid to buy power at wholesale and generation companies (GenCos) who offer to sell power at wholesale. These trading activities take place within a two-settlement (real-time and day-ahead) energy market system administered by a not-for-profit independent system operator (ISO), with congestion managed by LMP. The power flows resulting from these trading activites are constrained by the physical characteristics of an underlying AC transmission grid.

AMES experiments have been conducted using multi-period versions of a commonly used 5-bus ISO training case and a standard 30-bus IEEE test case. Key experimental treatment factors have included GenCo learning capabilities, the form of GenCo supply offers, the price-sensitivity of LSE demand bids, and price caps imposed by the ISO for the mitigation of market power.

One experimental finding has been the relative ease with which the GenCos can learn to exercise market power through economic and physical capacity withholding, even when LSE demand bids are 100 percent

➢ **Traders**
- Buyers = Load-Serving Entities (LSEs)
- Sellers = Generating Companies (GenCos)
- Learning capabilities

➢ **Independent System Operator (ISO)**
- Day-ahead hourly scheduling via bid/offer-based DC optimal power flow (OPF)
- System reliability assessments

➢ **Two-settlement process**
- Day-ahead energy market (double auction, financial contracts)
- Real-time energy market (settlement of differences)

➢ **AC transmission grid**
- LSEs and GenCos located at various buses across the grid
- Congestion managed via locational marginal pricing (LMP)

Figure 11.3   *Core features of FERC's wholesale power market design that have been incorporated into the AMES Wholesale Power Market Testbed*

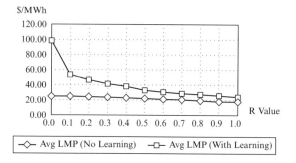

Figure 11.4   *Average LMP outcomes on day 1000 for the 5-bus test case with and without GenCo learning as the price-sensitivity of demand varies from 0% (R = 0.0) to 100% (R = 1.0)*

price sensitive (Li et al., 2010). As seen in Figure 11.4, this capacity with-holding results in a rise in LMP levels that is particularly dramatic for treatments in which the price-sensitivity of demand is low.

Another experimental finding involves 'ISO net surplus' collections in day-ahead energy markets (Li and Tesfatsion, 2011). ISO net surplus is determined each hour as the difference between the LMP payments received by the ISO from energy buyers (the LSEs) and the LMP pay-ments distributed by the ISO to energy sellers (the GenCos). Congestion arising on a transmission grid in any hour necessarily results in separation

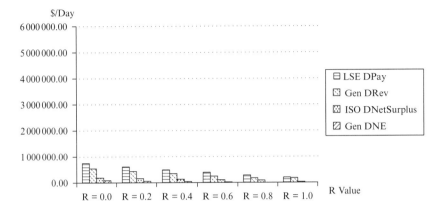

Figure 11.5   *No-Learning Treatment: LSE payments, GenCo revenues, ISO net surplus, and GenCo net earnings on day 1000 for the benchmark (no learning) 5-bus test case as the price-sensitivity of demand varies from 0% (R = 0.0) to 100% (R = 1.0)*

between the LMPs at two or more transmission grid bus locations, which in turn necessarily results in a non-negative ISO net surplus collection for that hour.

As indicated by the experimental findings reported in Figures 11.5 and 11.6, ISO net surplus and GenCo net earnings are simultaneously enhanced in circumstances unfavorable to market efficiency: namely, when demand exhibits low price sensitivity and GenCos have learning capabilities permitting them to exploit this lack of price sensitivity. The truly surprising finding here is just how substantial the net surplus collections of the not-for-profit ISO can be in these circumstances: similar in size to GenCo net earnings, and in some cases even exceeding GenCo net earnings.

Empirical investigations confirm that ISO net surplus collections in actual North American energy regions operating under LMP can indeed be substantial (Li and Tesfatsion, 2011). For example, in 2008 these ISO net surplus collections ranged from US$121 million in New England (ISO-NE) to US$2.66 billion in the Mid-Atlantic States (PJM).

11.6.3   Agent-Based Storage and Management of Information

A real-world example where ABM principles enable a dramatic simplification in system design is in the storage and management of information (Borrill, 2005).

Enterprise information storage systems have traditionally been designed

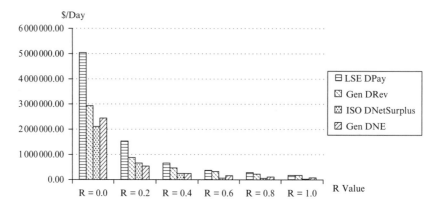

*Figure 11.6   Learning Treatment: average LSE payments, GenCo
revenues, ISO net surplus, and GenCo net earnings on day
1000 for the 5-bus test case with GenCo learning as the price-
sensitivity of demand varies from 0% (R = 0.0) to 100% (R
= 1.0)*

in a top-down manner by a human architect. This architect receives inputs
in the form of system requirements, feasible technologies, and available products, from which a 'blueprint' is created and presented to an
information technology (IT) team for implementation.

Unfortunately we have now gone far beyond the ability of any individual expert or expert team to anticipate the evolving information storage
requirements of a dynamic enterprise. As illustrated in Figure 11.7, this
has led in practice to the need to incrementally overlay existing storage
systems with new functions, resulting in unwieldy and inefficient systems
with hard-to-predict performance characteristics and brittle response to
perturbations (failures, disasters, attacks).

The result is an ongoing complexity crisis in the storage and IT industries. Chief information officers are frequently trapped between a rock and
a hard place. They are compelled to employ and train an ever-increasing
number of IT administrators to manage the overall operation of the
many disparate subsystems comprising their information storage systems.
Because of the centralized design of these systems, the administrators are
naturally seduced into managing such systems from a single 'crow's nest'
perspective, a tactic popularly referred to as 'all behind one pane of glass'.
The similarity between this centralized management design, the 'client-
server' architectural style of most software engineers, and the God's-Eye
View (GEV) adopted in traditional systems modeling, is not coincidental.

The resulting price in complexity paid by this GEV design practice

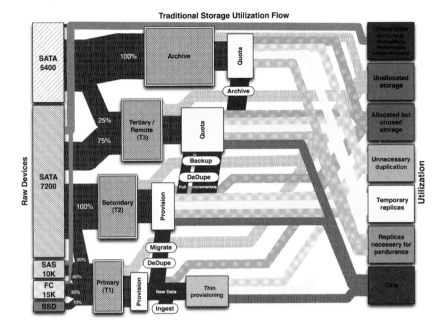

Note: Raw resources on the left (storage devices) are utilized by subsystems that manage primary, secondary, tertiary and archival storage by means of various discrete functions that tend to be poorly integrated. Resulting resource utilization is shown on the right.

Figure 11.7   A traditional enterprise information storage system

shows up when we try to scale these systems. Scaling increases the number, connectivity, and diversity of a system's elements, and results in cognitive overload for the administrators in the crow's nest whenever a non-routine failure or error occurs. This is particularly apparent during crises, such as equipment failures, natural disasters, and criminal or terrorist attacks (both physical and cyber).

A common defensive tactic has been to ensure there is only 'one throat to choke', meaning that a single vendor is made responsible for the entire information-storage operation in order to eliminate finger-pointing when things inevitably go wrong. However, this tactic involves major risk because the vendor is then in a monopoly position relative to the enterprise; it can dictate prices for its services and products, and it can take its time when developing needed upgrades, because the enterprise is a captive customer.

What this traditional approach to information storage has done, in effect, is to build human administrators into the systems while at the same time reducing their achievable reliability. Human beings are notoriously error-prone and often induce failure modes by their own inadvertent actions. Human beings are also bandwidth limited; they have limited cognitive ability to respond appropriately to large system perturbations occurring in short periods of time. Traditional information storage systems are thus prone to disaster, and recovery from these disasters – particularly for large systems – has proven to be very complex and time-consuming. Moreover, recovery can involve significant collateral damage to the businesses involved as well as to the local economy as commercial operations are curtailed until these and other IT systems are restored to their intended state of operation.

A primary motivation for considering the redesign of traditional information storage systems has been to find a way to dramatically reduce the time to recover these systems after a disaster. Recognizing that information storage systems inevitably evolve into complex systems encompassing many distributed interacting subsystems, researchers have converged on an alternative architecture based on ABM design principles to address the many 'wicked' problems that occur in such environments (Borrill, 2008).

This alternative ABM-based information storage system architecture is schematically depicted in Figure 11.8. The architecture operates in a manner similar to a 'network automaton' (Smith et al., 2009) in which resources grow and migrate as needed through an evolving network, driven by nearest-neighbor rendezvous and interactions. For the storage system, the individual (autonomous, encapsulated) storage cells represent the deployed units of hardware. Initially these storage cells are identical and substitutable. The system then auto-configures; storage cells form nearest-neighbor relationships with their peers and recursively build (and continue to evolve) the network topology. Given this physical infrastructure, it becomes trivial to deploy storage objects (files) over the infrastructure that are each treated as an agent – that is, as an abstract storage object encapsulating data, metadata and if–then rules for (meta)data disposition conditional on the occurrence of certain events. Examples of such storage objects include regular files, virtual machine images, databases, and media such as pictures or movies.

The agents (storage objects) in the resulting ABM-based information storage system can freely roam, replicate and evaporate down to some specifiable minimum number able to guarantee data persistence in the face of system perturbations. The relationship of an abstract file agent to its dynamically evolving set of peer replicas enables the ABM to respond in ways that no programmer or administrator would ever have the time, attention or ingenuity to invent. Moreover, while the underlying methods that drive agent interactions can be exceedingly simple (ingest, push, pull,

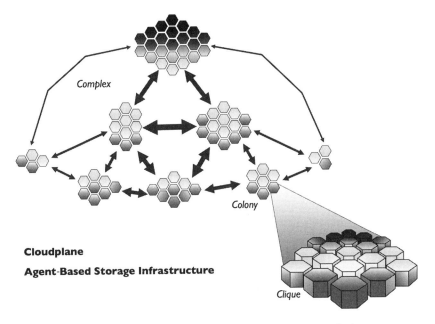

Note: The resulting system has a substantially simpler architecture yet displays greater robustness to perturbations and greater adaptivity to the evolving needs of geographically dispersed human users. The heatmap expresses one form of emergent behavior, namely, the most recently used data remain at the front of the network while the least recently used data migrate to the rear of the network.

Figure 11.8   An enterprise information storage system based on ABM design principles

evaporate), they can also produce rich examples of emergent behaviors. For example, as indicated by the heatmap depiction in Figure 11.8, data can migrate automatically across a system's resources (even if geographically distributed) on the basis of latest time of use, resulting in the creation of a self-tiered network.

Another advantage of information storage systems built in accordance with ABM principles is that their relatively simple architecture facilitates performance testing under normal lifecycle-management scenarios as well as under emergency disaster-recovery scenarios. In particular, it is relatively straightforward to copy the real system configuration into an ABM simulator that models the same resources, agents and network topology (extracted from instrumentation in the real system), using the same rules as the real system.

This simulator can then be used to conduct various 'what-if' experiments that would be prohibitively expensive or disruptive to carry out on the real system. For example, the simulator might be used to investigate the direct effects of system disturbances on bandwidth, capacity and recovery time, and to provide guidance for improving the robustness of the system against such disturbances. It might also be used to improve system efficiency by identifying ways to reduce connectivity or resource usage while at the same time maintaining essentially the same service capabilities at levels visible to human users.

Furthermore, disaster preparedness in personnel training, emergency procedure planning and other social phenomena under disaster scenarios could easily be built into the simulation. This would permit the testing of personnel responses to unusual events, including their necessary interactions with the data storage system as they initially evacuate their posts and as they later return to these posts to reinstate service to their customers.

11.7   CONCLUSION

This chapter has taken readers on a brief guided tour of ABM. Although applicability for the social sciences has been stressed, we have also touched on intriguing connections with ongoing methodological developments in constructive mathematics, computability theory, cosmology, and quantum physics.

It is perhaps unsettling to realize that the foundations of all of these disciplines are currently in ferment. The uncomfortable truth is that our universe is not the perfectly ordered and deterministic place envisioned by Laplace and Hilbert but the rich, unruly and largely uncomputable world of Kurt Gödel, Alonzo Church, Alan Turing, Errett Bishop and David Deutsch. What a wondrous development it would be if a methodology such as ABM, specifically designed for the study of complex interactive systems, were to enable common light to be shed across these seemingly disparate disciplines.

ACKNOWLEDGMENTS

The authors thank Rob Axtell, Julian Barbour, Daniel Goroff, Matheus Grasselli, Fotini Markopoulou, Simone Severini and Lee Smolin for insightful discussions and kind generosity in responding to questions. The collaboration of Michael Honig and Kenneth Steiglitz on Figure 11.1 is also gratefully acknowledged.

NOTES

1. Detailed discussions of the ABM methodology in relation to the social sciences can be found in Epstein (2006), Gilbert (2007), Macy and Willer (2002) and Tesfatsion and Judd (2006). Annotated pointers to online ABM readings, research groups and software resources can be found in Axelrod and Tesfatsion (2010) and Tesfatsion (2010a).
2. Object-oriented programming (OOP) represents 'objects' as encapsulated bundles of data and methods. ABMs are now commonly implemented either directly in OOP languages or by means of toolkits based on OOP languages. Nevertheless, the current structure of these languages is overly rigid for many ABM purposes in terms of the permitted forms of encapsulation, distribution, interagent communication and the envisioned degree of object autonomy (Jennings, 2000). Although work-arounds are possible, ABM researchers would surely benefit from having a 'new kind of programming' built from scratch with greater input from social scientists. Indeed, many initiatives along these lines are already under way (Tesfatsion, 2010b).
3. Alternatively, 'true' random data can be streamed directly into ABM experiments in place of PRNG-generated data, a possibility that raises interesting philosophical questions.
4. Cloud computing is Internet-based computing. Cloudbursting permits a computational load to expand dynamically into additional resources in other private or public clouds as needed.
5. According to Soare (1996), 'a *computation* is a process whereby we proceed from initially given objects, called inputs, according to a fixed set of rules, called a program, procedure, or algorithm, through a series of steps and arrive at the end of these steps with a final result, called the output'.
6. Given a formal language $\mathscr{L}$ consisting of formulas (propositions) well-constructed in accordance with some prescribed syntax, a deductive system expressed in $\mathscr{L}$ consists of axioms $L \subseteq \mathscr{L}$ together with a set of binary relations (rules of inference) on L that can be used to derive the theorems (conclusions) of the system (Dalen, 2008).

REFERENCES

Albert, Réka and Albert-László Barabási (2002), 'Statistical Mechanics of Complex Networks', *Reviews of Modern Physics*, **74** (January), 47–97.

Ambos-Spies, Klaus and Peter A. Fejer (2006), 'Degrees of Unsolvability', Unpublished Manuscript, March.

Axelrod, Robert and Leigh Tesfatsion (2010), *On-Line Guide for Newcomers to Agent-Based Modeling in the Social Sciences*, www.econ.iastate.edu/tesfatsi/abmread.htm.

Axtell, Robert L. (2001), 'Effects of Interaction Topology and Activation Regime in Several Multi-Agent Systems', in Scott Moss and Paul Davidsson (eds), *Multi-Agent Based Simulation*, Lecture Notes in Computer Science, Volume 1979/2001, Berlin/Heidelberg: Springer-Verlag, pp. 33–48.

Axtell, Robert L. (2003), 'Economics as Distributed Computation', in Hiroshi Deguchi, Keiki Takadama and Takao Terano (eds), *Meeting the Challenge of Social Problems via Agent-Based Simulation*, Tokyo: Springer, pp. 3–23.

Barbour, Julian (2001), *The End of Time: The Next Revolution in Physics*, Oxford, UK: Oxford University Press.

Barbour, Julian (2009), *The Nature of Time*, March. http://arxiv.org/abs/0903.3489.

Barr, Jason M., Troy Tassier, Leanne J. Ussher, Blake LeBaron, Shu-Heng Chen and Shyam Sunder (2008), 'The Future of Agent-Based Research in Economics: A Panel Discussion', *Eastern Economic Journal*, **34**, 550–565.

Batty, Michael (2005), *Cities and Complexity: Understanding Cities with Cellular Automata, Agent-Based Models, and Fractals*, Cambridge, MA: MIT Press.

Binder, Philippe (2008), 'Theories of Almost Everything', *Nature*, **455**, 884–885.
Borrill, Paul (2005), 'Autopoietic File Systems: From Architectural Theory to Practical Implications', Vanguard Conference, San Francisco, CA, January.
Borrill, Paul (2008), 'Smart Data and Wicked Problems,' Vanguard Conference, Atlanta, February, http://www.replicus.com/.
Bridges, Douglas (2009), 'Constructive Mathematics', *The Stanford Encyclopedia of Philosophy*, Summer 2009 edn, Edward N. Zalta (ed.), plato.stanford.edu/archives/sum2009/entries/mathematics-constructive.
Bridges, Douglas (1999), 'Constructive Mathematics: A Foundation for Computable Analysis', *Theoretical Computer Science*, **219**, 95–109.
Chang, Myong-Hun, and Joseph E. Harrington, Jr. (2006), 'Agent-Based Models of Organizations', in Leigh Tesfatsion and Kenneth L. Judd (eds), *Handbook of Computational Economics: Volume 2, Agent-Based Computational Economics*, Handbooks in Economics Series, Amsterdam: North-Holland/Elsevier, pp. 1273–1337.
Chen, Shu-Heng and Bin-Tzong Chie (2007), 'Modularity, Product Innovation, and Consumer Satisfaction: An Agent-Based Approach', in Hujun Yin, Peter Tino, Emilio Corchado, Will Bryne and Xin Yao (eds), *Intelligent Data Engineering and Automated Learning – IDEAL 2007*, Berlin/Heidelberg: Springer-Verlag, pp. 1053–1062.
Cioppa, Thomas M., Thomas W. Lucas and Susan M. Sanchez (2004), 'Military Applications of Agent-Based Simulations', *Proceedings of the 36th Winter Simulation Conference*, New Orleans, LA, pp. 171–180.
Dalen, Dirk (2008), *Logic and Structure*, 4th edn, Berlin/Heidelberg, Springer-Verlag.
Darema, Frederica (2005), 'Grid Computing and Beyond: The Context of Dynamic Data Driven Applications Systems', *Proceedings of the IEEE: Special Issue on Grid Computing*, **93**(3), 692–697.
Dawid, Herbert (2006), 'Agent-Based Models of Innovation and Technological Change', in Leigh Tesfatsion and Kenneth L. Judd (eds), *op. cit.*, pp. 1235–1272.
Devaney, Robert L. and Linda Keen (eds), (1989), *Chaos and Fractals: The Mathematics Behind the Computer Graphics*, Providence, RI: American Mathematical Society.
Döring, Andreas and Chris J. Isham (2010), '"What is a Thing?": Topos Theory in the Foundations of Physics', in Robert Coecke (ed.), *New Structures for Physics*, Lecture Notes in Physics, Vol. 813, Heidelberg: Springer, pp. 753–941.
Eberbach, Eugene, Dina Goldin and Peter Wegner (2004), 'Turing's Ideas and Models of Computation', in Christof Teuscher (ed.), *Alan Turing: Life and Legacy of a Great Thinker*, Berlin/Heidelberg: Springer-Verlag, pp. 159–194.
Epstein, Joshua M. (2006), *Generative Social Science: Studies in Agent-Based Computational Modeling*, Princeton, NJ: Princeton University Press.
Farmer, J. Doyne, Martin Shubik and Eric Smith (2005), 'Economics: The Next Physical Science?', *Physics Today*, September, 37–42.
FERC (2003), *Notice of White Paper*, US Federal Energy Regulatory Commission, Washington, DC, April.
Gilbert, Nigel (2007), *Agent-Based Models*, Quantitative Applications in the Social Sciences, Vol. 153, London: SAGE Publications.
Gilbert, Nigel, Andreas Pyka and Petra Ahrweiler (2001), 'Innovation Networks – A Simulation Approach', *Journal of Artificial Societies and Social Simulation*, **4**(3), www.soc.surrey.ac.uk/JASSS/4/3/8.html.
Goldin, Dina Q., Scott A. Smolka and Peter Wegner (eds), (2006), *Interactive Computation: The New Paradigm*, Berlin/Heidelberg: Springer-Verlag.
Grimm, Volker and Steven R. Railsback (2005), *Individual-Based Modeling and Ecology*, Princeton, NJ: Princeton University Press.
Herlihy, Maurice and Nir Shavit (2008), *The Art of Multiprocessor Programming*, Burlington, MA: Morgan Kaufmann.
Huang, Jun, Nick R. Jennings and John Fox (1995), 'An Agent-Based Approach to Health Care Management', *Applied Artificial Intelligence*, **9**(4), 401–420.

Jennings, Nicholas R. (2000), 'On Agent-Based Software Engineering', *Artificial Intelligence*, **117**, 277–296.

Joskow, Paul (2006), 'Markets for Power in the United States: An Interim Assessment', *Energy Journal*, **27**(1), 1–36.

Laubenbacher, Reinhard, Abdul S. Jarrah, Henning Mortveit and S.S. Ravi (2009), 'A Mathematical Formalism for Agent-Based Modeling', in Robert A. Meyers (ed.), *Encyclopedia of Complexity and Systems Science*, Berlin/Heidelberg: Springer-Verlag, pp. 160–176.

Laughlin, Robert B., and David Pines (2000), 'The Theory of Everything', *Proceedings of the National Academy of Sciences, USA*, **97**(1), 28–31, http://www.pnas.org/content/97/1/28. abstract.

Laughlin, Robert B., David Pines, Joerg Schmalian, Branko P. Stojković and Peter Wolynes (2000), 'The Middle Way', *Proceedings of the National Academy of Sciences, USA*, **97**(1), 32–37.

LeBaron, Blake and Leigh Tesfatsion (2008), 'Modeling Macroeconomies as Open-Ended Dynamic Systems of Interacting Agents', *American Economic Review Papers and Proceedings*, **98**(2), 246–250.

Li, Hongyan, Junjie Sun and Leigh Tesfatsion (2010), 'Testing Institutional Arrangements via Agent-Based Modeling: A US Electricity Market Application', in Herbert Dawid and Willi Semmler (eds), *Computational Methods in Economic Dynamics*, Berlin/Heidelberg: Springer-Verlag, pp. 135–58.

Li, Hongyan and Leigh Tesfatsion (2011), 'ISO Net Surplus Collection and Allocation in Wholesale Power Markets under Locational Marginal Pricing', *IEEE Transactions on Power Systems*, **26**(2), 627–641.

MacLane, Saunders (1998), *Categories for the Working Mathematician*, 2nd edn, New York, NY: Springer-Verlag.

Macy, Michael W. and Robert Willer (2002), 'From Factors to Actors: Computational Sociology and Agent-Based Modeling', *Annual Review of Sociology*, **28**, 143–166.

Markopoulou, Fotini (2000), 'The Internal Description of a Causal Set: What the Universe Looks Like from the Inside', *Communications in Mathematical Physics*, **211**(3), 559–583, http://arxiv.org/abs/gr-qc/9811053.

Markosian, Ned (2010), 'Time', Stanford Encyclopedia of Philosophy, http://plato.stanford. edu/entries/time/.

Nagel, Kai and Peter Wagner (2006), *Traffic Flow: Approaches to Modelling and Control*, New York: John Wiley & Sons.

Newth, David and David Cornforth (2009), 'Asynchronous Spatial Evolutionary Games', *BioSystems*, **95**(2), 120–129, http://www.ncbi.nlm.nih.gov/pubmed/18926874.

Parker, Dawn C., Steven M. Manson, Marco A. Janssen, Matthew J. Hoffman and Peter Deadman (2003), 'Multi-Agent Systems for the Simulation of Land-Use and Land-Cover Change: A Review', *Annals of the Association of American Geographers*, **93**(2), 314–337.

Prasse, Michael and Peter Rittgen (1998), 'Why Church's Thesis Still Holds: Some Notes on Peter Wegner's Tracts on Interaction and Computability', *Computer Journal*, **41**, 357–362.

Price, Hew (1996), *Time's Arrow & Archimedes' Point*, Oxford: Oxford University Press, http://www.usyd.edu.au/time/price/TAAP.html.

Rovelli, Carlo (1996), 'Relational Quantum Mechanics', *International Journal of Theoretical Physics*, **35**, 1637–1678.

Rovelli, Carlo (2008), 'Forget Time', http://www.fqxi.org/community/forum/topic/237.

Smerlak, Matteo (2006), 'Relational Quantum Mechanics', Internship Report, Ecole normale supérieure de Lyon, 17 September.

Smith, Adam (1776), *An Inquiry into the Nature and Causes of the Wealth of Nations*, reprinted (1976) in William B. Todd (ed.), Glasgow Edition of the Works and Correspondence of Adam Smith, Vol. 1, Oxford: Oxford University Press.

Smith, David M.D., Jukka-Pekka Onnela, Chiu Fan Lee, Mark Fricker and Neil F. Johnson (2009), 'Network Automata: Coupling Structure and Function in Real-World Networks', arXiv:physics/0701307v3[physics.soc-ph].

Smolin, Lee (2002), *Three Roads to Quantum Gravity*, New York: Basic Books.
Soare, Robert I. (1996), 'Computability and Recursion', *Bulletin of Symbolic Logic*, **2**, 284–321.
Strogatz, Steven (2003), *Sync: The Emerging Science of Spontaneous Order*, 1st edn, New York: Hyperion.
Tesfatsion, Leigh and Kenneth L. Judd (eds), (2006), *Handbook of Computational Economics: Volume 2, Agent-Based Computational Economics*, Handbooks in Economics Series, Amsterdam: North-Holland/Elsevier.
Tesfation, Leigh (2010a), *Agent-Based Computational Economics (ACE) Homepage*, www.econ.iastate.edu/tesfatsi/ace.htm.
Tesfation, Leigh (2010b), *ACE/CAS General Software and Toolkits*, www.econ.iastate.edu/tesfatsi/acecode.htm.
Tesfation, Leigh (2010c), *Verification and Empirical Validation of Agent-Based Computational Models*, www.econ.iastate.edu/tesfatsi/EmpValid.htm.
Tesfation, Leigh (2010d), *Agent-Based Computational Economics: Key Application Areas*, www.econ.iastate.edu/tesfatsi/aapplic.htm.
Tesfatsion, Leigh (2010e), *Agent-Based Computational Economics Research Area: Learning and the Embodied Mind*, http://www.econ.iastate.edu/tesfatsi/aemind.htm.
Tesfatsion, Leigh (2010f), *AMES Wholesale Power Market Testbed Homepage*, www.econ.iastate.edu/tesfatsi/AMESMarketHome.htm.
Tosic, Predrag T. (2005), 'Cellular Automata for Distributed Computing: Models of Agent Interaction and Their Implications', *IEEE Transactions on Systems, Man and Cybernetics*, **4**, 3204–3209.
van Fraassen, Bas C. (2010), 'Rovelli's World', *Foundations of Physics*, **40**(4), 390–417.
Velupillai, K. Vela (2010), *Computable Foundations for Economics*, New York: Routledge.
von Hayek, Friedrich A. (1948), *Individualism and Economic Order*, Chicago, IL: University of Chicago Press.
von Neumann, John (1951), 'The General and Logical Theory of Automata', in Lloyd A. Jeffress (ed.), *Cerebral Mechanisms in Behavior – The Hixon Symposium*, New York: John Wiley & Sons, pp. 1–41.
Wolfram, Stephen (2002), *A New Kind of Science*, Champaign, IL: Wolfram Media.
Wolpert, David H. (2008), 'Physical Limits of Inference', *Physica D*, **237**, 1257–1281.

12 Computing in economics
K. Vela Velupillai and Stefano Zambelli

12.1 A PREAMBLE

> Computing is integral to science – not just as a tool for analyzing data, but as *an agent of thought and discovery*. (Denning, 2010, p. 369, italics added)

No one economist – although he was more than just an economist – considered, modelled and implemented the idea of 'computing . . . as an agent of thought and discovery' better or more systematically, in human problem solving, organization theory, decision making in economics, models of discovery, evolutionary dynamics, and much else of core relevance to economic theory, than Herbert Simon.[1] In these two senses computing is clearly an epistemic and epistemological agent. On the other hand, the computer is undoubtedly also a 'tool for analyzing data', an aspect precisely and perceptively characterized by Richard Stone and Alan Brown in their pioneering work on *A Computable Model of Growth*:[2]

> Our approach is quantitative because economic life is largely concerned with quantities. We use computers because they are the best means that exist for answering the questions we ask. It is our responsibility to formulate the questions and get together the data which the *computer* needs to answer them. (Stone and Brown, 1962, p.viii; italics in original)

Remarkably – though not unexpectedly, at least to us[3] – 34 years later, we find two of the undisputed pioneers of real business cycle (RBC) theory, the core constituent of the stochastic dynamic general equilibrium[4] (SDGE) model, considered one of the two dominant, frontier, 'schools' of macroeconomics, defining and asserting the meaning of a computational experiment in economics as follows (Kydland and Prescott, 1996, p. 67):

> In a computational experiment, the researcher starts by posing a well-defined *quantitative question*. Then the researcher uses both theory and measurement to construct a model economy that is a *computer representation* of a national economy . . . The researcher then calibrates the model economy so that it mimics the world along a carefully specified set of dimensions. Finally, the *computer* is used to run experiments that answer the question.

Enormous developments in the theoretical and practical technology of the computer have made a tremendous impact on economic methodology in general, but also in economic theory in particular. It must be emphasized that these references are to the digital computer. There are also analogue and hybrid computers[5] that can be harnessed for service by the economist[6] – or any other analyst, in many other fields – to realize the intentions indicated by Stone and Brown, and Kydland and Prescott, as well as to act as 'an agent of thought and discovery'. Indeed, in many ways, the analogue computer should be more suitable for the purposes of the economic analysts simply because theorizing in economics is in terms of real numbers and the underpinning mathematics is, almost without exception, in terms of real analysis.[7] The seemingly simple observations above capture one of a handful of insightful visions that the ubiquity of the computer has conferred upon the intellectual adventurer in economics – in particular the epistemically oriented economist. Stone and Brown, and Kydland and Prescott seem to appeal to the raw quantitative economic analyst to respect the language and architecture of the computer in pursuing precise numerical investigations in economics.

However, as noted above, economic theorists tend to 'formulate the questions' in the language of a mathematics that the digital computer does not understand – real analysis – but 'get together the data' that it does, because the natural form in which economic data appears or is constructed is in terms of integer, natural or rational numbers. The transition between these two domains remains a proverbial black box, the interior of which is occasionally viewed, using the lenses of numerical analysis, recursion theory or constructive mathematics. With the possible exception of the core of economic theory, that is, general equilibrium theory, in its incarnation as computable general equilibrium (CGE) theory, and the newer fields of computable and constructive economics, there have been no systematic attempts to develop any aspect of economics in such a way as to be consistent with the use of the computer, respecting its mathematical, numerical and, hence, also its epistemological – 'as an agent of thought and discovery' – constraints.

Somewhat surprisingly, the adherents and aficionados of Leif Johansen's classic work on *A Multi-Sectoral Study of Economic Growth* (Johansen, 1960 [1974]) claim that this was 'the first CGE model' (Dixon and Parmenter, 1996, p. 6).[8] Their rationale for this claim is the following (p. 6; last two italics, added):

[The Johansen model] was *general* in that it contained . . . cost minimizing industries and utility-maximizing household sectors . . . His model employed market *equilibrium* assumptions in the determination of prices. Finally, it was *computable* (and *applied*). It produced a *numerical*, multi-sectoral description of growth in Norway using Norwegian input-output data and estimates of household price and income elasticities derived using Frisch's . . . additive utility method.

This is an untenable claim;[9] but we will not attempt at a substantiation of our counter-claim in this chapter, reserving it for a different, more focused, exercise. Here our aim is to structure and organize the computing tradition in economics in the age of the digital computer. For this reason, we accept, *pro tempore*, this claim by Dixon and Parmenter (and like-minded economists). Yet, we cannot refrain from raising at least half an eyebrow at the notion of equating the notion of computable with numerical. This was not the equivalence that underpinned the way the Arrow–Debreu general equilibrium (ADGE) was turned into the formal, rigorous, CGE model of Scarf, which will be discussed below in section 17.4.

In note 2 we claimed that the Computable[10] Growth Model that was being developed at the Department of Applied Economics, at Cambridge, within the Cambridge Growth Project framework under the direction of Richard Stone, was one that was parallel in aims and structure to the Johansen exercise. Surely, then, this model has a claim to be a 'joint first' CGE exercise, with the Johansen MSG model (except for minor details on the way the 'price and income elasticities' were derived)? Unsurprisingly, this claim, too, has been asserted by no less an authority than Graham Pyatt (1992, p. 246; italics added):

> By the end of the [1950s], a new release of creative energies was evident with the launch of the Cambridge Growth Project . . . The central idea was to synthesize demand analysis with input–output in an exercise which paralleled the work in Norway of Leif Johansen and *can be seen in retrospect as an immediate precursor of applied or general equilibrium models.*

This claim – that the Cambridge Growth Project work 'can be seen in retrospect as an immediate precursor of applied or general equilibrium models' – is at least as untenable as the previous claim by Dixon and Parmenter (1996). Here too, we accept this (untenable) claim, *pro tempore*, for the specific purpose of the aims of this chapter. Here, too, what 'emerged' as the applied general equilibrium modelling tradition, directly down the ADGE and (Scarf) CGE line, had nothing whatsoever to do with the way the Cambridge Growth Project modelling exercise was implemented. In the Cambridge Growth Project tradition – as well as the Johansen MSG exercise – the starting points were the necessary balances intrinsic to social accounting matrices (SAM). The numerical methods that were used to iterate towards the necessary balances in a SAM did not imply the computability of the model as a whole; nor did it have anything to do with the theoretical – economic and mathematical – underpinnings in an ADGE model.

Suppose, now, we teach our students the rudiments of the mathematics of the digital computer – that is, recursion theory and constructive mathematics – simultaneously with the mathematics of general equilibrium theory – that is, real analysis. As a first, tentative, bridge between these three different kinds of mathematics, let us also add a small dose of lectures and tutorials on computable and constructive analysis, at least as a first exposure of the students to those results in these fields that have bearings at least on computable general equilibrium theory à la Scarf. Such a curriculum content will show that the claims and, in particular, the policy conclusions emanating from applied general equilibrium theory are based on untenable algorithmic mathematical foundations. This is true in spite of the systematic and impressive work of Herbert Scarf, Rolf Mantel and others who have sought to develop some allegedly constructive[11] and computable foundations in core areas of general equilibrium theory. In this precise mathematical sense, the epistemic and epistemological status of applied claims and assertions – for example, in policy domains, especially with anchorings in one or both of the fundamental theorems of welfare economics – are, to put it mildly, questionable. Some of these points are discussed in section 17.4, below.

In this chapter we have decided to eschew any description or discussion of the various uses of numerical methods in economic analysis. We have computable reasons for this decision. Most of the models of economic analysis – whether micro or macro, game theory or industrial organization (IO) theory – are founded on real analysis underpinned by set theory plus the axiom of choice. Results obtained in this framework are seriously deficient in numerical content. To infuse numerical content via numerical methods does not make the theories computational in any rigorous sense. In fact, there is – provably – almost no meaningfully approximate connection between a 'rigorously' proved, say, equilibrium, and its numerically computed approximation, despite many claims to the contrary, even at the frontiers of economic analysis.

In the spectacular developments achieved in dynamical systems theory in the second half of the twentieth century, the digital computer played a decisive part. However, there is a close connection between algorithms and dynamical systems via numerical analysis. The use of the digital computer to study continuous dynamical systems requires the analyst or the experimenter first to discretize the system to be studied. The discretization processes for non-linear dynamical systems are often intractable and undecidable. On the other hand, paradoxically, until very recently the mathematical foundation for numerical analysis was not developed in a way that was consistent with the mathematical foundation of the digital computer – that is, computability theory. As a result we have, in economics, a plethora of attempts and claims about computational economics that are not well founded on recursion theoretic, constructive or numerical analysis based on formal algorithmic foundations. Now, there are at least two ways out of the dilemma faced by the computational economist. Either be rigorous about the theory of approximations and numerical analysis in discretizing the continuous; or, look for a mathematical foundation for numerical analysis taking heed of the following observations remarks by Blum et al. (1998) (which we will refer to as BCSS):

> There is a substantial conflict between theoretical computer science and numerical analysis. These two subjects with common goals have grown apart. For example, computer scientists are uneasy with calculus, whereas numerical analysis thrives on it. On the other hand numerical analysts see *no use for the Turing machine.* The conflict has at its roots another age-old *conflict,* that *between the continuous and the discrete.* Computer science is oriented by the digital nature of machines and by its discrete foundations given by Turing machines. For numerical analysis, systems of equations and differential equations are central and this discipline depends heavily on the continuous nature of the real numbers . . .
>
> Use of Turing machines yields a unifying concept of the algorithm well formalized . . .
>
> The situation in numerical analysis is quite the opposite. Algorithms are primarily a means to solve practical problems. *There is not even a formal definition of algorithm in the subject . . .*
>
> A major obstacle to reconciling scientific computation and computer science is the present view of the machine, that is, the digital computer. As long as the computer is seen simply as a finite or discrete subject, it will be difficult to systematize numerical analysis. We believe that the Turing machine as a foundation for real number algorithms can only obscure concepts.
>
> Towards resolving the problem we have posed, we are led to expanding the theoretical model of the machine to allow real numbers as inputs. (Blum et al., 1998, p. 23; italics added)

This is a strategy that is a compromise between using an analogue computer and a digital one, on the one hand, and, on the other, between accepting either constructive or computable analysis and classical real analysis. The model of computation developed with great ingenuity by Smale and his co-workers may well be the best way to retain much of classical mathematical economics while still being able to pose and answer meaningfully questions about decidability, computability and computational complexity – and to retain numerical meaning in the whole framework.

Yet, we are not convinced at all that the BCSS model is of much relevance to the issue of computable foundations for numerical analysis. Our reasons are as follows.

First, what is wrong with the analogue model of computation on the real numbers and why was it not invoked to provide the mathematical and physical foundation for numerical analysis by the authors of the BCSS model? This is particularly relevant in this chapter, given that a noble analogue computing tradition existed – and flourished – in economics, in different eras of the development of the subject.

Second, what is wrong with the computable and recursive analytic model, with its rich complexity and theoretic analysis of classic optimization operators routinely used in economic theory (optimal control, dynamic programming, and so on); of the perennial paradoxes of the initial value problem on ordinary differential equations and their solution complexities and of much else in a similar vein?

Third, we do not think there is any historical or analytical substance to the Newtonian vision frequently invoked as a backdrop against which to justify the need for a new mathematical foundation for numerical analysis.

Fourth and finally, there is an important strand of research that has begun to interpret numerical algorithms as dynamical systems; from this kind of interpretation to a study of undecidability and incompleteness of numerical algorithms is an easy and fascinating frontier research topic within the framework of computable analysis, which owes nothing to, and has no need for, the BCSS kind of modelling framework – even though there are claims to the contrary in Blum et al. (1998) regarding such issues.[12] This is also a point of relevance for the problem of being rigorous about the theory of approximations and numerical analysis in discretizing the continuous. It is not just a question about accurate or rigorous discretizations of a real analytic model for implementation on a digital computer; but we will have to leave it at that, for now.

Therefore, against the general backdrop provided in this preamble, we will concentrate only on the four areas of algorithmic behavioural economics, computable general equilibrium theory, computable economics and agent-based computational economics in discussing the role of computation in economics. With this in mind, in section 12.2, an ultra-brief outline of the computing tradition in economics is given. In sections 12.3 to 12.6, algorithmic behavioural economics, computable general equilibrium theory, computable economics and agent-based computational economics are outlined and critically discussed, as far as possible in methodological and epistemological terms. The concluding section, titled 'Towards an epistemology of computation in economics', is squarely epistemological in the vision we try to cultivate, from the lessons of approximately six decades of machine computing traditions in economics – both theoretical and applied.

Before concluding the preamble it may be apposite to ask a simple, but obvious, question: what is a computation?[13] In a sense there is a simple, concise, answer to this question. A computation is that which is implementable via a Turing Machine. But that leads to further questions: are there other models of computation that are richer in some sense – in the nature of the data analysable, in the kind of processing speeds, in the class of computable functions, and so on? Mercifully, the Church–Turing thesis obviates the need for any such elaboration: any and every computation that is implementable by a Turing Machine answers all such questions unambiguously: every model of computation is formally equivalent with respect to each of these – and many other – questions. There remains, of course, the notion of computation intrinsic to constructive mathematics, where there is no invoking of anything similar to a Church–Turing thesis. We will have to leave any discussion of this important issue for another exercise. It means, of course, that the answer to the question, 'What is a computation?' may be unambiguous.

12.2   THE MACHINE COMPUTING TRADITION IN ECONOMICS

> The Method I take to do this, is not yet very usual; for instead of using only comparative and superlative Words, and intellectual Arguments, I have taken the course (as a Specimen of the Political Arithmetick I have long aimed at) to express my self in Terms of *Number, Weight, or Measure* . . .
>
> Now the Observations or Positions expressed by *Number, Weight, and Measure*, upon which I bottom the ensuing Discourses, are either true, or not apparently false, and which if they are not already true, certain, and evident, yet may be made so by the Sovereign Power, *Nam id certum est quod certum reddi potest*, and if they are false, not so false as to destroy the Argument they are brought for; but at worst are sufficient as Suppositions *to shew the way to that Knowledge I aim at*. (William Petty, Preface to *Political Arithmetick*, 3rd edn, 1690;[14] italics (non Latin) added)

Petty, 'to shew the way to that Knowledge [he] aimed at' – that is, for reasons of epistemics and epistemology – aimed 'to express [himself] in Terms of Number, Weight or Measure', a tradition nobly inherited and resolutely preserved and enhanced by his physiocratic and classical economic successors. Calculating, estimating, comparing, constructing and reasoning with numerical ratios, averages, series, tables areas, volumes and so on – in short, 'analysing data', whether natural or artificial

– underpinned much inference and some deduction is the way our classical and physiocratic predecessors came to policy precepts. However, with the exception of Charles Babbage and, possibly, Jevons, till Irving Fisher (1892 [1991]), in 1891, constructed his 'remarkable hydraulic [analogue computing] apparatus for calculating equilibrium prices' (Brainard and Scarf, 2005, p. 57),[15] resorting to actually constructed machine models of computing in economics seems to have remained an isolated example. Fisher's own description of the functioning of his hydraulic analogue computing machine clarifies an important feature of such computations: their independence from any intermediation via numerical analysis:

> The [hydraulic] mechanism just described is the physical analogue of the ideal economic market.[16] The elements which contribute to the determination of prices are represented each with its appropriate rôle and open to the scrutiny of the eye. We are thus enabled not only to obtain a clear and analytical *picture* of the interdependence of the many elements in the causation of prices, but also to employ the mechanism as an instrument of investigation and by it, study some complicated variations which could scarcely be successfully followed without its aid. (Fisher, 1892 [1991], p. 44)

There were, of course, the famous computing machine metaphors used by Walras, Pareto and then, inspired by Barone, in the important 'Socialist Calculation Debate', most comprehensively summarized, both critically and constructively, by Hayek (1935, 1940). Lange, returning to the theme over 30 years later, in his Dobb Festschrift chapter on 'The Computer and the Market' (Lange, 1967), muddied the issue by unscholarly and unsubstantiable claims for the possibilities of a digital computer (having, in the meantime, also forgotten that the initial discussions were with reference to analogue computing machines and, in particular, the metaphor of the market as an analogue computer). None of the participants had any technical knowledge of the mathematical underpinnings of computing; in a sense understandably so, since the mathematical foundations of computing were being placed on a rigorous basis just during those very years that the debate was at its height.[17]

Analogue computing techniques in economics had the proverbial stillbirth. There was a flurry of activities in the late 1940s and early 1950s, at the hands of A.W.H. (Bill) Phillips, Richard M. Goodwin, Herbert A. Simon, Robert H. Strotz, Otto Smith, Arnold Tustin, Roy Allen, Oscar Lange and a few others. Phillips built his famous MONIAC[18] hydraulic national income machine at the end of the 1940s and it was used at many universities – and even at the Central Bank of Guatemala – for teaching purposes and even as late as the early 1970s Richard Goodwin, at Cambridge University, taught one of us elementary principles of coupled market dynamics using such a machine. Strotz and his associates, at Northwestern University, built electro-analogue machines to study inventory dynamics and non-linear business cycle theories of the Hicks–Goodwin varieties. Otto Smith and R.M. Saunders, at the University of California at Berkeley, built an electro-analogue machine to study and simulate a Kalecki-type business cycle model. Roy Allen's successful textbooks on macroeconomics and mathematical economics of the 1950s – extending into the late 1960s – contained pedagogical circuit devices modelling business cycle theories (see Allen, 1959, especially Ch. 9; and Allen, 1967, especially Ch. 18). Arnold Tustin's highly imaginative, but failed textbook attempt to familiarize economists with the use of servomechanism theory to build analogue machines as models of economic dynamics (Tustin, 1953), and Oscar Lange's attractive, elementary, expository book with a similar purpose (Lange, 1970) also suffered the fate of 'stillbirth', at the dawn of the digital computing age.

Humphreys (2009) refers to non-linear business cycle theories[19] as examples of computational 'studies' that straddle 'the pre-computational era and the era of computational economics', claiming that there is no sharp dividing line between the two eras. This claim can be substantiated by a more finessed study of the particular example of a canonical non-linear business cycle equation, using – as was, indeed, actually done – analogue computing machines as in the 'pre-computational era' and comparing it with its study using a digital computing machine of the 'era of computational economics'.

The example we have chosen here encapsulates a noble tradition of computation in economics in every sense of this concept, to study a precisely specified mathematical system on both analogue and digital computers. It is, in a precise sense, also a substitute for an analytical study (because such a study is provably 'unlikely' to succeed in any meaningful way). Moreover, it can be viewed as an explicit example of an epistemological tool to interpret the results (most of which were unexpected), finally, to gain insight into the link between a computing machine and its theory and the theory of non-linear dynamical systems. The latter point is turning out to be the most significant from the point of view of the epistemology of computation, since the interaction can only be explored by representing the one system by the other – and, therefore, even an exploration into a new domain: studying the repertoire of digital machine behaviour with analogue computing machines, and vice versa.

Consider, therefore, the following equation, representing a classical Keynesian non-linear multiplier-accelerator model of the dynamics of national income, y:

$$\varepsilon \dot{y}(t) + (1 - \alpha)y(t) = \phi[\dot{y}(t - \theta)] + \beta(t) + l(t) \qquad (12.1)$$

Now, there are at least six different ways to investigate solutions to this non-linear difference-differential equation:

- in old-fashioned analytical modes;
- using non-standard analysis;
- graphically, that is, in terms of the geometry of dynamic behaviour, as usually done in the qualitative theory of differential equations;
- by the method of equivalent linearization;
- using an electro-analogue computer;
- using digital computers.

It is, of course, only the last two alternatives that are of relevance in this discussion. Assuming, for example, $\beta(t) + l(t)$ a constant[20] and reinterpreting $y(t)$ as a deviation from the unstable equilibrium of (12.1) $\beta(t) + l(t)/1 - \alpha$ one obtains a mixed non-linear difference-differential equation:

$$\varepsilon\dot{y}(t + \theta) + (1 - \alpha)y(t + \theta) = \phi[\dot{y}(t)] \tag{12.2}$$

In the first case, expanding (12.2) by a Taylor series approximation and retaining only the first two terms, one obtains the famous (unforced) Rayleigh (van der Pol)-type equation:

$$\ddot{y} + \left[\frac{\chi(\dot{x})}{\dot{x}}\right]\dot{x} + x = 0 \tag{12.3}$$

With this approximated reformulation began an 'industry' in the endogenous theory of the business cycle, where the cardinal desideratum was the existence of a unique, stable, limit cycle, independent of initial conditions. All four desiderata were violated when the approximations were more precise – in a purely technical sense – and the analysis proceeded via studies by means of analogue and digital computing machines. Even more interestingly, the insights obtained from an analogue computing machine study provided hints in setting up a computing study of (12.1) by means of digital computing machines.

Now, using an electro-analog computer, it was found, in Strotz et al. (1953), that the approximation of (12.1) retaining the first four terms of a Taylor series expansion, generated 25 limit cycles, and a potential for a countable infinity of limit cycles with further higher-order terms included in the approximations. Moreover, in its original formulation, one of the desired criteria for the non-linear formulation of the endogenous model of the business cycle, was to generate self-sustaining fluctuations, independent of initial conditions. This latter property was lost when the approximation was made more precise.

Next, coupling two equations of type (12.3), via the Phillips Electro-Mechanical-Hydraulic Analogue Computing Machine (Goodwin, 1953), Goodwin and Phillips were able to generate – unexpectedly – the quasi-periodic paradox (see Abraham, 1985). Neither Goodwin, nor Phillips, who did the coupled-dynamics computation on the Phillips Machine, had any clue – theoretical or otherwise – about interpreting and encapsulating this outcome in any economic theoretical formalization. The key point is that they were surprised by the outcome and did not know how to interpret it when it emerged. This is where the richness of the epistemology of computation manifests itself most dramatically. There was no macrodynamic theory to which they could relate the observed behaviour, which was contrary to expected behaviour.

Finally, one of us – Zambelli (2010) – repeated the exercise but this time on a digital computer. Our results came as a surprise to us: although we can confirm the results in Strotz et al. (1953), the outcomes are richer and more varied and we would have no idea which way to proceed, if we are wedded to an equilibrium norm to which the results have to conform.

It goes without saying that one of the key differences between analogue and digital computing is that in the latter the intermediation between the continuous and the discrete is achieved by means of numerical procedures; this intermediation is circumvented in the analogue tradition. In this sense, there is a sharp difference between 'the pre-computational era and the era of computational economics'. Much of what is routinely referred to as computational economics in the modern era is simply variations on the theme of numerical analysis, without any anchoring in the mathematical theory of the computer, whether digital or analogue.

12.3   CLASSICAL BEHAVIOURAL ECONOMICS

If we hurry, we can catch up to Turing on the path he pointed out to us so many years ago. (Simon, 1996, p. 101)

12.3.1   A Brief Note on Classical versus Modern Behavioural Economics

Herbert Simon combined and encapsulated, in an intrinsically dynamic, decison-theoretic framework, a computationally founded system of choice and decision, both entirely rational in a broad sense. 'Computational' has always meant 'computable' in the Turing sense, at least in our reading of Simon's magisterial writings. In particular, in the context of bounded rationality, satisficing and their underpinnings in the architecture of human thinking, it was the path broached by Turing that guided Simon's fundamental contributions. In this section we try, in fairly precise and formal ways, to suggest computable foundations for boundedly rational choice and satisficing decisions. In a nutshell, the aim is to reformulate bounded rationality and satisficing in a computable framework so that their intrinsic (complex) dynamics is made explicit in as straightforward a way as possible.

Bounded rationality, satisficing and decision problems are the basic foundational pillars on which what we refer to as classical or algorithmic behavioural economics rests. A minor digression on the distinction between classical or algorithmic behavioural economics (CBE[21]) and modern behavioural economics (MBE) may be useful to place the discussion in context.

The defining works of CBE were the three pioneering contributions by Herbert Simon (and his close early collaborators, Alan Newell and Cliff Shaw); Simon (1955, 1956) and Simon et al. (1958). These three defining contributions to CBE were brought to an initial completion in the monumental book on *Human Problem Solving* by Newell and Simon (Newell and Simon, 1972).

Meanwhile, almost simultaneously, contrary to current attributions, the seeds were laid by Ward Edwards for what is now an orthodox vision of behavioural economics – which we refer to as 'modern behavioural economics' (MBE)[22] – starting from the work of Leonard Savage, who had himself become a believer in De Finetti's approach to probability. The three defining, absolutely pioneering contributions, by Ward Edwards, works presaging the subsequent works by Nobel Laureate Daniel Kahneman (and Amos Tversky) on 'prospect theory', a key foundational basis for modern behavioural economics, were Edwards (1954, 1961) and Edwards et al. (1963).[23]

Both traditions emerged from the infelicities in the axiomatic treatment of rationality that came to underpin expected utility maximization, emanating from the ground-breaking work of von Neumann and Morgenstern. Both found the framework and basis provide by von Neumann and Morgenstern wanting in realism – of a basic sort – and lacking in consistency in some of the underpinnings. For example, Edwards found the lack of consistency between a subjective theory of utility and an objective theory of probability that underpinned expected utility maximization. Edwards sought a 'reconciliation' via an appeal and a utilization of the emerging De Finetti-based theory of subjective probability theory that Savage was developing just about at that time. The flaw detected, and perceptively tackled by Edwards, persists in the post-prospect theory of behavioural economics, now called modern behavioural economics. These issues will be discussed, critically and exhaustively, in the relevant introductions to the respective volumes envisaged in this series.

Simon's starting point was computational cognitive science, in its psychological variants, and its confrontation with the theories of decision making that economists were developing, applying and refining, all of which were variations on the theme of the von Neumann–Morgenstern starting point, further developed by Nash and Arrow–Debreu. The key notion was computationally underpinning rational decision making, thereby naturally and intrinsically taking into account the theoretical limits that come with computability theory. In addition, this framework came with natural measures of computational complexity and they were imaginatively, and with great originality, incorporated into the kind of theories of decision making that Simon developed within the formal framework of what is called, in metamathematics and mathematical logic, decision problems (of which optimization is a special case).

From the line of research initiated with single-handed determination by Ward Edwards we have seen the emergence of modern behavioural economics, behavioural finance, behavioural game theory and behavioural neuroeconomics.

From the work initiated by Herbert Simon, we have seen the emergence of rich and deep concepts like bounded rationality and satisficing, and wholly refreshing fields like evolutionary growth theory, at the hands of classical behavioural economists like Richard Nelson and Sidney Winter; adaptive economic dynamics by Richard Day; 'models of discovery' by Simon and his many associates; the problem of causality and evolution in semi-decomposable systems by Simon and others; and much else.

12.3.2   Classical Behavioural Economics: Computable Foundations

A decision problem asks whether there exists an algorithm to decide whether a mathematical assertion does or does not have a proof; or a formal problem does or does not have an algorithmic solution. Thus the characterization makes clear the crucial role of an underpinning model of computation; secondly, the answer is in the form of a yes/no response. Of course, there is the third alternative of 'undecidable', too, but that is a vast issue outside the scope of this chapter. It is in this sense of decision problems that we interpret the word 'decisions' here.

As for 'problem solving', we shall assume that this is to be interpreted in the sense in which it is defined and used in the monumental classic by Newell and Simon (1972).

Finally, the model of computation is the Turing model, subject to the Church–Turing thesis. To give a rigorous mathematical foundation for bounded rationality and satisficing, as decision problems,[24] it is necessary to underpin them in a dynamic model of choice in a computable framework. However, these are not two separate problems. Any formalization underpinned by a model of computation in the sense of computability theory is, dually, intrinsically dynamic.

Remark 1   *Decidable–Undecidable, Solvable–Unsolvable, Computable–Uncomputable, and so on are concepts that are given content algorithmically.*

Now consider the Boolean formula:

$$(x_1 \vee x_2 \vee x_3) \wedge (x_1 \vee \{\neg x_2\}) \wedge (x_2 \vee \{\neg x_3\}) \wedge (x_3 \vee \{\neg x_1\})$$

$$\wedge (\{\neg x_1\} \vee \{\neg x_2\} \vee \{\neg x_3\}) \tag{12.4}$$

Remark 2   *Each subformula within parenthesis is called a clause; the variables and their negations that constitute clauses are called literals; It is 'easy' to 'see' that for the truth value of the above Boolean formula to be $t(x_i) = 1$ all the subformulas within each of the parenthesis will have to be true. It is equally 'easy' to see that no truth assignments whatsoever can satisfy the formula such that its global value is true. This Boolean formula is unsatisfiable.*

Problem 3   SAT – the satisfiability problem.
Given m clauses, $C_i (i = 1, \ldots m)$, containing the literals (of) $x_j (j = 1, \ldots n)$, determine if the formula is $C_1 \wedge C_2 \wedge C_3 \ldots \wedge C_m$ satisfiable.
    Determine means 'find an (efficient) algorithm'. To date it is not known whether there is an efficient algorithm to solve the satisfiability problem – that is, to determine the truth value of a Boolean formula. In other words, it is not known whether $SAT \in P$. But:

Theorem 4 $SAT \in NP$

Definition 5   *A Boolean formula consisting of many clauses connected by conjunction (that is, $\wedge$) is said to be in conjunctive normal form (CNF).*

Finally, we have Cook's famous theorem:

Theorem 6   *Cook's Theorem: SAT is NP–Complete.*

It is in the above kind of context and framework within which we are interpreting Simon's vision of behavioural economics. In this framework optimization is a very special case of the more general decision problem approach. The real mathematical content of *satisficing*[25] is best interpreted in terms of the satisfiability problem of computational complexity theory, the framework used by Simon consistently and persistently – and a framework to which he himself made pioneering contributions.

Finally, there is the computably underpinned definition of bounded rationality.

Theorem 7 *The process of rational choice by an economic agent is formally equivalent to the computing activity of a suitably programmed (Universal) Turing Machine.*

Proof By construction. See *Computable Economics* (Velupillai, 2000, 3.2, pp. 29–36).

Remark 8 *The important caveat is 'process' of rational choice, which Simon – more than anyone else – tirelessly emphasized by characterizing the difference between 'procedural' and 'substantive' rationality; the latter being the defining basis for Olympian rationality (Simon, 1983, p. 19), the former that of the computationally underpinned problem solver facing decision problems. Any decision – rational or not – has a time dimension and, hence, a content in terms of some process. In the Olympian model the 'process' aspect is submerged and dominated by the static optimization operator. By transforming the agent into a problem solver, constrained by computational formalisms to determine a decision problem, Simon was able to extract the procedural content in any rational choice. The above result is a summary of such an approach.*

Definition 9 *Computation universality of a dynamical system. A dynamical system – discrete or continuous – is said to be capable of computation universality if, using its initial conditions, it can be programmed to simulate the activities of any arbitrary Turing Machine, in particular, the activities of a Universal Turing Machine.*

Lemma 10 Dynamical systems capable of computation universality can be constructed from Turing Machines.

Proof See Velupillai (2000).

Theorem 11 *Non-maximum rational choice. No trajectory of a dynamical system capable of universal computation can, in any 'useful sense'* *(see Samuelson's Nobel Prize lecture, Samuelson, 1970), be related to optimization in the Olympian model of rationality.*

Proof   See Velupillai (2000).

Theorem 12   *Boundedly rational choice by an information processing agent within the framework of a decision problem is capable of computation universality.*

Proof   An immediate consequence of the definitions and theorems of this subsection.

Remark 13   *From this result, in particular, it is clear that the boundedly rational agent, satisficing in the context of a decision problem, encapsulates the only notion of rationality that can 'in any useful sense' be defined procedurally.*

We have only scratched a tiny part of the surface of the vast canvas on which Simon sketched his vision of a computably underpinned behavioural economics. Nothing in Simon's behavioural economics – that is, in classical behavioural economics – was devoid of computable content.

We should not end this subsection on classical behavioural economics without also indicating where the framework that we have developed falls short of encapsulating the deep and full force of Simon's visions. One important narrowness of vision in our approach is the concentration on time computational complexity. The key results here, which we have used above, are theorems 4 and 6, particularly the latter, that is, Cooke's celebrated theorem that SAT is NP-Complete. Now, because SAT is NP-Complete, it is reasonable to believe that it is unsolvable with a polynomial time algorithm. On the other hand, SAT is solvable even with a linear space algorithm. The theorem in space computational complexity that corresponds to Cooke's fundamental theorem in time computational complexity is, arguably, 'Savitch's theorem' (see Velupillai, forthcoming). We have neglected this theorem and also did not discuss the implications of the following series of plausible – not, as yet, entirely definite – series of inclusion relations:

$$P \subseteq NP \ PSPACE = NPSPACE \ EXPTIME$$

We should have asked ourselves the obvious question: why didn't Herbert Simon ever occupy himself, ever, with the *P vs NP* question (one of the seven 'Clay Millennium Problems')? We think a plausible answer to this (counterfactual) question is that Simon was intrinsically more interested in space computational complexity, as the domain in which human problem solving was best considered.

An additional subsection here should generalize the definition of satisficing in terms of the SAT problem in space computational complexity. When that task is undertaken it will be possible to go beyond Chess – a paradigmatic canvas on which Simon sketched many of his conjectures on human problem solving – and begin to try to study GO in terms of the notions of classical behavioural economics. This is especially and challengingly so because GO is known to be 'PSPACE-hard', but not known, as yet, to be 'PSPACE-complete'.

12.4   COMPUTABLE GENERAL EQUILIBRIUM THEORY[26]

> It is not natural for 'A implies B' to mean 'not A or B', and students will tell you so if you give them the chance . . . [W]e should not be surprised to find that certain classically accepted modes of inference are no longer correct. The most important of these is the principle of the excluded middle – 'A or not A'. Constructively, this principle would mean that we had a method which, in finitely many purely routine steps, would lead to a proof or disproof of an arbitrary mathematical assertion A. Of course we have no such method, and nobody has the least hope that we ever shall. It is the principle of the excluded middle that accounts for almost all of the important unconstructivities of classical mathematics. (Bishop, 1985, pp. 3, 10–11)

The main culprits – although not the only ones – in the failure of so-called computable general equilibrium (CGE) theory to be computable or constructive are the 'classically accepted modes of inference'. Unfortunately, to the best of our knowledge, none of the practitioners of CGE, nor any one of its 'offshoots' or alleged 'generalizations' – such as applied general equilibrium (AGE) theory, recursive competitive equilibrium (RCE) or dynamic general equilibrium (DGE) theory – are aware of the uncomputability and non-constructivity of their equilibria; *a fortiori*, they seem entirely uninterested in why this is so.[27]

One of the great achievements of mathematical economics in the twentieth century was the Walrasian economic equilibrium existence proof of Arrow and Debreu (1954). It is listed as the seventh of ten significant[28] achievements in applied mathematics in Piergiorgio Odifreddi's overall list of the 30 great solved problems of *The Mathematical Century* (2004). Its extension to dynamics is listed as the eighth of 18 problems for the twenty-first century – in 'Hilbertian mode' – by Steve Smale (1998). Given its undoubted and acknowledged significance in the intellectual canvas of twentieth-century mathematical economics, economic theory and applied mathematics, it is not surprising that attempts have been made, most notably by Herbert Scarf, to devise algorithmic methods to compute Arrow–Debreu equilibria. These attempts have resulted in the development of an independent discipline of computable general equilibrium (CGE) theory. It will not be an exaggeration to claim that, till Scarf's pioneering work on CGE theory and modelling, the Arrow–Debreu achievements remained in the realm of pure theory – whether of economics or mathematics; after Scarf, it is, surely, also a significant chapter in applied mathematics.[29]

On the other hand, the key feature of the CGE research program is its schizophrenic nature: all of the mathematical economic theory of general equilibrium is practised in the domain of real analysis, and founded on set theory plus the axiom of choice. However, all of the computational content of CGE is allegedly based on constructive mathematics (although the 'computable' in CGE may suggest a basis in recursion theory). This schizophrenia is ostensibly resolved by an appeal to what is known as Uzawa's equivalence theorem (Uzawa, 1962). Debreu's admirably concise acknowledgement of the importance of Uzawa's equivalence theorem is a testimony to the 'bridging role' it plays, between economic equilibrium existence theorems and fixed-point theorems (Debreu, 1982, pp. 719–720):

> [The equilibrium existence] theorem establishes the existence of a price vector yielding a negative or zero excess demand as a direct consequence of a deep mathematical result, the fixed-point theorem of Kakutani. And one must ask whether the . . . proof uses a needlessly powerful tool. This question was answered in the negative by Uzawa (1962) who showed that [the theorem] directly implies Kakutani's fixed-point theorem.

Scarf's insight was, then, to utilize algorithms that had been developed to approximate (Brouwer's) fixed-point theorem – invoking Uzawa's equivalence theorem – to determine approximations to (Walrasian or Arrow–Debreu) equilibria. Scarf himself was well aware that these were not 'approximations' of a useful nature (unless conjoined to those intangible non-formal concepts like intuition, experience and insight):

> In applying the algorithm it is, in general, *impossible* to select an ever finer sequence of grids and a convergent sequence of subsimplices. An algorithm for a digital computer must be basically finite and cannot involve an infinite sequence of successive refinements . . . *The passage to the limit is the non-constructive aspect of Brouwer's theorem*, and we have no assurance that the

subsimplex determined by a fine grid of vectors on S contains or is even close to a true fixed point of the mapping. (Scarf, 1973, p. 52; italics added)

Scarf, however, misses an important point here: it is not 'the passage to the limit' that 'is the nonconstructive aspect of Brouwer's theorem' implying non-assurance of useful approximations; it is, instead, the intrinsic undecidable disjunctions that characterize the Bolzano–Weierstrass theorem. In one of only two of the standard textbooks on mathematical general equilibrium theory where the Uzawa equivalence theorem is explicitly discussed (Cornwall, 1984; Starr, 1977), Starr's clear and detailed presentation of the proof of Brouwer's fixed point theorem is based on the excellent and almost elementary exposition in Tompkins (1964, particularly, pp. 424–427). There, in turn, the appeal to the Bolzano–Weierstrass theorem is made almost as if with a magician's wand:[30]

> Making [the] assumption [that given any simplex *S*, there are subdivisions that are arbitrarily fine] we can now finish the proof of Brouwer's fixed-point theorem. We take an infinite sequence of subdivisions of *S* with *mesh*, that is, length of the longest one-dimensional edge, approaching **0**. From each subdivision, we *choose* one simplex that carries all labels, and in this simplex we *choose* a single point. We thus have an infinite sequence of points in the original simplex *S*, and *we can choose a subsequence that converges to a single point*. This point .. is the limit point of the sequence of all vertices of all the simplexes from which the points of the convergent subsequence were originally *chosen*. (Tompkins, 1964, p. 427; all italics, except the first one, are added)

The deceptive use of the word 'choose' in the above description of mathematical processes conveys the impression that the 'choices', in each case, are algorithmically implementable. However, it is only the first use of the word 'choose' and the implied choice – that is, choosing simplexes from increasingly fine subdivisions – that can be algorithmized constructively. The part that invokes the Bolzano–Weierstrass theorem, that is, 'Choosing a subsequence that converges to a single point' – incidentally, this point is the sought after fixed-point of the Brouwer theorem – entails undecidable disjunctions and as long as any proof relies on this aspect of the theorem, it will remain unconstructifiable.[31]

Why, then do two of the most renowned practitioners of applied general theory, especially in its policy aspects, John Shoven and John Whalley (1992), make the following explicit claim:

> The major result of postwar mathematical general equilibrium theory has been to demonstrate the existence of such an equilibrium by showing the applicability of mathematical fixed point theorems to economic models . . . Since applying general equilibrium models to policy issues involves computing equilibria, these

fixed point theorems are important: It is essential to know that an equilibrium exists for a given model before attempting to compute that equilibrium . . .

The weakness of such applications is twofold. First, they provide *non-constructive rather than constructive proofs of the existence of equilibrium*; that is, they show that equilibria exist but do not provide techniques by which equilibria can actually be determined. Second, existence per se has no policy significance . . . Thus, fixed point theorems are only relevant in testing the logical consistency of models prior to the models' use in comparative static policy analysis; such theorems do not provide insights as to how economic behavior will actually change when policies change. *They can only be employed in this way if they can be made constructive* (i.e., be used to find actual equilibria). *The extension of the Brouwer and Kakutani fixed point theorems in this direction is what underlies the work of Scarf . . . on fixed point algorithms* . . . (ibid., pp. 12, 20–21; italics added)

Those who claim that they work with 'computable' general equilibrium models – the self-proclaimed followers of Leif Johansen, mentioned in the opening section, for example, and a host of applied general equilibrium, policy-motivated theorists and applied economists – continue to anchor their work on an appeal to formal Arrow–Debreu equilibrium theory or its CGE variant. For example such a claim is most explicitly made in Part II of Dervis et al. (1982). The exact claim is that the equilibria they – and others – compute, using their versions of general equilibrium models, can be linked to, and theoretically substantiated by, the Arrow–Debreu equilibrium of pure theory. Thus (Dervis et al., 1982, p. 153, italics added):

[I]t is reasonable to ask if, in fact, a solution exists [for the CGE model] and, if so, whether or not it is unique. Most applied model builders, in contrast to theorists, have not worried too much about general existence problems. After all, a solution is *numerically computed* and an existence proof may appear unnecessary. The models are always quite well behaved and, given that very general existence proofs have been established for theoretical models of which CGE models form a rather *well-behaved subset*, it is reasonable to expect that nonexistence problems will not arise in practice.

This is complete nonsense.

The Arrow–Debreu equilibrium is provably uncomputable, from the point of view of both the mathematics of constructivism and recursion theory. The equilibria computed by any and every computable general equilibrium model used for development policy exercises – or those that are linked to, and derived from, variations of the Johansen model – have nothing whatsoever to do with the theoretical equilibria of general equilibrium theory. The technical results of these untenabilities, infeasibilities and infelicities are rigorously demonstrated in Velupillai (2006) and (2009).

Computable general equilibrium theory has no grounding in computability or constructivity. Claims by applied general equilibrium theorists of any variety that their work is anchored in any form of CGE is vacuous from a theoretical computational point of view. At best, exercises by applied general equilibrium theorists can be considered ad hoc numerical exercises, seeking consistency and balance in accounts. Nothing more – especially nothing in theoretical anchors of any sort – is warranted. As long as a methodology theorizes in a kind of mathematics that is devoid of numerical meaning and computationally vacuous and relies on a schizophrenic appeal to a mathematics that is grounded in computational feasibilities, any claim of computability, constructivity or numerical feasibility must remain dubious, at best.

12.5 COMPUTABLE ECONOMICS

> [W]e want to stress that solutions that are not *effectively computable* are not properly solutions at all. (Arrow et al., 1958, p. 17; italics added)

In computable economics, as in any computation with analogue computing machines or in classical behavioural economics, all solutions are based on effectively computable methods. Thus computation is intrinsic to the subject and all formally defined entities in computable economics – as in classical behavioural economics – are, therefore, algorithmically grounded.

12.5.1 Briefly . . .

Given the algorithmic foundations of computability theory and the intrinsic dynamic form and content of algorithms, it is clear that this will be a 'mathematics with dynamic and algorithmic overtones'.[32] This means, thus, that computable economics is a case of a new kind of mathematics in old economic bottles. The 'new kind of mathematics' implies new questions, new frameworks, new proof techniques – all of them with algorithmic and dynamic content for digital domains and ranges.

Some of the key formal concepts of computable economics are, therefore: solvability and Diophantine decision problems, decidability and undecidability, computability and uncomputability, satisfiability, completeness and incompleteness, recursivity and recursive enumerability, degrees of solvability (Turing degrees), universality and the Universal Turing Machine and computational, algorithmic and stochastic complexity. The proof techniques of computable economics, as a result of the new formalisms, will be, typically, invoking methods of: diagonalization, the halting problem for Turing Machines, Rice's theorem, incompressibility theorems, Specker's theorem, recursion theorems. For example, the recursion theorems will replace the use of traditional, non-constructive and uncomputable, topological fixed point theorems, routinely used in orthodox mathematical analysis. The other theorems have no counterpart in non-algorithmic mathematics.

In the spirit of pouring new mathematical wines into old economic bottles, the kind of economic problems of a digital economy that computable economics is immediately able to grant a new lease of life are the classic ones of computable and constructive existence and learning of rational expectations equilibria, computable learning and complexity of learning, computable and bounded rationality, computability, constructivity and complexity of general equilibrium models, undecidability, self-reproduction and self-reconstruction of models of economic dynamics (growth and cycles), uncomputability and incompleteness in (finite and infinite) game theory and of Nash Equilibria, decidability (playability) of arithmetical games, the intractability (computational complexity) of optimization operators; and so on.

12.5.2   Formally . . .

Suppose the starting point of the computable economist whose visions of actual economic data, and its generation, is the following:

Conjecture 14   *Observable variables are sequences that are generated from recursively enumerable but not recursive sets, if rational agents underpin their generation.*

An aside: In 1974 Georg Kreisel posed the following problem:

> We consider theories . . . and ask if every sequence of natural numbers or every real number which is well defined (*observable*) *according to the theory* must be recursive or, more generally, *recursive in the data* . . . Equivalently, we may ask whether any such sequence of numbers, etc., can also be generated by an ideal computing or Turing Machine if the data are used as input. The question is certainly not empty because most objects considered in a . . . theory are not computers in the sense defined by Turing. (Kreisel, 1974, p. 11)

The above conjecture has been formulated after years of pondering on Kreisel's typically thought-provoking question. More recently, a reading of Osborne's stimulating book (1977) was also a source of inspiration in the formulation of the conjecture as an empirical disciplining criterion for computable economics.

The conjecture is also akin to the orthodox economic theorist and her handmaiden, the econometrician, assuming that all observable data emanate from a structured probability space and the problem of inference is simply to determine, by statistical or other means the parameters that characterize their probability distributions. If, therefore, the computable economist's starting point is the above conjecture then it follows that:

Theorem 15   *Only dynamical systems capable of computation universality can generate sequences that are members of sets that are recursively enumerable but not recursive.*

Theorem 16   *Only dynamical systems capable of universal computation can extract patterns inherent in arbitrary, digitally generated, data, without assuming their generation by an underlying probability model.*

Corollary 17   *Asymptotically stable dynamical systems are not capable of computation universality.*

Proposition 18   *Only dynamical systems capable of computation universality are consistent with the 'no arbitrage' hypothesis.*

Theorem 19   *Rational economic agents in the sense of economic theory are equivalent to suitably indexed Turing Machines; that is, decision processes implemented by rational economic agents – viz., choice behaviour – is equivalent to the computing behaviour of a suitable indexed Turing Machine.*

Put another way, this theorem states that the process of rational choice by an economic agent is equivalent to the computing activity of a suitably programmed Turing Machine. This is exactly parallel to the formalization with which choice in classical behavioural economics is implemented.

Conjecture 20   *Dynamical systems capable of computation universality can persist in disequilibrium configurations for long time periods.*

Theorem 21   *(Rabin, 1957). There are games in which the player who in theory can always win cannot do so in practice because it is impossible to supply him with effective instructions regarding how he should play in order to win.*

The next item has been mentioned twice already in this chapter; but I restate it here just for completion.

Theorem 22   *Undecidability of Hilbert's tenth problem. There is no algorithm which, for a given arbitrary Diophantine equation, would tell whether the equation has a solution or not.*

Theorem 23   *Halting problem for Turing Machines. Suppose we are given a Turing Machine computable function $f_n(m)$. Then there is no general algorithm for determining, for arbitrary $n \geq 0$ and $m \geq 0$, whether $f_n(m)$ is defined.*

Theorem 24   *Rice's theorem. Let C be a class of partial recursive functions. Then C is not recursive unless it is the empty set, or the set of all partial recursive functions.*

Claim 25   *Validity of the Church–Turing thesis on effective calculability.*

Theorem 26   *Specker's theorem in computable analysis (Specker, 1949, pp. 145–158). A sequence exists with an upper bound but without a least upper bound.*

Theorem 27   *The Pour-El–Richards theorem (Pour-El and Richards, 1979). There exists an ordinary differential equation (ODE) s.t: $\phi'(t) = F[t, \phi(t)]$ with $\phi(0) = 0$, s.t: $F(x,y)$ is computable on the rectangle $[0 \leq x \leq 1, -1 \leq y \leq 1]$, but no solution of the ODE is computable on any interval $[0, \delta]$, $\delta \geq 0$*

Theorem 28   *Fixed point theorem. Suppose that $\Phi: F_m \to F_n$ is a recursive operator (or a recursive program P). Then there is a partial function f_ϕ that is the least fixed point of Φ.*

Theorem 29 $\Phi(f_\phi) = f_\phi$;
If $\Phi(g) = g$, then $f_\phi \subseteq g$.

Remark 30   *If, in addition to being partial, f_ϕ is also total, then it is the unique least fixed point.*

Finally, related to invariance theorems in the domain of algorithmic complexity theory and the fixed point theorem of classical recursion theory, we have the recursion theorem, essential for understanding self-reproduction and self-reconstruction (for computable growth theory):

Theorem 31   *Recursion theorem. Let T be a Turing Machine that computes a function:*

$$t: \Sigma^* \times \Sigma^* \to \Sigma^* \tag{12.5}$$

Then, there is a Turing Machine R *that computes a function:*

$$r: \Sigma^* \to \Sigma^* \tag{12.6}$$

such that, $\forall \omega$:

$$r(\omega) = t(< R >, \omega) \tag{12.7}$$

where, $<R>$: denotes the encoding of the Turing Machine into its standard representation as a bit string; and the *(star) operator denotes its standard role as a 'unary operator' defined as: $A^* = \{x_1, x_2, \ldots x_K | k \geq 0, \forall x_i \in A\}$.

The idea behind the recursion theorem is to formalize the activity of a Turing Machine that can obtain its own description and, then, compute with it. All malicious 'hackers', perhaps with no knowledge of this theorem, are invoking this theorem every time they generate viruses. More seriously, this theorem is essential, too, for formalizing, recursion theoretically, a model of growth in a digital economy and to determine and learn, computably and constructively, rational expectations equilibria. The fixed point theorem and the recursion theorem are also indispensable in the computable formalization of policy ineffectiveness postulates, time inconsistency and credibility in the theory of macroeconomic policy. Even more than in microeconomics, where topological fixed point theorems have been indispensable in the formalizations underpinning existence proofs, the role of the above fixed point theorem and the related recursion theorem are absolutely fundamental in what I come to call computable macroeconomics.

Anyone who is able to formalize these theorems, corollaries and conjectures and work with them – and accept the claim – as those that are to discipline economic theoretical criteria, would have mastered all the necessary mathematics of computable economics. Unlike so-called computable general equilibrium theory and its offshoots, computable economics – and its offshoots – are intrinsically computational and numerical.

12.6   AGENT-BASED COMPUTATIONAL ECONOMICS

> It is suggested that a system of chemical substances, called morphogens, reacting together and diffusing through a tissue, is adequate to account for the main phenomena of morphogenesis . . .
> Most of an organism, most of the time, is developing from one pattern into another, rather than from homogeneity into a pattern. One would like to be able to follow this more general process mathematically also. The difficulties are, however, such that one cannot hope to have any very embracing *theory* of such processes beyond the statement of the equations. It might be possible, however, to treat a few particular cases in detail with the aid of a digital computer . . . The essential disadvantage of the method is that one only gets results for particular cases . . . The morphogen theory of phyllotaxis, to be described . . . in a later paper, will be covered by this computational method. Non-linear equations will be used. (Turing, 1952, pp. 37, 71–72)

The origins of what has become agent-based computational methods can be traced to the pioneering works of Turing on morphogenesis (1952), von Neumann on the theory of self-reproducing automata (1966), and Ulam on non-linear dynamics (Fermi et al., 1955; Stein and Ulam, 1964). A 'second generation' of pioneers were Conway (Berlekamp et al., 1982) and Wolfram (1985), the former directly in the von Neumann tradition and the latter straddling the von Neumann and Ulam traditions – that is, working on the interface between cellular automata modelling and dynamical system interpretation of the transition equations.

Remarkably, there was an independent tradition in economics, pioneered by Richard Goodwin (1947), in his computational studies of coupled markets, which directly inspired Herbert Simon's (1952) approach to the computational study of evolutionary dynamics in terms of semi-decomposable linear systems.

Sadly, none of these classics have had the slightest impact on the current frontiers of agent-based computational economics (see, for example, Tesfatsion and Judd, 2006). Had any awareness of the classics, their frameworks, the questions they posed, the tentative answers they obtained and the research directions they suggested had been absorbed, even in some rudimentary way, many of the exaggerated claims and assertions of the advocates of agent-based computable economics would have been less absurd, more measured and, surely, also humbler in the expectations of what this line of computational research could and must achieve. An example of the utterly untenable claim of a senior advocate of agent-based computational economics may convey our sadness of the lack of anchoring in the classics more vividly. In his chapter, titled 'Agent-Based Macro'

(Tesfatsion and Judd, 2006, p. 1626; italics added), Axel Leijonhufvud asserts that:[33]

> Agent-based computational methods provide *the only way* in which the self-regulatory capabilities of complex dynamic models can be explored so as to advance our understanding of the adaptive dynamics of actual economies.

Quite apart from the many undefined – even formally undefinable– concepts in this remarkably unscholarly statement, the extraordinary claim that 'agent-based computational methods provide *the only way*' to understand anything, let alone of the 'adaptive dynamics of actual economies', must make the scientific spirit of Goodwin and Simon writhe in intellectual pain, not to mention the noble ghosts of Ulam, von Neumann and Turing.

What are 'agent-based computational methods'? Do they transcend Turing Machine computation? If so, how – and why? How does one link a computationally implemented method with a complex dynamical system, even assuming that it is possible to define such a thing unambiguously and consistently with the dynamics of a computation?

On the other hand, agent-based computable economic practice is closely tied to the belief that such models are capable of generating so-called 'emergent phenomena', in the sense that their existence cannot be predicted from the underpinning laws of individual agent interactions. Very little scholarship on the rich tradition of philosophical, epistemological, computational and dynamic research – with a solid contribution to the epistemology of simulation (see Weissert, 1997) – on 'emergence' is manifested in the frontier research by agent-based computational economists (a paradigmatic example of inflated claims and deficient scholarship on agent-based computational modelling, the tortuous concept of 'reductionism' and the possibility of so-called 'emergent aggregative phenomena' can be found in Delli Gatti et al., 2008).

No better characterization of the practice of agent-based computational economists can be given than the one by Arthur Burks (see Burks, 1970, p. xviii), on a related 'procedure for investigating cellular spaces':

> The investigator starts with a certain global behavior and wants to find a transition function for a cellular automaton which exhibits that behaviour. He then chooses as subgoals certain elementary behavioral functions and proceeds to define his transition function piece-meal so as to obtain these behaviors . . .
>
> The task of searching for a transition function which produces a specified behavior is an arduous task because there are so many possible partial transition functions to explore.

The formal difficulties of 'searching for a transition function' are provably intractable, at best; algorithmically undecidable, in general. Even when found, depending on the way the data generating process is characterized, whether the transition function – when viewed as a finite automaton – 'halts' at the prescribed state is again, in general, algorithmically undecidable. Correspondingly, when viewed as a dynamical system, whether the global behaviour is an attractor, or is in a particular basin of attraction of the dynamical system, is algorithmically undecidable. Whether a set of initial conditions, for the transition function, can be algorithmically determined such that their halting state is the desired global behaviour, or such that the global behaviour is in the basin of attraction of the transition function as a dynamical system, is decidable only for trivial sets. And so on.

Suppose we succeed in finding such a transition function – as many agent-based computational economists claim they can, and have – and want to characterize it either in terms of computability theory or as a dynamical system. Suppose, also, that we ask the questions the pioneers asked: the feasibility of self-reproduction, self-reconstruction, evolution, computation universality, decidability of limit sets of the transition function when interpreted as a dynamical system, whether the transition function, viewed as an finite automaton, is subject to the halting problem, and so on. At the least, any reasonable notion of 'emergence' requires unambiguous answers to most of these questions – all of which are, in general, subject to algorithmic undecidabilities.

Agent-based computational economics is vacuous from an epistemological point of view, when viewed either from the point of view of computation theory or from a dynamical systems point of view, contrary to many and varied claims. We locate the vacuity in the lack of anchoring in the noble traditions broached by the pioneers. That the Fermi–Pasta–Ulam problem remains impervious to analysis, computational experiments or dynamical system explorations should be a lesson for those economists who think they have found a panacea to all modelling ills. Above all, it is strange that the overwhelming majority – if not, in fact, all – of agent-based computational economists are not aware of the disciplining criteria with which the pioneers embarked on computational explorations in cellular space. This is why agent-based computational economics is essentially an exploration of cellular spaces with finite automata that do not have the power of Turing Machines – that is, the transition functions that are routinely used for cellular space exploration by agent-based computable economists are not partial recursive functions, if indeed many, or any, of them are even aware of such finessed distinctions between classes of functions; there is certainly no evidence of any such awareness in any of the contributions in Amman et al. (1996), Tesfatsion and Judd (2006) or in Delli Gatti et al. (2008).

12.7 TOWARDS AN EPISTEMOLOGY OF COMPUTATION IN ECONOMICS

> Do we overpass . . . the Turing–Church 'barrier' and compute the uncomput-
> able? Not exactly. We just move the discussion in another territory[:] that of
> *processes that handle information*. This syntagma is so general that in these
> terms 'everything is a computation'; it is a matter of point of view ('for every
> process there is an observer which can interpret the process as a computation').
> (Păun, 2008, p. 345)

'Does nature compute?' is a question natural scientists ask with increasing
frequency. The differential equations, or maps, that seem to characterize
the dynamical systems of nature are hardly ever analytically 'solvable'.
Either we must try to devise and evolve an epistemology to come to terms
with 'unsolvability' and, therefore, accept a 'truth deficit' – that 'true' solutions are inherently unreachable – or find other ways to represent nature's
processes. One such alternative way is to interpret nature's processes as
computations. But computations, too, may not 'halt'. A master dynamical
system theorist outlined the dilemma cogently:

> We regard the computer as an 'oracle' which we ask questions. Questions
> are formulated as input data for sets of calculations. There are two possible
> outcomes to the computer's work: either the calculations rigorously confirm
> that a phase portrait is correct, or they fail to confirm it . . . The theory that
> we present states that if one begins with a structurally stable vector field, *there
> is input data that will yield a proof that a numerically computed phase portrait is
> correct. However, this fails to be completely conclusive from an algorithmic point
> of view, because one has no way of verifying that a vector field is structurally
> stable in advance of a positive outcome.* Thus, if one runs a set of trials of increas-
> ing precision, the computer will eventually produce a proof of correctness of a
> phase portrait for a structurally stable vector field. Presented with a vector field
> that is not structurally stable, the computer *will not confirm* this fact; it will only
> fail in its attempted proof of structural stability.[34] *Pragmatically, we terminate
> the calculation when the computer produces a definitive answer or our patience is
> exhausted.*
>   The situation described in the previous paragraph is analogous to the ques-
> tion of producing a numerical proof that a continuous function has a zero . . .
> Numerical proofs that a function vanishes can be expected to succeed only
> when the function has qualitative properties that can be *verified* with finite-
> precision calculations. (Guckenheimer, 1996, pp. 154–155, italics added)

We have discussed and described alternative visions of computation in
economics. What, then, if the economy is itself a computer? Do economic
processes, whether aggregative or not, embody the results of a computation? Do we, as economists, observing the economy's computational
processes, impute computability properties to the economy? Analogous

to Guckenheimer's thought experiment, if the data set generated by the economy as a computer is recursively enumerable but not recursive, inferences about the computability properties of the economy will remain incomplete. On the other hand, if we – as observers – feed the economy with data sets that are also recursively enumerable but not recursive, then whether the economy, as a computer, will be able to process it in a definitive way will remain unknown for an indeterminate period.

Whether definitive knowledge of the structure of the economy can be obtained by observing its processes will depend on the metaphors we use to characterize it; for example, characterizing the economy as a finite automaton or a dynamical system whose limit sets are stable limit points makes it easy to infer structural properties by observations of the outcome of its processes. This is the standard approach to modelling and inference of economic dynamics.

In the computable approach to economics, the starting point is that the economy is a Turing Machine and the data it generates forms a set that is recursively enumerable but not recursive. If so, what can be inferred about the structure of the economy may only be explored by Turing Machine computation, without any guarantee that a definitive answer will be obtained. Computation in economics becomes epistemologically meaningful only when the economic modeller, using computational metaphors to analyse the data generated by the economy, begins to accept, at least *pro tempore*, that the economy is itself a computer. This is the natural mode of interaction between the economy and the classical behavioural economist and the computable economist; it is not the natural mode for the CGE theorist, nor for the agent-based computational economist. This is why there is a serious epistemological deficit in the practice of the latter two classes of economists.

ACKNOWLEDGEMENTS

We are greatly indebted to the editors for the kind invitation to contribute and the immense patience with which they tolerated the various ways in which we transcended generous deadlines. The title has metamorphosed into the ultra-simple final form it has taken, having begun its life as 'Computational economics', become the 'Computational paradigm in economics', then 'Computational economics, computable general equilibrium theory and computable economics' and, finally, 'Classical behavioural economics, computable general equilibrium theory, computable economics and agent-based computational economics'. Each of the transitional titles seemed, at least to the authors, to emphasize particular kinds of ways the notion of machine computation, and its underpinning theory, were implemented in a variety of economic theories. To avoid any such connotation it seemed best to choose as neutral a title as possible, without losing focus on the main theme which is, of course, the foundations of the methodology of computing in economics. We are deeply indebted to our two graduate students, Selda Kao and V. Ragupathy, for invaluable logistical and intellectual help. Alas, they refuse to take any blame for the remaining infelicities.

NOTES

1. When we refer to 'classical behavioural economics', it is to the kind of computationally underpinned research programme in these fields broached by Simon that will be meant (see Velupillai, forthcoming; Langley et al., 1987; Newell and Simon, 1972; Simon, 1947, 1955, 1956, 1977, 1979, 1983, 1986, 1989, 1996, 1997).
2. It is little recognized by one wing of so-called computational economists (for example Dixon and Parmenter, 1996) that the research program of the Cambridge Growth Project under the direction of Richard Stone emerged independently of – even prior to – Johansen's justly famous work on a computational Multi-Sectoral Growth Model (see Johansen, 1960 [1974]).
3. 'Not unexpectedly' because newclassical scholarship on traditions and foundations – whether of the doctrine historical variety in economics or of knowledge of mathematical traditions – is both selectively doctrinaire and unusually narrow, bordering on being comprehensively ahistorical.
4. We prefer what we think is the more descriptively correct 'recursive macroeconomics' (see Ljungqvist and Sargent, 2000) for this 'school' (in the sense of Phelps, 1990) macroeconomics. The recursive in this description and encapsulation of 'newclassical macroeconomic methodology' refers to the notion of recursion in the sense of intuitive iteration that underpins filtering, Markov decision processes and dynamic programming associated with the names of Kalman, Wald and Bellman. The rational agent is, thus, formally equivalent to an optimal signal processor in Newclassical Macroeconomics. This should be contrasted with Simon's computational behavioural agent as an information processing system (IPS) and the algorithmically rational agent (ARA) of computable and constructive economics. The latter two notions are grounded in formal recursion theory or constructive mathematics. The notions of recursive and iteration in recursive macroeconomics have nothing whatsoever to do with the rigorous notion of recursive, recursion and iteration in recursion theory, constructive mathematics.
5. Not to mention quantum, DNA and other physical and natural computers that are beginning to be realized at the frontiers of theoretical technology.
6. Charles Babbage, viewed in one of his many incarnations as an economist, can be considered the only one to have straddled both the digital and analogue traditions. There is a story to be told here, but this is not the forum for it. We shall reserve the story for another occasion.
7. Real analysis, as used by the mathematical economist, in turn, founded on set theory plus the axiom of choice, whether explicitly acknowledged or not.
8. This claim is repeated in a curiously uninformed and seriously incomplete expository chapter on computational economics by Paul Humphreys in an otherwise prestigious recent *Handbook* (Humphreys, 2009).
9. Our stance on this issue is reflected exactly by the view held by our friend, Lance Taylor. After attending the recent 50th anniversary celebrations of the Johansen Model, held in Oslo, Lance wrote as follows to the first author (e-mail, 27 August 2010): [Most

participants at the] conference in honor of the 50th anniversary of Johansen's MSG model [held in Oslo in May, were] thinking that Leif was taking off from Arrow–Debreu when in fact he was doing disaggregated macro planning, moving around the numbers in a set of accounts that they had been constructed to satisfy. There is certainly no mention of A–D in his book.

10. Computable, in this context, is simply numerical in the same sense in which it was referred to in Dixon and Parmenter (1996), above.

11. I should mention that Douglas Bridges, a mathematician with impeccable constructive credentials, made a couple of valiant attempts, one of them with Fred Richman, to infuse a serious and rigorous dose of constructivism at the most fundamental level of mathematical economics (see Bridges, 1982; Bridges and Richman, 1991).

12. Primarily in relation to the decidability problems of the Mandelbrot and Julia sets, as posed by Penrose (1989, p. 124ff.).

13. A splendid and characteristically clear, simple – yet deep – discussion of this question can be found in Davis (1978).

14. Accessed at: http://www.marxists.org/reference/subject/economics/petty/.

15. As Scarf, (1967, p. 207), points out: 'In *Mathematical Investigations in the Theory of Value and Prices*, published in 1892, Irving Fisher described a mechanical and hydraulic analogue device intended to calculate equilibrium prices for a general competitive model . . . At least two versions of Fisher's device were actually constructed and apparently performed successfully . . . The equipment seems remarkably quaint and old-fashioned in this era of high-speed digital computers.'

16. In an early analogue approach to the study of macroeconomic dynamics, Strotz et al. (1951, p. 557) indicated the nature of what they mean by 'analogue' in these contexts (italics added): 'If a single group of equations can be written which defines the *assumed performance* for two separate systems (each of which within itself represents an orderly or definable behavior), one system may be called the complete analogue of the other.' Obviously, Fisher's system satisfies this condition – as would any analogue computing system, by definition.

17. Unless one expected such true economic scholars, before the kind of mathematization of economics that we are familiar with now, to be familiar with Brouwerian constructive mathematics, which was reaching its zenith, also during those very years.

18. Monetary National Income Analogue Computing Machine.

19. In an earlier note we referred to this chapter as curiously uninformed and seriously incomplete. A concrete example of the reason for us to characterize it as such is his reference to Krugman (1996) for references to 'nonlinear business cycle theories'. Anyone who takes seriously this kind of flippant, frivolous, reference and does check up on Krugman's booklet, would find the strange claim (ibid., p. 7): 'I may be the only economist in my generation who has even heard of [these non-linear business cycle theories].' Krugman is 57 years old; we could easily list a dozen eminent economist of his generation, give or take a few years, who are seriously competent in non-linear business cycle theories of the Goodwin–Kaldor–Hicks era, developing it at some of the current frontiers of macroeconomic theory.

20. If $\beta(t) + l(t)$ was not assumed a constant, the obdurate forced version of (12.1) would have to be confronted, without any hope of a disciplined solution even with the help of computing machines, whether analogue or digital.

21. We would have preferred to refer exclusively to algorithmic behavioural economics and, therefore, ABE. However, ABE has become one of the usual ways to refer to agent-based economics; hence we opt for CBE.

22. The beginning of MBE is generally identified with Thaler (1980), for example by Camerer et al. (2004, p. xxii).

23. A discerning reader would already have noticed that five of the six classic contributions were published in frontier psychological journals. One possibly obvious inference from this elementary observation may well be that the two classes of contributions emerged independently, focussing on those cognitive aspects that were neglected in more

orthodox economic theory of decision making, by individual agents and in organizations. But this inference – we think – would be most misleading.

24. The three most important classes of decision problems that almost characterize the subject of computational complexity theory, underpinned by a model of computation in general, are the P, NP and NP-Complete classes. The model of computation, in general, is the Nondeterministic Turing Machine Model. Concisely, but not quite precisely, they can be described as follows: P denotes the class of computable problems that are solvable in time bounded by a polynomial function of the size of the input; NP is the class of computable problems for which a solution can be verified in polynomial time; a computable problem lies in the class called NP-Complete if every problem that is in NP can be reduced to it in polynomial time.

25. In Simon (1997, p. 295), Simon clarified the semantic sense of the word 'satisfice', by revealing the way he came to choose the word: 'The term "satisfice", which appears in the *Oxford English Dictionary* as a Northumbrian synonym for "satisfy", was borrowed for this new use by H.A. Simon (1956) in 'Rational Choice and the Structure of the Environment' [that is, Simon (1956)]'.

26. Entirely for reasons of space we do not deal with the burgeoning field of algorithmic game theory from the point of view of the methodology of computation as conceived in this chapter. However, all of the strictures that are presented here 'against' the computable foundations of CGE apply, *pari passu*, to the claims and assertions of algorithmic game theory. Computing the uncomputable, deciding the undecidable and completing the incompletable is endemic in mathematical economics, of every variety.

27. Perhaps Fred Richman's perceptive reflection suggests the exact reason for these peculiar blinkers: 'Even those who like algorithms have remarkably little appreciation of the thoroughgoing algorithmic thinking that is required for a constructive proof. This is illustrated by the nonconstructive nature of many proofs in books on numerical analysis, the theoretical study of practical numerical algorithms. I would guess that most realist mathematicians are unable even to recognize when a proof is constructive in the intuitionist's sense. It is a lot harder than one might think to recognize when a theorem depends on a nonconstructive argument. One reason is that proofs are rarely self-contained, but depend on other theorems whose proofs depend on still other theorems. These other theorems have often been internalized to such an extent that we are not aware whether or not nonconstructive arguments have been used, or must be used, in their proofs. Another reason is that the law of excluded middle [LEM] is so ingrained in our thinking that we do not distinguish between different formulations of a theorem that are trivially equivalent given LEM, although one formulation may have a constructive proof and the other not' (Richman, 1990).

28. Odifreddi, 2004, #3.7 in Chapter 3, pp. 122–125.

29. Thus meriting inclusion in Odifreddi's list (op. cit.) as a significant contribution to applied mathematics.

30. In the clear and elementary proof of the Brouwer fix point theorem given in Starr's textbook (op. cit.), the appeal to the Bolzano–Weierstrass theorem is made when proving the KKM theorem (p. 62). In Scarf's own elegant text (op. cit.) invoking of this theorem occurs, during the proof of Brouwer's theorem, on p. 51: 'As the vectors are increasingly refined, a convergent subsequence of subsimplices *may be found*, which tend in the limit to a single vector x*' (italics added). Scarf is careful to claim that the required subsequence 'may be found', but does not claim that it can be found algorithmically. One may wonder: if not found algorithmically, then how?

31. Over 50 years ago, when Brouwer returned to the topic of his famous theorem with an Intuitionist version of it, he made the trenchant observation that seems to have escaped the attention of mathematical economists: '[T]he validity of the Bolzano–Weierstrass theorem [in intuitionism] would make the classical and the intuitionist form of fixed-point theorems equivalent' (Brouwer, 1952, p. 1). The invalidity of the Bolzano–Weierstrass theorem in any form of constructivism is due to its reliance on the law of the excluded middle in an infinitary context of choices (see also Dummett, 1977, pp. 10–12).

32. 'I think it is fair to say that for the main existence problems in the theory of economic equilibrium, one can now bypass the fixed point approach and attack the equations directly to give existence of solutions, with a simpler kind of mathematics and even mathematics with dynamic and algorithmic overtones' (Smale, 1976, p. 290).
33. When one of us first read this extraordinary statement, his mind went back to the witticism with which Dennis Robertson reacted when he supposedly first heard of revealed preference (Robertson, 1952, p. 19): 'Dare I confess that when I first heard this term . . . I thought that perhaps to some latter-day saint, in some new Patmos off the coast of Massachusetts, the final solution of all these mysteries had been revealed in a new apocalypse?'
34. A reader equipped with the standard knowledge of classical recursion theory would immediately invoke the distinction between recursive and recursively enumerable sets to make precise sense of this important observation.

REFERENCES

Abraham, Ralph (1985), 'Is There Chaos Without Noise', P. Fischer and William R. Smith (eds), *Chaos, Fractals, and Dynamics*, New York, USA, Basel, Switzerland: Marcel Dekker, pp. 117–121.

Allen, R.G.D. (1959), *Mathematical Economics*, 2nd edn, London: Macmillan.

Allen, R.G.D. (1967), *Macro Economic Theory: A Mathematical Treatment*, London: Macmillan.

Amman, Hans M., David A. Kendrick and John Rust (eds) (1996), *Handbook of Computational Economics*, Vol. 1, Amsterdam: North-Holland.

Arrow, Kenneth J. and Gerard Debreu (1954), 'Existence of an Equilibrium for a Competitive Economy', *Econometrica*, **22**, 265–290.

Arrow, Kenneth J., Samuel Karlin and Herbert Scarf (1958), *The Nature and Structure of Inventory Problems*, in Kenneth J. Arrow, Samuel Karlin and Herbert Scarf (eds), *Studies in the Mathematical Theory of Inventory and Production*, Stanford, CA: Stanford University Press.

Berlekamp, Elwyn R., John H. Conway and Richard K. Guy (1982), *Winning Ways for your mathematical plays – Volume 2: Games in Particular*, London: Academic Press.

Bishop, Errett A. (1985), 'Schizophrenia in Contemporary Mathematics', in Murray Rosenblatt (ed.), *Errett Bishop: Reflections on Him and His Research*, Contemporary Mathematics, Vol. 39, Providence, RI: American Mathematical Society, pp. 1–32.

Blum, Lenore, Felipe Cucker, Michael Shub and Steve Smale (1998), *Complexity and Real Computation*, New York: Springer-Verlag.

Brainard, William C. and Herbert E. Scarf (2005), '*How to Compute Equilibrium Prices in 1891*', in Robert W. Dimand and John Geanakoplos (eds), *Celebrating Irving Fisher – The Legacy of a Great Economist*, Oxford: Blackwell Publishing, pp. 57–83.

Bridges, Douglas (1982), 'Preferences and Utility: A Constructive Development', *Journal of Mathematical Economics*, **9**(1–2), 165–185.

Bridges, Douglas and Fred Richman (1991), 'A Recursive Counterexample to Debreu's Theorem on the Existence of a Utility Function', *Mathematical Social Sciences*, **21**(2), 179–182.

Brouwer, Luitzen E.J. (1952), 'An Intuitionist Correction of the Fixed-Point Theorem on the Sphere', *Proceedings of the Royal Society London*, **213**(5), 1–2.

Burks, Arthur W. (ed.) (1970), *Essays on Cellular Automata*, Urbana, IL: University of Illinois Press.

Camerer, Colin F., George Loewenstein and Matthew Rabin (eds) (2004), *Advances in Behavioral Economics*, Princeton, NJ: Princeton University Press.

Cornwall, Richard R. (1984), *Introduction to the Use of General Equilibrium Analysis*, Amsterdam: North-Holland.

Davis, Martin (1978), 'What is a Computation?', in Lynn Arthur Steen (ed.) *Mathematics Today: Twelve Informal Essays*, New York: Springer-Verlag, pp. 241–267.

Debreu, Gerard (1982), 'Existence of Competitive Equilibrium', in Kenneth J. Arrow and Michael D. Intrilligator (eds), *Handbook of Mathematical Economics, Volume II*, Amsterdam: North-Holland, pp. 697–743

Delli Gatti, Domenico, Edoardo Gaffeo, Mauro Gallegati, Gianfranco Giulioni and Antonio Palestrini (2008), *Emergent Macroeconomics – An Agent-Based Approach to Business Fluctuations*, Milano: Springer-Verlag Italia.

Denning, Peter J. (2010), 'The Great Principles of Computing', *American Scientist*, **98**(5), 369–372.

Dervis, Kemal, Jaime de Melo and Sherman Robinson (1982), *General Equilibrium Models for Development Policy*, Cambridge: Cambridge University Press.

Dixon, Peter B. and B.R. Parmenter (1996), 'Computable General Equilibrium Modelling for Policy Analysis and Forecasting', in Hans M. Amman, David A. Kendrick and John Rust (eds), *Handbook of Computational Economics, Volume 1*, Amsterdam: North-Holland.

Dummett, Michael (1977), *Elements of Intuitionism*, Oxford: Clarendon Press.

Edwards, Ward (1954), 'The Theory of Decision Making', *Psychological Bulletin*, **51**(4), 380–417.

Edwards, Ward (1961), 'Behavioural Decision Theory', *Annual Review of Psychology*, **12**, 473–498.

Edwards, Ward, Harold Lindman and Leonard J. Savage (1963), 'Bayesian Statistical Inference for Psychological Research', *Psychological Research*, **70**(3), 193–242.

Fermi, Enrico, John Pasta and Stanislaw Ulam (1955), *Studies of Non Linear Problems*, Los Alamos Preprint, LA-1940, May.

Fisher, Irving (1892 [1991]), *Mathematical Investigations in the Theory of Value and Prices*, Fairfield, NJ: Augustus M. Kelley.

Goodwin, Richard M. (1947), 'Dynamical Coupling with Especial Reference to Markets Having Production Lags', *Econometrica*, **15**(3), 181–204.

Goodwin, Richard M. (1953), 'Static and Dynamic Linear General Equilibrium Models', in Netherlands Economic Institute (ed.), *Input-Output Relations*, N.V., Leiden: H.E. Stenfort Kroese, pp. 54–87.

Guckenheimer, John (1996), 'Phase Portraits of Planar Vector Fields: Computer Proofs', *Experimental Mathematics*, **4**(2), 153–165.

Hayek, F.A. von (1935), *Collectivist Economic Planning – Critical Studies on the Possibilities of Socialism*, London: Routledge & Kegan Paul.

Hayek, F.A. von (1940), 'Socialist Calculation: The Competitive "Solution"', *Economica*, New Series, **7**(26), 125–149.

Humphreys, Paul (2009), 'Computational Economics', in Harold Kincaid and Don Ross (eds), *The Oxford Handbook of Philosophy of Economics*, Oxford: Oxford University Press, pp. 371–385.

Johansen, Leif (1960 [1974]), *A Multi-Sectoral Study of Economic Growth*, 2nd enlarged edn, Amsterdam: North-Holland.

Kehoe, Timothy J., T.N. Srinivasan and John Whalley (eds) (2005), *Frontiers in Applied General Equilibrium Modelling: In Honour of Herbert Scarf*, Cambridge: Cambridge University Press.

Kreisel, Georg (1974), 'A Notion of Mechanistic Theory', *Synthese*, **29**, 11–26.

Krugman, Paul (1996), *The Self-Organizing Economy*, Oxford: Blackwell Publishers.

Kydland, Finn E. and Edward C. Prescott (1996), 'The Computational Experiment: An Econometric Tool', *Journal of Economic Perspectives*, **10**(1), 69–85.

Lange, Oskar (1967), 'The Computer and the Market', in C.H. Feinstein (ed.), *Socialism, Capitalism & Economic Growth – Essays Presented to Maurice Dobb*, Cambridge: Cambridge University Press, pp. 158–161.

Lange, Oskar (1970), *Introduction to Economic Cybernetics*, London: Pergamon Press.

Langley, Pat, Herbert A. Simon, Gary L. Bradshaw and Jan M. Zytkow (1987), *Scientific*

Discovery: Computational Explorations of the Creative Process, Cambridge, MA: MIT Press.

Lawvere, F. William and Stephen H. Schanuel (1997), *Conceptual Mathematics: A First Introduction to Categories*, Cambridge: Cambridge University Press.

Ljungqvist, Lars and Thomas J. Sargent (2000), *Recursive Macroeconomic Theory*, Cambridge, MA: MIT Press.

Newell, Allen and Herbert A. Simon (1972), *Human Problem Solving*, Englewood Cliffs, NJ: Prentice-Hall Inc.

Odifreddi, Piergiorgio (2004), *The Mathematical Century: The 30 Greatest Problems of the Last Hundred Years* (tr. by Arturo Sangalli), Princeton: Princeton University Press.

Osborne, Maury F.M. (1977), *The Stock Market and Finance from a Physicist's Viewpoint*, Minneapolis, MN: Crossgar Press.

Păun, Gheorghe (2008), 'From Cells to (Silicon) Computers and Back', in *New Computational Paradigms- Changing Conceptions of What is Computable*, New York: Springer Science. pp. 343–371.

Penrose, Roger (1989), *The Emperor's New Mind: Concerning Computers, Mind, and the Laws of Physics*, Oxford: Oxford University Press.

Phelps, Edmund S. (1990), *Seven Schools of Macroeconomic Thought*, Oxford: Clarendon Press.

Pour-El, Marian Boykan and Ian Richards (1979), 'A Computable Ordinary Differential Equation Which Possesses No Computable Solution', *Annals of Mathematical Logic*, **17**, 61–90.

Pyatt, Graham (1992), 'In Memoriam: Sir Richard Stone, KT, CBE, ScD, FBA – 1913–1991', *Review of Income and Wealth*, **32**(2), 245–248.

Rabin, M.O. (1957), 'Effective Computability of Winning Strategies', in M. Dresher, A.W. Thicker and P. Wolfe (eds), *Contributions to the Theory of Games, Vol. III*, Annals of Mathematical Studies No. 39, Princeton, NJ: Princeton University Press, pp. 147–157.

Richman, Fred (1990), 'Intuitionism as Generalization', *Philosophia Mathematica*, **14**, 124–128.

Robertson, Dennis H. (1952), 'Utility and All That', in *Utility and All That – and Other Essays*, London: George Allen & Union, pp. 13–41.

Samuelson, Paul Anthony (1970), 'Maximum Principles in Analytical Economics', in *Les prix Nobel en 1970*, Stockholm: The Nobel Foundation, pp. 273–288.

Scarf, Herbert E. (1967), 'On the Computation of Equilibrium Prices', *Ten Economic Studies in the Tradition of Irving Fisher*, New York: John Wiley & Sons, pp. 207–230.

Scarf, Herbert E. (1973), *The Computation of Economic Equilibria*, New Haven, CT, USA and London, UK: Yale University Press.

Shoven, John B. and John Whalley (1992), *Applying General Equilibrium*, Cambridge: Cambridge University Press.

Simon, Herbert A. (1947), *Administrative Behavior*, New York: The Free Press.

Simon, Herbert A. (1952), 'The Architecture of Complexity', *Proceedings of the American Philosophical Society*, **106**(6), 467–482.

Simon, Herbert A. (1955), 'A Behavioural Model of Rational Choice', *Quarterly Journal of Economics*, **69**(1), 99–118.

Simon, Herbert A. (1956), 'Rational Choice and the Structure of the Environment', *Psychological Review*, **63**, 129–38.

Simon, Herbert A. (1977), *Models of Discovery – and Other Topics in the Methods of Science*, Dordrecht: D. Reidel Publishing Company.

Simon, Herbert A. (1979), *Models of Thought: Volume I*, New Haven, CT: Yale University Press.

Simon, Herbert A. (1983), *Reason in Human Affairs*, Oxford: Basil Blackwell.

Simon, Herbert A. (1986), 'Rationality in Psychology and Economics', *Journal of Business*, **59**(4), Pt. 2, S209–S224.

Simon, Herbert A. (1989), *Models of Thought: Volume II*, New Haven, CT: Yale University Press.

Simon, Herbert A. (1996), 'Machine as Mind', in Peter Macmillan and Andy Clark (eds), *Machines and Thought – The Legacy of Alan Turing*, Vol. 1, Oxford: Oxford University Press, pp. 81–101.

Simon, Herbert A. (1997), 'Satisficing', in *Models of Bounded Rationality, Vol. 3 – Empirically Grounded Economic Reason*, Cambridge, MA: MIT Press, pp. 295–298.

Simon, Herbert A., Allen Newell and J.C. Shaw (1958), 'Elements of a Theory of Problem Solving', *Psychological Review*, **65**(3), 151–166.

Smale, Steve (1976), 'Dynamics in General Equilibrium Theory', *American Economic Review*, **66**(2), 288–294.

Smale, Steve (1998), 'Mathematical Problems for the Next Century', *Mathematical Intelligencer*, **20**(2), 7–15.

Specker, Ernst (1949), 'Nicht Konstruktive beweisbare Sätze der Analysis', *Journal of Symbolic Logic*, **14**, 145–158.

Starr, Ross M. (1977), *General Equilibrium Theory: An Introduction*, Cambridge: Cambridge University Press.

Stein, P.R. and Stanislaw M. Ulam (1964), 'Nonlinear Transformation Studies', Warsaw: Rozprawy Matematyczne, Institute of Mathematics of the Polish Academy, pp. 3–20.

Stone, Richard and Alan Brown (1962), 'Foreword', in Richard Stone and Alan Brown, *A Computable Model of Economic Growth*, A Programme for Growth No. 1, London: Chapman & Hall.

Strotz, R.H., J.F. Calvert and N.F. Morehouse (1951), 'Analogue Computing Techniques Applied to Economics', *AIEE Transactions*, **70**(1), 557–563.

Strotz, R.H, J.C. McAnulty and J.B. Naines, Jr. (1953), 'Goodwin's Nonlinear Theory of the Business Cycle: An Electro-Analog Solution', *Econometrica*, **21**(3), 390–411.

Tesfatsion, Leigh and Kenneth L. Judd (eds) (2006), *Handbook of Computational Economics – Agent-Based Computational Economics*, Vol. 2, Amsterdam: North-Holland.

Thaler, Richard (1980), 'Toward a Positive Theory of Consumer Choice', *Journal of Economic Behavior and Organization*, **1**(1), 39–60.

Tompkins, Charles B. (1964), 'Sperner's Lemma and Some Extensions', in E.F. Beckenbach (ed.), *Applied Combinatorial Mathematics*, New York: John Wiley & Sons, pp. 416–455.

Turing, Alan (1952), 'The Chemical Basis of Morphogenesis', *Philosophical Transactions of The Royal Society of London*, Series B, Biological Sciences, **237**(641), 37–72.

Tustin, Arnold (1953), *The Mechanism of Economic Systems: An Approach to the Problem of Economic Stabilisation from the Point of View of Control-System Engineering*, Cambridge, MA: Harvard University Press.

Uzawa, Hirofumi (1962), 'Walras' Existence Theorem and Brouwer's Fixed Point Theorem', *Economic Studies Quarterly*, **8**(1), pp. 59–62.

Velupillai, Kumaraswamy (2000), *Computable Economics*, Oxford: Oxford University Press.

Velupillai, K. Vela (2006), 'The Algorithmic Foundations of Computable General Equilibrium Theory', *Applied Mathematics and Computation*, **179**(1), 360–369.

Velupillai, K. Vela (2009), 'Uncomputability and Undecidability in Economic Theory', *Applied Mathematics and Computation*, **215**(4), 1404–1416.

Velupillai, K. Vela (forthcoming), 'Computable and Dynamical Systems Foundations of Bounded Rationality and Satisficing', *ASSRU DP*.

von Neumann, John (1966), *Theory of Self-Reproducing Automata*, (edited and completed by Arthur W. Burks), Urbana, IL: University of Illinois Press.

Weissert, Thomas P. (1997), *The Genesis of Simulation in Dynamics: Pursuing the Fermi-Pasta-Ulam Problem*, New York: Springer-Verlag.

Wolfram, Stephen (1985), 'Undecidability and Intractability in Theoretical Physics', *Physical Review Letters*, **54**(8), 735–738.

Zambelli, Stefano (2010), 'Flexible Accelerator Economic Systems as Coupled Oscillators', *Journal of Economic Surveys*, **25**(3), 608–633.

PART IV

EVOLUTION AND EVOLUTIONARY ECONOMICS

13 A philosophical perspective on contemporary evolutionary economics

Geoffrey M. Hodgson[1]

13.1 INTRODUCTION

Although there are many precursors, the modern wave of evolutionary economics began in the 1980s, particularly after the publication of Richard Nelson's and Sidney Winter's (1982) *Evolutionary Theory of Economic Change*. In the following years much of the work in this genre was applied and policy-oriented. Theoretical developments have been significant, but there has not yet been convergence on an integrated approach (Silva and Teixeira, 2009). It is partly for this reason that there has been an intensifying debate since the 1990s on evolutionary principles and the underlying ontological assumptions of evolutionary economics.

The aim of this chapter is to examine the philosophical communalities and divergences that have been revealed in the literature. Seven sections follow. Section 13.2 sketches the historical background. It notes that despite the looseness and imprecision of the term 'evolution', there is an identifiable international network or 'college' of 'evolutionary economists' whose work can be placed under philosophical scrutiny. Section 13.3 considers the philosophical differences in broad terms and directs attention to ontology as the basis of much relevant agreement and dispute. Section 13.4 considers a number of ontological communalities in evolutionary economics. It is followed by two sections on ontological divergences. Of these, section 13.6 outlines the ontology of complex population systems. This lays the ground for the discussion of generalized Darwinism in section 13.7. The final section shows that some of the key disputes within evolutionary economics derive not from incompatible propositions but from different levels of abstraction within a single ontological framework. A strategy for the reconciliation of apparent differences is thus revealed.

13.2   HISTORY AND MEANINGS

Any consideration of the philosophical aspects of evolutionary economics immediately faces the problem that the term has been used historically in a wide variety of ways. The first use of the term 'evolutionary economics' in English was probably by Thorstein Veblen (1898, p. 398). Although Veblen was one of the founders of the original institutional economics, his followers abandoned his Darwinian legacy (Hodgson, 2004). While they retained the word 'evolutionary', it was used to refer more broadly to development and change, as with the Association for Evolutionary Economics in the USA.

Joseph Schumpeter famously described capitalist development as an evolutionary process. Work influenced by Schumpeter is also described as 'evolutionary economics' as evidenced by the title of the *Journal of Evolutionary Economics*, published by the International Joseph Schumpeter Society. Much work in the tradition of Nelson and Winter, particularly concerning industrial dynamics, is identified within this genre.

The Austrian School of economists is often described as 'evolutionary', as portrayed in Carl Menger's theory of the evolution of money and other institutions, and by the extensive use of evolutionary ideas in the later works of Friedrich Hayek. In addition, the economics of assorted writers such as Adam Smith, Karl Marx, Alfred Marshall and others are sometimes described as 'evolutionary' in character. Finally, evolutionary game theory is a prominent recent development in mainstream economics.

There is no good reason to claim than any one approach has greater claim to the 'evolutionary' mantle than another. Consideration of philosophical underpinnings is thus greatly complicated by this diversity of analysis and lack of consensus over meaning. In particular, there is nothing in the etymology or usage of the term 'evolution' that necessarily connotes Darwinism. The word was used long before Charles Darwin; it was first applied to natural phenomena by the German biologist Albrecht von Haller in 1744. Darwin himself used the word sparingly.

'Evolution' is a term of wide meaning, often connoting little more than development or change. This is especially the case in modern French and some other languages, where 'evolution' or its equivalent is used frequently in everyday parlance to refer to any process of development, often referring to single entities. In English its usage is less common, and it sometimes refers more restrictively to natural selection, but there is no warrant to insist on that narrower meaning.

In the social sciences as a whole, the term 'evolution' fell out of favour between the two world wars. The term did not become more widespread until after the publication of Kenneth Boulding's (1981) *Evolutionary*

Economics, Richard Nelson and Sidney Winter's (1982) *An Evolutionary Theory of Economic Change* and Friedrich Hayek's (1988) *Fatal Conceit* (which developed evolutionary ideas from some of Hayek's earlier works from the 1960s and 1970s).

This shift in usage is clear from the bibliometric evidence. The number of articles or books on economics (in English) with the word 'evolution' (or derivatives) in their title or subtitle leapt from none in the 1940s and 15 in the 1970s to 75 in the 1980s (Hodgson, 2004, p. 416). From 1990 the count has increased well into the hundreds (Silva and Teixeira, 2009).

Although the books by Boulding, Hayek, and Nelson and Winter all incorporated Darwinian ideas, their use was qualified, reluctant or even inexplicit (Hodgson, 1993, 1999). Being the most influential of the three, Nelson and Winter's (1982) volume mentioned Darwin only once in passing, ignored Veblen, and claimed a pre-eminently 'Schumpeterian' influence for its approach. Yet their theory embodied Darwinian processes of variety-creation, information inheritance and selection. They even drew an analogy between routines and genes. But ironically Joseph Schumpeter eschewed the use of Darwinian ideas in economics and all biological analogies (Hodgson, 1993; Witt, 2002; Andersen, 2009).

Although the word 'evolution' became popular, and Darwinian ideas were stalking in the shadows, many economists remained reluctant to go so far as Veblen and tackle economic evolution with the core principles of Darwinism. Nazism, racism, eugenics and other horrors of the twentieth century had repelled many social scientists from any use of ideas from biology (Degler, 1991). This resistance is still apparent today.

Despite this, by the 1990s it was possible to write of an international network or 'invisible college' of 'evolutionary economists' who, despite their differences of approach, were focusing on the problem of analysing structural, technological, cultural and institutional change in economic systems (Verspagen and Werker, 2003; Witt, 2008; Silva and Teixeira, 2009). Reference within this informal college is typically made to a variety of alleged precursors such as Schumpeter, Hayek, Marshall and Veblen, but the evolutionary college is too amorphous and eclectic to warrant a description in terms of a single mentor or school. Notably, although this college has many outposts in Asia, Australasia and the Western Hemisphere, it is particularly strong in Europe.

Despite its internal heterogeneity and lack of consensus on key issues, the networks, journals and forums that developed after the late 1980s created a scattered but linked community of scholars addressing common problems and overlapping research agendas. They were also united by their common dislike of the static and equilibrium approaches that dominated mainstream economics.

Despite the lack of a commonly agreed theoretical framework, evolutionary economists began to make considerable headway in the application of their ideas to empirical and policy matters. Evolutionary economics quickly established an impressive research programme and had a major impact on economic policy, particularly in the areas of technology policy, corporate strategy and national systems of innovation (Dosi et al., 1988).

Consequently it is possible to identify a loose community of 'evolutionary economists' and proceed to examine the philosophical issues that underlie both their achievements and their disputes. This task is further facilitated by a growing discourse within 'evolutionary economics' on philosophical questions.

13.3   PHILOSOPHICAL DIFFERENCES BROADLY CONSIDERED

Scientific reasoning occurs on different levels, and disputes can occur on one or more of these. There is the ontological level concerning assumptions about the nature of reality; the epistemological level concerning how knowledge is gained and justified; the heuristic level concerning how problems are framed; and the methodological level concerning theoretical explanations and their construction. I indicate below that ontology is the most important for understanding differences of approach within evolutionary economics.

But there are important epistemological and methodological divergences as well. The ancient epistemological dispute between rationalism (deduction) and empiricism (induction) is reflected within evolutionary genres in the contrast between the axiomatic approach of evolutionary game theory and, on the other hand, the more empirically oriented research.

Intermediate epistemological positions are possible. Darwin himself saw theory as a necessary prerequisite of empirical investigation: 'without the making of theories I am convinced there would be no observation' (F. Darwin, 1887, Vol. 2, p. 315). Alfred Marshall (1920, p. 29) quoted and endorsed Gustav Schmoller's statement that: 'Induction and deduction are both needed for scientific thought as the left foot and the right foot are both needed for walking.' Similarly, the approach adopted by Richard Nelson and others combines elements of grand theory with extensive empirical investigation (Nelson and Winter, 1982; Malerba et al., 1999). Alongside the theoretical features of his earlier work, Nelson (2006, p. 491) has gone so far as to express qualified support for generalizing Darwinian principles to cover social evolution. Nevertheless, this epistemological divide between induction and deduction, and attempts to establish inter-mediate positions, are familiar throughout the history of economics and further exploration in general terms would add little that is new.

A major methodological difference concerns whether social phenomena can eventually be explained largely in biological terms (for example Hirshleifer, 1977), or whether biological influences or constraints are too important to be ignored alongside additional cultural influences (Veblen, 1899; Boyd and Richerson, 1985; Camerer et al., 2005), or whether biological influences are so unimportant that they generally can be ignored in considering human potential (Rose et al., 1984). Underling this issue are important ontological assumptions about causal relations (Hodgson, 2007a), particularly concerning the causal links between human biology and individual preferences and beliefs. It is possible that some denials of biological influences on preferences or beliefs are grounded on an ontological dualism, where the realms of human society and thought are somehow causally disconnected from biology and nature.

Once again, ontological issues lie beneath the surface. This has led to a growing literature on the ontology of evolutionary economics (Foss, 1994; Herrmann-Pillath, 2001; Hodgson, 2002; Dopfer and Potts, 2004; Vromen, 2004; Hodgson and Knudsen, 2006; Witt, 2008). For these and other reasons the primary focus of this chapter is on ontology. I turn to this in the following sections.

13.4   PRIMARY ONTOLOGICAL COMMUNALITIES WITH SOME SECONDARY DIVERGENCES

What is the nature of the world to which the principles of evolutionary economics apply? Among contemporary evolutionary economists there is universal agreement on five important features. But as we shall see below, basic agreement on the fifth feature within the evolutionary college is combined with some important additional differences of stress or interpretation, in addition to further differences explored in the next section.

First, and above all, it is a world of change. But this change is not merely quantitative or parametric: it involves qualitative changes in technology, organizations and the structure of the economy (Schumpeter, 1934). The equilibrium orientation of much mainstream economics is criticized precisely for its limited ability to embrace such qualitative change (Klaes, 2004).

Second, an important feature of economic change is the generation of novelty. Variety and its replenishment through novelty and creativity is a central theme of contemporary evolutionary economics. Nicolai Foss

(1994, p. 21) argues that evolutionary economics of the type developed by Giovanni Dosi, Richard Nelson, Sidney Winter, Ulrich Witt and others is concerned with 'the transformation of already existing structures and the emergence and possible spread of novelties'. Accordingly, Witt (1992, p. 3) writes: 'for a proper notion of socioeconomic evolution, an appreciation of the crucial role of novelty, its emergence, and its dissemination, is indispensable'. And Witt (2009) addresses novelty in more depth.

Novelty drives technological and institutional evolution. But by its nature it is unpredictable (Popper, 1960) and implies a unidirectional arrow of time. Consequently modern evolutionary economists are generally cautious about the possibilities for prediction and regard the predictions of mainstream economists as typically grounded on a neglect of novelty, uncertainty and surprise.

Third, evolutionary economists stress the complexity of economic systems. There are various definitions of ontological complexity, but many invoke the key idea of causal interaction between a number of entities with varied characteristics (Saviotti, 1996). Such complex ontologies involve non-linear and chaotic interactions, further limiting predictability. They create the possibility of emergent properties and further novelties. And generally the combination of novelty and complexity make many evolutionary changes irreversible (Dosi and Metcalfe, 1991).

Fourth, human agents have limited cognitive capacities. Especially given the complexity, uncertainty and ongoing change in the real world, agents are unable to fully understand what is going on or what is likely to happen. They are unable to obtain a fully-specified set of options and decisions are based of simpler rules of thumb rather than comprehensive rational deliberation. As Herbert Simon (1957) put it, there is 'bounded rationality'.

Fifth, just as Darwin showed that intricate and complex phenomena can emerge without God or design, so evolutionary economists adopt the insight of Friedrich Hayek and others that many human institutions and other social arrangements evolve spontaneously through individual interactions, without an overall planner or blueprint.

But universal acceptance of the importance of self-organization or undesigned order does not mean unanimity on its ontological details or its explanatory significance. One crucial problem is whether markets or exchange are the universal ether of human interaction (from which spontaneous order emerges), or whether markets and contracts depend significantly on other institutions (such as the state) whose evolution has to be explained, which may in fact involve a significant measure of planning or design, as well as spontaneity (Vanberg, 1986; Hodgson, 1993, 2009). Differences of view over the latter issue lead to a variety of policy positions over the roles of states or markets in the evolutionary college, which I do not begin to explore here.

There is also a divergence over whether the idea of self-organization is sufficient to explain social evolution (Foster, 1997, p. 444), or is an 'abstract, general description of evolutionary processes' (Witt, 1997, p. 489), or has to be supplemented by other major mechanisms such as selection (Kauffman, 1993; Hodgson and Knudsen, 2006, 2010; Aldrich et al., 2008; Geisendorf, 2009).

13.5   FIRST PRIMARY ONTOLOGICAL DIVERGENCE: DUALISM VERSUS MONISM

There are two major areas of (overt or covert) ontological dispute within the evolutionary college. The first concerns monism versus dualism. The second concerns the demarcation of entities within the evolving system, and the impact of that demarcation on theory construction. These two divergences are addressed sequentially in this and the following section.

The ontological dispute between monism and dualism is central to philosophy and has major (but often unacknowledged) implications for the social sciences. Ontological dualism asserts that mind (or spirit) and matter are disconnected and fundamentally distinct kinds of substances. By contrast, monists uphold that ultimate reality is entirely of one kind of substance, and accordingly there is potential causal interaction between any one segment of reality and another.

Most modern monists describe the stuff of reality as matter. By contrast there is an alternative idealist-monist tradition that sees ideas as the essential stuff of the universe, as recently posited by evolutionary economists Kurt Dopfer and Jason Potts (2008, p. 3).

Emergentist materialism is a relatively nuanced version, and does not deny the reality of mind. It upholds that material reality is structured on different levels, resulting from complexities of interaction and emergent properties (for example Bunge, 1977, 1979). Mario Bunge (1980) classifies Darwin as an emergentist materialist. Darwin saw the human mind and intentionality as themselves caused – rather than insignificant, as some misinterpreters suggest – and hence potentially subject to causal explanation (Dennett, 1995; Hodgson, 2004). Partly for this reason, Darwinism had an early impact on philosophy, psychology and the social sciences (James, 1890; Veblen, 1898; Dewey, 1910).

By contrast, some economists deny that intentions and beliefs are caused, on the grounds that to assume otherwise would undermine the reality of human agency or spontaneity. Hence, George Shackle (1986

[1988], pp. 281–282) posits the 'uncaused cause' and Lanse Minkler (2008, p. 21) argues for an individual 'free of external causes'. Jack Vromen (2001) ably counters such arguments: the fact that intentions are somehow caused or determined does not mean that human agency is any less substantial or real. If our intentions are caused it does not mean that we are released from responsibility for our actions. And even if they were uncaused it would not mean that individual responsibility was real (Dewey, 1894 [1967–72]; Hodgson, 2004, pp. 61–62).

Sometimes reflecting an implicit dualism, much of social science takes preferences, reasons or beliefs as given. This 'folk psychology' obscures a much more complex neurophysiological reality. It cannot adequately explain the origins of preferences, reasons and beliefs. Commonplace 'mind-first' explanations of human behaviour are unable to explain adequately such phenomena as sleep, memory, learning, mental illness, or the effects of chemicals or drugs on our perceptions or actions (Bunge, 1980; Damasio, 1994; Rosenberg, 1995; Kilpinen, 1999).

Witt (2008) emphasizes the importance of the divergence between monism and dualism for evolutionary economics. He points out that much theorizing in the Schumpeterian and Nelson–Winter traditions fails to examine possible biological influences on economic phenomena, such as the impact of the human genetic endowment on human capabilities and behaviour. But to be fair, this neglect does not necessarily stem from ontological dualism. It could flow from a monist ontology combined with a view that human nature is highly malleable, and that genetic constraints are of lesser explanatory importance. Whether the latter view is valid is a different matter. Its veracity or falsehood cannot be determined without empirical enquiry.

Witt stresses not only ontological monism but also the significance of understanding the causal and constraining roles of the human genetic endowment in social science. On this basis Witt (2004, pp. 131–132) establishes the 'continuity hypothesis' according to which natural evolution has 'shaped the ground, and still defines the constraints, for man-made, or cultural, evolution . . . economic evolution can be conceived as emerging from, and being embedded in, the constraints shaped by evolution in nature'. But this important idea predates Darwin and modern evolutionary theory. For example, Auguste Comte (1853, Vol. 2, p. 112) wrote: 'Biology will be seen to afford the starting point of all social speculation in accordance with the analysis of the social faculties of Man and the organic conditions which determine its character.' Today the idea that the natural world shapes and conditions the social has become commonplace, even among social scientists. The problem is that social scientists disagree on the nature, impact and relevance of the genetic constraints.

The continuity hypothesis directs our attention at possible biological determinants of human behaviour. But contrary to one of its supporters (Cordes, 2006), there is nothing in this hypothesis that overturns the different idea that Darwinian principles can be generalized to embrace social evolution (as outlined later below). For Witt his approach does not overturn generalized Darwinism, but neither does it require it.

13.6 SECOND PRIMARY ONTOLOGICAL DIVERGENCE: A POPULATION ONTOLOGY

A second ontological divergence is less prominent in the history of philosophy, although it was discussed by Alfred N. Whitehead (1929). I suggest the term 'plurality principle' to refer to an ontological plurality of demarcated entities. This is not the same as ontological pluralism, which refers to multiple, disconnected kinds of being, and of which ontological dualism is one example. Instead it 'conveys the notion of disjunctive diversity . . . There are many "beings" in disjunctive diversity' (Whitehead, 1929, p. 31). The plurality principle is consistent with monism because the plurality of entities could be made of the same substance. It upholds that reality consists of many demarcated entities, and each entity is different (at least in terms of its timing or position) from every other entity.

Whitehead influenced systems theory, where notions of system and subsystem are ubiquitous (Miller, 1978). In turn there may be sub-subsystems, and so on. Entities within populations may themselves contain populations, leading to a more complex ontology. In any case the problem here is to define and account for the boundaries and integrity of each entity or subsystem in the plurality. This task is very tricky, and there is no consensus on a clear definitional formula. The plurality principle relies on the existence of sufficient integrity and coherence within multiple entities, including sufficient interdependence of each entity and its components, to establish boundaries between multiple entities and establish a plurality of (sub)systems.

A population ontology is a special plurality of demarcated entities. There are many individually different and demarcated entities, grouped in populations according to some shared characteristics. Obvious examples would be industries containing firms, and hence such a population ontology will be recognized by most evolutionary economists. Divergences in the college occur partly because of different degrees of ontological salience given to the plurality principle and the role it plays in the development of theory.

Consider, for example, the question of endogenous versus exogenous change. In his studies of economic evolution, Schumpeter (1934, p. 63) repeatedly emphasized the sources of change 'from within'. Other evolutionary economists, including Witt (1992) and Esben Sloth Andersen (1994), have followed this definitional emphasis on a self-transforming economic system. For this claim of endogenous change to be meaningful there must be some notion of a bounded system that does not itself exhaust the universe. If there is nothing without that system, then the claim that change is driven from within is trivial. So where do the boundaries lie? One passage is illuminating. Witt (2008, p. 551) writes:

> Consider something that evolves, be it the gene pool of a species, a language spoken in a human community, the technology and institutions of an economy, or the set of ideas produced by the human mind. Although such entities can change over time in response to exogenous . . . forces . . . their genuinely evolutionary feature is that they are capable of transforming themselves endogenously over time . . . In the biological domain, for instance, the crucial processes are genetic recombination and mutation.

Notice first that the first sentence refers to 'something that evolves' (despite several items on the list clearly having multiple members). This establishes the foremost boundary around the whole 'something' or the 'set', and downplays any additional boundaries around individual members of any set. In other words, the population characteristics of any set are given less emphasis. Second, there is no explanation given why self-transformation (of one entity) is more 'genuine' than other forms of evolution (such as those that involve multiple entities). Third, population characteristics are overlooked even when Witt turns to biology for illustration. Accordingly, the last quoted sentence concerning 'the biological domain' sympotomatically omits any mention of natural selection.[2]

Importantly, selection is meaningful only within an ontology of populations of multiple entities. Consequently 'population thinking' becomes necessary (Mayr, 1976, 1982, 1988). A corollary of the plurality principle is that evolution in a population can involve not only the immanent transformation of individual entities, but also changes resulting from interactions with other entities, as well as with their environment. Once we have an ontology involving such populations, then questions arise not only concerning the development of each individual entity, but also how each entity interacts with others, and why some entities survive longer and are more successful in some sense than others.

This ontological consideration is relevant for another group of researchers, which overlap to some degree with the evolutionary college. Much of 'complexity theory' addresses not complex phenomena in general, but a particular form of complexity typically described by John Holland (1992), Brian Goodwin (1994), Stuart Kauffman (1995), Ralph Stacey (1996,

2003), Brian Arthur et al. (1997) and many others as a 'complex adaptive system'. Although many accounts address singular systems, often these are made up of multiple interconnected entities. In complex adaptive systems theory a number of agents interact with each other and together form a system that adapts to its environment. Consideration of whether a particular object of analysis involves a population ontology is relevant for this literature as well.

13.7   FROM COMPLEX POPULATION SYSTEMS TO GENERALIZED DARWINISM

Population ontologies involving further important characteristics are described as 'complex population systems' (Hodgson and Knudsen, 2006, 2010; Aldrich et al., 2008). By definition, complex population systems contain multiple varied (intentional or non-intentional) entities that interact with the environment and each other. They face immediately scarce resources and struggle to survive, whether through conflict or cooperation. They are mortal or degradable and thus engaged in a 'struggle for existence' (Darwin, 1859, pp. 62–63). They adapt and may pass on information to others, through replication or imitation. (Information here is defined very broadly, in the Shannon–Weaver sense of conditional dispositions or coding that can be transmitted to other entities and cause a response.) Examples of complex population systems are plentiful both in nature and in human society, despite their special definitional features. They include every biological species, from amoeba to humans. And importantly for the social scientist, they include human organizations, as long as we regard organizations as cohesive entities having some capacity for the retention of information. An economic example is an industry involving cohesive organizational entities such as business firms. In this manner, the common ontological features of all complex population systems, including in nature and human society, are established, without ignoring the huge differences of detail between them.

The evolution of any complex population system must involve the three Darwinian principles of variation, selection and retention (Campbell, 1965). These abstract principles do not themselves provide all the necessary details, but nevertheless they must be honoured, for otherwise the explanation of evolution will be inadequate. In particular, investigations into complex population systems must address: (1) the sources and replenishment of variety in the population; (2) how information is passed from one entity in the population to another; and (3) why some entities are more successful in surviving or passing on information than others. These three explanatory requirements map onto the three core Darwinian principles of variation, replication and selection. To make this move, these Darwinian principles have to be defined in sufficiently abstract and general terms, so that they are no longer confined to the biological domain (Hull, 1988; Hull et al., 2001; Hodgson and Knudsen, 2010).

Consider these explanatory requirements in more detail. First, there must be some explanation of how variety is generated and replenished in a population. In biological systems the answers – established since Darwin's death – involve genetic recombination and mutations. By contrast, the evolution of social institutions involves innovation, planning and other mechanisms very different from the detailed processes found in biology (Crozier, 2008).

Second, there must be an explanation for how useful information concerning solutions to particular adaptive problems is retained and passed on. This requirement follows directly from our assumptions concerning the broad nature of complex population systems, wherein there must be some mechanism by which adaptive solutions are copied and passed on. In biology, these mechanisms often involve genes and DNA. In social evolution, we may include the very different replication or imitation of habits, customs, rules and routines, all of which may carry solutions to adaptive problems.

Third, and not least, there must be an explanation of the fact that entities differ in their longevity and fecundity. In given contexts, some entities are more adapted than others, some survive longer than others, and some are more successful in producing offspring or copies of themselves. This is the principle of selection. In its abstract definition, selection involves an anterior set of entities, each interacting with its environment and somehow being transformed into a posterior set where all members of the posterior set are sufficiently similar to some members of the anterior set, and where the resulting frequencies of posterior entities depend upon their properties in the environmental context (Price, 1995). Through selection, a set of entities, a population, will gradually adapt in response to the criteria defined by an environmental factor. Even when both variety-creation and selection involve human agency, as is often the case in the human domain, the two processes are quite distinct. Innovation is about the creation of new variations, whereas selection is about how they are tested in the real world. It is important to emphasize that although fitness characteristics play a role in selection, in neither the biological nor the social world is the outcome necessarily optimal, efficient or desirable (Dupré, 1987; Hodgson, 1993; Gould, 2002).

What is suggested here is that core abstract Darwinian principles themselves have a wider application than to biology alone. Darwin (1859, 1871) himself proposed that they might apply to the evolution of language and morality, as well as to biological organisms. Consideration of such a generalized Darwinism has a long history, including Veblen (1899), Donald T. Campbell (1965) and Richard Dawkins (1983).

But because the ontological presumptions of a complex population system are not universal, Dawkins's use of the term 'universal Darwinism' is misleading. That is why several authors prefer the term 'generalized' Darwinism (Hodgson and Knudsen, 2006, 2010; Aldrich et al., 2008; Stoelhorst, 2008).

Second, it is important to emphasize that while Darwinian principles are employed, generalized Darwinism does not mean that social evolution is explained largely or wholly in biological terms. Indeed, the principles would apply to social evolution even if there were no significant genetic change. Darwinian principles are instead applied to socio-economic units, including organizations and their component customs or routines.

Third, generalized Darwinism is not a matter of biological analogies. It rests instead on purported ontological communality. Analogies take phenomena and processes in one domain as reference points for the study of similar phenomena or processes in another domain. Differences are regarded as dis-analogies. Social evolution is clearly dis-analogous to genetic evolution, because of the very different entities and mechanisms of replication (Crozier, 2008).

By contrast, generalization in science starts from a deliberately copious array of different phenomena and processes, without giving analytical priority to any of them. Where possible, scientists adduce shared principles. Given that the entities and processes involved are very different, these common principles will be fairly abstract and will not reflect detailed mechanisms unique to any particular domain. The very triumph of successful generalization is in the face of real and acknowledged differences at the level of detail (Kitcher, 1981).

13.8 CONCLUSION: A STRATEGY OF RECONCILIATION

From this perspective, a central feature of Witt's (2008) argument requires further thought. Witt (2008, pp. 551–555) distinguishes between two 'heuristic strategies', namely a 'generic concept of evolution' involving the 'twin concept' of 'novelty emergence and dissemination' and 'generalized Darwinian concepts'. He combines these two heuristics with the ontological split between monism and dualism to form a two-by-two matrix of types of evolutionary economics.

A problem with this configuration is that, contrary to Witt, generalized Darwinism is not simply a heuristic strategy but also, more importantly, it rests on specific ontological presuppositions. When we examine these pre-suppositions it is clear that Witt's 'generic concept of evolution' does not exclude generalized Darwinism. The latter also embraces the vital issue of 'novelty emergence and dissemination'. Hence contrary to a possible interpretation of Witt's two-by-two matrix there is no dichotomy between Witt's 'generic concept of evolution' and the ontology of generalized Darwinism: the latter is a special case of the former.[3]

Cordes (2006) and Witt (2008, p. 559) warn of the dangers in adopting generalized Darwinism because it is 'domain specific'. But its principles are not specific to biology alone: they are specific to all complex population systems, including human society.

Obversely, one might warn of the dangers of confining ourselves to ontologies that are too domain-general. Witt's 'generic concept of evolution' involves an ontology of singular 'somethings' that evolve. But for much analysis in the social domain it is important to get inside these 'somethings' and acknowledge their internal difference in terms of multiple entities. If multiple entities were fully acknowledged, then Witt's 'generic concept of evolution' would cease to be generic in the fullest sense. In particular, the failure to acknowledge multiple entities means that the nature of the process of diffusion of novelty must be considered within the whole, not from demarcated entity to entity. Similarly, this 'generic concept of evolution' cannot accommodate competition between different entities, without ceasing to be generic.

It is not clear how much can be built upon this extremely general ontological specification without adding additional features. In practice, it would seem that any application of this 'generic concept of evolution' to economic evolution must adopt a series of specific modifications that render the concept no longer generic. Furthermore, the more abstract of these modifications – such as the specification of an ontology of populations – are likely to move in the direction of complex population systems, as defined above. Witt's 'generic concept of evolution' is not wrong but insufficient.

Of course, there are many further important modifications that make the ontology even more specific than that of the complex population system. Important additional features that have to be brought into the picture at some stage are human intentionality, the capacity of humans for mental analysis and prefiguration, the nature of human sociality and cooperation, social institutions, and the development of different types and technologies of information transmission (Hodgson and Knudsen, 2010). This means that the generalized Darwinian framework is also insufficient, but not that it is wrong (Hodgson and Knudsen, 2006). To make any progress we have to move through several nested ontological specifications and levels of analysis (Hodgson, 2001, pp. 329–330).

Consequently it seems possible to reconcile conflicting positions in this recent and intense dispute. Witt (2008, p. 559) complains that generalized Darwinism relies on abstract principles that apply to evolutionary biology and are then 'claimed to govern evolutionary processes in all spheres of reality'. If this were true it would apply *a fortiori* to Witt's 'generic concept of evolution' as well.

The fact that both generalized Darwinism and Witt's 'generic concept of evolution' apply to both biological and social evolution does not make them invalid. We are addressing abstract common principles that apply to both domains. This has been recognized by several leading evolutionary economists. As Sidney Winter (1987, p. 617) writes:

> In sum, natural selection and evolution should not be viewed as concepts developed for the specific purposes of biology and possibly appropriable for the specific purposes of economics, but rather as elements of the framework of a new conceptual structure that biology, economics and other social sciences can comfortably share.

J. Stanley Metcalfe (1998, pp. 21–22) developed this point in more detail:

> That evolution is a core concept in biology does not mean that it is an inherently biological concept. Evolution can happen in other domains providing that conditions for an evolutionary process are in place. Thus, as economists applying evolutionary ideas to economic phenomena, we can learn from the debates on evolutionary biology in order to understand better the logical status of concepts such as fitness, adaptation and unit of selection without in any sense needing to absorb the associated biological context.

Metcalfe (p. 36) continues:

> Nothing I have said is intrinsically a matter of biological analogy, it is a matter of evolutionary logic. Evolutionary theory is a manner of reasoning in its own right quite independently of the use made of it by biologists. They simply got there first . . .

Both these authors hint at Darwinism without mentioning it by name. They also show explicitly that leading evolutionary economists start from general, abstract principles that apply to both biological and social evolution. The latter is also true of Witt (2008). This common ground suggests the possibility of reconciliation on some fundamental issues, while retaining a creative diversity of detailed approaches.

The first step in the strategy of reconciliation proposed here is to acknowledge that Witt's 'generic concept of evolution' and generalized Darwinian principles apply to both social and economic evolution, by virtue of their overlapping ontological stress on novelty and change. The further ontological presuppositions of generalized Darwinism are a special case of Witt's 'generic concept of evolution'. The second step is to understand that they are on different levels of abstraction. The third is to acknowledge that no single level of abstraction is adequate to approach the details and specificities involved.

While both Witt's 'generic concept of evolution' and generalized Darwinian principles apply, it is clear that the detailed mechanisms in society and nature are very different. Darwinism thus provides a metatheoretical framework, within which specific, detailed explanations must be placed. Darwinism, as such, cannot provide all the answers. Similar remarks apply to Witt's 'generic concept of evolution'.

The challenge for both generalized Darwinism and Witt's 'generic concept of evolution' is to show that they can have an important impact on the development of middle-range theory and serve as a useful guide for empirical enquiry. As Sandra Silva and Aurora Teixeira (2009) reveal, empirical work in evolutionary economics is relatively scarce, and there is a need to redirect the evolutionary research agenda. But theoretical frameworks are always necessary to guide empirical enquiry, and some consensus on theoretical fundamentals should empower this mission. A common recognition of the overlapping and nested ontologies discussed above, combined with a shared acknowledgement that vital matters of detail must always be added, provides a route towards reconciliation of apparently conflicting positions and a means of joining forces and framing shared problems in empirical analysis and middle-range theory construction.

Given these developments, the possibility emerges that evolutionary economics begins to generate a theoretical paradigm that can rival mainstream theory. This involves the shared evolutionary assumptions of a changing complex world that generates novelty. Agents therein have limited memories and cognitive capacities and assume that the rationality of others is similarly bounded (Hodgson, 2007b). The work of Nelson and Winter (1982) has already generated extensive discussion of the role of routines in storing information within organizations (Becker, 2008). More broadly, generalized Darwinian principles point to the need to examine different mechanisms of information retention and transmission between institutions, and the conditions of informational replication that have the potential to generate greater complexity (Hodgson and Knudsen, 2010). Witt (2008, 2009) and others enhance this theoretical agenda of information transmission and complexity-generation, by pointing to the wellspring of novelty and examining the extent to which biological factors frame economic evolution. The overall promise here is for an economics that transcends static theory and accommodates a richer picture of the complexities and specificities of economic change.

NOTES

1. The author is very grateful to John Davis, Wade Hands, Dick Nelson and Ulrich Witt for especially helpful comments on preceding versions of this chapter.
2. In a written comment on a previous version of this paper, Witt explained that he omitted selection here 'because it reduces variety rather than creating it'. This may be true of subset selection but not generally of successor selection. Subset selection simply means the elimination of some members of a set. By contrast, in successor selection – which is important in both natural and social evolution – new entities are created alongside others that expire (Price, 1995; Hodgson and Knudsen, 2010, Ch. 5).
3. In a written comment on a previous version of this paper, Witt clarifies that while the choice between columns of his matrix (between monism and dualism) is dichotomous, the row choice between the two different 'heuristics' is 'not a dichotomy but a difference'.

REFERENCES

Aldrich, Howard E., Geoffrey M. Hodgson, David L. Hull, Thorbjørn Knudsen, Joel Mokyr and Viktor J. Vanberg (2008), 'In Defence of Generalized Darwinism', *Journal of Evolutionary Economics*, **18**(5), 577–596.

Andersen, Esben Sloth (1994), *Evolutionary Economics: Post-Schumpeterian Contributions*, London: Pinter.

Andersen, Esben Sloth (2009), *Schumpeter's Evolutionary Economics: A Theoretical, Historical and Statistical Analysis of the Engine of Capitalism*, London, UK and New York, USA: Anthem.

Arthur, W. Brian, Steven N. Durlauf and David A. Lane (eds) (1997), *The Economy as an Evolving Complex System II*, Redwood City, CA: Addison-Wesley.

Becker, Markus C. (ed.) (2008), *Handbook of Organizational Routines*, Cheltenham, UK and Northampton, MA, USA: Edward Elgar.

Boulding, Kenneth E. (1981), *Evolutionary Economics*, Beverly Hills, CA: Sage Publications.

Boyd, Robert and Peter J. Richerson (1985), *Culture and the Evolutionary Process*, Chicago: Chicago University Press.

Bunge, Mario A. (1977), *Treatise on Basic Philosophy*, Vol. 3, *Ontology I: The Furniture of the World*, Dordrecht: Reidel.

Bunge, Mario A. (1979), *Treatise on Basic Philosophy*, Vol. 4, *Ontology II: A World of Systems*, Dordrecht: Reidel.

Bunge, Mario A. (1980), *The Mind–Body Problem: A Psychobiological Approach*, Oxford: Pergamon.

Camerer, Colin F., George Loewenstein and Drazen Prelec (2005), 'Neuroeconomics: How Neuroscience Can Inform Economics', *Journal of Economic Literature*, **43**(1), 9–64.

Campbell, Donald T. (1965), 'Variation, Selection and Retention in Sociocultural Evolution', in Barringer, H.R., G.I. Blanksten and R.W. Mack (eds), *Social Change in Developing Areas: A Reinterpretation of Evolutionary Theory*, Cambridge, MA: Schenkman, pp. 19–49.

Comte, Auguste (1853), *The Positive Philosophy of Auguste Comte*, 2 vols, transl. Harriet Martineau from the French volumes of 1830–42, London: Chapman.

Cordes, Christian (2006), 'Darwinism in Economics: From Analogy to Continuity', *Journal of Evolutionary Economics*, **16**(5), 529–541.

Crozier, G.K.D. (2008), 'Reconsidering Cultural Selection Theory', *British Journal of the Philosophy of Science*, **59**(3), 455–479.

Damasio, Antonio R. (1994), *Descartes' Error: Emotion, Reason, and the Human Brain*, New York: Putnam.

Darwin, Charles R. (1859), *On the Origin of Species by Means of Natural Selection, or the Preservation of Favoured Races in the Struggle for Life*, 1st edn, London: Murray.

Darwin, Charles R. (1871), *The Descent of Man, and Selection in Relation to Sex*, 2 vols, 1st edn, London: Murray.
Darwin, Francis (ed.) (1887), *Life and Letters of Charles Darwin: Including an Autobiographical Chapter*, 3 vols, 3rd edn, London: John Murray.
Dawkins, Richard (1983), 'Universal Darwinism', in D.S. Bendall (ed.), *Evolution from Molecules to Man*, Cambridge: Cambridge University Press, pp. 403–425.
Degler, Carl N. (1991), *In Search of Human Nature: The Decline and Revival of Darwinism in American Social Thought*, Oxford, UK and New York, USA: Oxford University Press.
Dennett, Daniel C. (1995), *Darwin's Dangerous Idea: Evolution and the Meanings of Life*, London, UK and New York, USA: Allen Lane and Simon & Schuster.
Dewey, John (1894), 'The Ego as Cause', *Philosophical Review*, **3**(3), 337–341; Reprinted (1967–72) in Jo Ann Boydston (ed.), *John Dewey: Early Works 4*, Carbondale, IL: Southern Illinois University Press, pp. 96–105.
Dewey, John (1910), *The Influence of Darwin on Philosophy and Other Essays in Contemporary Philosophy*, New York: Holt.
Dopfer, Kurt and Jason Potts (2004), 'Evolutionary Realism: A New Ontology for Economics', *Journal of Economic Methodology*, **11**(2), 195–212.
Dopfer, Kurt and Jason Potts (2008), *The General Theory of Economic Evolution*, London, UK and New York, USA: Routledge.
Dosi, Giovanni, Christopher Freeman, Richard Nelson, Gerald Silverberg and Luc L.G. Soete (eds) (1988), *Technical Change and Economic Theory*, London: Pinter.
Dosi, Giovanni and J. Stanley Metcalfe (1991), 'On Some Notions of Irreversibility in Economics', in Pier Paolo Saviotti and J. Stanley Metcalfe (eds), *Evolutionary Theories of Economic and Technological Change: Present Status and Future Prospects*, Reading, MA: Harwood, pp. 133–159.
Dupré, John A. (ed.) (1987), *The Latest on the Best: Essays on Evolution and Optimality*, Cambridge, MA: MIT Press.
Foss, Nicolai Juul (1994), 'Realism and Evolutionary Economics', *Journal of Social and Evolutionary Systems*, **17**(1), 21–40.
Foster, John (1997), 'The Analytical Foundations of Evolutionary Economics: From Biological Analogy to Economic Self-Organisation', *Structural Change and Economic Dynamics*, **8**(4), 427–451.
Geisendorf, Sylvie (2009), 'The Economic Concept of Evolution – Self-Organization or Universal Darwinism?', *Journal of Economic Methodology*, **16**(4), 359–373.
Goodwin, Brian C. (1994), *How the Leopard Changed its Spots: The Evolution of Complexity*, London: Weidenfeld & Nicholson.
Gould, Stephen Jay (2002), *The Structure of Evolutionary Theory*, Cambridge, MA: Harvard University Press.
Hayek, Friedrich A. (1988), *The Fatal Conceit: The Errors of Socialism. The Collected Works of Friedrich August Hayek, Vol. I*, ed. William W. Bartley III, London: Routledge.
Herrmann-Pillath, Carsten (2001), 'On the Ontological Foundations of Evolutionary Economics', in Kurt Dopfer (ed.), *Evolutionary Economics: Program and Scope*, Boston: Kluwer, pp. 89–139.
Hirshleifer, Jack (1977), 'Economics from a Biological Viewpoint', *Journal of Law and Economics*, **20**(1), 1–52.
Hodgson, Geoffrey M. (1993), *Economics and Evolution: Bringing Life Back Into Economics*, Cambridge, UK and Ann Arbor, MI, USA: Polity Press and University of Michigan Press.
Hodgson, Geoffrey M. (1999), *Evolution and Institutions: On Evolutionary Economics and the Evolution of Economics*, Cheltenham, UK and Northampton, MA, USA: Edward Elgar.
Hodgson, Geoffrey M. (2001), *How Economics Forgot History: The Problem of Historical Specificity in Social Science*, London, UK and New York, USA: Routledge.
Hodgson, Geoffrey M. (2002), 'Darwinism in Economics: From Analogy to Ontology', *Journal of Evolutionary Economics*, **12**(2), 259–281.
Hodgson, Geoffrey M. (2004), *The Evolution of Institutional Economics: Agency, Structure and Darwinism in American Institutionalism*, London, UK and New York, USA: Routledge.

Hodgson, Geoffrey M. (2007a), 'Taxonomizing the Relationship Between Biology and Economics: A Very Long Engagement', *Journal of Bioeconomics*, **9**(2), 169–185.

Hodgson, Geoffrey M. (2007b), 'Evolutionary and Institutional Economics as the New Mainstream?', *Evolutionary and Institutional Economics Review*, **4**(1), 7–25.

Hodgson, Geoffrey M. (2009), 'On the Institutional Foundations of Law: The Insufficiency of Custom and Private Ordering', *Journal of Economic Issues,* **43**(1), 143–166.

Hodgson, Geoffrey M. and Thorbjørn Knudsen (2006), 'Why We Need a Generalized Darwinism: and Why a Generalized Darwinism is Not Enough', *Journal of Economic Behavior and Organization*, **61**(1), 1–19.

Hodgson, Geoffrey M. and Thorbjørn Knudsen (2010), *Darwin's Conjecture: The Search for General Principles of Social and Economic Evolution*, Chicago, IL: University of Chicago Press.

Holland, John H. (1992), 'Complex Adaptive Systems', *Daedalus*, **121**(1), 17–30.

Hull, David L. (1988), *Science as a Process: An Evolutionary Account of the Social and Conceptual Development of Science*, Chicago, IL: University of Chicago Press.

Hull, David L., Rodney E. Langman and Sigrid S. Glenn (2001), 'A General Account of Selection: Biology, Immunology and Behavior', *Behavioral and Brain Sciences*, **24**(3), 511–573.

James, William (1890), *The Principles of Psychology*, 2 vols, 1st edn, New York, USA and London, UK: Holt and Macmillan.

Kauffman, Stuart A. (1993), *The Origins of Order: Self-Organization and Selection in Evolution*, Oxford, UK and New York, USA: Oxford University Press.

Kauffman, Stuart A. (1995), *At Home in the Universe: The Search for Laws of Self-Organization and Complexity*, Oxford, UK and New York, USA: Oxford University Press.

Kilpinen, Erkki (1999), 'What is Rationality? A New Reading of Veblen's Critique of Utilitarian Hedonism', *International Journal of Politics, Culture and Society*, **13**(2), 187–206.

Kitcher, Philip (1981), 'Explanatory Unification', *Philosophy of Science,* **48**, 507–531.

Klaes, Matthias (2004), 'Evolutionary Economics: In Defence of "Vagueness"', *Journal of Economic Methodology*, **11**(3), 359–376.

Malerba, Franco, Richard R. Nelson, Luigi Orsenigo, and Sidney G. Winter (1999), '"History Friendly" Models of Industry Evolution: The Computer Industry', *Industrial and Corporate Change*, **8**(1), 3–40.

Marshall, Alfred (1920), *Principles of Economics: An Introductory Volume*, 8th edn, London: Macmillan.

Mayr, Ernst (1976), *Evolution and the Diversity of Life: Selected Essays*, Cambridge, MA: Harvard University Press.

Mayr, Ernst (1982), *The Growth of Diological Thought: Diversity, Evolution, and Inheritance*, Cambridge, MA: Harvard University Press.

Mayr, Ernst (1988), *Toward a New Philosophy of Biology: Observations of an Evolutionist*, Cambridge, MA, USA and London, UK: Harvard University Press.

Metcalfe, J. Stanley (1998), *Evolutionary Economics and Creative Destruction*, London, UK and New York, USA: Routledge.

Miller, James G. (1978), *Living Systems*, New York: McGraw-Hill.

Minkler, Lanse P. (2008), *Integrity and Agreement: Economics When Principles Also Matter*, Ann Arbor, MI: University of Michigan Press.

Nelson, Richard R. (2006), 'Evolutionary Social Science and Universal Darwinism', *Journal of Evolutionary Economics*, **16**(5), 491–510.

Nelson, Richard R. and Sidney G. Winter (1982), *An Evolutionary Theory of Economic Change*, Cambridge, MA: Harvard University Press.

Popper, Karl R. (1960), *The Poverty of Historicism*, London: Routledge & Kegan Paul.

Price, George R. (1995), 'The Nature of Selection', *Journal of Theoretical Biology*, **175**, 389–396.

Rose, Steven, Leon J. Kamin and Richard C. Lewontin (1984), *Not in Our Genes: Biology, Ideology and Human Nature*, Harmondsworth: Penguin.

Rosenberg, Alexander (1995), *The Philosophy of Social Science*, 2nd edn, Boulder, CO: Westview Press.

Saviotti, Pier Paolo (1996), *Technological Evolution, Variety and the Economy*, Aldershot, UK and Brookfield, VT, USA: Edward Elgar.

Schumpeter, Joseph A. (1934), *The Theory of Economic Development: An Inquiry into Profits, Capital, Credit, Interest, and the Business Cycle*, Cambridge, MA: Harvard University Press.

Shackle, George L.S. (1986), 'The Origination of Choice', in Israel M. Kirzner (ed.), *Subjectivism, Intelligibility and Economic Understanding: Essays in Honour of Ludwig M. Lachmann on his Eightieth Birthday*, London: Macmillan, pp. 281–287; reprinted in Shackle, George L.S. (1988), *Business, Time and Thought: Selected Papers*, ed. Stephen F. Frowen, London: Macmillan.

Silva, Sandra Tavares and Aurora A.C. Teixeira (2009), 'On the Divergence of Evolutionary Research Paths in the Past 50 Years: A Comprehensive Bibliometric Account', *Journal of Evolutionary Economics*, **19**(5), 605–642.

Simon, Herbert A. (1957), *Models of Man: Social and Rational. Mathematical Essays on Rational Human Behavior in a Social Setting*, New York: Wiley.

Stacey, Ralph D. (1996), *Complexity and Creativity in Organizations*, San Francisco, CA: Berrett-Koehler.

Stacey, Ralph D. (2003), *Strategic Management and Organisational Dynamics: The Challenge of Complexity*, 4th edn, Harlow: Prentice Hall.

Stoelhorst, Jan Willem (2008), 'The Explanatory Logic and Ontological Commitments of Generalized Darwinism', *Journal of Economic Methodology*, **15**(4), 343–363.

Vanberg, Viktor J. (1986), 'Spontaneous Market Order and Social Rules: A Critique of F.A. Hayek's Theory of Cultural Evolution', *Economics and Philosophy*, **2**(1), 75–100.

Veblen, Thorstein B. (1898), 'Why Is Economics Not an Evolutionary Science?', *Quarterly Journal of Economics*, **12**(3), 373–397.

Veblen, Thorstein B. (1899), *The Theory of the Leisure Class: An Economic Study in the Evolution of Institutions*, New York: Macmillan.

Verspagen, Bart and Claudia Werker (2003), 'The Invisible College of the Economics of Innovation and Technological Change', *Estudios de Economía Aplicada*, **21**(3), 393–419.

Vromen, Jack J. (2001), 'The Human Agent in Evolutionary Economics', in John Laurent and John Nightingale (eds), *Darwinism and Evolutionary Economics*, Cheltenham, UK and Northampton, MA, USA: Edward Elgar, pp. 184–208.

Vromen, Jack J. (2004), 'Conjectural Revisionary Economic Ontology: Outline of an Ambitious Research Agenda for Evolutionary Economics', *Journal of Economic Methodology*, **11**(2), 213–247.

Whitehead, Alfred N. (1929), *Process and Reality: An Essay in Cosmology*, Cambridge: Cambridge University Press.

Winter, Sidney G., Jr (1987), 'Natural Selection and Evolution', in John Eatwell, Murray Milgate and Peter Newman (eds), *The New Palgrave Dictionary of Economics*, Vol. 3 London: Macmillan, pp. 614–617.

Witt, Ulrich (ed.) (1992), *Explaining Process and Change: Approaches to Evolutionary Economics*, Ann Arbor, MI: University of Michigan Press.

Witt, Ulrich (1997), 'Self-Organisation and Economics – What is New?', *Structural Change and Economic Dynamics*, **8**, 489–507.

Witt, Ulrich (2002), 'How Evolutionary is Schumpeter's Theory of Economic Development?', *Industry and Innovation*, **9**(1–2), 7–22.

Witt, Ulrich (2004), 'On the Proper Interpretations of "Evolution" in Economics and its Implications for Production Theory', *Journal of Economic Methodology*, **11**(2), 125–146.

Witt, Ulrich (2008), 'What is Specific about Evolutionary Economics?', *Journal of Evolutionary Economics*, **18**, 547–575.

Witt, Ulrich (2009), 'Propositions about Novelty', *Journal of Economic Behavior and Organization*, **70**, 311–320.

14 Economics in a cultural key: complexity and evolution revisited
Kurt Dopfer

14.1 THE RISE OF EVOLUTIONARY ECONOMICS

The last three decades have seen an upsurge in the number of publications addressing themes that have come to be grouped under the heading of 'evolutionary economics'. In a recent bibliometric account comprising the abstracts of articles published in all economic journals over the past half-century, Sandra Silva and Aurora Teixeira have been documenting the impressive magnitudes and structural dynamic of this trend – a trend that has accelerated tremendously in the last two decades, considering that 90 per cent of this body of research is recorded as having been published after 1990 (Silva and Teixeira, 2009; EconLit database). There have been related accounts, emphasizing the interpretation and assessment of these trends, that have not shied away from a discourse about the general applicability and adequacy of the term 'evolutionary' itself (Dolfsma and Leydesdorff, 2010; Witt, 2008; Hanappi, 1994; Hodgson, 1993).

In its paradigmatic outlook, the essential difference of evolutionary economics from the neoclassical mainstream is that it gives priority to dynamic rather than static analysis and, more specifically, puts behavioural, institutional, technological and other explanatory variables centre stage (rather than exogenous ones) when coping with dynamics. It was a great moment for the science of economics, and for evolutionary economics in particular, when the book by Richard Nelson and Sidney Winter entitled *An Evolutionary Theory of Economic Change* appeared in 1982. In their trailblazing contribution, they set out two perspectives: a general one, addressing foundational issues, and a particular one, relating to the construction of specific theoretical models. Addressing the former, they state (Nelson and Winter, 1982, p. 4) that: 'a major reconstruction of the theoretical foundations of our discipline is a precondition for significant growth in our understanding of economic change.'

They acknowledge (p. 399) that they are 'developing a general way of theorizing about economic change'. In turn, their particular endeavour is 'with exploring particular models and arguments, consistent with that approach, focusing on particular features or issues about economic change' (p. 399). When assessing the two, they state (p. 399), significantly:

> Of the two parts of the endeavor, we view the development of the general theoretical approach as by far the more important. The particular models are interesting in their own right, but we regard them primarily as examples of the class of models consistent with our proposed way of theorizing.

The significance of their book lies in the fact that it succeeds in providing an alternative to neoclassical economics by furnishing essential cues for a new 'way of theorizing'.

14.2　EVOLUTIONARY ECONOMICS IN THE FUTURE

When assessing developments in the field since the publication of this book, two trends warrant particular attention. First, there has been a considerable falling short in the ensuing efforts to attain the former of the two goals. Most of the publications, worthy though they are, have concentrated on devising and refining particular models and theoretical positions, with much less effort being devoted to the goal of constructing viable foundations for the approach. The lack of underpinning has not just left much valuable work unstructured and unrelated, it has also rendered the new discipline as a whole generally weak in terms of its competition with the mainstream.

Second, there has been a growing recognition that the search for better foundations should be informed by integration rather than isolated developments along author-focused approaches based, for instance, on the works of Joseph Schumpeter, Thorstein Veblen, Friedrich Hayek or Alfred Marshall. This applies even to Schumpeter's work, which has probably contributed more to the foundations of the new approach than that of any other author (Hanusch and Pyka, 2007). Marking the boundaries of a modern Schumpeter programme, Andreas Pyka and Horst Hanusch (2006, p. 4) note: 'that strand of literature which is concerned with industry evolution and technological progress . . . can be coined Neo-Schumpeterian economics'.

Since Nelson and Winter's work bears strong imprints of Schumpeter's thinking, what Nelson and co-author Davide Consoli have said recently when addressing the overall scope of the discipline is particularly noteworthy (Nelson and Consoli, 2010, p. 665):

Many contemporary economists who consider themselves evolutionary theorists have in mind a narrower and a broader goal. The narrower goal is to meet what we will call 'Schumpeter's challenge', which is to create a theoretical framework capable of analyzing innovation-driven economic growth. While it might be suggested that this narrow goal is rather broad, the still broader goal is no less than the replacement of neoclassical theory with a theoretical alternative . . .

Schumpeter's approach, which originally represented the general reference point, is now seen as a narrow approach in view of a new, broader vision of the discipline. Esben Andersen's (2008, p. 1) general assessment may mirror a view held widely in this school of thought: '[E]volutionary economics has moved beyond Schumpeter's strand . . . and has also moved beyond Marshall and Veblen and many other pioneers'.

Although the extended scope has not yet coalesced into a solid, unified theoretical framework, it has already been providing, as will be shown, enormously fertile ground for developing, testing and experimenting with new theoretical approaches, simulation techniques, statistical methods, ways of organizing and collecting data and mathematical representations.

14.3   NATURAL HISTORY: HIERARCHY OF EVOLVED COMPLEXITY

From a global perspective, the question is this: what makes entities specifically economic ones, distinctively different from non-economic ones? Economic entities are part of a natural history that has evolved into a hierarchy of levels with differing complexity. Although complexity scientists have variously addressed the issue of how to define and validate the hierarchy of evolved complexity (Lane, 2006; Holland, 1998), few contributions have been forthcoming so far from the camp of economists, with the notable exception of John Foster (2005).

Construed in elementary terms, the natural hierarchy can be seen as being composed of physical (or physiochemical), biological and cultural levels. Significantly, economic entities are phenomena that, in their evolved complexity, belong to the cultural – not to the physical, biological or any other – level of complexity. To claim empirical validity, economic entities need to be portrayed in such a way that they take into account the characteristics of the level of complexity to which they belong. Economics in this way is, in a very fundamental sense, a cultural science.

14.4   THE NATURAL SCIENCES AS A TOOLBOX

Although empirical validity is clearly of major concern for science, there is another desideratum of equal significance. Scientific statements stand out over non-scientific ones in their logical rigour, formal elegance and openness to falsification. To qualify for appellation as 'scientific', a particular toolbox is required, involving analytical language, various forms of logic, mathematical representation, statistical methods and modelling techniques. In their search for an adequate toolbox, proponents of evolutionary economics have turned variously to physics and to biology.

The physics-based approach to economics has benefited much from the early work on complexity done at the Santa Fe Institute (Anderson et al., 1988; Arthur et al., 1997). Through the application of modern physics, the work acquired the status of a 'new' heterodox economics. The new assumptions of non-linearity, feedback, discrete parameters and iteration stood in stark contrast to the well-behaved world of mechanics that informs the neoclassical canon. These nucleic activities have developed into a broader programme under the label 'complexity science' or 'complexity economics' (Colander et al., 2010; Rosser, 2010). The complexity approach – arguably the sister discipline of evolutionary economics – has branched into various special strands, in particular into econophysics and econobiology. The generality of the concept has evoked the broad vision of a 'transdisciplinary approach' (Rosser, 2010).

The toolbox of physics has provided mathematical representations for modelling various kinds of economic phenomena, ranging from laser-based synergy for modelling the emergence of collective preferences, fashion patterns or self-organization in firms (Weidlich, 2000; Haken, 2005) to multi-particle physics for modelling the behaviour of various markets, particularly financial ones (Schweizer, 2003; Lux and Kaizoji, 2007), complex regularities of socio-economic networks and collectives (Hollingsworth and Müller, 2008; Sornette, 2008), and to percolation theory for modelling spatial dynamics (Brenner, 2004) or the diffusion of technology under conditions of various consumer demand characteristics (Silverberg and Verspagen, 2005a).

The physics-based models display generally high mathematical abstraction, precision and consistency. To achieve this they use methods that were developed to represent phenomena the complexity of which is lower than that for economic ones. These tools work within a range of empirical assumptions, and importing them into economics necessarily means accepting their particular array of assumptions. Accordingly, the need arises to explain what exactly justifies treating economic particles as if they were physical particles with low complexity, and how those then relate to others in the entirety of an economic unit that typically displays features of high complexity. Models of a physico-mathematical nature are premised on a great empirical distance – that between dead matter and economic life – thereby rendering evident the need to justify their empirical content. The methodological crux is this: the empirical distance is great, making the problem large; and, simply because it is large, solutions aimed at vindicating it become difficult. The size of the problem paralleled by the ensuing difficulty to solve it may well represent a major limitation on the development of physics-based economics into an empirically attractive variant.

14.5   BIOLOGY: PARADIGMATIC SIGNPOST AND TOOLS FOR ECONOMICS

The proximity of biology and economics – both deal with living systems – has inspired economists in two fundamental ways. First of all, biology has served as paradigmatic orientation in a world ruled by mechanics. The founding fathers of the discipline, particularly Veblen and Marshall, entertained the vision of economics as a science drawing deep inspiration from biology (Veblen, 1898; Marshall, 1890). The two great precursors held quite different views about how economics should be reconstructed, but they were united in what they were against: the mechanics of neoclassical economics.

Biology may provide paradigmatic guidance for economics in terms of both its static and its dynamic problems. Concerning economic statics (defined as the logic of coordination), biology provides a paradigmatic pillar in the form of the living system approach as, for instance, universalized into 'general system theory' by Ludwig von Bertalanffy (Bertalanffy, 1968; Kapp, 1976). The historical dynamic of that system, as its second pillar, is captured by the concepts of ontogeny and phylogeny. The common denominator is biological knowledge, say G. In a state of ontogeny, an organism performs life-maintaining operations on the basis of a given G. In phylogeny, G changes over time. Gottfried Leibniz, an early discoverer of evolution, spoke – dissenting from Isaac Newton's continuity of equilibrium – of a continuity of change (Leibniz, 1714 [1991], calling it 'Continuity Principle'; Öser, 1974; also Witt, 2004).

The prefix 'biological' in knowledge can, like a constant in mathematics, readily be dropped, and then we get a universal concept of knowledge and of operation. Applied to economics, this means that we have two major levels of theoretical analysis:

- operational level: ongoing operations based on given knowledge.
- knowledge level: structure and evolution of knowledge governing operations.

Evolutionary economics deals with the structure and evolution of knowledge for economic operations. Neoclassical economics analyses ongoing economic operations under the assumption of given knowledge.

Biology is useful as more than just a paradigmatic signpost; it also renders practical services. Like physics, it provides a toolbox incorporating modelling techniques, mathematical representations and statistical procedures. Applying this toolbox, a range of conceptual, theoretical and simulation models have been devised, including genetic algorithm and genetic computing (Alander, 2009), game-theoretic models and replicator dynamics (Gintis, 2009; Metcalfe, 2005), evolutionary growth and percolation models (Kwasnicka and Kwasnicki, 2006; Silverberg and Verspagen, 2005b) and fitness landscape models (Frenken, 2006). These models shed light on the richness of life in economics in a mathematical form borrowed from biology.

The issue, again, is whether the mathematical representations adequately portray the complexity that is characteristic of economic phenomena. The complexity of life is closer to that of economic phenomena than dead matter, but there is still an empirical distance to be justified (Windrum et al., 2007; Geisendorf, 2007; Foray and Steinmueller, 2001). For instance, genetic algorithm and genetic computing models posit knowledge in terms of algorithms, prompting questions about the extent to which a completely determined technical sequence can capture evolution; Stuart Kaufmann's 'NK fitness landscapes' depict biological environments, inviting the question as to whether or in what way these portray characteristics of economic landscapes with complementary-defined structures anchored in the division of labour and knowledge; and replicator models dealing with genetic knowledge transmission call for clarification as to whether or how empirically meaningful economic knowledge transmission is without considering the behavioural key concept of adoption upon which all communication is premised.

Biology-based models, like physics-based models, require an explanation as to why biological phenomena, such as genes, organisms, replication or selection, should represent the complexity of economic phenomena. There has been an extensive discussion revolving around 'universal Darwinism', a concept introduced by biologist-philosopher Daniel Dennett (1995). It got a warm reception from some economists (Hodgson, 2002; Hodgson and Knudsen, 2006; Aldrich et al., 2008), but little approval from others, who criticized either the weak evidence of homologies, or the irrelevance of its questions (Levit et al., 2010; Witt, 2008, 2004; Nelson, 2006; Cordes, 2006; Vromen, 2007), or the lack of integration of other relevant concepts such as self-organization (Geisendorf, 2009; Buenstorf, 2006). It must suffice here to conclude with a general assessment: the discussion has furnished little in the way of systematic practical criteria to evaluate the question of whether, or to what extent, it is warranted to apply biological models or representations to a clearly defined class of economic cases.

The difficulties with establishing systematic procedures have led some economists to discard a transdisciplinary perspective altogether. Nelson and Winter, whose work has set the pace for much of the significant debate in the last three decades, have pointed out that they generally start with theoretical propositions and use any tools or language that are fit for a particular purpose of economic theorizing. Unlike advocates of universal Darwinism, they contend (Nelson and Winter, 1982, p. 11): 'We emphatically disavow any intention to pursue biological analogies for their own sake, or even for the sake of progress toward an abstract, higher-level evolutionary theory.' Stanley Metcalfe takes the same course when he asserts (Metcalfe, 2005, p. 392) that the various evolutionary concepts employed in economics, 'have nothing inherently to do with biology and related disciplines'.

Indeed, why should one rule out the use of methods, analytical models or mathematical representations if they are useful in economics but lack empirical corroboration in biology? Universal Darwinism cannot set the theoretical agenda of economics. To state that self-generated change and selection are important in economics means preaching to the converted, and to investigate whether or not Darwinian principles hold in physics as they do in biology is, though intellectually highly fascinating, of no great concern for economists. The assessment reached from a practical vantage point is this: encountering universal Darwinism with agnosticism not only allows us to retain the precious legacy of Darwin's work, it also opens up biology as a rich field for economists, ranging from Ludwig von Bertalanffy's grand general system theory to more recent (neo-Lamarckian) approaches involving epigenetics, which explain the adoption of information – the core of a communication-based evolutionary behavioural economics – in a way that Darwinism does not (Knottenbauer, 2009).

14.6   ECONOMICS AS CULTURAL SCIENCE

Economics belongs to the cultural level of the evolved natural hierarchy of complexity. In order to acknowledge the complexity of economic phenomena it is necessary to state them in terms of the complexity of that level.

Looking at the research that has been carried out in evolutionary economics, it is clear that there have been few efforts to confront the problem head-on. The main reason for this reluctance may lie in the difficulties inherent in devising methods, mathematical representation and statistical tools adequate to cope with the level of complexity that the cultural level expounds. In the approach to economic complexity, recourse has been had – as has been pointed out – to lower levels of complexity 'as if' they were the levels that economic phenomena displayed. I am proposing that, if economics is to be empirically meaningful, the starting point of any theoretical endeavour has to be the cultural level, not the physical or biological level. Based on this theoretical premise, any tool may be chosen that renders adequate service.

While there is no broad discourse on economics as a cultural science, some groundwork has been forthcoming from the evolutionary camp. Though still scanty, it may well provide a rough skeleton of a future theoretical agenda setting the pace for further developments. The research includes works by Carsten Herrmann-Pillath (2010), Jason Potts (2008), Richard R. Nelson (2008), Ngai-Ling Sum and Bob Jessop (2011) and Michael Hutter and David Throsby (2008).

The domain of human culture comprises two major constituencies: *Homo sapiens* and cultural artefacts. Captured in their essentials, both are carriers of knowledge: *Homo sapiens* of subjective (subject-related) knowledge and cultural artefacts of objective (object-related) knowledge. This nucleic view of the cultural level yields a classification that is, in many and important ways, useful for economic theory construction and modelling. It distinguishes between carrier and knowledge on the one hand, and between subjects and objects on the other.

Knowledge is used in various cultural contexts. The specificity of and differences between cultural contexts are defined by the kinds of operations that are performed. In this way, economics is defined as the discipline dealing with the cultural context governing economic operations. Economic operations include production, consumption and transaction. This insight starts to put some flesh on the bones of the earlier distinction of the knowledge level and the operational level, specifying the former as cultural knowledge and the latter as economic operations. Cultural knowledge becomes economically relevant – that is, economic knowledge – when used in the context of economic operations.

14.7 *HOMO SAPIENS OECONOMICUS*

Homo sapiens and cultural artefacts thus acquire particular meanings in the economic context. *Homo sapiens* – in his economic operations – gets specified as a particular disciplinary construal: *Homo sapiens oeconomicus* (HSO; Dopfer, 2004). Seizing upon this concept, various specifications may be allowed for, depending on the faculties required for particular problem solving in economic environments. Essentially, HSO operates in an economic environment that embraces highly complex structures and is subject to continuous novelty-driven change. HSO, accordingly, may be seen as a 'complex individual', coping with problems of structural complexity (Davis, 2008, 2003), or as '*Homo creativus*', meeting the challenges of unpredictable qualitative change in economic environments (Foster, 1987). The former construal may prove particularly useful as an assumption for complexity models, the latter as an assumption for evolutionary models.

Other primates create culture, but *Homo sapiens* – and, for that matter, HSO – excels in three fundamental ways. First, man is a knowledge maker. This faculty unfolds as a process the characteristics of which may be captured by a trajectory that is composed of three phases:

- Phase 1: origination of knowledge.
- Phase 2: adoption of knowledge (perception, understanding, learning).
- Phase 3: retention of knowledge for ongoing economic operations.

Second, *Homo sapiens* can combine different pieces of knowledge into a whole. This faculty is exercised not only on the basis of reacting to environmental conditions but also on that of imagination independent of those external conditions. The cognitive autonomy enables complex knowledge anticipation. Third, humans can share their imagination. Symbolic language is a powerful tool for doing so. Shared imagination, as it unfolds in the process of the generation, adoption and retention of knowledge, lies at the heart of economic evolution.

14.8 MATERIAL CULTURE IN ECONOMICS

With *Homo sapiens*, cultural objects acquire their operational meaning when posited in an economic context. Operationally specified, these represent commodities, products or goods, or similarly operationally specified objects.

By way of an exemplar, archaeologists are excavating objects at a site that furnishes a record of material culture. They apply methods of stratification, which highlight the history of objects, and of geographic information systems (GISs) and related techniques, which place the findings in their spatial context. The material account is visible, measurable and quantifiable, but in itself says nothing about the rationale of the organization of the objects and about their operational use. Although archaeologists agree widely on the usefulness of modern stratification methods, the GISs and related techniques, they are split in their views as to whether or in what way it should be of concern to an archaeologist to give meaning to the objects or, instead, simply to leave them as material witnesses untouched by hermeneutic endeavours.

For the present analysis, it is particularly interesting that efforts have been under way to construct the discipline as evolutionary archaeology employing explanatory schemes from biology, such as Darwinism. These attempts have been challenged on the grounds that the explanations were based on wrong analogies to biology – though, in this process, they have left in limbo the principal question, as to whether or how to explain the material record in general. Starting from the cultural (rather than the biological) level, an approach has been suggested that relates cultural artefacts to human cognition, highlighting the co-evolution of objects and cognition (van der Leeuw and McGlade, 1997). This new kind of complexity-based evolutionary archaeology takes as its departure point the cultural level. It employs principles from biology, such as Darwinian selection, whenever they fit a particular explanatory purpose; but it does not construct archaeology from biology. Given this cultural platform, operational economic contexts may be identified, and the discipline of economics may be given a systematic home in archaeology. Complexity-based evolutionary archaeology, in turn, would seem to be the most natural home for evolutionary economics, which generally emphasizes long-run views and empirical evidence.

In neoclassical economics, cultural objects have no qualitative attributes. It makes for the universality of the demand and supply model in its partial and general equilibrium variants that it abstracts from any characteristics. Qualitative differences between commodities are translated into quantitative differences stated in price ratios of commodities. Heterogeneity turns into homogeneity. The neoclassical model operates not only with the assumption of a representative agent but also – significantly – with that of a representative commodity.

In contrast, evolutionary complexity economics works with both heterogeneous agents and heterogeneous commodities. Admittedly, there are types of multi-agent models that work with heterogeneous agents but retain the assumption of homogeneous commodities, as when analysing the fish market of Marseilles (Kirman and Vignes, 1991). Although these models shed light on market equilibrium under the condition of a single kind of commodity, such as stocks, or indeed fish, they fail to provide new insights when there are many different kinds of commodities. In the case of the economy as a whole (or an equivalent macro context), when, typically, many markets connect qualitatively in complementarities, the assumption of heterogeneous commodities is mandatory. As with an excavation site in archaeology, an economy is composed of heterogeneous objects, and constructing the whole can be accomplished only by putting together the pieces with all their distinct attributes.

14.9   BIMODAL METHODOLOGY

Economic operations are anchored in knowledge. An understanding of the nature of the structure and of the evolution of knowledge is therefore the key to an understanding of economic operations. A clear analytical exposition of this concept would therefore appear to represent a sensible starting point for the construction of an economic theory or model.

In its archetypical form, knowledge may be seen as representing a knowledge-bit. This elementary analytical unit has two essential properties. On the one hand, it is an idea; it embodies semantic content. As idea, it is timeless and spaceless. On the other hand, ideas do not reside in a Platonic heaven, but are always physically actualized; they have a carrier. Ideas are actualized by matter and energy in time and space. The knowledge-bit therefore typically possesses – ontologically – a bimodal nature (Dopfer and Potts, 2008).

Acknowledging this ontologically anchored characteristic has important implications for the way methodology is approached. Ideas are not observable. They cannot be measured with a metre rule but, instead, have to be interpreted in terms of their meaning – for example, as function or task. The appropriate procedure for coping with qualitative attributes, such as product or technological characteristics, is hermeneutics. In turn, knowledge in its physical actualization is observable. It can be measured on a metric scale and quantified. Its methodology is statistics and other such quantitative measurement.

Conceiving the elementary unit of the knowledge-bit in the entirety of its properties calls for recognition of both quality and quantity: for a bimodal methodology. A monomodal methodology aims either at only a qualitative empirical account or at only a quantitative one. It would be a mistake to associate traditional economics with quantification and distinguish it from evolutionary and complexity economics as an approach that deals only with qualitative analysis. The difference is that the latter strand is premised on concepts such as technological heterogeneity or product characteristics, conducting quantification in recognition of these qualitative attributes. Traditional economics lacks any such hermeneutic guidance. It is therefore good at aggregation (notwithstanding the well-known problems that accompany it), but fails entirely in accounting for structure. Evolutionary economics retains qualitative attributes and, rather than rejecting any aggregation, it performs it in recognition of the qualitatively structured data.

14.10   FROM MICRO TO MACRO

The knowledge approach stands in close kinship with the system approach. A system may be defined as relations between component parts, and knowledge, if conceived of in a very generalized manner, defines both. In this way, the economy as a knowledge-defined macro-system is composed of interrelated knowledge-defined micro-systems.

In simple models, the micro units are treated like physical particles (rather than systems) with fixed behavioural propensities. Complex models, in turn, treat the micro units themselves as systems, and, as a consequence, the macro-system of the economy is composed of interrelated micro-systems. There is a system hierarchy, with an upper level consisting of the total system and a lower level of multiple subsystems. Coping with the intricacies of system hierarchy poses major challenges for complexity science and complexity economics (Lane, 2006).

The analytical problems are compounded when dealing with several levels. Given a continuum of levels, the complexity in the analysis may be reduced by keeping the component parts simple, for instance, as in the mentioned case, by working with non-systemic micro units. Heading in the opposite direction, higher levels may be accounted for by specifying the micro unit, for instance by allowing for HSO in his systemic or similar characteristics. A theory of the firm may thus work with either a simple or a complex model of HSO. Viewed from the angle of its assumptions, it will be either a simple or a complex theory of the firm (Leibenstein, 1976; Frantz, 1997).

14.11   COMPLEXITY MEETS EVOLUTION: MESO

Looking at the economy through the lens of complexity science, we see it as system. Accordingly, the analytical focus here is on aspects such as hierarchy, structure, relations and complementariness. In this way it is, basically, a static view. The further question, then, is this: how does this macro-system move in time? How does the economy as complex system evolve?

We get a first clue when recalling that the micro unit is involved in the process of the generation, adoption and retention of knowledge seen as a trajectory (section 14.7). Change occurs in the form of a micro trajectory actualized within the boundaries of a subsystem – for example a firm. Since the novel knowledge variant introduces a novel component into an extant structure, structural change takes place. This is an important result; and it is here, where complexity-based analysis usually ends, that evolutionary economics steps in.

From an evolutionary angle, the micro units are, in their process-dynamic, not closed but open systems. Novel knowledge variants cross the boundaries of the generating carrier, 'spilling over' into the environment. Knowledge is encoded and decoded by carriers, and transmitted by communication.

The hallmark of the bimodality assumption is that a single knowledge-bit can be actualized many times. It can be actualized not just by a single carrier but by many carriers; for instance a technology can be adopted by many firms. A single actualization of a knowledge-bit may be possible, but it would be a special case, as opposed to the general case of many actualizations. Introducing the evolutionary perspective, the analytical unit for the construction of an evolutionary macro is not a single knowledge-bit (a single idea, a single actualization) but, rather, a single idea and many carriers actualizing it. The analytical unit is one knowledge-bit and many actualizations. Evolutionary complexity expounds as both 'one-ness' and 'many-ness'.

This leads us to a theoretical architecture of economics in which the received micro–macro dichotomy collapses. 'Micro' is a member of a population, and it is not the micro unit but, rather, a population of micro units that is the component part of 'macro'. One may circumvent the population by heading directly from micro to macro, but this represents a valid procedure only if one is dealing with the uniform single-actualization case or if the aim is to ignore the aspects of process altogether.

As this 'component part' is neither micro nor macro, there is a gap in our terminology. Recognizing the intermediate nature of this analytical unit, we may call it, without challenging our vocabulary excessively, 'meso'. The upshot of the meso unit is the duality of its defining characteristics: it is a structure component and a process component. It is a structure component in that it connects as single knowledge-content or idea with other such components (section 14.13), and a process component in that it expounds the logic of its physical actualization in time and space (section 14.14).

14.12   ARCHITECTURE: MICRO–MESO–MACRO

The architecture of an evolutionary complexity-based economics is starting to take shape. Its constituent domains are these: micro, meso and macro. The major building block from which macro is constructed is meso. The construction work can start by specifying what the two constituencies of knowledge consist of: knowledge content and actualization process. Constructing macro from knowledge content, we get structure in its semantic characteristics, as ideas; let us call it the 'deep' macro structure (section 14.13). Constructing macro from actualization processes, we obtain an inferable structure as it unfolds along the trajectories of the generation, adoption and retention of knowledge; we may call this the 'surface' macro structure (section 14.14).

14.13   INVESTIGATING STRUCTURAL COMPLEXITY

Knowledge content may come in two guises: as a single knowledge-bit or as a structured knowledge composite actualized in a carrier. Depending on which one we choose as our assumption, we will get quite different models.

On the one hand, a meso model may be constructed by turning to the composite knowledge actualized in a carrier – for example a firm. A meso population is then composed of many carriers, such as firms. The macro is construed analogously, from a composite of carrier-defined meso units. It represents the visible surface structure of macro. Most current strands, such as multi-agent models and industrial sector dynamic models, operate on the basis of carriers or agents. In models of the former type the theoretical specification of meso does not play an essential role (Tefsatsion, 2002), but it is a constituent aspect in the latter (Pyka et al., 2006; Pyka and Fagiolo, 2007; Castellacci, 2009).

On the other hand, meso may be viewed as being composed of single knowledge-bits, such as a technology. Unlike in the preceding case, the meso population is now not composed of carriers but, rather, of actualizations of a single knowledge-bit. In this way, for instance, a single technology has a population of actualizations. Models that operate upon single knowledge-bits (rather than carriers) include learning, selective adoption and path-dependent models, as addressed in the following section.

Employing knowledge-bits as the building block, macro emerges as a deep knowledge structure or division of knowledge. The methodological cornerstone of this analysis is mereology. Though not conducted under this label, there is a body of literature (scanty as it is) that explicitly recognizes its theoretical significance (Helmstädter, 2003; Langlois, 2002; Antonelli, 2008). By way of an example, producing a car requires the assembly of various components that stand in complementariness to each other. In contrast, a carrier-based composite approach allows us only to analyse interdependences stated in terms of inputs and outputs – for instance, as a Leontief inverse matrix. Neither the input mix nor the output end result provides any information as to how the component parts are combined. As can be seen, therefore, the conventional composite approach fails to serve as an appropriate basis for depicting the 'deep' structure of knowledge in an economy.

Micro knowledge-bits or carriers may be assembled into a subsystem; or, similarly, a game-theoretic social context may be singled out for partial analysis (Elsner, 2010; Hayden, 2008). In this way, a further level (besides micro and macro) in the continuum of levels of the system hierarchy may be introduced. Analogously, a level of sub-aggregates in a continuum marked by micro (no aggregation) and macro (total aggregation) may be allowed for. Assuming a single (systemic, aggregation) level, it will show up as an intermediate level, and the label 'meso' may be assigned to it.

Within our framework, for an analytical unit to qualify as meso, two conditions have to be met. On the one hand, the construal must be identified as a component part of a structure. It is inessential that the structure component itself expounds structural features (though this assumption is consistent with the concept). On the other hand, the structure component must be stated in terms of a process dealing with the generation, selective adoption and retention of knowledge.

Although in-depth system analysis, game theory or differentiated aggregation procedures are themselves useful, they fail to provide essential cues for a theoretical construction of an evolving macro structure unless they explicate its role as structure component and, as is shown subsequently, as process component.

14.14 THE EVOLUTIONARY CORE

While a systemic account focuses on the synchronic aspects of an economy, evolutionary analysis aims at an enquiry into its diachronic aspects. Dealing in the following with the latter, meso – as building block for macro – needs to be identified as a process component. Until this juncture, change has been viewed as occurring within micro – for example a firm – representing its dynamic as a micro trajectory. The concept of trajectory applied to micro may serve as a blueprint for dealing with the meso dynamic – with the only, albeit essential, difference relating to adoption. In the first phase the two concepts match, but in the second phase (dealing with the adoption of knowledge) the distinction is between microscopic and macroscopic – or 'mesoscopic' – adoption. Again, the trajectory may be construed by employing either a single carrier or a single knowledge-bit actualized in distinct populations.

As a master model, the meso trajectory looks as follows:

1. Origination of new knowledge.
2. Macroscopic adoption of new knowledge.
3. Retention of new knowledge.

An enormous amount of work has been done on the various aspects of the trajectory dynamic. In the most recent work, a trend may be observed away from the analysis of 'isolated trajectories' towards looking at 'embedded trajectories', which work out their dynamic in a structured or network environment (Potts, 2000).

With regard to the first phase, novelty generation, though usually considered the engine of economic growth, is still for the most part an under-researched topic (Witt, 2009; Grebel, 2009; Encinar and Muñoz, 2006). An intriguing aspect concerns the complex dynamic relationship between structural complementariness and the generation of novelty, as captured by the concept of 'generative relationship' and micro–meso–macro innovation clusters (Lane and Maxfield, 2005; Brette and Mehier, 2008).

There is a vast literature related to the second phase, the diffusion and macroscopic adoption of knowledge. The work embraces broadly conceived diffusion models (Buenstorff and Klepper, 2009; Klepper, 1997), selection models (van den Bergh and Gowdy, 2009; Knudsen, 2002), path-dependence and network life cycle models (David, 2005; Martin and Sunley, 2006; Arthur, 2009; Pyka, 2000) and learning and networking models (Dosi et al., 2005). These models address different aspects of the meso dynamic, but they all share the feature of conceiving it in a structured environment or network.

The third phase embraces the fields of habits, skills and routines and, in general, the field of institutions. The literature on these topics has expanded ever since the publication of the seminal 1982 contribution by Nelson and Winter (Lazaric and Raybaut, 2005; Becker, 2008). Further developments may be expected along the line of the original strands of American institutionalism – a theoretical potential that is far from being exhausted (Nelson, 2008; Hodgson, 2007; Nelson and Nelson, 2002).

14.15   LOOKING TO THE FUTURE

Schumpeter remarked 100 years ago that economic statics was already well developed and that what was therefore needed was the development of an economic dynamics. Developments in the discipline took a different course, however. The theoretical efforts of the last 100 years or so have resulted in a monumental edifice of economic statics, lacking anything comparable on the side of economic dynamics. The exceptions were (besides Schumpeter's own contribution) the various post-war economic growth theories. While these theories, particularly in their vintage as endogenous growth theories and post-Keynesian models, have furnished important insights, they are built on premises that make it difficult to address economic growth as an endogenously self-generating, self-adapting and continuously self-restructuring process.

A theory conducive to coping with this core problem requires the introduction of a vehicle that allows us to deal with both process and structure. Since structure and process are not isolated but, rather, two sides of a single phenomenon, the meso vehicle would seem to render a useful service in tackling this problem. Although the construction of macro along these lines is still in its infancy, interesting work has already been forthcoming in terms of addressing economic growth as a self-generating process in its causal nexus with a continuous restructuring of the economy (Metcalfe et al., 2006; Saviotti and Pyka, 2004, 2008; Cantner and Krüger, 2008; Malerba, 2006; Silverberg and Verspagen, 2005a).

Further groundwork will be needed to secure the sustainability of this theoretical course. This will include, on the one hand, further theoretical work on the basic relationship between the levels of micro, meso and macro, as well as on taxonomies relating to the various kinds of knowledge and of carriers. Work on the micro–meso–macro architecture may be advanced in various ways such as, for instance, by adopting a unified rule approach that advances taxonomy and the theoretical exposition on the basis of the concept of (complex and evolving) generic rules (Dopfer and Potts, 2008; Dopfer, 2005; Dopfer et al., 2004). Further groundwork is needed, on the other hand, concerning the methods for empirical research (Ostrom and Basurto, 2011; Ostrom, 2005). Enquiring into complex evolving systems requires both quantification and hermeneutic methods. These methods apply to empirical data that at any one time have a structure, calling for a Linnean type of taxonomy, and that over time are continuously changing, calling for a Darwinian type of taxonomy. Cladistic and related taxonomies have emerged as a way of reconciling the demands of structural complexity and evolution when charting empirical data (Allen, 2005; Andersen, 2008; Cantner and Pyka, 2001). Scientific advances will be made in the future in this new camp – as they will, arguably, in much of science – along a co-evolutionary path, with theory, method and empirical work receiving their appropriate share of the recognition.

ACKNOWLEDGEMENTS

The author gratefully acknowledges valuable comments and suggestions by Cristiano Antonelli, Stefania Bandini, Georg D. Blind, Stephan Boehm, Wolfram Elsner, Peter Fleissner, Carsten Herrmann-Pillath, Thomas Grebel, Magnus Pirovino, Mike Richardson, Manuel Wäckerle and Hermann Schnabl.

REFERENCES

Alander, J.T. (2009), 'An Indexed Bibliography of Genetic Algorithms in Economics', Vaasa Paper, University of Vaasa, Finland.

Aldrich, H.E., G.M. Hodgson, D.L. Hull, T. Knudsen, J. Mokyr and V.J. Vanberg (2008), 'In Defence of Generalized Darwinism', *Journal of Evolutionary Economics*, **18**(5), 577–596.

Allen, P.M. (2005), 'Understanding Social and Economic Systems as Evolutionary Complex Systems', in K. Dopfer (ed.), *The Evolutionary Foundations of Economics*, Cambridge: Cambridge University Press, pp. 431–458.

Andersen, E.S. (2008), 'Fundamental Fields of Post-Schumpeterian Evolutionary Economics', DRUID (Danish Research Unit for Industrial Dynamics) Working Paper no. 08-25. Copenhagen and Aalborg: Copenhagen Business School and Aalborg University.

Anderson, P.W., K.J. Arrow and D. Pines (eds) (1988), *The Economy as an Evolving Complex System*, Reading, MA: Addison-Wesley.

Antonelli, C. (2008), *Localised Technological Change: Towards the Economics of Complexity*, London: Routledge.

Arthur, B.W. (2009), *The Nature of Technology: What It Is and How It Evolves*, New York: Free Press.

Arthur, B.W., S.N. Durlauf and D.A. Lane (eds) (1997), *The Economy as an Evolving Complex System II*, Reading, MA: Addison-Wesley.

Becker, M. (2008), *Handbook of Organizational Routines*, Cheltenham, UK and Northampton, MA, USA: Edward Elgar.

Bertalanffy, L. von (1968), *General System Theory: Foundations, Development, Applications*, New York: George Braziller.

Brenner, T. (2004), *Local Industrial Clusters: Existence, Emergence and Evolution*, London: Routledge.

Brette, O. and C. Mehier (2008), 'Building on the "Micro–Meso–Macro" Evolutionary Framework: The Stakes for the Analysis of Clusters of Innovation', in W. Elsner and H. Hanappi (eds), *Varieties of Capitalism and New Institutional Deals: Regulation, Welfare and the New Economy*, Cheltenham, UK and Northampton, MA, USA: Edward Elgar, 227–249.

Buenstorf, G. (2006), 'How Useful is Generalized Darwinism as a Framework to Study Competition and Industrial Evolution?', *Journal of Evolutionary Economics*, **16**(5), 511–527.

Buenstorf, G. and S. Klepper (2009), 'Heritage and Agglomeration: The Akron Tyre Cluster Revisited', *Economic Journal*, **119**, 705–733.

Cantner, U. and I.J. Krüger (2008), 'Micro-heterogeneity and Aggregate Productivity Development in the German Manufacturing Sector: Results from a Decomposition Exercise', *Journal of Evolutionary Economics*, **18**(5), 119–133.

Cantner, U. and A. Pyka (2001), 'Classifying Technology Policy from an Evolutionary Perspective', *Research Policy*, **30**(5), 759–775.

Castellacci, F. (2009), 'The Interactions between National Systems and Sectoral Patterns of Innovation', *Journal of Evolutionary Economics*, **19**(3), 321–347.

Colander, D., R.P.F. Holt and J.B. Rosser (2010), 'The Complexity Era in Economics', Working Paper no. 1001, Middlebury, VT: Middlebury College.

Cordes, C. (2006), 'Darwinism in Economics: From Analogy to Continuity', *Journal of Evolutionary Economics*, **15**(5), 529–541.

David, P.A. (2005), 'Path Dependence in Economic Processes: Implications for Policy Analysis in Dynamical Systems Contexts', in K. Dopfer (ed.), *The Evolutionary Foundations of Economics*, Cambridge: Cambridge University Press, pp. 151–194.

Davis, J.B. (2003), *The Theory of the Individual in Economics: Identity and Value*, London: Routledge.

Davis, J.B. (2008), 'Complex Individuals: The Individual in non-Euclidian Space', in H. Hanappi and W. Elsner (eds.), *Advances in Evolutionary Institutional Economics: Evolutionary Mechanisms, Non-Knowledge and Strategy*, Cheltenham, UK and Northampton, MA, USA: Edward Elgar, pp. 123–142.

Dennett, D.C. (1995), *Darwin's Dangerous Idea: Evolution and the Meaning of Life*, London: Penguin Books.

Dolfsma, W. and L. Leydesdorff (2010), 'The Citation Field of Evolutionary Economics', *Journal of Evolutionary Ecoonomics*, **20**(5), 645–664.

Dopfer, K. (2004), 'The Economic Agent as Rule Maker and Rule User: *Homo sapiens oeconomicus*', *Journal of Evolutionary Economics*, **14**(2), 177–195.

Dopfer, K. (ed.) (2005), *The Evolutionary Foundations of Economics*, Cambridge: Cambridge University Press.

Dopfer, K., J. Foster and J. Potts (2004), 'Micro–Meso–Macro', *Journal of Evolutionary Economics*, **14**(2), 263–279.

Dopfer, K. and J. Potts (2008), *The General Theory of Economic Evolution*, London: Routledge.

Dosi, G., L. Marengo and G. Fagiolo (2005), 'Learning in Evolutionary Environments', in K. Dopfer (ed.), *The Evolutionary Foundations of Economics*, Cambridge: Cambridge University Press, pp. 255–338.

Elsner, W. (2010), 'The Process and a Simple Logic of 'Meso': Emergence and the Co-evolution of Institutions and Group Size', *Journal of Evolutionary Economics*, **20**(3), 445–477.

Encinar, M.-I. and F.-F. Muñoz (2006), 'On Novelty and Economics: Schumpeter's Paradox', *Journal of Evolutionary Economics*, **16**(3), 255–277.

Foray, D. and W.E. Steinmueller (2001), 'Replication of Routine, the Domestication of Tacit Knowledge and the Economics of Inscription Technology: A Brave New World?', paper presented at conference in honour of Richard R. Nelson and Sidney G. Winter, Aalborg, 12 June.

Foster, J. (1987), *Evolutionary Macroeconomics,* London: Unwin Hyman.

Foster, J.(2005), 'From Simplistic to Complex Systems in Economics', *Cambridge Journal of Economics*, **29**(6), 873–892.

Frantz, R. (1997), *X-Efficiency: Theory, Evidence and Applications*, 2nd edn, Norwell, MA: Kluwer Academic.

Frenken, K. (2006), 'A Fitness Landscape Approach to Technological Complexity, Modularity, and Vertical Disintegration', *Structural Change and Economic Dynamics*, **17**(3), 288–305.

Geisendorf, S. (2007), *Are Genetic Algorithms a Good Basis for Learning Models?* paper for Agent-Based Economics no. 2007–5, Kassel: University of Kassel.

Geisendorf, S. (2009), 'The Economic Concept of Evolution: Self-organisation or Universal Darwinism?', *Journal of Economic Methodology*, **16**(4), 361–375.

Gintis, H. (2009), *The Bounds of Reason: Game Theory and the Unification of the Behavioral Sciences*, Princeton, NJ: Princeton University Press.

Grebel, T. (2009), 'Technological Change: A Microeconomic Approach to the Creation of Knowledge', *Structural Change and Economic Dynamics*, **20**(4), 301–312.

Haken, H. (2005), 'Synergetics: From Physics to Economics', in K. Dopfer (ed.), *The Evolutionary Foundations of Economics*, Cambridge: Cambridge University Press, pp. 70–85.

Hanappi, H. (1994), *Evolutionary Economics*, Aldershot: Avebury.

Hanusch, H. and A. Pyka (eds) (2007), *Elgar Companion to Neo-Schumpeterian Economics*, Cheltenham, UK and Northampton, MA, USA: Edward Elgar.

Hayden, F.G. (2008), 'Circular and Cumulative Causation and the Social Fabric Matrix', *Journal of Economic Issues*, **42**(2), 389–397.

Helmstädter, E. (ed.) (2003), *The Economics of Knowledge Sharing: A New Institutional Approach*, Cheltenham, UK and Northampton, MA, USA: Edward Elgar.

Herrmann-Pillath, C. (2010), *The Economics of Identity and Creativity: A Cultural Science Approach*, St Lucia: University of Queensland Press.

Hodgson, G.M. (1993), *Economics and Evolution: Bringing Life Back into Economics*, Cambridge: Polity Press.

Hodgson, G.M. (2002), 'Darwinism in Economics: From Analogy to Ontology', *Journal of Evolutionary Economics*, **12**(3), 259–281.

Hodgson, G.M. (2007), 'The Revival of Veblenian Institutional Economics', *Journal of Economic Issues*, **41**(2), 325–340.

Hodgson, G.M., and T. Knudsen (2006), 'Why We Need a Generalized Darwinism and Why a Generalized Darwinism is Not Enough', *Journal of Economic Behavior and Organization*, **61**(1), 1–19.

Holland, J. (1998), *Emergence: From Chaos to Order*, Reading, MA: Addison-Wesley.

Hollingsworth, R. amd K.H. Müller (2008), 'Transforming Socio-economics with a New Epistemology', *Socio-economic Review*, **6**, 395–426.

Hutter, M. and D. Throsby (2008), *Beyond Price: Value in Culture, Economics and the Arts*, Cambridge: Cambridge University Press.

Kapp, K.W. (1976), 'The Open System Character of the Economy and its Implications', in K. Dopfer (ed.), *Economics in the Future: Towards a New Paradigm*, London: Macmillan, pp. 90–105.

Kirman, A.P. and A. Vignes (1991), 'Price Dispersion: Theoretical Considerations and Empirical Evidence from the Marseilles Fish Market', in K.J. Arrow (ed.), *Issues in Contemporary Economics: Proceedings of the Ninth World Congress of the International Economic Association, Athens, Greece*, Vol. I, *Markets and Welfare*, New York: New York University Press, pp. 160–185.

Klepper, S. (1997), 'Industry Life Cycles', *Industrial and Corporate Change*, **6**(1), 145–181.

Knottenbauer, K. (2009), 'Recent Developments in Evolutionary Biology and Their Relevance for Evolutionary Economics', Paper on Economics and Evolution no. 0911, Jena: Max Planck Institute of Economics.

Knudsen, T. (2002), 'Economic Selection Theory', *Journal of Evolutionary Economics*, **12**(3), 443–470.

Kwasnicka, H. and W. Kwasnicki (2006), 'Evolutionary Modeling and Industrial Structure Emergence', in J.-P. Rennard (ed.), *Handbook of Research on Nature Inspired Computing for Economy and Management*, Vol. I, Hershey, PA: IGI Global, pp. 281–300.

Lane, D.A. (2006), 'Hierarchy, Complexity, Society', in D. Pumain (ed.), *Hierarchy in Natural and Social Sciences*, Berlin: Springer-Verlag, pp. 81–119.

Lane, D.A. and R. Maxfield (2005), 'Ontological Uncertainty and Innovation', *Journal of Evolutionary Economics*, **15**(1), 3–50.

Langlois, R. (2002), 'Modularity in Technology and Organization', *Journal of Economic Behavior and Organization*, **49**(1), 19–37.

Lazaric, N. and A. Raybaut (2005), 'Knowledge, Hierarchy and the Selection of Routines: An Interpretative Model with Group Interactions', *Journal of Evolutionary Economics*, **15**(4), 393–421.

Leibenstein, H. (1976), 'Micro–Micro Theory, Agent–Agent Trade, and X-efficiency', in K. Dopfer (ed.), *Economics in the Future: Towards a New Paradigm*, London: Macmillan, pp. 53–68.

Leibniz, G.W. (1714 [1991]), *Monadologie*, Pittsburgh, PA: University of Pittsburgh Press.

Levit, G.S., U. Hossfeld and U. Witt (2010), 'Can Darwinism Be "Generalized" and of What Use Would This Be?', Paper on Economics and Evolution no. 1007, Jena: Max Planck Institute of Economics.

Lux, T. and T. Kaizoji (2007), 'Forecasting Volatility and Volume in the Tokyo Stock Market: Long Memory, Fractality and Regime Switching', *Journal of Economic Dynamics and Control*, **31**(6), 1808–1843.

Malerba, F. (2006), 'Innovation and the Evolution of Industries', *Journal of Evolutionary Economics*, **16**(1), 3–23.

Marshall, A. (1890), *Principles of Economics*, Vol. I, London: Macmillan.

Martin, R. and P. Sunley (2006), 'Path Dependence and Regional Economic Evolution', *Journal of Economic Geography*, **6**(4), 395–437.

Metcalfe, J.S. (2005), 'Evolutionary Concepts in Relation to Evolutionary Economics', in K. Dopfer (ed.), *The Evolutionary Foundations of Economics*, Cambridge: Cambridge University Press, pp. 391–430.

Metcalfe, J.S., J. Foster and R. Ramlogan (2006), 'Adaptive Economic Growth', *Cambridge Journal of Economics*, **30**(1), 7–32.

Nelson, R.R. (2006), 'Evolutionary Social Science and Universal Darwinism', *Journal of Evolutionary Economics*, **16**(5), 491–510.

Nelson, R.R. (2008), 'What Enables Rapid Economic Progress: What are the Needed Institutions?', *Research Policy*, **37**(1), 1–11.

Nelson, R.R. and D. Consoli (2010), 'An Evolutionary Theory of Household Consumption Behavior', *Journal of Evolutionary Economics*, **20**(5), 665–687.

Nelson, R.R. and K. Nelson (2002), 'On the Nature and Evolution of Human Know-how', *Research Policy*, **31**(5), 719–733.

Nelson, R.R. and S.G. Winter (1982), *An Evolutionary Theory of Economic Change*, Cambridge, MA: Harvard University Press.

Öser, E. (1974), *System, Klassifikation, Evolution: Historische Analyse und Rekonstruktion der Wissenschaftstheoretischen Grundlagen der Biologie*, Vienna: Braumüller.

Ostrom, E. (2005), *Understanding Institutional Diversity*, Princeton, NJ: Princeton University Press.

Ostrom, E. and X. Basurto (2011), 'Crafting Analytical Tools to Study Institutional Change', *Journal of Instutional Economics*, **7**(3), 317–43.

Potts, J. (2000), *The New Evolutionary Microeconomics: Choice, Complexity and Adaptive Behaviour*, Cheltenham, UK and Northampton, MA, USA: Edward Elgar.

Potts, J. (2008), 'Economic Evolution, Identity Dynamics and Cultural Science', *Cultural Science*, **1**(2), available at: http://cultural-science.org/journal/index.php/culturalscience/article/viewArticle/16/54.

Pyka, A. (2000), 'Informal Networking and Industrial Life Cycles', *Technovation*, **20**(11), 25–35.

Pyka, A. and G. Fagiolo (2007), 'Agent-based Modelling: A Methodology for neo-Schumpeterian Economics', in H. Hanusch and A. Pyka (eds), *Elgar Companion to Neo-Schumpeterian Economics*, Cheltenham, UK and Northampton, MA, USA: Edward Elgar, pp. 467–487.

Pyka, A., N. Gilbert and P. Ahrweiler (2006), 'Simulating Knowledge-Generation and Distribution Processes in Innovation Collaborations and Networks', Discussion Paper no. 287, Augsburg: University of Augsburg.

Pyka, A. and H. Hanusch (eds) (2006), *Applied Evolutionary Economics and the Knowledge-Based Economy*, Cheltenham, UK and Northampton, MA, USA: Edward Elgar.

Rosser, B. (2010), 'Is a Transdisciplinary Perspective on Economic Complexity Possible?', *Journal of Economic Behavior and Organization*, **75**(1), 3–11.

Saviotti, P.P. and A. Pyka (2004), 'Economic Development by the Creation of New Sectors', *Journal of Evolutionary Economics*, **14**(1), 1–36.

Saviotti, P.P. and A. Pyka (2008), 'Micro and Macro Dynamics: Industry Life Cycles, Inter-sector Coordination and Aggregate Growth', *Journal of Evolutionary Economics*, **18**(2), 167–182.

Schweizer, F. (2003), *Brownian Agents and Active Particles: Collective Dynamics in the Natural and Social Sciences*, Berlin: Springer-Verlag.

Silva, S.T. and A.A.C. Teixeira (2009), 'On the Divergence of Evolutionary Research Paths in the Past 50 Years: A Comprehensive Bibliometric Account', *Journal of Evolutionary Economics*, **19**(5), 605–642.

Silverberg, G. and B. Verspagen (2005a), 'Evolutionary Theorizing on Economic Growth', in K. Dopfer (ed.), *The Evolutionary Foundations of Economics*, Cambridge: Cambridge University Press, pp. 506–539.

Silverberg, G. and B. Verspagen (2005b), 'A Percolation Model of Innovation in Complex Technology Spaces', *Journal of Economic Dynamics and Control*, **29**(1–2), 225–244.

Sornette, D. (2008), 'Interdisciplinarity in Socio-economics, Mathematical Analysis and Predictability of Complex Systems', *Socio-Economic Review*, **6**, 27–38.

Sum, N.-L. and B. Jessop (2011), *Towards a Cultural Political Economy: Taking the Cultural Turn in Economics*, Cheltenham, UK and Northampton, MA, USA: Edward Elgar.

Tesfatsion, L. (2002), 'Agent-based Computational Economics: Growing Economics from the Bottom Up', *Artificial Life*, **8**(1), 55–82.

van den Bergh, J.C.J.M. and J.M. Gowdy (2009), 'A Group Selection Perspective on Economic Behavior, Institutions and Organizations', *Journal of Economic Behavior and Organization*, **72**(1), 1–20.

van der Leeuw, S.E. and J. McGlade (eds) (1997), *Archaeology: Time, Process and Structural Transformations*, London: Routledge.

Veblen, T. (1898), 'Why is Economics not an Evolutionary Science?', *Quarterly Journal of Economics*, **12**(4), 373–397.

Vromen, J. (2007), 'Generalized Darwinism in Evolutionary Economics: The Devil is in the Details', paper on Economics and Evolution no. 0711, Jena: Max Planck Institute of Economics.

Weidlich, W. (2000), 'Sociodynamics: An Integrated Approach to Modelling in the Social Sciences', in K. Dopfer (ed.), *Economics, Evolution and the State: The Governance of Complexity*, Cheltenham, UK and Northampton, MA, USA: Edward Elgar, pp. 120–139.

Windrum, P., G. Fagiolo and A. Moneta (2007), 'Empirical Validation of Agent-based Models: Alternatives and Prospects', *Journal of Artificial Societies and Social Simulation*, **10**(2).

Witt, U. (2004), 'On the Proper Interpretation of "Evolution" in Economics and its Implications for Production Theory', *Journal of Economic Methodology*, **11**(2), 125–146.

Witt, U. (2008), 'What is Specific about Evolutionary Economics?', *Journal of Evolutionary Economics*, **18**(5), 547–575.

Witt, U. (2009), 'Novelty and the Bounds of Unknowledge in Economics', *Journal of Economic Methodology*, **16**(4), 361–375.

15 Heterogeneous economic evolution: a different view on Darwinizing evolutionary economics
Jack Vromen[1]

15.1 INTRODUCTION

Recently proponents declared their Generalized Darwinism to be the emerging *communis opinio* in evolutionary economics (Hodgson, 2010). Given that over the last decade Generalized Darwinism has met strong resistance from within certain quarters of evolutionary economics (see Witt, 2004, 2007; Bünstorf, 2006; Cordes, 2006; Schubert, 2009), this (alleged) convergence on a received view on how to Darwinize evolutionary economics is remarkable. This agreement might well turn out to be a Pyrrhic victory for Generalized Darwinism's proponents, however. As I argued elsewhere (Vromen, 2007, 2010), the price for gaining acceptance in the evolutionary economics community seems to be that proponents had to settle on a version of Darwinism that is so general and abstract that 'Darwinism' seems to have lost its definite and discriminating contours. Indeed, the sort of Darwinism we are left with seems so diluted that it is not worth fighting for. It seems that its principles are so much emptied from their content and substance that they are of little if any use in guiding further theory construction.

Fortunately there seems to be an alternative view on Darwinizing evolutionary economics in the offing that does not have this drawback. In his recent book, Peter Godfrey-Smith (2009) develops a useful taxonomy for distinguishing Darwinian from non-Darwinian processes and, within the former category, for distinguishing the degree to which processes are Darwinian. This taxonomy is developed to come to grips with the vast heterogeneity of evolutionary processes in biology. But, as Godfrey-Smith himself suggests, it can also be used to come to grips with the perhaps even greater heterogeneity in processes of cultural evolution. In this chapter I first introduce Godfrey-Smith's taxonomy and contrast it with Hodgson and Knudsen's version of Generalized Darwinism. I then take a closer look at an argument that proponents of Darwinizing culture (and social science) advance to counter an objection that opponents have often voiced: the Darwinist model of biological evolution is too simple to do justice to culture and cultural evolution. This 'biological evolution is not simple either' counterargument is analyzed from the perspective of both Generalized Darwinism and that of Godfrey-Smith's taxonomy. After that a specific argument is critically scrutinized that Hodgson and Knudsen put forward to show the inevitability of invoking Darwinian principles in acceptable explanations of evolutionary processes in economic systems. Again, this is contrasted with Godfrey-Smith's take on the usefulness of Darwinism in both biological and cultural evolution. Finally, the issues are taken up of whether there are social replicators and of whether replicator dynamic can be applied also in the absence of social replicators. This relates to the long-standing debate between proponents and opponents of Darwinizing culture about the relevance of the observation that discrete entities such as genes, which are copied with high fidelity, seem to be rare (if not non-existent) in the cultural domain.

15.2   THE RECEIVED VIEW ON DARWINIZING EVOLUTIONARY ECONOMICS

Attempts to Darwinize evolutionary economics (see Aunger, 2000) have met resistance from within the field of evolutionary economics (Witt, 2004, 2007; Bünstorf, 2006; Cordes, 2006; Schubert, 2009). But now it seems that the field has reached an agreement about what sort of Darwinism is acceptable and perhaps even necessary (Hodgson, 2010). In a nutshell, the crux of this 'received view' is that the three Darwinian principles – variation, replication and selection – should be given an abstract and general interpretation (see also Aldrich et al., 2008; Hodgson and Knudsen, 2010a). A Generalized Darwinism is based on a recognition of ontological communalities between the biological and the economic (or, more broadly, the cultural) domain,[2] while acknowledging that there are also huge differences in the ('details' of the) mechanisms that bring about variation, replication and selection in the two domains. It is acknowledged, for example, that in the cultural domain intentionality plays an important role in the production of variation and in selection, that replication is often mere retention of information and that, if there is genuine transmission of information from the one cultural interactor to the other, the fidelity typically is lower than in genetic inheritance.

By identifying variation, replication and selection as the key ingredients in Darwinism, proponents of Generalized Darwinism such as, notably, Hodgson and Knudsen (2006, 2010a) seem to place themselves in the 'classical' tradition of attempts to give generic descriptions of Darwinian evolution through natural selection (Godfrey-Smith, 2009). Important forerunners in this tradition are Lewontin (1970) and Lewontin (1985). In this tradition, variation, heredity and differential fitness are seen as separately necessary and jointly sufficient conditions for evolutionary change through natural selection to occur. Hodgson and Knudsen also argue, however, that further refinements and clarifications of these Darwinian principles are needed. One such refinement is the requirement that interactors and replicators are to be identified. By imposing this requirement, Hodgson and Knudsen put themselves also in another tradition of attempts to give generic descriptions of Darwinian evolution pioneered by Dawkins (1976) and further developed by Hull (1980): the replicator approach (Godfrey-Smith, 2009). The replicator approach insists that for some evolutionary process to qualify as Darwinian there must be replicators involved. Replicators are entities that induce the production of copies of themselves. The paradigm examples of replicators in biological evolution are genes. Hodgson and Knudsen argue that in the economic domain, habits (of individual persons) and routines (of organizations such as firms) are replicators. Hull defines 'interactors' as cohesive entities that interact with each other, causing reproduction to be differential. Individual organisms are paradigm examples of interactors in Darwinian biological evolution. Hodgson and Knudsen argue that firms are interactors in the economic domain.

Hodgson (2002, 2004) rightly argues that Darwinism is thoroughly committed to causation and to causal explanation. Darwinism forbids postulating an entity or phenomenon that enters the scene as a *deus ex machina* (or as an 'uncaused cause'). For each entity or phenomenon postulated, it must be possible (at least in principle) to show that it has been produced in earlier causal processes. In Dennett's (1995) felicitous wording, whereas it is admissible to invoke cranes in evolutionary explanations, referring to skyhooks is inadmissible. Thus, contrary to a common and tenacious misunderstanding, Darwinism does not rule out intentional (or purposeful) action. Darwinism does insist, though, that the capacity for intentional action must have been produced in earlier evolutionary processes (Vromen, 2001). In the same spirit, natural selection itself is to be conceived of as a causal mechanism. Or, to be more precise, natural selection is to be conceived of as a recurring cycle of three mechanisms: one that produces (and replenishes) variation, one that does the selecting and one that takes care of the replication (Darden and Cain, 1989). Similarly, Hull argues that natural selection is not one causal process, but two: one of interaction (in which interactors are put to the test of environmental selection) and one of replication (in which replicators are transmitted).

Hodgson and Knudsen hold that the three Darwinian principles must necessarily be invoked in any adequate causal explanation of evolution in complex population systems.[3] But they also argue that invoking the three Darwinian principles is insufficient for providing adequate causal explanations. Taken together the three Darwinian principles form a meta-theory. To arrive at empirically meaningful middle-range theories, auxiliary hypotheses will have to be added to the three Darwinian principles. And the auxiliary hypotheses added will have to do justice to the peculiarities of the phenomena in the domain at issue. The contribution of the Darwinian meta-theory in constructing middle-range theories is an heuristic one: it directs theorists to look specifically at the details of how the mechanisms of variation, replication and selection (or, alternatively, those of interaction and replication) are implemented in some particular domain.

There is much to be admired and recommended in Hodgson and Knudsen's treatment of Generalized Darwinism. They rightly stress that Darwinism is firmly committed to population thinking (Mayr, 1976; Metcalfe, 1988). Rather than thinking in terms of fixed types and immutable essences, as in typological and essentialist thinking (modes of thinking, it can be said, that we are more accustomed to), Darwinism takes changes in populations of heterogeneous entities as its starting point. Among the many other merits of Hodgson and Knudsen's treatment is also a thoughtful analysis of how social structure, which arguably is important in economic systems, can be fitted into the Darwinian meta-theory. Hodgson and Knudsen also argue convincingly that their Generalized Darwinism steers clear from justifying optimality claims and also from genetic determinism and biological reductionism. It is indeed one of the attractive features of Generalized Darwinism that it allows for the possibility that processes of cultural evolution can go against biological imperatives. Generalized Darwinism grants that there can be more or less autonomous processes of economic evolution in their own right, leading to outcomes that run against the 'interests' of our 'selfish genes'. Hodgson and Knudsen also seem to recognize the many significant disanalogies between phenomena and processes in the biological and economic domain. They rightly sense that any rendering of 'Darwinism' that tries to deny or conceal the profound differences between those domains is bound to fail.

The latter comes at a price, however. To accommodate legitimate concerns about significant differences between biological and cultural evolution (at the level of detail, Hodgson and Knudsen assure us), Hodgson and Knudsen are compelled to give a very general and abstract rendering of Darwinism. It seems that their Generalized Darwinism does not rule out 'selection' understood as conscious, deliberate choice, for example, and 'replication' as mere retention or as systematically biased transmission. Indeed, it seems their rendering becomes so general and abstract that the Darwinian principles are bereft of much if not all of their substance. We are left, it seems, with a diluted (or watered-down) version of Darwinism. The problem with this is that it not only tends to lose its discriminating power (the set of non-Darwinian dynamic processes tends to be empty). It also seems to put all the explanatory work on the auxiliary domain-specific hypotheses that have yet to be added to the three Darwinian principles. The devil is in the detail, as the saying goes (Vromen, 2007, 2010). And since the principles are emptied from almost all of their substance, it also seems that the three Darwinian principles are not able to give much ('heuristic') guidance in the search for the auxiliary domain-specific principles. Of course, all this does not show that attempts to base further theory construction in evolutionary economics on the three abstract Darwinian principles are doomed to fail. What it rather shows is that the three abstract Darwinian principles are not of much use as a basis for further theory construction.[4]

15.3   A DIFFERENT VIEW: GODFREY-SMITH'S TAXONOMY

Godfrey-Smith (2009) presents a different view on Darwinism.[5] Like Hodgson and Knudsen, Godfrey-Smith also takes Lewontin's (1970, 1985) classical descriptions of Darwinism, in terms of the three conditions (or principles) of variation, inheritance and differential fitness,[6] as his point of departure. But he works this out in a way that deviates from Hodgson and Knudsen's at two critical points. First, while Godfrey Smith takes Lewontin's classical approach to describe the key tenets of Darwinian evolution through natural selection as a useful starting point for further distinctions and refinements, he criticizes and ultimately rejects Dawkins's and Hull's replicator approach. Second, he argues that additional requirements have to be added to Lewontin's 'minimal' description to arrive at a more substantive form of Darwinism that is able to explain cumulative evolution of novel structures.

Godfrey-Smith criticizes and ultimately rejects Dawkins's and Hull's replicator approach for various reasons. One is that it provides an 'agential' view on evolutionary processes, with hidden 'selfish' interests and machinations, which is often misleading. The most important reason, though, it that it suggests that Darwinian evolutionary change through natural selection is impossible without replicators. Godfrey-Smith (2000) points out that this suggestion is false. All that is needed for evolutionary change through natural selection to occur is that offspring resemble their parents to a greater degree than that they resemble non-related individuals from the population.

One might be tempted to conclude from this that this plays into the hands of Hodgson and Knudsen. After all, Hodgson and Knudsen argue that the, by itself correct, observation that replication tends be less faithful in cultural evolution than in biological evolution does not undermine their project of Darwinizing social science. Isn't this exactly what we can conclude from Godfrey-Smith's main objection against the replicator approach (see Kincaid, 2009)? It is true that the mere (alleged) fact that the fidelity in social transmission tends to be lower than that in genetic inheritance does not by itself vitiate the classical Darwinian approach in the social sciences (in terms of variation, replication and differential fitness). But in Godfrey-Smith's view this fact does undermine the replicator approach. Following Dawkins (1976), Godfrey-Smith insists that the notion of replicator implies a process of high-fidelity copying. If high-fidelity copying is lacking, there are no replicators. And then the replicator approach does not apply. More importantly, Godfrey-Smith argues that Darwinism imposes rather stringent requirements on the sorts of processes in which 'parents' produce their 'offspring'. 'Reproduction is at the center of Darwinism' (Godfrey-Smith, 2009, p. 69): a crucial presupposition in Darwinism is that parents are actively causally involved in the production of their offspring. Sexual reproduction in biology, in which the parents copulate and produce a fertilized egg, probably is the first example that comes to mind here. As Godfrey-Smith argues, the presupposition is important for distinguishing Darwinian evolutionary processes from other processes, such as processes of growth. Mere retention or persistence of traits in individuals is also a different sort of process. Godfrey-Smith argues that when there is retention instead of genuine reproduction, the minimal requirements of Darwinism are not met. In Godfrey-Smith's vocabulary, minimal Darwinian populations then shade into marginal (or partial) Darwinian populations.

According to Godfrey-Smith, the minimal requirements of Darwinism are not met either when the primary causal action in 'reproduction' is not with the parents but with the offspring. He argues that the latter is often the case in social transmission. Thus, in imitating (or 'socially learning' from) others, the primary causal action is with the 'offspring'. The imitators rather than the ones that are imitated do the 'copying'. Often imitators do not only (consciously or unconsciously) decide what trait to 'copy', but also whom to 'copy'. It is possible that imitators put together their own behavioral traits by selectively copying traits from various role models. In such a case, the imitator (as 'offspring') blends traits from various 'parents'. This differs from genetic inheritance, in which genes of parents are passed on their offspring as discrete units. What is more, the cultural 'parents' selected need not stand out in terms of social prestige or reputation. Imitators might be inclined to safely stay 'in the middle' by choosing

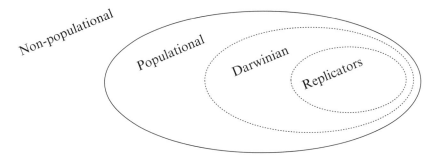

Figure 15.1 Different shades of Darwinism

'average' role models (that is, in Boyd and Richerson 1985's vocabulary, there might be a conformism-based bias in social transmission).

It is important to see that Godfrey-Smith is not contrasting peculiarities of cultural evolution with a straightforward and simple neo-Darwinian model of biological evolution. His point is not that whereas that simple model does fit all of biological evolution, it does not fit anything of cultural evolution. His point is rather more subtle. We can find different shades of Darwinism in both domains. Over the last decades it has become abundantly clear, he thinks, that the simple neo-Darwinian model does not fit the full complexity of biological evolution either (more on that below). Yet Godfrey-Smith does maintain that there are good reasons (such as the ones alluded to above) to believe that relatively many processes of cultural evolution do not meet the minimal requirements of Darwinism. At best these processes shade into marginal Darwinian ones. Sometimes, however, processes of cultural change are not even populational in character.[7] Members of organizations such as firms might lack the degree of autonomy that is characteristic of populations, for example. In general, Godfrey-Smith argues, the more networks of interaction feature role asymmetries, the less population-like they are (Godfrey-Smith, 2009, p. 149). Given the ubiquity of role asymmetries in societies, this would severely restrict the scope of Darwinism in the social sciences. Godfrey-Smith presents the Venn diagram shown in Figure 15.1 to illustrate the relevant distinctions.

Thus processes that are populational in character comprise more sorts of processes than Darwinian processes, which in turn comprise more sorts of processes than the ones in which replicators feature.

There is one more relevant category in Godfrey-Smith's view on Darwinism that deserves special mentioning: 'paradigm Darwinian populations'. Paradigm Darwinian populations form a subcategory of minimal Darwinian populations in that they are populations in which key parameters in minimal Darwinian populations assume particular values. One such key parameter is the degree to which reproductive success of members of populations depends on their 'intrinsic properties'. The relevant contrast here is with drift. Drift is taken to be evolutionary change that occurs randomly, by chance or by accident. Being struck by lightning or by an earthquake is a paradigmatic example. To some evolutionary theorists (cf. Sober, 1984) drift is an evolutionary force alongside others, such as notably natural selection. In Godfrey-Smith's view, however, drift is a situation in which the dependence of differences in reproductive success of members of a population on differences in their intrinsic properties (that is, properties that in the absence of the accident would determine differential reproductive success) is low. Another crucial parameter is the degree to which there are bottlenecks in reproduction. A bottleneck is a narrowing that marks the divide between generations. In the extreme case this narrowing means that one single cell (such as an egg) links generations in reproduction. Yet another parameter is fidelity in copying. We saw that this degree need not be high in minimal Darwinian populations. But in paradigm Darwinian populations copying is high-fidelity. Thus paradigm Darwinian populations form a subset of the set of replicators in the Venn diagram depicted in Figure 15.1.

Paradigm Darwinian populations are populations that not only satisfy the three requirements of minimal Darwinian populations but that in addition have high dependence of differential reproductive success on intrinsic properties, have a high degree of 'bottlenecking', and have high fidelity in replication.[8] The introduction of the notion of a paradigm Darwinian population does not serve classificatory purposes only. It does not only provide a benchmark for telling how Darwinian a population is. It also is meant to single out populations for which so-called 'origin explanations' can be given. Godfrey-Smith contrasts origin explanations with distribution explanations. Distribution explanations can only explain how and why the distribution of certain, already existing variants in a population changed. Origin explanations can do more: they can also explain why some population has come to contain the variants in the first place. In particular, they can explain the cumulative evolution of novelty.

Given that natural selection is often characterized as some sort of a filtering mechanism that can only trim the set of pre-existing variants, this might come as a surprise. How can natural selection generate novel structures if all it can do is weed out 'unfit' variants? Godfrey-Smith's answer is that natural selection may change the population-level background against which new mutations appear. Consider the evolution of the human eye, for example. Let us assume that natural selection cannot increase the probabilities that the right type of mutations occur for the human eye to be produced. But what natural selection can do is to 'prepare' the population so that when the right types of mutations occur they eventually result in the production of the eye. Natural selection can increase the number of independent 'slots' in which mutations will give us the eye (Godfrey-Smith, 2009, p. 50). For natural selection to be able of doing that, certain requirements have to be met. Drift should play a negligible role, fidelity in copying should be high and there should be a high degree of 'bottlenecking'. In short, the more that populations approximate paradigm Darwinian populations, the more likely it is that origin explanations can be given.

Summing up now, Godfrey-Smith's view implies that both biological and cultural evolution are heterogeneous.[9] In some cases there is high-fidelity replication. Then replicators are involved. Replicators are not necessary for Darwinian evolutionary change through natural selection to take place, however. The minimal requirements of variation, replication and differential fitness can be met while replicators are non-existent. But it seems more stringent requirements have to met for natural selection to be able to ('cumulatively') produce novelty. High fidelity in replication seems to be one of them. Thus we have different shades or degrees of Darwinism. Sometimes populations also shade into marginal or partial Darwinian populations, or outright non-Darwinian populations. The minimal requirements of Darwinism are not met when there is no reproduction of the right causal sort, for example (if 'parents' are not causally responsible for the resemblance with their 'offspring', for example, or if there is only persistence or retention). And sometimes there can be gradual change in entities (such as firms) that do not even qualify as populations, let alone as Darwinian populations.

15.4 THE 'BIOLOGICAL EVOLUTION IS NOT SO SIMPLE EITHER' ARGUMENT

Perhaps the most common objection against attempts to Darwinize the social sciences is that Darwinism does not fit cultural phenomena and processes. The basic idea is that the processes envisaged in Darwinism are too simple to do justice to the complexities of processes in the cultural domain. Thus it is sometimes argued that in the cultural domain we do not have discrete entities like genes that act as replicators. In social learning there can be a lot of 'blending': individuals can choose to put together traits that they selectively pick from different role models. And insofar as we have replication at all in cultures, it is often of the horizontal rather than the vertical type: whereas parents pass on their genes only to their biological offspring in biological evolution, in cultural evolution there is social transmission of traits also between individuals of the same generation that are genetically unrelated. Children do not learn just from their biological parents, for example, but also from their peers and other role models. These are just a few of the many dis-analogies between biological and cultural evolution that have been pointed out by critics of Darwinizing the social sciences.

This objection is sometimes answered by what can be called the 'biological evolution is not so simple either' counterargument (see Hull, 1988; Mesoudi et al., 2006; Crozier, 2008; Hodgson and Knudsen, 2006; Wenseleers et al., forthcoming). This counterargument runs as follows. Critics of a Darwinian approach in the social sciences implicitly assume that the simple (neo-Darwinian) model that they take to be Darwinian fits biological evolution. In this simple model variants are traits of individual organisms that are heritable, inheritance (via genetic transmission) is only vertical and perfectly faithful ('like begets like'), fitness differences translate perfectly into differences in reproductive success, and new variants enter through gene mutations that are blind or random. Cultural evolution might be too complex for this poor, simplified understanding of Darwinism to be fitting. But the same can be said also about biological evolution. The poor, simplified understanding of Darwinism does not fit much of biological evolution either. Especially with bacteria, for example, we now know that there is also horizontal transmission of genetic information. Ergo: the argument is flawed that Darwinism is to be resisted in the social sciences because cultural evolution is much more complex than biological evolution.

The logic of the counterargument is impeccable. A crucial premise in the critics' argument is that Darwinism as they understand it fits biological evolution. The critics think they spot dis-analogies between biological and cultural evolution, whereas in fact they only spot dis-analogies between cultural evolution and a particular version of Darwinism that they take to be representative of biological evolution. If it is indeed the case that the premise is factually false, as proponents of Generalized Darwinism argue, then the conclusion (that Darwinism as they understand it does not fit cultural evolution) might be false as well. Ergo: Generalized Darwinism cannot be discarded on the basis of alleged, but non-existing dis-analogies.

It should be clear by now where proponents of Generalized Darwinism believe the critics go wrong: the critics read too much into 'Darwinism'. The understanding of Darwinism by the critics is not general and abstract enough. On a more general and abstract understanding of Darwinism, Darwinism might fit many more (and perhaps even all) processes of biological evolution through natural selection. And indeed this is exactly what biologists and philosophers like David Hull with their abstract rendering of Darwinism have been trying to accomplish. Their claim is furthermore that their rendering of Darwinism is general and abstract enough to account also for at least some evolutionary processes outside the biological domain (such as processes of cultural evolution).

Still, for all its 'impeccability', there seems to be something strange about the counterargument. It seems that critics are not really interested in whether or not some version of Darwinism can be formulated that fits all instances of biological evolution. What they are really interested in is whether or not Darwinism gives a clear and simple model to study cultural evolution. They are not really helped by being told that in order to accommodate all processes of biological evolution Darwinism should be understood in a more general and abstract way than what they took Darwinism to be. They thought (and perhaps hoped) that Darwinism gives a rather clear and simple model. But now they learn that Darwinism does not give anything of the sort. Instead of a clear and simple model, Generalized Darwinism provides them with a very general and abstract description that is explicitly aimed at covering diverse processes and phenomena.

Critics might wonder why we would like to have such a general and abstract rendering of Darwinism in the first place. What is so desirable about a formulation of Darwinism that is able to accommodate a multitude of biological evolutionary processes, if it is admitted that there are significant differences between evolutionary processes in the biological domain? Obviously, such a formulation would slide over such differences. What is the use of a formulation of Darwinism that blurs rather than highlights such differences? If proponents of Generalized Darwinism are correct in their observation that a simple model of Darwinism does not fit many processes of biological evolution either (and it seems they are correct), why not draw the alternative conclusion that there is no clear model of Darwinism that can do justice to all processes of biological evolution through natural selection?[10]

It seems that is the conclusion Godfrey-Smith is drawing. Rather than searching for a watered-down version of Darwinism that is able to cover all known instances of biological evolution through natural selection (and that 'flattens out' all those instances as equally Darwinian), he is looking for a clear conception of a minimal Darwinian population to distinguish Darwinian processes from not quite (marginal) Darwinian ones, and within the first category for a clear conception of a paradigm Darwinian population to distinguish between populations that are more or less (paradigmatically) Darwinian. Whether or not cultural evolution harbors many paradigm Darwinian populations remains an open, as yet unresolved question. The merit of Godfrey-Smith's approach is that we at least have a clear understanding of what paradigm Darwinian populations are. Instead of stretching 'Darwinism' so as to cover as many dynamic processes as possible, we keep to a relatively simple and clear model. Just as there are some dynamic processes in the biological domain that are not Darwinian (or only marginally Darwinian at best, and some are not even populational – such as the cells in organisms), there are dynamic processes in culture (and economies) that are not populational (let alone Darwinian).

In the end this is a matter of what we want abstract formulations of Darwinism to do for us. Godfrey-Smith argues that two different desires have spurred attempts to give abstract formulations of Darwinism. One desire is to capture all genuine cases of natural selection in a summary description. The other is to describe a clear, simple and causally transparent machine. Often it has gone unnoticed that there have been these two different desires (Godfrey-Smith, 2009, p. 4). As a consequence it has not been acknowledged either that there is a trade-off between what is required to meet the two desires: since the total set of cases of natural selection is rather messy, heterogeneous and complex, meeting the desire to cover all cases of natural selection goes at the cost of the simplicity, transparency and clarity of the resulting description: 'As the summaries get sharper and function better as recipes, they start to omit cases. As they become more inclusive, they break down as recipes' (Godfrey-Smith, 2009, p. 27).

In their version of Generalized Darwinism, Hodgson and Knudsen seem to be led more by the first than by the second desire. In Hodgson and Knudsen (2010a, p. 22) they describe the difference between generalizing and analogical reasoning as follows. Analogical reasoning takes phenomena and processes in one domain as reference points for the study of similar phenomena and processes in another domain. Generalizing does not prioritize analytically any domain. It rather takes a deliberately copious array of phenomena and processes (possibly in different domains) and tries to adduce shared principles. It is clear that Hodgson and Knudsen believe that they themselves are engaged in generalizing rather than analogizing. This is roughly the same, I venture, as what Godfrey-Smith calls the desire to give a summary description of all cases of natural selection. By contrast, critics who stress the dis-analogies between biological and cultural evolution are interested in whether or not analogical reasoning is apt. They conceive of Darwinism not as a summary description of all cases of evolution through natural selection, but as a description of a simple, clear and transparent mechanism; a description that was first given in evolutionary biology.

Thus it seems Hodgson and Knudsen's Generalized Darwinism does not provide what critics of Darwinism believe Darwinism (if adequate, or useful, or fruitful) ideally should provide: a clear and simple model for how to study processes of cultural (or more specifically economic) change. As an analogy for studying economic evolution, the critics find the simple model wanting. But what else could the contribution of Darwinism to economics be other than offering a clear and simple model to study processes of economic change? A summary description of ontological communalities between processes and phenomena in various domains is not what made Darwinism an interesting candidate approach or framework to look at in the first place. For all its shortcomings as an analogy, the simple model has at least the merit of being clear and substantive. That merit seems to be missing from Hodgson and Knudsen's version of Generalized Darwinism.

15.5   THE 'DARWINIAN PRINCIPLES MUST BE INVOKED' ARGUMENT

> An adequate explanation of the evolution of such as system [a complex population system; JJV] *must* involve the three Darwinian principles of variation, inheritance and selection . . . Otherwise the explanation of evolution will be inadequate. (Hodgson and Knudsen, 2010a, p. 31)

Hodgson and Knudsen (2010a) argue that adequate explanations of evolution of complex population systems must refer to the three Darwinian principles of variation, inheritance (or replication) and selection. Reference to the principles is said to be inevitable. Invoking the three principles is not sufficient to give complete explanations of evolution in such systems, however. To that effect, domain-specific auxiliary hypotheses have to be added. But no adequate explanation of evolution can do without invoking the three Darwinian principles.

Let us have a closer look at how Hodgson and Knudsen argue (Hodgson and Knudsen, 2010a, pp. 30–31). They first make plausible that in complex population systems variation, inheritance and selection are present. 'Complex population systems' are defined abstractly and loosely as systems comprised of a variety of entities that interact with each other. Thus variation is part of complex population systems by definition. Hodgson and Knudsen argue that there is also selection in the sense that entities in such systems are mortal and degradable. The entities have to compete for locally scarce resources. Finally, Hodgson and Knudsen assume that the entities have the capacity to retain and pass on workable solutions (acquired in the struggle for existence) to others. In other words, there is also replication. After Hodgson and Knudsen establish that variation, inheritance and selection are omnipresent in complex population systems,[11] they go on assuming that for each of these – variation, inheritance and selection – a distinct mechanism (or distinct sets of mechanisms) is working. Thus we have a mechanism for the creation (and replenishment) of new variation, a mechanism for replication and one for selection. Finally they present the 'crucial step in the argument': an adequate explanation of evolution in complex population systems must involve the three Darwinian principles (cf. 'each principle is an explanatory requirement', ibid., p. 31).

What Hodgson and Knudsen seem to do here is to infer the necessity of invoking the three Darwinian principles in explanations of processes in complex population systems from the (alleged) ubiquitous existence of variation, replication and selection in those systems. This inference is dubious if not fallacious, however. The mere presence of certain things in some system does not ensure the importance (or relevance) of these things in explanations of phenomena and processes in the system. Take atoms, for example. Assuming that complex population systems always consist of matter and that the presence of matter always involves the presence of atoms, atoms are always necessarily present in such systems. Yet it is clear that adequate explanations of the evolution of such systems need not refer to atoms. If anything, adequate explanations are likely not to refer to atoms. Or consider another example closer to the subject matter of economics. Hedström (2005) argues that adequate explanations of social phenomena must refer to individual persons and their (inter) actions (rather than to institutions and social structure) because individual persons and their (inter)actions are always necessarily involved in the production of social phenomena. Sperber (2010) rightly observes that this is a non sequitur. There are many other things involved (at different levels of description) in social phenomena than individual persons and their interactions; their mere presence does not grant any of them explanatory primacy. Indeed, given their emphasis on the importance of social structure, I am pretty sure that Hodgson and Knudsen would readily agree that even though individual persons are always necessarily present whenever there are social phenomena, often not individual persons and their interactions but social positions, roles and institutions are the adequate level of analysis in explanations of social phenomena.

Note also that the claim at stake here – that in systems in which the three principles are present, adequate explanations must involve the three principles – is a stronger claim than that, taken together, the three principles are a sufficient condition for evolution through natural selection. The latter weaker claim can be rephrased as follows: in any system in which the three conditions are met, evolution through natural selection necessarily occurs (see Lewontin, 1970, 1985; Dennett, 1995). Thus the three principles are often seen as a recipe for Darwinian evolution (Godfrey-Smith,

2009).[12] This latter claim is weaker than Hodgson and Knudsen's claim that adequate explanations must involve the three principles because it does not imply that natural selection is the only mechanism working in complex population systems. There might be other mechanisms working in complex population systems than (paradigmatic) Darwinian natural selection, such as drift and migration. The weaker claim that the presence of the three principles is a recipe for Darwinian evolution does not imply either that natural selection dominates or overrides the possible working of other 'forces'. Indeed, other forces might override the working of natural selection.

A simple economic ('toy') example shows why in such a case explanations in terms of the three Darwinian principles would not be adequate. Suppose that firms in, say, the automobile industry differ in profitability. Suppose also that the conditions of variation, replication and selection are all met. Imagine that the firms vary with respect to the traits that they are selected for. The traits are perfectly heritable. Firms are of the same size and the number of spinoff firms that 'parent' firms found is proportional to their profitability. Then, *ceteris paribus*, 'natural selection' will see to it that the market share of more profitable firms increases at the cost of that of less profitable firms (this is an example of what Hodgson and Knudsen call 'successor selection'). Now suppose that the more profitable firms are geographically concentrated in a particular area and that that area is hit by an earthquake. The earthquake causes fatal losses for the hitherto more profitable firms, which in turn increases the market share of the hitherto less profitable firms (or, to be strict, of their traits). It seems that evolution in such a system is clearly not adequately explained in terms of variation, inheritance and selection. The effects of 'natural selection' are overridden here by drift (assuming that events such as earthquakes are paradigm examples of drift).

Thus adequate explanations of evolution in complex population systems need not, and perhaps sometimes should not, involve the three Darwinian principles. But it might still be that the three principles must be invoked to explain particular sorts of evolutionary processes. Perhaps the *explananda* of Darwinian explanations should be delineated more precisely (Stoelhorst, 2008). Perhaps explanations of the evolution of adaptive complexity must involve the three Darwinian principles. Sometimes it seems Hodgson and Knudsen have something like this in mind. They argue, for example, that for the evolution of (ordered and adapted) complexity, and for important transitions in the mode of replication (especially social organization: social structures, rules, positions and institutions), we need the existence of replicators and interactors. Without social replicators, social evolution would be less sophisticated than biological evolution, and would have a more limited potential for the evolution of a more complex phenomenon. (Hodgson and Knudsen, 2010a, p. 71). Given that we continuously witness the evolution of more complex phenomena in economic systems, they argue, there must be 'economic' replicators.

I think that there are several issues at stake here that should be distinguished carefully. One is whether adequate explanations of the evolution of adaptive complexity must involve variation, replication and selection. This does not seem to be the case. To see this let us return to the automobile industry example. In the absence of drift and other confounding factors, Darwinian evolution through 'natural selection' led to a particular outcome in our simple toy example. Here, in this specific example, it can be perhaps maintained that an adequate explanation must involve variation, replication and selection.[13] But it is easy to see that the same outcome can result via very different sorts of causal processes. Instead of 'parent' firms founding spinoff firms with exactly the same traits, firms now simply retain their traits over time. The growth of firms is proportional to their profitability. Then again the traits of the most profitable firms will eventually come to prevail in the industry. Thus we have the same particular outcome, but this time without any replication (this is an instance of what Hodgson and Knudsen call subset selection).

It can be argued that the deviation from the Darwinian variation – replication – selection framework in this second example is only minor. The only thing that has to be replaced, it seems, is 'replication' by 'retention'. But now consider a third example: all firms in the industry imitate the superior traits of the most profitable firms (and assume, for the sake of argument, that they can perfectly copy and implement the traits). Again the outcome will be that only the superior traits will come to prevail in the industry. But now all the relevant causal action is with the offspring firms, rather than with the parent firms. And it seems that 'replication' (or social transmission) is doing all the causal work here. Unlike in the first two examples, there is no active causal role here for selection, at least not in the sense of the test of environmental selection. This rendering seems to square well with how Hodgson and Knudsen would render this third example. Hodgson and Knudsen would probably classify such a causal process as diffusion. In their classification, diffusion is a subcategory not of selection but of replication, since the traits transmitted are not (yet) subjected to the test of environmental selection.[14] (this can be said to be pre-empted in this particular case). We can think of many more causal routes via which the same outcome may be produced. Thus all firms might individually learn (that is, unlike the social learning in the third example, independently of each other) that the traits of the most profitable firms are the superior ones. Or firms from other industries might found new firms with the superior traits in the automobile industry (which would be an example of migration, not natural selection).[15] In sum, contrary to what Hodgson and Knudsen argue, adequate explanations of the evolution of adaptive complexity need not involve variation, replication and selection. There seem to be other causal pathways via which adaptive complexity can be produced than the one involving variation, replication and selection.

15.6   SOCIAL REPLICATORS?

It might be objected that the outcome in all these examples is not an instance of adaptive complexity: the outcome for sure is adaptive, but it is not complex. And it might be added that it is exactly for the cumulative evolution of increased complexity that we need replication and replicators. Without replication and replicators, Hodgson and Knudsen seem to suggest, what is momentarily gained in previous evolutionary processes (in terms of increased complexity) is subsequently lost. This seems to be similar to Godfrey-Smith's argument that we need more than minimal Darwinian populations, namely ideally paradigm Darwinian populations with high-fidelity replication, for the cumulative evolution of novel phenomena. But Godfrey-Smith reserves this argument for biological evolution. He questions the relevance of the argument for explaining adaptive complexity in cultural systems. It seems that one of the central messages of Williams (1966), that Darwinian natural selection is the only mechanism in biology that we know of that can produce adaptive complexity, still stands. But for cultural evolution things might well be different. As Godfrey-Smith rightly argues, in a cultural context we are dealing with intelligent agents who can accumulate skills and information by a variety of means (Godfrey-Smith, 2009, p. 163). 'Replication' and 'replicators' in a substantive sense, implying that 'parents' are actively causally involved in the material reproduction of 'offspring' that almost perfectly resemble their parent with respect to the relevant traits, do not seem to be required. In cultural evolution, skills and information might not only be retained in various memory systems in individual persons, but also in artifacts and various systems of social organization (see Hutchins, 1995; Clark, 1998), for example.

Here is where the difference between Godfrey-Smith's view and Hodgson and Knudsen's 'received view' seems to have real bite. We saw that Godfrey-Smith emphasizes that there is huge heterogeneity in both biological and cultural evolution. Hodgson and Knudsen agree. The difference between the two seems to be that whereas Hodgson and Knudsen tend to call all of these Darwinian, Godfrey-Smith reserves 'Darwinian' for a subset only (and allows – with his notions of minimal and paradigm Darwinian populations – for distinguishing different degrees of Darwinism within the subset). When it comes to explaining a particular *explanandum* – cumulative evolution of novelty and adaptive complexity – however, it seems that Hodgson and Knudsen agree with Godfrey-Smith that something like paradigm Darwinian populations (and surely more than just minimal Darwinian populations) are required. But Godfrey-Smith confines this argument to biological evolution only. In cultural evolution cumulative evolution of novelty and adaptive complexity might occur through completely different sorts of causal pathways (pathways not involving replicators in any meaningful sense, in particular). By contrast, Hodgson and Knudsen seem to assume that the argument also applies across the board to cultural evolution.

Evolutionary economists in the tradition of Nelson and Winter (1982) have always been keen to criticize 'orthodox' (or mainstream) economics for its assumptions of 'hyper-rationality'. And rightly so. But they should not make the opposite failure of downplaying the cognitive powers of human beings. They should not and need not deny that individual persons (and sometimes also collectives of individuals) are at least sometimes capable of anticipating future contingencies and of making reasonable plans. Likewise they need not deny that there are many more ways for people to accumulate knowledge and wisdom than to instruct and teach their 'offspring'. Arguably, assuming that the evolution of adaptive complexity requires faithful copying also in cultural evolution is to fall into the trap of relying on unfounded analogies between biological and cultural evolution. Godfrey-Smith does not fall into this trap. But it is not so clear in this specific case that Hodgson and Knudsen also evade the trap.

Hodgson and Knudsen do acknowledge vast differences between biological and cultural evolution (like the ones just indicated). This makes it all the more remarkable that at places they seem to insist on the existence of 'faithful social replicators' (Hodgson and Knudsen, 2010a, p. 70). Copying error is said to have a cumulative destructive effect on the evolution of complexity (ibid., p. 102; see also Hodgson and Knudsen, 2010b). What is more, they seem to impose severe requirements on things to qualify as replicators. They build upon previous conceptual work done by Sterelny et al. (1996), Godfrey-Smith (2000) and Sperber (2000). From this work they derive three conditions that replicators have to meet: causal implication (the source must be causally involved in the production of the copy), similarity (the replicated entity must be or contain a replicator) and information transfer (the copy must inherit from the source the properties that make it relevantly similar to the source). To this, they add a fourth condition: conditional generative mechanisms (to make sure that replicators play the required instructive role in the ontogenetic development of the interactor; Hodgson and Knudsen, 2010a, pp. 96–97).

What is striking here is that Hodgson and Knudsen apparently believe that with the addition of the fourth condition they are able to salvage the replicator notion from recurrent objections voiced by critics. Godfrey-Smith and Sperber are such critics. They spell out the three conditions mainly to show how demanding and restrictive they are. Godfrey-Smith and Sperber want to point out that social replicators are rare, if not non-existent especially in cultural evolution. By contrast, Hodgson and Knudsen want to show that the social (or cultural) domain is rife with replicators. But by adding a fourth condition that has to be met, it seems that they further reduce the chances that social replicators exist. By doing so, it seems that they make their Generalized Darwinism a subset of Godfrey-Smith's set of replicators (which, recall, is for Godfrey-Smith a subset of Darwinism). Let us call this 'strict' interpretation of their Generalized Darwinism GD_S. This raises a problem of interpretation, however. Above I argued that viewed from the perspective of Godfrey-Smith's categorization, Hodgson and Knudsen's version of Generalized Darwinism is closer to what Godfrey-Smith calls the populational set (which, recall, comprises Darwinism as a subset) than to its subset of Darwinian populations. Let us call this broad interpretation of their Generalized Darwinism GD_B. Now which of these interpretations is the correct one?

There is textual evidence in Hodgson and Knudsen's writings for either interpretation. But GD_B seems to be the dominant one. A first indication for this is how Hodgson and Knudsen interpret the first condition for replicators, that of causation. This condition states that the source is causally implied in the production of the copy. A natural interpretation of this is that the parents materially reproduce the offspring. The causal action is with the parents. Above we saw that Godfrey-Smith insists that this is one of the hallmarks of Darwinism. And it is easy to think of possible examples of this in the cultural realm: biological parents trying to instill certain values in their children and teachers trying to instruct their pupils. As Godfrey-Smith observes, however, it seems that in most of cultural evolution the causal roles are reversed: the causal action is with the 'receiving' party. They decide whom and what to imitate (or whom and what to socially learn from). Thus in a sense, cultural children choose their own cultural parents. In such cases, the first condition, if given the natural interpretation, is not met.

But it seems that Hodgson and Knudsen want to give a very broad interpretation of this first condition. Stating that the source must be causally involved in the production of the copy is interpreted as demanding no more than that the source must serve as a model in the production of the copy. Without the existence of the source the copy could not have been produced. Thus understood the condition does not state that the sources must be causally responsible for the production of the copy (as is the case in genetic inheritance). Hodgson and Knudsen seem to interpret the second and third condition in a similarly loose way. They acknowledge that in the process of transmission, organizational routines are likely to undergo considerable modifications, for example. This does not prevent them from claiming that organizational routines are social replicators. Thus in Hodgson and Knudsen's interpretation of the second and third condition, copies apparently need not be very similar to their sources.[16] Yet other indications that Hodgson and Knudsen in the end opt for GD_B rather than GD_S can be readily given. For example, drift (understood as fitness-unrelated reproductive success of variants) is treated by them as part of Darwinian evolutionary processes (ibid., p. 26). Apparently, in their view 'Darwinism' does not entail a strong correlation between fitness and reproductive success.

Therefore it seems fair to say that the dominant theme in all the things that Hodgson and Knudsen say about the Darwinian principles (and especially about replicators) is that they should be understood in a highly abstract, general and broad way. Above I gave several examples of different causal processes in the automobile industry.[17] My point was that there might be various different causal processes leading to the same adaptive outcome and that in only one of them do all three Darwinian principles seem to be operating. This seemed to refute Hodgson and Knudsen's claim that adequate explanations of the evolution of adaptive complexity in complex population systems must involve the three Darwinian principles. But this presumed a somewhat strict reading of variation, replication and selection. On a more abstract, general and broader reading of the principles, it can be maintained that the three Darwinian principles are operating in all causal processes envisioned. Differences between the causal processes are then relegated to the domain of details. Only on such a broad reading, Hodgson and Knudsen's claim can be substantiated that adequate explanations of evolution of adaptive complexity in complex population systems must involve the three Darwinian principles. The claim then boils down to stating no more than that on a sufficiently abstract, general and broad interpretation of the three principles, adequate explanations of such evolutionary processes can be (re)formulated in terms of the three principles.[18]

15.7   REPLICATOR DYNAMICS WITHOUT REPLICATORS?

Thus far I discussed the adequacy and necessity of Darwinism in evolutionary economics in informal terms. Increasingly, discussions about the foundations of Darwinism and evolutionary theory are carried on in formal terms. Hodgson and Knudsen invoke the Price equation (see also Andersen, 2004 and Metcalfe, 2008). On a standard interpretation, the Price equation partitions evolutionary change over one generation into two components: a selection effect (normally represented in the equation as a covariance term) and a 'systematic transmission bias' effect (represented as an expectation term). In an economic context, 'market selection' might stand for the first effect. And innovations might be instantiations of the second effect. Hodgson and Knudsen use the Price equation to arrive at a generic understanding of 'selection'. They also argue that the equation can be used to verify empirically the effects of separate processes. And, as has been observed also by many other evolutionary theorists (see Okasha, 2007), they argue that the equation lends itself naturally to account for multilevel selection.

Here, in this section, I concentrate on another standard formal representation of Darwinian evolution through natural selection: the replicator dynamic (Taylor and Jonker, 1978).[19] The replicator dynamic and its properties are studied extensively in evolutionary game theory. At an intuitive level it is easy to see that the replicator dynamic neatly captures an idealized version of Darwinian evolution through natural selection. The replicator dynamic basically states that the growth rates of the strategies' frequencies in a population are a function of the strategies' relative fitness (that is, as compared to the population's average fitness). Thus, if some strategy has superior fitness (independent of the prevailing frequencies in the population), then natural selection will drive that strategy to fixation (so that, in the end, only that strategy survives in the population). It seems clear that one of the crucial idealizations in the replicator dynamic is that there is perfect-fidelity replication. The reference point seems to be asexual reproduction without any mutations. The assumption is that 'like begets like' (Maynard Smith, 1982).[20]

Given this standard depiction of the idealizations involved in the replicator dynamic, it is remarkable that Henrich and Boyd (2002) argue that the replicator dynamic is useful for studying population-level changes also if social transmission is biased systematically.[21] What is more, they even argue that the stronger the systematic biases in social transmission as compared to the force of selection, the more accurate the replicator dynamic tracks population-level patterns (see also Henrich et al., 2008). If Henrich and Boyd are right, the applicability of a standard modeling tool in evolutionary theorizing is not compromised by low-fidelity social transmission. It seems that their result would support the belief that Darwinism does not require high-fidelity copying. We would be entitled to maintain replicator dynamic even in the absence of replicators. Yet, as Claidière and Sperber (2007) point out convincingly, what Henrich and Boyd show falls short of drawing this (for Darwinism, comforting) conclusion. What Henrich and Boyd show at most is that under quite restrictive and arbitrary conditions it is possible that even in the presence of systematic transmission biases replicator dynamic nevertheless tracks population-level change accurately.

Let us have a closer look at Henrich and Boyd's argument. Claiming that replicator dynamic gets the patterns in population-level behavior right especially when the force of systematic transmission biases prevails over that of selection is surely counter-intuitive. So how do they go about arguing this? Claidière and Sperber (2007) correctly observe that when one looks through the math, Henrich and Boyd's results are in effect driven by two crucial assumptions:

1. There are a few strong attractors that 'deterministically' and quickly pull imitated representations towards these attractors.
2. Selection subsequently favors one of these attractors over the others so that eventually the favored attractor prevails in the population.

Henrich and Boyd give the 'toy' example of how people perceive the moon. Suppose there are different potential role models in the population whose perceptions of the moon range (in some sort of a continuum) from the one extreme belief that the moon is a self-aware, conscious entity with goals, emotions and motivations, to the opposite extreme belief that the moon is simply a big rock, lacking goals, emotions and motivations. Henrich and Boyd assume that social learners are naturally drawn to one of these opposite beliefs. Thus, when social learners imitate role models who are (on the continuum) more to the side of the former extreme belief, what they take over from their role models is not their particular beliefs but the extreme belief near to them. This is what it means to say that there are 'deterministic' strong cognitive attractors (see Sperber, 1996). The presence of such attractors imply a strong and systematic transmission bias (often called a content-based bias). If the two attractors indicated are indeed strong, it will not last long, until there are only two types left in the population: the one type holding the one extreme belief and the other one holding the opposite extreme belief. If then one type for whatever reason stands out as being the more attractive cultural model (because the bearers of it are more successful, or prestigious, for example) then selection will drive the population in the direction of that type. Thus, when (potential) cultural models holding the inanimate belief tend to be imitated more often than the (potential) cultural models holding the animistic belief, the first type will come to prevail in the population. This is precisely what the replicator dynamic predicts.

It is easy to see that Henrich and Boyd's results are quite sensitive to changes in the assumptions. And this is exactly what Claidière and Sperber (2007) set out to do. They show that the replicator dynamic fails to predict population behavior if the type of role model with the highest (social) fitness does not coincide with an attractor, for example. They furthermore show that it also makes a difference whether 'attraction' is taken to be probabilistic rather than deterministic. Claidière and Sperber also point out that assuming that there are strong attractors, as Henrich and Boyd (2002) do, amounts to postulating replicators. After all, once the strong attractors have done their work, we are left with only two types of cultural models whose beliefs are imitated with perfect fidelity. Thus, they conclude, Henrich and Boyd's results are an artifact of the peculiarities of their model. The results do not warrant the general conclusion that when the force of systematic transmission biases prevails over that of selection the replicator dynamic gets population-level behavior right.

What is perhaps more telling here, though, is that the two camps (who arguably can be taken to be the *fine fleur* of contemporary theorists about cultural evolution) agree on many substantive issues. They agree for example on what it means to say in this context of cultural evolution that the force of selection is relatively weak as compared with the force of attraction: social learners do not have a strong preference for the same cultural model(s), whereas the content-based transmission bias in their learning is strong. Thus 'selection' refers here to selective attention, the tendency for social learners to pay particular attention to some individuals more than others (Henrich et al., 2008). In short, it is the choice of the cultural model. Henrich and Boyd suggest that (weak) selective forces come into play only after the strong attractors have done their variation-reducing work. But strictly speaking this is misleading. In terms of time, selection comes first here and transmission comes second. First a cultural model is selected and then information is transmitted from the role model to the learner. Or perhaps it is even more appropriate to say that instead of two distinct processes, 'selection' and transmission, we have just one process. It is not that first a cultural model is picked and that only subsequently it is decided by the learner what trait to imitate. It seems this often comes in one fell swoop. An adolescent perceives the behavior of some other adolescent as 'cool', for example, and at once starts mimicking it (often without being aware of it).[22]

It seems that Claidière and Sperber are in agreement with Henrich and Boyd that this is how 'selection' and transmission typically intermingle in cultural evolution. Conversely, Henrich and Boyd seem to agree with Claidière and Sperber that social transmission is characterized not only by distribution-based biases (such as the conformity or prestige bias, relating to whom are learned from) but also by content-based biases (attractors, relating to what is learned). Indeed, it has become received wisdom that there is a panoply of different sorts of transmission biases in cultural evolution. But if all this is symptomatic of cultural evolution, standard causal interpretations of either the classical approach or the replicator approach to Generalized Darwinism do not seem to fit cultural evolution. These approaches do not seem to fit not only for the reason that 'replication' (let alone 'replicator') seems to be ill-suited. The standard causal interpretation of Darwinian evolution in terms either of three distinct mechanisms (variation, replication and selection) or of two mechanisms (interaction and replication) do not seem to capture the peculiarities of cultural evolutionary processes. As argued above, insofar as it is appropriate at all to invoke the three Darwinian principles in cultural evolution, they are aspects of the same process rather than three distinct processes. In one and the same process of social learning from some cultural model, new variants might pop up, the cultural model is (de facto) selected and information is transmitted. Likewise the portrayal of natural selection as interaction that causes replication to be differential does not seem to fit either. The only 'interaction' in social learning seems to be between role model ('parent') and learner ('child'), not between 'parents'. And the causes of differential 'replication' might be due more to content-based biases than to the social fitness of potential role models. In sum, it might be quite arbitrary and artificial to distinguish two or three mechanisms in processes of cultural evolution. That also implies that in its intended role as a heuristic device Darwinism might lead researchers seriously astray. It invites social theorists to look for two or three processes (or mechanisms) whereas there in fact there might only be one.

Henrich et al. suggest that many of their critics are simply mathematically illiterate (Henrich et al., 2008, footnote 1). That might well be true. They are also right in arguing that mathematical modeling might be very helpful in fleshing out the implications of particular assumptions; implications we fail to see without the modeling. In particular, it needs some formal modeling to see that the presence of considerable systematic biases in 'micro'-transmission does not rule out that patterns in population-level behavior are fairly accurately tracked by replicator dynamic. But it seems we really do not learn much from Henrich and Boyd's formal model about the scope of applicability of the replicator dynamic. It seems that with their model Henrich and Boyd draw attention to a logical possibility rather than to an empirically confirmed behavioral regularity. This is reminiscent of a lot of what has been going on in mathematical economics. Especially in the heydays of general equilibrium theory and social choice theory, mathematical economists excelled in proving yet another existence or (im)possibility theorem (or in proving the same theorem under less restrictive conditions). Much less attention was paid to how all this sophisticated formal work related to the real world. Do we in evolutionary economics want to go in the same direction?

Another aspect to the use of the Price equation and of the replicator dynamic should not go unnoticed. As Gardner (2009) argues, the Price equation can be used (and is actually used) to bolster rationality (that is, optimization or constrained maximization) based models (see Grafen, 2002). Similarly, the replicator dynamic has done a lot to justify the centrality of the Nash equilibrium as the solution concept in game theory (Mailath, 1998; Vromen, 2009). Khalil and Marciano (2010) argue that evolutionary economists who turn to (neo-Darwinian) evolutionary biology in order to get away from mechanistic Walrasian general equilibrium theory will not find what they are looking for. In fact, neo-Darwinism and Walrasian equilibrium rest on the same formal model (Joosten, 2006). Given all these conceptual and mathematical links between neo-Darwinian models and equilibrium-based standard economic models, it seems that neo-Darwinian models are of very little use for coming to grips with processes of cumulative evolution resulting in increased adaptive complexity and in novelty. Thus, if we seek an evolutionary economics that is able to come to grips with the latter – and friends and foes of Generalized Darwinism seem to agree that we should seek such models – the equations mentioned might steer us in the wrong direction.

Precisely because the equations are so general and multi-interpretable they might also be used in many other ways. For very different causal processes they might accurately track population-level behavior. If we insist that our explanations should get the actual causal processes at least roughly right, however, it seems that the equations have limited applicability. This seems to hold especially (but not only) for cultural evolution. Their applicability in cultural evolution seems to be severely limited by the pervasiveness of asymmetries in social roles, for example.

15.8 CONCLUSIONS

On closer inspection, it is not so clear that the 'biological evolution is not simple either' argument can be used to unnerve the objection that

Darwinian models are too simple to do justice to the complexity of culture. The argument could as well be turned against proponents of Darwinizing culture: if Darwinian models are also too simple to do justice to the complexity of biology, then it seems we need more complex models than Darwinian ones to come to grips with cultural and biological evolution alike. We saw that instead of coming up with a more satisfactory model, Hodgson and Knudsen seem to be looking for a summary description of Darwinian evolution through natural selection that is general and abstract enough to cover almost all possible processes of change in both domains. Thus it is not just that in their hands 'Darwinism' tends to become a 'catch-all' term. Generalized Darwinism does not offer a clear simple and substantive model for how to start studying economic evolution either.

Similar doubts arose with respect to Hodgson and Knudsen's 'the three Darwinian principles must be invoked' argument. The argument can only be defended on a sufficiently general, abstract and broad understanding of the three Darwinian principles. If the principles are understood in a stricter sense, then at most the claim can be defended that the three principles must be invoked to explain particular sorts of processes in complex population systems: those in which novelty and adaptive complexity cumulatively evolve. Sometimes it seems that Hodgson and Knudsen insist on high-fidelity copying in replication for exactly this reason: without high-fidelity copying such processes would be impossible. It seems Godfrey-Smith develops a similar argument. But he confines the scope of the validity of this argument to biological evolution only. In cultural evolution, he suggests, novelty and adaptive complexity can be produced also in other, distinctly non-Darwinian sorts of processes.

There seems to emerge a consensus among theorists of cultural evolution that social transmission is typically characterized by various systematic biases. Not only is what social learners take over from their role models mostly at best an imperfect copy of what they imitate, but whom they select as their role models tends to be systematically biased as well. We saw that even in such cases of clear absence of replicators, the replicator dynamic might be able to predict population-level behavior pretty well. We also saw, however, that this seems to be a 'possibility result' at best that only obtains when rather peculiar conditions are met. What is more, the actual causal mechanisms involved in such processes of cultural evolution seem to be markedly different than the ones in biological evolution. It is not just that we find different instantiations (or implementations) of mechanisms of variation, replication and selection (or of interaction and replication) in cultural evolution; it is not even clear that we find distinct mechanisms of variation, replication and selection (or of interaction and replication) in cultural evolution at all. If so, following the ('heuristic') lead of Generalized Darwinism (that is, look out for such distinct mechanisms in cultural evolution), would steer researchers in counter-productive directions.

Compared with the diluted concept of Generalized Darwinism, Godfrey-Smith's concept of Darwinism has a definite shape and is discriminating. Godfrey-Smith's distinctions between populations and non-populations, between minimal Darwinian populations and marginal (or partial) Darwinian populations, which are not quite Darwinian, and between minimal Darwinian populations and paradigm Darwinian populations, are useful to classify different cases of change in both biological and cultural evolution. They give us at least a rough and ready idea in what sorts of cases application of Darwinian principles makes sense. The other side of the coin is that Godfrey-Smith's distinctions suggest in what sorts of cases we are advised to look for non-Darwinian principles. But Godfrey-Smith's taxonomy does not give fool-proof directions and does not make for a full-fledged theory. Here the situation is the same as with Generalized Darwinism: much domain-specific substance is yet to be added and success is not guaranteed. As before, the devil is in the detail and the proof of the pudding is in the eating.

NOTES

1. Comments by Geoff Hodgson and Thorbjørn Knudsen are gratefully acknowledged. All remaining errors are mine.
2. Implicitly, it is assumed that the economic domain is a subdomain of the cultural domain and that the biological and cultural domain can be carved up 'horizontally' as two adjacent, non-overlapping domains. The implications of the fact that the biological domain can be seen as part of the economic domain (brains, neurons and genes can be seen as constituent parts of the economic domain at different levels of organization, for example) are given scant attention (see Vromen, 2004). In this chapter I accept the implicit assumption for the sake of argument.
3. Complex population systems are systems that are populated by a great variety of different entities (Mayr, 1976) that interact with each other in non-trivial ways.
4. Generalized Darwinism might still be useful for other purposes, for example for facilitating cross-disciplinary communication (as it seems to provides a common 'language') and for unifying different theories. Since Hodgson and Knudsen themselves stress the heuristic function of Darwinism in further theory development, however, I confine my attention in this chapter to that function.
5. In my discussion, I shall refrain from making critical remarks. On the back cover of the book, Elisabeth Lloyd calls Godfrey-Smith's book 'a gem'. A gem it is: it is full of illuminating insights. But not many of the insights are worked out in great detail.
6. Note that Godfrey-Smith replaces Hodgson and Knudsen's third principle, selection, by differential fitness. I think Godfrey-Smith's is more accurate (as 'selection' does not appear then in both the *analysans* – evolution through natural selection; and the *analysandum* – variation, replication and differential fitness), but henceforth I will use both formulations interchangeably.
7. Again, Godfrey-Smith is not arguing that this is unique to cultural evolution. In

biological evolution, we also find ensembles of entities (such as the atoms in hemoglobin molecules) that do not constitute populations.

8. This list does not exhaust the list of crucial parameters that should have a high value for populations to qualify as paradigm Darwinian populations. But it gives the gist of the notion of a paradigm Darwinian population.

9. For a similar argument especially with respect to cultural evolution, see Sterelny (2006).

10. It would seem that we need a more general model with (paradigm) Darwinism as a special, limiting case. Kerr and Godfrey-Smith's (2009) generalization of the Price equation can be seen as exactly such an attempt. See Wenseleers et al. (forthcoming) for an interesting further discussion with a special focus on (alleged) differences between biological and cultural evolution.

11. Strictly speaking, Hodgson and Knudsen do not prove that besides variation, replication and selection are always ('necessarily') present in complex population systems. They rather trust that readers will recognize that in many different systems there is selection and replication (if 'selection' and 'replication' are understood sufficiently generally and abstractly).

12. Godfrey-Smith gives a simple example to show that this need not be true, though: it is possible that the differential fitness effects are exactly nullified by the systematically biased transmission effects (cf. the two terms in the Price equation exactly add up to zero) so that there is no net evolutionary change.

13. It should be noted, though, that the causal processes envisaged in this simple example can be described at other levels (for example at the level of individual persons and their interactions in particular social situations) in ways that do not refer (at least explicitly) to variation, replication and selection.

14. In this specific case it might be argued, though, that there is a subsequent stage of selection. It is just that in this specific case (as all firms are assumed to copy the superior traits flawlessly) the causal efficacy of selection is pre-empted. But below we will see examples of cultural evolution in which there is no subsequent stage of selection.

15. Hodgson and Knudsen (2010a) treat Klepper's (2002, 2007) insightful analyses of spinoff firms in the automobile industry as an example of organization-level replication of routines. But what Klepper rather wants to explain is why new (*de novo*) car manufacturing firms that are founded by dissatisfied members of 'old' firms tend to do better than old diversifying firms, and also why firms, tend to be spatially clustered. More importantly, Klepper is not at all assuming that there is high-fidelity replication of routines from parent firms to spinoff firms.

16. Hodgson and Knudsen (2010b) distinguish between copying fidelity and reading (and development) fidelity. They argue that whereas copying errors are absolutely fatal for the evolution of complexity, development errors (in the reading of the generative instructions) are not. As Hodgson and Knudsen seem to concede, however, copying fidelity seems to characterize the creation of new units by (and in) the same firm better than the ('real') social learning by the one firm from another firm.

17. It might be objected that it testifies to the explanatory (in the sense of unifying) power of Generalized Darwinism that it is so general that it can cover all these very different causal processes. But if we want Generalized Darwinism to (in the end) provide causal explanations, this does not seem to be a merit, as the relevant counterfactuals differ greatly from the one sort of causal process to the other (Godfrey-Smith, 2009, p. 153).

18. Brian Arthur (2009) argues convincingly that the Darwinian principles of variation and selection cannot explain how radically new technologies originate (in his view by combining and recombining already existing technologies). It is easy to see that on a sufficiently general, abstract and broad reading of especially 'variation' and 'replication', Arthur's own explanation of combinatorial evolution can be recast in terms of the three Darwinian principles (and thus Hodgson and Knudsen's claim can be rescued). But one wonders what is gained by doing so.

19. Page and Nowak (2002) show that if a mutation term is added to the replicator

dynamic, the resulting replicator-mutator equation is mathematically equivalent to the Price equation.
20. Maynard Smith's related notion of an evolutionarily stable strategy (ESS) investigates a counterfactual situation: what would happen if a single mutant strategy were to enter the population?
21. Henrich and Boyd also use the Price equation to make their case.
22. Of course, this is just one possible way in which social learning can work. There are many others.

REFERENCES

Aldrich, H.E., G.M. Hodgson, D.L. Hull, T. Knudsen and V.J. Vanberg (2008), 'In Defense of Generalized Darwinism', *Journal of Evolutionary Economics*, **18**(5), 577–596.
Andersen, E.S. (2004) 'Population Thinking, Price's Equation and Evolutionary Economic Analysis', *Evolutionary and Institutional Economics Review*, **1**(1), 127–148.
Arthur, W.B. (2009), *The Nature of Technology: What It Is and How It Evolves*, London: Penguin Group (Allen Lane).
Aunger, R. (2000), *Darwinizing Culture: The Status of Memetics as a Science*, Oxford: Oxford University Press.
Boyd, R. and P. Richerson (1985), *Culture and the Evolutionary Process*, Chicago, IL: University of Chicago Press.
Bünstorf, G. (2006), 'How Useful is Generalized Darwinism as a Framework to Study Competition and Industrial Evolution?', *Journal of Evolutionary Economics*, **16**(5), 511–527.
Claidière, N. and D. Sperber (2007), 'The Role of Attraction in Cultural Evolution: Reply to J. Henrich and R. Boyd, On Modeling Cognition and Culture', *Journal of Cognition and Culture*, **7**(1–2), 89–111.
Clark, A. (1998), *Being There: Putting Brain, Body, and World Together Again*, Cambridge, MA: MIT Press.
Cordes, C. (2006), 'Darwinism in Economics: From Analogy to Continuity', *Journal of Evolutionary Economics*, **16**(5), 529–541.
Crozier, G.K.D. (2008), 'Reconsidering Cultural Selection Theory', *British Journal for the Philosophy of Science*, **59**(3), 455–479.
Darden, L., and J. Cain (1989), 'Selection Type Theories', *Philosophy of Science*, **56**(1), 106–129.
Dawkins, R. (1976), *The Selfish Gene*, Oxford: Oxford University Press.
Dennett, D.C. (1995), *Darwin's Dangerous Idea*, London: Penguin Press.
Gardner, A. (2009), 'The Price Equation', *Current Biology*, **18**(5), R198–202.
Godfrey-Smith, P. (2000), 'The Replicator in Retrospect', *Biology and Philosophy*, **15**(3), 403–423.
Godfrey-Smith, P. (2009), *Darwinian Populations and Natural Selection*, Oxford: Oxford University Press.
Grafen, A. (2002), 'A First Formal Link between the Price Equation and an Optimization Program', *Journal of Theoretical Biology*, **217**(1), 75–91.
Hedström, P. (2005), *Dissecting the Social: On the Principles of Analytical Sociology*, Cambridge: Cambridge University Press.
Henrich, J. and R. Boyd (2002), 'On Modeling Cognition and Culture: Why Replicators are not Necessary for Cultural Evolution', *Journal of Cognition and Culture*, **2**(2), 87–112.
Henrich, J., R. Boyd and P.J. Richerson (2008), 'Five Misunderstandings about Cultural Evolution', *Human Nature*, **19**(2), 119–137.
Hodgson, G.M. (2002), 'Darwinism in Economics: From Analogy to Ontology', *Journal of Evolutionary Economics*, **12**(3), 259–281.
Hodgson, G.M. (2004), 'Darwinism, Causality and the Social Sciences', *Journal of Economic Methodology*, **11**(2), 175–194.

Hodgson, G.M. (2010), 'A Philosophical Perspective on Contemporary Evolutionary Economics', Papers on Economics and Evolution #1001, Max Planck Institute of Economics.

Hodgson, G.M. and T. Knudsen (2006), 'Why We Need a Generalized Darwinism, and Why Generalized Darwinism is Not Enough', *Journal of Economic Behavior and Organization*, **61**(1), 1–19.

Hodgson, G.M. and T. Knudsen (2010a), *Darwin's Conjecture: The Search for General Principles of Social and Economic Evolution*, Chicago, IL: University of Chicago Press.

Hodgson, G.M. and T. Knudsen (2010b), 'Generative Replication and the Evolution of Complexity', *Journal of Economic Behavior and Organization*, **75**(1), 12–24.

Hull, D.L. (1980), 'Individuality and Selection', *Annual Review of Ecology and Systematics*, **11**, 311–332.

Hull, D.L. (1988), *Science as a Process: An Evolutionary Account of the Social and Conceptual Development of Science,* Chicago, IL: University of Chicago Press.

Hutchins, E.L. (1995), *Cognition in the Wild*, Cambridge: MIT Press.

Joosten, R. (2006), 'Walras and Darwin: An Odd Couple?', *Journal of Evolutionary Economics* **16**(5), 561–573.

Kerr, B. and P. Godfrey-Smith (2009), 'Generalization of the Price Equation for Evolutionary Change', *Evolution*, **63**(2), 531–536.

Khalil, E.L. and A. Marciano (2010), 'The Equivalence of Neo-Darwinism and Walrasian Equilibrium: In Defense of Organismus Economicus', *Biology and Philosophy*, **25**(2), 229–248.

Kincaid, H. (2009), 'Social Sciences', in S. Psillos and M. Curd (eds), *The Routledge Companion to the Philosophy of Science*, London: Routledge, pp. 594–603.

Klepper, S. (2002), 'The Capabilities of New Firms and the Evolution of the US Automobile Industry', *Industrial and Corporate Change*, **11**(4), 645–666.

Klepper, S. (2007), 'Disagreements, Spinoffs, and the Evolution of Detroit as the Capital of the US Automobile Industry', *Management Science*, **53**(4), 616–631.

Lewontin, R.C. (1970), 'The Units of Selection', *Annual Review of Ecology and Systematics*, **1**, 1–18.

Lewontin, R.C. (1985), 'Adaptation', in R. Levins and R.C. Lewontin (eds), *The Dialectical Biologist*, Cambridge, MA: Harvard University Press, pp. 65–84.

Mailath, G.J. (1998) 'Do People Play Nash Equilibrium? Lessons from Evolutionary Game Theory', *Journal of Economic Literature*, **36**(3), 1347–1374.

Maynard Smith, J. (1982), *Evolution and the Theory of Games*, Cambridge: Cambridge University Press.

Mayr, E. (1976), 'Typological versus Populational Thinking', *Evolution and the Diversity of Life*, Cambridge: MA: Harvard University Press, pp. 26–29.

Mesoudi, A., A. Whiten and K.N. Laland (2006), 'Towards a Unified Science of Cultural Evolution', *Behavioral and Brain Sciences*, **29**(4), 329–383.

Metcalfe, J.S. (1988), 'Evolution and Economic Change', in A. Silberston (ed.), *Technology and Economic Progress*, London: Macmillan, pp. 54–85.

Metcalfe, J.S (2008), 'Accounting for Economic Evolution: Fitness and the Population Method,' *Journal of Bioeconomics*, **10**(1), 23–49.

Nelson, R.R and S.G. Winter (1982), *An Evolutionary Theory of Economic Change*, Cambridge, MA: Belknap Press of Harvard University Press.

Okasha, S. (2007), *Evolution and the Levels of Selection*, Oxford: Oxford University Press.

Page, K.M. and M.A. Nowak (2002). 'Unifying Evolutionary Dynamics', *Journal of Theoretical Biology*, **219**(1), 93–98.

Schubert, C. (2009), 'Darwinism in Economics and the Evolutionary Theory of Policy-making', Papers on Economics and Evolution #0910, Max Planck Institute of Economics Jena.

Sober, E. (1984), *The Nature of Selection*, Cambridge: MIT Press.

Sperber, D. (1996), *Explaining Culture: A Naturalistic Approach*, Oxford: Basil Blackwell.

Sperber, D. (2000), 'An Objection to the Memetic Approach to Culture', in R. Aunger (ed.), *Darwinizing Culture*, Oxford: Oxford University Press, pp. 163–173.

Sperber, D. (2010), 'A Naturalistic Ontology for Mechanistic Explanations in the Social Sciences', in P. Demeulenaere (ed.), *Analytical Sociology and Social Mechanisms*, Cambridge: Cambridge University Press, pp. 64–77.

Sterelny, K. (2006), 'Memes Revisited', *British Journal for the Philosophy of Science*, **57**(1), 145–165.

Sterelny, K., K.C. Smith and M. Dickison (1996), 'The Extended Replicator', *Biology and Philosophy*, **11**(3), 377–403.

Stoelhorst, J.W. (2008), 'The Explanatory Logic and Ontological Commitments of Generalized Darwinism', *Journal of Economic Methodology*, **14**(4), 343–363.

Taylor, P. and L. Jonker (1978), 'Evolutionarily Stable Strategies and Game Dynamics', *Mathematical Biosciences*, **40**, 145–156.

Vromen, J.J. (2001), 'The Human Agent in Evolutionary Economics', in J. Laurent and J. Nightingale (eds), *Darwinism and Evolutionary Economics*, Cheltenham, UK and Northampton, MA, USA: Edward Elgar, 184–208.

Vromen, J.J. (2004), 'Conjectural Revisionary Economic Ontology: Outline of an Ambitious Research Agenda for Evolutionary Economics', *Journal of Economic Methodology*, **11**(2), 213–247.

Vromen, J.J. (2007), 'Generalized Darwinism in Evolutionary Economics – The Devil is in the Details', Papers on Economics and Evolution #0711, Max Planck Institute of Economics, Jena.

Vromen, J.J. (2009), 'Advancing Evolutionary Explanations in Economics: The Limited Usefulness of Tinbergen's Four-Question Classification', in D. Ross and H. Kincaid (eds) *The Oxford Handbook of Philosophy of Economics*, Oxford: Oxford University Press, pp. 337–367.

Vromen, J.J. (2010), 'Ontological Issues in Evolutionary Economics: The Debate between Generalized Darwinism and the Continuity Hypothesis', in U. Mäki (ed.), *Handbook of the Philosophy of Science: Philosophy of Economics*, Amsterdam: Elsevier, pp. 673–699.

Wenseleers, T, S. Dewitte and A. De Block (forthcoming), 'Evolutionary Theories of Cultural Change', *Trends in Ecology and Evolution*.

Williams, G.C. (1966), *Adaptation and Natural Selection*, Princeton, NJ: Princeton University Press.

Witt, U. (2004), 'On the Proper Interpretation of "Evolution" in Economics and its Implications for Production Theory', *Journal of Economic Methodology*, **11**(2), 125–146.

Witt, U. (2007), 'Heuristic Twists and Ontological Creeds: Road Map for Evolutionary Economics', Papers on Economics and Evolution #0701, Max Planck Institute for Economics.

PART V

MACROECONOMICS

16 Recent developments in macroeconomics: the DSGE approach to business cycles in perspective

Pedro Garcia Duarte[1]

16.1 INTRODUCTION

In the late 1990s and early 2000s mainstream macroeconomists started seeing the fundamental disagreements they had about economic fluctuations vanish.[2] Increasingly they understood that there was a common framework through which they could analyze such issues as the effects of real and nominal shocks on real activity, how monetary and fiscal policies should be designed in order to maximize welfare, and the importance or not that governments commit to a pre-established set of policy actions, among many others.[3]

This new consensus in macroeconomics became known as the new neoclassical synthesis, after Goodfriend and King (1997), and it emerged from the combination of the dynamic general equilibrium approach of the real business cycle (RBC) literature with the nominal rigidities and imperfect competition of the new Keynesian models. As a result of these rigidities, these general equilibrium models predict that monetary disturbances do have lasting effects on real variables (such as real output) in the short run, even if the influence of these shocks on aggregate nominal expenditure can be forecast in advance (Woodford, 2003, pp. 6–10; Galí, 2008, pp. 4–6). This result contrasts to those coming from both the earliest new classical models, in which monetary shocks can have transitory real effects only if they are unanticipated; and the RBC literature, in most of which there is no room for a monetary stabilization policy because real and nominal variables are modeled as evolving independently of each other, usually in a context of price flexibility.[4] Having a general equilibrium macroeconomic model with microfoundations in which money is non-neutral in the short run, which implies that monetary policy has lasting effects similar to what is observed in the data, is the main motivation for using dynamic, stochastic general equilibrium (or DSGE) models to 'discuss the nature of desirable monetary policy rules' (Woodford, 2003, p. 7) and for taking them to the policymaking, quantitative arena (where having a 'scientific' way of making normative analysis is surely valued).

The key characteristics of this consensus framework in its most basic incarnation are the use of a DSGE model in which a continuum of infinitely lived agents (households and firms) solve intertemporal optimizing problems to choose how much to consume, to work, to accumulate capital, to hire factors of production and so on. For the modern mainstream economists, the time is past when macroeconomists could readily assume reduced-form relationships among aggregate variables – such as the consumption, investment, and liquidity preference functions upon which rests the IS-LM model of the old neoclassical synthesis. Nowadays these economists argue that what they understand to be the good standards dictate that such relationships ought to follow from first-order conditions of maximization problems. With the pervasive use of a representative agent in those models, modern macroeconomists feel comfortable in using the welfare of private agents (in fact, of the representative agent) as 'a natural objective in terms of which alternative policies should be evaluated' (Woodford, 2003, p. 12).[5] Therefore, they argue that because they have a general equilibrium macroeconomic model based on microfoundations they also have a normative framework for policy analysis that is immune to the famous critique of large-scale macroeconometric models of the 1960s and the 1970s made by Lucas (1976).[6] Therefore, DSGE models are appealing to these economists because they believe they can make 'scientific' welfare analysis, a point hinted by Solow (2000, p. 152, emphasis added) when he raised his reservations to the consensus macroeconomics:

> Another foundational question is whether agents in macro models should be described as making optimizing decisions or proceeding by rule of thumb. In my more optimistic moments I suspect that this dichotomy may be more apparent than real. By now, to assume that a representative consumer maximizes a discounted sum of constant-elasticity utilities subject to a lifetime budget constraint is practically to adopt a rule of thumb. . . . *But in my more pessimistic moments, I think that the only reason to insist on optimizing behavior is to get welfare conclusions that no one believes anyway*, the most spectacularly implausible one being that the observed business cycle is really an optimal adjustment to unexpected shocks to technology.

It is precisely because the standards held by mainstream macroeconomists are that one ought to derive macroeconomic models from microeconomic optimization problems, and because they want to apply their models to the data and policy analysis, that a trade-off emerges: they are willing to introduce as many shocks and frictions (habit formation in consumption, investment adjustment costs, sticky prices and wages, capital utilization, among others) into their models as they need for estimating them and for overcoming econometric issues such as identification of structural parameters, goodness of fit and forecasting performance – interestingly, so far few of these economists want to consider seriously whether they are really able to introduce such frictions in a structural way.[7] However, as argued by Chari et al. (2009), by enlarging their models this way macroeconomists introduce some shocks that are not invariant with respect to the alternative policies considered, thus making these models subject to the Lucas critique.

My goal in this chapter is to survey the main methodological innovations brought by the DSGE macroeconomics, with an emphasis on monetary economics. I start by showing the empirical facts that macroeconomists seek to reproduce through their models, and then I present briefly a very basic new Keynesian DSGE model. I then muse upon the current practices, their implications and what to expect from them in the near future. Finally, I briefly explore how the prevailing consensus is being challenged by the recent crisis: while the critics argue that the modern macroeconomics went into a dead-end road, mainstream macroeconomists defend their game as the only one available in the macroeconomics town.

16.2   WHAT ARE THE 'FACTS'?

As Christiano et al. (1999, p. 67) put it, in economics in general, and in macroeconomics in particular, one cannot use purely statistical methods because there is no data drawn from 'otherwise identical economies operating under the monetary institutions or rules we are interested in evaluating'. On the other hand 'real world experimentation is not an option' for macroeconomists. Therefore, the computer is the laboratory that macroeconomists use to perform experiments in structural models.[8] How to carry out such experiments? Modern macroeconomists follow Robert Lucas (1980) and look for a substantive shock whose effects on the economy are known with confidence, so that they can test models by comparing theoretical and observed effects of such shocks. These computational experiments are important not only for testing alternative economic policies but also for selecting 'good' macroeconomic models.[9]

Why do macroeconomists focus on monetary shocks instead of on the systematic actions of policymakers? The answer is that these actions reflect the effect of all shocks hitting the economy, including non-monetary ones. In other words, policymakers' systematic actions are endogenous responses to developments in the economy. It is exactly this endogeneity that makes useless an analysis of co-movements among variables as evidence of money non-neutrality. Moreover, as different models respond differently to a monetary shock, this shock can be used to select among alternative models given the evidence collected.

As the RBC literature had problems identifying a real shock and establishing its importance to business cycle fluctuations (see Hartley et al., 1997, pp. 44–46), monetary economists also struggled to build up facts that they wanted their models to replicate. In the early 1990s, Chris Sims (1992, p. 975) stated that: 'the profession as a whole has no clear answer to the question of the size and nature of the effects of monetary policy on aggregate activity' (echoed by Martin Eichenbaum, 1992, in his comments to Sims). Different approaches to identifying a monetary shock were on the way.[10] Romer and Romer (1989), ostensibly following Friedman and Schwartz (1963), proposed a narrative approach that tries to identify innovations in a monetary policy variable or instrument (say, money stock or interest rates) that can be attributed to an autonomous action by the monetary authority. They examined the records of the Fed's policy deliberations and determined the periods when the authority intended to change its instrument not as an endogenous response to developments in the economy. The authors then considered these dates as those when the authority in fact changed its policy instrument. Hoover and Perez (1994a) criticized, among other things, their identification assumptions and thus questioned the causal inference of this approach.[11]

The other strategies to identifying exogenous monetary shocks that are used most often could be broadly referred to as the vector autoregression (VAR) approach. It was first put forward by Sims (1980) as a criticism to the 'incredible' restrictions imposed by econometricians that used large-scale, structural macroeconometric models.[12] To avoid the necessity of imposing restrictions that are not based on 'sound economic theory or institutional factual knowledge . . . Sims proposed that macroeconometrics give up the impossible task of seeking identification of structural models and instead ask only what could be learned from macroeconomic data', with systems of reduced form equations 'used in innovation-accounting exercises and to generate impulse response functions' (Hoover, 1995, p. 6).[13]

However, if one is interested in recovering the structural parameters from the estimated reduced-form VAR, one still has to impose identification restrictions. The gist is to try to use economic theory as a guide to imposing tenable restrictions.[14] Then this VAR literature (known as structural VAR, SVAR) differs according to the strategy chosen for characterizing the economic effects of a monetary shock. One approach is to impose long-run restrictions. For instance, some economists believe that money (or monetary shocks) does not affect economic activity in the long run. Then macroeconometricians can use this theoretical result of money neutrality to impose restrictions in their VARs so that in them money does not affect output in the long run.

Another way, in contrast to the narrative approach, is to model explicitly the central bank's reaction function (usually referred to as a Taylor rule after John B. Taylor, 1993; see next section): a rule that describes how the authority would change its instrument (like the interest rate) given the evolution of some economic variables (like deviations of inflation from its desired target, and the output gap). It is important to notice here that a monetary shock is, according to this formulation, an exogenous movement on the nominal interest rate not related to changes in either inflation or output gap. So, this change in the interest rate is not a deliberate policy. Instead, as Leeper (1991, pp. 134–135) discusses, it rather represents aspects of policy behavior that stem 'from either the technology of implementing policy choices or the incentives facing policymakers' (p. 135). In the first case, the monetary authority controls its instrument only up to a random error (so, those changes are in fact control errors) because, for instance, the variables to which the interest rate responds are measured with errors – as if the policymaker has palsied hands when writing down the interest rate to be set. In the second case, that monetary shock is understood as responses to 'unmodeled or noneconomic shocks' (p. 135).

After modeling that reaction function, the macroeconometrician imposes the minimally necessary assumptions to identify the parameters of the central bank's feedback rule. Instead of long-run restrictions, a very common strategy is to impose contemporaneous restrictions: Christiano et al. (1999) assume that the monetary policy shock and the variables in the feedback rule are orthogonal (or independent of each other) – this is known as the recursiveness assumption. It means that in a given period t, 'the time t variables in the Fed's information set do not respond to time t realizations of the monetary policy shock' (Christiano et al., 1999, p. 68). Such an assumption allows the coefficients of the feedback rule to be consistently (but not efficiently) estimated by ordinary least squares and also to take the fitted residual as an estimate of the monetary policy shock.

However, the recursiveness hypothesis is controversial and alternative contemporaneous restrictions have been proposed by other authors (see Christiano et al., 1999, pp. 68–69). More recently, macroeconomists started employing more heavily Bayesian methods for estimating their models and for comparing them to the data – but here the identifying restrictions are usually imposed as restrictions on the prior distributions, and the focus is on comparing posterior distributions and their moments to those of the data.

Disagreements emerge not only with respect to which identification strategy to adopt, but also with respect to what variable should be used as the monetary policy instrument: a monetary aggregate or an interest rate. While this was more debated in the early 1990s (see Eichenbaum's 1992 comments on Sims, 1992), nowadays it is more standard to use the interest rate as the monetary policy instrument. This practice reflects in part the increasing adoption of explicit inflation targeting in many countries and the understanding that even non-inflation-targeting central banks nowadays implement their policy via movements of an interest rate.[15] Moreover, the use of monetary aggregates as instrument (and even as carriers of economic information) became less and less favored as financial innovations destroyed the stability of money demand functions in most developed economies.

Despite the still remaining controversies and alternative empirical approaches, mainstream macroeconomists treat a few features of the data as the facts that their models should replicate (Woodford, 2003, Chap. 3; Christiano et al., 2005; Galí, 2008, pp. 6–9).[16] Given their emphasis on a policy shock, the most common features are presented in terms of impulse response functions (IRFs), which describe the reactions of endogenous variables to an exogenous shock hitting the economy: although these functions are truly dependent on identifying assumptions imposed to VARs, these economists take them to be robust to alternative assumptions (thus allegedly these IRFs could be used to evaluate even models that share the same theoretical commitments as the ones used to identify the shock in the first place).[17]

The basic idea behind the use of IRFs to assess a model is that of a counterfactual experiment: the variables are considered to be initially in equilibrium when a particular shock (say, an exogenous, temporary decrease of the interest rate set by the central bank) temporarily hits the economy; then all variables will respond to this shock over time and eventually return to the original equilibrium. An impulse response function depicts the trajectory of each variable away from the equilibrium initially perturbed – therefore it is zero when the variable is in the original equilibrium and positive (negative) when the variable is above (below) its value in the initial equilibrium. So, the first empirical fact that mainstream macroeconomists believe to exist is that after a temporary exogenous reduction in the interest rate, both inflation and real output would increase over time in a hump-shaped pattern as in Figure 16.1.[18]

Another feature is that inflation tends not to respond to a monetary shock for over a year (four quarters), which is 'generally interpreted as evidence of substantial price rigidities' (Galí, 2008, p. 9). It reaches a peak around nine quarters and slowly returns to its initial equilibrium. Additionally, it is often found that inflation tends to decrease initially after such expansionary shock (or to rise after an exogenous increase in the interest rate), even if this effect may not be statistically significant. This apparent contradiction with the theoretical understanding that a fall

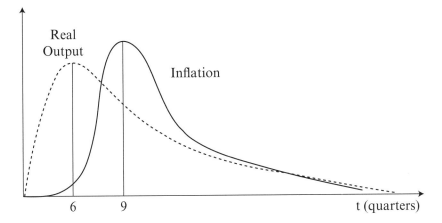

Figure 16.1 Empirical impulse response functions to a temporary expansionary monetary shock (a reduction of the nominal interest rate)

(rise) in the interest rate expands (contracts) aggregate demand and then increases (decreases) prices was labeled by Eichenbaum (1992, p. 1002) as the 'price puzzle' and it received much attention in the literature afterwards. The response of output is positive initially (though sometimes not statistically significant), it increases for about six quarters and it returns to the initial equilibrium only after ten quarters. Usually this estimated response of output is viewed as 'evidence of sizable and persistent real effects of monetary policy shocks' (Galí, 2008, p. 9).

Other features of the data macroeconomists discuss are (see Galí, 2008, pp. 6–9 for references): the liquidity effect, which tells us that a monetary aggregate will have to increase persistently in order to bring about a decline in the nominal interest rate; that other aggregate variables such as consumption and investment also exhibit a hump-shaped IRF to a monetary shock (Christiano et al., 2005); that the nominal interest rate tends to gradually return to its original value after a monetary shock; and as evidence of the presence of nominal rigidities, several studies found that the median duration of prices is from 4 up to 11 months (which tend to vary substantially across sectors of the economy or types of goods) and that the average frequency of wage changes is about one year (additionally, there is evidence showing asymmetries, meaning that wages are more rigid downwards than upwards).[19]

Once we are clear what the established facts are that macroeconomists use to assess their models, we can now explore a very basic version of a DSGE model.

16.3   A 'TOY' MODEL[20]

The basic set-up assumed in the new Keynesian, new neoclassical synthesis is that of a continuum of identical households and identical firms, which consume and produce a continuum of goods on the interval [0, 1], indexed by i. These assumptions not only allow one to work with a representative household and firm in a symmetric equilibrium, but also make, in such equilibrium, aggregate variables equal to their average and unitary values, as they are distributed over an interval of mass one. Moreover, the basic new Keynesian model is an Arrow–Debreu, general equilibrium model of complete asset markets. This means that agents can fully diversify idiosyncratic risks because they have access to a complete system of futures and insurance markets. The model sketched below is of a closed economy without capital accumulation. Therefore, it 'abstracts from the effects of variations in private spending . . . upon the economy's productive capacity' (Woodford, 2003, p. 242).[21] Nonetheless, there are several attempts to include these features into more complete versions of new Keynesian models (see Woodford, 2003, Ch. 5; Woodford, 2004; Galí, 2008, Ch. 7).

Another characteristic of the basic model is the absence of money. In fact, a key motivation of Woodford in his book is to challenge Sargent and Wallace's (1975) result that the price level is indeterminate when expectations are rational and the central bank follows an interest rate rule (that is, there are multiple equilibria under these circumstances). Woodford (2003) wants to show that determinacy of equilibrium does not depend on the particular way money is introduced in a general equilibrium framework: usually either by including real money balances in the utility function, or by assuming that goods ought to be purchased with money balances already held by consumers – that is, by imposing a cash-in-advance (CIA) constraint – or by assuming that money reduces transactions costs. That is his motivation to discuss what he calls a cashless economy, one in which these monetary frictions exist but are negligible, and to show that prices are uniquely determined in these economies when the monetary authority follows a certain class of interest rate rule (basically, one in which interest rate responds to current endogenous, non-predetermined variables), provided also that the fiscal policy is specified to support that equilibrium.[22] Therefore, more than being primarily concerned with the possibility that in the future electronic payment systems may displace the use of cash in the economy, Woodford wants to study monetary policy without control of a monetary aggregate.[23] So a salient feature of these models is not to have money: nominal rigidities are not necessary for characterizing equilibrium and they could be introduced if one is interested in tracking the money supply evolution that is associated with the equilibrium path of the nominal interest rate.

16.3.1 Households

Consumers offer a single type of work and work N_t hours in period t. They consume an aggregate of the continuum of existing goods, C_t, which is given by the following Dixit–Stiglitz aggregator (also known as the constant elasticity of substitution (CES) aggregator):[24]

$$C_t = \left(\int_0^1 C_{i,t}^{\frac{(\theta-1)}{\theta}} \, di \right)^{\frac{\theta}{(\theta-1)}}$$

where $C_{i,t}$ denotes the consumption of good i in period t, and $\theta > 1$ is the (constant) elasticity of substitution among the differentiated goods.

The representative consumer chooses how much to consume of each good, how much to save and how many hours to work in order to maximize his lifetime, discounted, expected utility. Assuming that the household's utility is separable between consumption and hours worked (or leisure), we obtain the following first-order condition for the intertemporal allocation of consumption (known as the Euler equation):

$$(1 + R_t)^{-1} = \beta \cdot \left\{ E_t \left[\frac{U_C(C_{t+1})}{U_C(C_t)} \cdot \frac{P_t}{P_{t+1}} \right] \right\} \tag{16.1}$$

where R_t is the short-term nominal interest rate, β is the discount factor households use to value future streams of utility, U_c denotes the marginal utility of consumption, E_t denotes the conditional-expectation operator (it is the expectations of a future variable conditional on the information set available at time t), and P_t is the general price level that aggregates prices of all intermediary goods, $P_{i,t}$, according to the following aggregator:

$$P_t = \left(\int_0^1 P_{i,t}^{1-\theta} \right)^{\frac{1}{(1-\theta)}}.$$

Additionally, by imposing the equilibrium condition that all markets clear, so that aggregate consumption equals aggregate output, $C_t = Y_t$, after we log-linearize that intertemporal condition around a steady-state with zero inflation we obtain:[25]

$$y_t = E_t(y_{t+1}) - \frac{1}{\sigma} \cdot [r_t - E_t(\pi_{t+1})] \tag{16.2}$$

where $\sigma > 0$ measures the intertemporal elasticity of aggregate expenditure, π_t is the inflation rate and where all other lowercase letters denote the percentage deviation of the original variable with respect to its steady state value: $x_t \equiv (X_t - \overline{X})/\overline{X} \cong \log(X_t/\overline{X})$, $\overline{X}$ being the steady-state value of any variable X_t. Equation (16.2) then describes how output (and consumption) evolves over time depending on the real interest rate (the nominal interest rate minus expected inflation, $r_t - E_t(\pi_{t+1})$), and is also known as the 'intertemporal IS equation' – although in this basic version the model does not have investment spending as in the textbook IS-LM model, and it usually also does not have a money demand function as in the IS-LM model (although there are nowadays the already mentioned standard ways of introducing it if one wishes).

16.3.2   Firms

There is a continuum of identical intermediary firms, each one being a monopolistically competitive supplier of one differentiated good. Their market power allows them to set their prices, but these are assumed to be sticky: following Calvo (1983) and Yun (1996), at each period each firm may reset their prices with probability $1 - \alpha$, independent of the time elapsed since the last time it has set its price. In other words, given that there is a continuum of firms on the interval [0, 1], each period there is a measure of firms that have not chosen their prices – a common assumption made is that these firms will just charge the price they set in the previous period – and a fraction $1 - \alpha$ of firms that have reset their prices. This implies that the average duration of a price contract is $(1 - \alpha)^{-1}$. Thus, people tend to calibrate the parameter α via the average duration found in the data (which is, as discussed in the previous section, from four to 11 quarters).

A firm that gets to set a new price today chooses the one that maximizes the sum of current and future profits that it would get if it never has a chance of readjusting them in the future. In a symmetric equilibrium, all suppliers that reset prices for their goods in a given period t face exactly the same maximization problem and, therefore, choose the same price, P_t^*. The other fraction α of the suppliers does not readjust prices and charges prices prevailing in the previous period. The aggregate price level can then be written as:

$$P_t = [\alpha \cdot P_{t-1}^{1-\theta} + (1 - \alpha) \cdot P_t^{*1-\theta}]^{\frac{1}{(1-\theta)}}$$

After a log-linearization of this equation and the first-order condition of suppliers that change prices, we obtain the so-called new Keynesian Phillips curve (NKPC):

$$\pi_t = \beta \cdot E_t(\pi_{t+1}) + \lambda \cdot mc_t \tag{16.3}$$

with mc_t denoting the (percentage deviation of) the economy's average real marginal cost. This equation tells us that inflation today depends only on the current marginal cost and on expected future inflation – it is entirely forward looking.[26] A more standard version of this equation is obtained by replacing the real marginal cost by some measure of economic activity. The details of this are discussed by Woodford (2003, Ch. 3) and Galí (2008, Ch. 3). Under certain circumstances, we can finally obtain:

$$\pi_t = \beta \cdot E_t(\pi_{t+1}) + \kappa \cdot (y_t - y_t^n) \tag{16.4}$$

where y_t is the percentage deviation of real output from its steady state level and y_t^n is its flexible price counterpart (known in this literature as the 'natural output'). The last term of equation (16.4) is commonly referred to as the 'output gap', but it is not the gap that many applied macroeconomists use in their models – the most common output gaps computed from the data are deviations of current output from some trend, either linear or non-linear (in the latter case people tend to use the Hodrick–Prescott filter to obtain such a gap). What these derivations tell us is that the new Keynesian Phillips curve ought to be assessed empirically using a very particular measure of output gap: given that one cannot observe this natural output, some macroeconomists proposed to approximate that output gap by the average level of unit labor cost (the share of wages on aggregate output; see Woodford, 2003, pp. 182–187 for details and references).

The Calvo price-setting – which is a time-dependent pricing rule because the timing of price changes is exogenous, that is, independent of the economy's phase in the business cycle, and every period a constant fraction of firms can choose their prices[27] – is clearly a building block of the DSGE approach to macroeconomics. It has recently been assessed empirically by Eichenbaum and Fisher (2007), but the main argument for its widespread use in modern macroeconomics is that it delivers simple solutions (no matter how ad hoc it may seem). In fact, because it is time dependent, Calvo pricing reduces the number of state variables in a DSGE model given that one does not need to keep track of when was the last time a firm has set its price. However, there is a growing literature advocating the use of a state-dependent pricing scheme, in which firms choose to reset prices based on the economic conditions at the time and the costs they have to incur in doing so. In favor of state-dependent pricing there is the argument not only that it is more realistic, but also that it captures important asymmetries over the cycle that Calvo does not because it is not state dependent and also because the solution methods used in conjunction with it are based on log-linearizations (see Dotsey and King, 2005; Devereux and Siu, 2007).

Besides the continuum of intermediary goods producers, there are in this economy firms that buy the differentiated goods produced and bundle them together and sell this final good to the consumers. The technology they use to produce the final good is a CES aggregator exactly analogous to that of the aggregate consumption. These firms are identical and operate in a perfectly competitive market. The zero-profit equilibrium condition gives us the formula for the aggregator of the general price level written before.

16.3.3   Monetary Policy

As mentioned before, monetary and fiscal policies are designed so that a unique equilibrium exists in a DSGE model[28] – thus, despite the fact that macroeconomists usually assess their models by checking the predicted effects of a monetary shock in them with those observed in the data, the systematic part of the monetary policy is crucial for the way the model behaves after a shock. Usually the fiscal policy is of a sort that implies that the government obeys its intertemporal budget constraint and that the monetary authority sets the short-run nominal interest rate according to a Taylor rule like:

$$r_t = \rho \cdot r_{t-1} + \phi \cdot \pi_t + y_t + \varepsilon_t \qquad (16.5)$$

in which ϕ is the relative weight that the central bank attaches to changes in inflation (or deviations of inflation from a target), viz. to changes in some measure of real activity such as output (or output gap); ρ measures the degree of interest rate smoothing, and ε_t is a monetary shock. Thus, equation (16.5) is based on the assumptions that the monetary authority decides the level of its instrument based on the inflation and output levels observed, and that the changes in the interest rate are smoothed over a number of periods instead of being made at once. There are many variants of such a rule, like including past or expected future values of inflation and output and so on.

If, as mentioned, the fiscal policy is assumed to obey the government's intertemporal budget constraint, then the determinacy of equilibrium (the existence of a unique equilibrium) depends on how aggressively the monetary authority responds to inflation. The intuition is that equilibrium will be unique if the monetary authority changes nominal interest rate more than proportionally to a given change of inflation, which amounts to a rise of the real interest rate as a response to an inflationary surge that prevents the economy from taking an off-equilibrium path in which expectations of future inflation are self-fulfilling. This imposes restrictions on the values that the parameters of the Taylor rule and is usually known as the 'Taylor principle' (see Woodford, 2001). If instead the fiscal policy violates that intertemporal constraint, then the equilibrium will be unique if the monetary authority passively generates seigniorage to finance fiscal deficits (thus accepting higher inflation).[29]

16.3.4 The Basic Model

Therefore, the basic DSGE model considered here is composed by an intertemporal IS relation (equation 16.2), a new Keynesian Phillips curve (equation 16.4) and a Taylor rule (equation 16.5). Usually equation (16.2) is rewritten in terms of the output gap that appears in the NKPC:

$$(y_t - y_t^n) = E_t(y_{t+1} - y_{t+1}^n) - \frac{1}{\sigma} \cdot [r_t - E_t(\pi_{t+1}) - r_t^n] \quad (16.6)$$

where $r_t^n \equiv \sigma \cdot E_t(y_{t+1}^n - y_t^n)$ is the so-called 'natural interest rate'.[30] The Taylor rule, when expressed in terms of the same output gap becomes:

$$r_t = \rho \cdot r_{t-1} + \phi \cdot \pi_t + (y_t - y_t^n) + v_t \quad (16.7)$$

Thus, the DSGE model expressed in terms of the output gap – the difference between the percentage change in real output from its steady state value and the percentage change in the natural (or flexible-price) level of output from its equilibrium level – is composed by equations (16.4), the new Keynesian Phillips curve, (16.6), the intertemporal IS curve, and (16.7), the Taylor rule.

16.3.5 What Does Such a 'Toy' Model Buy Us?

If one calibrates (or estimates) the parameters of this simple model, then solves and simulates it numerically, one can consider what mileage it can deliver. As is easy to see, we cannot go very far. For instance, after a temporary expansionary monetary shock (a one-time temporary decrease in v_t that makes the nominal interest rate be below its steady-state value), both inflation and output return to their initial equilibrium levels as soon as the shock dies out (Figure 16.2).[31]

The effects of the monetary shock on output and inflation presented in Figure 16.2 last about three quarters just because in this simulation I have calibrated the smoothing parameter, ρ, in the Taylor rule to be

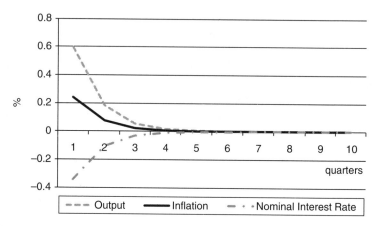

Note: In these figures, the horizontal axis represent the time periods (which in this case are quarters). The unit of the vertical axis is percentage points: for instance, when the monetary shock hits the economy in period 1, the inflation rate raises roughly 0.2% above its steady-state value.

Figure 16.2   Theoretical impulse response functions to a temporary expansionary monetary shock (a reduction of the nominal interest rate)

0.9. If I had set it to close to zero these effects would surely last less.[32] To use Frisch's (1933) terminology, the basic new Keynesian model has little persistency in its propagation mechanism beyond that assumed for the impulse (exogenous shock). Even when one makes its propagation mechanism more persistent, as in Figure 16.2, it is clear that this model does not reproduce those stylized facts that macroeconomists believe are present in the data (see Figure 16.1): the impulse response functions are not hump-shaped, the peak of the IRF of both inflation and output occur at the instant when the shock occurs, instead of inflation peaking later than output after not responding immediately for a short period following the shock, and they tend to return to zero faster than what is observed in the data.

Given the empirical failure of such a toy model, macroeconomists reverse engineer and add features to it, expanding their models in several ways. In order to get hump-shaped IRFs for consumption, investment (when a model does have capital) and output they introduce habit persistence on consumption (by adding past consumption as an argument of the utility function, meaning that the level of consumption you choose today depends on your habits of consumption in the recent past), adjustment costs to investment (which makes firms smooth out capital accumulation over time instead of adjusting it once and for all to a given shock) and capital utilization (each period firms choose not only how much capital to accumulate but also how much to use of the capital already accumulated). Price and wage stickiness are also assumed. In terms of inflation, the purely forward-looking new Keynesian Phillips curve (equation 16.4) cannot deliver a peak of inflation after the peak of output: that equation can be solved forward to imply, after imposing that $\lim_{j \to +\infty} \beta^j \cdot E_t \pi_{t+j+1} = 0$:[33]

$$\pi_t = \kappa \cdot \sum_{j=0}^{\infty} \beta^i \cdot E_t (y_{t+j} - y_{t+j}^n)$$

This equation tells us that the future peak in the output gap should be reflected in current inflation, implying that the effect on inflation should precede that on the output gap because, 'this equation states that the inflation response each quarter should be an increasing function of the output responses that are expected in that quarter and *later*' (Woodford, 2003, p. 206). This is the lack of inflation inertia that concerns macroeconomists. To correct this problem several attempts to introduce some kind of lagged inflation in the NKPC were made. It is common to introduce inflation indexation in the Calvo model by assuming that those firms that cannot set prices optimally index them to past inflation instead of charging the same price as the last period – and indexation here can be either full or partial (see Woodford, 2003, pp. 213–218; Cogley and Sbordone, 2008).[34] Another alternative is to introduce information stickiness in the manner of Mankiw and Reis (2002): 'information about macroeconomic conditions diffuses slowly through the population' (p. 1296) because there are either costs of acquiring new information or costs for agents to reoptimize their choices, which implies that pricing decisions are made based also on past information (that is, not all prices are currently set optimally based on the most up-to-date information set).[35] An alternative change to the standard Calvo pricing model is to assume that the new prices chosen by part of the firms do not take effect immediately but instead with a delay – so that they are optimally chosen based upon an earlier information set than the one available when they effectively take place (Woodford, 2003, pp. 207–13).

Recent incarnations of DSGE models with all those bells and whistles are presented in Christiano et al. (2005) and in Smets and Wouters (2003, 2007) (see also Woodford, 2003, Ch. 5). They not only contain enlarged models but also represent part of the recent trend in empirical macroeconomics, exactly the one criticized by Chari et al. (2009), as mentioned before.

16.4   CURRENT PRACTICES AND PROSPECTS

An important feature of modern economics in general is its appeal to computational methods (see Judd, 1998). If in the past the use of log-linear relations or of quadratic loss functions in evaluating alternative policies was justified as delivering easy solutions to complex dynamic problems, nowadays macroeconomists rely more heavily on numerical approximation techniques that allow them to use more general functions.[36] After Blanchard and Kahn (1980) and King and Watson (1998), macroeconomists increasingly adopted log-linear solution methods. One important advantage that helps explain their popularity is that these methods do not suffer from the 'curse of dimensionality': they can be applied to problems in which there are many state variables without imposing a great computational burden. It is crucial to notice that these are local methods for studying the existence and determinacy of equilibrium and the size of second moments of endogenous variables: they are accurate for 'small' shocks that perturb the economy in the neighborhood of the steady state. Moreover, given that the equilibrium conditions are linearized, second- or higher-order terms of the policy functions are disregarded, which implies that these methods cannot be used, for instance, either to perform welfare evaluations of alternative policies or to study risk premium in stochastic environments (Schmitt-Grohé and Uribe, 2004, p. 773).[37]

The toy model presented in the previous section had its equilibrium relations log-linearized around a particular point (a zero-inflation steady state); this turned the non-linear first-order difference equation for consumption (or output), equation (16.1), into a linear first-order difference equation given by equation (16.2); this approximation to (16.1) is accurate depending on the tightness of the neighborhood around the steady state that the variables fluctuate. The linear system of equilibrium equations, (16.4), (16.6) and (16.7), determine paths of output gap, inflation and nominal interest rate for given parameters and exogenous stochastic variables.[38]

The parameters of a DSGE model can be either calibrated or estimated. The original real business cycle literature promoted calibration as a method of obtaining numerical values for the parameters of the model. Usually it is done by evaluating the equilibrium conditions (like equations 16.4, 16.6 and 16.7) in a steady state that then imply that parameters are functions of steady-state variables; the numerical values of these variables are obtained by averages (or other moments) from the data. Alternatively, some parameters may be calibrated with microeconomic evidence (as elasticities for instance). In the new consensus, DSGE macroeconomics, it became a staple to estimate parameters. One way is to match the impulse response functions of a monetary (or some other) shock implied by the log-linearized model with those estimated in a VAR from the data – note that this literature relies on first-order approximations to the model solution and, thus, is subject to the limitations that are inherent to this solution method discussed earlier. While in principle all parameters could be estimated, Christiano et al. (2005), following Rotemberg and Woodford (1997), chose to calibrate a subset of parameters – about which there is more empirical evidence and alleged consensus on their numerical values, or because they are not identifiable econometrically – and estimate the other parameters of their model by minimizing the distance between theoretical and empirical impulse response functions. Another strategy that has recently become very popular in macroeconomics is to estimate a DSGE model with Bayesian techniques.[39] This is the approach taken by Smets and Wouters (2007), although they have also calibrated a few parameters that are hard to estimate or to identify in their model.

One way to see the new consensus macroeconomics is as a merger of the RBC and new Keynesian theories of business fluctuation – a rather local agreement instead of a global consensus in macroeconomics (Duarte, 2010) – brought about by their use of rational expectations in their models and their search for a particular kind of microfoundations to macroeconomics as an answer to the Lucas critique (see also Hoover, 2010b). As Woodford (2003, p. 11) wrote, macroeconomists want to use:

> structural relations that explicitly represent the dependence of economic decisions upon expectations regarding future endogenous variables . . . My preference for this form of structural relations is precisely that they are ones that should remain invariant (insofar as the proposed theory is correct) under changes in policy that alter the stochastic laws of motion of the endogenous variables.

The critical point is the clause 'insofar as the proposed theory is correct' (correct to a good enough approximation, given the solution methods employed in this literature): Hoover (2006) argues that the combination of the Arrow impossibility theorem and the general theory of the second best completely gut any claim that these models can make to having truly connected the private to social welfare.

Nonetheless Woodford (2003, p. 12, italics added) voices the arguments used by mainstream macroeconomists that see the search for microfoundations as a worthy enterprise not only because it allegedly addresses the Lucas critique and delivers invariant structural relations among aggregate variables, but also because it 'provides a *natural objective* in terms of which alternative policies should be evaluated': the welfare of private agents. If one is willing to ground structural macroeconomic relations on an intertemporal welfare maximization problem, it is natural, according to these macroeconomists, to take private welfare as the social welfare function – clearly, the widespread use of a representative agent in macroeconomics is particularly convenient because it sidesteps aggregation problems that plague the construction of a social welfare function from individual utility functions. Again, for them the time is past when macroeconomists felt comfortable assuming ad hoc (quadratic) welfare or loss functions. They now know how to derive them from the representative agent's utility function (Woodford, 2003, Ch. 6).

However, the log-linear solution methods discussed above are not useful for policy analysis: the welfare computed with log-linear approximations to the solution of a model cannot distinguish between two policies that imply the same steady state – all second- and higher-order moments that could discriminate those policies are not taken into account in such calculation of the welfare criteria. One way out was to make second-order approximations to the model's solution, as proposed by Schmitt-Grohé and Uribe (2004) among others. Another way is to make the steady state around which the model will be approximate be an efficient (Pareto optimal) equilibrium which then allows one to distinguish alternative policies implying the same steady state by making a first-order approximation to the equilibrium conditions together with a second-order approximation to the social welfare function for policy analysis (see Woodford, 2003, Ch. 6 and 8).

Everything seemed promising in mainstream macroeconomics: a synthesis guiding part of the theoretical work in the field and going quickly to the practice of central banks. The battles that recurrently happened in the past seemed indeed gone, at least for a group of economists who shared important methodological premises (Duarte, 2010). But the economic crisis of 2008–09 brought back criticisms of the ability of such models not only in giving warning signs in anticipation of a crisis but also in helping economies to recover. I do not think it is a big stretch to say that a great part of these criticisms targeted the DSGE incarnation represented by Christiano et al. (2005) and Smets and Wouters (2003, 2007) – and a few variations of it that several central banks were pursuing (see for instance Wren-Lewis, 2007). Not only were these models of a closed economy, identical agents and no involuntary unemployment, but they were also mostly without banks and any financial frictions (remember that these models assumed a complete asset market through which idiosyncratic risks are insured). Moreover, if one interprets the crisis as a shock that has hit the economy, one surely wonders how accurate local solution methods can be in this case as the economy will not fluctuate in a bounded neighborhood of a given initial steady state.

What is indeed surprising is that a few prominent mainstream macro-economists explicitly recognized the limitations of the new synthesis macroeconomics, much earlier than any signs of the current crisis could be identified, but often not very prominently so.[40] For instance, in an interview with Philipp Harms in August 2004, who asked Woodford if the concepts he proposed in his 2003 book 'apply to all countries alike', Woodford recognized that his macroeconomic models were not very suitable for developing countries, for example (p. 2):[41]

> What I am doing in the book is going through a framework that allows for vari-ations in order to take the models to particular circumstances. But the frame-work as a whole may be more easily tailored to some countries than to others. In particular, the analytical framework that I use relies a lot on the assumption that financial markets are highly developed and very efficient. This abstrac-tion is reasonably useful for many advanced economies now, but I would not say that with the same confidence for developing economies, where financial market imperfections are much larger and where many households and firms are constrained in their ability to borrow.

Robert Lucas (2004, p. 23) also clearly stated that:

> The problem is that the new theories, the theories embedded in general equilib-rium dynamics of the sort that we know how to use pretty well now – there's a residue of things they don't let us think about. They don't let us think about the US experience in the 1930s or about financial crises and their real consequences in Asia and Latin America. They don't let us think, I don't think, very well about Japan in the 1990s. We may be disillusioned with the Keynesian appa-ratus for thinking about these things, but it doesn't mean that this replacement apparatus can do it either. It can't.

But these were concerns timidly voiced. They did not prevent an increas-ing number of researchers, and the students they trained, from entering into what Ricardo Caballero (2010, p. 1) has called the '"fine-tuning" mode within the local-maximum of the dynamic stochastic general equi-librium world', instead of being in a '"broad-exploration" mode'. As a result, he continues, the core of mainstream macroeconomics 'has become mesmerized with its own internal logic that it has begun to confuse the precision it has achieved about its own world with the precision that it has about the real one' (ibid.).[42] This 'pretense-of-knowledge syndrome' has made several enthusiasts of the DSGE macroeconomics believe that they were getting close to good models for policy analysis, no matter that most of them were solved with local methods of approximation. Clearly, a more balanced conversation, in which dissenters could be heard, would have been more productive at least for perhaps forcing those enthusiasts to think carefully about the usefulness and limitations of their models.

With the crisis, the limitations of the consensus macroeconomics came to the fore, in newspapers, blogs, articles, and so on, as Katarina Juselius also point out in her contribution to this volume (Chapter 17). Just to take a few examples, Willem Buiter (2009), who has important academic and policymaking credentials,[43] argued in the *Financial Times* that modern macroeconomics has to be rewritten almost from scratch because it is simply incapable of dealing with economic problems during 'times of stress and financial instability', and he discussed a central point:

> The dynamic stochastic general equilibrium (DSGE) crowd saw that the economy had not exploded without bound in the past, and concluded from this that it made sense to rule out, in the linearized model, the explosive solution trajectories. What they were left with was something that, following an exogenous random disturbance, would return to the deterministic steady state pretty smartly.

The 18 July 2009 edition of *The Economist*, which had as the magazine cover a book titled 'Modern Economic Theory' melting down, included two articles criticizing modern macroeconomics and finance. A few issues later, Robert Lucas (2009) wrote his 'defence of the dismal science', where he argued that:

> both pieces were dominated by the views of people who have seized on the crisis as an opportunity to restate criticisms they had voiced long before 2008. Macroeconomists in particular were caricatured as a lost generation educated in the use of valueless, even harmful, mathematical models, an education that made them incapable of conducting sensible economic policy. I think this caricature is nonsense and of no value in thinking about the larger questions: What can the public reasonably expect of specialists in these areas, and how well has it been served by them in the current crisis?

Defending rational expectations and Fama's efficient-market hypothesis from the magazine's attacks, he added that:

> One thing we are not going to have, now or ever, is a set of models that forecasts sudden falls in the value of financial assets, like the declines that followed the failure of Lehman Brothers in September. This is nothing new. It has been known for more than 40 years and is one of the main implications of Eugene Fama's 'efficient-market hypothesis' (EMH), which states that the price of a financial asset reflects all relevant, generally available information. If an economist had a formula that could reliably forecast crises a week in advance, say, then that formula would become part of generally available information and prices would fall a week earlier. (The term 'efficient' as used here means that individuals use information in their own private interest. It has nothing to do with socially desirable pricing; people often confuse the two.)

Paul Krugman (2009) in his column in the *New York Times* asked: 'how did economists get it so wrong?' He argued that modern economists have mistaken the beauty of their models for truth, he discussed the state of macroeconomics and finance, and criticized the defensive argument these economists use that the crisis could not have been predicted:

> In recent, rueful economics discussions, an all-purpose punch line has become 'nobody could have predicted . . .' It's what you say with regard to disasters that could have been predicted, should have been predicted and actually were predicted by a few economists who were scoffed at for their pains.

The list of voices from both sides are too numerous to represent them all here: there were letters written to answer the questions that Queen Elizabeth II asked economists during her visit to the London School of Economics on 5 November 2008; mainstream economists circulating short texts attacking the critics of modern macroeconomics; even more blog posts; hearings with economists to the Committee on Science and Technology of the US House of Representatives; and so on.[44] In any case, economists, dead and alive, have been put on the spot by the media.[45]

More broadly, the lack of confidence brought by the crisis led some economists to rethink the widespread assumptions of complete markets, rational expectations (see De Grauwe, 2010), stability of equilibrium, the mechanistic ways that (and relevance of) money was introduced, and the use of a representative agent in macroeconomic models. Two things are important in this respect. First, it does not mean that macroeconomists of the new synthesis simply ignored all these aspects: there has been work in bringing financial frictions and banks into business cycle models, in open economies, extensions to have a richer labor market, work on learning and expectations (see Evans and Honkapohja, 2001), on asymmetric information, and so on. The crisis may value and increase the research in these areas and make them more central to the theory and practice of business cycle fluctuations. Second, it is unclear how much of these criticisms will be taken as a resurrection of 'old dissenting voices' to formal models in economics and thus be set aside as unimportant: for instance, V.V. Chari (2010, p. 2) has recently claimed that DSGE models are the only game in the macroeconomics town, while Blanchard et al. (2010, p. 10) argued that 'most of the elements of the precrisis consensus, including the major conclusions from macroeconomic theory, still hold'.[46] So the question that remains is whether the most recent crisis will invite mainstream macroeconomists to be more flexible in applying their methods of analysis and to rethink some of their assumptions and methods that in previous years have been increasingly seen as natural or correct by definition.

NOTES

1. I am very grateful to the editors of this *Companion*, Wade Hands and John Davis, not only for inviting a historian of economics interested in macroeconomics to contribute to this volume, but also for continually supporting me to explore very recent developments in macroeconomics and for providing invaluable editorial guidance and comments to the first draft. Kevin Hoover went far beyond his duties as a referee and made detailed and very sharp comments and suggestions on a previous draft, to which I am not sure I have done full justice. Needless to say that any remaining errors and inaccuracies are my own.

2. It is important to be clear that this chapter is about the branch of macroeconomics concerned with business cycle fluctuations: the fluctuations in and determinants of the level of business activity, interest and exchange rates, and inflation, basically. It will not discuss the growth literature or other topics.

3. See Duarte (2010) for a discussion on how mainstream macroeconomists understood the emergence of such consensus, and how narrow it is.

4. Duarte (2010) explains that one of the differences between new classical and RBC economists is that the latter build models without money not only because they estimate that technological shocks explain most of US business cycle fluctuations in the period after the Korean War, but also because they argue that prices are countercyclical (meaning that price changes result from shifts of the aggregate supply along a given aggregate demand – thus, monetary shocks should not matter because they change aggregate demand along a given aggregate supply) and that monetary aggregates do not lead the cycle (denying the monetarist view that money is important over the cycle). Therefore, RBC theorists left aside monetary shocks and focused on real shocks such as changes in technology (see also Hoover, 1988). However, in the early 1990s this literature moved towards including money and other features previously ignored in their dynamic general equilibrium models (see Cooley, 1995).

5. There are clearly economists who dissent from the pervasive use of optimizing dynamic general equilibrium models with a representative agent, such as Robert Solow, Axel Leijonhufvud and Joseph Stiglitz, just to cite a few (see Duarte, 2010, who provides these and other references). Kevin Hoover (2010a) takes up critically the issue of microfoundations of macroeconomics.

6. Lucas's point was that reduced-form, estimated macroeconomic models (such as the large-scale macroeconometric models of the time) cannot be used to evaluate the consequences of alternative policies. The reason is that these models may fail to reflect the underlying decision-problems of agents: their estimated parameters would change when a different policy is implemented, because agents change their behavior in response to the new policy. Therefore, one cannot take the estimated macroeconomic model as given and simply use it to evaluate alternative policies. The pervasive use of microfounded models with a representative agent is justified by mainstream economists as the way to answer the Lucas critique. However, as Hoover (2006, p. 147) argues: 'many economists seem to read the Lucas critique as if it implies that we can protect against non-invariance simply by applying microeconomic theory. But, of course, what it really implies is that we are safe if we can truly model the underlying economic reactions to policy. Are we confident enough in the highly stylized microeconomics of textbooks to find the promise of security in the theory itself, absent convincing empirical evidence of its detailed applicability to the problem at hand? I think not.'

7. Consider, for instance, the introduction of price stickiness à la Calvo (that we shall discuss later). Is it the case that the optimization problem of the firms setting prices can be considered the same under any policy regime? Are the parameters here structural, that is, invariant to such regimes? These are the kind of questions that mainstream economists tend to be silent about.

8. Macroeconomists early in the post-war period saw computers, then recently available,

as an important laboratory for testing alternative policies to be prescribed (Duarte, 2009).

9. Duarte and Hoover (2011) explore the role of shocks in present-day macroeconomic modeling and model selection, showing that they were elevated to a starring role after the new classical macroeconomics and the VAR literature.

10. See further references to these approaches in Bernanke and Mihov (1998), and in Christiano et al., (1999, pp. 68–69), Walsh (2003, Ch. 1) and Uhlig (2005). For a more complete presentation of the state of the art in empirical macroeconomics, see Fabio Canova's (2007) textbook and also Bernanke et al. (2005).

11. Hoover and Perez (1994a) argue that the Romers' approach cannot discriminate between monetary and non-monetary shocks; they show through simulations that the narrative approach cannot distinguish a world in which the Fed only announces it will act, without effectively doing so, from one in which the authority in fact acts; finally, they demonstrate that the dynamic simulation methods used by the Romers are inappropriate for causal inference. Hoover and Perez do not take a stand on whether or not money matters, but they argue that the Romers' approach cannot guide us in answering this question. See also Romer and Romer's (1994) response and Hoover and Perez's (1994b) rejoinder. Later, Romer and Romer (2002) would again use their narrative approach, being silent about these criticisms.

12. For advances on the research of structural econometric models after the Lucas critique, see Fair (1994) and Ingram (1995).

13. Stock and Watson (2001), Canova (2007, Ch. 4) and Zha (2008) present a useful survey on VARs.

14. Often the arguments used to specify the contemporaneous structure of VARs are very causal, such as because financial markets clear more quickly than any other market, innovations that affect these markets would affect the other markets after a period of time. Sometimes a more structured theory is used, but usually through highly simplified models with numerous arbitrary elements. Therefore, in fact, this literature uses ad hoc assumptions to impose restrictions on the VARs, taking the level of 'ad hoc-ness' to be the least acceptable. I thank Kevin Hoover for calling my attention to this.

15. Central banks in several countries have often implemented monetary policy through interest rate management. What is a recent trend is the use of explicit interest rate rules either in inflation targeting regimes or just through a Taylor rule. Advocacy of such rules long predates the DSGE macroeconomics – as Woodford's intentional revival of Wicksell in his 2003 book exemplifies.

16. Most of the findings discussed here refer to the United States or to Europe.

17. This emphasis on shocks and thus on IRFs distinguishes the new neoclassical synthesis (new Keynesian) models from the original RBC literature. In the latter, models were usually assessed empirically in terms of their ability to replicate co-movements among aggregate variables that were observed in the data.

18. This figure is presented here just as a qualitative illustration of the (point estimate of the) impulse response functions after an expansionary monetary shock. See Christiano et al. (1999, 2005) for the estimated IRFs shown with their confidence intervals.

19. See Katarina Juselius, Chapter 17 in this volume, for a critical assessment of the empirical performance of DSGE models.

20. I here follow Woodford (2003, Ch. 2–4) and Galí (2008, Ch. 3). See these references for a complete description of the new Keynesian model and all its equilibrium conditions. As a matter of simplifying the exposition I ignore all stochastic terms present in Woodford (2003).

21. This model with consumers who own the differentiated firms and with no capital stock is also known as an economy of 'yeoman farmers'.

22. Because he focuses on equilibrium implemented by monetary policies specified in terms of interest-rate rules, Woodford (2003, p. 25) seeks 'to revive the earlier approach of Knut Wicksell'. For a historical analysis of Woodford's book, see the mini-symposium published in the *Journal of the History of Economic Thought*, **28**(2), 2006.

23.   Usually, the concern with the development of electronic payment systems is that they may eventually supplant cash and checks. This may cause problems if the price level in a general equilibrium is to be determined by the equilibrium between demand and supply of the medium of exchange. Woodford's point is to argue that general equilibrium models can have determinate price level even if there is no demand for money (cash). Hoover (1988, pp. 94–106) discusses a related point: that electronic payment systems may supplant cash, but it will not displace money in the economy.

24.   The Dixit–Stiglitz aggregator is the most commonly used. An alternative also used in the literature is the aggregator proposed by Miles Kimball (1995): $\int_0^1 G(C_{i,t}/C_t) = 1$, with G being an increasing and strictly concave function, with $G(1) = 1$. This formulation allows one to treat the elasticity of substitution among differentiated goods variable and dependent of the goods' relative price. It is easy to see that the Dixit–Stiglitz (CES) aggregator is a particular case of Kimball's:

$$G(C_{i,t}/C_t) = (C_{i,t}/C_t)^{\frac{(\theta-1)}{\theta}}.$$

25.   Equation (16.2) is the result of a first-order Taylor approximation of the Euler equation (16.1) around the non-stochastic steady state of zero inflation (an equilibrium in which all variables grow at a constant rate and in which all stochastic disturbances are not present). Sometimes it is convenient to apply logarithms on both sides of an equation, like the Euler, and then do a first-order Taylor expansion on the resulting equation, which delivers exactly the same linear condition. This is why macroeconomists talk about 'log-linearizations'.

26.   Rotemberg (1982) presents a model with quadratic costs of price adjustment, in which he obtains an identical curve as the NKPC. DSGE macroeconomists sometimes use this as an argument in defense of Calvo's staggered pricing: if one considers Calvo as too unrealistic, we could still keep using it, for its simplicity, given that the same Phillips curve is obtained in a model with quadratic costs of price adjustment (supposedly a bit more realistic).

27.   Another type of time-dependent price stickiness model is that of Taylor (1980), in which a firm sets its price every nth period. In the Calvo staggered price-setting model this timing of price changes is random: in each period a firm has a given probability of setting its price that is independent of the last time it has readjusted its price.

28.   As Mehrling (1996, p. 79) wrote, given that dynamic models usually exhibit 'many equilibrium paths that are not saddle-point stable', 'the theory of policy consists in identifying policies that change the *set* of equilibria and rule out the worst ones'. In this light, what the DSGE macroeconomists do is to characterize the economy with not only the discipline of equilibrium, but in fact the discipline of a unique equilibrium. Policies that imply either that there are multiple equilibria or no equilibrium in their general equilibrium models are not interesting, because those economists are usually interested in evaluating how the economy moves from one equilibrium to another (that can be also the initial equilibrium) after a shock or a policy regime change: if the economy is in an initial steady state, is hit by a shock and the model tells us that it can go to any element of a set of equilibria, how can we analyze this situation (both in a positive as well as in a normative sense)?

29.   Leeper (1991) discusses in a very clear way these issues in a simple monetary model with flexible prices. See Woodford (2003, pp. 252–261) and Galí (2008, Ch. 3–4) for this discussion in a new Keynesian framework (monetary model with staggered price-setting).

30.   If I have not ignored the stochastic terms considered by Woodford (2003), they would be collected in this natural interest rate.

31.   The parameters of the model were calibrated for quarterly data. Therefore, the time unit in the graphs to follow and their analysis is a quarter. The values of the parameters calibrated are: $\beta = 0.99$; $\kappa = 0.1$; $\sigma = 1$; $\varphi = 3$; $\rho = 0.9$. Although these numbers are consistent with some steady-state moments and in line with values used in the literature

32. (for the US and Europe), the point here is just to present qualitatively the impulse response functions implied by the toy model.

32. The qualitative effects of a monetary shock in this basic model are mostly invariant to alternative Taylor rules that one could consider. Galí (2008, Ch. 3), explores in more detail additional simulations with this model.

33. To solve (16.4) forward just replace π_{t+1} on the right-hand side for equation (16.4) evaluated one period ahead and proceed making iterated substitutions.

34. With indexation, firms change prices every period, although just a fraction of them choose the optimal price to set. Again, convenient simplicity and better fit to data is what DSGE macroeconomists use to justify indexation, leaving aside the issue of whether or not this assumption makes the model subject to the Lucas critique.

35. It is worth pointing out that Mankiw and Reis (2002), following the literature of the time, criticized the new Keynesian Phillips curve and promoted the empirical relevance of their own model based on one major piece of evidence: a correlation between inflation acceleration (usually $\pi_t - \beta \cdot \pi_{t+1}$, but they used an alternative measure) and output gap. The problem is that they used as such a gap a series of detrended real output (by a Hodrick–Prescott filter) instead of the 'true' gap implied by the model, the difference between output and its natural level (which can be approximated by unit labor costs, as already mentioned). By using the incorrect output gap, they follow an earlier empirical literature that found such correlation to be positive in the data, while the new Keynesian Phillips curve (NKPC) implies that it ought to be negative. The positive correlation was used as an argument against the NKPC, but other papers showed that when one approximates the output gap by an indicator of the marginal costs (the unit labor cost), that correlation turns out to be positive in the data, as the model predicts. See Galí (2008, pp. 60–61) for references.

36. I explored elsewhere (Duarte, 2009) how this argument of solutions feasibility played out in the use of a quadratic loss function by monetary economists in the post-war period.

37. Additionally, these methods rely on continuity and differentiability assumptions that make them inappropriate for models where there are occasionally binding constraints.

38. Once the parameters are assigned numerical values the model can be solved with computer programs as those of Schmitt-Grohé and Uribe (2004) or with 'Dynare' (http://www.dynare.org/).

39. See An and Schorfheide (2007) and Canova (2007, Ch. 9–11) for details and further references.

40. Perhaps Solow was more active in raising his reservations to the DSGE literature, and had even argued with some of its advocates (see Duarte, 2010).

41. This interview was published in the Swiss National Bank Study Center Gerzensee *Newsletter*, in January 2005, and is available at Woodford's webpage: http://www.columbia.edu/~mw2230/SGZInterview.pdf (accessed 8 September 2010).

42. A similar point is made by David Colander (2010), who goes beyond and associates the popularity of DSGE macroeconomics as being also a result of funding policies in American academia.

43. Buiter obtained his PhD in economics at Yale in 1975. He is a professor of political economy at the Centre for Economic Performance (London School of Economics, LSE), currently with a joint appointment at the University of Amsterdam, and chief economist of the Citigroup in London, UK. Among many other positions, from 1995 to 1997 he was senior adviser, Chief Economist's Office, at the European Bank for Reconstruction and Development, and in the period of 2006–08 he was a member of the European Central Bank Shadow Council.

44. Links to some of these documents are available in the post I wrote to the blog *History of Economics Playground* ('The crisis and mathematics in economics', 16 August 2009), http://historyofeconomics.wordpress.com/2009/08/16/the-crisis-and-mathematics-in-economics/. The first letter to the Queen is available at http://media.ft.com/cms/3e3b6ca8-7a08-11de-b86f-00144feabdc0.pdf. The Hearings to the US

House of Representatives, with Robert Solow, Sidney Winter, Scott Page, V.V. Chari and David Colander, are available at http://science.house.gov/publications/hearings_markups_details.aspx?NewsID=2916. Colander et al. (2008), Lawson (2009), Leijonhufvud (2009) and Skidelsky (2009, especially Ch. 1–2) all side with the critics of modern economics (see other articles in the special volume of the *Cambridge Journal of Economics*, 2009, **33** (4)).

45.   There is a series of interesting interviews that John Cassidy, of the *New Yorker*, made with eight Chicago economists early in 2010, which are available at: http://www.newyorker.com/online/blogs/johncassidy/chicago-interviews/

46.   Chari (2010, 2) claimed that 'any interesting model must be a dynamic stochastic general equilibrium model. From this perspective, there is no other game in town . . . A useful aphorism in macroeconomics is: 'If you have an interesting and coherent story to tell, you can tell it in a DSGE model. If you cannot, your story is incoherent.'

REFERENCES

An, Sungbae, and Frank Schorfheide (2007), 'Bayesian Analysis of DSGE Models', *Econometric Reviews*, **26**(2–4): 113–172.

Bernanke, Ben S., Jean Boivin and Piotr Eliasz (2005), 'Measuring the Effects of Monetary Policy: A Factor-Augmented Vector Autoregressive (FAVAR) Approach', *Quarterly Journal of Economics*, **120**(1), 387–422.

Bernanke, Ben S. and Ilian Mihov (1998), 'Measuring Monetary Policy', *Quarterly Journal of Economics*, **113**(3), 869–902.

Blanchard, Olivier J., Giovanni Dell'Ariccia, and Paolo Mauro (2010), 'Rethinking Macroeconomic Policy', IMF Staff Position Note (SPN/10/03), 12 February 2010. http://www.imf.org/external/pubs/ft/spn/2010/spn1003.pdf, accessed 20 February 2010.

Blanchard, Olivier J. and Charles M. Kahn (1980), 'The Solution of Linear Difference Models under Rational Expectations', *Econometrica*, **48**(5), 1305–1311.

Buiter, Willem (2009), 'The Unfortunate Uselessness of Most "State of the Art" Academic Monetary Economics', *Financial Times*, 3 March, http://blogs.ft.com/maverecon/2009/03/the-unfortunate-uselessness-of-most-state-of-the-art-academic-monetary-economics/, accessed 5 March 2009.

Caballero, R.J. (2010), 'Macroeconomics after the Crisis: Time to Deal with the Pretense-of-Knowledge Syndrome', *Journal of Economic Perspectives*, **24**(4), 85–102.

Calvo, Guillermo (1983), 'Staggered Prices in a Utility Maximizing Framework', *Journal of Monetary Economics*, **12**(3), 383–398.

Canova, Fabio (2007), *Methods for Applied Macroeconomic Research*, Princeton, NJ: Princeton University Press.

Chari, V.V. (2010), 'Testimony before the Committee on Science and Technology', Subcommittee on Investigations and Oversight, US House of Representatives, 20 July, Washington, DC, http://science.house.gov/publications/hearings_markups_details.aspx?NewsID=2916, accessed 13 October 2010.

Chari, Varadarajan V., Patrick J. Kehoe and Ellen R. McGrattan (2009), 'New Keynesian Models: Not Yet Useful for Policy Analysis', *American Economic Journal: Macroeconomics*, **1**(1), 242–266.

Christiano, Lawrence J., Martin Eichenbaum and Charles L. Evans (1999), 'Monetary Policy Shocks: What Have We Learned and to What End?', in John B. Taylor and Michael Woodford (eds), *Handbook of Macroeconomics*, Amsterdam: North-Holland, pp. 65–148.

Christiano, Lawrence J., Martin Eichenbaum and Charles L. Evans (2005), 'Nominal Rigidities and the Dynamic Effects of a Shock to Monetary Policy', *Journal of Political Economy*, **113**(1), 1–45.

Cogley, Timothy and Argia Sbordone (2008), 'Trend Inflation, Indexation, and Inflation

Persistence in the New Keynesian Phillips Curve', *American Economic Review*, **98**(5), 2101–2126.

Colander, David (2010), 'Written Testimony of David Colander', House Committee on Science and Technology, US House of Representatives – Subcommittee on Investigations and Oversight, 20 July, Washington, DC, http://science.house.gov/publications/hearings_markups_details.aspx?NewsID=2916, accessed 13 October 2010.

Colander, David, Peter Howitt, Alan Kirman, Axel Leijonhufvud and Perry Mehrling (2008), 'Beyond DSGE Models: Toward an Empirically Based Macroeconomics', *American Economic Review, Papers and Proceedings*, **98**(2), 236–240.

Cooley, Thomas F. (ed.) (1995), *Frontiers of Business Cycle Research*, Princeton, NJ: Princeton University Press.

De Grauwe, Paul (2010), 'The Scientific Foundation of Dynamic Stochastic General Equilibrium (DSGE) models', *Public Choice*, **144**(3–4), 413–43.

Devereux, Michael B. and Henry Siu (2007), 'State Dependent Pricing and Business Cycle Asymmetries', *International Economic Review*, **48**(1), 281–310.

Dotsey, Michael and Robert G. King (2005), 'Implications of State-Dependent Pricing for Dynamic Macroeconomic Models', *Journal of Monetary Economics*, **52**(1), 213–42.

Duarte, Pedro G. (2009), 'A Feasible and Objective Concept of Optimal Monetary Policy: The Quadratic Loss Function in the Postwar Period', *HOPE*, **41**(1), 1–55.

Duarte, Pedro G. (2010), 'Not Going Away? Microfoundations in the Making of a New Consensus in Macroeconomics', Working Paper, University of São Paulo.

Duarte, Pedro G. and Kevin Hoover (2011), 'Observing Shocks', CHOPE Working Paper No. 2011-09, Duke University, http://papers.sssn-com/sol3/papers.cfm?abstract_id=1840705.

Eichenbaum, Martin (1992), 'Comments: "Interpreting the Macroeconomic Time Series Facts: The Effects of Monetary Policy" by Christopher Sims', *European Economic Review*, **36**(5), 1001–1011.

Eichenbaum, Martin and Jonas D.M. Fisher (2007), 'Estimating the Frequency of Price Re-Optimization in Calvo-Style Models', *Journal of Monetary Economics*, **54**(7), 2032–2047.

Evans, George W. and Seppo Honkapohja (2001), *Learning and Expectations in Macroeconomics*, Princeton, NJ: Princeton University Press.

Fair, Ray (1994), *Testing Macroeconomic Models*, Cambridge, MA: Harvard University Press.

Friedman, Milton and Anna J. Schwartz (1963), *A Monetary History of the United States, 1867–1960*, Princeton, NJ: Princeton University Press.

Frisch, Ragnar (1933), 'Propagation Problems and Impulse Response Problems in Dynamic Economics', *Economic Essays in Honour of Gustav Cassel: October 20th, 1933*, London: George Allen & Unwin, pp. 171–205.

Galí, Jordi (2008), *Monetary Policy, Inflation, and the Business Cycle – An Introduction to the New Keynesian Framework*, Princeton, NJ: Princeton University Press.

Goodfriend, Marvin and Robert G. King (1997), 'The New Neoclassical Synthesis and the Role of Monetary Policy', *NBER Macroeconomics Annual*, **12**, 231–283.

Hartley, James E., Kevin D. Hoover and Kevin D. Salyer (1997), 'The Limits of Business Cycle Research: Assessing the Real Business Cycle Model', *Oxford Review of Economic Policy*, **13**(3), 34–54.

Hoover, Kevin D. (1988), *The New Classical Macroeconomics: A Sceptical Inquiry*, Oxford: Basil Blackwell.

Hoover, Kevin D. (1995), 'The Problem of Macroeconometrics', in Kevin D. Hoover (ed.), *Macroeconometrics – Developments, Tensions, and Prospects*, Boston, MA: Kluwer Academic Publishers, pp. 1–12.

Hoover, Kevin D. (2006), 'A Neowicksellian in a New Classical World: The Methodology of Michael Woodford's Interest and Prices', *Journal of the History of Economic Thought*, **28**(2), pp. 143–149.

Hoover, Kevin D. (2010a), 'Idealizing Reduction: The Microfoundations of Macroeconomics', *Erkenntnis*, **73**(3), 329–347.

Hoover, Kevin D. (2010b), 'Microfoundational Programs', Working paper, http://papers. sssn.com/sol3/papers.cfm?abstract_id=1562282, accessed 8 September 2010.

Hoover, Kevin D. and Stephen J. Perez (1994a), 'Post Hoc Ergo Propter Once More an Evaluation of "Does Monetary Policy Matter?" in the Spirit of James Tobin', *Journal of Monetary Economics*, **34**(1), 47–74.

Hoover, Kevin D. and Stephen J. Perez (1994b), 'Money May Matter, but How Could You Know?, *Journal of Monetary Economics*, **34**(1), 89–99.

Ingram, Beth F. (1995), 'Recent Advances in Solving and Estimating Dynamic, Stochastic Macroeconomic Models', in Kevin D. Hoover (ed.), *Macroeconometrics – Developments, Tensions, and Prospects*, Boston, MA: Kluwer Academic Publishers, pp. 15–46.

Judd, Kenneth (1998), *Numerical Methods in Economics*, Cambridge, MA: MIT Press.

Kimball, Miles S. (1995), 'The Quantitative Analytics of the Basic Neomonetarist Model', *Journal of Money, Credit and Banking*, **27**(4, Part 2), 1241–1277.

King, Robert and Mark Watson (1998), 'The Solution of Singular Linear Difference Systems Under Rational Expectations', *International Economic Review*, **39**(4), 1015–1026.

Krugman, Paul (2009), 'How Did Economists Get It So Wrong?', *New York Times*, 2 September, http://www.nytimes.com/2009/09/06/magazine/06Economic-t.html?_r=1&em =&pagewanted=all, accessed 11 September 2009.

Lawson, Tony (2009), 'The Current Economic Crisis: Its Nature and the Course of Academic Economics', *Cambridge Journal of Economics*, **33**(4), 759–777.

Leeper, Eric M. (1991), 'Equilibria Under "Active" and "Passive" Monetary and Fiscal Policies', *Journal of Monetary Economics*, **27**(1), 129–147.

Leijonhufvud, Axel (2009), 'Out of the Corridor: Keynes and the Crisis', *Cambridge Journal of Economics*, **33**(4), 741–757.

Lucas Jr, Robert E. (1976), 'Econometric Policy Evaluation: A Critique', *Carnegie-Rochester Conference Series on Public Policy*, **11**, 19–46.

Lucas Jr, Robert E. (1980), 'Methods and Problems in Business Cycle Theory', *Journal of Money, Credit and Banking*, **12**(4), 696–715.

Lucas Jr, Robert E. (2004), 'My Keynesian Education', in Michel De Vroey and Kevin D. Hoover (eds), The IS-LM Model: Its Rise, Fall, and Strange Persistence, *HOPE,* **36** (Annual Supplement), 12–24.

Lucas Jr, Robert E. (2009), 'In Defence of the Dismal Science', *The Economist*, 6 August. http://www.economist.com/node/14165405?story_id=14165405, accessed 10 August 2009.

Mankiw, N. Gregory and Ricardo Reis (2002), 'Sticky Information versus Sticky Prices: A Proposal to Replace the New Keynesian Phillips Curve', *Quarterly Journal of Economics*, **117**(4), 1295–1328.

Mehrling, Perry (1996), 'The Evolution of Macroeconomics: The Origins of Post-Walrasian Macroeconomics', in David Colander (ed.), *Beyond Microfoundations: Post Walrasian Macroeconomics*, Cambridge: Cambridge University Press, pp. 71–86.

Romer, Christina D. and David H. Romer (1989), 'Does Monetary Policy Matter? A New Test in the Spirit of Friedman and Schwartz', *NBER Macroeconomics Annual*, **4**, 121–184.

Romer, Christina D. and David H. Romer (1994), 'Monetary Policy Matters', *Journal of Monetary Economics*, **34**(1), 75–88.

Romer, Christina D. and David H. Romer (2002), 'The Evolution of Economic Understanding and Postwar Stabilization Policy', NBER Working Paper 9274, October.

Rotemberg, Julio (1982), 'Monopolistic Price Adjustment and Aggregate Output', *Review of Economic Studies*, **49**(4), 517–531.

Rotemberg, Julio and Michael Woodford (1997), 'An Optimization-Based Econometric Framework for the Evaluation of Monetary Policy', in Ben S. Bernanke (ed.), *NBER Macroeconomics Annual*, Cambridge: MIT Press, pp. 297–346.

Sargent, Thomas J. and Neil Wallace (1975), '"Rational" Expectations, the Optimal Monetary Instrument, and the Optimal Money Supply Rule', *Journal of Political Economy*, **83**(2), 241–254.

Schmitt-Grohé, Stephanie and Martín Uribe (2004), 'Solving Dynamic General Equilibrium

Models Using a Second-Order Approximation to the Policy Function', *Journal of Economic Dynamics and Control*, **28**(4), 755–775.

Sims, Christopher A. (1980), 'Macroeconomics and Reality', *Econometrica*, **48**(1), 1–48.

Sims, Christopher A. (1992), 'Interpreting the Macroeconomic Time Series Facts: The Effects of Monetary Policy', *European Economic Review*, **36**(5), 975–1000.

Skidelsky, Robert (2009), *Keynes: The Return of the Master*, New York: Public Affairs.

Smets, Frank and Raf Wouters (2003), 'An Estimated Dynamic Stochastic General Equilibrium Model of the Euro Area', *Journal of the European Economic Association*, **1**(5), 1123–1175.

Smets, Frank and Raf Wouters (2007), 'Shocks and Frictions in US Business Cycles: A Bayesian DSGE Approach', *American Economic Review*, **97**(3), 586–606.

Solow, Robert M. (2000), 'Toward a Macroeconomics of the Medium Run', *Journal of Economic Perspectives,* **14**(1), 151–158.

Stock, James H. and Mark W. Watson (2001), 'Vector Autoregressions', *Journal of Economic Perspectives*, **15**(4), 101–115.

Taylor, John B. (1980), 'Aggregate Dynamics and Staggered Contracts', *Journal of Political Economy*, **88**(1), 1–23.

Taylor, John B. (1993), 'Discretion versus Policy Rules in Practice', *Carnegie-Rochester Conference Series on Public Policy*, **39**, 195–214.

Uhlig, Harald (2005), 'What Are the Effects of Monetary Policy on Output? Results From an Agnostic Identification Procedure', *Journal of Monetary Economics*, **52**(2), 381–419.

Walsh, Carl E. (2003), *Monetary Theory and Policy*, 2nd edn, Cambridge: MIT Press.

Woodford, Michael (2001), 'The Taylor Rule and Optimal Monetary Policy', *American Economic Review*, **91**(2), 232–237.

Woodford, Michael (2003), *Interest and Prices: Foundations of a Theory of Monetary Policy*, Princeton, NJ: Princeton University Press.

Woodford, Michael (2004), 'Inflation and Output Dynamics with Firm-Specific Investment', Working Paper, http://www.columbia.edu/~mw2230/capital.pdf, accessed 20 Feburary 2010.

Wren-Lewis, Simon (2007), 'Are There Dangers in the Microfoundations Consensus?', in Philip Arestis (ed.), *Is There a New Consensus in Macroeconomics?* New York: Palgrave Macmillan, pp. 43–60.

Yun, Tack (1996), 'Nominal Price Rigidity, Money Supply Endogeneity, and Business Cycles', *Journal of Monetary Economics*, **37**(2), 345–370.

Zha, Tao (2008), 'Vector Autoregressions', in Steven N. Durlauf and Lawrence E. Blume (eds), *The New Palgrave Dictionary of Economics*, 2nd edn, Basingstoke: Palgrave Macmillan, http://www.dictionaryofeconomics.com/article?id=pde2008_V000066, accessed 20 January 2010.

17 On the role of theory and evidence in macroeconomics

Katarina Juselius[1]

17.1 INTRODUCTION

Economists frequently formulate an *economically* well-specified model as the empirical model and apply statistical methods to estimate its parameters. In contrast, statisticians might formulate a statistically well-specified model for the data and analyze the statistical model to answer the economic questions of interest. In the first case, statistics are used passively as a tool to get some desired estimates, and in the second case, the statistical model is taken seriously and used actively as a means of analyzing the underlying generating process of the phenomenon in question.

The general principle of analyzing statistical models instead of applying methods can be traced back to R.A. Fisher. It was introduced into econometrics by Trygve Haavelmo (1944) and operationalized and further developed by Hendry and Mizon (1993), Hendry (1987), Johansen (1995), Juselius (2006), and followers. Haavelmo's influence on modern econometrics has been discussed, for example, in Hendry et al. (1989) and Andersen (1991).

Because few observed macroeconomic variables can be assumed to be fixed or predetermined a priori, Haavelmo's approach to econometrics requires a probability formulation of the full process that generated the data. Thus, the statistical model has to be based on a full system of equations. The computational complexities involved in the solution of such a system were clearly prohibitive at the time of Haavelmo's monograph when even the estimation of a multiple regression was a non-trivial task. In today's computerized world, it is certainly technically feasible to adopt Haavelmo's guidelines to empirical econometrics. Although the technical difficulties have been solved long ago, most articles in empirical macroeconomics do not seem to follow Haavelmo's general principles, despite being stated very clearly in his monograph.

I shall argue here that the cointegrated vector autoregressive (hereafter CVAR) approach offers a number of advantages as a general framework for addressing empirical questions in (macro)economics without violating Haavelmo's general probability principle. I shall also argue that the

CVAR approach is likely to meet Summers's 1991 critique (Summers, 1991) on many points. He claimed in his article titled 'The Scientific Illusion in Empirical Macroeconomics' that empirical economics has exerted little influence on the development of economic theory and provided little new insight on economic mechanisms. As an illustration, he mentioned empirical analysis of representative agent models, which involves estimating a few deep parameters characterizing preferences and technology. He contrasted this analysis with sophisticated statistical techniques that impose minimal theoretical constraints on the data, as exemplified by a vector autoregressive (VAR) model à la Sims. Summers argued that both approaches have been unable to explain the inherently richer and more complicated macroeconomic reality. He concluded that less formal examination of so-called stylized facts (correlations, mean growth rates, graphs) has resulted in more fruitful economic research. Almost 20 years have passed since Summer's critique and this seems a good opportunity to revisit his main arguments. Has the marriage between theory and evidence improved? Has empirical economics become more enlightening?

One of the key developments after Summers's critique was the so-called dynamic stochastic general equilibrium (DSGE) modeling of the macroeconomy. These models combine the assumptions of a representative agent and the 'Rational expectations hypothesis' (REH) together with a dynamic stochastic structure à la Sims's VAR. The added dynamics and stochasticity render the models more flexible than earlier representative agent models. Nonetheless, in the way that they are practiced, one may say that the DSGE approach gives the primary role to the theory model and a subordinate role to the VAR. In this sense the DSGE model embodies the principle of pre-eminence of theory over empirics or what I shall call the 'theory-first' approach. Hardly surprisingly, not everyone in the profession was prepared to adopt the theory-first approach exemplified by the DSGE models as the best way to describe and understand our complex empirical reality. Many methodologically oriented scholars were vigorously debating the role of theory and empirical evidence in macroeconomics as illustrated by the discussions in Backhouse and Salanti (2000a, 2000b) and Colander (1996, 2000, 2001, 2006). These debates however, seemed, only to have a marginal (if any) effect on the empirical practice of the economics profession. At the beginning of the new century the popularity of the DSGE models in graduate programs and among editors of top economics journals and researchers at central banks suggested that economics as a science had finally converged to a state of unanimity regarding both theory and how to apply it to data.

This view was challenged when the crisis struck with a suddenness that took most economists, central bankers and politicians by complete surprise. Obviously, standard models must have lacked important features as they failed to warn their users about the growing vulnerability of the macroeconomy to the crisis. As the crisis accelerated, the chorus of critical voices became a tsunami that washed over newspapers, blogs, and so on. The debate on how to do economics was again fresh and alive. See for example discussions in Colander et al. (2008, 2009), Katlesky (2009), Leijonhufvud (2009), Krugman (2009), Cochrane (2009), Juselius (2009a, 2011a) and Lawson (2009). Summers's critique of the scientific value of empirical models in economics seems as relevant as it was 20 years ago.

I shall here question the pre-eminence of theory over empirics in economics and argue that empirical econometrics needs to be given a more important and independent role in economic analysis, not only in order to have some confidence in the soundness of our empirical inferences, but also to uncover empirical regularities that can serve as a basis for new economic thinking.

In the first part of this chapter I contrast the theory-first approach with what I call the data-first approach as a way of bridging economic theory and empirical evidence. To fix ideas, I make use of the article 'Taking a DSGE Model to the Data Meaningfully' (Juselius and Franchi, 2007), which provides a detailed discussion of 'A Method for Taking Models to the Data' (Ireland, 2004a). Since the discussion can be seen as a critical attack on Ireland's article, I would like to stress that it was chosen because it was well documented, all results are reproducible, and it uses sophisticated econometrics.

I then argue that one important reason why the DSGE theory-first approach does not seem to have resolved Summers's critique is that it does not properly account for the pronounced non-stationarity, such as unit root persistence and breaks, typical of economic data, neither from a theoretical nor an econometric point of view. To have some confidence in the soundness of the inference being made, the number of stochastic trends has to be tested, not just assumed; parameter constancy has to be checked, not just assumed; dynamics have to properly fit the data, and so on. I demonstrate that these features can be modelled and tested with the (cointegrated) VAR model and argue that the non-stationarity of the data has strong implications for how to model expectations and for the *ceteris paribus* clause in economic models. This data-first approach shows how economic theory can be confronted with the basic regularities in the data, thereby exposing lack of empirical relevance and sometimes even inconsistencies.

In the second part of the chapter, I discuss how a statistically adequate VAR analysis often delivers additional (often theoretically puzzling) results. If these are taken seriously, they can generate new economic hypotheses that subsequently can be tested on new data. Thus, a VAR analysis based on full information maximum likelihood analysis of the data can be used to test prior hypotheses and to generate new ones, thereby replacing 'simple stylized facts' such as correlations, graphs, and so on with more sophisticated facts that better describe the non-stationary world in which individual decisions and market outcomes unfold. By doing so, it has the potential of providing a basis for new economic thinking.

17.2   THEORY-FIRST VERSUS DATA-FIRST

The basic dilemma of empirical macro modeling is that the reality behind the available macroeconomic data is so much more rich and complex than the often narrowly analyzed problem being modeled by the theory. How to treat these 'additional' features of the data, which often go against the *ceteris paribus* assumptions of the economic model, has divided the profession into the proponents of the so-called specific-to-general versus general-to-specific approach to empirical economics. To emphasize my subsequent arguments I shall here call them theory-first versus data-first. For a detailed methodological discussion of the two approaches, see for example Gilbert (1986), Hendry (1995, 2009), Juselius (2006), Pagan (1987) and Spanos (1995, 2006, 2009).

The former, more conventional, approach starts from a mathematical formulation of a theoretical model and then expands the model by adding stochastic components. The aim is to estimate the parameters of a 'stylized' economic model, while ignoring the wider circumstances under which the data were generated. These factors are then dumped into the residual term, causing its variance to be large. This practice has important implications for the power of empirical testing, often leading to a low ability to reject a theory model even when it provides a poor description of the basic regularities in the data. As a result, competing theory models are often not rejected despite being tested against the same data. See Cooley and Leroy (1985) for an early discussion. Furthermore, the statistical inference in such models is usually based on a number of untested and empirically questionable assumptions so the 'significance' of estimated parameters may lack scientific meaning.

This approach is strongly influenced by the legacy of the pre-eminence of theory, which presumes that the basic economic mechanisms can be pre-specified, that is, we know which variables are exogenous, which are adjusting when the system has been pushed out of steady state by exogenous shocks, how various interventions have affected the system, and so on. Econometrics in this case play the subordinate role of 'quantifying' theoretically meaningful parameters assumed to be empirically relevant on a priori grounds. This approach can only be defended if the probabilistic assumptions comprising the underlying statistical model are satisfied vis-à-vis the data in question (Spanos, 2009). If not, it produces empirically irrelevant and possibly misleading results.

The data-first approach starts from an explicit stochastic formulation of all data (selected on the basis of the theory model in question) and then reduces the general statistical model by simplification testing. It answers the economic questions of interest by embedding the economic model within the statistical model and uses strict statistical principles as a criterion for a good empirical model. In this case, the statistical model ties economic theory to the data when it nests both the data-generating process and the theoretical model, so that the parameters of the theoretical model can be derived from the parameters of the statistical model (Hoover et al., 2008).

It recognizes from the outset the weak link between the theory model and the observed reality. For instance few, if any, theory models fully allow for basic characteristics of macroeconomic data such as path-dependence, unit-root non-stationarity, structural breaks, shifts in equilibrium means, and location shifts in general growth rates. Such empirical features of economic data are generally at odds with the prevailing theory-first paradigm, which assumes a few constant structural parameters describing technology and preferences, REH and some ad hoc dynamics. In contrast, the data-first methodology works by allowing the empirical regularities in data to speak as freely as possible about underlying theoretical relationships, thereby allowing us to discriminate between empirically relevant and irrelevant theories, but also to discover new evidence for which prior hypotheses have not yet been formulated. All this will be discussed in the next sections using Ireland (2004a) as an illustrative case study.

17.3   IRELAND'S DSGE MODEL: A FIRST CHECK

The hypothesis that aggregate technology shocks alone drive business cycle fluctuations is a key feature of the real business cycle (RBC) model discussed in Ireland (2004a). More specifically, the model assumes a utility-maximizing representative agent, who chooses between consumption and total hours worked in an economy subject to a constant returns to scale technology described by a Cobb–Douglas production function. The latter is defined for capital and labor subject to labor-augmented technological progress, which is assumed to have grown with a constant rate over the examined period 1948–2002. Capital and total factor productivity are assumed to be unobserved and generated from cumulated identical shocks. The model describes a closed economy without a government sector.

To take the highly non-linear RBC model to the data, Ireland applies log-linearization around theoretical steady-state values making use of the following basic assumptions: (1) total factor productivity follows a first-order stationary autoregressive model; and (2) the growth rate of labor-augmenting technological progress is constant over time. The implications of these assumptions are that: (1) trend-adjusted output, consumption, investment and capital are stationary around their steady-state values; (2) the rate of labor-augmenting technological progress is constant and results in identical linear trends in output, consumption, investment and capital; and (3) technology shocks are pushing both total factor productivity (TFP) and capital. The model's three equations (output, consumption and labor) are made 'more flexible' by adding a VAR(1) process. Most model parameters are estimated using a Kalman filter non-linear optimization routine that can handle the singularity of the model.[2] The exceptions are the parameters for depreciation rate and the discount rate, which are calibrated. The estimated structural parameters are constrained to satisfy the restrictions implied by theory.

The reported estimates are claimed to be maximum likelihood (ML) estimates. But ML requires that the assumptions underlying the model are correct. Thus, they have to be checked, not just assumed. In this context it is useful to draw a distinction between substantive and statistical assumptions (Spanos, 2009) as their respective validity has different implications for inference. The substantive assumptions pertain to the centuries-old issue of the realism of economic theories, whereas the statistical assumptions pertain to the reliability of the statistical inference. Because the Ireland article did not report tests of these assumptions, Juselius and Franchi (2007) first replicated all results reported in Ireland's article and then performed a detailed check of the statistical and some of the substantive assumptions.

Parameter constancy is one of the substantive assumptions: if parameters are structural they ought to remain constant despite changes in policy regimes. Over the sample period, the US economy experienced a major policy regime shift around 1979. In a footnote, Ireland mentions that parameter constancy before and after this date has been tested and rejected. Nonetheless he disregarded this evidence, because parameter estimates were 'quite similar' before and after that date.

The stationarity assumption needed for the log-linearization around the constant steady states can be assessed based on estimates of the characteristic roots of the model, of which the largest were 0.9987, 0.94 and 0.88.[3] A root of 0.9987 is admittedly less than one, but in practice indistinguishable from a unit root. Even a root of 0.94 is pretty close to unity, suggesting an additional source of pronounced persistence in the data.

One consequence of the assumption of identical deterministic growth rates for output, consumption and capital, when the actual rates differed markedly, and stationarity, when there are near unit roots in the data, can be inferred from Figure 17.1.[4] The deviations from the assumed steady-state values are very persistent and systematically either positive or negative. Except for hours worked, they never cross the zero line over a period of 50 years.

The statistical misspecification tests of Ireland's model showed that the null hypotheses of residual normality, no autocorrelation and no autoregressive conditional heteroskedasticity (ARCH) were rejected for essentially all variables. Furthermore, the cross correlogram showed significant correlations between the errors which are assumed independent. Thus, the first set of diagnostic tests revealed clear violations of the distributional assumptions. Hence, the probability model is not correctly specified; the reported statistical inference is not maximum likelihood and the p-values calculated from standard normal distributions (t, F, and χ^2) may be completely unreliable. In particular, the assumption that data are stationary, when in fact they are very close to being non-stationary, is likely to make all inference on steady-state values meaningless (see Johansen, 2006).

There is, however, an easy solution to the problem of unit roots in the data and its effect on inference. By transforming the data into stationary components using differencing and cointegration (see, for example, Engle and Granger, 1987; Hendry, 1987, 2009; Johansen, 1988, 1995; Juselius, 2006) standard inference would apply again. This is also the preferred solution in Ireland (2004b). That the assumed probability model was not correctly specified does not as such imply that the assumed RBC model is incorrect. Therefore, Juselius and Franchi (2007) examine whether the RBC hypothesis is a good description of US business cycles by recasting the basic hypotheses in the Ireland model as statistical tests in a well-specified cointegrated VAR (CVAR) model.[5]

17.4   THE RBC HYPOTHESIS: A CVAR CHECK

17.4.1   A Theory-Consistent CVAR Scenario

To test the basic RBC assumptions underlying Ireland's DSGE model formulation, we need to formulate all basic (substantive and statistical) assumptions as testable hypotheses on the VAR model. Such a theory-consistent VAR scenario can be seen as a bridge between the theory model

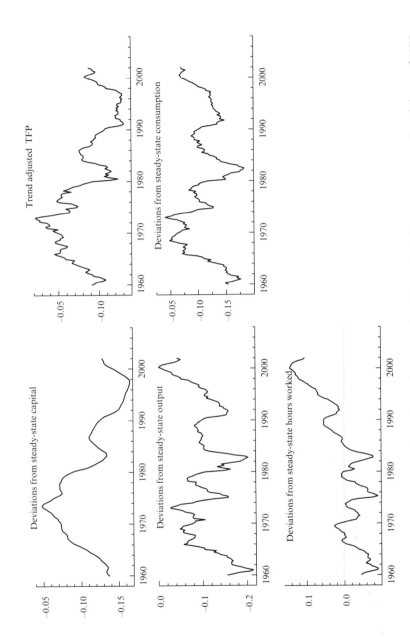

Figure 17.1   Deviations from trend-adjusted steady-state values for capital, income, consumption, labor and TFP

and the VAR and is a summary of necessary conditions on the data for the model to be empirically relevant.

One of the roots (associated with total factor productivity) was very close to unity and was approximated with a unit root, that is, we assume that total factor productivity, a_t, is a unit root stochastic process instead of an AR(1) with a near unit root:

$$a_t = a_{t-1} + \varepsilon_t = \sum_{i=1}^{t} \varepsilon_i + a_0, \tag{17.1}$$

where ε_t is a permanent TFP shock. The cumulation of these shocks, $\sum_{i=1}^{t} \varepsilon_i$, is called a (first-order) stochastic trend and describes the development of total factor productivity over time. A variable containing a first-order stochastic trend is called integrated of order one, in short I(1). The difference between a first-order stochastic and a deterministic linear trend is that the permanent increments of a stochastic trend change randomly, whereas those of a deterministic trend are constant over time.

When two variables share the same cumulated permanent shocks we say that the two variables are cointegrated. For example, if capital and income share the same TFP stochastic trend (17.1) it implies that they have followed the same long-run stochastic growth path and are therefore likely to be causally associated. In a growing economy, many variables would contain a linear deterministic trend. But as the source of the linear increment is generally unidentified, the fact that two variables share a linear deterministic trend does not imply that they are causally related (Yule, 1926). Therefore, finding significant cointegration is a much more demanding and relevant measure of long-run association than a significant regression relationship. For an expository introduction to integration and cointegration see Hendry and Juselius (1999, 2000).

Furthermore, an important advantage of classifying data according to their order of integration, I(0), I(1) and I(2)[6] is that it allows us to classify variables and relations according to their 'persistency profiles', that is, we can discriminate between relations which exhibit pronounced persistence and relations which do not (Juselius, 2010, 2011b). For example, the strong persistence visible in the graphs of the steady-state errors in Figure 17.1 suggests that: (1) the long-run path of Ireland's data is not adequately described by a common deterministic trend; and (2) the steady-state errors contain unexplained persistence that suggests serious misspecification.

Assuming one stochastic trend and three cointegration relations, a theory-consistent CVAR scenario for Ireland's model is given by (17.2) and (17.3). It is useful to start with the formulation of the pushing forces:

$$
\begin{bmatrix} y_t \\ c_t \\ h_t \\ k_t \end{bmatrix} = \begin{bmatrix} d_1 \\ d_1 \\ 0 \\ d_1 \end{bmatrix} [a_t] + \begin{bmatrix} b_1 \\ b_1 \\ 0 \\ b_1 \end{bmatrix} [t] + \begin{bmatrix} v_{1,t} \\ v_{2,t} \\ v_{3,t} \\ v_{4,t} \end{bmatrix}
\tag{17.2}
$$

where y_t is the log of output, c_t is the log of consumption, h_t is the log of hours worked, k_t is the log of capital, $a_t = \sum_{i=1}^{t} \varepsilon_i$ is the sum of total factor productivity shocks and v_t is a stationary moving average (MA) process. It implies: (1) a non-stationary Cobb–Douglas production function, $y_t - \theta k_t - (1 - \theta) h_t$ is $I(1)$; (2) a stationary consumption–income ratio, $c_t - y_t$ is $I(0)$, (3) a stationary capital–income ratio, $k_t - y_t$ is $I(0)$; and (4) that hours worked is stationary, h_t is $I(0)$. Thus, under scenario (17.2) the three cointegration relations should correspond to the relations in (2)–(4).[7] According to Ireland's model, shocks to technical progress should explain the development over time in TFP and capital, whereas output, consumption and labor would be adjusting (that is, endogenous). The latter can be formulated in the following equilibrium error correcting model:

$$
\begin{bmatrix} \Delta y_t \\ \Delta c_t \\ \Delta h_t \\ \Delta k_t \end{bmatrix} = \begin{bmatrix} \alpha_{11} & \alpha_{21} & \alpha_{31} \\ \alpha_{12} & \alpha_{22} & \alpha_{32} \\ \alpha_{13} & \alpha_{23} & \alpha_{33} \\ \alpha_{14} & \alpha_{24} & \alpha_{34} \end{bmatrix} \begin{bmatrix} (c - y - \mu_{01})_{t-1} \\ (k - y - \mu_{02})_{t-1} \\ (h - \mu_{03})_{t-1} \end{bmatrix} + \begin{bmatrix} b_1 \\ b_1 \\ 0 \\ b_1 \end{bmatrix} + \begin{bmatrix} \varepsilon_{1,t} \\ \varepsilon_{2,t} \\ \varepsilon_{3,t} \\ \varepsilon_{4,t} \end{bmatrix}
$$

$$\tag{17.3}$$

The scenarios (17.2) and (17.3) comprise a set of necessary conditions that need to be supported by the data for the Ireland RBC model to pass a first test of empirical relevance.

17.4.2   A CVAR Reality Check of Ireland's Model

An unrestricted VAR(2) model in levels was first estimated and tested for misspecification, and then revised accordingly. The null of constant parameters for the periods 1960:1–1979:4 and 1981:2–2002:1 was, however, strongly rejected: the assumption that the structural parameters are constant over time did not seem tenable with the information in the data. The VAR analysis was, therefore, done separately for the two periods and produced the following general results: (1) The first period was fairly well described by the estimated model, but the second period less so;[8] (2) in both periods there seemed to be at least two stochastic trends (rather than one), one of which was associated with permanent shocks to consumption and the other to labor; (3) a trend-stationary Cobb–Douglas production function with plausible coefficients seemed to work well in the first, but not in the second period; (4) hours worked was found to be non-stationary against the stationarity assumption in Ireland's model.

Altogether, the results suggested that total factor productivity and technological progress might have been well approximated by a linear trend in the first period but not in the second, and that it was demand shocks rather than shocks to TFP that have triggered off US business cycles. Thus, the information in the data seemed more consistent with a Keynesian than an RBC explanation of US business cycles. When this is said, the CVAR results should only be considered tentative, as a better model specification is clearly needed. This is particularly so for the second period where the results were based on an econometrically unsatisfactory model.

Thus, the conclusion reached in Ireland's article (that the real business cycle theory model is able to explain the long business cycles in the US post-war period) was not based on correct statistical inference and the conclusion was reversed when based on a well-specified CVAR model. In spite of the sophisticated dynamic and stochastic specification, Ireland's DSGE model seemed to lack important features needed to account properly for the complexity of the economic reality: The basic predictions from Ireland's DSGE model fell outside the confidence bands of the empirical reality.

17.4.3   Pulling Sophisticated Empirical Facts Out of Data

Summers (1991) concluded his critique by claiming that a less formal examination of empirical facts has generally resulted in more fruitful economic research. While possibly useful, such stylized facts are nevertheless too coarse and can even be misleading when data are non-stationary, because simple correlation coefficients and mean growth rates are only well defined for stationary, but not for non-stationary data (Yule, 1926).

The unrestricted VAR model, properly specified and tested, can be seen as a convenient summary of the covariances of the data (Hendry and Mizon, 1993; Juselius, 2006, Ch. 3) and, therefore, represents the reality we would like our theoretical model to describe. But, because the VAR is heavily overparametrized, it is not very informative as such. Its usefulness derives from its ability to reduce the number of parameters until further restrictions significantly change the value of the likelihood function. If correctly done, the final parsimonious VAR model would describe regularities in the data without suppressing any relevant information and, therefore, would provide a set of 'statistical regularities' that the theoretical model should explain in order to be empirically relevant.

In particular, by combining differenced and cointegrated data, the CVAR model offers a natural way of analyzing economic data as short-run variations around moving long-run equilibria. Longer-run forces are themselves divided into the forces that move the equilibria (pushing forces, which give rise to stochastic trends) and forces that correct deviations from equilibrium (pulling forces, which give rise cointegrating relations). Interpreted in this way, the CVAR has a good chance of nesting a multivariate, path-dependent data-generating process and relevant dynamic macroeconomic theories. One could say that the CVAR model gives the data a rich context in which they are allowed to speak freely (Hoover et al., 2008). See also Møller (2008) for a detailed exposition of how to translate basic concepts of macroeconomic models into testable concepts of the CVAR model.

The CVAR analysis of Ireland's DSGE model illustrates this latter point. When data were allowed to speak freely, they spoke about a number of empirical regularities that had been silenced by prior restrictions: the number of stochastic trends were two or three in the data, but one in Ireland's model; the two driving forces originated from shocks to consumption and labor in the data, but from TFP and capital in Ireland's model; the lag order of the VAR was two in the data, but one in Ireland's model; the variables were trend non-stationary in the data, but trend-stationary in Ireland's model; there was strong evidence of structural breaks in the data, whereas a constant DSGE structure was assumed in Ireland's model.

An advantage of analyzing the Ireland data separately for the period before and after 1980 was that it gave an opportunity to compare similarities and differences between the two periods and, therefore, to get a first idea of which economic mechanisms had changed and why. In particular, it was possible to demonstrate that income, consumption, labor and capital did a reasonable job in 'explaining' business cycle movements in the first period (though with a Keynesian flavor), but a much less satisfactory one in the more recent period indicating that some important information is missing in the theoretical set-up. Section 17.6 will argue that it is the world wide deregulation of financial markets that has influenced US savings and investment decisions and this information is missing in the present set-up.

17.5   ECONOMIC MODELING AND NON-STATIONARY DATA

The lack of empirical support may not come as a big surprise to economists, who would argue that their models are not meant to be close approximations to the economic reality. Many would argue that by adding new features to these models they will gradually improve.[9] I would like to challenge this view and argue that the strong evidence of non-stationarity in data points to a more fundamental problem with many economic models which are intrinsically developed for a stationary world despite containing some added-on persistence and dynamics. As will be discussed below, non-stationarity has strong implications for important aspects of economic models, such as expectations, risk versus uncertainty, and the robustness of policy conclusions to the empirical validity of the *ceteris paribus* clause.

17.5.1   The Role of Expectations in a Non-stationary World

The strong evidence of (near) unit roots and (structural) breaks in economic variables and relations suggests that economic behavior is often unpredictable. In such a non-stationary world Clements and Hendry (1999, 2008) show that forecasts from constant-parameter theory models, assumed to be correct from the outset, are likely to perform poorly. Since rational expectations models imagine economic agents who are able recursively to foresee future outcomes with known probabilities, they are inconsistent with the prevalence of structural breaks in the data (Hendry and Mizon, 2011). Indeed, these models have often often failed to describe macroeconomic data satisfactorily. The strong prevalence of non-stationarity in economic time series, in itself, is evidence that we do not know in which direction the future is moving. To act as if we do would indeed be highly irrational. In the words of Keynes (1937):

> By 'uncertain' knowledge, let me explain, I do not mean merely to distinguish what is known for certain from what is only probable. The game of roulette is not subject, in this sense, to uncertainty . . . The sense in which I am using the term is that in which the prospect of a European war is uncertain, or the price of copper and the rate of interest twenty years hence . . . About these matters there is no scientific basis on which to form any calculable probability whatever. We simply do not know.

But, if rational expectations have to go, what should replace them? Frydman and Goldberg (2007, 2008, 2011) provide an alternative approach dubbed 'imperfect knowledge economics' (IKE), which recognizes that the process driving outcomes in modern economies changes at times and in ways that no one can specify ahead of time up to a random error. Such change arises in part because individuals's forecasting strategies, which play an important role in driving market outcomes, change in ways that they themselves, let alone an economist, cannot fully pre-specify.

IKE holds out the possibility that although change in modern economies does not unfold mechanically, it may exhibit qualitative regularities that can be modeled both theoretically and empirically. Because IKE models impose qualitative restrictions on change, it generates qualitative implications which, though testable, are looser than those derived under REH. Johansen et al. (2010), Juselius (2010) and Frydman et al. (2008) find that the implications of REH-based models of nominal and real exchange rates are strongly rejected in favor of IKE-based models.

One of the key implications of Frydman and Goldberg's (2007, 2008, 2009) IKE model of asset markets is that imperfect knowledge can lead to greater persistence in asset price fluctuations than implied by REH-based models. Thus the IKE model is able to explain the long swings in asset prices away from and toward benchmark levels that characterize asset markets.

17.5.2 The *Ceteris Paribus* Clause and Non-stationarity

It is a common practice to simplify a theory model by using the *ceteris paribus* clause, 'everything else unchanged'. However, the empirical relevance of the *ceteris paribus* assumption in a theory model is likely to be strongly affected by the order of integration of the *ceteris paribus* variables. If they are stationary, the conclusions are more likely to remain robust than if they are non-stationary. This is because a non-stationary *ceteris paribus* variable if included in the empirical model is likely to influence the cointegration results and, therefore, the conclusions of the model's steady-state behavior. Since no variables can be kept artificially fixed in the real economy, the empirical problem needs to be addressed in the context of 'everything else changing' and the impact of the *ceteris paribus* variables needs to be brought into the analysis by conditioning.

Consider, for example, the empirical CVAR analysis of Ireland's RBC model discussed in section 17.4.2. In particular, it demonstrated that the first period up to 1979 was reasonably well described by two pulling and two pushing forces, though with a Keynesian rather than a RBC explanation of US business cycles. For the more recent period the chosen information set was not sufficient: there was only weak evidence of cointegration, suggesting that some important determinants are missing. This can be illustrated with the graphs of the first two cointegration relations, the first

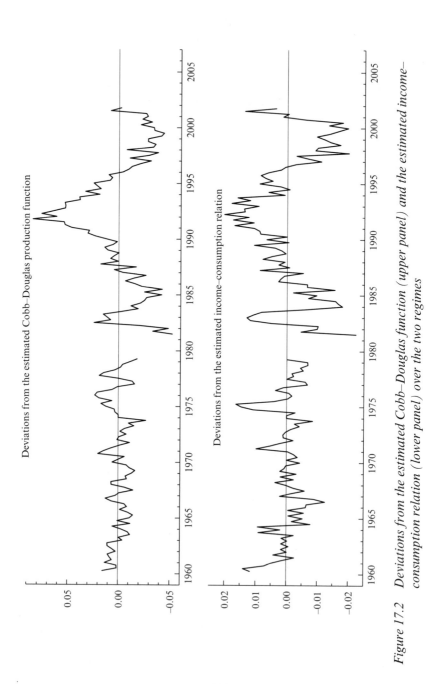

Figure 17.2   Deviations from the estimated Cobb–Douglas function (upper panel) and the estimated income–consumption relation (lower panel) over the two regimes

one describing deviations from a homogeneous Cobb–Douglas relation, the other from the consumption–income ratio. There is a striking difference between the two periods: in the first period, deviations from fundamental long-run values are reasonably modest; in the second, these are characterized by long and persistent swings.

Because a major difference between the two periods is the deregulation of financial markets in the mid-1980s, a first hypothesis that springs to mind is the importance of long swings in asset prices. This would be consistent with the IKE theory discussed above as well as with the notion of reflexivity (Soros, 1987) suggesting that such pronounced movements away from long-run benchmark values may strongly affect aggregate behavior in the real economy and vice versa.

However, if the information set is increased by new variables, for example by financial and housing wealth, reflecting booms and busts of global financial markets, previous empirical conclusions may not remain unchanged. For example, in the enlarged model it may very well be empirical shocks to financial or housing wealth that are now pushing the system, rather than shocks to consumption and hours worked. Therefore, equating a residual with an autonomous shock, as is frequently done, can be totally misleading unless the model contains all relevant variables.[10]

Such concerns are, however, easily met as it is straightforward to increase the information set, building on previously obtained results (the cointegration property is invariant to changes in the information set) thereby learning systematically how sensitive previous conclusions are to the *ceteris paribus* clause. Thus, the CVAR story is not claimed to be 'structural' in the usual sense, albeit it often has a lot of empirical content. This is contrary to Ireland's DSGE analysis which tells a 'structural' story, but with little empirical content.

17.6   'SHERLOCK HOLMES' ECONOMETRICS

More than a quarter of a century ago, when Søren Johansen and I started working on the CVAR approach, I was taken by the beauty of this model, its rich structures and its potential for addressing highly relevant questions within a stringent statistical framework. What I did not expect was that the data consistently refused to tell the stories they were supposed to. After many frustrating attempts, it seemed that I had the choice of either forcing data to tell a theoretically acceptable story or approaching the complex reality without the guide of a reliable theory. I chose the latter and started using the cointegrated VAR model in the spirit of Sherlock Holmes, an experience that best can be described as a long sequence of 'why's.

Though economic puzzles are probably harder to solve than crimes, I believe it is in the Sherlock Holmesian spirit that a well-structured empirical CVAR analysis can inspire new economic thinking. It is based on the following important principles: (1) data are allowed to speak as freely as possible against a background of not just one but several theories; (2) falsification is considered more important than verification; and (3) results that go against conventional wisdom are considered more interesting than confirmatory results.

It has a Marshallian rather than a Walrasian flavor, expressed by Kevin Hoover as:

> The Walrasian approach is totalizing. Theory comes first . . . The Marshallian approach is archaeological. We have some clues that a systematic structure lies behind the complexities of economic reality. The problem is how to lay this structure bare. To dig down to find the foundations, modifying and adapting our theoretical understanding as new facts accumulate, becoming ever more confident in our grasp of the super structure, but never quite sure that we have reached the lowest level of the structure. (Hoover, 2006)

As an illustration, I shall give a brief account of such a Sherlock Holmesian CVAR process and discuss how it has generated new hypotheses that may inspire new economic thinking.

17.6.1   Puzzling Features in the Data

Based on standard economic models it is often difficult to explain all the pronounced persistence in economic data, in particular such persistence that seems to originate from other sources than those associated with shocks to technology, preferences and money supply. Also, structural breaks are common in economic data but are puzzling viewed from standard REH-based theoretical models. Such breaks can sometimes be handled econometrically by equilibrium mean shifts or changes in mean growth rates but, as Ireland's RBC model analysis illustrated, can also be of such fundamental character that a split sample analysis is required.

What do we find when analyzing data using the CVAR in the spirit of Sherlock Holmes? A robust finding is that an important regime shift seems to have occurred at the beginning of the 1980s. Few models of the macroeconomy are able to pass statistical tests of parameter constancy for the periods before and after 1980. The the main reason is that the division into exogenous and endogenous forces seems to have undergone a change: a new type of persistence influencing the number and the origin of the stochastic trends seems to influence the data after this date.

Most economists would believe that the change in US monetary policy was the reason for the change. But data consistently refused to tell such a story. However, digging down into the data gave some other clues: the real exchange rates, the real interest rates, and the term spreads were exhibiting a pronounced persistence that seemed untenable with stationarity, as illustrated by the graphs in Figures 17.3, 17.4 and 17.5.[11] The inability to reject the unit root hypothesis suggested that many basic parity conditions, such as the purchasing power parity (PPP), the uncovered interest rate parity, the domestic and international Fisher parity and the 'expectations hypothesis' for the term spread were not working as standard REH-based theory would predict. As these variables can be associated with financial market behavior, it seemed plausible that this persistence was associated with the worldwide deregulation of financial markets. The hypothesis that the 'new' puzzling persistence in our macro models is due to speculative behavior in financial markets was suggested by Sherlock Holmesian VAR analyses some 20 years ago.

17.6.2 Empirical Regularities in the Financial Markets

As the recent and previous financial crises have demonstrated, the boom-and-bust behavior in the stock market and the market for foreign exchange is likely to have a strong impact on the real sector of the economy. Such behavior is hard to explain with REH-based models and has, therefore, often been considered puzzling. In particular, the long swings behavior of real exchange rates under currency floats has puzzled economists.[12] Figure 17.3, upper panel, illustrates why: the nominal exchange rate moves in long persistent swings around relative prices. That nominal exchange rates exhibit long swings in periods of currency float, whereas relative prices do not, explains why nominal and real exchange rates tend to resemble each other.

Such persistent movements away from competitive long-run fundamental values are almost bound to have a strong impact on price competitiveness among tradables. In the absence of equilibrium-correcting nominal exchange rates, one would, therefore, expect goods prices to equilibrium-correct. But the high variability with which nominal exchange rates move prevents prices from taking the full burden of adjustment. Therefore, to restore equilibrium in the goods market, nominal interest rates would have to compensate for these persistent swings in the real exchange rates, producing a similar persistence in nominal interest rates. The latter is illustrated in the upper panel of Figure 17.4, which exhibits long and persistent swings in the US–German long-term interest rate differential. Similar persistent swings can be shown for short-term interest rate differentials, albeit with greater variability. Figure 17.5 demonstrates that also the short–long

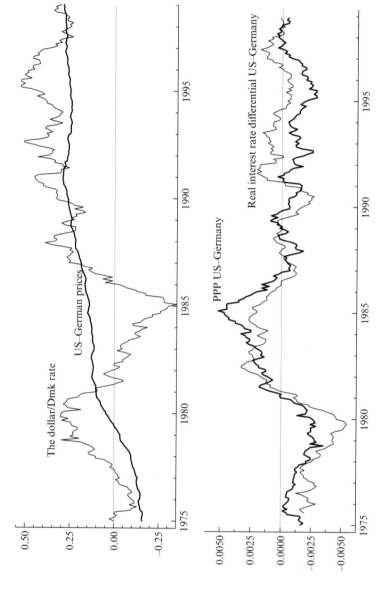

Figure 17.3 *Mean adjusted relative prices and the nominal exchange rate (upper panel) and the real exchange rate and the real interest rate differential (lower panel) between US and Germany*

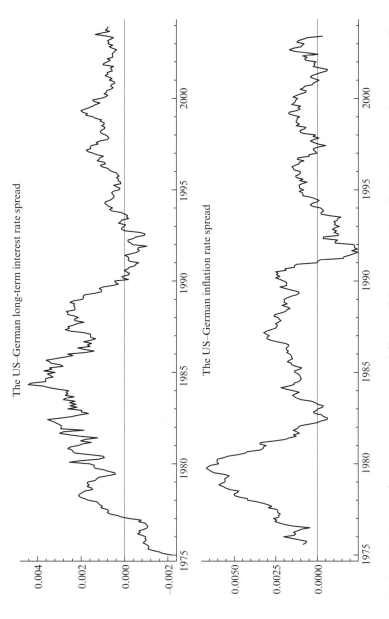

Figure 17.4 US–German long-term interest rate differential (upper panel) and US–German inflation rate differential (lower panel)

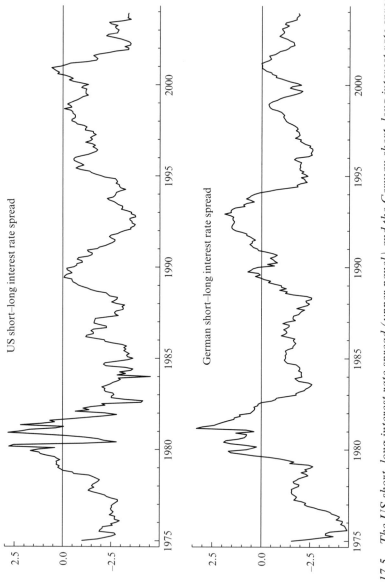

US short–long interest rate spread

German short–long interest rate spread

Figure 17.5 *The US short–long interest rate spread (upper panel) and the German short–long interest rate spread (lower panel)*

spreads exhibit a similar persistence. Based on a CVAR analysis of five US zero coupon bonds, Giese (2008) finds that the term spreads are nonstationary but cointegrated, and that shocks to the level and the slope of the term structure are pushing the system.

To dig deeper into these data regularities, Johansen and Juselius (1992) and Juselius (1995) first tested a number of hypotheses related to the purchasing power parity (PPP) and uncovered interest rate parity (UIP) based on US–UK data. This was followed up by a similar study of US–Japanese data (Juselius and MacDonald, 2004) and one of US–German data (Juselius and MacDonald, 2007). All of them find that the persistent movements in the real exchange rate are compensated by similar persistent movements in the interest rate differential (either short term or long term).

How can this be empirically and theoretically understood? Obviously, prices and nominal exchange rates differ in one important respect: nominal exchange rates are primarily being determined in the speculative market for foreign exchange based on future expectations of capital gains, whereas prices of tradables are determined in an internationally highly competitive goods market. That prices and nominal exchange rates behave differently has, of course, also been recognized by many REH-based models such as the Dornbush and Frankel overshooting type of models (Dornbusch, 1976; Dornbusch and Frankel, 1995) some of which allow for persistence in the real exchange rate (Benigno, 2004; Engel and West, 2006; Galí and Monacelli, 2005). But, Juselius (2009b) finds that the swings in the real exchange rate are too persistent for the REH-based models to tell an empirically credible story. The long swings remain a puzzle in these models. In contrast, the IKE-based models proposed by Frydman and Goldberg (2007, 2008) seem to provide a remarkably good fit. See Frydman et al. (2008) and Juselius (2009b).

To test the two competing theories Juselius (2010) formulated a theory-consistent CVAR scenario for REH-based and IKE-based monetary models. The scenario analysis shows that under REH the real exchange rate and the real interest rate differential are each I(0) or at most near I(1), whereas under IKE they are I(1) or near I(2) and cointegrate to stationarity. One important testable difference is that the degree of persistence is one degree higher under IKE than under REH. Strong evidence for the IKE-based model is found in Frydman et al. (2008), Johansen et al. (2010), and Juselius (2010).

In the stock market, the efficient market hypothesis is one of the theoretical cornerstones of financial behavior. It has often been formulated as a random walk hypothesis of stock prices, which has been tested and often not rejected. The random walk hypothesis, however, is much too simplistic as a description of financial market behavior and as a test of the EMH. A more sophisticated formulation was given in the seminal article by Campbell and Shiller (1987) relying on a REH present value model for stock prices and nominal exchange rates. The model is based on the assumption that both prices and dividends are first-order difference stationary and that parameters are constant over the full sample period.[13]

In a still ongoing project, the author of this chapter applied the CVAR model to the Shiller data and obtained the following tentative results: (1) a constant equilibrium relationship over the entire sample 1934–2008 is strongly rejected, but reasonably constant subsamples can be found; (2) first-order difference stationarity is rejected in favor of second-order difference stationarity; (3) dividends alone cannot explain movements in stock prices, earnings are also needed; (4) stock prices tend to fluctuate in a boom and bust fashion around the price–earnings ratio; (5) earnings are influenced by the price–dividend ratio and are error-correcting toward the price–earnings ratio. Thus, rising earnings lead to rising stock prices, and rising stock prices has a positive 'long-run' effect on earnings which, therefore, feed back on stock prices.

These empirical regularities, though still tentative, resemble many of those found in the foreign currency markets and suggests that an IKE-based model might also work well in the stock market. For example, under IKE, we would expect that financial behavior is non-constant over time, that endogenously loss-averse agents produce near I(2) persistent swings in asset prices, and that this would likely imply strong feedback effects between prices, dividends and earnings. This is what the data show.

17.6.3   Financial Markets and Macroeconomic Modeling

Speculative behavior in the foreign exchange market (through its impact on the real exchange rate, the real interest rate and the term spread) is bound to have strong implications for macroeconomic modelling and policy. This is also the story macroeconomic data tell. The non-stationarity of the term spread and the real interest rate (and indirectly the real exchange rate) is likely to have a strong impact on monetary policy and its transmission mechanism. Empirical results in Juselius (1992, 1996, 1998a, 1998b, 1999, 2001, 2004, 2006), Juselius and Toro (2005) and Juselius and Johansen (2006) demonstrate that standard transmission mechanisms for how changes in monetary instruments affect the system are seriously impaired by the interference of financial market behavior.

The non-stationarity of the real exchange rate and the real interest rate have been shown to have a strong impact on domestic wage and price setting[14] with important implications for fiscal policy. For example, Juselius (2006, 2011b) and Juselius and Ordóñez (2009) provide strong empirical evidence. Further evidence supporting the importance of these findings for policy can be found in Bjørnstad and Nymoen (2008), Fanelli (2008) and M. Juselius (2008), showing essentially no empirical evidence in support of the new Keynesian Phillips curve model favored by central banks all over the world.

The effect of stock prices on the real economy is also potentially large through their impact on earnings. The latter is likely to have a strong impact on financial and housing wealth and, thus, on consumption and investment behavior. The results in Tabor (2009) suggest that this may explain why the domestic variables of the Ireland model were not able to explain the data variation over the more recent period.

Thus, the stories that data tell when allowed to speak freely seem to reject REH-based models, to be consistent with an IKE based framework, and to suggest significant interaction between the financial and real sectors of the economy. I am convinced that a Sherlock Holmesian type of approach has the ability to inspire new economic thinking in empirically relevant directions.

17.7   CAN WE TRUST THE STORIES DATA TELL?

Claiming that one can learn anything from data analysis is often considered controversial in economics. Many economists would argue that unless the empirical model is constrained by theory from the outset, one would not be able to make sense of the results: without the mathematical logic of the theory model, one opens up possibilities of quackery. For example, as some of the CVAR results reported in Juselius and Franchi (2007) were less straightforward to interpret, one might ask, as one of the referees did, whether at the end of the day DSGE modeling with interpretable theory is to be preferred to VAR modeling without theory. No doubt many economists would be sympathetic to such a view, and sometimes for good reasons: there is an abundance of bad VAR applications in the literature. These give the impression of having been applied mechanically (pressing the VAR button) rather than asking sharp and precise questions about the economy. Ireland's VAR(1) process was just an add-on to the RBC model without any attempt to use it as a source of valuable data information.

Such VAR modeling has nothing to do with a maximum-likelihood-based VAR analysis. To claim that the statistical analysis is based on full information maximum likelihood requires that the model satisfactorily describes all aspects of the data. This means that the researcher must carefully check for many things: have there been shifts in mean growth rates or in equilibrium means? Are the effects of interventions, reforms, and changing policy properly modelled? Is the sample period defining a constant parameter regime? Is the information set correctly chosen? and so on. The accuracy of the results depends on all this being correct in the model. To make the necessary analysis to develop a satisfactory model is a time-consuming and tedious process that depends upon the researcher's judgment and expertise and has nothing to do with pressing the VAR button. But without such checking, the results can be (and often are) close to useless and if they are taken seriously by policymakers, even worse than worthless.

It is, therefore, important to emphasize that a statistically adequate VAR analysis has to obey equally strict scientific rules as an analysis of a mathematical model in economics. In principle there is no arbitrariness in such empirical analyses, as Spanos (2009) points out. However, objectivity can only be achieved provided data are not constrained from the outset in theoretically prespecified directions as it would otherwise be impossible to know which results are due to the assumptions made and which are the empirical facts. The only way the methodology works properly is by allowing the data to speak as freely as possible about empirical regularities. This is, of course, not the same as letting the data speak without any theory, which generally would not produce anything useful.

Another frequent argument is that the quality of economic data is too low. I agree that economic time series data seldom correspond exactly to the theoretical concepts of a theory model. For example, the representative agent's income, consumption and hours worked in Ireland's model has little in common with the various measurements of aggregate income, private consumption and total hours worked that are used in his empirical analysis. While, admittedly, macro data are contaminated with measurement errors, such errors may not be of great concern for the more important long-run analysis, unless they are systematic and cumulate to non-stationarity. Whatever the case, theoretically correct measurements do not exist and, hence, cannot be used by politicians and decision makers to react on.

17.8   THE ROLE OF EVIDENCE AND THEORY IN MACROECONOMICS: A CONCLUDING DISCUSSION

For more than a decade, the DSGE modelling has been the preferred way of doing empirical macroeconomics. But although the models have become a lot more sophisticated over time, they were not able to warn policymakers about the approaching crisis in 2007, the worst in almost a century.

This failure revealed almost painfully that extant economic models are seriously lacking when it comes to understand out-of-equilibrium behavior. As the Dahlem report (Colander et al., 2009) expressed it: 'When the crisis struck policy makers were essentially left to grope in the dark without much guidance for how to ride out the crises. They could only hope that their costly policy measure would have the intended effect.'

Why did the models perform so badly, exactly when reliable advice was most urgently needed? I have argued that one reason these models fail to describe macroeconomic behavior adequately is that they are generally based on information rich agents with 'rational expectations' and, therefore, are consistent with fast adjustment back towards equilibrium when pushed away by exogenous shocks. One could say that if the REH hypothesis was a good description of how economic agents behave, data would not have exhibited the persistent behavior away from long-run steady states that preceded the recent crisis. The fact that the empirical analysis of Ireland's model at a first glance seemed impressive, despite its strong empirical rejection, is therefore a warning against drawing conclusions from models based on many untested assumptions. Strong economic priors imposed on the data without testing may say more about the beliefs of the researcher than the state of the economic reality. The ultimate question is, therefore, whether we can afford to let economic policy be guided by beliefs which are not strongly backed up by empirical evidence.

But can we do better? The fact that economic data are often well described by CVAR models may suggest that empirically relevant economic models need to be formulated as dynamic adjustment models in growth rates and equilibrium errors, the so-called equilibrium correction models. See, for example, Hendry (1987, 1995) and Juselius (2006). Such models are inherently consistent with the idea that unanticipated shocks cumulate over time to generate stochastic trends in the variables. However, the fact that basic long-run relationships such as purchasing power parity, real interest rates, uncovered interest rate parity, the term spread, the consumption–income ratio, the capital–income ratio, the labour–income ratio, the natural rate of the Phillips curve, and so on often exhibit a pronounced persistence untenable with stationarity, suggests that empirically relevant models need to be formulated in acceleration rates, medium-run relations between growth rates, and dynamic rather than static long-run relations. In the econometrics jargon it means that we should formulate models for an I(2) rather than an I(1) world.

The economic rationale for choosing such models is that an imbalance (a disequilibrium error) in one sector of the economy cannot develop into a persistent movement unless compensated by something else. For example, the persistent out-of-equilibrium behavior of the US-German real exchange rate was possible because of a compensating movement in the relative real interest rates. On the other hand, a persistent movement in the real interest rate is likely to generate persistent movements elsewhere, for example in the unemployment rate. Therefore, to understand the pronounced persistence of economic time-series we need to unwind the mechanisms that have generated it. By its ability to uncover empirically stable combinations of individually persistent (equilibrium) errors, cointegration analysis is potentially a very efficient procedure in this respect. It suggests where to start digging.

But the persistence of static equilibrium errors have implications for economic modeling that takes us even further. In such disequilibrium situations, the mathematical logic of the CVAR model tells us that the adjustment back towards long-run sustainable equilibrium states will entail growth rates that move in a similarly persistent manner (Kongsted, 2005; Juselius, 2006). The implication is that we need to move from a framework of static to dynamic equilibrium relationships, in particular, when the horizon of the analysis is the medium run of say five or six years. The fact that we find static equilibrium errors to be unstable (non-stationary) does not preclude the existence of stable relationships; it just moves the discussion of stability to a higher level. In this sense, a standard static long-run relation can be seen as a special case of a more general dynamic equilibrium relation.

Can a DSGE model be empirically assessed? Many of these models would also allow for permanent shocks that cumulate to stochastic trends, for example shocks to technology and preferences. But, in this case, the non-stationarity of the data is incorporated in the model by assuming an exogenously given stochastic trend. A crucial difference between the two approaches is that the number of stochastic trends is estimated in the CVAR model, not assumed, and the presumption that one of them is a technology trend would be formulated as a testable restriction on the parameters of the CVAR model rather than imposed from the outset. But, because the general structure of a DSGE and a CVAR model is similar, the former can in principle be formulated as a submodel within the CVAR and is, therefore, testable as illustrated for the DSGE model in Ireland (2004a). That most assumptions underlying the model were rejected and the conclusions reversed seem to illustrate Tony Lawson's claim that 'models that get "the right results" and "address interesting questions" may nevertheless turn out to be misleading and empirically irrelevant' (Lawson, 2009).

I have argued here that one reason the DSGE models did so poorly in forecasting the financial and economic crisis of 2007–09 was because they ignored the importance of interactions between the financial and the real sectors of the economy. Would CVAR modeling have done better? The crisis was a consequence of equilibrium errors that were allowed to cumulate over a fairly long period without a proper warning system which, at an early stage, would have signaled that the system was moving seriously out of equilibrium. Already many years before the bubble burst, CVAR analyses showed that the relative house–consumption price relationship exhibited very pronounced non-stationary behavior and that this was (primarily) facilitated by increasing financial wealth. Prior to the bursting of the bubble, the house–consumption price ratio increased almost exponentially, signaling that house prices were moving far away from their sustainable level as given by the very low levels of Consumer Prices Index (CPI) inflation and interest rates. This would have been absolutely the last moment for the authorities to react to prevent the subsequent disaster. But the fact that the extraordinarily high level of house prices was sustainable only by a record high credit expansion, and extraordinarily low levels of nominal interest rates and inflation rates, should have been a reason for concern much earlier.

My point here is that in order to prevent the next crisis, we need a proper understanding of the disequilibrium forces at the macro level. Markets are infinitely inventive and it is almost impossible to foresee what could generate the next crisis. Unless we build up a good macroeconomic understanding and a reliable signaling system, it is very likely that the next crisis will come as an equally big surprise. One way of avoiding this happening is to learn from the data in a systematic and structured way using available theories and hypotheses, but at the same time being open to signals in data suggesting that there are mechanisms we do not yet understand. By embedding the theory model in a broader empirical framework, the empirical analysis should be able to point to possible pitfalls in macroeconomic reasoning, and at the same time to generate new hypotheses for how to modify too narrowly specified theoretical models. The clues to present and previous crises are hidden in the historical data and we need to take them much more seriously than is usually done.

NOTES

1. Useful comments by Michael Goldberg, Søren Johansen and Mikael Juselius are gratefully acknowledged.
2. Because the technology shock is the only source of randomness in the model, the model is stochastically singular.
3. The simulation in Johansen (2006) shows that with a root of 0.9987, at least 5000 observations are needed to get close to the correct size of a test on the steady-state value.
4. These were not reported in Ireland, but derived from his model.

5. Gross capital formation is used as a measure of capital instead of the Ireland variable which was generated to fit the RBC hypothesis.
6. Transitory shocks which do not cumulate are called I(0), permanent shocks which cumulate once are called I(1), and permanent shocks that cumulate twice are called I(2).
7. A similar transformation of the theoretical model into growth rates and cointegration is suggested in Ireland (2004b).
8. The second period contained a lot more persistence, and as will be illustrated below it is questionable whether there is any cointegration.
9. To cite an anonymous discussant to Spanos (2009): 'I don't think DSGE modelers don't care about the empirical support of their theories; they just have a different metric to assess the usefulness of their theories. If the standard metric rejects the model, just choose a different metric.'
10. This points to the importance of not just assuming that the model contains all basic relevant variables, but checking whether this is the case, for example by using automatic search procedures such as autometrics (Hendry and Krolzig, 2005).
11. The fact that the literature abounds with econometric tests suggesting that the unit root hypothesis can be rejected does not make the pronounced persistence in the data disappear. It may, however, say something about the way econometrics is used to illustrate prior beliefs, rather than as a tool for discovery.
12. These are known as the PPP puzzle, the long swings puzzle and the nominal exchange rate disconnect puzzle (Rogoff, 1996).
13. Shiller (2000), in a critique of EMH, concluded that financial markets are essentially driven by irrational exuberance. But under this hypothesis, we would essentially have to give up understanding financial market behavior and how to best cope with it.
14. This provides evidence for some important hypotheses in Phelps (1994).

REFERENCES

Andersen, T.W. (1991), 'Tryggve Haavelmo and Simultaneous Equation Models', *Scandinavian Journal of Statistics*, 18, 1–19.
Backhouse, R.E. and A. Salanti (2000a), 'Macroeconomics and the Real World: Volume 1: Econometric Techniques and Macroeconomics', Oxford: Oxford University Press.
Backhouse, R.E. and A. Salanti (2000b), 'Macroeconomics and the Real World: Volume 2: Keynesian Economics, Unemployment, and Policy', Oxford: Oxford University Press.
Benigno, G. (2004), 'Real Exchange Rate Persistence and Monetary Policy Rules', *Journal of Monetary Economics*, **51**, 473–502.
Bjørnstad, R. and R. Nymoen (2008), 'The New Keynesian Phillips Curve Tested on OECD Panel Data', *Economics: The Open-Access, Open-Assessment E-Journal*, **2**(23), http://www.economics-ejournal.org/economics/journalarticles/2008-23.
Campbell, J.Y. and R. Shiller (1987), 'Cointegration and Tests of Present Valus models', *Journal of Political Economy*, **95**(5), 1062–1089.
Clements, M.P. and D.F. Hendry (1999), *Forecasting Non-Stationary Time Series*, Cambridge, MA: MIT Press.
Clements, M.P. and D.F. Hendry (2008), 'Economic Forecasting in a Changing World', *Capitalism and Society*, **3**, 1–18.
Cochrane, J. (2009), 'How Did Paul Krugman Get It So Wrong?', http://modeledbehavior.com/2009/09/11/john-cochrane-responds-to-paul-krugman-full-text/.
Colander, D. (ed.) (1996), *Beyond Microfoundations: Post Walrasian Macroeconomics*, Cambridge: Cambridge University Press.
Colander, D. (ed.) (2000), *The Complexity Vision and the Teaching of Economics*, Cambridge: Cambridge University Press.

Colander, D. (2001), *The Lost Art of Economics. Essays on Economics and the Economics Profession*, Cheltenham, UK and Northampton, MA, USA: Edward Elgar.

Colander, D. (ed.) (2006), *Post Walrasian Macroeconomics: Beyond the Dynamic Stochastic General Equilibrium Model*, Cambridge: Cambridge University Press.

Colander, D., M. Goldberg, A. Haas, K. Juselius, A. Kirman, T. Lux and B. Sloth (2009), 'The Financial Crisis and the Systemic Failure of the Economics Profession', *Critical Review*, **21**(3), 249–267.

Colander, D., P. Howitt, A. Kirman, A. Leijonhufvud and P. Mehrling (2008), 'Beyond DSGE Models: Toward an Empirically Based Macroeconomics', *American Economic Review*, **98**, 2.

Cooley, T.F. and S.F. Leroy (1985), 'Atheoretical Macroeconometrics: A Critique', *Journal of Monetary Economics*, **16**(3), 283–308.

Dornbusch, R. (1976), 'Expectations and Exchange Rate Dynamics', *Journal of Political Economy*, **84**(7), 1161–1174.

Dornbusch, R. and J.A. Frankel (1995), 'The Flexible Exchange Rate System: Experience and Alternatives', in S. Borner (ed.), *International Finance and Trade*, London: Macmillan, reprinted in J.A. Frankel (ed.), *On Exchange Rates*, Cambridge, MA: MIT Press.

Engel, C. and K. West (2006), 'Taylor Rules and the Deutschemark–Dollar Real Exchange Rate', *Journal of Money, Credit and Banking*, **38**, 1175–1194.

Engel, R.F. and C.W.J. Granger (1987), 'Cointegration and Error Correction: Representation, Estimation, and Testing', *Econometrica*, **55**(2), 251–276.

Fanelli, L. (2008), 'Evaluating the New Keynesian Phillips Curve under VAR-based Learning', *Economics: The Open-Access, Open-Assessment E-Journal*, **2**(33), http://www.economics-ejournal.org/economics/journalarticles/2008-33.

Frydman, R. and M. Goldberg (2007), *Imperfect Knowledge Economics: Exchange rates and Risk*, Princeton, NJ: Princeton University Press.

Frydman, R. and M. Goldberg (2008), 'Macroeconomic Theory for a World of Imperfect Knowledge', *Capitalism and Society*, **3**(1), http://bepress.com/cas/vol3/iss3/art1.

Frydman, R. and M. Goldberg (2009), 'Financial Markets and the State: Price Swings, Risk, and the Scope of Regulation', *Capitalism and Society*, **4**(2), http://bepress.com/cas/vol4/iss2/art2.

Frydman, R. and M. Goldberg (2011), *Beyond Mechanical Markets: Risk and the Role of Asset Price Swings*, Princeton, NJ: Princeton University Press.

Frydman, R., M. Goldberg, K. Juselius, and S. Johansen (2008), 'Imperfect Knowledge and a Resolution of the Purchasing Power Parity Puzzle: Empirical Evidence', Working Paper 08-31, University of Copenhagen.

Galí, J. and T. Monacelli (2005), 'Monetary Policy and Exchange Rate Volatility in a Small Open Economy', *Review of Economic Studies*, **72**, 707–734.

Giese, J.V. (2008), 'Level, Slope, Curvature: Characterising the Yield Curve in a Cointegrated VAR Model', *Economics: The Open-Access, Open-Assessment E-Journal*, **2**(28), http://www.economics-ejournal.org/economics/journalarticles/2008-28.

Gilbert, C.L. (1986), 'Professor Hendry's Econometric Methodology', *Oxford Bulletin of Economics and Statistics*, **48**, 283–307.

Haavelmo, T. (1944), 'The Probability Approach to Econometrics', *Econometrica*, **12**(Supplement), 1–118.

Hendry, D.F. (1987), 'Econometric Methodology: A Personal Perspective', in T.F. Bewley (ed.), *Advances in Econometrics*, Cambridge, MA: Cambridge University Press, Chapter 10.

Hendry, D.F. (1995), *Dynamic Econometrics*, Oxford: Oxford University Press.

Hendry, D.F. (2009), 'The Methodology of Empirical Econometric Modeling: Applied Econometrics Through the Looking-Glass', in T.C. Mills and K. Patterson (eds), *Palgrave Handbook of Econometrics, Vol. 2*, London: Macmillan, pp. 3–67.

Hendry, D.F. and K. Juselius (1999), 'Explaining Cointegration Analysis. Part 1', *Energy Journal*, **21**(1), 1–42.

Hendry, D.F. and K. Juselius (2000), 'Explaining Cointegration Analysis. Part 2', *Energy Journal*, **22**(1), 1–52.

Hendry, D.F. and H-M. Krolzig (2005), 'The Properties of Automatic Gets Modelling', *Economic Journal*, **115**, C32–C61.

Hendry, D.F. and G.E. Mizon (1993), 'Evaluating Econometric Models by Encompassing the VAR', in P.C. Phillips (ed.), *Models, Methods and Applications of Econometrics*, Oxford: Blackwell, pp. 272–300.

Hendry, D.F. and G.E. Mizon (2011), 'What Needs Rethinking in Macroeconomics', *Global Policy*, **2**(2), 176–183.

Hendry, D.F., A. Spanos and N.R. Ericsson (1989), 'The Contributions to Econometrics in Trygve Haavelmo's "The Probability Approach in Econometrics"', *Socialøkonomen*, **43**(11), 12–17.

Hoover, K. (2006), 'The Past as Future: The Marshallian Approach to Post Walrasian Econometrics', in D. Colander (ed.), *Post Walrasian Macroeconomics: Beyond the Dynamic Stochastic General Equilibrium Model*, Cambridge: Cambridge University Press, pp. 239–257.

Hoover, K., S. Johansen and K. Juselius (2008), 'Allowing the Data to Speak Freely: The Macroeconometrics of the Cointegrated VAR', *American Economic Review*, **98**, pp. 251–255.

Ireland, P.N. (2004a), 'A Method for Taking Models to the Data', *Journal of Economic Dynamics and Control*, **28**(6), 1205–1226.

Ireland, P.N. (2004b), 'Technology Shocks in the New Keynesian Model', *Review of Economics and Statistics*, **84**(4), 923–936.

Johansen, S. (1988). 'Statistical Analysis of Cointegration Vectors', *Journal of Economic Dynamics and Control*, **12**(213), 231–254.

Johansen, S. (1995), *Likelihood-Based Inference in Cointegrated Vector Autoregressive Models*, Oxford: Oxford University Press.

Johansen, S. (2006), 'Confronting the Economic Model with the Data', in D. Colander (ed.), *Walrasian Macroeconomics: Beyond the Dynamic Stochastic General Equilibrium Model*, Cambridge: Cambridge University Press, pp. 287–300.

Johansen, S. and K. Juselius (1992), 'Testing Structural Hypotheses in a Multivariate Cointegration Analysis of the PPP and the UIP for UK', *Journal of Econometrics*, **53**, 211–244.

Johansen, S., K. Juselius, R. Frydman and M. Goldberg (2010), 'Testing Hypotheses in an I(2) Model With Piecewise Linear Trends. An Analysis of the Persistent Long Swings in the Dmk/$ Rate', *Journal of Econometrics*, **158**, 117–129.

Juselius, K. (1992), 'Domestic and Foreign Effects on Prices in an Open Economy. The Case of Denmark', *Journal of Economic Policy Modelling*, **14**, 401–428; reprinted (1995) in Ericsson and J.S. Irons (eds), *Testing Exogeneity*, Advanced Texts in Econometrics, Oxford: Oxford University Press, pp. 161–190.

Juselius, K. (1995), 'Do Purchasing Power Parity and Uncovered Interest Rate Parity Hold in the Long Run? An Example of Likelihood Inference in a Multivariate Time Series Model', *Journal of Econometrics*, **69**(1), 211–240.

Juselius, K. (1996), 'An Empirical Analysis of the Changing role of German Bundesbank after 1983', *Oxford Bulletin of Economics and Statistics*, **58**, 791–817.

Juselius, K. (1998a), 'Changing Monetary Transmission Mechanisms Within the EU', *Empirical Economics*, **23**, 455–481.

Juselius, K. (1998b) 'A Structured VAR under Changing Monetary Policy', *Journal of Business and Economics Statistics*, **6**, 400–412.

Juselius, K. (1999), 'Models and Relations in Economics and Econometrics', *Journal of Economic Methodology*, **6**(2), 259–290.

Juselius, K. (2001) 'European Integration and Monetary Transmission Mechanisms: The Case of Italy', *Journal of Applied Econometrics*, **16**, 341–358.

Juselius, K. (2004), 'Inflation, Money Growth, and I(2) Analysis', in A. Welfe (ed.) *Contributions to Economic Analysis. New Directions in Macromodelling: Essays in Honor of J. Michael Finer*, Bingley: Emerald, pp. 69–106.

Juselius, K. (2006), *The Cointegrated VAR Model: Methodology and Applications*, Oxford: Oxford University Press.

Juselius, K. (2009a), 'Special Issue on Using Econometrics for Assessing Economic Models – An Introduction', *Economics: The Open-Access, Open-Assessment E-Journal*, 3(2009–28).

Juselius, K. (2009b), 'The Long Swings Puzzle. What the Data Tell When Allowed to Speak Freely', in T.C. Mills and K. Patterson (eds), *The New Palgrave Handbook of Econometrics, Vol. 2*, London: Macmillan, pp. 349–384.

Juselius, K. (2010), 'Testing Exchange Rate Models Based on Rational Expectations versus Imperfect Knowledge Economics: A Scenario Analysis', Working Paper, Economics Department, University of Copenhagen.

Juselius, K. (2011a), 'Time to Reject the Privileging of Economic Theory over Empirical Evidence? A Reply to Lawson', *Cambridge Journal of Economics*, 35(2), 423–436.

Juselius, K. (2011b), 'Imperfect Knowledge, Asset Price Swings and Structural Slumps: A Cointegrated VAR Analysis of Their Interdependence', Department of Economics, University of Copenhagen, Discussion papers 10-31; forthcoming in Phelps, E. and Frydman, R. (eds), *Microfoundations for Macroeconomic Theory*, Princeton, NJ: Princeton University Press.

Juselius, K. and M. Franchi (2007), 'Taking a DSGE Model to the Data Meaningfully', *Economics-The Open-Access, Open-Assessment E-Journal*, 2007-4, http://www.economics-ejournal.org/economics/journalarticles/3007-4.

Juselius, K. and Johansen, S. (2006), 'Extracting Information from the Data: A European View on Empirical Macro', in D. Colander (ed.), *Post Walrasian Macroeconomics: Beyond the Dynamic Stochastic General Equilibrium Model*, Cambridge: Cambridge University Press, pp. 301–334.

Juselius, K. and R. MacDonald (2004), 'The International Parities Between USA and Japan', *Japan and the World Economy*, 16, 17–34.

Juselius, K. and R. MacDonald (2007), 'International Parity Relationships Between Germany and the United States: A Joint Modelling Approach', in A. Morales-Zumaquero (ed.), *International Macroeconomics: Recent Developments*, New York: Nova Science Publishers, pp. 79–104.

Juselius, K. and J. Ordóñez (2009), 'Balassa-Samuelson and Wage, Price and Unemployment Dynamics in the Spanish Transition to EMU Membership', *Economics: The Open-Access, Open-Assessment E-Journal*, 3(4), http:/www.economics-ejournal.org/economics/journalarticles/2009-4.

Juselius, K. and J. Toro (2005), 'The Effect of Joining the EMS. Monetary Transmission Mechanisms in Spain', *Journal of International Money and Finance*, 24, 509–531.

Juselius, M. (2008), 'Testing the New Keynesian Model on US and Euro Area Data', *Economics: The Open-Access, Open-Assessment E-Journal*, 2(24), http://www.economics-ejournal.org/economics/journalarticles/2008-24.

Katlesky, A. (2009), 'Goodbye, Homo Economicus', *Prospect Magazine*, 157, 26 April.

Keynes, J.M. (1937), 'General Theory of Employment', *Quarterly Journal of Economics*, 51(2), 209–223.

Kongsted, H.C. (2005), 'Testing the Nominal-to-Real Transformation', *Journal of Econometrics*, 124, 205–225.

Krugman, P. (2009), 'How Did Economists Get It So Wrong?', column in *New York Times*, 6 September, http://www.nytimes.com/2009/09/06/magazine/06Economic-t.html?_r=4.

Lawson, T. (2009), 'The Current Economic Crisis: Its Nature and the Course of Academic Economics', *Cambridge Journal of Economics*, 33, 759–777.

Leijonhufvud, A (2009), 'Out of the Corridor: Keynes and the Crisis', *Cambridge Journal of Economics*, 33(4), 741–757.

Møller, N.F. (2008), 'Bridging Economic Theory Models and the Cointegrated Vector Autoregressive Model', *Economics: The Open-Access, Open-Assessment E-Journal*, 2(36), http://www.economics-ejournal.org/economics/journalarticles/2008-36.

Pagan, A.R. (1987), 'Three Econometric Methodologies: A Critical Appraisal', *Journal of Economic Surveys*, 1, 3–24.

Phelps, E. (1994), *Structural Slumps*, Princeton, NJ: Princeton University Press.
Rogoff, K. (1996), 'The Purchasing Power Parity Puzzle', *Journal of Economic Literature*, **34**, 647–668.
Shiller, R.J. (2000), *Irrational Exuberance*, New York: Broadway Books.
Soros, G. (1987), *The Alchemy of Finance*, New York: John Wiley & Sons.
Spanos, A. (1995), 'On Theory Testing in Econometrics: Modeling with Nonexperimental Data', *Journal of Econometrics*, **67**, 189–226.
Spanos, A. (2006), 'Econometrics in Retrospect and Prospect', in T.C. Mills and K. Patterson (eds), *Palgrave Handbook of Econometrics*, Vol. 1, London: Macmillan, pp. 3–58.
Spanos, A. (2009), 'The Pre-Eminence of Theory versus the European CVAR Perspective in Macroeconometric Modeling', *Economics: The Open-Access, Open-Assessment E-Journal*, **3**(10), http://www.economics-ejournal.org/economics/journalarticles/2009-10.
Summers, L. (1991), 'The Scientific Illusion in Empirical Macroeconomics', *Scandinavian Journal of Economics*, **93**, 129–148.
Tabor, N.M. (2009), 'The Effect of Financial Markets on US Consumption: A Cointegrated VAR Approach. 1954–2008', Masters thesis, Department of Economics, University of Copenhagen.
Yule, U. (1926), 'Why Do We Sometimes Get Nonsense-Correlations Between Time Series? A Study in Sampling and the Nature of Time Series', *Journal of the Royal Statistical Society*, **89**, 1–63.

18 Methodological issues in Keynesian macroeconomics
Roger E. Backhouse and Bradley W. Bateman

18.1   INTRODUCTION

The crisis of 2007–8 brought the name of John Maynard Keynes back into public discourse. Faced with a real prospect of a slide into a depression comparable with the 1930s, Keynesian ideas helped to provide an explanation of what had happened, a reason for taking action to expand demand, and a way to legitimate the budget deficits that arose as a result of propping up a banking system that was on the brink of collapse. Clearly, because of his role as Chairman of the Federal Reserve System (the Fed) from 1987 to 2006, in fostering the ideology that led up to the crisis, the paradigmatic statement of this position will be Alan Greenspan's confession, testifying before a House of Representatives Committee on 23 October 2008, that he had found a flaw in his ideology: that his belief that free competitive markets were the best way to organize economies could not be sustained. However, a fuller statement of such a view can be found in the writing of another economist whose view was changed as a result of the crisis, Richard Posner:

> Some conservatives believe that the depression is the result of unwise government policies. I believe it is a market failure. The government's myopia, passivity, and blunders played a critical role in *allowing* the recession to balloon into a depression . . . but without any government regulation we would still, in all likelihood, be in a depression. We are learning from it that we need a more active and intelligent government to keep our model of a capitalist economy from running off the rails. The movement to deregulate went too far by exaggerating the resilience – the self-healing powers – of laissez-faire capitalism. (Posner, 2009)

Posner went on to use Keynesian ideas to justify a program of macroeconomic intervention to prevent the crisis from developing into a major depression.

But what of economic theory? After all, Keynes's *General Theory* (1937) offered not a revolution in policy but a revolution in economic theory. New theories take time to develop, so it would be unreasonable to expect to see new theories to have developed since the onset of the recent crisis, but it is not clear whether economists have been convinced that new theories are needed. There are prominent advocates of a return to Keynes, some of whom have gone so far as to claim that the crisis demonstrates the bankruptcy of the prevailing approach to macroeconomic theory. Paul Krugman (2009) has called upon economists to 're-embrace Keynes', arguing that current macroeconomic models have completely failed to take account of the possibility of speculative bubbles that may collapse. Willem Buiter has written of, 'The unfortunate uselessness of most "state of the art" academic monetary economics', contending that the model that has dominated the field for the past two decades is inherently flawed (Buiter, 2009).

If the crisis has revealed the inadequacy of much macroeconomic theory, what is the way forward? One would be to decide that the problem lies solely with the models that have been pursued and that there is no need for methodological change. One could, for example, start with the approach represented by Michael Woodford's *Interest and Prices* (2003), widely taken as the definitive statement of the status quo in macroeconomics before the crisis, modifying it to take account of banking and the financial sector. Such an approach is presumably feasible, given that there exists a substantial literature on bubbles. However, given that the core of the dominant approach is the dynamic stochastic general equilibrium (DSGE) model, based on assumption of a representative agent, a world in which it is hard to see a real role for money, let alone problems that arise from the incompatibility of different agents' plans, it is not clear whether such an approach is feasible without changing, or at least qualifying, the underlying methodology. Grafting on to the DSGE model such features of the world as are necessary to make sense of financial crisis might well be taken to imply a new method.

18.2   NEW KEYNESIAN METHODOLOGY

This strategy, of starting with the accepted model and 'bolting on' features that make it compatible with reality, is the one pursued by new Keynesian macroeconomists when confronted with the new classical macroeconomics. In the 1970s, Robert Lucas (1972), Robert Barro (1974) and the advocates of what came to be called the new classical macroeconomics, took to its limit the ideas of individually rational behaviour and perfect competition. This led inexorably to the assumptions of rational expectations (why would agents not take account of information that would enable them to make better decisions?) and continuous market clearing (if markets were not in equilibrium, agents could not be maximizing their utility), leading to anti-Keynesian conclusions, of which Lucas's (1976) policy invariance result was the most widely cited (see Introduction to Hoover, 1999). In the early 1980s, after empirical work had cast doubt on Lucas's monetary shocks theory of the business cycle, the new classical macroeconomics was largely superseded by 'real business cycle' theory (see, for example, Kydland and Prescott, 1982), which differed primarily in assuming that shocks were real, not monetary, but which shared the same basic approach. In particular, unlike either macroeconomists or general equilibrium theorists of the 1950s and 1960s, these two approaches to macroeconomics developed rigorous micro-foundations through adopting the device of the representative agent, thereby eliminating problems that might arise only in worlds where agents were heterogeneous.

This approach represented a much deeper challenge to Keynesianism than the 'monetarism' that Milton Friedman had been advocating since the mid-1950s. Monetarism, with its focus on targeting the growth rate of the money supply and its critique of discretionary stabilization policy, had challenged Keynesian policies. It also challenged the way in which econometric models were constructed and used to formulate policy. But though they might differ over the certain parameter values, such as the interest elasticity of the demand for money, or over the stability of key parameters, most monetarists worked within a theoretical framework that was shared with Keynesians. Friedman (1970), when pushed to write down his theoretical framework, used the IS-LM model, which had long served as the analytical foundation of Keynesianism (see Gordon, 1974 for discussion of this article). Friedman himself had much in common with Keynes (see Backhouse and Bateman, 2012).

Faced with the much more radical theoretical challenge posed by the new classical macroeconomics and real business cycle theory, the Keynesians had two choices. One was the approach best represented by Edmond Malinvaud (1977) who concluded from the experience of 'stagflation' that markets could not possibly be working properly: that the perfect competition model had to be abandoned in favor of a model of markets that were out of equilibrium. This was an approach that fitted well with the way Keynesian theory had been developing over the previous decade, which had seen the creation of models of systematic market failure – models of 'general disequilibrium' (for example Solow and Stiglitz, 1968; Barro and Grossman, 1971). Such an approach had the merit not only of reconciling models with experience but it also addressed basic conceptual problems with the theory of general competitive equilibrium (Arrow, 1959). However, the alternative choice to these models of general disequilibrium, and the one out of which the new Keynesian economics emerged, was to accept what might be termed the new classical methodology (that is, theorizing based on rational, optimizing agents) but to modify the theory in ways that would generate Keynesian phenomena. Here there was a significant divergence between Europe and the United States.

In the United States, new classical ideas were widely accepted. Lucas and Sargent (1978) felt sufficiently confident to claim that it was by then a simple matter of fact that Keynesian theory was fundamentally flawed. Two years later Lucas summed up the position of Keynesian economics by claiming:

> One cannot find good, under-forty economists who identify themselves or their work as 'Keynesian'. Indeed, people even take offense if referred to as 'Keynesian'. At research seminars, people don't take Keynesian theorizing seriously any more; the audience starts to whisper and giggle at one another. (Quoted in Dixon, 1992, p. 1273)

This may have involved significant hyperbole (at least outside Chicago and Rochester) but it is indicative of a rapid and profound change in attitudes within the profession towards not only the content of macroeconomics but the methods by which macroeconomic research should be undertaken.

American new Keynesians accepted much of this. Attempting to define the new Keynesian macroeconomics at the end of the 1980s, Gregory Mankiw and David Romer (1991, p. 1) conceded that the new classical macroeconomists were right to argue that Keynesian economics was flawed and that macroeconomics had to be built on firm microeconomic foundations. However, rather than accept that markets cleared continuously, with all the policy conclusions that followed, they found reasons why markets might behave differently. American new Keynesians developed theories about price and wage stickiness: menu costs, long-term labor contracts, implicit contracts, staggered setting of wages and efficiency wages. They also developed theories of credit market imperfections and theories of monopoly, extending to both labor markets (union power) and product markets. However, beneath this entire literature was the assumption that these factors affected only the short-run behavior of the economy: it did not challenge the new classical claim that in the long run the Phillips curve must be vertical and classical neutrality results would apply. New Keynesian theorists were just explaining why the short-run Phillips curve might be flat, causing adjustment to shocks to be protracted and involving potentially high costs in terms of unemployment and lost output.

In Europe, on the other hand, skepticism about the new classical macroeconomics was more pervasive. Reasons are no doubt complex, but a significant factor must have been the different unemployment experience of Europe during the 1980s – after the second oil shock of 1979–80, unemployment remained high several years after US unemployment had declined, making it far less obvious that it should be modeled as being a short-run phenomenon. Some Europeans turned to supply-side explanations, explaining persistent high unemployment in terms of more generous social security systems and labor market rigidities: the term 'Eurosclerosis' was coined. But others saw European unemployment as casting doubt on market-clearing models. Theories of 'hysteresis' in which high unemployment raised the equilibrium rate of unemployment were developed. Imperfect competition models were taken far more seriously than in the United States, involving elements of monopoly in product as well as labor markets. For example, Oliver Hart proposed 'A Model of Imperfect Competition with Keynesian Features' (1982). Such models showed how economies could get stuck in situations of high unemployment. Others explored how the unemployment rate at which inflation would be stable might be determined within the system (see, for example, Jackman et al., 1991). Though they accepted the framework of a long-term unemployment rate, around which there would be fluctuations determined by aggregate demand, they did not take this long-term rate as being independent of the short-term behavior of the system, but as a property of the same model.

For Joseph Stiglitz, one of the American new Keynesian theorists of the 1970s, it was experience of the East Asian financial crisis, while in his role as head of the World Bank, that brought home the fact that the world did not work according to the paradigm of perfectly competitive markets. He argued that, given the possibility of bankruptcy, which became very real indeed in the 1997 East Asian crisis, the policies of credit restriction being advocated by the International Monetary Fund (IMF) were the reverse of what was needed: they increased the risk of bankruptcy and the need for liquidity, deepening the crisis. The financial crisis and the accompanying exchange rate collapses precipitated depressions in a part of the world that had been seen by many as a model of how capitalist economies should be run (Stiglitz, 2002, 2003). For Japan, a near neighbor of Thailand and the other countries hit by the crisis, the property boom of the 1980s had already given way to a decade of stagnation, prompting Paul Krugman (1999) to talk of a return to 'depression economics'. The experience of Asia (and Latin America a few years earlier) had shown that the concerns that had motivated Keynes's *General Theory* were still real, and that Keynesian economics augmented with modern conceptual tools, such as Stiglitz's theories of asymmetric information, could be used to work out appropriate policy responses.

The crisis of 2007–08 bore out those fears, making some new Keynesian economists bolder in developing alternatives to orthodoxy. George Akerlof and Robert Shiller (2009) have argued that macroeconomics needs to take on board insights from 'behavioral economics' that support Keynesian conclusions in a way that standard models do not. Though behavioral economics echoes earlier work on consumer and investor sentiment by psychologists such as George Katona at the University of Michigan's Survey Research Center, it became much more widely noticed in the 1990s when experimental economics became much more widespread and when there developed a large literature on behavioral finance.

Writing in the immediate aftermath of the 2007–08 financial crisis, Akerlof and Shiller (2009, p. ix) took up Keynes's view that much economic activity is driven by what Keynes called 'animal spirits', the spontaneous urge to do something rather than nothing:

> People have noneconomic motives. And they are not always rational in pursuit of their economic interests. In Keynes' view these *animal spirits* are the main cause for why the economy fluctuates as it does. They are also the main cause of involuntary unemployment.

Akerlof and Shiller contended that the Keynesians who came after Keynes had good reasons to keep as close as possible to neoclassical economics, so as to make converts as quickly as possible, but the result was that animal spirits got watered down. It became harder to argue that government was needed to keep the economy stable and to find arguments to counter those who believed in free markets. Behavioral economics made it possible to develop the role of animal spirits in the economy in a way the early Keynesians had been unable to do, creating a theory that was much less vulnerable to free-market attacks (Akerlof and Shiller, 2009, p. xi). Akerlof and Shiller are arguing that the methodology of macroeconomics needs to be reconsidered.

18.3   POST-KEYNESIAN METHODOLOGY

The crisis also provided seeming vindication for the position of post-Keynesians who have long opted for a more radical rejection of orthodox economics. Hyman Minsky, an economist whose claims concerning the inherent instability of capitalism had been dismissed by most economists, though not by post-Keynesians, suddenly became fashionable (we leave aside the question of whether he should be considered a post-Keynesian, or one of a kind). Not only do post-Keynesians join new Keynesians in dismissing the denial by new classical economics that involuntary unemployment is even a meaningful concept, but they also reject as insufficiently radical the new Keynesian response of explaining Keynesian phenomena by adducing reasons why wages and prices may not adjust to bring about full employment. For example, Paul Davidson has argued that the crisis vindicates his long-argued claim that the statistical characteristics of the world render conventional modeling techniques inappropriate (Davidson, 2009). Post-Keynesians have taken up the claim that Keynes made when defending his book against the critics assembled in the *Quarterly Journal of Economics*, that:

> Actually, however, we have, as a rule, only the vaguest idea of any but the most direct consequences of our acts . . . The sense in which I am using the term [uncertainty] is that in which the prospect of a European war is uncertain, or the price of copper and the rate of interest twenty years hence, or the obsolescence of a new invention, or the position of private wealth-owners in the social system in 1970. About these matters there is no scientific basis on which to form any calculable probability whatever. We simply do not know . . . I accuse the classical economic theory of being itself one of these pretty, polite techniques which tries to deal with the present by abstracting from the fact that we know very little about the future. (Keynes, 1937, pp. 213–215)

Post-Keynesian economics is thus based on a commitment to certain beliefs about the world, notably the existence of uncertainty that cannot be reduced to probability, and that this irreducible uncertainty renders rational decision making, as understood in mainstream economics, inapplicable. However, there is little agreement on how to translate such beliefs into a workable method. Perhaps the most radical proponent of this position was G.L.S. Shackle (1973), whose views arguably amounted to nihilism as to the prospects for scientific economics. A common theme in post-Keynesian methodology has been that of pluralism, but despite the extensive talk of the need to analyze 'open systems' (see, for example, Dow, 1996; Jespersen, 2009), it is not clear how that is translated into a distinctive method for developing Keynes's insights into a usable theory.

Perhaps the clearest recent statement of the post-Keynesian position is Paul Davidson's *The Keynes Solution* (2009). For Davidson, the so-called ergodic axiom – 'the presumption that data samples from the past are equivalent to data samples from the future' (2009, p. 37) – provides a clear dividing line between Keynes, who rejected it, and post-war Keynesians such as Paul Samuelson who argued that without it economists could not enter the realms of science. Davidson therefore argues that being a Keynesian means completely rejecting mainstream Keynesianism: the new Keynesians are using techniques that make sense only in an ergodic world.

A more subtle defense of such a position is found in Robert Skidelsky's *Keynes: The Return of the Master* (2009). Drawing on his intimate knowledge of Keynes's life, Skidelsky (2003) perceptively notes that Keynes was a moral scientist, for whom science and ethics could never be completely separated. He acknowledges that there is 'no single Keynesian way out of a depression', and 'no single Keynesian system of political economy' identifying the Keynesian element in economic policy simply 'to make sure aggregate demand is sufficient to maintain a full-employment level of activity' (Skidelsky, 2009, p. 169–170). Yet Skidelsky rejects new Keynesian economics on much the same grounds as Davidson, claiming that its flaw is that though it may assume asymmetric information and though it may identify systematic market failures, it assumes that someone has perfect information (Skidelsky, 2009, p. 44–45). Neither does behavioral economics solve the problem. He sums up the failure of conventional explanations in the following words:

> The New Keynesian solution is to say that people are rational but have informational problems. Another is simply to say that human behavior is irrational, and therefore efficient markets don't exist. This is the thrust of behavioral economics. But the epistemological source of such irrationality is unexplored. The adoption of 'irrationality' as a general explanation for all 'abnormal' distributions smacks of theoretical panic. Another line of retreat is to say, with Alan Greenspan, that disasters such as the present are (unexplained) once-in-a-century events, and that most of the time markets behave in a perfectly rational way. None of these explanations gets to the heart of the matter, because they all leave out the influence of irreducable uncertainty on behavior. (Skidelsky, 2009, p. 46)

To find a way forward, Skidelsky thus turns not to economic theory, but to Keynes's discussions of the ethics of capitalism and his politics. His conclusion is that the economics profession needs reform, so as 'to protect macroeconomics from the encroachment of the methods and habits of mind of microeconomics' by separating, at least at postgraduate level, the teaching of the two subjects. Microeconomics should be taught in business schools and the role of mathematics in macroeconomics should be sharply reduced by requiring students to spend half their time on another subject, such as history, sociology or anthropology (Skidelsky, 2009, p. 189). Even though one might think that his belief in the importance of conventions and other devices for dealing with uncertainty would lead him to endorse behavioral economics, Skidelsky ends up rejecting mainstream macroeconomics as completely as Davidson and on essentially the same grounds.

Post-Keynesianism is much broader than the positions represented by Davidson and Skidelsky (for other recent interpretations see Hayes, 2006; Jespersen, 2009). The post-Keynesian literature contains, for example, extensive critiques of the notion of equilibrium as used in most macroeconomics (whether new classical or new Keynesian), of the need to analyze economies that are operating in historical time and of the need to view economic agents as social agents rather than isolated individuals. These form additional reasons for the post-Keynesian view that the new

Keynesians are too close to the new classical economics. However, the importance of uncertainty about the future, that cannot be modeled using a probability distribution, which Davidson and Skidelsky represent so clearly, remains fundamental to the difference between new Keynesian and post-Keynesian economics.

18.4   KEYNES AND KEYNESIANISM

There is no doubt that the methodology implicit in the *General Theory* (Keynes, 1973) is far removed from that of modern economics. As is well known, Keynes had great doubts about the use of mathematics in economics (O'Donnell, 1999), and he was skeptical about the modeling being undertaken by econometricians such as Tinbergen (Lawson and Pesaran, 1979). His theorizing was not based on the assumption that individuals were rational in the sense that the term is used in modern microeconomics, and whilst he did adopt the assumption of perfect competition, it is arguable that this was far from essential to his conclusions (and may even have been a reason why subsequent commentators found fault with his theory) and was probably adopted so as to concede as much as possible to his potential critics. Instead, he based his theory on behavior he had observed during a career in which he had acquired considerable experience of the workings of government, financial institutions and financial markets. The result was that subsequent generations of economists felt the need to develop what, in their eyes, were more rigorous micro-foundations and to operationalize his theory using econometric techniques such as those developed at the Cowles Commission in the 1940s. Much of the history of macroeconomics since 1945 has been the history of this process of reworking Keynesian ideas – deriving new theories of consumption, investment and the demand for money, and new models of unemployment equilibrium. Because these developments have generally involved the construction of formal mathematical models, in which consumers and firms optimize subject to constraints, the apparent gap between them and the ideas found in the *General Theory* itself has increased.

The result is that it is easy to see a gulf between Keynes and most of contemporary macroeconomics since 1945 that lends a certain plausibility to the post-Keynesian position. Keynes did present himself as a radical critic of the status quo, claiming to do for economics what Einstein had done for physics, and in recasting his ideas in the algebra of maximizing individuals, the mainstream of post-war macroeconomics was certainly moving in directions that Keynes had not gone. However, Keynes's distance from what became the dominant methods in post-1945 macroeconomics should not be exaggerated. Donald Moggridge (1986, p. 369) has pointed out that Keynes often used a revolutionary rhetoric to garner attention for his later work by increasing the probability that it would become controversial; and as David Laidler (1999) has argued, the *General Theory*, notwithstanding Keynes's radical language, built on work that had been undertaken on the business cycle by a wide-ranging community of economists during the 1920s and 1930s. The packaging of these ideas and some of the interpretations he placed on them may have been novel, but the main components of his theoretical framework were all to be found in the previous literature. Furthermore, though for a modern economist the book is non-mathematical, it was considered a mathematical work by many of his contemporaries. Algebra may have been thin on the page, but the book was emphatically that of a mathematician, for the argument was structured around functions and schedules: take away those elements of his theory that were expressed in such language and little would remain of his argument (Backhouse, 2010). This may have increased the attractiveness of his book to the younger generation that took up his ideas in the 1940s, some of whom attached great importance to mathematics as a means of developing economic analysis (Paul Samuelson is the most notable example).

More importantly, Keynes did not try to control the use of his ideas, provided that people had understood the essentials. Orthodoxy was anathema to him and he had no interest in replacing the old orthodoxy with a new one. He encouraged both John Hicks and Roy Harrod, both of whom developed comparatively 'neoclassical' models of the *General Theory*, as well as the more radical Joan Robinson (see Backhouse and Bateman, 2010). Equally significantly, even in his 1937 article, where he is so bold in staking out his claim to be creating economics anew, there are important signs of caution.

This should serve as a warning to contemporary economists laying claim to Keynes's mantle. Clearly post-Keynesians are right when they point to the importance Keynes attached to uncertainty and to his discontent with 'classical' orthodoxy. Yet this did not stop him building theories using components taken from his predecessors; neither did he condemn the construction of theories that were more formal than his own. He might express technical reservations about Tinbergen's econometric methods, and he had confidence in his own intuitions about data, but he attached great importance to statistics and the methods needed to analyze them (Bateman, 1990). In 1944–45, he even served as President of the Econometric Society. It is thus hard to imagine him having a post-Keynesian view of how economic inquiry should be conducted. The new Keynesian exploration of alternative ways to explain the failure of markets to clear echoes his explorations of money illusion and his catalogue of reasons why wage cuts might not reduce unemployment contains ideas that have been explored by new Keynesian and new classical followers alike (for example, even the Phelps–Lucas 'island' model formalizes an idea found in the *General Theory*).

The Keynesianism that perhaps resonates most closely with the way Keynes argued in the *General Theory* is the recent turn to behavioral theories, not withstanding the fact that, as Davis (2003) has argued, much modern behavioral economics is individualistic, in contrast with socially embedded individuals that Keynes's less formal analysis could accommodate. Though he might use ideas related to profit maximization – his supply function (the aggregate supply price) and his labor demand curve are straightforward implications of profit maximization in perfectly competitive markets – the discussions of financial markets and the determinants of investment turn not on profit maximization but on the psychology of investors. Faced with a future about which they know nothing, investors may assume that the future will be much like the past, or they will fall back on conventions, or the beliefs of other investors (Keynes, 1973, Ch. 12) These resonate with the use of psychology by economists such as Akerlof and Shiller (2009), with their discussions of phenomena such as attitudes toward fairness, money illusion, myopia and herding. It seems safe to conjecture that Keynes, with his typically Bloomsbury interest in psychology, would have been fascinated by the work on which this literature is based, even if he might have asked critical questions of it, as he was critical of Tinbergen's econometrics. Yet it would be a mistake to conclude that this is the 'true' Keynesianism, for the essence of Keynes's position was his flexibility and his reluctance to be constrained by a specific approach. Today's macroeconomists need to find their own way forward, not to try to turn the clock back to 1936, 1937 or any other date.

18.5   THE WAY FORWARD

Suppose that we were to wind the clock back to 1983 and imagine that someone revealed that in the course of the next 25 years there will be a series of very large speculative bubbles in world stock markets, each followed by a painful bursting of the bubble, in which billions of dollars of wealth will be destroyed (see Bateman, 2004). Suppose further you were told that many mainstream economists will declare that this bubble is not a bubble at all, but merely a reflection of the rational expectations of investors who understand the emerging 'new economy', and it will take the prospect of a collapse of the entire financial system and a repeat of the Great Depression to dent that confidence. Finally, suppose you are told that after several of these bubbles have burst, a marginal group of economic theorists who had been talking about speculation, bubbles and irrational economic behavior for many years will gain considerable stature in the profession and dramatically increase their presence in mainstream journals. Suppose you are even told that these previously marginalized theorists will be praised, in a Nobel lecture, as the bright future of macroeconomic modeling, resurrecting the important insights of Keynes and able to explain macroeconomic phenomena that 'classical' theorists could not explain (Akerlof, 2002, p. 367).

If you had been told all this, and you knew that the person telling it to you was correct, what school of thought would you have named as the likely beneficiary of the bursting of the bubble? Only five years earlier, Paul Davidson had launched the *Journal of Post Keynesian Economics*, and the previous year Hyman Minsky (1982) had just published *Can 'It' Happen Again? Essays on Instability and Finance*. But despite being the most uncompromising skeptics about the new classical macroeconomics, rejecting its methods more uncompromisingly than the new Keynesians wished to do, and despite emphasizing the importance of financial instability, uncertainty, and bubbles, it was not the post-Keynesians but the proponents of behavioral macroeconomics and behavioral finance – two offshoots of literature in economics and psychology that were nascent but already well established in 1984 – that were the beneficiaries of events. Minsky's reputation rose after 'it' nearly did happen again in 2008, but this was for his apparent farsightedness, not because he pointed to a new way to do economics. The success of behavioral finance is undoubtedly linked to the rise of behavioral and experimental methods more generally, and is connected to views about what it means to be scientific, but insofar as there is interest in behavioral ideas in macroeconomics it is presumably because it appears to offer a new methodology for finding evidence that might adjudicate between the new classical and the Keynesian conceptions of how the economy operated.

Behavioral finance is not the same as behavioral macroeconomics, which is much more limited in both acceptance and achievements. However, the story of finance in the past decade or so carries a methodological lesson for macroeconomics. Behavioral economics was taken up not because it represented a vision of the world, but because it offered a set of techniques that economists believed might be used to understand the behavior of financial markets (and might be used to make money). For all its limitations, the merit of behavioral economics is that it offers a new set of tools which may, in due course, resolve some of the problems that other methods have not.

This is not to say that behavioral economics is necessarily the way forward, let alone the only way in which Keynesian theory may be developed. It is not even the approach favored by the majority of new Keynesians. For example, Stiglitz, probably the new Keynesian with the most prominent public profile since his denunciation from the World Bank of IMF policies in 1997, has continued to rely on theoretical arguments about asymmetric information, seeing this as confirmed by recent events in financial markets, without seeing any reason to turn in the same direction as Akerof and Shiller (see Stiglitz and Greenwald, 2003). Behavioral economics and the economics of asymmetric information may be proposed by their authors as offering new paradigms in economics, but whether such hopes will be realized is something that can be judged only after the event. This is where we part company with those such as Colander (1996) or King (2009) who try to forecast the basis on which a new paradigm is or is not likely to emerge.

It may well be that, rather than one approach dominating, all theories have to be used as partial accounts that elucidate some problems whilst distracting from others. If theories are not intended to be theories of everything, but only partial accounts that identify particular mechanisms that may be operating in the world, it may be legitimate and even necessary to explore models based on abstractions. It may well be the case that the mainstream emphasis on the necessity for formal 'microfoundations' for macroeconomic theories is misplaced, and it may be essential for policy-making to rest on judgment, informed both by economic models and by understanding of psychological, political and social factors that cannot be captured in those models, but this does not imply that it is possible to dispense with theory. It may even be possible to learn some things from representative-agent DSGE models even if, in ruling out phenomena such as coordination failures (if agents are identical and far-sighted, their behavior must be coordinated), they are treacherous guides to macroeconomics in general. Such an eclectic view is consistent with Keynes's own practice, which resembled that of a physician concerned with diagnosing illness and appropriate remedies rather than a pure scientist, seeking a unified theory of everything (Hoover, 2006). To be consistent with Keynes's own position, Keynesian methodology has to reflect his broader ethical and political concerns, that lay close to the surface of all his policy interventions, and his willingness to theorize creatively using whatever he thought the best tools available for the problem in hand, for to do otherwise would be to risk creating a new orthodoxy, something to which he was resolutely opposed.

REFERENCES

Akerlof, George A. (2002), 'Behavioral Macroeconomics and Macroeconomic Behavior', *American Economic Review*, **92**(3), 411–433.

Akerlof, George A. and Robert Shiller (2009), *Animal Spirits*, Princeton, NJ: Princeton University Press.

Arrow, Kenneth J. (1959), *Towards a Theory of Price Adjustment*, in A. Abramovitz (ed.), *The Allocation of Economic Resources*, Stanford, CA: University of California Press, pp. 41–51.

Backhouse, Roger E. (2010), '"An Abstruse and Mathematical Argument": the Use of Mathematical Reasoning in the *General Theory*', in B.W. Bateman, T. Hirai and C. Marcuzzo (eds), *The Return of Keynes: Keynes and Keynesian Policies in the New Millennium*, Cambridge, MA: Harvard University Press, pp. 133–147.

Backhouse, Roger E. and Bradley W. Bateman (2010), 'Whose Keynes?', in R. Dimand, R. Mundell and A. Vercelli (eds), *Keynes's General Theory: A Reconsideration after Seventy Years*, London: Palgrave Macmillan.

Backhouse, Roger E. and Bradley W. Bateman (2012), '"The Right Kind of an Economist": Friedman's view of Keynes', in T. Cate (ed.), *Keynes's* General Theory: *Seventy-Five Years Later*, Cheltenham, UK and Northampton, MA, USA: Edward Elgar.

Barro, Robert J. (1974), 'Are Government Bonds Net Wealth?', *Journal of Political Economy*, **82**, 1095–1117.

Barro, Robert J. and Herschel I. Grossman (1971), 'A General Disequilibrium Model of Income and Employment', *American Economic Review*, **61**, 82–93.

Bateman, Bradley W. (1990), 'Keynes, Induction and Econometrics', *History of Political Economy*, **22**, 359–379.

Bateman, Bradley W. (2004), 'A History of Post Keynesian Economics since 1936 (Review)', *History of Political Economy*, **36**(3), 581–583.

Colander, David C. (ed.) (1996), *Beyond Microfoundations: Post-Walrasian Economics*, Cambridge: Cambridge University Press.

Buiter, Willem (2009), 'The Unfortunate Uselessness of Most "State of the Art" Academic Monetary Economics', *Financial Times* blog, 3 March, http://blogs.ft.com/maver ecom/2009/03/the-unfortunate-uselessness-of-most-state-of-art-academic-monetary-econo mics/.

Davidson, Paul (2009), *The Keynes Solution: The Path to Global Economic Prosperity*, London: Palgrave.

Davis, John B. (2003), *The Theory of the Individual in Economics: Identity and Value*, London: Routledge.

Dixon, Huw (1992), 'Review of Mankiw and Romer, *New Keynesian Economics*', *Economic Journal*, **102**, 1272–1275.

Dow, S.C. (1996), *The Methodology of Macroeconomic Thought: A Conceptual Analysis of Schools of Thought in Economics*, Cheltenham, UK and Brookfield, UT, USA: Edward Elgar.

Friedman, Milton (1970), 'A Theoretical Framework for Monetary Analysis', *Journal of Political Economy*, **78**(2), 193–238.

Gordon, Robert A. (ed.) (1974), *Milton Friedman's Monetary Framework*, Chicago, IL: University of Chicago Press.

Hart, Oliver D. (1982), 'A Model of Imperfect Competition with Keynesian Features', *Quarterly Journal of Economics*, **97**(1), 109–38.

Hayes, Mark G. (2006), *The Economics of Keynes: A New Guide to the General Theory*. Cheltenham, UK and Northampton, MA, USA: Edward Elgar.

Hoover, Kevin D. (1999), *The Legacy of Robert Lucas, Jr.*, 3 vols, Intellectual Legacies in Modern Economics 3, Cheltenham, UK and Northampton, MA, USA: Edward Elgar.

Hoover, Kevin D. (2006), *Doctor Keynes: Economic Theory in a Diagnostic Science*, in R.E. Backhouse and B.W. Bateman (eds), *The Cambridge Companion to Keynes*, Cambridge: Cambridge University Press, pp. 78–97.

Jackman, Richard, Richard Layard and Stephen J. Nickell (1991), *Unemployment: Macroeconomic Performance and the Labour Market*, Oxford: Oxford University Press.

Jespersen, Jesper (2009), *Macroeconomic Methodology: A Post-Keynesian Analysis*, Cheltenham, UK and Northampton, MA, USA: Edward Elgar.

Keynes, John Maynard (1937), 'The General Theory of Employment', *Quarterly Journal of Economics*, **51**, 209–223.

Keynes, John Maynard (1973), *The General Theory of Employment, Interest and Money*, London: Macmillan.

King, John E. (2009), 'Heterodox Macroeconomics: What Exactly Are We Against?', in L. Randall Wray and Matthew Forstater (eds), *Keynes and Macroeconomics after 70 Years*, Cheltenham, UK and Northampton, MA, USA: Edward Elgar, pp. 3–19.

Krugman, Paul (1999), *The Return of Depression Economics*, London: Allen Lane.

Krugman, Paul (2009), 'How Did Economists Get It So Wrong?', *New York Times*, 6 September, http://www.nytimes.com/2009/09/06/magazine/06Economic-t.html?_r=2.

Kydland, Finn E. and Edward C. Prescott (1982), 'Time to Build and Aggregate Fluctuations', *Econometrica*, **50**(6), 1345–1370.

Laidler, David E.W. (1999), *Fabricating the Keynesian Revolution: Studies of the Inter-War Literature on Money, the Cycle, and Unemployment*, Cambridge: Cambridge University Press.

Lawson, Tony and Hashem Pesaran (1979), *Keynes' Economics: Methodological Issues*, London: Routledge.

Lucas, Robert E. (1972), 'Expectations and the Neutrality of Money', *Journal of Economic Theory*, **4**, 103–124.

Lucas, Robert E. (1976), 'Econometric Policy Evaluation: A Critique', in K. Brunner and A. Meltzer (eds), *The Phillips Curve and Labor Markets: Carnegie-Rochester Conference Series in Public Policy*, Amsterdam: North-Holland.

Lucas, Robert E. and Thomas J. Sargent (1978), *After Keynesian Macroeconomics*, Boston, MA: Federal Reserve Bank of Boston.

Malinvaud, Edmond (1977), *The Theory of Unemployment Reconsidered*, Oxford: Basil Blackwell.

Mankiw, N. Gregory and David Romer (1991), *New Keynesian Economics*, 2 vols, Cambridge, MA: MIT Press.

Minsky, Hyman P. (1982), *Can 'It' Happen Again? Essays on Instability and Finance*, New York: M.E. Sharpe.

Moggridge, Donald E. (1986), 'Keynes and His Revolution in Historical Perspective', *Eastern Economic Journal*, **12**, 357–369.

O'Donnell, R. (1999), 'Keynes and Formalism', in C.G. Harcourt and P.A. Riach (eds), *A 'Second Edition' of the General Theory*, London: Routledge, pp. 95–119.

Posner, Richard A. (2009), *A Failure of Capitalism: The Crisis of '08 and the Descent into Depression*, Cambridge, MA: Harvard University Press.

Shackle, George L.S. (1973), *Epistemics and Economics*, Cambridge: Cambridge University Press.

Skidelsky, Robert (2003), *John Maynard Keynes, 1883–1946: Economist, Philosopher, Statesman*, London: Macmillan.

Skidelsky, Robert (2009), *Keynes: The Return of the Master*, London: Allen Lane.

Solow, Robert M. and Joseph E. Stiglitz (1968), 'Output, Employment and Wages in the Short Run', *Quarterly Journal of Economics*, **82**, 537–560.

Stiglitz, Joseph E. (2002), *Globalization and its Discontents*, London: Allen Lane.

Stiglitz, Joseph E. (2003), *The Roaring Nineties: Seeds of Destruction*, London: Allen Lane.

Stiglitz, Joseph E. and Bruce Greenwald (2003), *Towards a New Paradigm in Monetary Economics*, Cambridge: Cambridge University Press.

Woodford, Michael (2003), *Interest and Prices: Foundations of a Theory of Monetary Policy*, Princeton, NJ: Princeton University Press.

19 The dismal state of macroeconomics and the opportunity for a new beginning
L. Randall Wray

19.1 INTRODUCTION

The Queen of England famously asked her economic advisors why none of them had seen 'it' (the global financial crisis) coming. Obviously the answer is complex, but it must include reference to the evolution of macroeconomic theory over the post-war period – from the 'Age of Keynes', through the Friedmanian era and the return of neoclassical economics in a particularly extreme form, and finally on to the 'new monetary consensus' with a new version of fine-tuning. The story cannot leave out the parallel developments in finance theory – with its efficient markets hypothesis – and in approaches to regulation and supervision of financial institutions. Even if the early post-war 'Keynesian' economics had little to do with Keynes at least it had some connection with the world in which we actually live. What passed for macroeconomics on the verge of the global financial collapse had nothing to do with reality. It is difficult to see that anything taught as macroeconomics in the best-selling textbooks in 2007 will survive. It is as relevant to our economy as flat earth theory is to natural science – warranting a small footnote in the history of economic thought. In short, expecting the Queen's economists to foresee the crisis would be like putting flat earthers in charge of navigation for NASA and expecting them accurately to predict points of re-entry and landing of the space shuttle.

19.2 POST-WAR DEVELOPMENT OF MAINSTREAM MACROECONOMICS

Many authors have previously questioned the degree to which 'Keynesian' theory and policy actually followed Keynes's *General Theory* (GT). In 1937 John Hicks had created the IS-LM model to present Keynes's theory in a simple framework that could be used to compare 'Keynesian' and 'classical' results. Immediately after the war, macroeconomists set out to 'marry' the 'Keynesian' IS-LM model with the old pre-Keynesian microeconomic theory based on individual rational utility and profit maximization – in other words, on the neoclassical approach to the behavior of firms and consumers.[1] Paul Samuelson called it the 'neoclassical synthesis' and it became the foundation for macroeconomics taught in classrooms (Samuelson, 1973). Macro theory continued to develop through the 1960s as James Tobin's portfolio balance approach, Don Patinkin's labor market, and the Phillips curve were added to Hicks's IS-LM model (see Patinkin, 1965; Minsky, 1986). Likewise, 'Keynesian' policy gradually developed over the post-war period, finally taking hold in the administration of President Kennedy. And Milton Friedman developed monetarism as a 'laissez-faire' counterpoint (Friedman, 1969; Brunner, 1968). Still, even his approach was easily integrated within the neoclassical synthesis so that the 'great debate' between 'Keynesians' and 'monetarists' was reduced to differences over parameters (interest rate elasticity of investment and income elasticity of money demand) and policy prescriptions (discretionary interest rate targets or money growth rules).

Yet many important aspects of Keynes's GT were absent (Keynes, 1964). For example, the synthesis version of Keynes never incorporated true uncertainty or 'unknowledge', and thus deviated substantially from Keynes's treatment of expectations in Chapters 12 and 17 of the GT. It essentially reduced Keynes to sticky wages and prices, with non-neutral money only in the case of fooling.[2] The stagflation of the 1970s ended the great debate between 'Keynesians' and 'monetarists' in favor of Milton Friedman's rules, and set the stage for the rise of a succession of increasingly silly theories rooted in pre-Keynesian thought. As Lord Robert Skidelsky (Keynes's biographer) argues: 'Rarely in history can such powerful minds have devoted themselves to such strange ideas' (Skidelsky, 2009, p. xiv).

First, new classical theory restored the most extreme version of neoclassical economics, with continual market clearing (including full employment) and 'rational expectations' that ensures economic agents do not make persistent errors. This makes it impossible to fool rational actors in the manner Friedman supposed, since expectation formation is forward-looking and is based on the correct model of the economy. This also means that non-random policy has no effect at all because agents immediately figure out what policymakers are doing and adjust their own behavior in an optimal manner. Money matters only temporarily, while agents gather the information necessary to distinguish real from nominal prices. Fiscal policy does not matter at all – for example, deficit spending is completely crowded-out because taxpayers know they will have to pay down government's debt later so begin saving immediately (Ricardian equivalents). Still, new classical theory's explanation of the business cycle depended on short-run non-neutrality of money (the misperception of rising nominal prices as rising relative prices).

'Real business cycle' theory took the final step to eliminate any effect of money by making the business cycle a function only of real variables. The most important is random and large fluctuations of productivity. In this way, the Great Depression was explained not as a fault of errant monetary policy – as Friedman had done – but rather as a negative productivity shock. Because workers were suddenly less productive, their real wage fell. At the lower real wages, they decided to take more leisure. This is suboptimal only if they misperceive a change of nominal wages as a change of real wages – a mistake that could only be temporary. Hence, involuntary unemployment did not rise during the Great Depression – rather, people took long vacations. All behavior is always optimal, all markets always clear – indeed, the observed business cycle is not a cycle at all, rather, the economy follows a 'random walk with drift'. (The economy follows a constant growth rate trend until it is shocked so that it instantly adapts to a new trend rate of growth.) Government should not do anything about what we have called recessions or depressions because these are actually optimal responses to random shocks. You can see why Lord Skidelsky labels these theories 'strange' – the suffering of the unemployed in the Great Depression was an 'optimal' response because workers preferred standing in bread lines over working at lower real wages. Those who developed these ridiculous theories actually got Nobel Prizes for this work.[3]

Developments in finance theory mirrored the evolution of mainstream economic theory in the sense that like money, finance also became irrelevant (Fama, 1970). So long as markets are efficient, all forms of finance are equivalent. Financial institutions are seen as intermediaries that come between savers and investors, efficiently allocating savings to highest-use projects. Evolution of financial practices continually reduces the 'wedge' between the interest rate received by savers and that paid by investors – encouraging more saving and investment. Domestic financial market deregulation (under way since the mid-1960s in the US) as well as globalization of international financial markets plays a key role in enhancing these efficiencies and, hence, in promoting growth. The key conclusion is that if market impediments are removed, finance becomes 'neutral'. Further, markets will discipline financial institutions; hence, self-regulation is enough because it will align incentives to produce safe practices.

In recent years a 'new' neoclassical synthesis (often called the 'new monetary consensus') was developed, adopting most of the 'strange ideas' but obtaining 'Keynesian'-style results by reviving sticky wages and prices. Again, Skidelsky nicely skewers the new orthodoxy: 'Having swallowed the elephant of rational expectations, they strained at the gnat of the continuous full employment implied by it, and developed theories of market failure to allow a role for government' (Skidelsky, 2009, p. xv). Unlike the early post-war Keynesian policy that advocated use of fiscal policy to fine-tune the economy, this version elevated monetary policy to that role. By this time, however, mainstream economists had given up on attempts by central banks to control the money supply – Friedman's preferred target – and replaced that with control over the interest rate (Wray, 2004).

The goal was the same. Following a strategy known as the Taylor rule, the central bank would adjust its interest rate target based on deviation of actual inflation rates from targets as well as the output gap (differential between potential output and actual output). For example, if inflation is higher than desired and if actual output exceeds potential output, then the central bank raises interest rates to cool the economy. This is really just a slightly updated Phillips curve notion – if the unemployment rate gets too low, inflation results – but with far more concern shown for inflation than unemployment. Some advocates go a bit further, actually proposing specific inflation rate targets (completely ignoring unemployment outcomes) – with several central banks around the world explicitly adopting such targets. In any event, the belief is that all government really needs to do is to keep inflation low – by itself, that will promote robust growth that will keep the economy close to full employment. There is also the belief that monetary policy is highly potent – central banks can keep inflation on target (say, 1–2 per cent per year), which by itself will fine-tune the economy.

Mainstream economists thought it all worked splendidly through 2007. Central bankers around the world congratulated themselves for keeping inflation low. Federal Reserve System (Fed) Chairman Alan Greenspan was known as the 'Maestro', and was proclaimed to be not only the greatest central banker ever, but also the most powerful human on earth. When he retired, the chairmanship mantle was handed over to Ben Bernanke, who promoted the idea of the 'great moderation'. By keeping inflation low, the world's central bankers had promoted economic stability (the 'moderation'). Since everyone in the economy knew central bankers were committed to stability, all expected stability, and hence we would have stability. All that was now necessary was to manage expectations. Markets knew the central banks would keep inflation low, and knew that if there were any economic hiccups, the central banks would quickly act to restore stability. That, itself, provided confidence – it was known as the 'Greenspan put' and then as the 'Bernanke put', the idea that the Chairman of the Fed would prevent anything bad from happening. Real-estate prices boomed, commodities prices bubbled, stock markets rose and

Wall Street's financial institutions recorded terrific profits (Wray, 2008a, 2009).

Well, it worked until it didn't – more precisely, it failed spectacularly beginning in spring 2007 as the world's economy slipped into the worst crisis since the 1930s (only a few nations escaped – notably China, which had not allowed unfettered financial markets). The major central banks moved to reassure markets that they were in charge. Yet, it became apparent that lowering interest rates – essentially to zero – had no impact. The crisis grew worse, with rising unemployment, falling retail sales, the worst collapse of real-estate markets since the Great Depression, and with one financial institution failing after another. The Fed lent reserves, bought toxic waste assets and guaranteed private institution liabilities, while the Treasury followed suit with its own bailouts, including effectively nationalizing the US auto industry. Total US government spending, lending and guarantees (including those by the Fed and Treasury) grew to more than $20 trillion (substantially larger than gross domestic product, GDP) – all with little success (Cassidy, 2008; Chancellor, 2007; Wray, 2009). As this chapter was being written, more than three years into the crisis, many economists and policymakers were projecting a 'double-dip' – that is, a collapse back into recession – and many argued that the biggest banks were still massively insolvent. So much for 'maestros' and 'great moderations' and 'laissez-faire'.

The global crisis exploded reigning orthodoxy. Among those theories and claims that should no longer be taken seriously by any macroeconomist we must include: rational expectations and continuous market clearing; new classical and real business cycle approaches; neutral money; the new monetary consensus, the Taylor rule and the great moderation; the efficient markets hypothesis; Ricardian equivalents and other versions of the policy irrelevance doctrine; and claims made by advocates of deregulation and self-regulation. None of these ideas should be taught in any serious economics course – they are no more relevant to economic theory than are bloodletting techniques to the study of medicine.

To be sure, we have been here before. The Great Depression also exploded the reigning orthodoxy. Keynes offered a revolution in thought. Unfortunately, that revolution was aborted; or, at least, co-opted by 'synthesizers' who borrowed only the less revolutionary aspects of his theory and then integrated these into the old neoclassical approach. The important insights of Keynes were never incorporated in mainstream macroeconomics. Eventually, neoclassical theory was restored. It is now time to throw it out, to see what should be recovered from Keynes, and to update Keynes's theory to make it relevant for the world in which we actually live.

19.3 KEYNES'S REVOLUTION: THEORY AND METHODOLOGY

The central proposition of the *General Theory* can be simply stated as follows: *Entrepreneurs produce what they expect to sell, and there is no reason to presume that the sum of these production decisions is consistent with the full employment level of output either in the short run or in the long run* (Forstater and Wray, 2008). Moreover, this proposition holds even in conditions of perfect competition and flexible wages, even if expectations are always fulfilled, and even in a stable economic environment. In other words, Keynes did not rely on sticky wages, monopoly power, disappointed expectations, or economic instability (due, for example to 'exogenous' shocks) to explain unemployment. While each of these conditions could certainly make matters worse, he wanted to explain the possibility of equilibrium with unemployment even under the conditions most favorable to the neoclassical model.

Keynes's approach begins with a focus on the entrepreneurial decision – each firm produces what it expects to sell – rather than on the consumer who maximizes utility through time. That entrepreneurial decision is based on a comparison between the costs incurred to produce now against the proceeds expected to be received in the future. A decision to produce is simultaneously a decision to employ and to provide incomes to workers. It probably also commits the firm to a stream of payments over some time period (since firms usually borrow to finance production costs). Production will not be undertaken unless the expected proceeds exceed by a sufficient margin the costs incurred today and into the future. Both the costs and the revenues accrue in the form of money. If the comparison of estimated costs and expected revenues is deemed unfavorable, production is not undertaken and income is not generated. There is no reason to believe that the result of all of these individual production decisions will be full employment of labor resources. Note also that because production begins and ends with money, Keynes rejects the notion of neutrality of money – in an important sense, the purpose of production is money (Keynes called this a monetary theory of production; Marx designated this 'M–C–M': the entrepreneur begins with money, produces commodities, and hopes to end up with more money).[4]

Keynes required only three conditions to ensure the possibility of equilibrium with unemployment: historical time, autonomous spending and existence of a non-producible store of value. With historical time, the past is more or less known, but cannot be changed; decisions taken today depend on outcomes that depend in turn on past decisions as well as on outcomes expected in the future; and the future cannot be known now.

Each of these considerations represents an important deviation from most orthodox analysis. Mistakes cannot be easily eliminated through 'recontracting'; hysteresis and cumulative causation are pervasive phenomena; decisions must be taken without the possibility of knowing what the future might bring. At least a portion of spending depends on expectations of the future, rather than on today's income – allowing individual spending to be less than, equal to, or greater than income. Both income and spending are in monetary terms; income received but not spent allows accumulation of money balances. Again, money matters.

For Keynes (1964), money is an asset with 'special properties': nearly zero carrying costs, elasticity of substitution and elasticity of production. Zero carrying costs mean that it costs nothing to hold money – unlike, say, holding wheat, which would incur storage costs as well as wastage (some wheat will spoil or be lost to pests). Zero elasticity of substitution means that if you really want to hold money, there are no close substitutes to satisfy your demand. The last characteristic means that when the demand for money rises, labor is not diverted to its production. So long as there is at least one asset that is not produced by labor, it can become a bottomless sink of purchasing power, overturning Say's Law and subverting any market forces to return the system to full employment. Note that it is not important that these conditions hold strictly – there are some carrying costs of money and there are substitutes (you could hold government bonds, or bank certificates of deposit). What matters is the degree – money does have a low carrying cost, substitutes are imperfect, and almost no labor is involved in producing money (a tiny bit is required to print currency; banks have loan officers and tellers who work to create bank money). For these reasons, preference for money creates a barrier to expanding production up to the full employment point.

As mentioned, Keynes did not need to assume that expectations had been disappointed, causing production to fall temporarily below the full employment level. Indeed, after publication of the GT, he argued that he could have assumed that expectations are always fulfilled and still he would have obtained the same results. All that is necessary is that entrepreneurs cannot be sure that their expectations will be fulfilled. It is the uncertainty that generates a preference for liquid assets and thus a barrier to achieving full employment. Nor does the outcome require instability. While some of Keynes's best-known passages (especially those in Chapter 12 of the GT) do refer to 'whirlwinds of speculation' and other examples of instability, his favorite explanation of equilibrium with unemployment utilized a static model in which expectations – both short run and long run – are held constant, uninfluenced by outcome. Again, firms produce only what they expect to sell at profit, and it is not necessary for them to have been disappointed or to be subject to unstable economic forces in order for the sum of their individual production decisions to leave some labor resources unutilized.

Keynes famously remarked that no one in a neoclassical world would hold money because there could be no value to holding a riskless (hence, low return) asset. This was later confirmed by Frank Hahn (1983), who lamented that there is no room for money in any rigorous orthodox model. Charles Goodhart (2008) insists that the possibility of default is central to any analysis of a money-using economy. As decisions about production made today commit entrepreneurs to payments in the future, there is the possibility that they will not be able to meet contractual terms. However, orthodox models explicitly rule out default, implying that all IOUs are risk-free, thereby eliminating any need for the monitoring services provided by financial institutions. Not only is there no room for money in these models, but there is also no need for banks or other financial intermediaries. Financial instability is also ruled out, not – as in Keynes – because instability is unnecessary to demonstrate the desired results, but because absence of the possibility of default requires perfect foresight or complete and perfect markets so that all outcomes can be hedged.

Thus, these mainstream macro models cannot incorporate the real-world features that Keynes included: animal spirits and degree of confidence, market psychology and liquidity preference. By contrast, Keynes's basic model is easily extended to account for heterogeneous credit ratings, to allow default to affect expectations, and to include 'contagions' and other repercussions set off by default of one large economic entity on its commitments. The best example of such extensions is the work of the late Hyman Minsky, who developed the 'financial instability hypothesis' (Minsky, 1986; Papadimitriou and Wray, 1998). According to Minsky, the economy emerged from World War II with a very robust financial system – hardly any private debt (it had been wiped out in the Great Depression) and lots of safe and liquid federal government debt (due to deficit spending during World War II). This allowed relatively rapid economic growth without borrowing by households and firms. Various New Deal and post-war reforms also made the economy stable: a safety net that stabilized consumption (social security, unemployment compensation, welfare and food stamps); strict financial regulation; minimum-wage laws and support of unions; low-cost mortgage loans and student loans, and so on. In addition, memories of the Great Depression discouraged risky behavior.

Gradually all that changed – the memories faded, financial institutions got around regulations, the anti-government movement replaced regulation with deregulation, unions lost power and government support, globalization introduced low-wage competition and increased uncertainties, and the safety net was chronically underfunded (Minsky and Whalen, 1996). Minsky believed the transformation would have occurred even without those changes, as profit-seeking firms and financial institutions would take on greater risks with more precarious financing schemes. Financial crises and recessions became more frequent and more severe, but the New Deal institutions and reforms helped the economy to recover relatively quickly from each crisis. Thus, debts built up and fragility grew on trend over the entire post-war period. This made 'it' (another Great Crash like the one that occurred in 1929) possible again. Minsky died in 1996, but it is clear that the current crisis unfolded in a manner consistent with his projections. Indeed, many have called this a 'Minsky crisis' and his name has become almost a household word – at least among those who are studying the crisis that began in 2007 (Cassidy, 2008; Chancellor, 2007). In other words, Minsky did 'see it coming' because, unlike mainstream economists, his theory included the possibility that the economy would evolve toward instability. Further, finance and money matter in his theory – as in Keynes, money is never neutral. He takes Keynes further by adding a detailed analysis of financial operations.

Keynes (1964, Ch. 2) had addressed stability issues when he argued that if wages were flexible, then market forces set off by unemployment would move the economy further from full employment due to effects on aggregate demand, profits and expectations. This is why he argued that one condition for stability is a degree of wage stickiness in terms of money. (Incredibly, this argument has been misinterpreted to mean that sticky wages cause unemployment – a point almost directly opposite to Keynes's conclusion.[5]) Minsky extended Keynes by arguing that if the economy ever were to achieve full employment, this would generate destabilizing forces restoring unemployment. Minsky believed that the main instability experienced in a modern capitalist economy is a tendency toward explosive euphoria. High aggregate demand and profits that can be associated with full employment raise expectations and encourage increasingly risky ventures based on commitments of future revenues that will not be realized. A snowball of defaults then leads to a debt deflation (debtors default on their debts, which are assets of creditors) and high unemployment unless there are 'circuit breakers' that intervene to stop the market forces. The main circuit breakers, according to Minsky are the 'Big Bank' (central bank as lender of last resort) and 'Big Government' (countercyclical budget deficits) interventions (Minsky and Ferri, 1991; Minsky, 1986).

Finally a technical note on Keynes's method. Roger Backhouse (2010) has provided an excellent defense of Keynes's method, in particular his reluctance to use mathematical models. (Keynes was a good mathematician, and his PhD thesis – later published – was on probability theory.)

The earliest reviews of the GT actually complained about Keynes's excessive use of mathematics in the book – something the modern reader finds surprising because there are few equations (all using simple math) and only one diagram. But this is not simply because economics came to rely so heavily on mathematics. Backhouse shows that the GT is actually permeated by a mathematical way of thinking – beginning with intuition and clear thinking, with details added later as Keynes constructed incomplete models, explained mostly verbally. Keynes believed there were too many qualifications, reservations, adjustments and interdependencies that precluded specification in formal mathematics. In other words, to keep his theory general he had to keep it somewhat vague.

It was precisely because post-war 'Keynesian' economics translated the GT into algebra that it became too simplistic and specific to be relevant to our complex world. The post-1970s developments further mathematized economics in an attempt to make it ever more rigorous. Ironically, the math became more complex but the 'economy' analyzed had to be made increasingly simple. By doing so, it became concomitantly irrelevant to the complex world in which we live. The methodology adopted by orthodoxy was precisely the opposite of Keynes's methodology – it strove to have a 'general' theory that begins from well-specified assumptions ('axioms'), supposedly free from the institutions, culture and habits of any specific economy. In that way, the theory could be applied to any behavior – even non-human behavior – at all times and places. In its most extreme version, orthodox economics became a branch of the 'decision sciences', adopting methodological individualism and studying the way an optimizing 'agent' (typically, Robinson Crusoe) would allocate consumption across time.

By contrast, Keynes's GT was general but at the same time institution-specific. It concerned a capitalist (or entrepreneurial) economy, that is to say one in which the purpose of production is money (production begins with money on the expectation of realizing even more money). Further, it concerns an economy operating in historical time, where the past cannot be changed and the future cannot be known. It applies to decision-making in an uncertain world. His methodology has been described by Jan Kregel (1976) as one of 'shifting equilibrium' – taking expectations as given we can determine the point of effective demand (defined, as above, as the level of output and employment that would be achieved at the aggregate level if entrepreneurs were to produce the amount they expect to sell). Each change of expectations produces a new point of equilibrium (point of effective demand). There are no forces to drive this economy to the full employment level of effective demand; indeed, the dynamics are such that full employment is an unstable equilibrium as it changes expectations in a destabilizing manner (recall Minsky's arguments about the tendency toward explosive euphoria).[6]

19.4   KEYNES AND POLICY

Keynes had long rejected the notion of laissez-faire, writing a pamphlet titled *The End of Laissez-Faire* in 1926 (Keynes, 1926 [2009]). Not only did he argue against that the claim that some 'invisible hand' could guide self-interested individuals to behave in the public interest, but he also denied that these individuals even knew their own self-interest. He went further, arguing that the notion of laissez-faire had never really been embraced by economists. Rather it was adopted by ideologues. To be sure, in that 1926 piece Keynes did not provide a convincing rebuttal to the laissez-faire doctrine, nor did he provide a policy solution. His theory of effective demand had to wait another decade. It was only with his publication of the GT that Keynes made it clear why the invisible hand would fail, and why government had to play a positive role in the economy.

Keynes's impact on post-war policy was at least as great as his impact on theory. Of course, it is questionable whether much of the policy that was called Keynesian really had strong roots in Keynes's GT. Still, the influences of Keynes's work on domestic fiscal and monetary policy, on the international financial system, and on development policy – especially in Latin America – cannot be denied. If we take the central message of the GT as the proposition that entrepreneurial production decisions cannot be expected to generate equilibrium at full employment, then the obvious policy response is to use government to try to raise production beyond the level 'ground out' by market forces. Unfortunately, 'Keynesian' policy was eventually reduced to overly simplistic metaphors such as 'pump-priming' and 'fine-tuning' that would keep aggregate demand at just the right level to maintain full employment. It is now commonplace to claim that Keynesian policy was tried, but failed.

In practice, post-war policy usually consisted of measures to promote saving and investment. The first was wholly inconsistent with Keynes, based instead on the neoclassical loanable funds view that saving 'finances' investment; the second was based on a multiplier view, that while somewhat consistent with Keynes's explication of the determination of the equilibrium level of output, relied on overly simplistic views of entrepreneurial expectation formation while ignoring important stability questions. First, there is no reason to believe that the demand (or multiplier) effect of investment will be sufficient to absorb the additional capacity generated by the supply effect of investment. There are a number of related avenues of research – ranging from Alvin Hansen's stagnation thesis (modern capitalism tends to stagnate due to lack of investment opportunities), to a Keynesian 'disproportionalities' argument that such gross policy measures would generate the wrong mix of productive capacity relative to demand, and to the Harold Vatter and John Walker view that sustaining adequate rates of growth through time would require continuous growth of the government sector relative to growth of the private sector (Wray, 2008b).

Second, attempting to maintain full employment by stimulating private investment would shift the distribution of income toward owners of capital, worsening inequality and thereby lowering the society's propensity to consume – one of the problems addressed by Keynes in Chapter 24 of the GT. For example, work based on Michal Kalecki's (1971) profit equation shows how higher investment rates generate higher profit rates, and shifts the distribution of income toward entrepreneurs and away from workers. There are also two kinds of sectoral issues raised. A high investment strategy will tend to favor capital-intensive industries, shifting the distribution of income toward higher-paid and unionized workers. The sectoral balances approach implicitly adopted by Minsky (1963) in his earliest work, and developed in detail by Wynne Godley carries the Kalecki analysis further by examining the implications for financial balances implied by spending growth (Godley and Wray, 2000). For example, an expansion led by private sector deficit spending (with firms borrowing to finance investment in excess of internal income flows) implies that the government and/or the external sector will record equivalent surpluses (a government budget surplus and/or a capital account surplus). This then raises sustainability issues as private debt will grow faster than private sector income. Indeed, this is exactly what happened in the decade after 1996 in the US (and some other nations), helping to create the overindebtedness that led to the financial crisis (Wray, 2003b).

Third, Minsky's financial instability hypothesis raises related concerns. Over the course of an economic boom that is led by investment spending, private firms stretch liquidity (income flows are leveraged by debt, and the ratio of safe assets to liabilities rises), leading to increasingly fragile financial positions. Combining the financial instability hypothesis with the Godley sectoral balances approach, it is apparent that the government budget plays an important role in cooling a boom: rapid growth of income moves the government budget toward balance and even to a surplus. The mostly unrecognized flip-side to a government sector surplus is a private sector deficit (holding the foreign balance constant), so 'improvement' of government balances (lower budget deficits) must mean by identity that non-government balances become more precarious (smaller surpluses). Followers of the work of Minsky and Godley were thus amused by positive reactions to the Clinton-era budget surpluses, and the predictions that all federal government debt would be eliminated over the coming decade and a half. It was no surprise that the Clinton surpluses killed the boom and morphed into budget deficits, since the budget automatically moves toward larger deficits in a slump, maintaining profit flows and strengthening private balance sheets that accumulate net wealth in the form of safe government bonds (Wray, 2003b).

Hence, the heterodox approach that follows Keynes and Minsky is skeptical that the private sector can be a reliable engine of growth. It is also skeptical of a 'pump-priming' approach to government policy. Rather, policymaking is going to have to be specific, with well-formulated regulations to constrain private firms and with well-targeted government spending. The wholesale abandonment of regulation and supervision of the financial sector has proven to be a tremendous mistake. Left to supervise itself, Wall Street created complex and exceedingly risky financial instruments that allowed it to burden households and non-financial firms (as well as state and local governments) with debt (Wray, 2009). Wall Street also managed to shift the distribution of income toward its traders and CEOs – just before the financial crash, the financial sector captured 40 percent of all corporate profits in the US. The debt to GDP ratio rose to 500 percent (versus 300 percent in 1929 on the eve of the Great Depression). Income inequality rose to levels not seen since 1929 – with poverty rising in the midst of plenty. Even though Wall Street was booming, real economic growth was not particularly good in the period before the crash; and the average real wage of workers was no higher than it had been back in the early 1970s. And while official unemployment was relatively low, unmeasured unemployment and underemployment has been rising on trend (Wray, 2003a). It is clear that fundamental reform of the financial sector – on a scale similar to what was done in the 1930s – will be required to get the American economy back on track. A similar story can be told about all the advanced capitalist economies.

In addition, we need to do something about the rest of the economy to create jobs and rising living standards. If heterodox economists do not believe that 'fine-tuning' is possible, what can be done? First, policy should address the obvious areas that have been neglected for more than three decades as well as new problems that have emerged. America's public infrastructure is entirely inadequate – with problems ranging from collapsing bridges and levees, to overcrowded urban highways and airports, an outdated electrical grid and lack of a high-speed rail network. Global warming raises new problems that need to be addressed: moving to cleaner energy production, expanding public transportation, retrofitting buildings to make them energy efficient, and reforestation. In all of these areas, government must increase its spending – either taking on the projects directly or subsidizing private spending. Because this spending will help to make America more productive, the spending will be more effective than general pump-priming and will not suffer from the drawbacks discussed above.

Still, it is likely that even if all of these projects are undertaken, millions of workers will be left behind. First, there is no reason to believe that the additional demand for labor will be sufficient to create enough jobs; second, there can be a skills mismatch, problems of discrimination (against ethnic groups, by gender, against people with disabilities, and against people with low educational attainment or criminal records), and geographic mismatch (jobs need to be created where the unemployed live). For this reason, many heterodox economists have revived Minsky's call for an 'employer of last resort' (Minsky, 1965; Wray, 1998; Kelton and Wray, 2004; Harvey, 1989). Minsky argued that only the federal government can offer an infinitely elastic demand for workers – hiring anyone ready and willing to work – at a decent wage. This is also called a job guarantee program. The idea is that the federal government provides funding for a basic (living) wage with benefits. Creation and administration of the program as well as supervision of the workers in the program could be highly decentralized to local not-for-profit agencies, community development organizations, and state and local governments. The program would take 'workers as they are' – designing jobs to fit the workers' needs and abilities. There would be no skills or education requirement, although all jobs would provide training and perhaps even basic education. Jobs would be created where the workers live. Flexible work arrangements could be made (such as part-time jobs) to fit the needs of working mothers (and even students of working age). The jobs could include some of those listed above (retrofitting homes with insulation, for example) but would be expanded to include provision of public services – child and aged care, 'meals on wheels' (delivering hot meals to the aged, infirm and those otherwise confined to their homes due to disabilities), playground and subway supervision, litter clean-up, and so on.

All of this could require more government spending (although it is possible that reducing spending in areas that do not generate jobs and that do not enhance US production and living standards would partially offset the additional spending). While orthodoxy fears budget deficits (with many arguing that they only 'crowd out' private spending), heterodox economists argue that orthodoxy conflates government budgets with household budgets. A sovereign government's budget is not like the budget of a household or firm. Government issues the currency, while households and firms are users of that currency. As the chartalist or 'modern money' approach explains, modern governments actually spend by crediting bank accounts (Bell, 2000; Wray, 1998). It really just amounts to a keystroke, pushing a key on a computer that generates an entry on someone's balance sheet. Government can never run out of these keystrokes. Remarkably, even the Chairman of the Fed, Ben Bernanke, testified to Congress that the Fed spends through simple keystrokes – hence could afford to buy as many assets as necessary to bail out Wall Street's banks. All that is necessary is to recognize that the Treasury spends the same way, and then Washington's policymakers could stop worrying about 'affordability' of the types of programs that everyone recognizes to be necessary: public infrastructure investment, 'green' investments to reduce global warming, and job creation. To be sure, this is not a call for 'the sky is the limit' spending by government. Too much spending will be inflationary and could cause currency depreciation. Government spending must be well targeted and must not be too large. How big is too large? Once productive capacity is fully used and the labor force is fully employed, additional spending would be inflationary.

This is also called the 'functional finance' approach to policy, developed by Abba Lerner (1943, 1947). Policy should be directed to resolving problems, raising living standards and achieving the public purpose as defined by the democratic process. There should be no pre-conceived budgetary outcome – such as a balanced government budget over a year or over the cycle. In other words, the goal should be to use the government's 'purse' to achieve the public purpose – not to mandate any specific dollar amount for spending or for its deficit. This does not mean that government spending on programs should not be constrained by a budget – Congress needs to approve the budgets for individual programs, and then hold program administrators accountable for meeting the budgets. The purpose of budgeting is not to ensure that the overall federal government budget balances, but rather to reduce waste, graft and corruption. Budgeting is one means of controlling projects to help ensure that they serve the public interest. Unlike the case of a household or firm, the sovereign government can always 'afford' to spend more on a program – but that does not mean it should spend more than necessary.

In conclusion, most economists 'didn't see it coming' because their approach to economics denies that 'it' could happen. The neoclassical approach that provides the foundation for all mainstream macroeconomics is applicable only to an imaginary world, an economy focused on market exchange based on a barter paradigm. Money and finance are added to the model as an afterthought – they really do not matter. Because an invisible hand guides rational individuals who have perfect foresight toward an equilibrium in which all resources are efficiently allocated, there is little role for government to play.

The current crisis has shown this approach to be irrelevant for analysis of the economy in which we live. By contrast, the Keynesian revolution that began with the GT offered an alternative that does allow us to understand the world around us. Keynes's different methodological approach allowed him to develop a theory that was at the same time 'general' but also 'specific' in the sense that it incorporated those features of the capitalist (entrepreneurial) economy that cause it to move toward crisis. Economists working in that tradition did see 'it' coming, and they have offered policy advice that would help to get the economy back on track and to reform it not only so that it would be more stable, but also so that it would operate in the interest of most of the population.

NOTES

1. Throughout this section I will provide only a brief overview of the main tenets of orthodox approaches, and will spare the reader detailed citations. Thorough summaries as well as references are provided in many commonly used macroeconomics textbooks. The Samuelson (1973) text is useful for the 'Keynesian' neoclassical synthesis; for the post-1970s developments the text by Mankiw (2008) is good for undergraduates while the Snowden and Vane (2006) text provides a more advanced examination.
2. Workers and/or firms would be fooled temporarily by an increase in nominal wages and prices, mistaking it for an increase in real wages or prices – thus, temporarily supplying more labor and/or output. This was supposed to be caused by an increase of the money supply. In the Lucas version, such 'fooling' can occur only if the increase of the money supply is unanticipated (which requires that it is random and therefore unpredictable).
3. It is not commonly known that the Nobel Prize in economics is actually awarded by the Bank of Sweden – the prize in economics is not a real Nobel Prize, but the economists who win do like to call themselves Nobel laureates. Of course, that does not mean that their research is not worthy of an award.
4. This is not to say that orthodoxy has completely ignored money. Indeed, as discussed above, all but the real business cycle approach tried to find a way to make money matter – that is, to make it 'non-neutral'. However, money was never introduced in a convincing manner – as Hahn's lament (p. 459) makes clear. None of the orthodox approaches makes money the object of production. In Keynes's terminology, the subject of orthodox economics is not an entrepreneurial economy, so although money might be used it is not essential.
5. To be clear, in the more orthodox versions of Keynes (both the neoclassical synthesis as well as the new Keynesian economics) unemployment is caused by sticky wages (and prices). If wages were perfectly flexible, markets would eliminate unemployment by lowering the real wage. Hence, in these versions of Keynes, the choice is either to make wages more flexible, or to use policy to ameliorate the suffering caused by unemployment. By contrast, in Keynes's theory, greater flexibility of wages would likely cause unemployment to rise. For Keynes, relative stability of wages actually improves stability of markets.
6. So by contrast with orthodox methodology, Keynes's methodology makes room for issues such as path-dependency, hysteresis, true uncertainty and expectation formation in situations of 'unknowledge'.

REFERENCES

Backhouse, Roger E. (2010), 'An Abstruse and Mathematical Argument: The Use of Mathematical Reasoning in the *General Theory*', in Bradley W. Bateman, Toshiaki Hirai and Maria Cristina Marcuzzo (eds), *The Return to Keynes*, Cambridge, MA and London, UK: Belknap Press of Harvard University Press, pp. 133–147.

Bell, Stephanie (2000), 'Do Taxes and Bonds Finance Government Spending?', *Journal of Economic Issues*, **34**, 603–620.

Bell, Stephanie (2001), 'The Role of the State and the Hierarchy of Money', *Cambridge Journal of Economics*, **25**(2), 149–163.

Brunner, Karl (1968), 'The Role of Money and Monetary Policy', *Federal Reserve Bank of StLouis Review*, **50**(July), 9.

Cassidy, John (2008), 'The Minsky Moment', *New Yorker*, 4 February, www.newyorker.com, accessed 29 January 2008.

Chancellor, E. (2007), 'Ponzi Nation', *Institutional Investor*, 7 February.

Fama, E.F. (1970), 'Efficient Capital Markets: A Review of Theory and Empirical Work', *Journal of Finance*, **25**(2), 383–417.

Forstater, Mathew and L. Randall Wray (eds) (2008), *Keynes for the Twenty-First Century: The Continuing Relevance of The General Theory*, London: Palgrave Macmillan.

Friedman, M. (1969), 'The Optimum Quantity of Money', in M. Friedman (ed.), *The Optimum Quantity of Money and Other Essays*, Chicago, IL: Aldine, pp. 1–50.

Godley, Wynne and L. Randall Wray (2000), 'Is Goldilocks Doomed?', *Journal of Economic Issues*, March, 201–206.

Goodhart, Charles A.E. (2008), 'Money and Default', in Mathew Forstater and L. Randall Wray (eds), *Keynes for the Twenty-First Century: The Continuing Relevance of The General Theory*, London: Palgrave Macmillan, pp. 213–223.

Hahn, Frank (1983), *Money and Inflation*, Cambridge, MA: MIT Press.

Harvey, Phillip (1989), *Securing the Right to Employment*, Princeton, NJ: Princeton University Press.

Kalecki, M. (1971), 'The Determinants of Profits', in M. Kalecki (ed.), *Selected Essays on the Dynamics of the Capitalist Economy*, Cambridge: Cambridge University Press, pp. 78–92.

Kelton, Stephanie and L. Randall Wray (2004), 'The War on Poverty after 40 Years: A Minskyan Assessment', Public Policy Brief, Levy Economics Institute of Bard College, No. 78.

Keynes, John Maynard (1926), *The End of Laissez-Faire*, republished (2009) in *The End of Laissez-Faire: The Economic Consequences of the Peace*, BN Publishing, at http://www.amazon.com/End-Laissez-Faire-Economic-Consequences-Peace/dp/1607960869.

Keynes, John Maynard (1964), *The General Theory of Employment, Interest and Money*, New York, USA and London, UK: Harcourt Brace Jovanovich.

Kregel, J.A. (1976), 'Economic Methodology in the Face of Uncertainty: The Modeling Methods of Keynes and the Post-Keynesians', *Economic Journal*, **86**(342), 209–225.

Lerner, Abba P. (1943), 'Functional Finance and the Federal Debt', *Social Research*, **10**, 38–51.

Lerner, Abba P. (1947), 'Money as a Creature of the State', *American Economic Review*, **37**, 312–317.

Mankiw, Gregory (2008), *Brief Principles of Macroeconomics*, 5th edn, Mason, OH: Cengage Learning.

Minsky, Hyman P. (1963), 'Discussion', *American Economic Review*, **53**(2), 401–412.

Minsky, Hyman P. (1965), 'The Role of Employment Policy', in Margaret S. Gordon (ed.), *Poverty in America*, San Francisco, CA: Chandler Publishing Company, pp. 175–200.

Minsky, Hyman P. (1986), *Stabilizing an Unstable Economy*, New Haven, CT: Yale University Press.

Minsky, Hyman P. and P. Ferri (1991), 'Market Processes and Thwarting Systems', Levy WP 64.

Minsky, Hyman P. and C. Whalen (1996), 'Economic Insecurity and the Institutional Prerequisites for Successful Capitalism', Levy WP 165.

Papadimitriou, Dimitri B. and L. Randall Wray (1998), 'The Economic Contributions of Hyman Minsky: Varieties of Capitalism and Institutional Reform', *Review of Political Economy*, **10**(2), 199–225.

Patinkin, Don (1965), *Money, Interest and Prices*, 2nd edn, New York: Harper & Row.

Samuelson, Paul (1973), *Economics*, 9th edn, New York: McGraw-Hill.

Skidelsky, Robert (2009), *Keynes: The Return of the Master*, New York: Public Affairs, Perseus Books Group.

Snowden, Brian and Howard R. Vane (2006), *Modern Macroeconomics: Its Origins, Development and Current State*, Cheltenham, UK and Northampton, MA, USA: Edward Elgar.

Wray, L. Randall (1998), *Understanding Modern Money: The Key to Full Employment and Price Stability*, Northampton, MA: Edward Elgar.

Wray, L. Randall (2003a), 'Can a Rising Tide Raise All Boats? Evidence from the Kennedy-Johnson and Clinton-era expansions', in Jonathan M. Harris and Neva R. Goodwin (eds), *New Thinking in Macroeconomics: Social, Institutional and Environmental Perspectives*, Cheltenham, UK and Northampton, MA: Edward Elgar, pp. 150–181.

Wray, L. Randall (2003b), 'The Perfect Fiscal Storm', *Challenge*, **46**(1), 55–78.

Wray, L. Randall (2004), 'The Fed and the New Monetary Consensus: The Case for Rate Hikes, Part Two', Public Policy Brief, Levy Economics Institute, No. 80.

Wray, L. Randall (2008a), 'Lessons from the Subprime Meltdown', *Challenge*, **51**(2), 40–68.

Wray, L. Randall (2008b), 'Demand Constraints and Big Government', *Journal of Economic Issues*, **42**(1), 153–173.

Wray, L. Randall (2009), 'The Rise and Fall of Money Manager Capitalism: A Minskian Approach', *Cambridge Journal of Economics*, **33**(4), 807–828.

PART VI

THE ECONOMICS PROFESSION, THE MEDIA AND THE PUBLIC

20 The spontaneous methodology of orthodoxy, and other economists' afflictions in the Great Recession

Philip Mirowski

20.1 AN ANATOMY OF CHAGRIN

It is never a life-affirming experience to be the guest of honor at a status-degradation ceremony; but ever since Plato and Boethius, one source of solicitude has been the consolations of philosophy. A grounding in philosophy has often permitted those of a contemplative turn to weather the brickbats and reversals of cruel fate. One may disagree or not with such notions of the nobility of stoicism, but the spectacle of victims deficient in such consolations flailing away at their fate must be conceded a less edifying phenomenon. It may also constitute a topic in cognitive psychology, something we shall explore shortly.

This chapter contemplates one such disaster, the reactions of the economics profession to the economic crisis which began in 2007. No sane person could welcome a worldwide economic contraction; but the economics profession was particularly vulnerable to scorn and derision with its onset, because the orthodox majority had been boasting of unprecedented success in guaranteeing prosperity during the first decade of the millennium, often under the rubric of 'The Great Moderation'.[1] Furthermore, the economists had grown so confident in their orthodoxy that they had driven out most rival views and approaches from the richest and most powerful academic settings. This relative homogeneity of their disciplinary convictions helped to set the stage for what has become a rolling come-uppance. Once the contraction proceeded in earnest in 2008, it became commonplace in newspapers, blogs and symposia at various universities to query openly why these economists had apparently been caught unawares. Disparagement grew sharper as time passed, such as in movies like Charles Ferguson's *Inside Job* (2010). Individual economists have responded with a bewildering array of diagnoses, qualifications and bald excuses, in ephemeral blogs and interviews, but also in durable print. How can an observer extract signal from noise in order to come to understand the modern predicament of economics? Has it all really been just a flash in the pan? How did economists acquit themselves during the shellacking? As the reader will appreciate, this is eminently a methodological question; but by 2008 the economists were bereft of methodological and philosophical resources to inform their responses.

After a brief flirtation in the 1960s and 1970s, the grandees of the economics profession took it upon themselves to express openly their disdain and revulsion for the types of self-reflection practiced by 'methodologists' and historians of economics, and to go out of their way to prevent those so inclined from occupying any tenured foothold in reputable economics departments.[2] It was perhaps no coincidence that history and philosophy were the areas where one found the greatest concentrations of skeptics concerning the shape and substance of the post-war American economic orthodoxy. High-ranking economics journals, such as the *American Economic Review*, the *Quarterly Journal of Economics* and the *Journal of Political Economy*, declared that they would cease publication of any articles whatsoever in the area, after a prior history of acceptance.

Once this policy was put in place, then algorithmic journal rankings were used to deny hiring and promotion at the commanding heights of economics to those with methodological leanings. Consequently, the greybeards summarily expelled both philosophy and history from the graduate economics curriculum; and then, they chased it out of the undergraduate curriculum as well. This latter exile was the bitterest, if only because many undergraduates often want to ask why the profession believes what it does, and hear others debate the answers, since their own allegiances are still in the process of being formed. The rationale tendered to repress this demand was that the students needed still more mathematics preparation, more statistics and more tutelage in 'theory', which meant in practice a boot camp regimen consisting of endless working of problem sets, problem sets and more problem sets, until the poor tyros were so dizzy they did not have the spunk left to interrogate the masses of journal articles they had struggled to absorb. How this encouraged students to become acquainted with the economy was a bit of a mystery – or perhaps it telegraphed the lesson that you did not need to attend to the specifics of actual economies (Klamer and Colander, 1990). Then, by the 1990s there was no longer any call for offering courses in philosophy or history of doctrine, since there were very few economists with sufficient training (not to mention interest) left in order to staff the courses.[3] Methodology had been effectively defined as 'not economics'. As one of the original interviewers noted about a follow-up survey of economics graduate students at major departments just before the crisis:

> These students furthermore do not show a great deal of ability to reflect on their discipline. They are satisfied with the commonplace, the things that economists

conventionally say about their discipline. This cohort appears to be mindless, or at least resourceless, when it comes to reflections on the nature of their science. They have no literature to fall back on. (Klamer in Colander, 2007, p. 231)

Consequently, when the Great Mortification followed in the wake of the demise of the Great Moderation, both those occupying the commanding heights of the profession and those in the trenches were bereft of any sophisticated resources to understand their predicament comprehensively. In a pinch, many fell into a defensive crouch, falling back on the most superficial of personal anecdotes, or else the last refuge of scoundrels, the proposition that 'we' already knew how to handle the seemingly anomalous phenomena, but had unaccountably neglected to incorporate these crucial ideas into our pedagogy and cutting-edge research. Streaming video sometimes captured these pageants on the Internet.[4] It takes some thick skin not to cringe at the performance of four famous economists at the January 2010 meetings of the American Economics Association in Atlanta, in a session expressly titled, 'How Should the Financial Crisis Change How We Teach Economics?'[5] Three out of the four were not even bothered actually to address the posited question, so concerned were they to foster the impression that they personally had not been caught with their pants down by the crisis. The fourth thought that simply augmenting his existing textbook with another chapter defining collateralized debt obligations and some simple orthodox finance theory would do the trick.

For the ragged remnants of economic methodologists, it was a dreary sight to watch a few older economists rummaging around in the vague recesses of memories of undergraduate courses criticizing Milton Friedman's little 1953 benediction for believing whatever you pleased as long as it was neoclassical (Mäki, 2009), and coming up with nothing better than badly garbled versions of Popper and Kuhn. Of course quite a few had premonitions that something had gone very wrong, but the sad truth was that they were clueless when it came to abstract philosophical argument isolating just where the flaws in professional practice might be traced, and assessing the extent that they were susceptible to methodological remedies. Mired in banality, the best they could prescribe was more of the same. No wonder almost every eminent economist took their philosophical perplexity as a convenient occasion to settle internecine scores within the narrow confines of the orthodox neoclassical profession: MIT v. Chicago, blinkered econometrics v. blinkered axiomatics, New Keynesians v. New Classicals, Pareto suboptima v. rational bubbles . . .

In this chapter, I shall try not to pay much attention to such local settling of scores, but instead attempt to comprehend these responses as a case study in the social psychological problem of cognitive dissonance.

The father of 'cognitive dissonance theory' was the social psychologist Leon Festinger. In his premier work on the subject, he addressed the canonical problem situation which captures the predicament of the contemporary economics profession:

> Suppose an individual believes something with his whole heart . . . suppose that he is then presented with unequivocal and undeniable evidence that his belief is wrong: what will happen? The individual will frequently emerge, not only unshaken, but even more convinced of the truth of his beliefs than ever before. Indeed, he may even show a new fervor about convincing and converting people. (Festinger et al., 1956, p. 3)

This profound insight, that confrontation with contrary evidence may actually augment and sharpen the conviction and enthusiasm of a true believer, was explained as a response to the cognitive dissonance evoked by a disconfirmation of strongly held beliefs. The thesis that humans are more rationalizing than rational has spawned a huge literature (Fischer et al., 2008), one that gets little respect in economics. Cognitive dissonance and the responses it provokes goes well beyond the literature in the philosophy of science that travels under the rubric of 'Duhem's thesis', in that the former plumbs response mechanisms to emotional chagrin, whereas the latter sketches the myriad ways in which auxiliary hypotheses may be evoked in order to blunt the threat of disconfirmation. Philosophy of science reveals the ways in which it may be rational to discount contrary evidence; but the social psychology of cognitive dissonance reveals just how elastic the concept of rationality can be in social life. Festinger and his colleagues illustrated these lessons in his first book (1956) by reporting the vicissitudes of a group of Midwesterners they called 'The Seekers' who conceived and developed a belief that they would be rescued by flying saucers on a specific date in 1954, prior to a great flood coming to engulf Lake City (a pseudonym). Festinger documents in great detail the hour-by-hour reactions of the Seekers as the date of their rescue came and passed with no spaceships arriving and no flood welling up to swallow Lake City. At first, the Seekers withdrew from representatives of the press seeking to upbraid them for their failed prophecies, but soon reversed their stance, welcoming all opportunities to expound and elaborate upon their (revised and expanded) faith. A minority of their group did fall away, but Festinger notes that they tended to be lukewarm peripheral members of the group before the crisis. Predominantly, the Seekers never renounced their challenged doctrines. At least in the short run, the ringleaders tended to redouble their proselytizing, so long as they were able to maintain interaction with a coterie of fellow covenanters.

In a manner of speaking, the legacy of renunciation of philosophy and methodology led much of the orthodox economics profession to behave in ways rather similar to the Seekers from 2008 onwards. The parallels between the Seekers and the contemporary economics profession are, of course, not exact. The Seekers were disappointed when their world didn't come to an end; economists were convinced their Great Moderation and neoliberal triumph would last forever, and were disappointed when it did appear to come to an end. The stipulated turning point never arrived for the Seekers, while the unsuspected turning point got the drop on the economists. The Seekers garnered no external support for their doctrines, indeed, quitting their jobs and contracts prior to their Fated Day; the economists, on the other hand, persist in being richly rewarded by many constituencies for remaining stalwart in their beliefs. The public press was never friendly towards the Seekers; it only turned on the economists with the financial collapse. (There are already signs it may be reverting to its older slavish adoration, however.) But nonetheless, the shape of the reactions to cognitive dissonance were amazingly similar. The crisis, which at first blush might seem to have refuted most everything that the economic orthodoxy believed in, was in the fullness of time more often than not trumpeted from both the Left and the Right as reinforcing their adherence to neoclassical economic theory. Thus was made manifest the 'spontaneous methodology of the economics profession'.

20.2   THE UNHEALTHY OBSESSION WITH PREDICTION

Easily the number one topic in the immediate aftermath of the financial crisis of 2008 was: why didn't economists see it coming? For the median layperson, this was symptomatic of the frequent misconception that the primal *raison d'être* of the economics profession is to give them investment advice. For journalists, it simply reprised the way they had been treating economic professionals all along as soothsayers for hire. But beneath the surface, this conviction that it was the professional responsibility of economists to predict such calamities in fact conjured deep unresolved philosophical issues concerning the very essence of economics, which were triggered when many members of the profession felt impelled to respond to the cascade of derision.

The journalist's complaint was broadcast from a number of platforms in normal times more respectful and subservient to economists, such as *Business Week*:

> Economists mostly failed to predict the worst economic crisis since the 1930s. Now they can't agree how to solve it. People are starting to wonder: What good are economists anyway? . . . To be fair, economists can't be expected to predict the future with any kind of exactitude. The world is simply too complicated for that. But collectively, they should be able to warn of dangers ahead. And when disaster strikes, they ought to know what to do. Indeed, people pay attention to economists at times like this precisely because of their bold claim that they know how to prevent the economy from sliding into a repeat of the Great Depression. But seven decades after the Depression, economists still haven't reached consensus on its lessons. (Coy, 2009)

At first, a few candid members of the profession opted to second the judgment of the journalists with respect to the crisis. One of most heartfelt, because it was cast in the format of an apology, was by Uwe Reinhardt at Princeton:

> If, like every university, the American Economic Association had a coat of arms, its obligatory Latin banner might read: *'Est, ergo optimum est, dummodo ne gubernatio civitatis implicatur.'* ('It exists, therefore it must be optimal, provided that government has not been involved.') . . .
> These thoughts occurred to me as I attended the American Economic Association's annual conference in San Francisco over the weekend. It offered a humongous smorgasbord of eloquent theory, clever econometric tricks, illuminating empirical insights and a few standing-room-only panel discussions on the shocking surprises the real economy served up as the economics profession was otherwise preoccupied during the past two decades or so.
> Fewer than a dozen prominent economists saw this economic train wreck coming – and the Federal Reserve chairman, Ben Bernanke, an economist famous for his academic research on the Great Depression, was notably not among them. Alas, for the real world, the few who did warn us about the train wreck got no more respect from the rest of their colleagues or from decision-makers in business and government than prophets usually do. (Reinhardt, 2009)

Far from merely echoing the antipathy of the man in the street, this refrain that the profession had suffered real failure by not predicting the crisis bore some real resonance among the rank and file for three substantive reasons. The first derived from the existence of the only self-identified methodological paper most contemporary economists had ever heard of, Milton Friedman's 'Methodology of Positive Economics' (1953). Even those who had never actually read it nonetheless were possessed of some vague notion that Friedman had stated that the truth of assumptions did not matter, just the success of predictions which the models emitted. I will bypass whether that was the 'real' or correct reading of Friedman's message (Mäki, 2009); the point here is rather that the Friedman dispensation had become one expedient in the lazy economist's playbook, in the odd situation that they actually had to defend the 'scientific character' of what they were doing to a semi-literate audience. So the failure to predict the crisis tended to discomfit the last vestiges of what passed for philosophy in the training of the modern economist; concurrently, it also made 'Chicago' look bad. No one wanted to reopen the old 'unrealism of assumptions' debate, which the profession believed to have relegated to the dustheap of doctrinal history long ago. Hence, making a big deal of failed predictions summoned up a submerged world of humiliation that most economists would rather just avoid.

And then there was the second nagging source of relevance. It was a little-discussed attribute of the economics profession that, even in the last decade, many economists made their livings by producing predictions of one sort or another. Although it had become de rigueur in the commanding heights of reputable academic ivory towers to sneer at the very possibility of successful prediction (see below), the truth of the matter was that down in the trenches, where most economists lived, dealing in prediction was a bread-and-butter activity (Sherden, 1998).

'Prediction' had become the stereotypical outcome of most quotidian economic research, even though most players realized it merely signified a stylized denouement. As one MIT student reported (in Colander, 2007, p. 241):

> There is a sentiment here from people I have talked to that if they want a model we can give them a model. We sit down and make up a model, and we play with it until it gives us the empirical result that we find, even though you could as easily written down a model that would have given a different result. We have even had seminar speakers say, 'Oh, I worked on a model that predicts it; of course I could have written down a model that predicts the opposite, but why would I do that?' In general, you can write down a model that predicts just about anything.

If you worked for a firm or the government, you were simply expected to produce predictions like clockwork, and with a straight face. If you had aspirations to be a public intellectual, then one could not write op-eds or appear on television or radio without being importuned to predict something or other. If you did not comply, you would not be invited back; there were hundreds lined up, willing to prognosticate. The entire quotidian public discourse of professional economists continuously revolved around predictions, whatever they might say to one another in university seminars or academic papers. It is significant that careful inquiry into economists' predictions had revealed a rather dismal track record long before the crisis had hit:

- The forecasting skill of economists is on average about as good as uninformed guessing. Predictions by the Council of Economic Advisors, Federal Reserve Board, and Congressional Budget Office were often worse than random.
- Economists have proven repeatedly that they cannot predict the turning points in the economy.
- No specific economic forecasters consistently lead the pack in accuracy.
- No economic forecaster has consistently higher forecasting skills predicting any particular economic statistic.
- Consensus forecasts do not improve accuracy (although the press loves them; so much for the wisdom of crowds).
- Finally, there is no evidence that economic forecasting has improved in recent decades (Sherden, 1998).

Again, if this track record were widely known already to have been so very poor, then missing the onset of the crisis should not have caused such consternation on its own. Or conversely, the profession could set about writing down little models that could 'retrospectively' have predicted the crisis, doing what worked in the past. Neither of those eventualities got to the heart of the uproar about 'failures of prediction' in the public press. Rather, the crisis brought to consciousness for the lay public the portent that there was a specific bias in the orientation of the profession, a bias that ruled out of bounds predictions of the sorts of global system-wide breakdowns which had galvanized those living through 2008–10. Hence what the clientele thought they were buying – a sort of neutral reconnaissance of the near future – did not correspond very well with what the economists had been proffering.[6]

And that leads us to the third Pandora's Box opened by the mortification of failed prediction. Skipping over detail, it is sufficient to point to the fact that orthodox theories of macroeconomics since the 1980s had grown obsessed with the issue of prediction. Whereas earlier models in American Keynesianism had been constructed to be backward-looking (distributed lags, moving averages, and so on) both orthodox finance theory and the new macroeconomics adopted the neoclassical position that bygones are bygones, and from the so-called 'permanent income hypothesis' onwards, therefore all relevant decisions were based upon expectations of the future. Furthermore, the rational expectations school and the later dynamic stochastic general equilibrium models insisted that expectations were formed with the very same neoclassical models and econometric techniques that the orthodoxy endorsed. Thus the orthodoxy had effectively conflated the prediction of the economist with the predictions of the agent, and elevated it as a central theme of modern economic theory (Sent, 1998). There had always been pockets of resistance to this audacious theoretical move, but the crisis brought the qualms out into the open by suggesting that agents should not rely so heavily on the clones of the 'rational' economists to ground their expectations. It was not intentional, but the hue and cry over failed prediction tore the scabs off a number of repressed and forgotten wounds in the philosophy of the 'rational economic agent'. This may explain why the journalists were so keen to indict the leaders of the 'rational expectations' movement hard on the heels of the financial collapse.

The best evidence that the accusations of failed prediction were so minacious that they provoked a triumph of indignation over complacency can be found in the wildly bipolar reactions of economists to the indictment: one coterie insisted that economists were vindicated by the successful predictions of the few and the canny; whereas another insisted instead that good economists never claimed to be able to predict the economy in the first place. Viewed as a totality, this exemplified a larger tendency for the profession as a whole simultaneously to assert A and not-A in response to calumny.

The gambit to search for 'successful predictors' amongst the economists seemed to have originated with journalists. Economists sat up and took more notice of the rebukes published in the magazine *The Economist* (2009) than the other news magazines, if only because those articles softened the condemnation with various potential excuses that the complaints found elsewhere had gone 'too far', and that the allegations only had partial validity. With regard to the accusation that 'most economists failed to see the crisis coming', *The Economist* averred that some had indeed issued warnings, and explicitly named Robert Shiller, Nouriel Roubini and the 'team at the Bank for International Settlements'.

This set off the starting gun for a veritable silly season of all manner of economists being proposed as vindicated prophets and unappreciated soothsayers, as though the prescience of the few would redeem the dimwittedness of the many. This race to populate the Nostradamus Codex continued for more than a year, encompassing even an online ballot to vote for the best crisis prognosticator.[7] A motley cavalcade of economists then jostled in an unseemly fashion to put themselves forward as having somehow anticipated the crisis, across not just from the orthodoxy, but spanning the political gamut from Libertarians to Left Post-Keynesians.[8] But worse, the scrum began to unfocus the definition of the moving object that stood as the appropriate target for prediction. In the rush to judgment, anyone who said or wrote anything about some kind of bubble or imbalance or financial instability sometime in the 2000s suddenly sought to be credited as rivalling the Oracle at Delphi, engaging in the most exquisite augury. Some Nobel winners in particular pushed this gambit well beyond the breaking point, eliding prediction proper, and instead suggesting that anyone who had ever produced a mathematical model mentioning bank runs or financial fraud or irrational expectations or debt deflation or [fill in the blank] was proof positive that the economics profession had not been caught unawares. It helped if the interlocutor stopped paying attention to what had been taught in the macroeconomics classes across the most highly ranked economics departments. It got so bad after a while that any mention of market failure or departure from equilibrium was supposed to function as a 'get out of jail free' card in 2009. Here is one illustrative example:

> Q: There's been lots of criticism, for example from Paul Krugman, that the economics profession did not foresee the crisis. But from the way you're talking, it seems there are existing models that predict that these crises will happen, and it's a question of how you respond.
> A: I don't accept the criticism that economic theory failed to provide a framework for understanding this crisis. Indeed, the papers we're discussing today show pretty clearly why the crisis occurred and what we can do about it. The sort of economics that deserves attack is Alan Greenspan's idealized world, in which financial markets work perfectly well on their own and don't require government action. There are, of course, still economists – probably fewer than before – who believe in that world. But it is an extreme position and not one likely to be held by those who understand the papers we're talking about. (Maskin, 2009)

Of course, the unstated lesson was that no one with a gold-plated ivy union card (Greenspan was awarded a belated PhD by New York University in 1977) whom acknowledged the 'best journals' as revealed doctrine was caught unawares by the crisis. This whole quest to identify the predictive elect amongst the economists was therefore very rapidly driven to Bedlam, partly because it was so mendacious, but also because it twisted the meaning of predictive success beyond all recognition. In a sort of Protestant Reformation, everyone was sanctioned to read and interpret the Revealed (Journal) Scripture and the crisis portents in their own idiosyncratic manner, and then enjoy absolution, so long as they pledged their troth to the One True neoclassical economics.

Lest the reader get the impression that this was the only retort to the accusation that economists had failed in predicting the crisis, they should be apprized that there was also a Counter-Reformation movement. Primarily it was located amongst those economists found at the sharp end of the journalists' stick, the high-profile leaders of the rational expectations macroeconomics movement. In the heat of the downdraft, magazines like *Business Week* and *The Economist* were not shy in naming names: 'Count Harvard's Robert Barro in this camp, along with Chicago's Robert E. Lucas, Arizona State's Edward C. Prescott, and the University of Minnesota's Patrick J. Kehoe and V.V. Chari' (Coy, 2009). It was seconded in a broadside from Willem Buiter:

> Most mainstream macroeconomic theoretical innovations since the 1970s (associated with such names as Robert E. Lucas Jr., Edward Prescott, Thomas Sargent, Robert Barro etc., and the New Keynesian theorizing of Michael Woodford and many others) have turned out to be self-referential, inward-looking distractions at best. Research tended to be motivated by internal logic, intellectual sunk capital and aesthetic puzzles of established research programmes rather than by a powerful desire to understand how the economy works . . . the manifest failure of the EMH [efficient-market hypothesis] in many key asset markets was obvious to virtually all those whose cognitive abilities had not been warped by a modern Anglo-American PhD education. (Buiter, 2009)

Their intellectual leader, Robert Lucas, was quick to respond in the pages of *The Economist* that critics were holding economists to a standard that their own theories tell them they could never meet. In other words, economics tells us that economists will never be good predictors:

> One thing we are not going to have, now or ever, is a set of models that fore-casts sudden falls in the value of financial assets, like the declines that followed the failure of Lehman Brothers in September. This is nothing new. It has been known for more than 40 years and is one of the main implications of Eugene Fama's 'efficient-market hypothesis' (EMH), which states that the price of a financial asset reflects all relevant, generally available information. If an econo-mist had a formula that could reliably forecast crises a week in advance, say, then that formula would become part of generally available information and prices would fall a week earlier . . . *The Economist*'s briefing also cited as an example of macroeconomic failure the 'reassuring' simulations that Frederic Mishkin, then a governor of the Federal Reserve, presented in the summer of 2007. The charge is that the Fed's FRB/US forecasting model failed to predict the events of September 2008. Yet the simulations were not presented as assur-ance that no crisis would occur, but as a forecast of what could be expected conditional on a crisis not occurring. (Lucas, 2009)

Patently, in the Counter-Reformation, economists should never have been expected to predict the really bad stuff: that was the sole province of The Market, the greatest information processor known to humanity. Furthermore, critics in the lay audience do not appreciate what it means when we offer you a 'model': it only 'predicts' in limited situations which resemble the ones the model was built for. *Caveat emptor.*

One index of the extent of disruption within the profession induced by the crisis was that economists no longer felt compelled to defer humbly to

Nobelist Robert Lucas as they had before 2008, but rushed to go on record to dispute this 'defense' of the profession. *The Economist* was happy to provide a special blog on which they could register their dissent.[9] Some insisted that the heart of the problem was the efficient-markets hypothesis. Brad de Long suggested Lucas was changing his tune as the crisis evolved. Others, like Harvard's Robert Barro, propounded the proposition that the proof of the pudding was not in the success of the prediction, but instead what the clientele would pay for: 'Like Bob Lucas, I have a hard time taking seriously the view that the financial and macroeconomic crisis has diminished economics as a field. In fact, the crisis has clearly raised the demand for economic services and economists. There is no more counter-cyclical occupation than economist.' This only served to pour gasoline on the blogosphere.

The line quickly hardened within the Counter-Reformation that the orthodox 'efficient-markets hypothesis' had been confirmed by the crisis, and that economists had never borne the onus of predicting much of anything at all. This comes out quite clearly in the *New Yorker* interviews with Chicago economists:

John Cassidy: *I asked Fama how he thought the theory, which says prices of financial assets accurately reflect all of the available information about economic fundamentals, had fared.*
Eugene Fama: I think it did quite well in this episode. Stock prices typically decline prior to and in a state of recession. This was a particularly severe recession. Prices started to decline in advance of when people recognized that it was a recession and then continued to decline. There was nothing unusual about that. That was exactly what you would expect if markets were efficient.
Many people would argue that, in this case, the inefficiency was primarily in the credit markets, not the stock market – that there was a credit bubble that inflated and ultimately burst.
I don't even know what that means. People who get credit have to get it from somewhere. Does a credit bubble mean that people save too much during that period? I don't know what a credit bubble means. I don't even know what a bubble means. These words have become popular. I don't think they have any meaning . . .
Back to the efficient markets hypothesis. You said earlier that it comes out of this episode pretty well. Others say the market may be good at pricing in a relative sense – one stock versus another – but it is very bad at setting absolute prices, the level of the market as a whole. What do you say to that?
People say that. I don't know what the basis of it is. If they know, they should be rich men. What better way to make money than to know exactly about the absolute level of prices.
So you still think that the market is highly efficient at the overall level too?
Yes. And if it isn't, it's going to be impossible to tell. (Cassidy, 2010)

And then there is the Cassidy interview with John Cochrane:

The two biggest ideas associated with Chicago economics over the past thirty years are the efficient markets hypothesis and the rational expectations hypothesis. At this stage, what's left of those two?
John Cochrane: I think everything. Why not? Seriously, now, these are not ideas so superficial that you can reject them just by reading the newspaper. Rational expectations and efficient markets theories are both consistent with big price crashes. If you want to talk about this, we need to talk about specific evidence and how it does or doesn't match up with specific theories.
In the United States, we've had two massive speculative bubbles in ten years. How can that be consistent with the efficient markets hypothesis?
Great, so now you know how to define 'bubbles' for me. I've been looking for that for twenty years. (Cassidy, 2010)

If one imagines the faint echoes of the Seekers after they were left stranded by the flying saucers, then perhaps you begin to comprehend how complaints that economists did not foresee the crisis are not going to change anyone's mind in economics.

20.3   SOMETHING IN THE 'PROTECTIVE BELT' TO SACRIFICE

Without going into detail, it had been taken for granted in the philosophy of science of 1970s–1980s vintage that older Popperian stories of empirical refutation of well-entrenched theories by stark crucial experiments had no counterparts in the actual history of science. First, renegade Popperians like Imre Lakatos and Paul Feyerabend pointed out that seeming disconfirmations were often shifted to expendable auxiliary theories in what Lakatos himself called the 'protective belt'. Later philosophers and science studies scholars may have found Lakatos a bit mechanical, yet explored even more roundabout ways that the threat of empirical refutation could be deflected or redirected away from a set of doctrines or models deemed at the core of a particular science. Much attention was devoted to the ways in which revision was permitted at the boundaries and outskirts of research programs, as well as at the various interfaces between theoretical and empiricist communities. There was a time when economic methodologists explored similar tactics in the history of economics;[10] but those atrophied with the expulsion of methodology and history of economics from the curriculum.

It would not be germane here to defend or resuscitate Lakatos; it nevertheless seems apparent that when vibrant research programs encounter big potential disconfirmations, a lively topic of conversation revolves around what subtheories or discrete programs might be jettisoned so that the global program might perdure unscathed. This strategem is not a particularly devious or illegitimate concern; indeed, one might even regard it as Occam's Razor in action. The problem arises when someone has to evaluate the quality of the renunciation: was it too drastic, jettisoning baby with bathwater? Was it misguided, neglecting the ways in which different subsets of the program meshed, such that excision in one area has unanticipated effects in other parts of the program? And how much neutralization of empirical evidence should be allowed? Too many blank checks might lead to utter sterility, whereas too few indulgences might result in premature demise of a program with real promise. One of the lessons philosophy of science teaches is that scrupulous evaluation and restraint of sterilization of empirical counter-evidence is where the real quality control of research inheres.

The economists described in this section were not quite so inclined to insist that the orthodoxy had escaped scot-free from the ravages of the crisis, by contrast with the figures cited in the previous section. In the heat of the crisis, these were figures who enjoyed legitimacy at the pinnacles of the profession, yet in the crunch appeared to outsiders simultaneously as valiant rebels, peremptorily dispensing with theories which had brought the world economy crashing down around us. Not unexpectedly, whereas much of the wrangling about prediction tended to occur within the orbit of the University of Chicago, many of the current revisionists covered in this section went out of their way to excoriate Chicago economics. Yet, as with the previous case of prediction, all was not as it seemed. Sneering at Chicago should never be confused with making a clean break with orthodox economics. Venturing beyond the superficial impressions of the journalists who often championed one or another of these protagonists as our saviors, it will turn out whatever was 'new' was not very serious as a research program, and whatever really was serious was not in fact new. Hence, the widespread impression that 'the crisis has increased the vitality of economics' (Acemoglu, 2009, p. 3) turned out to be premature, to say the least.

Although many different ideas were floated from 2008 to 2010 about what types of conceptual revisions would best rectify the previous errors of economists, I shall here restrict myself to the top three proposals in terms of their overall popularity. Arrayed in order from most ambitious to least, they were: dispense with full neoclassical 'rationality' of agents; dispense with notions of the market as ideal information processor embodied in the efficient-markets hypothesis; and finally, simply dispense with the standard orthodox macroeconomic model taught in all contemporary orthodox graduate schools, dubbed the dynamic stochastic general equilibrium (DSGE) model. Although the reader may not care much about the intricate technical details, a quick reconnoiter of each will reveal the limited imagination that the economics profession could muster in the depths of its philosophical perplexity.

20.3.1 Ditching 'Rationality'

It has been fairly common in the annals of economic history to observe that in the wake of serious financial crises, observers tended to bewail a weakness in human cognition, attributing pecuniary disaster to a 'madness of crowds'. Eventually, eschewing structural explanations, all serious problems would conventionally tend to be traced back through intermediate 'bad choices' to moral or character flaws in particular individuals. Thus, it was no surprise that a pervasive and immediate response to 2008 was to blame the entire mess on a rabid outbreak of 'irrational exuberance'.

Unfortunately, madness often lodged in the eye of the beholder. When it came to orthodox economics, the term 'rationality' bore a very narrow and curious interpretation as the maximization of a utility function subject to constraints by an otherwise cognitively thin and emotionally deprived 'agent'. This unsatisfactory version of rationality had been the perennial subject of complaint and criticism from within and without economics since the 1870s; numerous defenses had been developed over the decades supposedly to neutralize those concerns. Hence, in economics, repudiation of 'rationality' meant in practice tinkering with the utility function and/or its maximization. The latest attempt at accommodation dated from the 1990s, introducing some amendments from narrow subsets of psychology (mostly decision theory) while keeping the basic maximization of utility framework intact: this had come to be called 'behavioral economics'. This purported enrichment of simpler concepts of rationality had even established a beachhead in the study of finance well before the crisis; its most prominent advocate in the prelapsarian era was Lawrence Summers, which might begin to signal that its revolutionary potential may not have been all that transformative. Mostly, in finance it produced models predicated upon the posited existence of a complement of stupid people, somewhat more charitably known as 'noise traders', who performed certain functions in financial markets (liquidity, smoothing of reactions to shocks) so that the neoclassically 'rational' agents could more readily find the 'true' or 'fundamental' values dictated by the prior orthodox theory. Nothing here substantially impugned the basic orthodox model.

Once the crisis hit, journalists predictably turned to accusing Wall Street of behaving irrationally (in the vernacular meaning), and economists of investing too much credence in the rationality of their agents. Two bestselling books were especially effective in broadcasting this line:

John Cassidy's *How Markets Fail* (2009) and Justin Fox's *Myth of the Rational Market* (2009). Some economists who had been strong advocates of behavioral approaches prior to the crash, Robert Shiller (2006) and Robert Frank (2009), leapt in with op-eds essentially blaming the entire crisis on cognitive weaknesses of market participants. This line became entrenched with the appearance of George Akerlof and Robert Shiller's *Animal Spirits* (2009a): displaying an utter contempt for the history of economic thought, they 'reduced' the message of Keynes's *General Theory* to the proposition that people get a little irrational from time to time, and thus push the system away from full neoclassical general equilibrium.[11] They wrote:

> The idea that economic crises, like the current financial and housing crisis, are mainly caused by changing thought patterns goes against standard economic thinking. But current crisis bears witness to the role of such changes in thinking. It was caused precisely by our changing confidence, temptations, envy, resentment, and illusions . . . (2009a, p. 4)

The timing was propitious, since at that juncture all sorts of people were casting about for something different in the way of economic analysis of the crisis. Nevertheless, when a few journalists read the book, the first thing they noticed was that it said very little substantive about the current crisis, for much of it had been written well before 2008. Brought up short, they began to doubt its pertinence. The second thing they noticed was it was full of overweening claims, but contained very little in the way of causal mechanisms. 'Animal spirits' boiled down to such timeworn neoclassical expedients as changing the utility function over time and calling it 'confidence' (while Chicago called it 'time-varying rates of discount'), appealing to sticky wages and prices while attributing them to 'money illusion' and concerns over fairness (which the neoliberals modeled as 'envy'), and suggestions that corruption would grow over the course of a long expansion (Chicago theorist Gary Becker theorized this the 'rational choice approach to crime'). Far from some brave venturesome foray into the unexplored thickets of real psychology by open-minded economists unencumbered by entrenched dogmas, this was just more of the same old trick of tinkering with the 'normal' utility function to get out the results you had wanted beforehand – something falling well short of the trumpeted dramatic divergence from standard economic theory.

This raised an objection that had long been a subject of discussion in the methodology literature: wasn't 'irrationality' in the neoclassical lexicon an oxymoron, since the moment one formalized it in the utility function, didn't it effectively get subsumed under some perverse version of meta-rationality? Richard Posner (2009b), an especially perceptive critic from the Right, pushed this point home in a review of *Animal Spirits*. The Akerlof–Shiller reply, deficient in philosophical sophistication, proved unable to confront this debility:

> When Posner asserts that it is not always easy to rule out that people are acting rationally – even if they seem not to be – he is of course right, for this is what most academic economists have thought. It is hard to disprove such a theory that people are completely economically rational because the theory is somewhat slippery: It doesn't specify what objectives people have or what their information really is. (Akerlof and Shiller, 2009b)

The problem with behavioral economists going gaga over 'irrationality' was that they conflated that incredibly complex and tortured phenomenon with minor divergences from their own overly rigid construct of pure deterministic maximization of an independent invariant 'well-behaved' utility function. Akerlof and Shiller could only condone an incongruously rationalist framing of their irrational exuberance. One can therefore appreciate misgivings that this core theory was so 'slippery' that it is not at all evident what the enthusiasm over 'behavioral economics' really amounted to. Two decades of behavioral research certainly has not resulted in any consensus systematic revisions of microeconomics, much less macroeconomics. Beyond wishful thinking, why should one even think that the appropriate way to approach a macroeconomic crisis was through some arbitrary set of folk psychological mental categories? Again, they had to admit that Posner had caught them putting the rabbit into the hat:

> Posner makes the interesting point that most behavioral economists – who study the application of psychology to economics – did not predict the economic crisis either. We would put this somewhat differently: There were very few behavioral economists who made forceful public statements that a crisis may be imminent. That is because there are very few behavioral economists who even specialized in macroeconomics, and so virtually none was willing to take the risk of making any definitive forecast. (Akerlof and Shiller, 2009b)

The plea that in the eventuality that behavioral economics had had more adherents, it would have done more of the things Akerlof promised, is hardly a compelling reason to get enthused about a line of research. Akerlof and Shiller were loathe to admit that they had not proffered any good conceptual reasons to believe that behavioral economics was even particularly relevant to the crisis. What this literature had to do with the genesis of credit default swaps, the rise of the shadow banking sector and the collapse of the manufacturing sector was entirely opaque. And however much Akerlof and Shiller protested that their politics was diametrically opposed to neoliberals like Reagan and Bush, what was their version of 'animal spirits' but tantamount to simply blaming the victims for the macroeconomic contraction? Shiller's previous books did indeed identify the housing bubble as a problem, but his 'solutions' always involved even more baroque securitizations of the assets in question (Shiller, 2006). In this, he rivaled the most avid neoliberal in his belief in the superior power of The Market to fix any problem.

The unbearable lightness of Akerlof's behavioral theory is nicely exemplified by the one paper that was repeatedly cited by bloggers and journalists during the crisis, his 'Looting: The Economic Underworld of Bankruptcy for Profit' (Akerlof and Romer, 1993). From reading the title, one would suspect it might deal with the phenomenon of running a financial institution into the ground given the temptations of short-term trading profits; like, say, Bear Stearns or Lehman Brothers. Few of its enthusiasts actually bothered to go so far as to read the model, however. In the MIT tradition, it was a purely deterministic little 'toy' model of a single firm over three periods, where assets are not bought or sold after the first period, and a little maximization exercise which argues that if the owners of the firm could pay themselves more than the firm is worth and then declare bankruptcy in period three, then they will do so. Accounting manipulation and regulatory forbearance (which were not described in any level of detail) are asserted to make this outcome more likely. Deposit insurance permits owners to offload costs of auto-destruction onto the government. This was then asserted to 'explain' the savings and loan crisis of the 1980s.

This displays all the hallmarks of the behavioral program touted by Akerlof and Shiller. First, a reputedly irrational behavior (looting banks by their owners) is rendered 'rational' through minor amendment of a simple orthodox maximization exercise by tinkering with the utility function of bank owners. Insights from professional psychology are absent. Macroeconomic phenomena are reduced to isolated individual choice in a manner far less sophisticated than in the reductionist rational expectations movement. Predictably, the model adds nothing to what simple intuition would suggest, given that the problem has been artificially restricted to a rudimentary cost–benefit exercise beforehand. Indeed, the model does not particularly illuminate the situation that nominally inspired it, since it does not encompass any of the specific institutional detail pertinent to the phenomenon; that is, it bypasses what precipitated the crisis at that particular juncture. It ignores the breakdown of Depression-era walls between depository and investment institutions, and neglects the spread of baroque securitization at the behest of finance economists, and the watershed of the 'originate and unload' business model for retail loans. But more to the point, their supposedly left-wing approach ends up backhandedly reproducing the conventional neoliberal story, as was pointed out by Gregory Mankiw in his published commentary:

> Although the two authors from Berkeley did not intend this paper to be a defense of Ronald Reagan and his view of government, one can easily interpret it in this way. The paper shows that the savings and loan crisis was not the result of unregulated markets, but of overregulated ones . . . The policy that led to the savings and loan crisis is, according to these authors, deposit insurance. (Akerlof and Romer, 1993, p. 65)

Hence, when some economists speculated that the orthodoxy would give way to a 'more realistic' behavioral economics in reaction to the crisis, it was primarily a symptom of the general unwillingness to entertain any serious departure from conventional arguments.[12] If anyone had bothered actually to read any of the leaders of the behavioral 'movement', they would have quickly realized that those economists went out of their way to renounce any ambitions to displace the orthodoxy. In one spectacularly badly timed compromise, Andrew Lo had sought to reconcile the findings of behavioral finance with the efficient-markets hypothesis (Lo, 2005). And behavioral economists could care less about the layered complexity of the human soul. Indeed, one need not look far to encounter their contempt for the academic psychology profession:

> I think we strive for parsimonious, rigorous theoretical explanations; this distinguishes us from the psychologists . . . Economists want a theory that provides a unifying explanation of these results whereas psychologists are much more willing to accept two different theories to explain these 'contradictory' results . . . I don't like the argument that everything is context dependent. That view lacks any grounding. In this regard, I really like the strong theoretical emphasis of economics and our desire for unifying explanations. It distinguishes us a lot from biologists and psychologists, and provides us with a normative anchor. (Fehr in Rosser et al., 2010, pp. 72–73)

If you asked behavioralists what all this tinkering with conventional neoclassical utility functions (which dated back to the very inception of the program in the 1880s) was supposed to portend, they would tell you in no uncertain terms that so-called behavioral economics 'is based not on a proposed paradigm shift in the basic approach of our field, but rather is a natural broadening of the field of economics . . . [it is] built on the premise that not only mainstream *methods* are great, but so too are mainstream economic *assumptions*' (Rabin, 2002, p. 659).[13]

So wherever did the vast bulk of commentators get the unfounded impression that behavioral economics was poised to deliver us from the previous errors of orthodoxy when it came to the economic crisis? Partly, it was the fault of a few high-profile economists like Shiller, Akerlof and

Krugman, whose own 'behavioral' credentials within the community were, shall we say, a bit shaky. But it also emanated from the vast scrum of journalists, primed to believe that when economists would just abjure 'rational choice theories', then all would become revealed. It got so bad that two bona fide behavioralists felt impelled to pen an op-ed for the *New York Times* absolving themselves of any responsibility to explain the crisis:

> It seems that every week a new book or major newspaper article appears showing that irrational decision-making helped cause the housing bubble . . . It's becoming clear that behavioral economics is being asked to solve problems it wasn't meant to address . . . Behavioral economics should complement, not substitute for, more substantive economic interventions [of] traditional economics. (Loewenstein and Ubel, 2010)

Ultimately, the more perceptive journalists acknowledged this: 'While behaviorists and other critics poked a lot of holes in the edifice of rational market finance, they haven't been willing to abandon that edifice' (Fox, 2009, p. 301). It is not even clear that they have been all that willing to bring themselves to look out the window. What 'behavioral economics' fostered was the warm glow of feeling that you had changed your economic stripes without having to change your mind, or your models. Like the Seekers.

20.3.2   Renunciation of the Efficient-Markets Hypothesis

For those living through the roller-coaster of 2008, and retrospectively searching for previous wrong turns, it seemed obvious to focus on the sector wherefrom disasters cascaded one after another like clowns piling out of an auto: namely, Wall Street. Not only had finance become the 400 pound gorilla of the US economy, accounting for 41 per cent of all corporate profits in 2007 (Stiglitz, 2010a, p. 7), but it was also the arena where economic theory had seemed to matter to a greater degree than elsewhere, given recourse to formal models to 'justify' all manner of activities, from securitization and options pricing to risk management.[14] Thus it was fairly predictable that some economists would look to finance theory as the locus of error, and rapidly settled upon a single doctrine to scapegoat, the one dubbed the 'efficient-markets hypothesis' [EMH]. Paul Krugman became a prominent spokesperson for this option in his notorious 'How Did Economists Get it so Wrong?' (2009):

> By 1970 or so, however, the study of financial markets seemed to have been taken over by Voltaire's Dr Pangloss, who insisted we live in the best of all possible worlds. Discussion of investor irrationality, of bubbles, of destructive speculation had virtually disappeared from academic discourse. The field was

dominated by the 'efficient markets hypothesis' . . . which claims that financial markets price assets precisely at their intrinsic worth given all publicly available information . . . And by the 1980s, finance economists, notably Michael Jensen of the Harvard Business School, were arguing that because financial markets always get prices right, the best thing corporate chieftains can do, not just for themselves but for the sake of the economy, is to maximize their stock prices. In other words, finance economists believed that we should put the capital development of the nation in the hands of what Keynes had called 'a casino'.

Journalists found the EMH irresistibly seductive to ridicule, with John Cassidy and Justin Fox attacking it at length. The journalist Roger Lowenstein declared: 'The upside of the current Great Recession is that it could drive a stake through the heart of the academic nostrum known as the efficient-market hypothesis.'[15] There was more than sufficient ammunition to choose from to rain fire down on the EMH, not least because it had been the subject of repeated criticism from within the economics profession since the 1980s. But what the journalists like Cassidy, Fox and Lowenstein, and commentators like Krugman, neglected to inform their readers was that the back and forth, the intellectual thrust and empirical parry had ground to a stand-off more than a decade before the crisis, as admirably explained in Lo and MacKinlay (1999):

There is an old joke, widely told among economists, about an economist strolling down the street with a companion when they come upon a $100 bill lying on the ground. As the companion reaches down to pick it up, the economist says 'Don't bother – if it were a real $100 bill, someone would have already picked it up.' This humorous example of economic logic gone awry strikes dangerously close to home for students of the Efficient Markets Hypothesis, one of the most important controversial and well-studied propositions in all the social sciences. It is disarmingly simple to state, has far-reaching consequences for academic pursuits and business practice, and yet is surprisingly resilient to empirical proof or refutation. Even after three decades of research and literally thousands of journal articles, economists have not yet reached a consensus about whether markets – particularly financial markets – are efficient or not.

What can we conclude about the Efficient Markets Hypothesis? Amazingly, there is still no consensus among financial economists. Despite the many advances in the statistical analysis, databases, and theoretical models surrounding the Efficient Markets Hypothesis, the main effect that the large number of empirical studies have had on this debate is to harden the resolve of the proponents on each side. One of the reasons for this state of affairs is the fact that the Efficient Markets Hypothesis, by itself, is not a well-defined and empirically refutable hypothesis. To make it operational, one must specify additional structure, e.g., investors' preferences, information structure, business conditions, etc. But then a test of the Efficient Markets Hypothesis becomes a test of several auxiliary hypotheses as well, and a rejection of such a joint hypothesis tells us little about which aspect of the joint hypothesis is inconsistent with the data. Are stock prices too volatile because markets are inefficient, or is it due to risk aversion, or dividend smoothing? All three inferences are consistent with the data. Moreover, new statistical tests designed to distinguish among them will no doubt require auxiliary hypotheses of their own which, in turn, may be questioned.

This imperviousness of an isolated hypothesis to empirical rejection, and the crucial role of auxiliary hypotheses in serving as a protective barrier, is familiar in the philosophy of science literature as 'Duhem's thesis'. The mere fact of deflecting disconfirmation off onto harmless auxiliary hypotheses is not prima facie an illegitimate ploy; it occurs in all the natural sciences. The issue was not that immunizing stratagems had been resorted to in this instance; rather, it was that the EMH had proven so rabidly tenacious within orthodox economics and in business schools, occupying pride of place for decades within both macroeconomics and finance, that economists had begun to ignore most modern attempts to disprove it. Perhaps it was not the localized cancer that its detractors had portrayed; maybe it was more akin to a symbiotic parasite that actually helped orthodox economics thrive. The lesson for crisis-watchers that I shall explore is that the EMH cannot be killed easily, and maybe not at all within the parameters of the current economics profession. That is one reason why non-economists need to be suspicious of claims like the pro-nunciation of the economist most famous for the 'reject the EMH' option, Joseph Stiglitz:

> [A] considerable portion of [blame] lies with the economics profession. The notion economists pushed – that markets are efficient and self-adjusting – gave comfort to regulators like Alan Greenspan, who didn't believe in regulation in the first place . . . We should be clear about this: economic theory never provided much support for these free market views. Theories of imperfect and asymmetric information in markets had undermined every one of the 'effi-cient market' doctrines, even before they became fashionable in the Reagan–Thatcher era. (Stiglitz, 2010b)

Pace Stiglitz, each blow just seemed to leave it stronger. One of the characteristics of the EMH which rendered it impervious to refutation was the fact that both proponents and critics were sometimes extremely cavalier about the meaning and referent of the adjective 'efficient'. Both Krugman and Stiglitz, for instance, in the above quotes simply conflate two major connotations of efficiency, namely, 'informational efficiency' and 'allocative efficiency'. The former is a proposition about the efficacy and exactitude of markets as information conveyance devices; the latter is a proposition that market prices correctly capture the 'fundamentals' and maximize the benefits to market participants by always representing the unique arbitrage-free equilibrium. It is sometimes taken for granted that the former implies the latter; this is the gist of the comment that one will never find loose $100 bills on the sidewalk. However, if one rephrased the claim to state that no one will ever find valuable unused information on the sidewalk, then the fallacy starts to become apparent.[16] In order to respect the significance of that distinction, in this section I deal with those who propose that the orthodoxy shed the information-processing version of the EMH in reaction to the crisis; while in the next I consider those who seek to dispense with allocative efficiency altogether.

The journalist and blogger Felix Salmon posed the critical question during the crisis: why did the EMH become the destructive love affair which the economics profession seemed unable to shake off?[17] To understand where the orthodox economics goes awry, one must become acquainted with a little bit of history. The role of the EMH should be situated within the broader context of the ways that neoclassical economics has changed over time.[18] In a nutshell, neoclassical economics looks very different now than it did at its inception in the 1870s. From thenceforth until World War II, it was largely a theory of the allocation of scarce means to given ends. Although trade was supposed to enhance 'utility', very little consideration was given to what people knew about commodities, or how they came to know it, or indeed, about how they knew much of anything else. The Socialist Calculation Controversy, running from the Great Depression until the Fall of the Wall, tended to change all that. In particular, Friedrich Hayek argued that the true function of The Market was to serve as the greatest information processor known to mankind. Although Hayek was not initially accorded very much respect within the American economics profession before the 1980s, nonetheless, the 'information processing' model of The Market progressively displaced the earlier 'static allocation' approach in the preponderance of neoclassical theory over the second half of the twentieth century. As one can appreciate, this profoundly changed the meaning of what it meant to assert that 'the market works just fine', at least within the confines of economics.[19] 'Efficiency', a slippery term in the best of circumstances, had come increasingly to connote the proposition that the market could package and convey knowledge on a 'need-to-know' basis in a manner which could never be matched by any human planner.

Once one recognizes this distinct trend, then the appearance of the EMH in Samuelson (1965) and Fama (1965) and its rapid exfoliation throughout finance theory and macroeconomics (Mehrling, 2010; Bernstein, 1992) becomes something more than just a fluke. The notion that all relevant information is adequately embodied in price data was one incarnation of what was fast becoming one of the core commitments of the neoclassical approach to markets. Of course, the fact that numerous ineffectual attempts were made along the way to refute the doctrine in specific instances (variance bounds violations, the end-of-the month effect, January effect, small cap effects, mean reversion, and a host of others) did not impugn the EMH so much as quibble over just how far the horizon would be extended. The EMH spawned lots of econometric empiricism, but surprisingly little alteration in the base proposition. The massive number of papers published on the EMH merely testified to the Protean character of the idol of 'market efficiency', which grew to the status of obsession within the American profession.

In the *Odyssey*, Proteus assumed a plethora of shapes to escape Menelaus; in the EMF, 'information' had to be gripped tight by neoclassical theory, because it kept squirming and changing shape whenever anyone tried to confine it within the framework of a standard neoclassical model. Few have been sensitive enough to the struggle to attend to its twists and turns, but for present purposes it will be sufficient that three major categories of cages to tame the beast have been: information portrayed as 'thing' or object, information reified as inductive index, and information as the input to symbolic computation (Mirowski, 2009). For numerous considerations here bypassed, they cannot in general be reduced one to another. The reason this matters to journalists' convictions that the crisis has invalidated the EMH is that the detractors mostly conform to the literature which treats information like a commodity, whereas the defenders repulse them from battlements of legitimation built largely from information as an inductive index. This may seem a distinction that only a pedant could love, but once clarified it goes a long way to demonstrating that the crisis will never induce the majority of neoclassical economists to give up on the EMH.

The standard-bearer for the denial of the *Kenntnisnahme über alles* EMH has been Joseph Stiglitz. Here it is important to acknowledge that Stiglitz deserves the respect of the Left because he has repeatedly taken political positions that have not ingratiated him with those in power, and often has been steadfast in his pessimistic evaluations of the crisis, when all the journalists wanted to hear was how the crisis was done, dusted and under control. He has been right more often about the gravity of problems that the crisis revealed than the thundering herd of economists claiming that they had sagely prophesied disasters.[20] And, in stark contrast to most of the figures encountered in this chapter, he has repeatedly gone on record stating that economists should bear some responsibility for the crisis. By these lights, Stiglitz has been an exemplary contrarian economist. Nonetheless, Stiglitz has simultaneously been a major defender of neoclassical economics, suggesting that the EMH is not all that central to the core doctrines of orthodoxy:

Normally, most markets work reasonably well on their own. But this is not true when there are externalities . . . The markets failed, and the presence of large externalities is one of the reasons. But there are others. I have repeatedly noted the misalignment of incentives – bank officers' incentives were not consistent with the objectives of other stakeholders and society more generally. Buyers of assets also have imperfect information . . . The disaster that grew from these flawed financial incentives can be, to us economists, somewhat comforting: our models predicted that there would be excessive risk-taking and shortsighted behavior . . . In the end, economic theory was vindicated. (Stiglitz, 2010a, pp. 150, 153)

This is what Krugman has called 'flaws-and-frictions' economics, and it comes perilously close to the standard response (encountered in section 20.3) that 'we already had models that told us the crisis was coming'. It follows that our first hesitation should be the one previously broached: so why weren't these models well represented in macro or micro textbooks and graduate pedagogy? Stiglitz is fully aware that there exists a tradition of oxymoronic 'New Keynesianism' which reprised a boring old story of sticky wages and prices in a neoclassical equilibrium, but he wants to suggest that there exists something else on offer which is more compelling. In Stiglitz's case, there is a special caveat: the models he has in mind are found mostly in his own previous publications. While there could be no academic prohibition against tooting your own horn, there is something less than compelling about claiming a generality for some idiosyncratic models where the novelty quotient is distinctly low. While Stiglitz has certainly earned the Nobel, he has not effectively staunched the intellectual trend of treating markets as prodigeous information processors; nor has he provided a knock-down refutation of the EMH. This has led to the distressing spectacle of Stiglitz, the great hope of the Left, openly defending the neoclassical approach to the crisis, while not really changing it all that much.

Stiglitz has admitted that his mission all along was to undermine free market fundamentalism from within:

[I]t seemed to me the most effective way of attacking the paradigm was to keep within the standard framework as much as possible . . . While there is a single way in which information is perfect, there are an infinite number of ways that information can be imperfect. One of the keys to success was formulating simple models in which the set of relevant information could be fully specified . . . the use of highly simplified models to help clarify thinking about quite complicated matters. (Stiglitz, 2003, pp. 613, 583, 577)

The way he has chosen to do this is to produce little stripped-down models which maximize standard utility or production functions, with a glitch or two inserted up front in the set-up. He has been especially partial to portraying 'information' as a concrete thing to be purchased, and 'risk' as standard density function with known parameters. There is no canonical Stiglitz 'general model', but rather a number of specialized dedicated exercises, one for each flaw and/or friction explored. Macroeconomics then simply becomes microeconomics with the subscripts dropped. This distinguishes Stiglitz from the small cadre of researchers in section 20.3.3 below, who are convinced that this 'representative agent' trick does not constitute serious macroeconomic theory.

In Stiglitz's academic writings, he stakes his claim to have refuted the EMH primarily on two papers, one co-authored with Sanford Grossman in 1980, and another co-authored with Bruce Greenwald in 1993.[21] The take-away lesson of the first was summarized in his Nobel lecture:

> When there is no noise, prices convey all information, and there is no incentive to purchase information. But if everybody is uninformed, it clearly pays some individual to become informed. Thus, there does not exist a competitive equilibrium. (2002, p. 395)

The second is proffered as the fundamental cause of the crisis in his (2010b):

> It perceives the key market failures to be not just in the labor market, but also in financial markets. Because contracts are not appropriately indexed, alterations in economic circumstances can cause a rash of bankruptcies, and fear of bankruptcy contributes to the freezing of credit markets. The resulting economic disruption affects both aggregate demand and aggregate supply, and it's not easy to recover from this – one reason that my prognosis for the economy in the short term is so gloomy.

Both of his crucial 'findings' are in fact based upon very narrow versions of what is a much more diversified neoclassical orthodoxy. It would indeed have been noteworthy if Stiglitz or his co-workers had provided a general impossibility theorem, say, along the lines of Gödel's incompleteness theorem or Turing's computability theorem, but Stiglitz has explicitly rejected working with full Walrasian general equilibrium (2003, pp. 580, 620), or Chicago's resort to transactions costs (p. 573), and does not seriously consider the game theorists' versions of strategic cognition. Indeed, it seems a rather heroic task to derive any general propositions from any one of his individual 'toy' models. Stiglitz himself admits this in when he is not engaged in wholesale promotion of his information program.[22] Instead, it is possible that 'simple' models serve mainly to cloud the issues that beset the half-century quest for a consensus economics of information.

Take, for instance, the Grossman–Stiglitz model (1980). The text starts out by positing information as a commodity that needs to be arbitraged (p.

393), but claims in a footnote (p. 397) that the model of knowledge therein is tantamount to the portrayal of information as inductive index, which is not strictly true, and then defines its idiosyncratic notion of 'equilibrium' as equivalence of plain vanilla rational expected utilities of informed and uninformed agents. Of course, 'for simplicity' all the agents are posited identical; how this is supposed to relate to any vernacular notions of divergences in knowledge is something most economists have never been poised to address. Many economists of a different political persuasion simply ignored the model, because they deemed that Stiglitz was not taking into account their (inductive, computational) version of 'information'. When Grossman offered his own interpretation of their joint effort, he took the position that the rational expectations model was identical to the approach in Hayek (1945), that: 'when the efficient markets hypothesis is true and information is costly, competitive markets break down', and that, 'We are attempting to redefine the Efficient Markets notion, not destroy it' (Grossman, 1989, p. 108). That seems closer to the median interpretation of Stiglitz's work in the profession as a whole.

Perhaps the most distressing aspect of Stiglitz's designated models that he believes starkly refute neoliberalism has been that, when you really take the trouble to understand them, they end up having nothing cogent to say about the current crisis whatsoever. Start with Grossman and Stiglitz (1980). The problems with the financial system in 2007 had nothing to do with participants lacking correct incentives to purchase enough 'information' which would have revealed the dodgy nature of the collateralized debt obligations (CDOs) and other baroque assets which clogged the balance sheets of the financial sector. Rather, the reams of information that they did purchase, from ratings agency evaluations to accounting audits to investment advice, was all deeply corrupted by being consciously skewed to mislead hapless clients and evade the letter of the law. Perhaps the 'information' was corrupted by the mere fact of being bought and sold. Since Stiglitz never comes within hailing distance of confronting epistemology in any of his models – he disdains philosophy as much as the next neoclassical – he never really deals with matters of truth and falsehood. Agents are just machines buying unproblematic lumps of information (or not).

And worse, the 'market failure' that he repeatedly diagnoses has nothing to do with what people mean by 'failure' in the vernacular. Stiglitz identifies 'market failure' with not realizing the full measure of utility which might have occurred in the standard neoclassical model – this is called 'Pareto optimality' in the trade – and exists in an imaginary universe utterly devoid of markets freezing up and the implosion of the assignment of credible prices across the board. Likewise, the Stiglitz–Greenwald paper has nothing whatsoever to do with the collapse of the financial sector in 2008. Using their own words: 'we showed that there were essentially always simple government interventions that could make some individuals better off without making anyone worse off. The intuition behind our result was that whenever information was imperfect, actions generated externality-like effects' (Stiglitz, 2009, p. 557). Stiglitz persistently conflates 'welfare loss' with system-wide economic failure: this travesty stands in stark contrast to the model-free occasions wherein Stiglitz perceptively analyzes the inconsistencies of concrete practices in real-world institutions, linking them to palpable dire outcomes. Pareto optimality was the last thing one needed to consult to try and understand the utter confusion and disarray accompanying the mad improvisations at the Federal Reserve System (the Fed) and the Congressional Troubled Asset Relief Program (TARP) appropriation in the depths of the crisis; it certainly would be impotent to clarify the types of 'government intervention' required to stem the collapse. Incredibly, the Greenwald–Stiglitz model does not even explicitly have any money in it, even though one core phenomenon of the 2008 meltdown was a credit crisis. Instead, their model identifies the central weakness of the capitalist system as a rational contraction of investment on the part of firms, not financial system collapse.[23]

Stiglitz repeatedly pronounces last rites over the EMH, but has little effect on the profession because he cannot see that what is sauce for the goose is sauce for the gander. 'The Chicago School and its disciples wanted to believe that the market for information was like any other market' (2010a, p. 268). Yet, that is the fundamental initial premise of his own models. 'The widespread belief in the EMH played a role in the Federal Reserve's failure. If that hypothesis were true, then there were no such thing as bubbles' (2010a, p. 269). But this just displays a deficiency of hermeneutic attention. As noted above, both the Fed and the profession can accept that the EMH, properly understood, and bubbles are entirely compatible – you just will not know you are in one till it bursts. And paraphrasing Bill Clinton, it all depends what you mean by 'bubble'. Does Joe Stiglitz really repudiate the neoliberal doctrine of the Marketplace of Ideas? 'The price mechanism is at the core of the market process of gathering, processing and transmitting information' (2010a, p. 266). It seems the answer is No. His evangelism consists of showering his political opponents with little models where the Cosmic Information Processor aka 'The Market' is beset with various formats of idiosyncratic noise, pesky little flaws and granular frictions. There is nothing fundamentally autodebilitating about the system, nor autodestructive in the Marketplace of Ideas.[24] But then, who in the elite of the orthodox economics profession ever thought otherwise?

The endless quest to dispatch the EMH almost constitutes the definition of 'empty gesture' within orthodox economics.

20.3.3   Abandon the DSGE Model

A third reaction to the crisis is to refrain from indictment of the global orthodoxy, and instead suggest that since the crisis was eminently a 'macroeconomic' event, the onus for failure must be narrowly restricted to that subset of the profession tasked with study of the macroeconomy; and furthermore, the correct response is simply to jettison the paradigmatic model found in contemporary macroeconomic textbooks, the so-called 'dynamic stochastic general equilibrium' [DGSE] model. The crisis, for this cadre, does not portend the 'death of economics', but just a garden variety 'model failure': so replace the model. We might think of this as the 'ounce of prevention' response. Now, I can imagine my audience rolling their eyes – even those willing to put up with a modicum of technical issues raised so far are not going to countenance a tedious discussion of a specific mathematical model, no matter how crucial to the self-image of the economics profession. And it is true that there is almost no commentary in the general press on the DSGE model, compared with breathless denunciations of 'rational economic man' and the EMH. But this option does even more directly call into question the commonplace notion that economists can learn from their mistakes.

This is exemplified by an event in 2010 that was literally unprecedented in the history of economic thought in America. Congressional testimony is regularly convened on all manner of issues of applied economics; and economists are regularly enjoined to testify. But never before, to my knowledge, has an entire session been convened to hold public hearings on criticism of a mathematical model produced by economic theory, not on its purported applications. Yet, on 20 July 2010 a kind of Star Chamber was convened to pillory the DSGE model.[25] The basic stance of the hearings was defined in the opening comments by Chairman Brad Miller:

> According to the model's most devoted acolytes, the model's insights rival the perfect knowledge Paul described in the First Letter to the Corinthians; but unlike the knowledge Paul described, DSGE's insights are available in the here and now. To be fair, DGSE and similar macroeconomic models were first conceived as theorists' tools. But why, then, are they being relied on as the platform upon which so much practical policy advice is formulated? And what has caused them to become, and to stay, so firmly entrenched? And, finally, the most important question of all: What do we get when we apply the various tools at our disposal to the urgent economic problems we're facing today?

This is how the committee staff described the DSGE model for a lay audience:

> The dominant macro model has for some time been the Dynamic Stochastic General Equilibrium model, or DSGE, whose name points to some of its outstanding characteristics. 'General' indicates that the model includes all markets in the economy. 'Equilibrium' points to the assumptions that supply and demand balance out rapidly and unfailingly, and that competition reigns in markets that are undisturbed by shortages, surpluses, or involuntary unemployment. 'Dynamic' means that the model looks at the economy over time rather than at an isolated moment. 'Stochastic' corresponds to a specific type of manageable randomness built into the model that allows for unexpected events, such as oil shocks or technological changes, but assumes that the model's agents can assign a correct mathematical probability to such events, thereby making them insurable. Events to which one cannot assign a probability, and that are thus truly uncertain, are ruled out.
>
> The agents populating DSGE models, functioning as individuals or firms, are endowed with a kind of clairvoyance. Immortal, they see to the end of time and are aware of anything that might possibly ever occur, as well as the likelihood of its occurring; their decisions are always instantaneous yet never in error, and no decision depends on a previous decision or influences a subsequent decision. Also assumed in the core DSGE model is that all agents of the same type – that is, individuals or firms – have identical needs and identical tastes, which, as 'optimizers', they pursue with unbounded self-interest and full knowledge of what their wants are. By employing what is called the 'representative agent' and assigning it these standardized features, the DSGE model excludes from the model economy almost all consequential diversity and uncertainty – characteristics that in many ways make the actual economy what it is. The DSGE universe makes no distinction between system equilibrium, in which balancing agent-level disequilibrium forces maintains the macroeconomy in equilibrium, and full agent equilibrium, in which every individual in the economy is in equilibrium. In so doing, it assumes away phenomena that are commonplace in the economy: involuntary unemployment and the failure of prices or wages to adjust instantaneously to changes in the relation of supply and demand. These phenomena are seen as exceptional and call for special explanation.

While skepticism concerning the DSGE is worn openly in this précis, it was nowhere near as scathing as the disparagement of the model that one hears in private and reads on blogs. Incredulity often focuses upon the presumption of a single immortal representative agent capturing the entire economy. For instance, at the Institute for New Economic Thinking (INET), I witnessed one famous economist compare coordination failures in DSGE models to the right hand losing track of what the left hand was doing, and the treatment of uncertainty in DSGE as tantamount to diagnosing the onset of Alzheimer's. You can just imagine the bizarre shapes that 'information' assumes in this solipsistic portrait: what can it mean for this god-like agent to learn anything? A good DSGE joke current on the blogs is: 'Based on all available information, I rationally expect DSGE models to suck for an infinite number of future periods; and because I am a representative agent, everybody agrees with me.'

So maybe economist jokes are not all that funny, but there are a few philosophical points to be extracted from the imbroglio. The first is that, within the profession, seeking out the Golden Mean does not guarantee intellectual credibility. The DSGE model was the product of a long series of compromises resulting in what was conceived as best-practice consensus, following a period in which participants had endured what they felt was three decades of bickering, discord and wrangling over the correct way to theorize in macroeconomics.[26] In the middle of the Noughties, embrace of the Great Moderation was coupled with declaration of the Great Macro Accord, and the DSGE model was its offspring. Complacency in the world of ideas replicated complacency in the world of policy. In another instance of bad timing, Olivier Blanchard, Chief Economist of the IMF, decreed: 'The state of macro is good . . . macroeconomics is going through a period of great progress and excitement, and there has been, over the past two decades, convergence in both vision and methodology' (2008, pp. 2, 26). 'DSGE models have become ubiquitous. Dozens of researchers are involved in their construction. Nearly every central bank has one, or wants to have one' (2008, p. 24). But perhaps the fact that the DSGE model was an attempt to be all things to all sides, a détente imposed from above, emitted from a very few 'top-ranked' economics departments rather than a voluntary truce taking hold organically. This had something to do with its clueless set-up for its vertiginous fall.

While there are some good historical summaries of how the rational expectations movement and the so-called 'Lucas critique' killed off the previous Keynesianism of the 1960s/1970s, there are very few sociological meditations on how economics got from there to the DSGE model. Starting out under the banner of 'consistency', it was insisted that neoclassical microeconomics and macroeconomics be fully interchangeable. Second, orthodox macroeconomists came to conflate 'being rational' with thinking like an orthodox economist. What this implied was that agents knew the one and only 'true model' of the economy (which conveniently was stipulated as identical with neoclassical microeconomics); and since they all knew the same thing, for practical purposes of the model, they were all alike in most relevant respects. Hence, far from congealing an intellectual travesty, it seemed plausible (not to mention mathematically convenient) to portray the entire economy as playing out between the ears of a single person. Thus the 'representative agent' fiction in fact constitutes a projection of deep commitments of the existing elite of the orthodox economics profession. That is why it became a shared presumption of neoliberals who believe in the natural healing powers of the market, as well as 'New Keynesians' looking for reasons why the economy falters.

Consensus is often mistaken for groupthink within the DSGE model, and this tends to mirror a sociological characteristic of the economics profession. Both the 'agent' in the DSGE model and in the American profession could not imagine an effective search for truth emerging out of substantial persistent disagreement over fundamentals. Agents in orthodox models are enjoined from 'agreeing to disagree'; and economists in good standing must knuckle under as well. The utter revulsion for anything smacking of real heterodoxy, combined with a fear of appearing 'unscientific' to outsiders, eventually led to a 'donnybrook' far more drastic than any embarrassment or compromised legitimacy that might have otherwise previously arisen from strident disagreement in the court of public opinion. Indeed, the effect of the crisis has been to bring those repressed disputes out into the open.

Once the presumption of omniscience broke down, then the consequences of the banishment of methodological self-scrutiny began to be felt. Both the criticisms and defenses of DSGE, at the Congressional hearings and elsewhere after the crisis onset, were distressingly unsophisticated, as one might expect as fallout from the ostracism of methodological thought. Robert Solow testified in Congress that DSGE models 'didn't pass the smell test', introducing a novel olfactory standard for scientific model choice. The defense of DSGE at the hearings by V.V. Chari equally reveals the paucity of resources (and rhetorical skills) possessed by contemporary economists:

> So, any interesting model must be a dynamic stochastic general equilibrium model. From this perspective, there is no other game in town. Modern macroeconomic models, often called DSGE models in macro share common additional features. All of them make sure that they are consistent with the National Income and Product Accounts. That is, things must add up. All of them lay out clearly how people make decisions. All of them are explicit about the constraints imposed by nature, the structure of markets and available information on choices to households, firms and the government. From this perspective DSGE land is a very big tent. The only alternatives are models in which the modeler does not clearly spell out how people make decisions. Why should we prefer obfuscation to clarity? My description of the style of modern macroeconomics makes it clear that modern macroeconomists use a common language to formulate their ideas and the style allows for substantial disagreement on the substance of the ideas. A useful aphorism in macroeconomics is: 'If you have an interesting and coherent story to tell, you can tell it in a DSGE model. If you cannot, your story is incoherent'.[27]

It is one thing to assert that you personally cannot imagine any other possible way to discuss the macroeconomy than the DSGE; it is quite another (in public, before a tribunal) to insist that no one else can either, without babbling incoherently. But of course there were alternatives studded throughout the literature, which had been proposed repeatedly by those seeking to exit the 'big tent' of orthodox macroeconomics.[28] This is not the appropriate venue to examine those proposals; rather, it is to ask – why are so many economists so loathe to let go of DSGE? All the usual considerations of inertia and sunk costs of intellectual commitment come into play; but there is something else as well. One way to understand such intransigence is to explore the possibility that excision of the DSGE cannot staunch the bleeding of the American economics profession; for these economists, renunciation of the DSGE is a slippery slope to the dissolution of the entire economic orthodoxy. *Après DSGE, la déluge.*

There were a few economists who had proposed that the monolithic coherence of macroeconomics and neoclassical microeconomics was a sham, but they were not accorded much respect, and were notably absent from the Congressional hearings. Perhaps the most prominent was the European economist Alan Kirman. He headed a group of scholars who issued the 'Dahlem report' (Colander et al., 2009) excoriating the economics profession early on in the crisis, and explained his own position in a widely read blog post (Kirman, 2009). Kirman suggested that the root problem with macroeconomics was really philosophical: the vaunted foundations of the DSGE model in full neoclassical general equilibrium were illusory. First, he cited some technical results dating from the 1970s stating that full general equilibrium analysis does not allow one to make much of any aggregate generalizations from the behavior of a diverse group of neoclassical agents; and furthermore, except under some strained special circumstances, one cannot guarantee the existence of a unique or stable general equilibrium.[29] The reason that DSGE models could pretend that there was a full macroeconomic equilibrium was that the fiction of a one-person economy was one of the few cases where (obviously) the individual is identical to the aggregate economy, and that existence proofs were available in that case for a unique stable equilibrium. To put it more bluntly, DSGE models were predicated upon the only arbitrary special case where neoclassical microeconomics and macro could be logically reconciled. Instead of drawing the conclusion that the marriage of micro and macro was doomed, and the DSGE a stillbirth, the profession had chosen to pledge its troth to an *outré* mutant case and call it the whole world. It would be as though a religious fanatic arranged to live in a hermetic world comprised only of Christian Scientist cyborgs, so that he need never encounter anyone who might call his faith in natural healing into question. As Kirman (2009) wrote: 'both the development of the DSGE model and the efficient markets hypothesis share a common feature – despite the empirical evidence and despite their theoretical weaknesses, their development proceeded as if the criticism did not exist'.

If there had been a contingent of methodologists integrated into the profession, they might have insisted that all the brouhaha about jettisoning the DSGE model was a weary sideshow, since the gnawing problem that the economic orthodoxy was intent on avoiding was gauging to what extent the crisis had voided the legitimacy of neoclassical microeconomics. Legions of macroeconomists were mobilized into action by the crisis not to address its dire consequences, but instead to obscure this threatening conclusion through smoke, mirrors and legerdemain. No one who wanted to maintain their position in academia would countenance the possibility that amputation of the DSGE would result in the patient bleeding to death. So instead they promoted endless consultations over the health of the DSGE – and even Congress was snookered into the pointless game.

This argument would begin by characterizing the two options promoted by economists who thought of themselves as orthodox macroeconomists after the crisis hit. The first was to insist that all that ridicule of the DSGE model was simply ignorant: all those aspects of the crisis that critics said could not be accommodated by the model, had in fact been fully taken into account somewhere in the journal literature.[30] You want heterogeneity of agents – we've done it. We've got models with frictions galore, and we have even coquetted with bounded irrationality. You claim there are big political divisions within macro, and that DSGE only describes neoliberal fantasies of self-regulating markets; but the 'freshwater–saltwater' divide is just an illusion. We've got DSGE models to conform to all ideologies. We even have a version of the model here and there that mentions banks and credit.[31] All those nagging complaints are baseless, and mired in an outdated impression of real business cycle theory back in the 1980s.

This option, while commonplace, is utterly unavailing. A methodologist would point out, as I have done, that the canonical DSGE assumes its canonical outlandish format in order to 'save' its microfoundations, viz., the non-negotiable prescription that macro and neoclassical microeconomics are one big unified theory. All these current fragmentary amendments to render the DSGE model more 'realistic', or perhaps more politically acceptable to the 'New Keynesians', are self-contradictory, since they attempt to mitigate or 'undo' the microfoundations which had been imposed by decree from the outset. It ends up being one more instance of economists asserting both A and not-A simultaneously. By thrusting the rabbit into the hat, then pulling it back out with a different hand, the economist merely creates a model more awkward, arbitrary and unprepossessing than if they had just started out explicitly to incorporate confused heterogeneous agents, dodgy banks, consciously duplicitous CDOs, informationally challenged markets, and all the rest of the usual suspects for the crisis, minus the neoclassical window dressing. If you allowed freedom of amendment to the DSGE in this manner, you would end up with models that violated the Lucas critique in a more egregious fashion than the earlier Keynesian models these macroeconomists love to hate. Thus, a 'more realistic DSGE' ends up as a contradiction in terms.

The second option, the one favored by the really high-profile attackers of DSGE like Robert Solow and Paul Krugman, was to roll back the clock to 1969, and pretend that the whole sequence of sordid developments leading up to DSGE never happened. Sometimes this was portrayed as a 'return to Keynes', although a historian might aver that the American profession was never all that enamored of the actual Keynes and his writings.[32] Nevertheless, this latter group was extrapolating from the heady days of late 2008, when all thoughts of DSGE were nowhere to be found. As the economic historian Greg Clark (2009) put it: 'The debate about the bank bailout, and the stimulus package, has all revolved around issues that are entirely at the level of Econ I. What is the multiplier from government spending? Does government spending crowd out private spending? . . . If you got an A in college Econ I, you are an expert in this debate: fully an equal of Summers and Geithner.'

This proposal was, if anything, even more implausible than the revision of the DSGE. Most macroeconomists would rather abandon the field than admit that all their technical sophistication was superfluous, and purge the lessons they learned at the feet of Robert Lucas and Thomas Sargent. The entire field was populated by people drilled in contempt for reading Keynes, and confirmed in their convictions that those 1960s-era models, like the old-fashioned IS-LM and Phillips curve, fully deserved to be tossed on the trash-heap of history. Yet, even if some magic wand waved away generations of inertia, there was no guarantee that if you re-ran the tape of history over one more time, starting once more in 1969, the neoclassical orthodoxy would not just end up rejecting all those 1960s-era models all over again. For Lucas and Sargent had a point: the earlier 'Keynesian' macroeconomics as it existed back then was logically incompatible with neoclassical microeconomic theory, and if something had to give, it would be Keynes, and not the Arrow–Debreu theory of general equilibrium, at least in America. Hence, by a circuitous route I arrive once more at the lesson of this section: the real bone of contention is not the DSGE model per se, but rather the pre-eminence of legitimacy of neoclassical microeconomics. The DSGE model is a herring of the brightest red.

One of the places where the 2010 Congressional hearing missed an opportunity at gaining an understanding of the true character of the path to dominance of the DSGE was in not inviting a historian and methodologist to provide meta-commentary upon the strange testimony offered by the invited participants. Not only would the missing witness have provided some context for the seemingly orthogonal positions voiced by Solow, Chari, Page and Winter, and pointed out that it was no accident that no substantial alternative to neoclassical theory had a place at the table; but she might have also suggested that the Congress (or its delegated agencies) itself deserved its own fair share of the blame for the rise to intellectual monopoly of the DSGE. To suggest where such testimony might have ventured, I here cite another occasion of testimony before the same House committee dating back to March 1981. Then the issue was a Reagan administration drive to cut the funding of economic research from the NSF. The speaker was Harvard economist Zvi Griliches:

> It is ironic and sad that whoever came up with these cuts does not even recognize that most of the recent 'conservative' ideas in economics – the importance of 'rational expectations' and the impotency of conventional macroeconomic policy, the disincentive effects of various income-support programs, the magnitude of the regulatory burden, and the arguments for deregulation – all originated in, or were provided with quantitative backing by NSF supported studies.[33]

Griliches was merely stating the obvious: economists produce the sorts of knowledge that its patrons desire, within the trajectory of its accumulated intellectual heritage; that list of patrons includes neoliberal elements within the government, with their allies in selected ranked economics departments. Congressmen today should not act as though the DSGE model and its precursors were somehow foisted upon unsuspecting regulators and an innocent public by imperious economists. Mostly, Americans just got what they paid for.

20.4   CONCLUSION

The most high-profile responses of famous economists to the crisis have been disappointing, both from a theoretical vantage point, and from the perspective of methodological sophistication. Taking that into account, perhaps it is no wonder that the cultural stock of the economics profession continues to sink.

NOTES

1. Federal Reserve System (Fed) Chair Ben Bernanke had begun in 2004 in speeches and writings to proclaim the onset of a 'Great Moderation' in the US macroeconomy since 1984 (Bernanke, 2004). Briefly, this was an assertion that economists had attained such an advanced understanding of the economy that macroeconomic fluctuations had been tamed relative to previous experience, and thus we had entered into a new era of capitalist stability and prosperity. His repeated citation of this thesis went some distance in explaining why Bernanke's Fed did essentially nothing to counter the worst financial abuses which led up to the crisis of 2007–08; Bernanke was insisting that the mortgage market was sound right up to the failure of Lehman Brothers. It is difficult to convey in any short space just how much the orthodox economics profession loved this thesis; so much so that it spawned a huge academic literature in its own right, one which has yet to be curtailed by events.
2. Here is not the place to document this trend, but see Paul Samuelson's setting the tone for the community in the 1970s: 'Those who can, do science; those who can't prattle on about its methodology' (quoted in Holcombe, 1989).
3. This dynamic is described from various vantage points in Weintraub (2002).
4. See, for instance, John Cochrane attacking Paul Krugman: http://www.youtube.com/watch?v=HO4E1bs4CbE; or Cochrane on the PBS News Hour, 17 February 2010: http://www.youtube.com/watch?v=7hQb1qkQUu0; or for some more nuanced defences of orthodoxy, see the speakers at the April 2010 meetings of the Institute for New Economic Thinking at: http://ineteconomics.org/video (last accessed 10 July 2010).
5. Available at: http://www.aeaweb.org/webcasts/assa2010.php.
6. 'It's not just that they missed it, they positively denied that it would happen' (Knowledge@Wharton, 2009).
7. I refer to the so-called 'Revere Prize' organized by the 'Real World Economic Review'. The winners are described at: http://rwer.wordpress.com/2010/05/13/keen-roubini-and-baker-win-revere-award-for-economics-2/.
8. See, for candidates from the Left, Galbraith (2009); while for candidates from the far right, consult http://www.freedomfest.com/2009/home.htm.
9. http://www.economist.com/blogs/freeexchange/lucas_roundtable. All quotes and paraphrasing in this paragraph come from this source.
10. Latsis (1976), Sent (1998), Mirowski and Hands (1998).
11. Although calling themselves 'Keynesians', their understanding of what Keynes wrote was so tenuous that they were called to account in this regard by Posner (2009b) and at http://dmarionuti-blogspot.com/2009/09/akerlof-shiller-animal-spirits-misnomer.html.
12. 'What's probably going to happen now – in fact, its already happening – is that flaws-and-frictions economics will move from the periphery of economic analysis to its center. There's a fairly well developed example of the kind of economics I have in mind: the school of thought known as behavioral finance' (Krugman, 2009).
13. Yet even this divergence went too far for the Old Guard of the orthodoxy (Arrow in Clarke, 2009).
14. The impression that economists were in some sense responsible for the existence of these markets became the pretense for the burgeoning literature on 'performativity' in the sociology of finance. See MacKenzie et al. (2007).
15. *Washington Post*, 7 June 2008.
16. This distinction has been a crucial component in some contemporary defenses of the EMH. See, for instance Szafarz (2009), or the Cassidy interview with Richard Thaler: 'I always stress that there are two components to the theory. One, the market price is always right. Two, there is no free lunch: you can't beat the market without taking on more risk. The no-free-lunch component is still sturdy, and it was in no way shaken by recent events: in fact, it may have been strengthened' (Cassidy, 2010).
17. http://blogs.reuters.com/felix-salmon/2009/08/11/why-the-efficient-markets-hypothesis-

510 *The Elgar companion to recent economic methodology*

caught-on/: 'Economists *are* scientists, after all. That which they can't explain, they turn into an axiom.'

18. The following three paragraphs are ridiculously telegraphed summaries of narratives found in Mirowski (2002, 2009).

19. Since the notion that The Market is uniquely better at information processing than any human mind is a core tenet of neoliberalism (Mirowski and Plehwe, 2009), this trend justifies the claim that the economic orthodoxy has become more neoliberal, and hence more conservative, over time.

20. This often attracts the disdain of other Nobel winners, here James Heckman: 'The whole profession was blindsided. I don't think Joe Stiglitz was forecasting a collapse in the mortgage market and large-scale banking collapses' (Cassidy, 2010). For some sensible Stiglitz observations on the state of affairs in 2010, see: http://www.hulu.com/watch/148219/foratv-economy-joseph-stiglitz-on-freefall-the-sinking-of-the-world-economy and http://www.businessinsider.com/joseph-stiglitz-were-probably-going-to-have-to-bail-out-the-banks-again-2010-7.

21. These are reprinted in (Stiglitz, 2009) as Chapters 21 and 26, respectively. Stiglitz identifies these as the key papers in his (2010a) and (2010b).

22. 'Unfortunately, we have not been able to obtain a general proof of any of these propositions. What we have been able to do is analyze an interesting example' (Grossman and Stiglitz, 1980, p. 395).

23. 'While Keynes was willing to let Animal Spirits serve as the *deus ex machina* to retrieve an explanation of investment variability, our theory provides a more plausible explanation of variability in investment' (Stiglitz, 2009, p. 647). 'Talking up animal spirits can only take you so far' (2010a, p. 256). These quotes exemplify why Stiglitz does not belong under our previous category of 'behavioral economics'.

24. This is why Stiglitz's repeated attempts to usurp the mantle of Hyman Minsky are deeply embarrassing; at least, if you had actually read Minsky. A serious attempt to refute neoliberalism would begin with acknowledgment of the ways in which markets undermine themselves in the course of 'normal' operations (for example Mirowski, 2010).

25. The Hearing Charter (quoted above) of the House Committee on Science and Technology and sworn testimony of economists Sidney Winter, Scott Page, Robert Solow, David Colander and V.V. Chari can be found at http://sciencedems.house.gov/publications/hearings_markups_details.aspx?NewsID=2876.

26. This is not the place to run through the tortured history of orthodox neoclassical macroeconomics, from the 'neoclassical synthesis' through Friedman's monetarism to 'New Classical' to 'real business cycles' to 'New Keynesians', and thus finally to DSGE. Some good sources on this massive literature are Quiggin (2010) and Mehrling (2010). As usual, the history is frequently accompanied by utterly naive methodological statements: 'the field looked like a battlefield. Researchers split in different directions, mostly ignoring each other, or else engaging in bitter fights or controversies. Over time however, largely because facts have a way of not going away, a largely shared vision of fluctuations and of methodology has emerged' (Blanchard, 2008, p. 2).

27. V.V. Chari, Testimony before the Committee on Science and Technology, Subcommittee on Investigations and Oversight, US House of Representatives, 20 July 2010. For a similar argument, see Kocherlakota (2010).

28. See, for instance, Colander et al. (2008), Meeusen (2010) and Howitt (2006, 2008).

29. For the curious, he was referencing the Sonnenschein–Mantel–Debreu theorems in microeconomics. See Rizvi (2006) for the relevant background.

30. This position is almost exactly repeated in the Chari testimony, and in Kocherlakota (2010), De Grauwe (2010) and Maskin (2009). All reactions in this paragraph are paraphrases of DSGE defenses found in these sources.

31. I shall indulge in just one example of how such protests were so misleading as to border on mendacity. The notion that DSGE models, which rarely incorporated money, much less a banking sector, could indeed handle a financial crisis, is often motivated by citation

of the Diamond–Dybvig model (Diamond and Dybvig, 1983), which is a model of a run on a solvent bank. Since most of the main institutions in the current crisis were insolvent, and not merely illiquid, this model turns out to be utterly irrelevant. Furthermore, since most DSGE models encompass a presumption of the EMH at base, and accept the Modigliani–Miller theorem, there are no functions for finance to perform in the models.

32. See, for instance, Mirowski (forthcoming).
33. Quoted in Scheiding and Mata (2010).

REFERENCES

Acemoglu, Daron (2009), 'The Crisis of 2008: Structural Lessons For and From Economics', CEPT Policy Insight no. 28.

Akerlof, George and Paul Romer (1993), 'Looting: The Economic Underworld of Bankruptcy for Profit', *Brookings Papers on Economic Activity*, **2**, 1–73.

Akerlof, George and Robert Shiller (2009a), *Animal Spirits*, Princeton, NJ: Princeton University Press.

Akerlof, George and Robert Shiller (2009b), 'Disputations: Our New Theory Of Macroeconomics', *New Republic*, http://www.tnr.com/article/books-and-arts/disputations-our-new-theory-macroeconomics.

Bernanke, Ben (2004), 'The Great Moderation', http://www.federalreserve.gov/Boarddocs/Speeches/2004/20040220/default.htm.

Bernstein, Peter (1992), *Capital Ideas*, New York: Free Press.

Blanchard, Olivier (2008), 'The State of Macro', NBER Working Paper 14259.

Buiter, Willem (2009), 'The Unfortunate Uselessness of Most "State of the Art" Academic Monetary Economics', *Financial Times* blog, 3 March, http://blogs.ft.com/maverecon/2009/03/the-unfortunate-uselessness-of-most-state-of-the-art-academic-monetary-economics/.

Cassidy, John (2009), *How Markets Fail*, New York: Farrar Strauss.

Cassidy, John (2010), 'Rational Irrationality', Chicago Interviews, *New Yorker*, 21 January, http://www.newyorker.com/online/blogs/johncassidy/chicago-interviews/.

Clark, Gregory (2009), 'Dismal Scientists: How the Crash is Reshaping Economics', *Atlantic*, February.

Clarke, Conor (2009), 'Interview with Kenneth Arrow', http://correspondents.theatlantic.com/mt-42/mt-tb.cgi/12601.

Colander, David (2007), *The Making of an Economist Redux*, Princeton, NJ: Princeton University Press.

Colander, David, Peter Howitt, Alan Kirman, Axel Leijonhufvud and Perry Mehrling (2008), 'Beyond DSGE Models', *American Economic Review, Papers and Proceedings*, **98**(2), 236–240.

Colander, David, H. Föllmer, A. Hads, M. Goldberg, K. Juselius, A. Kirman, T. Lux and B. Sloth (2009), *The Financial Crisis and the Systematic Failure of Academic Economists*, 'Dahlem Report', http://www.debtdeflation.com/blogs/wp-content/uploads/papers/Dahlem_Report_EconCrisis021809.pdf.

Coy, Peter (2009), 'What Good are Economists Anyway?', *Business Week*, 16 April.

De Grauwe, Paul (2010), 'The Scientific Foundation of DSGE Models', *Public Choice*, **144**, 413–443.

Diamond, Douglas and Philip Dybvig (1983), 'Bank Runs, Deposit Insurance and Liquidity', *Journal of Political Economy*, **91**, 401–419.

The Economist (2009), 'What Went Wrong with Economics?', 18 July.

Fama, Eugene (1965), 'The Behavior of Stock Market Prices', *Journal of Business*, **38**, 34–105.

Festinger, Leon, Henry Riecken and Stanley Schachter (1956), *When Prophecy Fails*, Minneapolis, MN: University of Minnesota Press.

Fischer, Peter, D. Frey, C. Peus and A. Kastenmüller (2008), 'The Theory of Cognitive Dissonance: the State of the Science', in Peter Muesburger, Michael Welker and Edgar Wunder (eds), *Clashes of Knowledge*, Berlin: Springer, pp. 189–199.

Frank, Robert (2009), 'Flaw in Free Markets: Humans', *New York Times*, 14 September.

Friedman, Milton (1953), 'The Methodology of Positive Economics', *Essays in Positive Economics*, Chicago, IL: University of Chicago Press; reprinted in Uskali Mäki (ed.) (2009), *The Methodology of Positive Economics*, New York: Cambridge University Press, pp. 3–44.

Fox, Justin (2009), *The Myth of the Rational Market*, New York: HarperCollins.

Galbraith, James K. (2009), 'Who Are these Economists, Anyway?', *Thought and Action*, Fall, 85–97.

Grossman, Sanford (1989), *The Informational Role of Prices*, Cambridge, MA: MIT Press.

Grossman, Sanford and Joseph Stiglitz (1980), 'On the Impossibility of Informationally Efficient Markets', *American Economic Review*, **70**, 393–408.

Hayek, Friedrich (1945), 'The Use of Knowledge in Society', *American Economic Review*, **35**, 519–530.

Holcombe, Randall (1989), *Economic Models and Methodology*, New York: Greenwood.

Howitt, P. (2006), 'The Microfoundations of the Keynesian Multiplier Process', *Journal of Economic Interaction and Coordination*, **1**, 33–44.

Howitt, P. (2008), 'Macroeconomics with Intelligent Autonomous Agents', in R. Farmer (ed.), *Macroeconomics in the Small and the Large*, Cheltenham, UK and Northampton, MA, USA: Edward Elgar, pp. 157–177.

Kirman, Alan (2009), 'Economic Theory and the Crisis', http://www.voxeu.org/index. php?q=node/4208.

Klamer, Arjo and David Colander (1990), *The Making of an Economist*, Boulder, CO: Westview.

Knowledge@Wharton (2009), 'Why Economists Failed to Predict the Financial Crisis', http://knowledge.wharton.upenn.edu/article.cfm?artcleid=2234.

Kocherlakota, Narayana (2010), 'Modern Macroeconomic Models as Tools for Economic Policy', *The Region*, 4 May, 5–21, Federal Reserve Bank of Minneapolis.

Krugman (2009), 'How Did Economists Get It So Wrong?', *New York Times Magazine*, http://www.nytimes.com/2009/09/06/magazine/06Economic-t.html.

Latsis, Spiro (ed.) (1976), *Method and Appraisal in Economics*, Cambridge: Cambridge University Press.

Lo, Andrew (2005), 'Reconciling Efficient Markets With Behavioral Finance: The Adaptive Markets Hypothesis', *Journal of Investment Consulting*, **7**, 21–44.

Lo, Andrew and Craig MacKinlay (1999), *A Non-Random Walk Down Wall Street*, Princeton, NJ: Princeton University Press.

Loewenstein, George and Peter Ubel (2010), 'Economics Behaving Badly', *New York Times*, 14 July.

Lucas, Robert (2009), 'In Defense of the Dismal Science', *The Economist*, 6 August.

MacKenzie, Donald, Fabien Muniesa and Lucia Siu (eds) (2007), *Do Economists Make Markets?*, Princeton, NJ: Princeton University Press.

Mäki, Uskali (ed.) (2009), *The Methodology of Positive Economics*, New York: Cambridge University Press.

Maskin, Eric (2009), 'Economic Theory and the Financial Crisis', interview with Sophie Roell, http://fivebooks.com/interviews/eric-maskin, accessed 7 August 2010.

Meeusen, Wim (2010), 'Whither the Microeconomic Foundations of Macroeconomic Theory?', http://webcache.googleusercontent.com/search?q=cache:FqRtjNQ9ZMcJ:www. wise.xmu.edu.cn/Master/News/NewsPic/20106309239228.pdf+Microeconomic+Foundat ions+%22Wim+Meeusen%22&cd=2&hl=en&ct=clnk&gl=us.

Mehrling, Perry (2010), 'A Tale of Two Cities', *History of Political Economy*, **42**, 201–220.

Mirowski, Philip (2002), *Machine Dreams: Economics Becomes a Cyborg Science*, New York: Cambridge University Press.

Mirowski, Philip (2009), 'Why There Is (As Yet) No Such Thing as an Economics of

Knowledge', in Harold Kincaid and Don Ross (eds), *Oxford Handbook of Philosophy of Economics*, Oxford: Oxford University Press, pp. 99–156.

Mirowski, Philip (2010), 'Inherent Vice: Minsky, Markomata, and the Tendency of Markets to Undermine Themselves', *Journal of Institutional Economics*, **6**, 415–443.

Mirowski, Philip (forthcoming), 'The Cowles Anti-Keynesians', in Pedro Duarte and Gilberto Lima (eds), *Microfoundations Reconsidered: The Relationship of Micro and Macroeconomics in Historical Perspective*, Cheltenham, UK and Northampton, MA, USA: Edward Elgar.

Mirowski, Philip and Wade Hands (1998), 'Harold Hotelling and the Neoclassical Dream', in Roger Backhouse, Daniel Hausman, Uskali Maki and Andrea Salanti (eds) *Economics and Methodology: Crossing Boundaries*, London: Macmillan, pp. 322–397.

Mirowski, Philip and Dieter Plehwe (eds) (2009), *The Road from Mont Pèlerin: The Making of the Neoliberal Thought Collective*, Cambridge, MA: Harvard University Press.

Posner, Richard (2009a), *A Failure of Capitalism*, Cambridge, MA: Harvard University Press.

Posner, Richard (2009b), 'Shorting Reason', *New Republic*, 15 April.

Quiggin, John (2010), *Zombie Economics*, Princeton, NJ: Princeton University Press.

Rabin, Matthew (2002), 'A Perspective on Psychology and Economics', *European Economic Review*, **46**, 657–685.

Reinhardt, Uwe (2009), 'An Economist's Mea Culpa', NYT Blog Economix, http://economix.blogs.nytimes.com/2009/01/09.

Rizvi, Abu (2006), 'The Sonnenschein–Mantel–Debreu Results after 30 Years', in P. Mirowski and W. Hands (eds), *Agreement on Demand: Consumer Theory in the 20th Century*, Durham, NC: Duke University Press.

Rosser, J.B., Richard Holt and David Colander (2010), *European Economics at a Crossroads*, Cheltenham, UK and Northampton, MA, USA: Edward Elgar.

Samuelson, Paul (1965), 'Proof That Properly Anticipated Prices Fluctuate Randomly', *Industrial Management Review*, **6**, 41–49.

Scheiding, Tom and Tiago Mata (2010), 'The Only Disinterested Source of Funds: Embedded Science, Lobbying, and the NSF's Patronage of Social Science', paper presented at 2010 meetings of History of Economics Society, Syracuse, NY.

Sent, Esther-Mirjam (1998), *The Evolving Rationality of Rational Expectations*, New York: Cambridge University Press.

Sherden, William (1998), *The Fortune Sellers*, New York: Wiley.

Shiller, Robert (2006), *Irrational Exuberance*, rev. edn, New York: Broadway.

Stiglitz, Joseph (2002), 'Information and the Change in Paradigm in Economics', *American Economic Review*, **92**, 460–501.

Stiglitz, Joseph (2003), 'Information and the Change in Paradigm in Economics', in R. Arnott, B. Greenwald, R. Kanbur and B. Nalebuff (eds), *Economics in an Imperfect World*, Cambridge, MA: MIT Press, pp. 569–639.

Stiglitz, Joseph (2009), *Selected Works*, Oxford: Oxford University Press.

Stiglitz, Joseph (2010a), *Freefall*, New York: Norton.

Stiglitz, Joseph (2010b), 'The Non-existent Hand', *London Review of Books*, 22 April.

Stiglitz, Joseph and Bruce Greenwald (1993), 'Financial Market Imperfections and Business Cycles', *Quarterly Journal of Economics*, **108**, 77–114.

Szafarz, Ariane (2009), 'How Did Crisis-Based Criticisms of Market Efficiency Get It So Wrong?', http://ideas.repec.org/p/sol/wpaper/09-048.html.

Weintraub, Roy (ed.) (2002), 'The Future of the History of Economics', Supplement to *HOPE*, **24**.

21 Invasion of the bloggers: a preliminary study on the demography and content of the economic blogosphere
Tiago Mata

INVASION

In the 1956 horror movie *The Invasion of the Body Snatchers*, a local doctor returns to his hometown of Santa Mira, after a trip to a medical convention.[1] He finds a town gripped by hysteria, where wives no longer recognize their husbands and fearful children flee from their parents. As one character spells out: 'There's no emotion. None. Just the pretense of it.' The distressed allege that 'body snatchers' are taking over the minds and bodies of neighbors and loved ones. With a skeptical and analytical mind, the doctor dismisses these anxieties until he sees the 'giant seed pods' that are replicating the town folk, including one that will resemble him. The doctor escapes.

The *Invasion* has been interpreted as an artifact of 1950s imagination, reflecting American society's anxiety and confusion in face of the 'Red Menace' and the 'atomic age'. Stuart Samuels (2010) in a celebrated reading of the movie argues that three themes inform its plot: conformity, paranoia and alienation. The protagonist battles to preserve his individuality, rejecting the drone state of mind of the 'snatched'. A rebel self opposes the social norm, which ambiguously can be the small town but also modernity. Although the term 'invasion' suggests an alien threat, the movie represents an insidious contagion, where the infected cannot be easily triaged from the healthy. And once the 'snatched' are victorious, the new world superficially does not differ much from the old, but it has been emotionally debased.

Setting up a horror fiction film, a dusty classic, as a prologue to a chapter about blogging in economics may appear to trivialize the phenomenon. Blogging should not be so easily dismissed. It has become a part of economists' engagement with policy debates and non-academic audiences. The imaginary of an *Invasion of the Body Snatchers* is invited by the morphing of the identity of economists, who have invented a virtual existence as bloggers, mediated by electronic media and wired into larger public networks. I structure my chapter by discussing first the growth ('contagion') and structure ('conformity') of the economic blogosphere. I then argue that this space has debated the economic crisis that began in 2007 with an anxiety for the status of economics ('paranoia'). Finally, I discuss to what extent new media is occasioning novel discourse and interventions of economists with non-academic audiences ('alienation'). The *Invasion of the Body Snatchers* offers me more than clever section headings. The 1956 imagination of the socio-technical was anxious and ambivalent; in contrast, present-day economists' confident use of new media is neither. Blogging caused no disruption, instead it has found a useful role for the economics profession, as a connector to traditional media.

CONTAGION: WHO AND WHEN

The first blogs began in the mid-1990s as the personal journals of technology insiders, with Justin Hall's links.net often referred as the first (Rosenberg, 2010).[2] 'Weblog' began to be recognized as a genre in 1997–9, at which time they also shortened in name (Blood, n.d.). As 'blog' entered the lexicon, as noun and verb, programmers began to design software for quicker and user-friendly posting as well as providing hosted server space, notably Pitas and Blogger in 1999. The latter was the most successful, being bought by Google in 2003 for an undisclosed sum. The number of platforms has continued to increase, for instance with some specializing in the posting of images (Tumblr) and microblogging (such as Twitter).

Over the years there have been many attempts to measure the blogosphere and track its growth. By 2000 it had become futile to attempt a comprehensive directory. A few ventures in 2004–5 made simple counts, and when in 2003, the National Institute for Technology in Liberal Education conducted a 'census' of blogs it found 2.8 million, of which 1.8 were estimated active, then it ordered its bots to stop queries (NITLE, 2003). Such figures are outdated. LiveJournal, one of the least popular blog platforms, has 18 million active accounts. BlogPulse from the Nielsen ratings corporation tracks over 120 million English language blogs.

Economists joined blogging late. The exception was Brad de Long who had been publishing short book reviews online in late 1999 which developed into a opinionated and fiery voice in 2000. Tyler Cowen and Alex Tabarrok began in August 2003. But the bulk arrived in 2005 and 2006. Mark Thoma has been posting since March 2005. Paul Krugman introduced his blog in September 2005, promising to complement his opinion columns with graphs and data (Krugman, 2005) – not really blogging, but it soon became that too. Gregory Mankiw started a year later, timidly, as an: 'experiment, primarily aimed at interacting with students in Ec 10, the large introductory economics class that I teach at Harvard. Other students and teachers using my textbooks may find it of interest as well' (Mankiw, 2006). While Mankiw was writing for students and colleagues, and promoting his textbook, Robert Reich began in April 2006 with 'A test from your son'. It read: 'Dad, I know you may feel tentative about me setting this up for you, but I couldn't resist. Blogs are a great way to reach an audience immediately' (Reich, 2006). As blogs were going 'professional' some of the traditional media publications followed: at *Time*, 'Curious Capitalist' fronted by Justin Fox started in September 2006.

If in 2005–06, economists discovered the blogosphere, the mass media and the public discovered economists in 2008 thanks to the financial and economic crisis. Between July and September, traffic surged from 80 percent to 250 percent for economics blogs – as many as 50 000 to 100 000 page views a day (Evans, 2009). A new sweep of blogs appeared at the same time. 'Baseline Scenario', one of the most read blogs today, opened in September 2008. The *New York Times*, which already hosted 'Freakonomics' and Krugman's blog, pooled its economic staff to author 'Economix: Explaining the Science of Everyday Life'. It's original authors were journalists: David Leonhardt and Catherine Rampell; accompanied by 'a panel of outside economic thinkers': Alan Krueger ('everything from the job market to terrorism to rock 'n' roll'), Edward Glaeser ('housing, crime, innovation, segregation and a host of other topics'), Bob McTeer ('inner workings of the Fed and macroeconomic policy'), Hung Huang ('the Oprah of China') and Uwe E. Reinhardt ('health care') (Economix, 2008a). The first post of 23 September 2008 stated the goal of making 'economics accessible and useful to people who otherwise find it frightening, confusing and/or useless' (Economix, 2008b). Two years on, and six more journalists are writing regularly. Of the initial panel of economists only Reinhardt and Glaeser stayed on; the new 'Daily economists' are Nancy Folbre, Simon Johnson and Casey Mulligan. Similar changes were occurring at Freakonomics, which increased both its economist and non-economist staff (with journalists and academics from history and law). The latest generation of economic blogs is more collaborative, drawing from a greater number of contributors of different backgrounds, and as I will show below it is also more visible.

We do not know how many blogs exist. Competition from new blogging genres, social media and hybridization with traditional media has made it increasingly difficult to differentiate blogs neatly from their kin. Like the 'body snatchers', one can see them everywhere.

CONFORMITY: HIERARCHY AND VISIBILITY

Despite their ubiquity, some patterns in the content and influence of blogs can be observed and discussed. Problems posed by digital proliferation spawn digital solutions. Personal blogs, social networking sites and search engines are all attractive deposits of data, that specially designed mining software can harvest and analyze for marketing purposes.[3] A more benign solution to the torrents of blogs and their diffused content are partial directories, which survey and stabilize a pack order in the blogosphere. Not unlike impact factors and their role in academic ranking, Technorati, the principal website for search and directory of blogs, measures 'authority'.

As of 5 October 2010, the 100 top blogs of Technorati had five economics entries: Real Time Economics from the *Wall Street Journal* ranked at 56, Paul Krugman's *New York Times* blog at 71, Brad DeLong's blog was at 80 as was Marginal Revolution, Naked Capitalism was at 95.[4] How have these rankings evolved, in particular in interaction with the current economic crisis? Technorati does not offer a tool for doing historical ranking comparisons. However, in November 2007 and in November 2008 I had done similar queries on Technorati. The measurements are not fully comparable since in October 2009 Technorati changed its algorithm that ranks blog 'authority'.[5] Comparing sites run by individual academic economists and sites hosted by traditional media, in 2007 the top blogs were by economists. Although the highest ranked was the Freakonomics blog at the *New York Times* (#233), it was followed by Greg Mankiw (#709), and Tyler Cowen and Alex Tabarrok's Marginal Revolution (#629). In the top 10 000 there were also: Dani Rodrik (#8,963), Mark Thoma (#3,962), and the elder statesmen Gary Becker and Richard Posner (#4,527). Only then came the blogs of the *Wall Street Journal* and *The Economist*. In late 2008, economists' success at winning over the blogosphere's attention was evident. Nearly all economists had climbed the ranking: Freakonomics was 57, Krugman's new blog was 80; Mankiw (#313), Cowen and Tabarrok (#547), Thoma (#653) and Rodrik (#7188) had gone up too. Yet, it was also evident that economists writing in the *New York Times* had greater 'authority'. At the time of writing, September–October 2010, economics blogs have increased in visibility but among them the ones that do best are sponsored by conventional media.

The three observation points suggest that the most successful, visible, blogs are written by media professionals, not laymen, not economists. Besides its 'authority' measurements in real time, Technorati also conducts yearly surveys of the blogosphere. The 2009 survey observed that as much as 35 percent of bloggers had traditional media experience, and one in four were employed by traditional media. The survey asked specific questions about the 'economic downturn' and noted that only 19 percent of bloggers had changed the content of their writing in response to it (Technorati, 2009). Blogs conform to stable reporting themes that have strong relationships with traditional media. Overwhelming US bloggers are highly educated, business minded and affluent. In 2008 it was estimated that has much as half of US bloggers had household incomes higher than $75 000 a year, 72 percent had college degrees and 42 percent had done graduate work (Technorati, 2008). The surveys also tell us something about the reasons behind blogging. While only one in five bloggers expects to see their opinions presented in (traditional) media, as much as three in five argue that blogging has increased their visibility within their profession. The surveys suggest that blogging is conforming to partnerships with longstanding media ventures, and that it serves supportive strategies to professional careers.[6]

PARANOIA: CRISIS TALK

What is most novel in blog writing is neither its protagonists nor its payoff. The online medium is distinctive for not being writing. In its linguistic practice online media is time-bound, spontaneous, loosely structured, socially interactive and immediately revisable (Crystal, 2006). It is closer to orality than to script.

In their original instantiation, blogs were modeled after personal journals, a private subject matter that was made instantly public, and potentially viral. Economists however have not pursued the private voice. They have used the blog medium in its function as 'filter' or as occasion for 'commentary'. From the ever-increasing online mass (and mess) of information, economic bloggers parse the credible from the dubious, and flag for attention analyses and data. Besides the economy of attention, which the previous section on ranking suggests is more bound to conventional and traditional reporting than one might have assumed, bloggers also comment. The filtering and the commentary functions are often brought together. The 10 September 2010, post 'Ever-expanding Government' in Krugman's *New York Times* blog is a good illustration.[7] The post reads:

> Menzie Chinn points out that government employment <u>has not, in fact, soared</u> [linked to post in econbrowser blog] under Obama; he gets the usual mass of hysterical comments accusing him of being naive, dishonest, whatever. Heh.
>
> Here's another one: compare real government purchases in stimulus-happy America and frugal, austere Germany (I've mentioned this before, but here's a chart):

[a Eurostat chart showing faster trending index of real government consumption in Germany compared to the USA]

It's worth noting that just to keep up with the trend in potential GDP, US government purchases would have to have risen about 6 percent over the period shown. As far as actual government spending on goods and services goes, as opposed to aid to individuals, we've had no stimulus at all – basically because of cutbacks at the state and local level. (Krugman, 2010)

Krugman in his post is addressing another blogger, Menzi Chinn, not the reading public which he somewhat derides: 'Heh'. Krugman is filtering in that he is signaling Chinn, and the Econobrowser post, as deserving attention and a visit, following the link. Although links may appear equivalent to references in an academic paper, they are invitations to travel, to follow the thread of information, and as such to manage the attention of readers. Alongside the filtering function, Krugman also comments. He lends support to Chinn's original claim with a graph from Eurostat which he interprets in writing. Blogging does not lend itself to elaborate argument or evidence; it is a medium for expressing approval or critique.

The tone of blogging is conversational, but a conversation that is enclosed. One of the more exciting possibilities of social media and blogging is that it might originate a new Habermasian public sphere, a space of free reasoned debate (Boeder, 2005). Unlike the coffee houses and salons of eighteenth-century gentlemen's society and the original public sphere, the blogosphere does not restrict access: anyone with an Internet connection can read the posting. The conversation could therefore be widely inclusive: of expert and lay, of all ages, gender and opinions. However, in practice it is far from this ideal. Bloggers respond to other bloggers, or react to newsprint, but bloggers rarely interact with the haphazard visitors to their sites and their often quirky comments.[8]

The politics of inclusion shape the language and themes of the conversation. One example is the *Financial Times* and Martin Wolf's 'The Economists' Forum'. The platform began in September 2006. It initially posted the leads of Wolf's and Lawrence Summers' (monthly) columns and added extensions and criticisms by the invited 'expert panelists'.[9] From December 2007 and under the shadow of the 'credit squeeze', a larger number of entries by invited columnists appeared, and from the summer of 2008 the entries to the forum increased manyfold.[10] In November 2008 it listed 70 contributors, and posting was no longer restricted to published columns in the *Financial Times*. The change was policy of the newspaper pressured by the emergence of competing initiatives (like Economix mentioned above) (Wolf, 2008). While the 'Wolf forum' can be read by anyone with a web connection, only contributors (and a few special guests) can post articles and comment. More recently, comments are being allowed to persons beyond the panel, but they must be emailed and sanctioned by Wolf and the webmaster. This restricted design was justified in the following terms:

> We are not aiming to provide a forum for unrestrained free speech, where anyone has the right to say anything. There are plenty of those elsewhere online. Rather, we want our site to host intelligent debate, where quality is more critical than quantity. This is not a cosy club where a tiny number of strident participants can dominate and intimidate others, but a place where everyone with something substantial and constructive to add feels comfortable in contributing. You remain free to criticise or contradict the views of FT writers.

With some disdain for the 'strident' discourse that fills the web, the 'Wolf forum' proposes a controlled solution to the choice of who can speak and when. It succeeds at fixing discourse to a language that is mostly inaccessible to the wider public but about right for *Financial Times* readers. Wolf includes economists with strong credentials who prove themselves to be articulate by writing to the printed *Financial Times*, in columns or letters to the editor. The 'Wolf forum' is only distinctive for making explicit what is elsewhere tacit. The conversation is everywhere circumscribed to recognized professionals. Anonymity is a feature of political or personal blogs; in the economic blogosphere it is distrusted.

A consequence of this protective frame are the themes that have gripped the imagination of the economic blogosphere in the past years of crisis. Bloggers respond to whatever is the buzz debate on the traditional media, but economist bloggers have in addition been preoccupied with the public status of their profession. When in the Fall of 2008, Alan Greenspan offered his *mea culpa* in Congress, economists at 'Wolf's forum' were quick to dissociate themselves from the man and his legacy (Greenspan, 2008). A more recent case saw Frederic Mishkin writing in self-defense for the way he was portrayed in a documentary interview that had yet to be aired (Mishkin, 2010).

Perhaps the most revealing controversy of the past couple of years was the debate initiated by *The Economist*'s special issue on 'What Went Wrong with Economics' (16 July 2009) and soon followed by Krugman's *New York Times Magazine* article on 'How Did Economists Get It So Wrong?' (6 September 2009). These two critical assessments appeared in print and in traditional media. Krugman's piece was seen as the most acerbic and explosive; it offered no words of redemption, which *The Economist* did, and it was penned by the profession's foremost public intellectual and a Nobel Laureate. The two most significant opponents of Krugman were John Cochrane from the University of Chicago, who posted a long reply on his website, and David Levine from Washington University in St Louis who wrote an open letter for the *Huffington Post* (Levine, 2009). Both responses accused Krugman of being out of touch with the latest literature and misrepresenting the views of his colleagues. Krugman acknowledged in his blog the 'anger' generated by his article but offered no substantive response. In blogs, the controversy prompted a torrent of reactions (a good number of them indexed in Thoma, 2009).

Commentary by bloggers on the crisis of economics was lengthier than usual. It was principally about how each blogger saw himself in the great divide that Krugman identified: saltwater versus freshwater, Keynesians versus New Classicals. It accepted the terms set in traditional media. Despite its seeming importance, and the strong feelings it evoked, like all subjects in the blogosphere it came and went. It raged for a week, but no more.

In closing, blogs are a medium that fails to pursue themes and conversations consistently. Bloggers react to external stimuli in conventional media, filter content and position themselves. This sorting role is not without merit, and informs public debate; but blogs are impaired at leading a discussion. Blogs, the rankings and standings, the network of links, identify and focus. As the respondents to Technorati's survey noted, the principal outcome of blogs' is awarding attention to its authors.

ALIENATION, OR WHY INVASIONS ARE NOT WHAT THEY USED TO BE

The great fear of the 1950s *Invasion of the Body Snatchers* was bureaucratic alienation, be it Bolshevism or the rationalization of social life in an atomic age. The individual feared a loss of the 'emotional self' to conformity and control. Blogs could have invited similar anxious imaginations. The new electronic media might erode professional solidarities and force upon economists alliances with political trends or social movements. The economist might lose his 'expert self'. The new science communication might penetrate the practices of research by requiring instantly translatable results in the same way that journalism's twice-daily news cycle has given way to real-time news production. If economic bloggers ever felt anxious about being alienated from the rest of their profession and from its standards of practice, they today show no caution, and they have good reason not to fear such futures.

Blogging competes for time that might be spent on research or teaching. But it has not disrupted hierarchy, the discourse or the practices of economists. Admission to the conversation remains carefully managed:

economists responding to fellow professionals, often with the support of traditional media that has sought out prominent scholars to bring legitimacy to its economic reporting. And in this lies a surprising observation: new media has been the site for a renewed encounter with traditional media. Journalists find in blogs a source of informants; even if they rarely (never) reference blog posts in their reporting, they will contact bloggers for elucidation and quotes.

The rise of economic blogs in the rankings of Internet attention can be explained by genuine interest by the public, for what economists might have to say about the current economic climate, but also by the promotional work of conventional media seeking to fill webpages of commentary and information. In the words of one European editor: 'I'm not working on a newspaper, I'm working in news' (cited in Mitchelstein and Boczkowski, 2009). The product is content offered in multiple media: video, audio, online print, newsprint, books and lectures. The emerging business models draw on a variety of print and online advertising and layered subscriptions where access to thematic reports and financial information can be obtained at a premium. Blogs are a free port of entry. As Gregory Mankiw in interview explains: 'I make no money from my blog, but I do make money selling books', and 'My publisher loves it that I do the blog' (Evans, 2009). Placed in the context of contemporary media and publishing, that some have characterized as 'infotainment', the purpose of blogging is publicity, for authors and their brand. As the public are drawn to the webpage of the *New York Times* in want of news, they find a link to its Freakonomics blog on the front page, with its trademark oranged apple. In the blog the reader discovers a new book, and that the old bestseller has found a new medium: they can learn of the production and watch a trailer of *Freakonomics*, the movie.

ACKNOWLEDGMENTS

I thank Martin Wolf, Alex Tabarrok, Tyler Cowen and Mark Thoma for answering my questions. All omissions and mistakes are my own.

NOTES

1.   There were remakes in 1978 and 2007, and several parodies and adaptations. The 1978 movie is distinct for its urban imaginary, and more explicit in its violence and suspense, and presenting the body snatchers as otherworldly. It also updates on racial and gender stereotypes. The 2007 movie recenters the story away from man–woman affection to a father–son relationship.

2. Fred Turner (2006) reveals a history between the people and ideas of the Bay Area counterculture and the emergent software and digital business ventures at Silicon Valley, as well as the new genres of reporting it elicited.
3. The *Wall Street Journal* has provided good coverage on the subject (Carr, 2010).
4. Note that these fluctuate a great deal: the next day (6 October) Naked Capitalism fell to rank 99, and was listed as one of the top falling blogs of the day.
5. From a transparent rule of counting links to blogs in a six-month moving wall, Technorati now uses an undisclosed set of rules that include trending subjects as well as links.
6. In-depth interview research comes to similar results but it portrays blogging as more productive of research insights, as opposed to only circulation (Kjellberg, 2010).
7. There is no ease in reproducing a blog post in print. Although one can create an online copy of Krugman's post in a few seconds, the printed page loses the links, the immediacy and the manipulation of images.
8. In a blog a 'post', a text by the author, can be accompanied by remarks of visitors to the site, which may or may not be registered, which may or may not be moderated, which often are from an anonymous readership.
9. In the eventful fall of 2008, the panel is made up of 37 economists from the USA, 18 from the UK, two based in Asia and the remainder divided between France, Germany and Ireland. Of these only 9 are corporate employed economists, the majority are professors of economics (49), with the rest working for policy think-tanks or governmental organizations. By December 2010, the panel numbered 53.
10. The process of transformation of the 'forum' into a blog is not very different from the evolution of Krugman's online space at the *New York Times*, at first only for supplementary material related to his columns, but later a more community-oriented, daily journal of thoughts and readings.

REFERENCES

Blood, R. (n.d.), 'Weblogs: A History and Perspective', http://www.rebeccablood.net/essays/weblog_history.html.
Boeder, P. (2005), 'Habermas' Heritage: The Future of the Public Sphere in the Network Society', *First Monday*, **10**(9), http://firstmonday.org/htbin/cgiwrap/bin/ojs/index.php/fm/article/view/1280/1200.
Carr, N. (2010), 'Tracking is an Assault on Liberty, With Real Dangers', wsj.com, http://online.wsj.com/article/SB10001424052748703748904575411682714389888.html.
Crystal, D. (2006), *Language and the Internet*, Cambridge: Cambridge University Press.
Economix (2008a), 'Meet Our First "Daily Economist" – NYTimes.com', http://economix.blogs.nytimes.com/2008/09/23/meet-our-first-daily-economist/.
Economix (2008b), 'Welcome to Economix – NYTimes.com', http://economix.blogs.nytimes.com/2008/09/23/welcome-to-economix/.
Evans, K. (2009), 'The New Stars of the Blogosphere', wsj.com, http://online.wsj.com/article/SB10001424052970203739404574288793998936838.html.
Greenspan, A. (2008), 'Alan Greenspan: A Response to My Critics', *Economists' Forum*, http://blogs.ft.com/economistsforum/2008/04/alan-greenspan-a-response-to-my-critics/.
Kjellberg, S. (2010), 'I am a Blogging Researcher: Motivations for Blogging in a Scholarly Context', *First Monday*, **15**(8), http://firstmonday.org/htbin/cgiwrap/bin/ojs/index.php/fm/article/view/2962/2580.
Krugman, P. (2005), 'Welcome – NYTimes.com', http://krugman.blogs.nytimes.com/2005/09/17/welcome/.
Krugman, P. (2010), '"Ever-expanding Government" – NYTimes.com, http://krugman.blogs.nytimes.com/2010/09/10/ever-expanding-government/.

Levine, D.K. (2009), 'An Open Letter to Paul Krugman', *Huffington Post*, http://www.huffingtonpost.com/david-k-levine/an-open-letter-to-paul-kr_b_289768.html.

Mankiw, G. (2006), 'Greg Mankiw's Blog: Welcome', http://gregmankiw.blogspot.com/2006/03/welcome.html.

Mishkin, F. (2010), 'The Economist's Reply to the "Inside Job"', *Economists' Forum*, http://blogs.ft.com/economistsforum/2010/10/the-economists-reply-to-the-inside-job/.

Mitchelstein, E. and P.J. Boczkowski (2009), 'Between Tradition and Change', *Journalism*, **10**(5), 562–586.

NITLE (2003), 'NITLE Weblog Census', http://www.knowledgesearch.org/census/.

Reich, R. (2006), 'Robert Reich's Blog: A Test from Your Son', http://robertreich.blogspot.com/2006/04/test-from-your-son.html.

Rosenberg, S. (2010), *Say Everything: How Blogging Began, What It's Becoming, and Why It Matters*, New York: Random House.

Samuels, S. (2010), 'Science Fiction as Social Commentary. The Age of Conspiracy and Conformity: Invasion of the Body Snatchers (1956)', in S. Mintz and R.W. Roberts (eds), *Hollywood's America: Twentieth Century America Through Film*, Chichester, UK and Malden, MA, USA: John Wiley & Sons, pp. 198–206.

Technorati (2008), 'Feature: State of the Blogosphere 2008 – Technorati', http://technorati.com/blogging/feature/state-of-the-blogosphere-2008/.

Technorati (2009), 'Feature: State of the Blogosphere 2009 – Technorati', http://technorati.com/blogging/feature/state-of-the-blogosphere-2009/.

Thoma, M. (2009), 'What's Wrong with Macroeconomics?', *Economist's View*, http://economistsview.typepad.com/economistsview/2009/09/whats-wrong-with-macroeconomics.html.

Turner, F. (2006), *From Counterculture to Cyberculture: Stewart Brand, the Whole Earth Network, and the Rise of Digital Utopianism*, Chicago, IL: University of Chicago Press.

Wolf, M. (2008), Email communication.

Index